THE SELECTED LETTERS OF
BERTRAND RUSSELL

VOLUME 1

THE SELECTED LETTERS OF
BERTRAND RUSSELL

═══

VOLUME I

THE PRIVATE YEARS, 1884–1914

EDITED BY

NICHOLAS GRIFFIN

Houghton Mifflin Company

Boston / New York / London

1992

For information about permission to reproduce
selections from this book, write to
Permissions, Houghton Mifflin Company,
215 Park Avenue South,
New York, New York 10003.

Library of Congress Cataloging-in-Publication Data
Russell, Bertrand, 1872–1970.
[Correspondence.   Selection]
The selected letters of Bertrand Russell / edited
by Nicholas Griffin.
p.   cm.
Includes bibliographical references (p.   ).
Contents: v. 1. The private years, 1884–1914.
ISBN 0-395-56269-4
1. Russell, Bertrand, 1872–1970 — Correspondence.
2. Philosophers — England — Correspondence.
I. Griffin, Nicholas.   II. Title
B1649.R94A4   1992
192 — dc20   91-47644
[B]   CIP

HAD 10 9 8 7 6 5 4 3 2 1

Contents

═══

Preface

I don't know how many of Russell's letters are currently in the Russell Archives, but forty to fifty thousand is a reasonable guess, and the number grows each year. While a number of them are perfunctory notes of no especial interest – thank-you letters and the like – many thousands are interesting, revealing, amusing, or in other ways valuable as part of a record of his life; and many are little masterpieces. The most difficult and time-consuming task in editing this selection of Russell's letters, therefore, has been choosing which ones to include.

In the first place, with one exception, I have included only those letters which have not previously been published in full. Russell included a number of letters in his *Autobiography* and a number of others have appeared elsewhere, typically small batches of letters to individual correspondents. (The Bibliographical Notes at the end of the book include titles of other collections of Russell's letters relevant to matters which come up in this volume.) The exception is Russell's first letter to Frege (letter 112), which has not only been repeatedly published but has become quite famous. To my surprise it was the only letter I could find about the Russell class paradox which was roughly contemporary with Russell's discovery of the paradox (even so, it was still written a year after the discovery). Since the class paradox occupied Russell's thoughts for much of the next decade, the letter could not well be left out.

A number of the letters I have included have already been quoted in print (sometimes at length), so certain passages may well appear familiar. But to the best of my knowledge, with the exception of the letter to Frege, none of the letters included here have been published before in their entirety

Another main concern was to choose letters which covered as many facets of Russell's life as possible and which would arrange themselves into a sort of epistolary biography. There were inevitably some difficulties here. Very few letters from Russell's childhood and adolescence have survived, and few also that relate directly to his undergraduate years at Cambridge.

A difficulty of another kind concerns Russell's philosophical work between 1900 and 1910. The importance of this work to his life, both at the time and afterwards, and to his position in the intellectual world, would justify the inclusion of many more letters on these topics. There are, moreover, a good, though not enormous, number of such letters in the Russell Archives. However, most of them are so technical that to have included them in greater numbers would have made this a book for specialists only. I have included a couple of examples of some of the less technical of the letters on the foundations of mathematics. The matters they deal with were at the centre of Russell's life at the time and to have omitted all reference to them would have been a serious distortion. I have offered as much help with understanding them as I could, though in such cases one feels that the explanation will only be clear to those who could read the letters without it. The reader who still feels unable to face these letters may skip them without serious loss, safe in the thought that the matters under discussion really are every bit as difficult as they seem and that there are many other letters, not included, which seem a good deal more difficult. Even the reader who cannot follow these letters might still gain from them a sense of the intellectual complexity and subtlety of the work that Russell was doing at this time, and in this volume I don't wish to do more than convey some sense of this to the general reader.

Even within these constraints there has been plenty to choose from. It would easily be possible to do this volume over again several times with an almost completely different selection of letters each time. For example, I have included just over seventy letters to Ottoline Morrell from the well-over one thousand that were written during the period covered by the volume. Not many of the thousand and more letters to Ottoline that I read but decided to leave out, were excluded for lack of quality or interest.

The text has been treated both lightly and informally. No record of either authorial or editorial emendations has been kept – emendations of both types are, in any case, few. Missing words have been supplied in square brackets. (Russell occasionally used square brackets himself and these have been changed to round brackets to avoid confusion.) Russell's very occasional spelling mistakes and slips of the pen have been silently corrected – except where they had some interest or attraction. For example, I have not corrected the childish spelling of his first letters, nor the misspelling of proper names which indicates that he was unfamiliar with them. (In these last cases the correct spelling will be found in the annotation.) Abbreviations (other than those conventionally found in print) have been silently expanded. Abbreviations of proper names are again an exception. On their first appearances they have been expanded using square brackets, but once they have become familiar they are left unchanged. Book titles and foreign phrases have been italicized. Russell's capitalization has been preserved. Occasionally, where there was some doubt as to what Russell wrote, the reading offered is followed by '[?]'. Very occasionally, where the text is garbled, I have had to resort to a '[*sic*]', if only to reassure the reader that there's been no editorial mistake.

Missing punctuation has been silently supplied, though only where it was necessary to make the text easily readable. (If Russell omits the commas in a list, I've let him get away with it. But if he omits the period at the end of a sentence, I've supplied it.) Russell makes frequent use of the long Victorian stop ('–') and for almost every purpose for which this exceptionally flexible punctuation device can be used. Most commonly it replaces a period or a paragraph break or, used often in conjunction with a period, indicates a break intermediate in strength between these two. My treatment of it has been eclectic. Generally where it was used instead of a period or a paragraph break I have substituted the now more conventional punctuation; where it was used in the third way mentioned above to supplement a period, I have kept it. With this exception, Russell's punctuation, like his spelling and his accidentals in general, is quite conventional and no literary flavour is lost by correcting the occasional mistake that escaped his vigilance.

The address and dates given on the letters have been printed in a uniform style throughout the volume. Town and county names have usually been omitted from the address where they were not needed to identify Russell's location. Thus 'Pembroke Lodge, Richmond Park, Surrey' becomes 'Pembroke Lodge' and 'Trinity College, Cambridge' becomes 'Trinity College'. Where locations and dates have had to be inferred they are printed in square brackets.

Russell's letters to Louis Couturat were written in French. Translating them poses different problems from those facing the translator of an author writing in his native language. I have not tried to capture the slight stiffness of Russell's generally very correct, but rather unidiomatic, French (though I fear I have succeeded all too well). The translation is fairly free: I have often chosen words which Russell would have been likely to use had he been writing in English in preference to those which are most naturally suggested by the French. When he was an attaché at the British Embassy in Paris Russell wrote that he was having difficulty with French standards of politeness. Such difficulties are evident when he comes to close his letters to Couturat. A literal translation of his ornate endings would read absurdly in English. Generally I have tried to offer some conventionally acceptable English closing which at the same time indicates something of the tone and topic of the French. (For example, I indicate whether Couturat is thanked or esteemed or whether Mme Couturat is included in the felicitations.)

In annotating the letters I've tried to identify those persons, places, events, and literary allusions which might not be obvious to the modern reader and to provide any background information on specific points which might be helpful in understanding the letters. Inevitably, some of Russell's references escaped me. The observant reader will note that more women remain unidentified than men. This reflects their relatively greater invisibility in the reference books. Although there were many women teaching and studying at Cambridge before 1914, they were not officially members of the University and thus are excluded from standard reference sources such as Venn's *Alumni Cantabrigienses*. Others cannot be identified because we have only their family names and not their married names. I was fortunate to discover that Una Birch became Dame Una Pope-Hennessy, for example. We stand in need of a *Biographical Dictionary of Wives* – listed by maiden name.

In addition to the annotation, I've provided a linking commentary between the letters. This, I hope, will enable them to be more easily read continuously, in the sort of way that a biography is read – though, of course, no collection of letters can achieve the continuous narrative that is possible in a biography. I have used the commentary to provide information about Russell's life which is not revealed in the letters, to introduce his more important correspondents, and to give, where possible, a brief account of their side of the correspondence.

The copyright in all the letters included here is owned by the Bertrand Russell Peace Foundation, Nottingham, England. The documents used are all in the Bertrand Russell Archives, at McMaster University, Hamilton, Ontario. In some cases the Russell Archives has the original letter, in others the Archives has photocopies or microfilms. The originals which are not at the Archives are at the following locations: Russell's letters to Louis Couturat are at the Bibliothèque de la Ville, La Chaux-de-Fonds, Switzerland; his letters to G. E. Moore and Gilbert Murray are at the Bodleian Library, Oxford; his letters to Ottoline Morrell are at the Harry Ransom Humanities Research Center, University of Texas at Austin. The Archives acquired copies of most of Russell's letters to Alys Russell from Barbara Strachey; the originals of these letters are now owned by Camellia Investments, London. Russell's letters to Helen Flexner are held among the Flexner Papers by the American Philosophical Society; those to Karin Costelloe by Anne Synge; and those to Ivy Pretious by Hallam Tennyson. The London School of Economics has the originals of Russell's letters to Beatrice Webb; and Harvard University the originals of his letters to Ralph Barton Perry. Letter 112, to Frege, is reprinted by permission of the publishers from *From Frege to Godel: A Source Book in Mathematical Logic, 1879–1931* by Jean Van Meijenoort, Cambridge, Mass.: Harvard University Press copyright © 1967 by the President and Fellows of Harvard College.

A number of people have helped in the preparation of this book. Chief among them is Sheila Turcon of the Bertand Russell Archives, who not only suggested the titles for the individual volumes, but read the whole book as it was being written and provided a constant stream of comments, criticism, and advice. I have benefited very greatly from her knowledge of Russell and his papers and from the discussions I've had with her about almost every aspect of the book. Kenneth Blackwell, the Russell Archivist, though as always very busy was, as usual, never too busy to help those researching in his Archives. I apologize for the number of times I've interrupted him and thank him for his help. In trying to come to an understanding of Ottoline Morrell I was fortunate in being able to discuss her with her biographer, Miranda Seymour, who was also kind enough to send me comments on those parts of the book which deal with her. I must confess that I found Morrell a difficult subject to deal with sympathetically: she does not come across vividly in her letters to Russell and she is now obscured by generations of caricatures. Yet she must have been a striking presence and her effect on Russell was extraordinary. I doubt that I have done her justice, but I shall be pleased if I have avoided adding to the caricatures.

In the labour of typing letters and finding annotations I've had the help of a number of people working part-time and usually for short periods. It's a pleasure to thank Elaine Azzopardi, Maria Cavicchioli, Lisa Lockley, Alison Miculan, Hector Parekh, Marion Trent, and Sheena Urbansky for their uncomplaining help. Alison Miculan also checked my translations of Russell's letters to Couturat. Thanks also to Albert Lewis and Richard Rempel of the Russell Editorial Project; to the reference staff at the Mills Library, McMaster University; and to Kathy Garay of Mills Library, Research Collections. A number of people in the UK responded to my inquiries about perplexing annotations: Diana Chardin (at the Trinity College Library, Cambridge), Charles Haynes, and, again, Miranda Seymour. Janice Brent, at Allen Lane, has always been very helpful with her editorial comments and suggestions. I fear my delays have placed a great strain on her patience.

The final stages in the preparation of this book have been greatly helped by research funding from the Social Sciences and Humanities Research Council of Canada. I am happy also to thank the Toshiba Corporation for lending a laptop computer which made the transcription of letters in the Archives much easier. Another extremely valuable computer aid was the Bertrand Russell Archives Correspondence Entry and Retrieval System (BRACERS), which permits machine searching of large parts of the Archives' inventory. This became available only during the later part of my work on the book, but it still saved me a great deal of time.

Finally, thanks to Cheryl Griffin with whom I discussed a great deal of the book and who tolerated its being written and to Richard Griffin whose summer holidays were delayed while it was finished.

Troy, Ontario   Nicholas Griffin
August 1991

Introduction: Some Family Background

The first Russell to make his mark on the political life of his country was Lord William Russell, who was executed in 1683 for attempting to assassinate Charles II and his brother, the future James II, in the Rye House Plot. There is some doubt as to whether there was an assassination plot and, if there was, whether William Russell was part of it. But these doubts did not prevent his becoming a hero to his family. From his life and death they took two very important lessons: First, that it was sometimes necessary to oppose established authority by illegal means. Second, that established authorities would rarely be overscrupulous in eliminating their political enemies. No family member learnt these lessons better than Bertrand Russell, who was born nearly two hundred years after his distinguished ancestor died.

It was, however, Bertrand Russell's grandfather, Lord John Russell (1792–1878), the third son of the sixth Duke of Bedford, who for a time put the Russells at the centre of British political life. Although he was twice Prime Minister (1846–52, 1865–6), John Russell's greatest political achievements came earlier. He entered Parliament as a Whig in 1813 after an unusual education for someone of his class and time. Ill-health saved him from a public-school education, and he was sent to the University of Edinburgh, where he studied philosophy, rather than to Oxford or Cambridge, where, in those days, he might have studied nothing at all. It may have been on account of this education that he grew up with a strong sense of public duty and a relatively weak sense of solidarity with his own class. These values were reflected prominently in his political career. His first important parliamentary speech was made, characteristically enough, in opposition to a suspension of habeas corpus. In the 1830s, as one of the most radical Whigs in Lord Grey's Cabinet, he was active in helping to put through Parliament the series of great Whig reforms that transformed the political life of Britain. Among the causes he especially championed were religious freedom, public education, and the elimination of the death penalty for a large number of offences.

His greatest achievement was the Parliamentary Reform Act of 1832. He had taken up the cause of parliamentary reform as early as 1819 and in the 1820s he converted the Whigs to the idea of extending the franchise and eliminating various electoral abuses. When the Whigs came to power in 1830 he was responsible for introducing the Reform Bill in Parliament. The skill with which he steered this very controversial piece of legislation through Parliament established his political reputation.

His reforming zeal continued when the Whigs were out of office in the early 1840s. He embraced Free Trade ahead of his own party and thereby enabled Peel, the Conservative prime minister, to repeal the Corn Laws against the wishes of a good segment of his party. But when Russell took over as prime minister in 1846 his weaknesses as an administrator showed. He managed some further reforms – including factory and public-health legislation – but he was unable to continue the series of great reforms of the 1830s. Further efforts to extend the franchise failed, as did efforts to solve Ireland's land problem. Party discipline had broken over the repeal of the Corn Laws and Russell had neither the political nor the personal strength to re-establish it among the Whigs.

The Whigs were still a party of aristocrats and Russell's lack of solidarity with his class was in this case a hindrance in rallying the party behind him. Nor did he have the popular talents which could rally the people behind the party – as Palmerston or Gladstone could. He was a shy, reserved man; introspective, intellectual, and often rather remote. His best speeches were those in which he could argue his case on some point of principle. Bulwer Lytton in his poem 'The New Timon' described these occasions, when 'languid Johnny glows to glorious John'. But to be a successful prime minister required something more and something Russell was unable to muster.

In 1835 John Russell had married Lady Ribblesdale, the widow of the second Lord Ribblesdale. She had four children from her first marriage and she had two more daughters, Georgiana and Victoria, with Russell. She died in 1838 giving birth to Victoria. In 1841 Russell married again. His second wife, Bertrand Russell's grandmother, was Frances Anna Maria Elliot, the second daughter of the Earl of Minto. She was twenty-five at the time of her marriage; Lord John was forty-eight. The difference in ages, however, was only part of their vast differences in experience. Fanny Elliot had been brought up at Minto in remotest Roxburghshire where the infrequent arrival of a package of new books from London was a major event. Her first regular experience of London life came in 1835 when her father was made First Lord of the Admiralty under Lord Melbourne. Thereafter, until the fall of the Whig government, she spent part of each year in London with her father. She was rarely at ease in the capital, and was always happy to be back at Minto – the rustic pleasures of which are celebrated in her journal. She was by no means lonely there, having nine brothers and sisters.[1] Marriage to Lord John inevitably meant residence in London and seeing much less of her family. It also meant that overnight she became the stepmother of six children, ranging in ages from three to fourteen. And, last but

1. Anyone who has been keeping track of Russell's family tree so far will begin to appreciate his enormous circle of aunts, uncles, and cousins, remote members of which occasionally figure in his letters.

not least, it meant that by the time she was thirty-one she was the prime minister's wife. All this was a dramatic change for a young woman who grew up in rural Scotland with little company outside her immediate family.

She was indeed intimidated by the domestic, social and political responsibilities she had taken on. But she faced all such problems with iron will-power and an unflinching sense of public duty. Her grandson was convinced that she did not marry for love, indeed that she had never been in love. This, like all speculations of the young about the youth of their elders, deserves to be treated with some scepticism. But she does appear to have been less than ardently interested in Lord John's advances. She refused him once and received the following woeful response, similar in its line of reasoning to letters her grandson would write some seventy years later:

> I deceived myself ... from a deep sense of unhappiness, and a foolish notion that you might throw yourself away on a person of broken spirits, and worn out by time and trouble. There is nothing left to me but constant and laborious attention to public business, and a wretched sense of misery, which even the children can never long drive away.[1]

Thereafter her parents mounted a campaign on his behalf – though, to give them their due, they seemed as much impressed by his gentleness and modesty as by his excellent pedigree and political connections. Rather quickly Fanny was persuaded and the marriage took place just over nine months after her refusal had consigned him to a life of misery and public duty. For her part, she seems to have thought of her husband as something like a national monument entrusted to her care.

Frances Russell, or Lady John Russell as she came to be called, was every bit as reserved as her husband, and equally prone to introspection, melancholy and anxiety. Her journals are filled with worries about affairs of state, the fortunes of the Whigs, her husband's career, his health, the health of their children. They hardly seem a very merry pair, even before a series of personal catastrophes plunged the household into the unrelieved gloom that coloured most of Bertrand Russell's childhood.

They had four children: John, William, Rollo, and Agatha. John, Viscount Amberley, the eldest and Bertrand Russell's father, was born in 1842. He seems to have inherited a double dose of Russell melancholy from his parents. It was said that Lord John's career was spoilt by a combination of rashness and timidity. All his children inherited the timidity; only John displayed much rashness – most importantly, when he married Kate Stanley, the high-spirited daughter of the second Lord Stanley of Alderley.

The Stanley temperament was as different from that of the Russells as is possible

1. Desmond MacCarthy and Agatha Russell, *Lady John Russell* (London, 1910), p. 36.

to imagine. The Russells were shy, priggish, religious, somewhat morbid. The Stanleys were high-spirited, free-thinking extroverts. Shyness was unknown among them, and they were contemptuous of the Russell timidity and, indeed, of much else. Bertrand Russell never knew his maternal grandfather, but he came to know and fear Lord Stanley's formidable wife. He compared the two families:

> My brother, who had the Stanley temperament, loved the Stanleys and hated the Russells. I loved the Russells and feared the Stanleys. As I have grown older, however, my feelings have changed. I owe to the Russells shyness, sensitiveness, and metaphysics; to the Stanleys vigour, good health, and good spirits. (*Autobiography*, vol. I, p. 35)

Taken together it was not a bad inheritance. He also left an extraordinary account of his maternal grandmother's Sunday lunches:

> She had an enormous family of sons and daughters, most of whom came to lunch with her every Sunday. Her eldest son [Henry] was a Mohammedan and almost stone deaf. Her second son, Lyulph, was a free thinker, and spent his time fighting the Church on the London School Board. Her third son, Algernon, was a Roman Catholic priest, a Papal Chamberlain and Bishop of Emmaus. ... At the Sunday luncheons there would be vehement arguments, for among the daughters and sons-in-law there were representatives of the Church of England, Unitarianism, and Positivism, to be added to the religions represented by the sons. When the argument had reached a certain pitch of ferocity, Henry would become aware that there was a noise, and would ask what it was about. His nearest neighbour would shout a biased version of the argument into his ear, whereupon all the others would shout 'No, no, Henry, it isn't that!' At this point the din became truly terrific. .... I used to go to these luncheons in fear and trembling, since I never knew but what the whole pack would turn upon me. (*Autobiography*, vol. I, p. 34)

A daughter raised in this exuberant and hard-hitting atmosphere might seem an unlikely bride for a Russell.

Apart from his choice of wife, Amberley showed his rashness in his political opinions. He had a brief parliamentary career, which Lord John supported, sending him letters full of fatherly advice about strategy and tactics. He won a by-election for the Liberals at Nottingham, but lost his seat shortly afterwards in the general election of 1868. He then stood for South Devon the following year and this put an end to his political career for good. The previous year he had agreed to be vice-president of the London Dialectical Society, a rationalist debating society devoted to the discussion of religious and moral issues. There was already some question about Amberley's candidature on the grounds that he was not a Christian. But much worse was to follow when it became known that he had spoken at a meeting in favour of birth control. There was an immediate scandal: the press accused him of advocating 'unnatural crimes' and by the time the Bishop of Liverpool preached a sermon against him he was supposed to have advocated infanticide. Needless to say, he was defeated.

While it was certainly rash of him to speak in favour of birth control just before an election, once the damage was done, his timidity prevented him from repairing it. The personal attacks on him in the South Devon election were extremely vicious and seem to have undermined his will to continue a public life. Perhaps, as his son suggests, he was anxious all along to leave politics and devote himself to scholarship. This, at any rate, was what he did. He retired to the country to write a book on religion. The book, *An Analysis of Religious Belief*, was completed just before his death and posthumously published. In it he reveals some affinity for Buddhism and defends some form of deism.

Kate Amberley was every bit as advanced in her thinking as her husband. Free-thinking in religion, she was a feminist, active in the women's suffrage movement, and, what was rare even among feminists, an advocate of universal suffrage. Her views on sexual morality were highly unconventional. In morality she seems to have been a utilitarian; she was in any case a close friend of John Stuart Mill, and was generally well known in Victorian radical circles. She and her husband travelled to the United States in the 1860s, armed with a letter of introduction from Mill to Emerson.

Their first child, John Francis Stanley ('Frank') Russell, was born in 1865, just nine months after their marriage. In 1868, almost immediately after their return from America, she gave birth to a daughter, Rachel. Rachel was one of twins, but the other was stillborn. Their third and last child was Bertrand. It seems they used contraceptives as well as advocated them, for Bertrand Russell put his birth down to the failure of a contraceptive. Kate was so persuaded of their efficacy that she denied she was pregnant until her fifth month.

The Amberleys always lived in the country. Just after their marriage they moved into Rodborough Manor, in Gloucestershire, a house owned by Lord John. Shortly after Rachel's birth, however, Lord John decided to sell Rodborough, and the Amberleys moved to Ravenscroft, a largish eighteenth-century house near Trelleck with ten bedrooms and forty unkempt acres. The location was one of great natural beauty but extremely remote. They moved there shortly after the débâcle of the South Devon election, and one suspects Amberley relished the isolation where he could lick his political wounds. He seems to have shut himself away in Ravenscroft with his family, their servants and an eccentric collection of tutors for their children.

Though the isolation was chosen, there seems a pervasive air of melancholy about Ravenscroft, with its uncared-for plantations and unfenced kitchen garden, but for a while they were happy enough there. It was there that Bertrand was born on 18 May 1872 at 5.45 on a bitterly cold afternoon. John Stuart Mill agreed to be the secular equivalent of a godfather to him.

The Amberleys made an unconventional household for themselves. For Frank they engaged a tutor, Douglas Spalding, who secured a place in the history of ethology as a result of experiments he conducted while in the Amberleys' employment. For the sake of these experiments chickens were allowed to roam over the house, including the drawing-room and library. And in June 1874 little Rachel Russell reported to her grandmother that 'Spaldy has got robins and a hive of bees in his room' (*The Amberley Papers*, vol. ii, p. 567).

The year of Bertrand's birth saw the first of a number of calamities which now fell quickly upon the Russells. Amberley's brother, Rollo, had to give up his career in the Foreign Office on account of failing eyesight. The next year Amberley himself had a seizure of some kind, which was diagnosed as epilepsy. He seems to have recovered well enough, though his hours of work were restricted and the episode unsettled him. The year after that his other brother, William, went mad and had to be put in an asylum, where he spent the rest of his life. But worse was to follow. To help him recover from his seizure Amberley went to Italy for the winter with Kate and Frank and Spalding. Rachel and Bertrand stayed with their grandparents in London. Returning from Italy in May, Frank developed diphtheria. He was isolated in London and nursed by Kate and soon recovered. When all seemed well, they travelled back to Ravenscroft with Rachel and Bertrand. But although Frank was no longer sick, he still carried the disease and in June Rachel caught it. Four days later Kate had it too. In Kate the disease developed rapidly and the doctors were unable to control it. She died on 28 June 1874. Rachel died on 3 July.

At the first sign of the disease in Rachel, Bertrand had been removed with his nurse to a farm on the edge of the Ravenscroft estate, and he escaped unscathed. So did Amberley, but he was utterly broken in spirit. For the next eighteen months he continued to work on his book on religion. He finished the book in November 1875 with some reflections on death and the terrible fate of those who continue to live 'when the joys of life are gone'. In December 1875 he caught bronchitis and on 9 January he, too, died.

Amberley had made provision for his two surviving children to be looked after by guardians. He was anxious that his children should avoid a religious upbringing and had designated two free-thinkers, T. J. Cobden-Sanderson and the ubiquitous Spalding, as guardians. The Russells might have accepted non-Christians as guardians – they had, after all, tolerated one as a daughter-in-law. But worse skeletons than this were found in the family closet when Amberley died. Bertrand Russell described them in his *Autobiography*:

> [Spalding] was in an advanced stage of consumption and died not very long after my father. Apparently upon grounds of pure theory, my father and mother decided that although he ought to remain childless on account of his tuberculosis, it was unfair to expect him to be celibate. My mother therefore allowed him to live with her, though I know of no evidence that she derived any pleasure from doing so. This arrangement subsisted for a very short time, as it began after my birth and I was only two years old when my mother died. (Vol. I, p. 17)

The medical rationale for this arrangement escapes me, but at least part of the romantic rationale was that Spalding was in love with Kate Amberley. (So, too, for that matter, was Cobden-Sanderson, but it is not known in his case whether romantic ardour overstepped the bounds of convention.)

The Russells' horror at discovering these facts can well be imagined. Forty years later the Duke of Bedford was still destroying correspondence that might have revealed the situation. Lord and Lady Russell moved quickly to get the will overturned. Cobden-Sanderson and Spalding were told by their counsel that there was little chance they could win a case against the Russells. As a result Frank and Bertie were made wards in Chancery and brought up by their paternal grandparents.

Lord John by this time was in his eighties and had retired from active politics. He was not in line for his father's Dukedom, but in 1861 Queen Victoria had made him an Earl, the title he handed on to his grandson. Lady John, now Countess Russell, was sixty-one. They lived in Pembroke Lodge, in Richmond Park, a house owned by the Queen but which she had lent to them since 1847. The house was a rambling, two-storey, eighteenth-century building with many additions set in eleven acres of grounds. To the west it had a commanding view from the Epsom Downs to Windsor Castle. It was there that Bertrand Russell spent his childhood and adolescence. 'Throughout the years during which I lived at Pembroke Lodge', he wrote, 'the garden was growing gradually more and more neglected. Big trees fell, shrubs grew over the paths, the grass on the lawns became long and rank, and the box-hedges grew almost into trees. The garden seemed to remember the days of its former splendour, when foreign ambassadors paced its lawns, and princes admired its trim beds of flowers. It lived in the past, and I lived in the past with it' (*Autobiography*, vol. I, p. 19).

Frank Russell, always an intractable child, had been sent off to Winchester by his parents. He continued there and was seen at Pembroke Lodge only during the school holidays. Bertie, however, had been his grandmother's favourite ever since he was a baby and she decided that she would bring him up at Pembroke Lodge herself with the help of a succession of tutors. Bertie remembered his grandfather only as an extremely old man, being wheeled around the garden in a bathchair or reading Hansard in his study. He died in 1878. Russell's grandmother was therefore the most important person in his early life. She had, in fact, very definite plans for him. He was made very much aware that he was the heir to the Liberal tradition and that this meant a life unselfishly devoted to public service. She expected him to take up a political career, and was deeply upset when he took up philosophy instead. It may very well have been, as George Santayana suspected, that she was training him to become prime minister, and given the family's position, it was hardly an absurd ambition.

Russell left a lengthy account of his grandmother in his *Autobiography*:

> She was a Scotch Presbyterian, Liberal in politics and religion (she became a Unitarian at the age of seventy), but extremely strict in all matters of morality. ... As a mother and a grandmother she was deeply, but not always wisely, solicitous. I do not think she ever understood the claims of animal spirits and exuberant vitality. She demanded that everything should be viewed through a mist of Victorian sentiment. ... Of psychology in the modern sense, she had, of course, no vestige. Certain motives were known to exist: love of country, public spirit, love of one's children, were laudable motives; love of money, love of power, vanity, were bad motives. ... Marriage was a puzzling institution. It was clearly the duty of husbands and wives to love one another, but it was a duty they ought not to perform too easily, for if sex attraction drew them together there must be something not quite nice about them. ... She disliked wine, abhorred tobacco, and was always on the verge of becoming a vegetarian. Her life was austere. She ate only the plainest food, breakfasted at eight, and until she reached the age of eighty, never sat in a comfortable chair until after tea. She was completely unworldly, and despised those who thought anything of worldly honours. (Vol. I, pp. 20–22)

Russell complained about her intellectual limitations, and no doubt her knowledge was limited. But her letters reveal a sharp, shrewd mind and a terse, elegant, occasionally cutting turn of phrase not unlike that of her grandson.

Her recent life, when Bertie moved to Pembroke Lodge, had been tragic. One son dead, another incurably insane, and a third unable to hold a job because of failing eyesight. Her daughter, the youngest of her four children, would later show signs of mental instability as well. Her husband died two years later. The things that had given her joy in life were all in the past. Frank was despaired of. Bertie was her only hope for the future and she put all her still considerable energies into his upbringing.

As a child he adored her, and he absorbed many of her values. But in the elderly atmosphere and isolation of Pembroke Lodge, surrounded by his grandmother's cloying and often manipulative devotion, he became a lonely and morbidly introspective child and a lonelier and even more morbid adolescent.

1. CHILDHOOD AND YOUTH

(1884–93)

The earliest of Russell's letters to have survived are three to his brother, Frank, written in 1884, the third of which is printed below. It was written while Russell was staying near his Uncle Rollo's house, Dunrozel, at Hindhead on the Surrey–Sussex border. Each summer during Russell's childhood, he and other members of the Pembroke Lodge household would spend three months at Hindhead. Rollo Russell (1849–1914) was Lord John Russell's third son. 'Auntie', Lady Agatha Russell (1853–1933), was Lord John's youngest daughter. Her engagement, to which Russell refers, was broken off when she became subject to insane delusions. She lived at Pembroke Lodge, a victim of her mother's virtue according to Russell (*Autobiography*, vol. i, p. 26).

[1]

Oeborne, Fernhurst,
Sussex
14 September 1884

My dear Frank

Granny told me I'd better write to you whilst I was heare [*sic*] at Oeborne. I came here on Monday and I'm going home again today. What do you think of Auntie's engagement? I can't bear it of course. Auntie says one ought to think of it as one more person to love, but then Auntie will go away.

Last Saturday Uncle Rollo, M. Rochat[1] and I went to the Isle of Wight; it was very nice indeed there. We started by the 10.49 from Haslemere, and got to Ryde, and from there we went to Bembridge, which is very pretty. We went to the sea-shore, where the tide was coming in very fast. Then we went to see the Roman Villa which was very interesting. There were big nails and beautiful mosaics and broken vases, and the skelletons [*sic*] of a Roman and a horse, found in an old well near there, and supposed to have been thrown in by the Britons when the Romans were leaving at the same time that they burnt the villa. Uncle Rollo has had all his potatoes dug up;

1. Bertie's Swiss tutor. Frank described him in his diary as 'an ungainly Swiss youth'.

there are a frightful lot. He's only going to keep two pigeons for the future, which is a great pity.

   Goodbye
      Your loving brother,
         Bertie

Of all the members of his family it was Uncle Rollo for whom Russell as a child had the greatest affinity. Russell's biographer describes him as 'an amiable and uncomplaining man' (Clark, *Russell*, p. 34). Rollo lived mainly at Pembroke Lodge from 1886, after the death of his first wife, until he remarried in 1891. He had given up a career in the Foreign Office owing to poor eyesight, and thereafter spent his time as an amateur scientist. He published a number of books on meteorology and medical matters, as well as the book of poems, *Break of Day*, which Russell refers to in letter 6. Like that of many Victorian amateurs, his work was well respected and he had contacts with some of the leading scientists of his day. He took Bertie to meet the physicist John Tyndall, for example. Rollo Russell's encouragement during the years he lived at Pembroke Lodge helped shape his nephew's scientific interests.

Despite their closeness, Russell's letters to his uncle seem curiously stilted. In part this must have been due to his age and the Victorian rigidity of family relations at Pembroke Lodge. In part, however, it was the result of the excessive shyness of both correspondents. All his life, according to Russell, Rollo suffered from 'a morbid shyness so intense as to prevent him from achieving anything that involved contact with other human beings' (*Autobiography*, vol. i, p. 24). Bertie's shyness, by contrast, was overcome once he had left Pembroke Lodge.

Russell's first letter to his uncle was written shortly after his thirteenth birthday. Rollo was then living at Dunrozel with his first wife, Alice Sophia. It gives a brief glimpse of Russell's daily life at Pembroke Lodge with his tutors. Mr Quirke was attempting to teach Russell to play the violin.

[2]

Pembroke Lodge
7 June 1885

Dear Uncle Rollo

   We got here all right on Thursday, in time for tea, and found that Mr Marshall, the new tutor, had already come. He seems very nice indeed. We had some lawn-tennis the day before yesterday, but yesterday it was so wet that the lines have almost entirely disappeared. He plays very well. I believe he's got about half a dozen silver cups which he got for matches. In three sets I didn't win a single game.

Have you seen any more adders? or found any lark's nests. The things in my kitchen garden are doing very well, the rain yesterday brought them forward immensely.

I hope Andrews will be able to catch the two hens soon, because otherwise I'm afraid they won't breed here at all this year.

Mr Quirke came yesterday, and he thinks I have fallen back seriously from not practising for so long.

There is not time to write any more as it's time to go to church. Please give my love to Aunt Alice.

Your loving nephew
Bertie

Russell's Christmas letter of 1886 introduces various members of his family for the first time. 'Grandmamma Stanley' was Russell's maternal grandmother, Henrietta Maria, Lady Stanley of Alderley (1807–95). She lived with her unmarried daughter, Maude, in a large house on Dover Street in London. She was a rather intimidating personage to the young Russell, who later described his desperate efforts to make a good impression on her. The only occasion on which they were successful was when he asked her for a copy of *Tristram Shandy* as a birthday present. On one occasion she sighed in despair, 'I have no intelligent grandchildren' (*Autobiography*, vol. I, pp. 32–3). 'Granny', Lady Frances Anna Maria Elliot, the dowager Countess Russell (1815–98), was Russell's other grandmother, Lord John Russell's second wife. She was mainly responsible for Russell's upbringing at Pembroke Lodge. Russell described her as 'Liberal in politics and religion . . . but extremely strict in all matters of morality' (*Autobiography*, vol. I, p. 20).

Rollo Russell's wife had died earlier in the year giving birth to a son, Arthur Russell (1886–1943). Rollo, together with his son, always referred to at this time as 'Baby', had moved back to live in Pembroke Lodge. At the time the letter was written, Rollo was evidently holidaying in Nice.

[3]

Pembroke Lodge
Christmas 1886

Dear Uncle Rollo

My letter will be too late to wish you a merry Christmas, but I will wish you a happy New Year. I am very sorry I never saw you to say goodbye; I did not know you were going till I was at Dover Street. I suppose it is very warm at Nice, isn't it? We have had skating here; to-day it is a splendid morning with a west wind and a hoar frost on the ground.

Jemmie[1] has gone home to Yorkshire for his holidays, and Ernest[2] stayed here a few days. Mr Ewen[3] has gone to Plymouth for a fortnight's holiday, so I am alone in the schoolroom. Auntie has given me a splendid book, called *A Child of the Revolution*, by the author of the *Atelier du Lys*.[4] Grandmamma Stanley gave me a Shakespeare, one in small volumes in a case; about as fine an edition as possible. Wasn't that a magnificent present?

Neither Granny nor Auntie has caught cold, in spite of the cold weather.

My examination finished on Friday,[5] and I have holidays now till Mr Ewen comes home, which is a very pleasant change.

It is curious how few holly-berries there are this year; I don't think I have seen one about the place. There are very few decorations about the house this year; I haven't even decorated the schoolroom, I didn't think about doing it till this morning.

It is a pity they are so slow telling one about the result of the Exam; they don't let one know till March; by that time all the excitement is over. It is time to get ready for church now, so goodbye

Your loving
Bertrand Russell

P.S. Baby is very flourishing, and has learnt a lot of tricks, such as blowing

1. James Hugh ('Jimmie') Baillie (1872–1956), one of Russell's few childhood friends. He used to stay at Pembroke Lodge, where he attended classes with Russell. Russell kept in touch with him in later years, visiting him in Vancouver in 1929 and corresponding with his family into the 1960s.
2. Ernest Logan, another friend who had attended Russell's kindergarten at Pembroke Lodge. Russell had learnt the facts of life from him a few years earlier.
3. John F. Ewen was the most sympathetic of Russell's tutors. From him Russell learnt for the first time of Karl Marx and non-Euclidean geometry. He had left by 1888, probably because he was thought to be undermining Russell's religious faith.
4. Margaret Roberts, a popular novelist of the time.
5. It is not clear what examinations these were.

the candle when he's told, clapping his hands, and a lot of things like that. I think blowing the candle is quite a new thing.

Aunt Agatha twice took Russell to visit Ireland, where he remembered going for walks with Michael Davitt, the nationalist leader who founded the Irish Land League. Russell's letter to his uncle from Ireland shows an entirely conventional interest in the scenery and a more unconventional interest in the politics of the country, then entering a phase of repression after the defeat of Gladstone's first Home Rule bill. It says much for the advanced political opinions of Pembroke Lodge that Auntie should want to play Irish revolutionary songs on the piano.

Powerscourt, in County Wicklow just south of Dublin, was a large estate, originally the site of a castle, but in 1887 occupied by a fine eighteenth-century mansion. The Dargle, a mountain stream that bounds the property, flows over a 400-ft cliff in the deer park to form one of the highest single-drop waterfalls in the British Isles.

[4]

Breslin's Hotel
7 August 1887

Dear Uncle Rollo

I have just got Granny's letter; please thank her very much for it. I think Auntie is going to write to her to-day.

We have had most lovely weather ever since we came, and it has never been too hot because of the sea.

Yesterday we drove to Powerscourt, which is a most lovely place. It began by a few drops of rain in the morning, but our usual driver was perfectly certain it would be fine, so we risked it, and it turned out a perfect day. There is a most splendid waterfall, where the Dargle falls a tremendous height over the rocks. We had our luncheon close to the waterfall, and were immediately surrounded by wasps, which didn't prevent our enjoying it immensely. Powerscourt is an immense place, that took us about an hour to drive through. It is full of most beautiful trees, with high hills, wooded right up to the top. On our way home, I got out and walked by a short cut through a most lovely wood, with the Dargle flowing at the bottom of it. There is a great deal of fine scenery about here, and it changes very suddenly from woods to wild rocky precipices, which is quite a different kind of beauty.

Granny says Caractacus[1] has grown very savage, which I am very sorry for; I wonder why he should take to biting, as he never used to. I suppose he isn't ridable now, is he?

We daren't talk Home Rule in the Hotel, as everybody, especially Mrs Breslin, seems to be very much against it. Auntie would like to play the Wearing of the Green, as we have a Piano here, only she is too much afraid of Mrs Breslin. She makes up for it by talks with our driver, who quite forgets about his horse and everything when he's having a conversation. Luckily it's a very quiet horse, that goes on quite steadily by itself. He doesn't think Home Rule will ever pass, but he has curious ideas of the good it will do if it does. All the pigs, cattle, etc. are to stay in the country, instead of being exported to England and America. He seems to think that the chief advantage of it.

Your letter to Port Rush arrived some days ago, but Granny's never came, though Auntie wrote to Port Rush to forward letters. Auntie thinks Granny must have left it in her blotting book, or done something like that.

This is a splendid place for bathing; they don't have bathing-machines all along the sand, but special places where one gets a box, and where they have planking all out into the sea to dive off. The men's place is in a little bay, where one is sheltered from the wind and the waves, and can swim very easily.

I have got a good way into *Castle Daly*,[2] which I like more and more. I have been reading *Midsummer Night's Dream* over again too; I don't think I like it quite as well as *Julius Caesar*.

Auntie wants to know if you have read of the meeting of the Landlords at Omagh; there is a lot about it in the Irish Papers.[3]

Auntie says, once for all, that she is as well as possible. If she'd thought you wanted to know how she looked, she would have had her photograph taken at the waterfall. I think she does look very well.

Your loving
　　Bertie

---

1. Caractacus was a donkey which had been Russell's pet at Pembroke Lodge. There is a picture in the Russell Archives of Russell as a small boy riding him.
2. A novel set in Ireland by the popular Victorian novelist Annie Keary.
3. *The Times*, at any rate, did not report it. In all probability it was a meeting called to protest at the passage in July 1887 of an Irish Land bill that made a number of concessions to the nationalists.

Very few of Russell's letters to Granny have survived, although it seems clear that his correspondence with her from Cambridge was both frequent and detailed. The following letter was written towards the end of Russell's second year. Some of the friends mentioned in it will appear more fully in later letters.

The Apostles were the prestigious, secret discussion group officially known as the Cambridge Conversazione Society. Its members often referred to it simply as 'The Society'. Russell had been elected to membership on 27 February 1892 and associated the Apostles with the 'greatest happiness of [his] time at Cambridge' (*Autobiography*, vol. i, p. 68). C. P. Sanger, G. L. Dickinson, and J. M. E. McTaggart were all members. The *Cambridge Observer* was a student newspaper with which Russell was involved along with some of his friends, including Sanger and Arthur George Tansley (1871–1955), who later became Professor of Botany at Oxford. The newspaper ran for twenty-one issues, published over three terms. It is not clear what, if anything, Russell wrote for it, since most articles were published anonymously. A review of *The Doll's House* did appear in the second issue over the initial 'M.', probably the work of one of Russell's friends, Stanley Victor Makower. Russell may or may not have had a hand in it. The Decemviri cannot be identified.

[5]

Trinity College
1 May 1892

Dearest Granny

What a glorious May-Day it has been! Quite an ideal one here, warm and springy and every way delightful. I hope the Anarchists have not been doing anything horrible in Paris[1] on such a day.

We have been quite busy getting ready the first number of the *Cambridge Observer*, though I personally have done very little beyond discussing a prospectus and sundry articles written by other people. I will certainly order it to be sent to you, as it will very likely not run more than a term you will not have much time to bear it.

I have been doing a fair amount of work, but not really much; I have also been out a great deal except on the afternoons when I have had to go to the dentist, who will I hope have finished in a week or two.

Sanger[2] is back now and is very interesting with the accounts of his

1. 'Anarchist outrages' were widely anticipated at the May Day demonstrations in Paris that year. None eventuated, however.
2. Charles Percy Sanger (1871–1930), one of Russell's close Cambridge friends. Like Russell, he was studying for part one of the Mathematical Tripos, but he switched to economics in his fourth year. A man of very diverse interests, he became a barrister.

Spanish travels in the Vac., as Spain is a country that quite few people go to and which I gather from him to be very uncivilized. He read a paper to the Apostles last night trying to make science independent of metaphysics but everybody present disagreed with him, and Dickinson,[1] a King's Don, finally demolished him even in his own (Sanger's) estimation. It was lucky for Sanger that McTaggart[2] is in Australia or he would probably have conclusively disproved Sanger's existence or done something equally frightful. – I have just been elected to the Trinity Tennis Club so I hope I shall play a good deal this term; all the Decemviri almost belong and play often.

Yesterday afternoon I went to town with Sanger and Tansley to see Ibsen's *Doll's House*, ostensibly for the purpose of criticizing it in our paper. I was prepared to dislike the play, but in spite of very bad acting I thought it powerful though full of faults. – A joint-stock criticism will probably be found in our 2nd number. (By the way, the terminal subscription is 3s. 6d. this term.)

Please tell Auntie the country here is charming just now; there are delightful woods full of flowers and birds, and nightingales in every hedge. But very soon we shall have the invasion of smart ladies, who are already beginning to appear in small numbers. – I hope you and Auntie are well and are having as delightful weather as we are.

Your affectionate grandson
Bertrand Russell

Russell sat his final examinations in mathematics, part one of the Mathematical Tripos, in May and June 1893. The examination papers of part one were divided into two groups: the first seven over a four-day period in May, followed, after an eleven-day break, by a further seven papers over a four-day period in June. The examinations, like the three years of coaching which led up to them, were extremely arduous. The next letter was written during the break between the two sets of papers. Russell was too pessimistic about his prospects: he was bracketed seventh Wrangler, the first of the three honours divisions. (All students were ranked in strict order of merit.)

'Aunt Gertrude' is Rollo's second wife, Gertrude Ellen Cornelia Joachim, a sister

1. Goldsworthy Lowes Dickinson (1862–1932), a classics don and man of letters who wrote widely on historical and political topics. He was among the so-called 'new dons' who brought about reform in nineteenth-century Cambridge.
2. John McTaggart Ellis McTaggart (1866–1925), recently elected a Fellow of Trinity, was just beginning a distinguished career as Cambridge's most important neo-Hegelian philosopher. He was the leading figure in the Apostles at this time.

of the Oxford Idealist philosopher Harold Joachim. They married in 1891 and went to live in Rollo's house, Dunrozel, at Hindhead.

[6]

Trinity College
21 May 1893

My dear Uncle Rollo

I hardly know how to thank you for your letter: it is so much too kind, so much kinder than I deserve. I can only hope and endeavour to be worthier of it in the future. – I think I am less morbidly introspective than I used to be; I have my time so much busier and more occupied than I used to that my thoughts are perhaps too much taken up with the work or pleasure of the moment; but I still try to know myself as well as I can, both for the sake of my own improvement and because I think it leads to a better understanding of, and a readier sympathy with, other people.

I have just come back from home where I spent two nights after finishing the 1st half of my Tripos. I found Auntie very far from recovered in mind, though in body she seems much better than before she went. But it is terrible how almost impossible any effort of mind seems to be to her still. – Granny is not at all strong yet, but will I hope be well again soon especially as Auntie is home again. – I found at home to my very great surprise a book of poems![1] What a secret you kept it! I read several of them with Granny and was extremely struck with them.

I would have written to you before this term only that I have been so exceedingly busy, working for my Tripos. I have had hardly any opportunity of comparing myself with the others in the 1st 3½ days, but as far as I can tell I have done about as I expected to do. I have still a week's hard work and then the 2nd 3½ days which is the really important part, the 1st being more or less elementary. I have no notion where I ought to be, except that I am not likely to be in the 1st 10.

I hope you and Aunt Gertrude are well. I had a letter from Arthur the other day: please give him my love and say I will write to him when I am not quite so busy.

Your affectionate nephew
Bertrand Russell

1. Presumably Rollo's *Break of Day*, just published.

2. ENGAGEMENT

(1893–4)

In 1889 Rollo had taken Bertie to visit some American neighbours of his near Hindhead. These were Robert and Hannah Pearsall Smith, rich Philadelphia Quakers who had been well known on both sides of the Atlantic as evangelical crusaders. In 1875 Robert's crusading days came to an abrupt end when he became the centre of a full-blown, widely publicized sex scandal – the result, apparently, of too literal an interpretation of St Paul's injunction to 'salute one another with a holy kiss'– which forced the family to return to America. By the 1880s, however, the scandal had died down enough to permit them to return to Britain, where they leased a large estate, Friday's Hill, between Fernhurst and Haslemere in Surrey. They had three children: The eldest, Mary, known in the family by her nickname 'Mariechen', was married to Frank Costelloe, an Irish barrister with political aspirations and philosophical interests. But in 1891 she startled the family by going off to Italy with Bernhard Berenson,[1] whom she married after Frank's early death in 1899. The second, Logan, became a literary connoisseur and stylist. In 1891 he graduated from Oxford and for the next few years spent his summers at Friday's Hill and his winters in Paris. Alys, although the youngest of the three, was still five years older than Russell. She was unattached and devoted to good works of various kinds, including temperance reform, feminism, and social work. Her seriousness and reticence, which contrasted with Mary's flamboyance, made a favourable impression on the priggish young Russell. He was also impressed by her independence, for she had been to college, crossed the Atlantic alone, and had her own work in the various social causes she supported. She was also kind to the extremely shy and awkward seventeen-year-old Russell.

By Russell's own account it was love at first sight (*Autobiography*, vol. i, p. 76). But, despite the fact that he made weekly visits to Friday's Hill during the summer months he spent at Dunrozel, he seems to have made no move to gain her affections until the summer of 1893. The reasons are not far to find. Russell must have realized that any romantic involvement on his part could hardly find favour with his family. In May 1893, however, he turned twenty-one. This brought him not only legal independence – making marriage against his grandmother's will a possibility – but financial independence as well. From his father's estate he inherited £20,000, a sum which brought in £600 a year, quite enough for a couple with modest needs to live

1. Berenson patriotically dropped the 'h' in 'Bernhard' during the First World War.

on comfortably. Within a month, Russell had started a correspondence with Alys and in December 1894 they were married.

His first letter gives little indication of his feelings. The fact that he couldn't have lunch with Alys because of Granny's demands is an indication of things to come.

[7]

Pembroke Lodge
11 June 1893

Dear Alys

I wish it were my duty to come to luncheon tomorrow but alas this is one of the cases where enlightened self-interest and universalistic hedonism part company: I must therefore stay at home and read Wordsworth's 'Excursion' to my grandmother who is in bed and unable to read much to herself. The same remark applies to Sunday; and indeed to all days until I go away again to work. There is therefore no likelihood of my seeing you again till September, unless you and Logan renew your visit to Cambridge, when you will find everybody very staid and sober and no sign of a drunkard anywhere; (or unless I could get away from Cambridge for a day or two). The former of these propositions is to be reflected upon.

Yours very sincerely,
Bertrand Russell

The results of Russell's Mathematical Tripos were announced in June. The relentless grind of part one had got him down, as the next letter indicates. In old age he was more forthright: he had come, he said, to think mathematics 'disgusting', 'a set of clever tricks by which to pile up marks in the Tripos' (*My Philosophical Development*, p. 38). Thus, instead of continuing with part two of the Mathematical Tripos, he turned in his fourth year to study philosophy for part two of the Moral Sciences Tripos. He spent the long vacation of 1893 at Cambridge reading philosophy and attending Henry Sidgwick's lectures on ethics. It is clear that he took to his new work with enthusiasm.

[8]

Trinity College
16 July 1893

My dear Uncle Rollo

I was very much ashamed when I got your letter to find I had forgotten your birthday: I remembered it a few days before and had been going to write you but somehow forgot at the right time. It is true we meet terribly seldom now: I do wish you would come someday to Cambridge: the Long [Vacation] would be just the best possible time: any Saturday to Monday you could spare, or any other time if that is impossible to you, would be delightful for me. I could put you up in College if you would like. Besides you have never seen my present rooms, which are very different from my old ones.

I am very glad you are going to read *Brand*: I think with the exception of the last act which seems to me almost unmeaning it is the greatest play of Ibsen's I know: and in parts is really as great as anything could be. I read it to Granny lately and she thought it wonderful too. – I hope I shall be able to come to Dunrozel sometime in September: I should like to do so very much if I can.

It is delightful doing work that I really like, as it was some time since I had ceased to care much for Mathematics. But a year seems a hopelessly short time to get through so much reading, especially as it is impossible to read many hours a day with profit because one has to let what has been read soak in and get absorbed, which is a slow process.

It was splendid in the Lakes: brilliant sunshine every day, nice walks over the hills taking one down to Ullswater and other Lakes. But it is very nice here too as almost all my friends are up. I *do* hope you will come some day.

I hope Arthur still gets on with his German governess and begins to get on with his German.

Your affectionate nephew
Bertrand Russell

Russell's hopes in letter 7 that Alys would visit him in Cambridge were fulfilled. In fact, she came twice, accompanied by a cousin as chaperon. The first visit seems to have been at the time his Tripos was announced; the second took place on 11–12 August. Russell's rather awkward excitement about the second visit is clearly evident in the following letter, both in the fussiness with which he plans the details and the absurd confusion over her accommodation. The letter has a long postscript (deleted here) correcting some misapprehension that had arisen regarding his views on sexual relations. The exact nature and cause of the misunderstanding cannot be identified, and the postscript indicates mainly the difficulty Russell found in making his personal feelings clear without giving offence – of which there will be much other evidence later. (Russell was so pessimistic about his chances of success with Alys, that he destroyed her first letters to him, feeling that to keep them would be to indulge a futile passion.)

'The Amoi' (Russell's fanciful Greek plural of 'Amos') comprised Maurice Sheldon Amos, his sister Bonté, and their mother. Maurice was studying Moral Science at Cambridge and was introduced to Russell by Alys's brother, Logan. Russell described him as 'my only link between Cambridge and Friday's Hill' (*Autobiography*, vol. I, p. 141). Mrs Amos knew Alys's mother through their common interest in religion and social work.

[9]

Trinity College
9 August 1893

Dear Alys

I am delighted you are coming. I have got lodgings for you in Trinity Street which I think ought to be fairly convenient but I was unable to get a room with two beds except at the Hotel where I thought you would very likely prefer not to be. I hope you will arrive to luncheon as then it will be possible to spend the afternoon on the river and get up to where it gets nice which otherwise would be impossible. Could you wire and let me know if you would like me to ask the Amoi to lunch and go up the river or not? One word, yes or no, would do. Or if not would you like to see them some other time and when. I would suggest the following trains.

Liverpool St	11.00–11.55
Cambridge	12.17–1.15
St Pancras	12.50
Cambridge	1.25
King's Cross	11.10–12.40
Cambridge	12.30–2.00

No later trains to be considered. My valuable time is valueless just now as I have done so much work already that I am grown incapable of any more for some time and want cheering up. You will find me in deep despair I assure you. So I must hope as it is my valuable time which is your consideration that you will not be so unkind as to consider it.

Yours very sincerely,
Bertrand Russell

P.S. On reading your letter over again I find it is at the Hotel you want rooms but I hope you will not greatly mind their being lodgings. I had a notion you had said lodgings in your letter.

In his diary Russell described Alys's visit to Cambridge on 12 August 1893 as 'the greatest day of my life hitherto' (*Papers*, vol. I, p. 62). He had persuaded her to stay on after her chaperon had left and they went alone on the river where they discussed love and marriage for the first time, though still in completely general terms. To facilitate discussion he had given her a little essay about marriage designed to prove that two people in a situation very much like theirs ought to marry in order to further the liberal tradition. In her letter of 16 August Alys had included a short reply, the 'paper' Russell refers to in the next letter, in which she argued in general terms against marriage and in favour of independence for women. Russell had argued that marriage and childbearing might interrupt a woman's work for ten years, but this time would not be wasted since it would be spent rearing the next generation of advanced liberals. Alys replied that women had hardly yet begun to make their mark in the world and could not afford a ten-year delay. In the next letter Russell counters with considerations drawn from political economy and neo-Hegelian metaphysics, but he did not write another paper. 'How absurd it would seem', he wrote (with some justice) in his diary, ' . . . to have to argue and argue on a question of social ethics before acquiring the minutest right to speak of one's own feelings!' (*Papers*, vol. I, p. 62).

[10]

Penrhos, Holyhead[1]
19 August 1893

Dear Alys

I was very glad of your letter and paper. I cannot write an answer to the latter till I get away from this conventional atmosphere. I should be too harsh upon conventional views if I wrote from here: besides I am unable to keep my moral sense untroubled in a place where virtue is identified with respectability.

I have however been thinking a great deal of what you said about independence: as a motive it is of course a non-moral one and might be overcome as you said by the non-moral motive of falling in love. But as an

1. Penrhos, on the Anglesey coast, was the second country home of Russell's uncle, Lyulph Stanley.

ideal, I am convinced it cannot stand a moment: in the practical regulation of one's life it occupies the same position in relation to the higher ideal that *laissez faire* did in relation to Socialism; that the individualist philosophy of last century does to the modern, which regards the only reality as Spirit, and the whole universe as a unity of spirits connected as the members of the body are in working together for a common end. I agree with all you say about the impossibility of love subsisting without immense mutual sacrifice: but no more can anything of value in itself. Where people have been moral and therefore accustomed to the daily and hourly renunciation of their desires for the sake of virtue only, perhaps either unknown to their companions or contrary to their judgment; surely in such a case it cannot be very hard to do so for the preservation of the one thing that makes life valuable from a selfish point of view.

It is a dangerous fallacy to suppose virtue an end in itself: virtue is the necessary means to the best ends, but is not itself an end. In McTaggart's pamphlet which I was looking for[1] he says (and proves) that there can be no virtue in heaven: 'Virtue like all other vices will have to be left outside the door of heaven.' I will write an answer to your paper if I can find arguments against it which would not be a repetition of the old ones. I stay here till August 25th.

Yours ever,
Bertrand Russell

On 13 September Russell had gone to stay for two days with Alys's family at Friday's Hill. On this occasion they had managed at last to speak of their personal feelings. Although Alys had continued officially to resist the idea of marriage, she had none the less given a number of encouraging hints in letters and conversation. Indeed, had she not, it is difficult to see how anything would have been accomplished. While at Friday's Hill Russell had got as far as a proposal which was neither accepted nor rejected. They did agree, however, to see each other more frequently and to have what they described as an 'intimate friendship', although (as the next letter shows) the distinction between this and an engagement was not always easy to explain to others. Indeed, explaining their relationship to members of their respective

---

1. *The Further Determination of the Absolute* (privately printed, 1893). McTaggart there argues that the Absolute is a system of spirits united by bonds of love. Russell had wanted to show Alys the pamphlet when she was in Cambridge but was unable to find it. At this time, Russell was just beginning to come under the influence of McTaggart's neo-Hegelian philosophy.

families was the cause of some difficulty. Alys's mother seems to have accepted the situation with equanimity, but Granny embarked upon a long campaign against their relationship which continued to the very eve of their marriage. In his *Autobiography* Russell gives a more ferocious account of his interview with Granny after his return from Friday's Hill (perhaps running together a number of such meetings):

> When I came home, I told my people what had occurred, and they reacted according to the stereotyped convention. They said she was no lady, a baby-snatcher, a low-class adventuress, a designing female taking advantage of my inexperience, a person incapable of all the finer feelings, a woman whose vulgarity would perpetually put me to shame. (*Autobiography*, vol. I, p. 82)

The contrast between this account, the accuracy of which is borne out by several later letters, and the account Russell gives in his next letter to Alys, indicates rather poignantly the way his loyalties were divided.

The reference to 'Walt' indicates another, less serious, difficulty. With his previous letter Russell had enclosed two extracts from Walt Whitman's *Leaves of Grass*: the first, from 'One Hour to Madness and Joy', an exuberant but, by Whitman's standards, none too explicit declaration of sexual love; the second, from 'Out of the Rolling Ocean the Crowd', was gentler and more resigned to separation. Alys's response was not encouraging: she much preferred the second to the first. Russell had described the first as true but immoral. He now had to withdraw the first part of this opinion, since Alys thought the passage expressed only abandonment to passion. Alys knew and corresponded with Whitman and took Russell to see his house when they visited the United States in 1896.

Another potential problem was Russell's need to confess some past mis-demeanour – his 'last and bitterest duty'. He did so when they met on 5 October. It is not clear what he had to confess but, to judge from Alys's letter of that date, its disclosure was an anticlimax. (See also letter 12 below.)

Russell's hopes of seeing more of Alys, at least in the immediate future, were somewhat dampened by the fact that, on the day he proposed to her, she received an invitation from Lady Henry Somerset to travel with her to a temperance convention in Chicago. Alys was much involved in temperance work and undertook the journey, although for some time it was not clear whether she would go or not. Lady Isabel Caroline Somers, daughter of the third Earl Somers, was born in 1851. After a scandalous divorce from Lord Henry Somerset whom she had married in 1872, she took up temperance work and became president of the British Women's Temperance Association, a Christian organization of which Hannah Pearsall Smith was treasurer. Lady Henry had known Russell's parents about the time he was born. Alys formed a close attachment to her.

[11]

Pembroke Lodge
21 September 1893

Dear Alys

Your letter arrived at supper, and my grandmother's enquiring who it was from formed a good opening for the conversation. As soon as my uncle was gone to see my Aunt Gertrude I told her. She is really too entirely wonderful and saint-like. I never before felt her goodness so much. She was of course a good deal pained but she did not utter one word of reproof or for a moment suggest the slightest blame to either of us. She said (to which I heartily agreed) that I was much too young to be engaged yet: she took exactly the opposite view from your mother's that if we meet and correspond often it is as good as an engagement: I tried to explain but found it impossible. I saw she thought you also were in love and I hardly dare explicitly undeceive her as I saw she would probably blame you if I did and that I couldn't have stood. I told her several times there was more affection on my side but I believe she thought that mere modesty, particularly as I had begun saying (was I not justified?) that we were both fond of each other: thinking to avoid the word love, but of course she did not observe the shade of difference. You remember we had determined to emphasize the difference as little as possible and throughout I never mentioned love. She told me, what I was greatly astonished to hear, that she had had a somewhat similar experience with my father, though nothing had then been said of love, and she had died. She said we were already very intimate and didn't need to know each other any better for our purposes, but when I said I felt it my duty to do otherwise she said no more. She is going to tell my uncle tomorrow and of course to write to your mother. She repeated all that she had said before and how she thought we ought not to write and meet regularly (which shows how completely unable she was to understand the situation), finally she promised never to say another word against our doings and I am happy to say never once doubted the morality of our motives. I gather she will neither help nor hinder our meeting.

The talk was painful, but I felt that no one was to blame, which made it much less so than it might have been; and the same feeling made her *much* less unhappy than she might have been: particularly as I assured her that it was at least as likely as not it would never come to marriage and if it did, at any rate not for many years. I feel *much* happier now all is in the open.

There was only one thing which was amusing, but that too had its sting: she said she had hoped Harold Russell[1] would have saved me from that danger! He of all people! I am very glad of what you tell me about your mother; but as for my caring less I don't think that is likely. You see I really have known you fairly well longer than you have me because there was all the time when I was shy and silent and the whole time I bottled up most of my thoughts because I couldn't help it.

I am glad you don't like the Walt: I don't either. It was really rather an excess of honesty to represent it as expressing what my feelings had ever been; but in any case I cannot see why one should be ashamed of any feeling which has not got the better of one's reason; it seems to me the stronger it is the more glad one should be to have conquered it and have made it help (as every conquered feeling does) to the formation of a stable character. Such intensity and concentration is scarcely likely to occur often so that one may feel a certain confidence of being always able to act reasonably.

The other quotation was pointed out to me by Logan: there is a resignation about it which I scarcely even can bring myself to wish to aspire to – though it is sublime.

I hope you will not be too much afraid of trusting your feelings: you know you have years and years to test them in and I shall never for an instant, however you may be, forget that one termination of our friendship is quite as likely as the other.

It would be hopeless to sacrifice an iota of your honesty for my grandmother's sake: besides I think the opportunity will not often occur. But she will never object to our meeting as much as we wish, as she knows I think it right. Bohemianism and river trips are not likely to commend themselves to our elders[2] and if there were ever a chance of meeting acquaintances it would be to be avoided: short of that I see only good in it; besides it ought to be allowable and someone must begin.

I should have been furious too about vaccination: it is the one opinion in the course of a long catechism in which I found favour with my Grandmother Stanley.

It *would* be nice if you didn't go to America. Don't let me shirk the last

1. One of Russell's cousins. He was the grandson of Lord John's brother, William. It is not known what he had done to set such a dire example.
2. In Alys's letter of 20 September she described how she had told her mother of their relationship. Her mother, she said, did not altogether approve of Bohemianism and river trips – a reference to their trip on the Cam in August when they had first spoken of marriage.

and bitterest duty: a confession of sins belonging to a self that is dead but which can be dead only to myself: no one else has a right to consider it so. This must be in conversation and you must compel me to it. When I am with you I cannot bring myself to the point but I think everything ought to be told, don't you?

I have read a great deal more of Green[1] and have much to say about him but not now.

Ever yours,
Bertrand Russell

If you wish my grandmother more clearly to understand your position say so: but I don't think it will do any good.

At the last moment it became clear that Alys would, after all, go with Lady Henry Somerset to Chicago. She left for Southampton on 6 October. The day before, Russell went to say goodbye and to make his confession. The last, at any rate, proved less traumatic to both sides than had been feared.

Russell, at this time, was wildly over-optimistic about his grandmother's attitude.

[12]

Pembroke Lodge
6 October 1893

My Dear Alys
Yesterday's conversation was so satisfactory that I have not thought of all the hosts of things left unsaid that usually occur to one. The sense of relief is so overpowering that it almost excludes for the moment the things that can be written about. – However I have really innumerable things to say.

I told my grandmother we had explored South London on trams, which did not to all appearances cause her any annoyance. She was visibly relieved that Logan had not had to be told. I think she is growing perfectly resigned and will not object to anything any more.

I hope you will like my novel:[2] the character of Irina seems to me quite a

1. T. H. Green's *Prolegomena to Ethics* (1883), a seminal work for the British neo-Hegelians. Alys had been reading it, too, apparently in preparation for tackling McTaggart's pamphlet.
2. Turgenev's *Smoke* in a German translation. The novel concerns the love affair between Litvinov and Tanya, which is brought to an end by Irina, Litvinov's former lover.

masterpiece, though it is a most annoying character as it always fails at the critical moment. Don't you think we could form a habit of always having some book going which we are both reading? Whether a novel or a more serious book wouldn't much matter. I think the next metaphysic book I shall read will be Paulsen's *Einleitung in die Philosophie* which I gather is easy and amusing, and is full of quotations of poetry and altogether more human and less dry than most Germans. I imagine also that its views are fairly orthodox. I wonder if it would amuse you to read it when you are back in England?[1] I shall have finished it by then and should be glad to lend it you if the German wouldn't annoy you.

I am hoping to do a fine solid term's work and feel more fit for a good grind than ever before. – I am now reading *Elle et Lui* by George Sand: it seems strange to English ideas to write about a piece of autobiography which appears on both sides to have been lived entirely with a view to making artistic capital out of it:[2] but the strangeness rather adds to the interest though it greatly diminishes one's belief in the reality of the feelings narrated – I fear I shall never understand the French as long as I live, though all other nations seem intelligible enough.

There was one thing you will perhaps think trivial I wanted to say yesterday but forgot entirely: the photograph you gave me does not seem to me the very least like you, in fact it makes you look both ugly and disagreeable; if I am to give you a photograph of myself I shall have to be photographed on purpose, as I never have been since I was eleven, when I was chubby and round and used to be called Fatty by my friends; would you think it a very reckless extravagance also to be photographed again? Some time.

Don't forget to give me your right address in Chicago. I am going up tomorrow instead of next day, so I shall get your letter at Cambridge. After that I shall have a very long time without a letter. – I hope you will have a comfortable journey and will not be ill and enjoy yourself in America. Tell me all about these things when you write from there.

I am looking forward very much to getting back to Cambridge and being able again to say what I think and not to mean what I say: two things which at home are impossible. Cambridge is one of the few places where one can talk unlimited nonsense and generalities without anyone pulling one up or confronting one with them when one says just the opposite next day. This

1. Although they did develop the habit of reading books together, Alys thought better than to start with Paulsen.
2. The novel is based on Sand's love affair with Alfred de Musset.

is perhaps a foolish pleasure but it is a wonderful relaxation when one has been very earnest all morning at one's work or one's novel.

I hope you will keep well and enjoy yourself and convert innumerable drunkards.

Ever yours,
    Bertrand Russell

I must stop for the post.

With no letter from Alys to answer, Russell turned to gossip from Cambridge. His remarks reveal something of the social ethos of the University in the 1890s. A degree of racism, for example, seems to have been entirely taken for granted, even by Russell. Russell, however, didn't take for granted the inferior status of women in the University. Although two women's colleges, Newnham and Girton, had been established, the women in them were not members of the University and had no standing on the all-important Tripos list, although they were allowed to sit the examination and could attend lectures outside their college (accompanied by a chaperon). Formerly, both activities had required special permission. Philippa Fawcett (1868–1948), to whom Russell refers, had shamed the University by being placed above the Senior Wrangler in the Tripos of 1890, though her result still carried no official recognition. For many years Russell played an unobtrusive role in furthering women's education at Cambridge: among other things he donated a large sum to Newnham College and for many years sat on its governing body.

The status of women also had a more practical bearing on his situation, for Alys continued to argue that women ought not to get married. Russell argued, on the one hand, that marriage need not interfere with work and, on the other, that not getting married might – for it was impossible to live by work alone. None the less, given prevailing social conditions, he took the choice between work and marriage as a serious dilemma for women, though one which he hoped could be overcome by an egalitarian marriage. Alys, influenced no doubt by the congeniality of her friendship with Lady Henry, replied that the dilemma might be evaded by women living together – an alternative which had not occurred to Russell. Apart from Russell's emphasis on the morbid effects of not marrying, the issues are still with us.

[13]

Trinity College
12 October 1893

Dear Alys

It is tiresome not to have a letter of yours to answer and still more to think what a long time it will be before I get one from you. It is most aggravating to find that, though one can disprove the reality of space and time in a few strokes of the pen after reading a little metaphysics, it makes no apparent difference to the malignity of their operations. When Time has condescended to move as far as till you come home again I shall have grown very impatient of it; although McTaggart has given it its death blow in an article in this month's *Mind*[1] it seems as vigorous as ever.

Fortunately I have no lectures on Saturdays so when I come up to town I shall be able to come in the morning. Maud Joachim[2] and I go to the same lectures now: she goes with a chaperon who sleeps peacefully through the lecture and wakes up with a start at the end. Poor thing! I believe she has been chaperoning people in the same course of lectures the last 10 or 15 years and must have grown intolerably bored to hear the old phrases and the old jokes endlessly repeated. My former coach Webb[3] refused to coach Miss Fawcett because he thought her chaperon wouldn't like his jokes, which certainly were of a somewhat doubtful character. Talking of jokes, I hear someone is writing a moral antidote to *Dodo*, called Don't-Don't.[4] If the book is worthy of its title it ought to be amusing.

Amos, Sanger and I are all doing Moral Science now: Crompton[5] says it is the first time there have been three English men doing it at once: formerly it was confined to women and black men (excuse the collocation). He is

1. 'Time and the Hegelian Dialectic', *Mind* (1893), pp. 490–504. Despite the respect which Russell accorded McTaggart's views at this time, he seems never to have been wholly convinced by any of McTaggart's arguments for the unreality of time.
2. A relative of the Idealist philosopher, Harold Joachim, who was now Rollo Russell's brother-in-law. She was taking the Moral Science tripos.
3. Like most students, Russell had hired a private coach to prepare him for the Mathematical Tripos. This was Robert Rumsey Webb (1850–1936), a Fellow of St John's College.
4. *Dodo* (1893) was an indiscreet society novel by E. F. Benson. The book, Benson's first, created a minor sensation, partly because of its gossipy nature but also because it was written by the son of the Archbishop of Canterbury.
5. Crompton Llewelyn Davies (1868–1935), Russell's closest friend at Cambridge. He had completed part two of the Classical Tripos in 1891. He later became a lawyer and for many years handled Russell's rather tangled legal affairs.

going abroad with his sister,[1] who seems to have suffered for the prevailing fault of women (you must forgive me: I really mean it), over-con-scientiousness; and is now knocked up with overwork and overworry. He seemed to regard her as an instance of the hopelessness of not marrying: he says she is always wishing for sympathy more than is possible for her to have and now is obliged to give up all her work for some time, to recruit her energy. I am annoyed at the utter insolubility of the problem: there seems no alternative for an educated woman but to give up marriage or to give up (for a time at least) work which may seem to be the most important thing in life. And yet I hardly think anybody, especially any woman, can or ought to live on work alone; I am convinced myself I should find it quite impossible and should break down, like Miss Llewelyn Davies, if I were to try.

But I can also well understand finding it terrible to give up work, though I am much too lazy by nature to mind a bit myself as long as I can keep my conscience quiet. And not to marry comes sooner or later to renouncing everything but work: it is only by marriage one can form ties for the future, for old age or even in most cases for middle age. When we are young we have most of us a spring of enthusiasm and hope and self-confidence which helps us through periods of dullness: but later in life, if the dullness settles down as the normal state of things, and we realize that all the rest of our life is to be colourless and cold, it must become almost impossible to preserve our energy and our generosity. And nothing on earth makes people so unsympathetic as solitude: the most sympathetic in old age I am sure are those who have had a chequered life of joys and sorrows, not those who have always had to fight against all their natural impulses and cravings. These, if they succeed in their attempt, become hard; if they fail, they become, like my aunt,[2] quite incapable of anything except regret, and without the energy which would enable them to profit, as some do, by sorrow.

However I hope and believe you agree now with all I have been saying, so it was perhaps rather superfluous. But I meant to emphasize that the craving for sympathy, unlike many others, grows and grows by repression till finally it is apt to become an overmastering passion which nothing can control or which if it is controlled may succeed in ruining the person who controls it. If you ever condescend to read Browning I would refer to the Queen in 'In a Balcony':

1. Margaret Llewelyn Davies (1861–1944). She became a prominent socialist and feminist. See page 294.
2. Agatha Russell.

There have been moments, if the sentinel,
Lowering his halbert to salute the Queen,
Had flung it brutally and clasped my knees,
I would have stooped and kissed him with my soul.

However this is Browning and I am by way of having got tired of him and never did approve of his philosophy, so I ought not to quote him.

Talking of philosophy, I have read rather more than half of Paulsen of whom I wrote before; he is very easy but very sentimental and popular: he reaches all the orthodox conclusions but by crude arguments which don't really prove his point. Moreover he makes some extraordinary distinction between knowledge and faith which seems to me to serve absolutely no purpose: so much faith is involved in our having knowledge even of Euclid, and faith is again so much conditioned by knowledge that it seems to me only to incline to scepticism to emphasize the distinction; and further it might make one think faith was more or less arbitrary, whereas it ought to be the aim of philosophy surely to systematize it and eliminate all that is the least arbitrary. However the book is pleasantly written and is very good at giving the orthodox views in a more or less popular form.

I wonder very much what sort of crossing you have had and whether you have enjoyed it: Lady Henry Somerset must be delightful from all I have heard from you. Do write and tell me all sorts of things about your doings and so on: I shall expect you to have written a very long letter from the ship. I shall not write to America again as I think you said you would not get a later letter; so I shall not write till I hear you are back in England. *Auf glücklichster Wiedersehen.*

Ever yours
Bertrand Russell

Three letters at last arrived from Alys in the USA. In them she raised for the first time the question of their religious differences: Russell was already a convinced agnostic, while Alys still held her mother's Christian beliefs. In her letters Alys had expressed the thought that Russell would eventually come to need a belief in God to sustain his work, because work alone was too austere to sustain itself and human relations were too insecure to sustain it. In his reply, Russell disabuses her of any hope that he would be easily converted, though he did minimize their differences in his remarks about faith in the previous letter and his advocacy of pantheism in the next. Despite tolerance on both sides, the matter was not so easily resolved – as later letters reveal.

Alys had an easier pupil when it came to art, despite Russell's tendency to boast of his philistinism. For all her puritanism and the tradition of Quaker plainness from which she came, Alys was much more at home in the art world than Russell. Her brother, Logan, lived much of the time in the artists' quarter in Paris, and her sister, Mary, had by this time already established her collaboration with Berenson. Her *Guide to the Italian Pictures at Hampton Court* was published in 1894. Russell, though somewhat reluctant to have his mind improved, was prepared at least to evince an interest in music – despite some philosophical cavils.

[14]

Trinity College
29 October 1893

Dear Alys

I shall have more time for writing today than I have on week days, so I will begin my letter now. – I am rewarded for my long fast by your three letters, which were as you may imagine most welcome: I only got the first on the 25th, and the time had begun to seem quite interminable. I won't complain of the shortness of the other two, as I know you must have had all your time thoroughly filled up. I too, having observed the arrival and departure of the mails in the papers, had hoped to get your first letter on Saturday last; the New York post must be very ill-managed or I should have got it then.

I am very glad you have enjoyed yourself: from all you say Lady Henry must be delightful, and of course you must enjoy seeing so many friends again. – I think I should have enjoyed the Temperance meetings, only I should have found it impossible to take them quite seriously: when I look at philanthropy from a distance it seems the only thing worth doing, and I think myself a worm to be engaged for instance in trying to prove that the view that a good will is absolutely good and the only ultimate good involves contradictions, as I have been doing all this last week;[1] but I know that everything in which human happiness or misery does not directly appear strikes me first on the laughable side when I see it close: especially if I have a hand in it myself.

I am afraid it is almost necessary we should have a good deal of discussion on theological questions: I am sorry because I shall unavoidably appear in a rather brutal light as I am so utterly out of sympathy with Christianity. It

1. See Russell's essay for Henry Sidgwick, 'The Relation of Rule and End', *Papers*, vol. I, pp. 216–17.

would be no use at all hoping that I shall ever believe that God is a Person: no reader of metaphysics could I think be brought to such a view: it is almost as much discredited in Philosophy as Circle Squaring in Mathematics. But I do not mean to put nothing in its place: on the contrary I am convinced that as soon as we begin to reflect seriously on religion we shall find Pantheism a far finer, a far more inspiring faith: so that the other appears almost as Atheism in comparison. But the idea of Pantheism is rather difficult: I should be very glad if you felt enough interested to read a little Metaphysics as I am confident you would soon be convinced of its superiority in every point of view. McTaggart said once in a letter to me that no religion involving a personal God could be a religion of love: and this view he made clear I think in his pamphlet. You will see that all its conclusions are only possible if you regard every man as God incarnate and God as existing only as incarnate in individual spirits. This opinion I think is the one on which modern philosophy is most unanimous: it is taught in lectures even, and the orthodox view is openly scouted by all who teach Metaphysics.

I agree with you that human relations and work can neither of them afford satisfaction by themselves without faith: faith is involved in belief in work, and without it the value of human relations is purely ephemeral: But the faith required is not the belief in this or that dogma, but rather in the perfectibility of the world and in the ultimate attainment of such perfection. But no amount of faith will I think make one happy without some more substantial source of joy: I have seen the very purest and strongest faith completely powerless against misfortune, and I think it would be so in my own case probably. But there is about great happiness something eternal which is satisfying even when the immediate cause of happiness is removed. The fact that such a thing is possible is such a revelation that it seems to make everything else endurable: especially when one is convinced that this feeling is not mere sentiment but can be supported by reason.

I shall be able to come next Saturday and spend the night, which *will* be delightful.[1] I shall probably be able to arrive about twenty to two at Grosvenor Road, but I may come earlier. I am very sorry you had not got my letter when you last wrote: it must have come the next day. I hope you will have written on the ship and post it from Liverpool. How delightful to be addressing a letter to you in England again.

I read about your storm in the papers and felt for you: I never experienced sea-sickness but I am sure it must be horrible. I am glad to hear of your

1. From America Alys had invited Russell for a weekend visit to her parents' London home, 44 Grosvenor Road, to see her after she returned.

swearing: it is a great relief. Exams taught me the habit as they teach it to every one who does Mathematics. The peculiar beauty of Mathematical exams is that one always sees how to do some valuable question just as the clock strikes, or worse still discovers a fallacy in a long piece of work one had thought sound.

It must have been very delightful for you to find so many women who were grateful for your mother's book:[1] respect and gratitude towards those one is fond of are even more delightful than towards oneself. – I will finish this letter tomorrow. – I should like very much to read your mother's book with you.

Monday – I have a letter from Logan, still in town and with no prospect of leaving. Doesn't this make it necessary you should explain matters more or less to him, if I am to come on Saturday?[2] You could of course say as much or as little as seemed necessary but something I should think would be unavoidable. – He is very much afraid of my becoming Hegelian and indulging in 'perfumed dreams': hatred of every kind of religion is his ruling passion just now. But I don't think perfumed dreams are much in my line, at least as things to be believed in.[3]

I had also a letter from your mother to tell me of your cablegram on starting home again, which was very kind of her. I hope you won't want to improve my mind too much: when it is one's business it doesn't strike one as nearly such a fine thing as it would if one were more practical in one's work. However if music can count as mental improvement all good music is always delightful to me, far more so than poetry or anything else of the kind. There was a glorious concert here last Wednesday which I should have regarded as transporting me to heaven for an hour and a half, if I hadn't reflected that music, being a process in time, will be impossible in heaven, in spite of the conventional harps.

I hope your journey will have been calmer than the voyage out; also that you had the journey with your friend which you hoped for. How interesting people are who have a problem in their life. I have begun to think very meanly of purely intellectual occupations, though I continue to enjoy them

1. Probably Hannah Whitall Smith's *The Christian's Secret of a Happy Life* (1875, and much reprinted). In her letter of 16 October Alys had suggested that they read it together. They never did.
2. Logan had still not been told about their relationship. Alys had suggested that Russell tell him, but in the event the task fell to Alys.
3. A few months later, Russell did become a Hegelian and remained one until 1898, though his direct debts to Hegel were slight. 'Perfumed dreams', however, were hardly part even of his Hegelian philosophy.

more than ever: but it seems as if all the practical things were so far more pressing and so far easier to get definite results in; so that I shall be rather glad when I am done with academical hair-splitting. *Auf baldiges Wiedersehen.*
Ever Yours
Bertrand Russell

Russell's overnight stay at 44 Grosvenor Road immediately after Alys's return went off smoothly – they had, Russell wrote on 7 November, a 'glorious two days' together. A further visit the following Saturday, however, was less idyllic. A number of problems had arisen. Logan had been told and had said that Alys was a goose to expect the affections of a twenty-one-year-old man to last. She had brushed aside the suggestion by reasserting the official version of her relationship with Bertie, that it was just an 'intimate friendship' and that the question of marriage would not arise for many years, if ever. But the official version was becoming harder to maintain. There could be no doubt that Russell was attracted beyond all bounds of 'intimate friendship'. Moreover, Alys herself, though officially scouting any suggestion of marriage, had given discreet but unmistakable hints that she was none the less considering the possibility. Logan's doubts about the permanence of Bertie's feelings for her, however, reinforced her own reflections about the insecurity of human relations in her letters from America. The doubts, once raised, were not easily quelled.

As so often in the next year, the crisis was precipitated by the intervention of Granny, who had no doubts as to where this lamentable relationship was tending. Granny had come up with a comprehensive set of proposals for parting the two: a six-month separation, followed by monthly meetings and monthly letters – a sufficient diet, she thought, for an intimate friendship. Alys, apparently, had at first agreed, but Russell had resisted (in what must have been a memorable engagement) and in the end had carried Alys with him. Alys wrote to him on 12 November saying that she could now trust that his feelings wouldn't change. It was the first test of their relationship and in surmounting it they suddenly found that a decisive step beyond intimate friendship had been taken. Bertie's passionate opposition to his grandmother's plan seems to have convinced Alys's family of his love for her. None the less, Russell was left with the feeling that he had browbeaten her, and forced her into accepting a situation that he desired but she did not.

[15]

Pembroke Lodge
12 November 1893

My dear Alys

There can be nothing more to tell later as I leave here before daybreak tomorrow and everybody is gone to bed now. I have been on the whole a good deal more successful here than I expected. I spoke very fully to my aunt telling her exactly how matters stood and how you and your mother felt: she however, although she had agreed with my grandmother before, entirely came round to my point of view and thought it was no use now not to meet: she had no difficulty in believing (what her own life has proved to her only too bitterly) that absence so far from making me think less would make my thoughts dwell all the more exclusively on the one subject. She quite believed after I had spoken fully that there was no chance of my affection ever diminishing. I have always found her extremely sympathetic but was surprised to find that ever since last Christmas she had thought I was in love though she didn't know with whom. So she of course readily believed I had subjected myself to a long course of self-examination and had already tried absence as a test: she said the best test was to imagine an insuperable obstacle: I told her till June I had imagined the obstacles insuperable and had thought only pain could result from my feelings: so then she was completely convinced. To be quite fair, she thought once a month *rather* often but very mildly. She really understood everything at least as well as I do myself and was inexpressibly good and kind.

My grandmother is of course still and always will be unable to understand the situation: but I found her feeling about our frequent meetings very much less strong than I had imagined: all she said was that she wouldn't take the responsibility of bringing them about, and would not say, when I asked her, that there was any harm in them: only she hoped we would not get bound in any way: but that I think is more because she doesn't want it to happen than for any other reason. She said *most* strongly it had never crossed her mind to blame either you or your mother in the very slightest degree for one moment: and she was very kind in saying she thought we had both acted very beautifully (that was her word) throughout. My Uncle, under the modernizing influence of his wife, has thought throughout and still thinks we had better meet just as often as we like.

So much for the opinion of others. I have realized today that I said yesterday a great many things of which I am heartily ashamed. I was taken unawares and I fear my masculine selfishness which I had hoped dead revived in terrible strength. I was rather taken aback and clutched at any and every argument available whether legitimate or not: my only excuse for having argued selfishly is that you were wanting to do it for my sake; this strikes me as coming to the same as saying I had a right to be selfish because you were being unselfish which doesn't seem very good reasoning. I don't know whether you noticed and regretted my selfishness yesterday, but at any rate it must have struck you afterwards: I can only say I regret it.

But I think really my argument without unduly selfish considerations was perfectly good: and I am confirmed in this opinion by having brought my aunt to think exactly as I do although before she thought differently. I need external sympathy because since I know I have made you unhappy I have lost faith in the rectitude of my own conduct. I feel such an unutterable brute to be so happy at your expense that I can't bear to think of it. If you are really going to have a bad conscience I will give up anything in heaven or earth – for I cannot believe we can lay the foundations of permanent happiness except by following the very best that is in us. Can you not lay the responsibility at my door? I am *perfectly* confident that it would be right to meet as often as may be (say once a month in term time and once a week in the Vac.) if only you would think so too. Cannot you accept the opinion of my aunt as that of an unprejudiced person and of one who has proved how well she understands by having seen and maintained since Christmas quite against my grandmother's opinion that things were as they were though I didn't know I had betrayed anything beyond sympathy for her: perhaps I understood her feelings too well. Do make up your mind that it would be quite useless for you to go against my firm and unalterable conviction as to what we ought to do, and that therefore your conscience may be at rest. My happiness *is* involved but is not endangered by the course I suggest. You know one always risks remorse whatever course one adopts as, in my experience at least, remorse depends far more on results than on conviction of having done wrong: and no act can quite certainly have good results. I have been much relieved and encouraged by conversation with my people: I wish I could pass on some of this encouragement to you. I have been perfectly open with them about your opinion and your mother's. Do write very soon when you have reflected on this letter and tell me your conscience is at rest or I shall have to give up the fruit of all this arguing which has been much the severest mental labour I ever engaged in. But this is no argument. It was wonderful how you argued yesterday. I could never had done it. Goodbye Alys.

Ever Yours,
Bertrand Russell

Alys had written reassuringly on the 12th immediately after the crisis and further reassurances were offered in her reply to the above. She also called on Russell to take up their case with Logan, who seemed still the only sceptic on the Pearsall Smith side. Granny, meanwhile, faced with the rejection of her ultimatum, had summoned Hannah Whitall Smith to an interview at Pembroke Lodge. With increased confidence in the relationship, Russell for the first time signed himself 'Bertie'.

[16]

Trinity College
17 November 1893

My dear Alys

I *was* glad of your two letters; it was so horrible to think of you as unhappy, and it hadn't occurred to me before that you might be, when I was so much the reverse that I couldn't imagine your being troubled about the rightness of our conduct. It is really impossible to make rules about a thing so entirely dependent on personal conditions. I wonder what my grandmother will have said to your mother: she is very persuasive and will very likely have changed the opinion of my uncle and aunt: but so long as there is no chance of your having any more doubts the whole of the rest of the world doesn't matter. I should be glad though if my grandmother could be satisfied that it is all right as I honour her almost to idolatry. What she is to any one in trouble, and how wonderfully she has borne her succession of the very worst sorrows, such as most people never experience, it is impossible to say. I think she will never be quite satisfied unless she could get to know you well enough to be really very fond of you: and I am almost afraid she is too old for that to be possible. But my aunt I think you would be sure to get on with.

I wonder you succeeded in winning over Logan. I had thought he was altogether too wise. I will try and express myself to him when I see him but I shall find it difficult as in all our conversations we have always been both of us very cynical and it is not easy suddenly to adopt a different tone. Also on all matters of feeling I do not wish to acquire a habit of expressing myself to men: it would not increase their respect for me and in most cases would be apt to destroy friendship. Men, or at any rate Englishmen, cease to value or believe in any feeling as soon as it is expressed: they think it a pose or an affectation. But these remarks I know do not apply to Logan. I sent him a bundle of old clothes and £16 which I collected from my friends: I believe he thought I had sent it all myself, judging from a letter I had this morning from him.[1] I hope your meetings have gone off successfully and that the young women were pleased with your speech.[2] Is it Temperance you have been talking on at your other meetings? I have been very busy this week: I have been writing a paper for the Society which I have called 'Can we be Statesmen?'[3] by which I meant, Can our political opinions be determined on reasonable grounds? I have come to the conclusion that it is quite impossible and I fear everyone will agree with me. I have also written an essay to prove our desires are not always for pleasure (for Sidgwick),[4] and have read a great deal about *der Dingbegriff* and kindred subjects. As I have also had to entertain my brother and play whist with him I have hardly had time to turn round. But nothing can deprive one of the night, which is the really best time for pleasant thoughts.

I shall hope for a letter from you on Monday and I will write again some time next week and tell you what time I shall arrive on Sunday. – It is a good thing your conscience is all right again: tell me all about what my grandmother said and whether you have continued to be quite happy.

Ever Yours
Bertie

On 19 November Alys gave Bertie a reassuring account of Hannah's meeting with Granny. Granny did extract an undertaking that Bertie and Alys would not meet more than once a month, but more frequent correspondence was permitted. The relationship flowed on uneventfully for a few letters. In fact, having come so close to declaring themselves engaged, they now retreated to the safer ground of an intimate friendship once more.

The next blow fell on 15 December when Alys abruptly cancelled their next meeting in order to go to stay at Eastnor Castle, Lady Henry Somerset's home near Ledbury, in a letter which gave unmistakable signs that she was having second thoughts about the relationship. It was the third meeting in a row that she had cancelled, and it threw Russell into despair. Yet, as in many of Alys's letters, the signs were ambiguous: she said she didn't know whether she would rather him be annoyed that she had cancelled or accept it patiently; she confessed to a desire to hold his hand and say intimate things when they were together; and she had suggested

1. Logan was collecting money and supplies to aid a miners' strike in Barnsley. Russell published the letter he refers to in his *Autobiography*, vol. I, p. 94.
2. In her letter, Alys had sent an impressive list of meetings at which she had to speak.
3. *Papers*, vol. I, pp. 79–82, apparently Russell's first paper to the Apostles.
4. See *Papers*, vol. I, pt V, for Russell's surviving papers for Sidgwick. It is difficult to identify one written at the right time which fits this description, however.

an alternative meeting the following week. Russell replied from his brother's home, Amberley Cottage near Maidenhead.

[17]

[Amberley Cottage, Maidenhead]
17 December 1893. 1 a.m.

My dearest Alys

All you do is right in my eyes but I confess your letter was a disappointment and it was some time before I could feel resigned. I got it in the presence of a set of people for most of whom I have no respect or affection and had a good deal of difficulty in concealing my feelings. For 4 hours after getting it I was not a moment alone and had no chance of reading it a second time: till I could be alone I could not feel resigned; I was more than usually anxious for a meeting as I have been unusually worried by the tone and atmosphere of Pembroke Lodge and other things. I cannot go to sleep till I have said some of what I have to say and this is all the paper I can find in my bedroom.[1] I can come on Friday from after luncheon till late evening or on Saturday for all day: I leave the choice to you. I see we must have an argument about how we are to meet, though all arguments are tiresome. Why should you not be frank about what is pleasant as we have been about what is unpleasant? Your case is utterly different from mine as I should have thought you must see: you were obviously not in love with me and to try to make you so when I might have caused you pain if I succeeded would have been atrocious. But nothing you could do will make me love you either more or less: always I love you with all the strength of emotion of which I am capable. And I never make any illusions to myself as to the permanence of your present feelings: every now and then I read over all your old letters and also the arrangement we made at Friday's Hill which I wrote down at the time to remember it better, so I am not likely to imagine you have promised anything you haven't promised and you have made no new promises since you went to America. And your feelings must of course be the most interesting subject on earth to me so it would be barbarous to be silent about them. You say it is not necessary to you that you should express yourself but it is to me more than to express my own because you know them now. And so divine a thing as the sympathy we have reached by your allowing yourself to say and shew what you felt cannot be wrong: merely to have known it is a religion and

1. The letter is written on a curious sheet of paper bearing Belgian postage, but no address.

redeems the world from its sordidness and misery by opening up infinite possibilities. Do not deprive me of moments which have been to me a revelation of a glory I had never dreamt of as possible even in heaven. Though I could not myself be happy if your feelings should change I could work with faith for others, knowing what life can give and so having hope for mankind. Such sympathy has to me an eternal value which would live even if you should cease to feel it.

But I must come back to what will seem to you better arguments. All our intercourse would be strained and unnatural if you are always repressing what you feel especially if I (as I cannot but do) am always saying how your love is the one thing I value. And I do not deceive myself: if I didn't realize how difficult it is to be sure of oneself I shouldn't have waited so long myself. But you see I had to take the first step which you have not to do. When once I had spoken I ought (if I was right in speaking) to be able to trust myself if at any future time you should come to return my affection: for you this caution is impossible since I am already in love. And if you do not express yourself I shall not know whether you have changed from what you now feel, and I shall look in all you say and write (as I have done all these months) for indications, which will destroy my peace of mind as I am sure to read the indications unfavourably whenever that is possible.

What do you mean about infinite patience? I can never need more than in the dreary years when I believed all life to be misery and even death a doubtful relief. Patience is easy when one hopes for and has a possible reward and such a reward! The difficult patience is the patience that expects no reward except the doubtful and temporary consciousness of having done right. I can never again have the crushing sense of solitude and isolation, the feeling that if I were known as I know myself I should be despised as I despised myself perhaps even abhorred as I abhorred myself. – You will not give me more pain by being unreserved now and afterwards withdrawing your love than by being reserved all the time. And I believe if you were ever to grow tired of me (which would not surprise me) I should know it at once without your saying anything either before or after. What *do* you mean about my finding you at the end not worth my patience? Goodnight Alys. God bless you. God bless you.

Yours eternally

Bertie

The next letter is explained by the following passage in Russell's *Autobiography* (vol. I, p. 82):

> At this time I kept a locked diary, which I very carefully concealed from everyone. In this diary I recorded my conversations with my grandmother about Alys and my feelings in regard to them. Not long afterwards a diary of my father's, written partly in shorthand (obviously for purposes of conceal-ment), came into my hands. I found that he had proposed to my mother at just the same age at which I had proposed to Alys, that my grandmother had said almost exactly the same things to him as she had to me, and that he had recorded exactly the same reflections in his diary as I had recorded in mine. This gave me an uncanny feeling that I was not living my own life but my father's over again, and tended to produce a superstitious belief in heredity.

[18]

Pembroke Lodge
19 December 1893

My dear Alys

Since I wrote to you last I have got hold of my father's journals: I send you some extracts: I have felt as if the book were another self speaking to me, so that it was almost uncanny: the very echo of my own thoughts, the repetition of the same events at the same age. I am glad I did not know any of the things I have found in the journal before: I could hardly have believed that I was not influenced by the knowledge. The journal is largely written in a sort of shorthand which I had never seen before so that I have had some difficulty in deciphering it; so I should be glad to have the extracts back on Friday as they give the key to the rest which I have not yet deciphered. I hope to find a letter from you in London this afternoon or at any rate this evening. I have completely got over the things that worried me at home and have been very happy in spite of your putting me off but I hope you will not have to do it often. In spite of what you say in your letter I know of course really you would not have liked me to be angry.

Ever yours
Bertie

Russell's anguished letter of 17 December produced a very contrite response from Alys at Eastnor Castle on 18 December. She asked him to be patient with her attacks of conscience about the rightness of their relationship. Such attacks would continue, she said, until she had finally made up her mind, but they should be combated by Russell's letters. Her moods of irritation would also recur, but he should ignore them unless she told him definitely that she no longer loved him. Meanwhile, she told him, she would respect him more if he were far more critical of her and urged him to point out her faults. Russell struggled, rather unsuccessfully, with this last injunction in the following letter.

[19]

40 Dover Street
19 December 1893. 10.30 p.m.

My Dear Alys

Your letter gave me great pleasure but also much food for reflection. The process of administering periodical *drugs* to your conscience is not at all to my taste: my letter was intended rather as a cordial than as a drug. As I am in a merry mood tonight I will begin at once to make all sorts of severe criticisms upon you. But seriously I don't think your conscience ought to wake up periodically and slumber the rest of the time: cannot you set it at rest once for all when you have made up your mind that a certain course of action is right? Doubt is a disease of which you have probably less experience than I have (at least I hope so), so that perhaps you have not yet learnt thoroughly how to conquer it where reason alone is unable (as it *always* is) entirely to remove it. My own method is to consider a question as impartially as I can for as long as it needs or as I can spare it, and then to decide as best I can, and by an act of will refuse to reconsider my decision until new facts come up. For so sceptical a nature as mine it is only by such a process that I can believe even a proposition of Euclid, much more than that one course of action is right and another is wrong. I can only speak for myself but I know that since I adopted this method I have gained greatly in stability and energy of purpose, though I have known that at bottom my opinions depended on an act of will (as I am ready to maintain on metaphysical grounds that everyone's do).

But I assure you it is not for want of *trying* to find faults in you that I have not found them: of course I will admit anything you like in the abstract, and once (about six weeks ago) I spent a day hunting for these faults with no effect, except that at night I dreamt you and Flora Russell[1] had come down to Pembroke Lodge and had there both done something very disgraceful (I

1. One of Russell's cousins. She was the granddaughter of Lord John Russell's brother, William.

forget what), so that a crowd of visitors who were in the drawing room would none of them speak to you: and that I was divided between the longing to tell you I didn't mind and the terror of seeming to play the magnanimous [*sic*]. But when I woke up I was no nearer being able to imagine you doing wrong than before, though my dream shews how great an effort I had made to imagine it. But I think I can criticize your intellect just as well as anybody else's: I suppose because it is not intellect I care about in people. However I will hunt for these microscopic abstract faults and tell you when I find them; I don't believe I am blind because in everything else except virtue I can be perfectly critical; and I have never known my critical faculty fail me when I have tried to exert it, as it is very strong, and often obtrudes itself in a most unwelcome manner (but not about you). You are not quite right about me: too much uncritical sympathy is bad for me too, and it would be immensely useful to me if you could find out and remind me of my faults. I know some of them: the worst I think is talking and thinking too much about myself: but I probably don't know those faults that are really my worst.

I know only too well the occasional feeling of irritation with whoever may happen to be by, so that I should never be surprised or pained at your exhibiting it or imagine it meant anything serious. I don't see why you should wish I cared less: it is because I care so much that I derive so much intense joy from it.

My grandmother I regret to say is still very uneasy about us, and to see her worried has worried me and I reflected for some time on the possibility of a way of diminishing her anxiety: but I fear there is none so I have put away the thought of her worry in the most approved manner of the thorough egoist. She and my aunt however are still more pained at my independence of their judgment on any practical subject: they think I ought to consult them about going to Germany[1] and so forth: it is a little odd that in deciding to go to Germany I should have to defend myself against the charge of too little concern for other people, and makes me laugh and wonder alternately. Perhaps they are right! Who knows? The fear of appearing to be biased is often a very powerful motive and I am almost certain it is my real motive in adhering to my former decision, though of course I would not adhere

1. Alys had conceived the idea that Russell ought to go away to Germany by himself for six months in order to have some experience of an independent life, and to test the constancy of his affection for her. He continued to resist the plan over several letters. In the end he went to study economics at the University of Berlin in January 1895 – but only after they were married, and they went together.

to it if I did not know that I had other motives in making the decision.

You must excuse my handwriting: both the pen and the ink are bad. I will come at two on Friday and can stay as late as ever you like. I don't know if there is a concert and I imagine we could hardly go to the play alone,[1] could we? But I will try to discover if there is any music.

By the way, my grandmother was either very forgetful or not quite frank when she told me she had had just the same kind of talk with my father about a girl whom he did not afterwards marry: this girl died when he was 20, I have seen his letters to her and there is no hint of love in them: in fact in one of them he calmly discusses the advisability of her marrying a certain man her people wanted her to marry, and objects on the ground that it would interfere with their friendship and says he would expect his wife to understand exactly the relation and interfere in no way. I found also thoughts on her death in his journal which were not at all those of a man in love. I was interested in all this as I have been so much struck by my likeness to my father that I feel as if I could appropriate his experience as experience for myself, thus making myself 33 instead of 21!

This letter is very dull and prosy but as my father says in one of his letters to this girl I have no fear that you will find it so. *A Vendredi.*

Ever Yours Affectionately

Bertie

The crisis of mid-December forced Alys to choose whether to continue the relationship. Once she had decided to continue, things between them went more smoothly. Russell gave her his mother's journals to read and Alys found them so engrossing that she forgot to go to her Temperance meeting. She suggested that they address each other with the intimate Quaker 'thee', which was used in her family. A children's party on New Year's Eve left her longing for children of her own. Russell was ecstatic.

1. There was a danger of their being seen together. Great care had to be taken to keep their meetings secret.

[20]

Pembroke Lodge
1 January 1894

My Dear Alys

What shall I say? My heart is too full for words: I am overcome by joy too wonderful to be expressed. Thy letter is divine. But how could I think thee had taken my love grudgingly? I have only wondered how thee could trust me as thee has done. There is nothing I would forget, nothing thee should wish me to forget, in all thee has said and done from the first. I have been wondering why I should be chosen out for such joy while others remain in misery: we must help each other to try and deserve it as far as possible. I have felt the last remnants of hatred and bitterness melting away in thy love: I will be filled with goodwill to all henceforth and not hate or despise those who are less fortunate than I am. It is delightful to think thee is as happy as I am; I have been living all day in a dream of heavenly joy. Dear Alys I cannot write any more only silence is adequate. I will write a common letter tomorrow. I am so glad thy mother liked me.

Ever thine affectionately
Bertie

On 4 January Russell visited Alys at Grosvenor Road. Russell wrote lyrically of their meeting in his *Autobiography*, for on that occasion they had their first kiss. 'Although she still said that she had not made up her mind whether to marry me or not, we spent the whole day, with the exception of meal-times, in kissing, with hardly a word spoken from morning till night, except for an interlude when I read *Epipsychidion* aloud' (*Autobiography*, vol. I, pp. 82–3). 'I had not foreseen', he said, 'how great would be the ecstasy of kissing a woman whom I loved' (p. 82). Shelley's *Epipsychidion*, a long love poem inspired by Emilia Viviani, became their special poem: Russell read it eight times in 1893 and 1894, twice aloud with Alys.

Despite the ecstasies of Alys's declaration of love and their first kiss at the beginning of the year, Alys's moods were still liable to fluctuate. In a letter in which she lamented that, although she was tired and everyone said she looked ill, she was stopping up late to write to Bertie, she discussed some possible points of friction in their future life together. Bertie, she thought, liked solitude whereas she enjoyed company and thought a home could only be justified by inviting the homeless to share it, like a sort of hotel. Bertie's response to this alarming proposal was tactful. Meanwhile the delicate business of informing their close friends continued.

[21]

Trinity College
16 January 1894
Tuesday night

Dearest Alys

It is handier for me to write at night so I make it an excuse for not waiting till tomorrow. I feel a beast to have induced thee to sit up late two nights running and made thee look and feel ill. I vow I won't let thee sit up so late again. If *I* had been any the worse I shouldn't mind so much, but instead I have been unusually lively and energetic, working, walking and talking a great deal more than usual: which makes me feel very selfish.

I am very glad Sister Lion[1] was pleased and also that thee told her, as it is not nice to have friends misjudge one. I think the difference of age is a very small matter: if other people hadn't said so much about it I am sure it would never have entered my head as of the slightest importance. And I fail to see any method thee can invent for 'taking advantage' of my youth even if thee were to set about to try to find one: seeing things are as they are.

I am afraid I am not of a sociable disposition (I can see how sleepy thee was as thee wrote 'socialable'), that is to say from earliest childhood I have had so much solitude that it has become a sort of necessity and I find myself oppressed by thoughts I have no time to think unless I have a good deal of solitary leisure. But I dare say this will wear off in time, and I like the society of people I am fond of above all things. I dare say I shouldn't mind a house-full of people provided I could only see them at meals and in the evening, but I have an awkward habit of getting unable to work if I have to see many strangers. But this too would very likely wear off. Any way I don't think it is quite a proper frame of mind to feel that the society of a small and carefully selected set of people is the greatest of pleasures, but that in whole, the rest of the world is a necessary evil. However the question will no doubt arrange itself when it arises. I may observe that I had always supposed thee had a sociable disposition till thee said thee hadn't the other day, so that it is not a disappointment to me. But I don't agree at all that a house is only justified by allowing homeless people to share it, if this cuts at the root of the first requisite in a home, which must always be domestic comfort and harmony.

---

1. Lucy Fitzpatrick (1869–1957), nicknamed 'Lion' on account of her mane of black hair. She was employed by Lady Henry Somerset in her philanthropic work and was a close friend of Alys, who had told her of her relationship with Bertie. Later she married (against Bertie's advice) Robert Phillimore, the son of a rich Liberal Law Lord. Russell remained friendly with her until her death (cf. *Autobiography*, vol. II, pp. 212–13).

But this is too big a subject to discuss in a letter. I have not thought much about it, and perhaps when I have I shall agree with thee. I had always immensely admired the way Friday's Hill was a home for the homeless, but I think it is only certain dispositions that are able to succeed in this kind of home.

I was more fortunate than thee, as I got Maurice[1] pretty easily to talk about thy visit (without my mentioning thee) and he told me thee was in good spirits and had talked much and well, but wretch! he could not repeat anything that had been said. If I had been in his place I would have repeated the whole conversation word for word. Fountain[2] is the man who posed as pretending to know everything while really knowing nothing (the fact being that he did know nearly everything). I am sorry he didn't talk, as he is amusing, only his manners annoy me at times.

It is delightful being back here again among all these nice people who take me for granted without criticism: such a repose! To my intense joy Crompton is up for all the term, more bubbling with wit than ever, and as always altogether delightful. For the first time he began talking of his experiences in the way of friendship etc. but they were very conventional and uninteresting. He said he had often begun to get fond of girls but always found he forgot them after a short absence: and he seemed to have discovered it was my 'greater constancy' that often made me depressed, at least so he was pleased to say. This conversation led me into several half-confidences from which he probably was able to draw general inferences, which I am glad of.

It seems to me the month will pass without any very great difficulty: I cannot tell thee how peaceful and happy I feel. As thee said, there is an undercurrent of joy that seems to make all the common daily tasks delightful and gives me unbounded energy, for work and for everything. I am hoping thee will feel the same. Now that I feel secure in thy love all the disturbing distracting tumultuous elements of my love seem to have vanished and to have left a feeling of pure, calm, intense happiness which never leaves me whatever I am doing. I feel sure that if we can keep each other's love through life, all duties will be easy and all difficulties will be as nothing – for as long as we love each other every possible sacrifice except of each other seems trifling. God bless thee Alys. Goodnight.

Ever thine affectionately

Bertie

1. Maurice Amos.
2. Possibly Henry Fountain, a Wrangler in the Mathematical Tripos of 1892. He became an official in the Board of Trade.

Alys objected strongly to Russell's views about domestic comfort and harmony. She found them stodgy. Russell's retraction followed in the next post.

[22]

Trinity College
21 January 1894. 1.30 a.m.

Dearest Alys

I must begin this letter with a complete recantation which will make thee think me very weak and vacillating. But indeed my first thoughts even on the simplest subjects are always perfectly childish and not the least real. I am *very* glad thee was annoyed with the 'comfort etc.'. I was too even as I wrote it and it is unintelligible to me what odd perversity made me put it down. Thee will find out in time that I have a great love of professing vile sentiments, I don't know why, unless it springs from long efforts to avoid priggery. Indeed I have thought a great deal the last days to try and find out what would be my tastes as to society: I have come to the conclusion (1) that it is quite impossible to tell (2) that I should like whatever thee liked, for I have always been very indifferent about everything inessential and I see no reason why I should change in this respect. But as to whether I should like our home to be a sort of hotel or not apart from thy wishes, I cannot tell· I think very likely I should. The reason I have hated casual society all these years is that I have always been in a state of internal uproar, and the effort of appearing otherwise was exhausting; and whenever I got away from people wild thoughts became more oppressive than if I had plenty of time to face them [*sic*]. I can hardly realize the state of mind I am in now or believe that I am still the same person: it seems so abnormal to be able to let my thoughts take their natural course without cursing God and myself: and I can hardly tell yet how my new state of mind may change me, but it probably will change my tastes considerably. I forgot when I wrote to thee last that I had always considered the very thing thee wishes as an important thing gained by marriage, and I think I even put it into my paper I once gave thee on this subject.[1] So thee will have to believe that it was simply an unacceptable perversity that made me write my last letter, and I think thee had better burn it and forget it and try to believe that this difference of tastes which was to be so serious is mostly chimerical, though I grant it is not plausible to say so. It is fortunate that I very seldom have to *act* on first thoughts and never do if I can help it, for if I did my acts would be far from creditable.

1. 'Die Ehe', *Papers*, vol. i, pp. 69–71.

But even if our tastes were materially different I do not think it would be *very* serious as one ought to have plenty of independence, far more than most married people do, and anyway my tastes are of such a flabby flexible nature that they very soon become those of anybody I am fond of. Tell me if this recantation satisfies thee and if thee believes it, for it is far from plausible as I said before.

I continue to feel perfectly calm and happy though I cannot say the week has passed particularly fast, and I had rather be at home with all its bothers and see thee once a week than here and see thee once a month.[1] I cannot yet persuade myself that my present state is as natural to me as the state I have been in ever since I ceased to be a child, more or less; but as the other did not interfere with my power of work I see no reason why thee should object to it. But I think really it all sprang from certain definite unsatisfied wants and is done with, now that they are satisfied, forever.

I am perfectly ready to be satisfied with the Paris plan:[2] what I care about is seeing thee and I don't much care *where*, so long as the essential thing is secured.

I don't see why thee shouldn't tell Lady Henry if thee makes her promise secrecy. I too long for somebody to talk to about thee but I am always withheld by distrust: I know no one I could bring myself to tell except Amos, and he I fear would be rather a sieve.

I have had a very great pleasure this evening as we have elected Marsh,[3] who is my best friend after Crompton. I have for some time thought him ready for election but I was afraid I was prejudiced by my affection for him so I waited for someone else to propose him. He and Crompton and I have been walking round the court in the moonlight arm in arm in almost

---

1. Their meetings were still rationed to one a month during term time and one a week during vacations.
2. They had planned to visit Italy together but they had abandoned this on Hannah's advice for fear of encountering Russell's relatives. The new scheme was that Russell would visit Rome with his aunt, Maude Stanley, and then call at Paris to see Logan, who was then living in Montparnasse. Alys would join him in Paris. The trip took place in March as planned.
3. Russell refers to the election of Edward Howard Marsh, a Trinity student reading classics, to the Apostles on the society's first meeting of the term. Eddie Marsh (1872–1953) had a distinguished career as a civil servant, primarily as Winston Churchill's private secretary, in which capacity he followed Churchill through many branches of the bureaucracy. He was also an art collector, patron, and connoisseur. Between 1912 and 1922 he edited five volumes of *Georgian Poetry*, in which many of the best poets of the period were represented. He remained friends with Russell until their differing views on the First World War provoked a breach.

complete silence, which was delightful – with the consciousness of this new bond to supply the need of words.

We had no paper, being the first proper meeting of the term: but chose subjects for Crompton to read next time. He is going to read on 'Liberty, what of the night?', i.e. Socialism, on which he is quite sound. We did not have very much discussion as the election of Marsh took a good time: after that we got on to a subject we all abbor but which we feel it a duty to discuss now and then, Vice and its regulation. The disagreeable impression was not dispelled for me till I got into the moonlight and Marsh and I quoted Shelley to each other. It is now two in the morning so I will finish this letter later in the day!

8.40 a.m. I have still 20 minutes before going to breakfast with the youngest Trevelyan,[1] an intelligent youth of 17, still in the materialist stage, which most people go through about then. I am a bit stupid, having scarcely slept I don't know why, and having startled my bedmaker almost out of her wits by going a walk round the court in the early dawn, before seven. I love the dawn more than any other time of day but hardly ever see it.

I have been going ahead with Lotze's *Metaphysik*, which is interesting but very stiff: I have been working steadily and I think fairly well, and on much less tobacco than formerly, as I am no longer in need of drugs! In the evenings I have been discussing various irrelevant subjects such as whether the universe (= God) can be conceived as a person, whether direction or the straight line ought to be considered fundamental in Geometry, how many fallacies there are in Herbert Spencer's proof that life-sustaining and life-producing actions are those and those alone which give pleasure, etc. etc. It is almost impossible not to feel perfectly calm in a place where people seriously think such subjects worth discussing, for they are *so* irrelevant!

I am beginning to be seriously alarmed about my Tripos as it is drawing near and I feel very ill-prepared: I never used to care a fig whether I did well in this one or not and always said I took it up as an amusement and expected to get a third class, but now I know thee will join with everybody else if I do badly and say I have been distracted by love, which will be untrue but

---

1. George Macaulay Trevelyan (1876–1962), the historian. He was the youngest of the three sons of Sir George Otto Trevelyan (the others were Charles Philips and Robert Calverley Trevelyan). Russell got to know all three while they were studying at Cambridge, but was especially friendly with Robert, his contemporary, and (later) with George. In 1894 G. M. Trevelyan was in his freshman year at Trinity. He was Regius Professor of Modern History at Cambridge from 1927 to 1940, and Master of Trinity from 1940 to 1951.

annoying. My great consolation is that Crompton got a second and everybody acknowledges he is really good at it.

I think I will send thee two letters one from my grandmother and one from my former governess, partly because they expound the situation at home better than I can, and partly because I am in a humour for mortifications (being taken with a fit of self-depreciation and also because thee thinks *far* too well of me) and both of them shew me in a rather unfavourable light. All I had said to my governess was that I thought we encouraged each other in opposition to my people and that it was harder for us to get on with them when we were together at home than when we were separate. I had not then the slightest idea of being vexed with her, and selfish brute! it never struck me I should give her pain, as it ought to have for I knew her feelings were very sensitive. But I must have the letters back when thee has read them. I am very glad to see I had misjudged my aunt: it was the result of temporary irritation.

I am very glad thy friend Sister Lion said nice things of me: I have liked *very* much what I have seen of her, and somehow feel as if I knew her much more intimately than men I have seen every day for years: I was never before struck as I have been this time by the difference between men and women in the way of sympathy and of ease in growing intimate.

Do write me a good long letter if thee has time: thee cannot think how I hunger for every crumb from thee. I am very glad thee has done a lot of work and has a good conscience.

Fare thee well
   Ever thine affectionately
    Bertie

P.S. Thee didn't say if the Shelley had arrived. I ordered it to be sent the day I came up.

Alys's enjoyment of social life was evident in her next letter, written after she'd attended a ball thrown by the artist, William Rothenstein. Although she normally dressed plainly and even unfashionably, she had attended the ball in a gown designed for her by Rothenstein and had clearly enjoyed being the centre of attention. Russell was evidently unperturbed by this, and even by her suggestion that they should delay getting married because she did not yet feel ready to leave her mother and because Russell should spend some time on his own getting started in his career.

It was Russell who raised the next stumbling-block, namely the question of their religious differences. While both Russell and Alys were prepared to tolerate each other's opinions, the question of how to educate their children could not be so easily resolved, since Russell thought it would be wrong to bring them up as Christians and Alys thought it would be wrong not to.

[23]

Trinity College
28 January 1894. 12.30 p.m.

Dearest Alys

Half our month is now gone: thank Heaven! And I have found this week go much faster than the last, chiefly I think because thy letters have been so delightful. I *do* wish I could have seen thee at Rothenstein's ball: all the time he was talking to thee of the dress he was going to design thee I was wishing I could have seen thee in it! And I am glad thee did not adhere to thy resolution of not dancing: why did thee make such a needlessly unkind resolve?

I don't know when I could be back from Rome: I shall probably leave here the afternoon of the 12th: shall I come to you for a night and home for a night and then go on the 14th or 15th? I imagine my Aunt Maude would go whenever I liked, but it seems to me I could hardly be back by the 29th in Paris, but I can't tell yet. I shall try and come as soon as possible.[1]

I told Amos, which was *most* delightful as he was as genuinely pleased and sympathetic: I wanted to tell him because I have always known what an unbounded respect he had for thee. I said I had been long in love with thee and he said 'I suppose in a sense everybody has been who's ever talked with her' which was just what I had always felt! only I never dared even to myself express such a sentiment, so I was delighted to have it said for me! Amos was simply filled with simple pleasure at the news. I can't distinctly remember the other characteristics besides a complex character and an absence of hyper-sensitiveness about the particular things I am most sensitive about. The chief was I think a reserve of moral power. I remember they were all such as pleased me to hear. But when I told him another time, in answer to a question of his, that thee was a Christian, he seemed to think that difference important: and indeed I am sure it is and we ought to keep it in mind. It would only become very serious I think if we had children to bring up: I could hardly reconcile it to my conscience to have children of mine brought up as

1. A trip to Rome with Maude Stanley was not likely to be the sort of trial one might have expected. She was by far the most sympathetic of Russell's relatives. Frank Russell called her 'the beloved confidant of the whole family' (*My Life and Adventures*, p. 9).

Christians. Has thee thought any more about religion lately? I cannot argue well with thee, for when I am with thee thy religion seems so right that I lose all wish to change it: and yet at other times I am so strongly anti-religious that I am afraid it might in future become serious. I suppose thee would admit that thy beliefs are not founded on reason, indeed that they are in flagrant contradiction to it: that they are in fact founded only on thy wishes, which thee would not accept as sufficient ground for an opinion about anything else, say conduct for example. Or does thee think they rest on more than wishes?

I cannot understand thy former theories about work being enough for happiness, as my own have always been so very different: I have regarded work sometimes as a bore, sometimes as an opiate, but never as having any connection with the serious part of life: serious from one's own point of view I mean of course, not from society's. I believe thee has always been far more dependent on the affection and sympathy of thy mother and thy friends than thee thought. Work alone could only be enough for a machine it seems to me, not for a human being. But perhaps I am too extreme on the other side.

I have been reading Hobbes and Spinoza, tomorrow I am going to read Descartes, on the subject of the passions; Spinoza is good, though one cannot help feeling that both of them write of a good many passions from hearsay and not from personal experience. And one thing strikes me very much as a change in this century as compared with any other: most people now (in the younger generation at any rate), whether they have much experience of passion or not, regard it as in itself, and apart from the practical inconveniences of it in present society, a good thing: a heaven without emotion, spent in passionless contemplation of propositions of Euclid, which seems to be Spinoza's ideal (though he calls it intellectual love of God to make it sound better), makes any modern shudder: a heaven without all-absorbing emotional love seems a far less desirable thing than earth with all its drawbacks. This opinion is not mine peculiarly, but that of almost all the younger people I know, and that of philosophers like Bradley.[1]

But I wish I had got hold of Spinoza two years ago instead of Thomas à Kempis:[2] he would have suited me far better: he preaches a rich voluptuous asceticism based on a vast undefined mysticism, which even now has seized

1. F. H. Bradley was widely regarded as the most important philosopher then working in Britain. His major work, *Appearance and Reality*, had just been published. McTaggart would have been chief among the 'younger people' Russell had in mind.
2. Russell seems to have been struck by Thomas à Kempis, the 'Voice from the Past' in George Eliot's *Mill on the Floss*, while reading the novel in the summer of 1890. For the

hold of my imagination most powerfully. Now I must go to lunch with Marsh.

We had a very good meeting last night: Marsh was duly initiated, and McTaggart, Dickinson and Wedd[1] were there. Crompton's paper was unfortunately very scrappy and unfinished: and I think we all agreed that it is impossible to deduce immediate Socialism from metaphysics as Crompton tried to do. We none of us of course discussed whether socialism in the near future is good or bad, that being a question of detailed knowledge, but all agreed that it is more near the heavenly state than any other (except Sanger). We mostly discussed the notion of an organism as applied to Society: we divided on Where does Socialism belong? Sanger voted Hell, most people voted Heaven, Crompton and I voted both Earth and Heaven. I got McTaggart to say empirical Utilitarianism was the only method for practice, as the idealist self-realization cannot be made for directly and we don't know how to make for it. In which I strongly agree, as did most people I think except Crompton.

I have been reading nothing but shop this week and have done a good deal of work: I have been trying to become thoroughly the creature of routine and make every day an exact repetition of every other, even to going the same solitary seven-mile walk every day, which is spent entirely in pleasant thoughts. I have been divinely happy all the week and the time left before next meeting is no longer so oppressively long as it seemed before. I hope thee is having successful meetings and that thee has told Lady Henry and that she has been sympathetic. Goodbye.

Ever thine affectionately
    Bertie

I will write Wed. evening next.

Alys misconstrued Russell's remarks about passion, thinking that he meant sensual passion, and, as a result, objected strongly to his giving passion an important place in his philosophy. She also took issue with his plans for bringing up their children as non-Christians and raised more general concerns about their religious differences.

rather obscure connection Russell drew between Thomas à Kempis and Spinoza see K. Blackwell, *The Spinozistic Ethics of Bertrand Russell* (1985), pp. 27–9.
1. Nathaniel Wedd (1864–1940). An excellent teacher, he was then a classics don at King's. According to his friend Dickinson, he was 'notorious for blasphemy ... and the reading of Baudelaire' (*The Autobiography of G. Lowes Dickinson*, p. 161).

More alarmingly, she now talked of putting off the marriage for three years, and even broached the possibility of their remaining friends if she decided not to marry. Faced with this prospect of catastrophe, Russell tried to be conciliatory. But he evidently found it less easy to compromise on this point than he had earlier in the month on their future domestic arrangements.

[24]

Trinity College
31 January 1894. 12 noon

Dearest Alys

I must begin my letter today although I cannot send it: I have so much to say which it will be a relief to have written. I have hosts of things to say on the question of our marriage but I think I will keep them till we meet. Only I must protest against thy doubting my power to fulfil our ideal. If anything thee did could annoy me I should be annoyed at thy doubting me in this matter. There is no fact in heaven or earth of which I am more absolutely certain than that I shall be able to carry it out. How can thee suppose, even if I were to convince myself we had been mistaken in our ideal, that I could so degrade myself in thy eyes as to prefer that we abandon it? And besides I am firmly convinced that it is right, and shall not allow myself to reconsider it: the greater the temptation the less I should believe any arguments that might suggest themselves. And also I must protest against identifying passion with sensuality: whatever my faults, I am not sensual, and I believe the temptation would not be greater to me, but rather less, than to most men. Besides as we come to care more and more, I don't believe caring with me will take the form of being more strongly tempted: on the contrary I have found love antagonistic to temptation: where nobler things are consistently in one's thoughts, a more base physical satisfaction seems so very mean and contemptible. If I did not love thee so much it would be harder, but it is just my love that makes it easy. And as to self-control I think I may say without undue boasting that I have had more practice in it than most people of my age, for the very reason that I have cared so much about things which duty interfered with. And this is not a thing I can imagine myself ever really caring about as I am so firmly convinced it would ruin all I value about our love. So I must beseech thee to trust me entirely in this matter: thee may and I shall be hurt if thee cannot.

As to religion, it is difficult to argue in a letter with a conviction of the sort thee describes and which I have heard other Christians speak of. Oddly enough only the other day Ward[1] (who began life as a dissenting minister) described as comparable to self-consciousness this very God-consciousness (as he called it) which thee describes, and mentioned Quakers as specially possessing it. He said (and I agree with him) that if anyone asserts such a God-consciousness, argument becomes useless: one can only tell oneself that their introspection is faulty, but that is not an argument to them.

It is not illogical to regard God as almighty in spite of the evil, only then he must be regarded as an almighty Fiend; he cannot even be viewed as partly good and partly bad, like the world he has made, but must be regarded as wholly and infinitely wicked, having done wrong without temptation, for omnipotence cannot be tempted.

I am afraid it is rather a mockery to say our friendship and the congeniality of our tastes would still be left if thee decided not to marry: I think I ought, if I could possibly bring myself to it, not to see thee for several years in that case, otherwise I should be unable to endure it. And our friendship could never again be very intimate for I should always have to be silent about the one thing I could not fail to be always thinking of when I was with thee. And all my feelings would have to be cased in an iron reserve which would make our intercourse far more strained and unnatural than if we had never been anything but friends, and even than our intercourse with other friends. And I should have thought the friendship part was already thoroughly established. Thee knows me better than anybody else does and I know thee better than I know anybody else: and I do not see how we could have failed to be friends if we had not been more.

Thursday, 12 noon. Ever since thy last letter the fear that thy feelings will change has seized my imagination so powerfully that I feel almost as certain of it as if it had already happened. I have always been superstitious and the form it takes is always believing that what I dread will happen. When thee was on thy way to America I was firmly convinced thy ship would sink though I knew statistically it was very improbable. But *this* fear had not got hold of my imagination before: I am afraid now it will stick there at least till our next meeting. It is folly I know to worry about what one can't affect one way or the other, but to know a feeling is folly never makes me feel it a bit less. I lay awake the greater part of Tuesday night going through in imagination the scenes and this life suggested by these fears: yesterday I went

---

1. James Ward (1843–1925), a Cambridge philosopher and psychologist, and the most influential of Russell's philosophy teachers. In fact, he had never been ordained as a minister, despite arduous efforts to quell doctrinal doubts. He turned to philosophy shortly after leaving his church.

a 15-mile walk, and in the evening stayed up till 1 talking with Amos about his moral difficulties: this was a soothing occupation and combined with one of the best concerts I ever heard succeeded in putting me to sleep. But this morning all my fears are back again: I must try a longer walk today.

I am rather ashamed of all these feelings and had meant to keep silence about them but they are too strong. I wish we were going to meet sooner: I believe another meeting will dispel them. But it will be good practice for me to get over them by myself and I will make great efforts; till I do I am almost incapacitated for work.

I am glad thee told Lady Henry and that she was pleased and said nice things about my parents. I do not remember Dibblen(?):[1] he sounds rather a beast from thy account. Sometimes I think all men are beasts. I have had a fit of Browning lately and have been reading 'In a Year' many times: it seems to me very splendid. I have a mood just now for humbling myself in thy eyes so I have settled to send thee in a day or two my scraps of a journal, in which I used to put down things I was ashamed to say to other people: for that very reason it says nothing but what is very true about me. There is very little of it and I think a few bits might amuse thee. But I am on the whole ashamed of it for several things.[2]

I wrote to my grandmother to say I was probably going to Rome: she had suggested my asking Crompton in the Easter Vac. but I said as I should not be very long at home it would be a pity to break into the family party: her reply is very skilful. She says 'I wished particularly to see a great deal of Mr C. D. and learn to know him intimately – and hoped to do so in the Easter vacation " 'gin I be spared" – but of course if you spend it abroad there's no use in thinking of it – and the summer is too far off to look forward to at 78. – Auntie was in bed all the days I was, and very sad it was for us to be alone and apart – and Dora[3] away. – It is very saddening and when I am not with her and forcing myself to be cheerful, I am very down-hearted I own. But don't say so in letters.' – I had not written about Paris, and as thee may imagine the wish to know Crompton grew very much after it was discovered Rome would interfere with it. But still it is touching to think of them alone in their separate beds, and I get very much puzzled sometimes.

I hope thee will manage to write tomorrow evening or Saturday morning,

1. George Binney Dibblee, a Fellow of All Souls, Oxford. He had proposed to Alys two and a half years earlier, and had recently turned up again at Friday's Hill.
2. The journal is published in *Papers*, vol. I, pp. 43–67.
3. Dora Bühler, formerly Russell's Swiss governess, now a more or less permanent member of the Pembroke Lodge household.

and that thee will have successful meetings. Thee needn't have apologized for Lady Henry's paper: I approve of it strongly and wish thee used it oftener. Now I am off for a walk. Fare thee well.

    Devotedly thine
    Bertie

Russell's involvement in the Apostles figures prominently in the next letter. He had been writing a paper for them ('Lövberg or Hedda', *Papers*, vol. 1, pp. 84–9) advocating the admission of women to the society. He had already broached the topic with Alys and received some suggestions from her (surprisingly, she had not been in favour) and now he enclosed a draft for her to read. Later on in the letter he gives an amusing account of the meeting held the previous night, which indicates the surprising ways in which McTaggart's neo-Hegelian metaphysics were insinuated into all Apostolic discussions.

Russell's well-known mastery of train timetables also reveals itself in the letter. Alys was travelling down to London from Birmingham and had suggested travelling via Cambridge so that Russell could join her from Cambridge to London. Russell practically suggested that he meet her train earlier on the line. The plans, though elaborately laid, came to nothing since Alys decided not to travel from Birmingham after all. In the end, they met at King's Cross.

[25]

Trinity College
25 February 1894

My dearest Alys

    I have so much to write about that I hardly know where to begin. What I have uppermost in my mind is this paper: I wrote a first draft of it this morning after reading thy suggestions, which thee will see I have woven into my argument in various places. I am sorry thee is so pessimistic: I don't think thee quite realizes that the people are not quite normal. I know I myself can argue with thee or before thee just as well if not better than at other times: and I believe in the Society I should not be exceptional in this. I think very few women would be elected probably, as very few have independent intellectual interests at all strongly developed: so that those who were elected would be exceptional. I for one, however keen I might be from the point of view of the world, would never go for anything I thought bad for the Society, as it is so far as I know unique in its way and quite invaluable. I enclose a poem of Dickinson's on the Society which expresses what we all feel about it. It seems to me much better than the passage about the Society in *In Memoriam*. (Tomlinson was our founder.)[1]

I enclose my rough draft, but I shall have to rewrite it as I see the end contradicts the beginning and yet I wish to keep both, so the argument will have to be remodelled. I was immensely interested by thy information, which was very largely news to me. If thee has any fresh criticisms to make on my paper I should be very glad of them: I wish thee could write it for me! But I don't think thee has much experience of people in whom intellect is very predominant, as it is apt to be with members of the Society (I myself am not at all typical): can't thee imagine Logan or (still more) Graham Wallas[2] being in love and yet just as good at discussion as at any other time?

As to Germany I think thy plan is good, and with some modifications I feel very much inclined to adopt it.[3] Only if I don't go for work I will not go to a country town like Tübingen: Amos was there last year and I know I should be bored to death. I could only stand being in a capital, and I think I would go first to Berlin and then to Vienna. Anyway there is no term between July and October I believe. Also I am not *at all* prepared to give up the month of mutual boredom in September which thee almost promised. I think I might after that stay on abroad till December, as nothing would be going on in Germany in the summer and I shouldn't get the real life of the place till October: everybody is away travelling. But our month in September seems to me most important: it will be the only chance of such a thing before marriage and will be divine.

I am determined to go to Germany, but chiefly because thee wishes it: thee and Logan are the only people who advise me to go, except for the sake of enjoyment, of having a good time; and thee knows that from that point

1. This was probably the dedicatory poem in Dickinson's *Poems* (privately printed, 1896). It was republished in his *Autobiography* (1973), pp. 233–5. Alys, quite sensibly, did not think much of it as poetry. Tennyson describes an Apostles' meeting in *In Memoriam*, LXXXVII; both he and Arthur Hallam were members. George Tomlinson (1801–63), who went on to become the Bishop of Gibraltar, founded the Apostles in 1820 as a religious discussion society.
2. Graham Wallas (1858–1932), sociologist, educator and at this time still a Fabian. In 1895 he took up a position at the London School of Economics. Alys was working in the British Museum as his research assistant.
3. Alys was still resolved that Russell should see something of the world on his own before they married. This idea had crystallized into a plan for him to spend some time at a German university (she fixed on Tübingen) studying either economics or politics. Russell continued to resist the idea.

of view it is a mere farce to pretend it would be a success. Though of course I shall be divinely happy all the time in the thought of our love; only less happy than nearer thee.

Thy last letter *was* heavenly: I cannot possibly say what joy it gave me. It is so glorious to feel I have made thee happier, so wonderful to think of thy love. My dearest, how can thee talk of being unworthy? I draw all my strength from thee. How can I do wrong with the thought of thy love, and the thought that thee cares whether I do right? But without thee I should be nothing.

It is a great joy to have got within the fortnight and indeed the time has gone much faster than before: now that I trust so absolutely in thy love the thought of it makes every moment glorious, so that even separation is easy when it is necessary. I was quite right to say 'any other 6 months' to thy mother: those 6 would have been absolutely unendurable and might for aught I know have been fatal. Ugh! the mere thought makes me shudder. Fancy if I were now still enduring a solitary existence and perhaps hearing from my people with manifest joy concealed under a decent cloak of condolence that thee was just starting for a year's trip round the world! However I only raise the thought for the pleasure of the contrast with the fact.

I will look out the trains from Birmingham as soon as the March Bradshaw comes out: but as it is about four hours' journey from Birmingham I will come to meet thee at Rugby or Bletchley according to the trains, and then thee can travel straight through from Birmingham to London. I dare say for 6d. the guard will lock thy carriage for as long as the train is in the station so thee will probably be able to keep it to thyself if thee travels 1st.

Last night Sanger read on Which Wagner? i.c. Music or Economics? i.e. Art or Social Duty?[1] He went for art, and so of course did McTaggart, merely because it appears at 1st sight the less virtuous course, and he has a childish love of naughtiness. So did Moore because he is a Stoic and thinks happiness doesn't depend on externals such as food and clothing. Teach the East-ender to appreciate art and he will be happy. Moore is colossally ignorant of life. Crompton and I maintained very fine emotions were to be got out of identifying yourself with any great movement, even if it did have some practical utility, but I differed from Crompton in thinking it would be a gain if one could devote oneself solely to the pleasures not directly dependent

1. The allusion in the title is to Richard Wagner the composer and Adolph Wagner the economist.

on benevolence. (These include love.) The discussion was hopelessly unsatisfactory, as all discussions on practical questions always are. McTaggart ran
his Absolute, as usual, and we protested it was useless, and if not, worked
the other way: but Marsh, being new and not knowing the trick, was
frightened at such an imposing machinery and was half converted to McTaggart. The odd thing about the Absolute is that it always goes against the
Chronicle[1] whatever that paper may happen to say. Also that when anybody
else uses it McTaggart says it can't be used. McTaggart has had his friend
Young (late of Balliol), the musician, staying with him.[2] He is I think one
of the most fascinating men I know, and plays the piano divinely. He played
a number of pieces out of *Parsifal*, with a running commentary explaining
the dramatic use of movements, which was very instructive. Does thee know
him? He spent I believe two years in Vienna and a good while in Berlin
studying music and told me a lot about both.

I should like my paper back in a day or two when thee has had time to
think of some objections to it. There are a few bits of Society slang I will
explain: *Real* is what relates to the Society, *phenomenal* everything and
everybody else. We all have to speak in turn and lots are drawn as to the
order: and we all speak from the *hearthrug*. I should like to have Dickinson's
poem back some time but there is no hurry about that.

I think the best plan for Germany will be to go for the end of June and
the whole of July (i.e. part of the summer term), and again from the middle
or end of October till Christmas, so as to be only there during term-time.
Then thee can come to Dresden at Christmas as thee had meant to do.

I am colossally busy this week, as besides my paper I have two papers to
do for Ward and as soon as they are done, an Essay for Stout:[3] but I hope
to manage it all successfully. I am also carrying on an Ethical controversy as
to Ethical Axioms: I have revolted from pure Hedonism which has annoyed
Sidgwick.[4] However I am dining with him tomorrow and hope to find him
still friendly.

It makes no difference whether I get thy letters morning or evening: either

1. Under the editorship of H. W. Massingham, the *Daily Chronicle* was the chief voice
of the radical 'new Liberals'. Subsequently, and under different editorship, it became the
mouthpiece of the Liberal imperialists.
2. Probably Dalhousie James Young, a classics student who graduated in 1889.
3. George Frederick Stout (1861–1944), with Sidgwick and Ward, the third of Russell's
philosophy teachers. Russell wrote at least three essays for Ward in February (see *Papers*,
vol. I, pp. 141–54). The paper for Stout cannot be identified.
4. See the paper 'Ethical Axioms' (*Papers*, vol. I, pp. 227–8) which Russell wrote for
Sidgwick.

way they come at the beginning of a spell of work, but they don't interfere with it when they are pleasant, which they always are now.

Goodbye my darling.

Thine devotedly,

Bertie

Russell's excitement and frustration sometimes reached fever pitch. In the next letter his agitation was compounded by the prospect of a visit to Grosvenor Road the next day. His unusually erratic handwriting betrays his restlessness.

Their earlier debate about Alys's desire to turn her house into a sort of hotel had led to discussions about their attitudes to other people. Alys, in many ways a more reserved person even than Russell at this time, had said that she always tried to bring others out rather than to express her own opinions. Indeed, she thought that in company one ought to talk about what interested other people, rather than about one's own interests – a moral precept which could not have happy consequences if widely adopted. Russell, of course, deplored her refusal to talk about herself (the most interesting subject in the world), but he did say that in practice he did very much the same, although, in his case, it was rather due to curiosity than to concern for the other person. Alys, in turn, characteristically deplored his lack of concern. His meeting with the Newnham students at Ward's dinner party provided an opportunity for observation.

Frank Russell's marital misadventures were a continual source of trouble. His first wife, Mabel Edith Scott, had left him three weeks after their marriage early in 1890. The legal consequences of this action continued bitterly for ten years. Mabel sought a legal separation on grounds of cruelty, accusing Frank, among other things, of having homosexual relations during the brief time they were together. This action failed and she then sued for restoration of conjugal rights, the hope being to extract a financial settlement of £1,000 a year in lieu of restoration. When this failed also, Lady Scott, Mabel's mother, spread the allegation of homosexuality and in 1897 was gaoled for criminal libel as a result. Since the various judgments were variously appealed, in one case up to the House of Lords, the entire process was spectacularly complicated and exceedingly bitter. A divorce settlement was eventually achieved in 1901, but only after further extraordinary adventures. By this time, however, Miss Morris with whom Frank appears here had been left behind. He describes but does not name her in his autobiography. He says there that he did not approve of her principles and felt that they were temperamentally unsuited for each other. In the end he ran away to America to escape her (Frank Russell, *My Life and Adventures*, p. 180). 'We are always bad at choosing wives,' Frank said, when Bertie told him of Alys (Clark, *Russell*, p. 46). At this time Frank was a partner in an electrical company, Swinburne & Co., at Teddington.

[26]

Trinity College
8 March 1894

My darling

I am so excited I can hardly sit still even to write to thee. I have never been in such a frame of mind before and I am sure it is a pity to allow it to occur but I can't help it. I have done no work (except lectures I have paid no attention to) since Monday and then I could not work in the morning but had to go to Ely on my bicycle and see the Cathedral to keep me quiet. I have been all day yesterday wandering round and round or pacing up and down my room like a beast at the Zoo, except when I had to entertain some ladies to lunch and tea and to go out to dinner with Ward in the evening. There I talked with a brilliant and voluble flippancy throughout dinner, an effect excitement often has on me. But after dinner I practised thy precepts and my own usual practice by getting a Newnhamite[1] whom I didn't know before to tell me all about her scruples of conscience in first coming up and about her feeling of inferiority to her younger sister who had stayed at home and looked after the housekeeping and all about her *Sturm-und-Drang Periode* before she came up and the effect of Newnham in changing her character and all sorts of most intimate things. I tried to observe myself and it seemed to me I had a large share of genuine sympathy besides the psychological interest but then it was a case for which sympathy was easy.

I am always coming upon odd contrasts but never in my life have I come upon such an extraordinary and dramatic one as I have had before me these last few days. This however as thee will see must remain a *dead* secret from everybody. The ladies I had to look after were a Mrs and Miss Morris: My brother has been for three years (as he told me about a week ago) hypothetically engaged to Miss Morris i.e. he has promised to marry her if he can ever get a divorce. She is in no sense a lady and very dull and not even pretty: she was once clerk in his electrical office which is how it happened. She has however I think some force of character and I do not despair of her being able to stand him if they ever bring it off. He is fond of her in his placid way: and has got her to go in for [the] Newnham entrance exam and hopes to get her in. I have been seeing them together the last few days and his affection chiefly takes the form of making her eat too much, but I suppose he is paying for Newnham or rather will pay if she gets in. But he says himself he is not the least impatient. Unfortunately circumstances made it

---

1. In his agitation Russell wrote 'Newmanhite'.

necessary for me to tell him about thee but I hated doing it. However, in all he said he was very sympathetic and appreciative but in half a minute he was off on his electrical shop again.

I am not calm enough to think about Germany now but it seems to me only one of thy arguments, that thee wants to test thy own feelings, is good, and that points the other way because I am sure it is not absence that is the test at least the more we are apart the more passionately we seem to love each other. Thee must know if thee is frank that it is perfect nonsense now to talk about my developing away from thee. I should do nothing but mental arithmetic in the way of intellectual activity, working out in my head the number of days, hours, minutes, or seconds till the end of the six months. But I don't pretend I have been consistent and of course the New Year would be quite soon enough to begin work. I know I shall go finally because as long as thee feels it to be right it must be done.

I should not go to Germany for August and September, but for a walking tour in Norway or something of that sort. Thee has I see come back to the six months of complete separation which had been so long given up. Thee may be right but nothing would be developed in me except moral force if I succeeded. Intellectually and physically the time would be noxious to me. And now I don't see intellectual questions through thy eyes at all. And if thee were to ask my friends or my lecturers I am sure they would tell thee my intellect has been unusually acute and keen lately. And I have developed far more in every way in the last six months than in the preceding three years.

However if thee is firm I shall go as I won't make thee go round the world!

This letter is very mad I'm afraid: but I am completely dominated by impatience (with an e this time) in a way I have never known anything like before. Thank God we meet tomorrow.

Goodbye. Goodbye, my darling,

Thine

Bertie

Alys was curious to see what sort of letter Russell wrote to Granny, so he obliged by sending her a copy of one. The original is lost but the copy (written on the back of a mathematics exercise) was preserved with Alys's papers. Although the letter repeats the events described in the previous letter to Alys, it does indicate the tone Russell was taking towards his family as the battle over his relationship with Alys continued. So, too, does the next letter to Alys, which described his grim reception at Pembroke Lodge when he returned home on 13 March. Granny had now been informed of Russell's plans to visit Logan in Paris and of the fact that he would meet Alys there. His plans now were to see Logan on his way out to Rome and call again on his way back, by which time Alys would be there. It is not clear what examinations he was sitting.

[27]

[Trinity College]
11 March 1894

Dearest Granny

I have just come back from the Pearsall Smiths, where my short stay was of course very delightful. I am very sorry indeed you do not think my future prospects bright, particularly as it must be painful to you: but I am the more persuaded that your fears are groundless, as I find from my father's journal that you had just as great fears about his marriage, which yet was as perfectly happy as any marriage could be, to judge by his journal and my mother's. So I do wish you could get rid of your fears, as I am sure they make you unnecessarily unhappy.

I was delighted to get even a pencil note from you, as it showed a great improvement in your health. I do hope when I come on Tuesday I shall find you with very little of your usual strength wanting. I shall have an exam paper here from 9 to 12, and shall have to buy my ticket to Rome on my way so I shall not arrive till about 4.30 probably.

Frank was here for two days last week, in very good health and spirits as usual; but I didn't see very much of him as we were both busy and one of the days I was dining with Dr Ward, my lecturer in Metaphysics, a delightful man, who began life as a Congregational minister but began to have doubts of orthodoxy and so came up to Cambridge and read Philosophy. I had a very pleasant dinner there and had some interesting talk with some pleasant Newnhamites – *A mardi*.

Your loving grandson
Bertrand Russell

[28]

Pembroke Lodge
14 March 1894

My Dearest

It was a joy to find thy letter on arriving here this afternoon. I am so glad thee has not yet felt the pain of parting: no more have I. Absence is least painful at first, because least realized. Besides I have been so busy since we parted that I have had no time to think much of thee except at nights and during intervals of dream in my exam; though the *feeling* of thy love is *always* with me and never ceases to give me joy whatever is happening. I too felt as though it were an eternity since we met, and as if a whole lifetime had been concentrated in those days. It *is* overwhelming to think of the bliss in store for us. I believe I *do* think it silly, but I too have been feeling a perfectly childish joy at being properly engaged, I don't know why, unless that every external symbol becomes delightful in such a matter, or unless it is a remnant of a conventional bringing-up. – I can still call up thy image vividly and when I am alone I can almost feel thy arms round me and so I can almost imagine we are not really parted; I hope this will last nearly till we meet again, which is very little over a fortnight, joyful change! I *do* think thee has let thy self go now, and to me it is far far more heavenly than ever before in consequence, and it is glorious to think thee has no more scruples or doubts.

I suppose I may as well write about my people, but it seems really irrelevant. I find my aunt will probably be glad at bottom when it becomes an engagement, though she will *say* it is a breach of faith and so on: but she knows what love means, and I spoke extremely openly to her today about the strength of my love and even told her (apparently without hurting her particularly) that if she and my grandmother *would* say nothing but things I didn't wish to hear about thee, it was natural I shouldn't wish to talk about thee and should get out of sympathy with them. I couldn't have said so to my grandmother, but my aunt understood. When I arrived I found them together: my grandmother immediately attacked me with: I *hear* Mr Logan does not live in the best society in Paris: I should think you had much better stay at a hotel in Paris, and not identify yourself too much with his friends. (Not snobbery, but Puritanism.) And my aunt chimed in and they were very decided on my staying at a hotel: with ill-concealed joy at having something ill-natured to say of poor Logan, though I don't believe they themselves were conscious of this feeling. I preserved a strict silence till they stopped.

Later on my grandmother began: I suppose matters between you and Miss Smith are where they were. *I:* Well, of course things drift more or less. *She:* Oh there was no question of drifting: I have her mother's promise in writing, and hers in words, that it was to be nothing but simple friendship. I suppose I ought to have got hers in writing too but I never thought of it. She is as much bound in honour as any human being can be not to let anything but simple friendship arise. Poor old woman! as though such things could be ruled by all the promises in the world! And I don't know, but I imagine she exaggerated the extent of the promises. However, though I tried to prepare both her and my aunt for the announcement of our engagement, I think it will be a great blow to my grandmother and that it will be long before she can forgive thee. Later on she spoke of 'Revolting daughters, as they are called: You see the joke?' without any smile herself at the joke.[1] – Both she and my aunt can hardly speak about the 'hateful controversy' as they call it. Both of them I think had made up their minds to be agreeable before I came, and my grandmother began by saying she would not a say a word on the subject, but the temptation to small nastinesses was too great. My grandmother, when she found I was going early tomorrow morning, said it was hardly worth while having come, but to this my aunt didn't assent. I have not had the slightest difficulty in keeping my temper, partly because the time is short and partly because nothing they can do matters a jot.

I am glad thee told Frank Costelloe[2] and very glad of his reason for having guessed. I fear, though I am ashamed to confess it, love has hardly had such a good effect on my manners: whenever I am away from thee I am more or less impatient, so that people get on my nerves with their slowness and with their petty silly interests: besides to get into the way of always exposing my inmost soul to thee makes me more sensitive and less ready to hide it from other people: so that though I have come to love my few best friends very much more than I ever did before, I hate my enemies worse and am more

1. Alys had had an article, 'A Reply from the Daughters', published in the *Nineteenth Century*. It was one of three articles the magazine published in 1894 on 'the revolt of the daughters', that is, on the growing unwillingness of unmarried daughters to devote their lives to looking after their parents. Lady Russell was so hostile to it that she wrote a satire, 'Livia, a Daughter', to which, lest anyone should miss its point, she added the subtitle: 'Suggested by an article in the *Nineteenth Century* by Miss A. P. S.' Although Granny labelled the manuscript 'For *Punch*', the magazine did not publish it and it is quite possible that the label was intended to indicate its tone rather than its destination.
2. The husband of Alys's sister, Mary, who continued to live close by the Smiths with his two children at 40 Grosvenor Road while Mary was with Berenson in Italy.

bored by the people I only mildly dislike: and in fact I have found all passions intensified when they arise at all, and have become altogether more excitable or perhaps it would be better to say more alive. This extends to intellect too: when I can think about intellectual matters I am sure my thought is quicker and more penetrating than it used to be, though of course I am less apt to think of them! But I have perhaps been a little unjust to myself, I think I have grown more ready to sympathize with everybody.

I remember vividly a discussion in the train with Costelloe, in which I said I meant to do Moral Science in my fourth year (it was before I was a freshman), and he said that would be too late for philosophy, as my mind would have been spoilt by the 'abstract quantum' (most untrue by the way: nothing is so useful in Philosophy as a mathematical training), so I asked him what that meant, and generally drew him out on philosophy and said almost nothing myself, so of course he thought me intelligent; I realized this method even at the time.

I shall not send a p.c. as I send my address and other details with this. I enclose a copy of a letter to my grandmother since thee is interested to see what sort of letter I write. But it is scarcely typical, as I have not usually the impertinence to hint she can ever be mistaken.

I hope to see Logan at dinner in Paris tomorrow.

Goodbye my darling: it is useless to repeat how utterly I am thine in every thought and word and deed, and how thy love is the one thing that makes this world more heavenly than any heaven I can imagine.

Thine,
   Bertie

My address will be *Hôtel Suisse, Rome*. Term begins April 20. Tripos begins May 21 and ends May 24. I will write again from Genoa [?] where we arrive Thursday evening.

The letter from Genoa, if Russell wrote one, did not survive, but he wrote again from Turin on the 15th and again from Rome on the 17th. Tourist impressions, however, were not his forte. Nor, despite the efforts of those around him, was he able to take a lively interest in the glories of Roman art and architecture.

[29]

Hôtel Suisse, Rome
17 March 1894

My Dearest

I have no letter yet, but I hope for one tomorrow. I will not finish this letter till tomorrow morning, but as I shall not have much time then I will begin it now. I don't know whether thee wants to know all about my first impressions of Rome, but I don't see how I can make them interesting. I am immeasurably delighted with the look of the people, and the streets, and everything in the trip: of the details I cannot judge and therefore I cannot enjoy them properly since I never know what I ought to like, except that it is sure not to be what my uncle the Monsignor[1] who acts as Cicerone, tells me I ought. However he agrees with me in hating ruins. But I have been almost converted to ruins since I have been here: some I have seen have been so exquisitely beautiful.

What is more important than ruins is that I saw Miss Dawson[2] this morning and we went a drive right out into the Campagna in hope of brigands, who however failed us. She had the kindness to say all sorts of delightful things to me about thee; and it *was* nice to be able to talk about thee *à cœur ouvert*: since it has ceased to be universally necessary, self-suppression is become more irksome to me: I suppose because silence about thee is more complete self-suppression than any I have ever had to practise before. I am afraid I forgot thy precepts and talked incessantly, and only about my own interests! However there was some excuse for me, and being thy friend she was probably more or less interested in my interests! At least that is how I justified myself to myself. She had a Baedeker marked by thy sister, which I greatly envied her. I do wish I could go about with her all day long instead of with these stiff inartistic aristocrats. Whatever else might have been to be hoped from my never having met thee, my grandmother might always have despaired of my marrying an aristocrat: their icy reserve (though I feebly try to ape it) would kill me to live with. And I do believe the frivolous life of society and idleness kills out every particle of seriousness from all the girls who were at all attractive, it is only the Mary Bennets among aristocrats who 'read great books and make extracts'.[3] I have such a host of smart relations here that I fear all my time will be taken up in social 'duties':

1. Algernon Stanley, the Bishop of Emmaus and a papal chamberlain. According to Russell, he was 'witty, fat, and greedy' (*Autobiography*, vol. I, p. 34).
2. Emily Dawson, one of Alys's cousins.
3. See *Pride and Prejudice*, ch. 2.

tomorrow e.g. I am going to two tea-parties and an evening party (the latter however at an Italian's). My uncle is in some ways invaluable, but in others rather a drawback.

I have made friends at the table d'hôte here with a German family, father, mother, and youth. The latter at first took me for an Italian, I suppose because of my lively excitable manner, he could hardly be persuaded I was English. I amused myself yesterday evening in trying to impress him in the hopes that he might remark afterwards to his people: 'Die Engländer sind ein grossartiges Volk, aber verrückt sind sie doch, gänzlich verrückt.'[1] Alas! I shall never know if I succeeded, but as far as I could judge I was fairly successful: I adopted a Byronic pose, which is a very easy one. This evening I sat next his mother, and was quite different: I got her to tell me her husband was Professor of Medicine in Tübingen, and she went on with naïve pride to tell how he had just completed all but the preface and index of a large work on medicine in five bulky volumes: thank God no one need read it who doesn't want to!

This is palpably a family without problems: if I see many more like it I shall be converted back to domesticity and the wife's sphere as the kitchen. Obviously the good woman was perfectly happy and devoted to her husband: dull I must confess she was, deadly dull: but I suppose he was sufficiently absorbed in his shop not to notice that. If I were as thee wishes me, absorbed in my work, I suppose I could be as easily pleased as this good man: and just think what a simplification it makes to solve the problem so, and not on the complicated mutual-adjustment system which we and people like us have to adopt! – These remarks was sarcusstical as Artemus Ward[2] says. There is similarly no Father-and-Sons problem in this family: the young man doesn't know what a problem is, in fact.

I have been struck also by an American lady of about 50 whom my aunt[3] made friends with. She of course related her whole family history to my aunt: she has been for some years a widow, and has spent her time in complete solitude, travelling and studying art. She says she has no friends in Europe: she would have had a companion, only an American young woman would have expected *her* to do all the packing, and would have complained if there had not been plenty of society provided for her and everything made pleasant.

---

1. Roughly: 'The English are a great people, but they are crazy, completely crazy.'
2. The pseudonym of the popular American humorist, Charles Farrar Browne (1834–67). In the character of Ward, the manager of a travelling side-show, Browne wrote articles and gave lectures on both sides of the Atlantic commenting on a wide variety of subjects in a *faux*-illiterate style marked by grotesque misspellings and puns.
3. Maude Stanley, who accompanied Russell on the trip.

This is the other side of the picture. The poor old lady doesn't seem to mind solitude, however, but seems extremely happy and is very charming. I made her quite fall in love with me by advising her, against her conscience, to buy a very expensive book of engravings of Raphael which she had had lent her and was showing us. But such a life seems to me unendurable. I realized however, in thinking of it, that even for my own purpose of understanding people, it is necessary to realize how to some people pictures can give enough pleasure to act as substitutes for friendship, though to me *nothing* could, and that understanding people involves understanding all their interests. But it would never occur to me to study pictures for their own sakes: the only real reason I would do it is because thee wants me to.

I will finish this letter tomorrow morning: I hope thee got my letter from Turin all right, but as it was only addressed in pencil I was afraid it might go wrong. I will write again on Tuesday evening or Wednesday morning.

Sunday Evening. The morning post is not yet come, but as I have to go out with my aunt to a Catholic function very soon I must finish now. Miss Dawson was greatly shocked to find me such a barbarian, and indeed I am not much in the mood for admiring the lifeless works of dead men: being in love with thee makes me in love with life and all that lives, in spite of what I said last time I wrote. But I do succeed in enjoying everything here very much, though I miss half the things thinking about thee. I realize how fruitless it would have been to have gone abroad for 6 months: for though I can throw myself into everything here, it is only half-heartedly and with the mental reservation 'only for a fortnight'. After that I should begin to get disgusted with it I believe.

I hope thee is having successful meetings. I don't know where this letter will find thee so I send it to Grosvenor Rd. I think of thee day and night, and count the days till we meet: only 10 more after to-day! Fare thee well my dearest. I am intensely happy in the thought of thy love, and I can't find words for my love but thee knows it, doesn't thee, without words.

    Thine

      Bertie

While Russell was in Rome, Alys and her mother had travelled to Paris to visit Logan and Russell joined them there for a few days on his way home. Russell remembered 'floating on the Seine at night near Fontainebleau with Alys beside me, while Logan filled the night with unbending cleverness'. Efforts to improve his appreciation of art by taking him to see galleries and artists were less successful, though Russell found the life of the American artists in Paris 'very free and delightful'

(*Autobiography*, vol. i, p. 83). For the first time, he could feel confident that Alys returned his love.

He returned to Pembroke Lodge on 7 April. His letter next day, and the one which follows it, reveal the poisoned atmosphere there. The battle over the marriage had now clearly escalated. Granny was incensed that they had seen each other in Paris and, while Russell was still in Rome, she had summoned Alys to Pembroke Lodge for questioning. Alys recorded this intimidating event in her diary:

> Reached Pembroke Lodge at 4 o'clock, and saw Lady Russell alone for half an hour, then Lady Agatha came in ... I left at 5, as the conversation was painful and very fruitless. They think I am behaving in a very dishonourable and indelicate manner in seeing so much of Bertie and writing twice a week. And they do not understand how I can 'pursue' him to Paris. I saw it was hopeless to argue with Lady R. so I only repeated that I could not see the thing as she did. (B. Strachey, *Remarkable Relations*, p. 135)

[30]

Pembroke Lodge
8 April 1894. 5.40 p.m.

My Dearest Alys,

It is a horrid necessity to have to collapse into letters again and I have hardly realized our parting enough yet to imagine the necessity. However fortunately it is not for long. I have had the scene with my Grandmother: it didn't happen the way I had hoped and was I fear rather a failure, though I said all I had contemplated saying and said nothing beyond my intentions. At first I tried to refuse discussing the matter, but she said she didn't want to 'discuss' it, only to have a little friendly talk about it. So I weakly let her go on, and she began again about promises and writing and so on. So I repeated that I 'felt' too much to hear her blame thee, and told her thy mother (not thee, who was out at the time) had told me about thy conversation with her, and didn't she understand that it made a difficulty in our relations (hers and mine) if she said those sort of things, and that not from thy mother's comments but from the actual words she had reported I couldn't help feeling she had been 'unkind' to thee. This word seemed to sting her like an adder, far more than I had anticipated: and so it did when I spoke about difficulty in our relations. To this she said in a voice half choked with tears (as her voice was throughout) that such difficulty was only on my side (which seemed to me natural enough, since she has hitherto been the aggressor), and to the other she replied in an agonized tone (which was perfectly real: if thee says she couldn't or shouldn't have felt so much thee will be falling into the same mistake she falls into) that though she had many times had to speak plainly to people in a similar situation before nobody had *ever* told her she was unkind. The idea of blame from a younger person is so foreign to her mind that my words seemed like a combination of sacrilege and cruelty. I went on to explain how very likely it might be a pity I should be so heart-and-soul in love at my age (a sop to Cerberus), but that it was a fact, that I felt the feelings she had characterized as unmanly, as she did again today, with the difference that she was forced to admit them real; and that as things were so, and as thee cared for me, it was useless to talk of leaving me free in her sense, since I couldn't live without thee. I further explained that even if we were technically engaged we should still of course break it off at once if either of us ceased to care, which seemed to meet with her warmest approval, so warm that I was sorry I had said it as it may lead her to keep a spark of hope even till we are married. She apologized a good deal: said she had thought she was doing thee such a kindness in speaking frankly to thee about everything (including thy article, which she mentioned), that she had felt much relieved in her conscience (or rather her temper, which faulty analysis mistook for conscience) by her talk with thee, but that now she regretted it: that she would write to ask thy mother to visit her, though I don't know what good she could hope from a visit. She utterly denied that ever she had hinted or insinuated or implied the shadow of a moral fault in thee either in talking to me or in talking to thee: she said it was hard she should be judged by the inaccurate report of a third person; that it was difficult to realize so sudden a change from the reasonable way I had talked in September (it was here I explained my unmanly feelings). She was terribly upset by my accusing her of unkindness, and in my grief at her pain I could remember none of the unkind things: I was tempted 1,000 times to crawl down but fortunately just avoided it. I explained I didn't suppose she was intentionally unkind, and that it gave me intense pain to say what I had said. Well, you can undo it, she said. I hesitated a moment and then said: I am afraid I can't. I assured her of my love, and throughout the scene kissed her at intervals and displayed, as indeed I felt when I saw her suffer, a very great deal of affection. But nothing will ever efface the effect of having been blamed by me. It was obvious she cared nothing for an affection which could be combined with such cruel words, though they seemed to me very mild compared to what I might have said. Finally I begged the subject might be closed between us, which also seemed to pain her, but after such a stab I think she will be chary of opening it again. I will tell her on Saturday of my intention of asking for an engagement. I believe she will not sleep a wink all night, and will probably be ill for some days; but I have said my say, and though I greatly fear she will never feel at ease with me now she knows I can think her guilty of a fault, I hope she will reflect on what I have said and come to see the reasonableness of it. I told her she couldn't see thy point of view, and gave her hints of my analogy about my aunt: but I was disarmed by her denial of facts, for which, at least to so great an extent, I was not wholly prepared. – I have not yet seen my aunt alone: they were greatly shocked to learn that I had all my meals with you and stayed at Logan's and travelled home with you.

10.30 p.m. This conversation was in the afternoon, and was fortunately interrupted by a visitor: I found it very exciting, so much so that when I tried to write some letters afterwards my hand shook almost too much to write legibly; my grandmother was painfully impressed by my excitement, but I didn't lose my self-control. And after a bit I felt much relieved, though I won't say it was my conscience which was relieved, as she would have said. Also I think it has had a good effect already: We had five minutes' more talk just before dinner, which began by her saying 'I have only to say I suppose I am a very foolish old woman; indeed I must have been to have spoken in a way which could be so misunderstood.' This I received in silence. After a bit she went on 'But I must beg you to understand our point of view a little better if you can: don't you see that when the last thing we had heard was that she was undecided and that it was only to be an intimate friendship, it is a little difficult suddenly to realize such a complete change; you see you never informed us that your relations had changed.' *I:* 'Well, you always refused to discuss it: you often said you couldn't speak about it, so of course I couldn't keep you informed how things were going.' She made efforts to deny this, but couldn't, and was impressed by its justice. I also reminded her of what she had said to me, that she ought to have got thy promise in writing instead of in words. She felt the unkindness of it (though she tried to explain it away), and finally had to admit 'promise' was not the right word. She said she had the highest opinion of thy moral character and had not meant to blame anything but thy judgment, and in conclusion said she might very likely come to regard this as a wholly fortunate thing, and the best thing that could have happened to me. Now that she has realized she runs a risk of losing my affection by the course she has adopted hitherto, she is ready to do almost anything to retain it, so that my words are having a very wholesome effect. I only hope she will not get ill with grief, but I scarcely dare to hope it. She also said incidentally in our last five-minutes' talk that she thought at times it was a pity, except for my aunt's sake, that she had recovered when she was so ill about a month ago; this was an attempt to soften me, and I expressed all the proper feelings in exclamations and embraces but abated no jot of my unkind words. She has completely adopted the lachrymose method, which shows that she feels it her last resource. If I can hold out against it, all will be well, and I have felt more at home this evening than I have, at home, for a long time. I have come to think what I said was perhaps the best after all, but I can't tell for some days. – I will finish this tomorrow, when I have thy letter. Fortunately the weather is glorious and the spring here delicious, and the immense content of having been so long with thee is still quite overpowering; so that though I was excited at the moment, I have not got worried or irritable and I believe I shall not get so at all this time.

Monday morning. My Darling – I have got thy letter and it *is* heavenly. I don't know what to say. It seems such an age since it was necessary to find *words* for the expression of love, that none of them seem any good. And yet thee has found lovely words for it: I wish I could too. I did know thee expected to be a bit bored in Paris, but I hardly thought it would come so soon.[1] I *do* hope thee is right in having no forebodings and I cannot help thinking thee is. But I am not sure whether thee won't get bored when thee knows my heart all through and through, and when I have no new words and phrases by which to make myself interesting! But like thee, I am in a sort of dazed state: I feel as one does coming in from out of doors into a dark room, and can distinguish nothing yet. Even my grandmother's suffering scarcely affects me. I seem numb to all feelings except what relate to thee my dearest. I am glad to be in such a dreamy state and I hope it will last till Sunday: it makes it perfectly easy to get through the day and do all one has to do. – I am too dreamy even to realize we are separated or what difference there would be if we were together. Everything (except thy letter) is just neutral and colourless. I think my capacity for emotion for the time being is almost worn out and no ordinary stimulus can arouse it.

I too have been writing letters hard: I found one from my uncle which I enclose: he had good ground of complaint but overstates his case.[2] However I crawled on the ground in my reply and I hope I satisfied him. – My grandmother is pale and tired but not ill today: her eyes swim in tears and she is on the point of a break down all the time, but I hope will not be ill.

I don't think we have ever discussed the Socialistic future of marriage. I have thought about it a good deal but have no clear ideas on it. One thing

1. In fact, Alys had said that she had expected to be bored by Paris, but wasn't.
2. Rollo had written with a list of letters he and Gertrude had sent to Russell over the past five weeks without getting a reply.

is clear to me, that the mother mustn't be eliminated whatever else may happen: Plato's plan[1] I am sure is no good. I cannot repeat any of Mr Zangwill's[2] new humour. I get on very well and have had long talks with Dora[3] and am going to try and take to philosophy and baccy again.

I have found a Shelley selections, which my aunt lent to Dora, given her by the man she loved. It is marked in pencil with the dates and places when he read the poems to her (or recited them); and others (such as 'That time is dead for ever child') are marked without any such comments. So is 'The unheeded tribute of a broken heart'. She marks only for sentiment, and exactly what I marked at 17; with the difference that she *has* a broken heart while I only played at having one. Poor woman! the whole story of her life is in her marks. There is a grim pathos about seeing 'That time is dead' and 'Love's Philosophy' next each other both marked by her.[4] What a universe between the two! And the most touching of all is that she always denies that she is fond of Shelley. – I feel as if I could bear any amount of bitterness from her now that I realize what she has suffered. – I hope thee will wake up to speak and not be bored with temperance.[5]

Goodbye my darling. I love thee love thee love thee a thousand times.

Thine devotedly

Bertie

1. Plato proposed that children, at least those of 'superior' parents, should be brought up by the state. (The children of 'inferior' parents were to be 'disposed of in secret'.) See the *Republic*, bk v, 460.
2. Israel Zangwill (1864–1926), the novelist, playwright, and Zionist. He was a friend of the Pearsall Smiths.
3. Dora Bühler (see letter 24).
4. 'Love's Philosophy' is a short poem of 1819 in which Shelley supports with varied examples the view that 'Nothing in the world is single'; 'That time is dead ... ' is the first line of a lament he wrote for Harriet Shelley, his first wife, who committed suicide in 1816; 'The unheeded tribute ... ' is from *Alastor* (1. 624).
5. Alys had a temperance meeting that day. She hoped in her letter that she would wake up from her dreamy state in time for it.

[31]

Pembroke Lodge
14 April 1894. 11.40 a.m.

My Dearest,

I was very glad of thy letter this morning and have now administered the
coup de grâce. The scene should have been exquisitely painful, but I seem to
be getting hardened to the infliction of pain, and my grandmother was not
surprised evidently, so that there was no sudden shock to her as there was
last time. I did not need any brutal method such as refusing to discuss the
matter or leaving the room. I told her with an air of quiet determination
that I had made up my mind during the week to ask thee to make it an
engagement. She repeated of course that she and my aunt and Uncle Rollo
were strongly of the opposite opinion and she would have supposed that
might have weighed for something with me, and she hoped it would with
thee (though she didn't really of course and I said one couldn't tell how thee
might feel, *perhaps* thee would see it as she did!). She talked about thy article,
and I admitted to please her that it would have been better if thee had said
something to shew thee realized there were happy mothers and daughters,
as I think now it would have been, as a matter of policy. But she said she
firmly believed we should be happy together, only she didn't know thee
enough to say positively. She repeated various old stories about other
members of the family, and what thy mother had told her about thy brother
who died.[1] I listened patiently, but as I have had the upper hand ever since
our last interview I had no need to excite myself or protest or do anything
particular. Of course I couldn't give her most of the reasons, but I said it
would change our relation only in name and would enable us to meet more
easily. Poor woman! She was much pained by my disregard of the unanimous
advice of the three of them, and I was sorry to find I had chosen a moment
when she was peculiarly sensitive, as she had just been writing to her son
in a lunatic asylum,[2] for his birthday; which was naturally an intensely
painful occasion as I believe she hardly ever writes to him. I didn't know
this or I would have spoken yesterday. – She said as thee was older thee
would of course have a great influence on me, and they would largely

1. Frank Pearsall Smith, who died of typhoid in 1872 at the age of eighteen.
2. George Gilbert William Russell (1848–1933). He went mad in 1874, although his
behaviour had for a long time been odd. (At least, Granny thought so – though the
behaviour she cited as evidence would be consistent with nothing worse than eccentricity.)
Russell came to think his insanity was caused by cruel practical jokes played on him by
his fellow army officers.

judge of the good or bad of our marriage from that! So thee must take care!

My uncle said very little except, reply to a hint of mine, that he would be very sorry if it became an engagement yet-a-while. He gave me the enclosed, asking me not to read it till I was pure[?].[1] It was marked 'private' I suppose in order that I should not shew it to thee, so it would be better not to tell anyone I have shewn it to thee. But he is mistaken in imagining it is a point of view which doesn't readily occur to me, as thee knows.

My grandmother again lamented that I have never read her any extracts from thy letters, but I cannot bring myself to do it, though there are often things which might quite well be read. But then there are also so often whole letters of which no word should be read to her, and it is a bad precedent to begin reading extracts.

She is now genuinely in favour of our marriage, and only wishes we would submit our feelings (or rather mine, for it never seems to occur to her thine might change) to some more severe test. She seemed to think it absurd to regard constant companionship as a test, though it seems to me the only one of any value as a preliminary to marriage, as it is the test which is applied in marriage, and is far more searching than absence, which besides may succeed in weakening a wholly desirable affection just as well as an undesirable one.

I *am* glad we meet tomorrow. I have been one of those whom 'time ambles withal'[2] all this week, and continue to feel perfectly placid though very anxious for tomorrow –

Goodbye my dearest
Thine most affectionately
Bertie

Russell no doubt hoped that by getting formally engaged he would force his family to accept the inevitable. Nothing could have been further from the truth; it convinced them, rather, 'that something drastic must be done' (*Autobiography*, vol. I, p. 83). The engagement was agreed upon in the third week of April, though it was decided that it wouldn't be announced until after Russell's Tripos in May. Losing no time, Russell's family put into effect a new plan and one which, Russell admitted, 'very nearly gave them the victory' (ibid.). Their intention was to show that marriage between Bertie and Alys was undesirable on eugenic grounds, since there were

1. The document Russell enclosed was a memorandum from his Uncle Rollo urging him not to disgrace the family tradition, and warning, rather obliquely, of the hereditary dangers of coming from such an old family.
2. *As You Like It*, III, ii, 328.

supposed to be several cases of insanity in both families. The family physician, Dr William Anderson, suitably instructed by Granny, was the chief 'expert' on these matters, although other doctors were brought in to corroborate his opinions.

Hints of this plan have already appeared in the preceding letters – the coincidence of Granny's birthday letter to mad Uncle Willy; the dark warnings in Uncle Rollo's memorandum; and the poignant glimpse of Aunt Agatha's Shelley, pathetically marked in her hours of insanity and despair. The plan was evidently carefully laid and involved the entire entourage at Pembroke Lodge. Further hints appear in the next letter as Russell's family sought information from the Smiths' American doctor about Alys's manic-depressive Uncle Horace. (Her dead brother, Frank, whose religious fits and enthusiasms suggested that there had been something peculiar about him, seems to have been dropped as a promising candidate for serious madness.) It is clear from the tone of the next few letters that Russell did not at first realize how serious this new campaign was to be. Granny did not reveal her hand at once – she was no doubt anxious not to jeopardize Russell's chances in his Tripos coming up in May. Once the exams were out of the way, however, she moved swiftly and dramatically. When it came, Russell found the blow devastating.

Even so, he had already taken the idea seriously enough to mention to Alys, in a letter she seems to have destroyed, the possibility of their having children by other people – an idea she hotly rejected in her reply. Russell apologizes for it in the next letter, written the same day. The discord was not serious, no doubt because Alys was able to make allowances for the strain Russell was under at Pembroke Lodge. In her reply to his apology she told him that he had not behaved like a cad but 'like the dearest goose in the world'.

[32]

Trinity College
24 April 1894. 9.00 p.m.

My Dearest

I must begin my letter tonight, though it will be no use sending it, because I have a fit of such unsufferable contempt for myself that I cannot rest till I have told thee what a worm I feel. As far as I can remember, everything I wrote in my last letter was contemptible and smug and self-satisfied. I suppose it came of being pleased about my work and absorbed in it. But I have been growing gradually more ashamed of it ever since, until I feel hardly worthy to write to thee even.

Thee must be beginning to find out my faults now with a vengeance and I feel as if to write the way I am writing now were as weak and despicable as the rest, but I can't help it. Thee must have known I didn't seriously mean to suggest any fault in thee, only my pen somehow carried me away as it sometimes does. Of course also I wasn't myself really anxious about the question of children: if I had been I couldn't have written in such a priggish fashion. But my people were so solemn, and they never spoke out, so that I had never discovered what it was they imagined about thy uncle, and I fancied they knew the bare facts.[1] Of course also I ought to have been in a position to satisfy them on the subject before speaking to thee in September, but seeing all appearances favourable as to health it didn't occur to me as necessary, though I am now convinced it would have saved bother if I had. However the subject is uninteresting and had better be forgotten. If thee will send me the address of your Philadelphia Doctor as soon as possible he will set my people's minds finally at ease.[2]

Even in my present mood I don't think there was much harm in my remark to Sanger: he has had my views on women too much drummed into him to have supposed I meant such a remark seriously and would have known it merely meant I didn't choose to discuss the subject. I did go on to repeat various things out of thy article as facts to be considered on the subject, my remark having disarmed criticism.[3]

I don't think I generalize about women from thee, as I am never inclined to take anybody as typical, having often found what bad mistakes one is liable to make from doing so. Besides I keep thee in such a special corner of my brain that I don't regard thee as any sort of type of anything but just thyself. I know too that the vast majority of men are hopelessly illogical, but logic is largely the result of education, particularly of a great deal of unsympathetic criticism of which women get less as a rule than men. And it is a platitude that women care more about people and less about abstract principles than men, which would naturally result from their being more

1. Alys's Uncle Horace (1837–1906) suffered alternating fits of depression and manic elation. During the latter he would involve himself in wild schemes and was the source of much embarrassment to his family, who generally preferred to have him depressed. The Russells had got hold of the idea that he was in an asylum.
2. Alys had called on Lady Russell the day before. Although all had seemed to go well, Lady Russell had raised the question of heredity and Alys had volunteered to put her in touch with the Pearsall Smiths' family doctor in Philadelphia.
3. The nature of this altercation is unclear. But it seems that Russell had discussed her article with Sanger and had failed to defend it adequately (perhaps agreeing with Sanger's criticisms). The particular phrase in dispute was Russell's 'she's a woman' which Alys complained was unworthy of his feminist principles and dangerous to use with a man like Sanger who didn't respect women as Russell did. Alys also accused Russell of generalizing about women on the basis of his experience of her. She seems to have thought that he had come to the conclusion that all women were illogical by this means.

sympathetic and affectionate. But I thoroughly realize that all such generalizations have hosts of exceptions, the more so as I am in the habit of making an exception of myself when I generalize about men.

I have continued to do a lot of work and have been still exceptionally fit. I think my grandmother had better know about my visit on Saturday and Sunday week: I don't want to conceal too much now, and a Saturday to Monday is such a recognized thing that it can't be supposed even by her to matter much to my work. I am very glad thee had a pleasant visit:[1] I also have had her playful remarks on thy article inflicted on me, and I also laughed and displayed the most lively amusement. I made very little defence of thee as I should certainly have lost my temper which it was very important not to do. But I said as much as I safely could. Thee is so much like my more real self to me that I have the same sort of diffidence about defending thee that I have about defending myself. I never do defend myself, or only when it is very important to justify myself (except to thee); but usually I make a joke of it, accept any criticism and give a psychological explanation of how I came to be so absurd; and I am much tempted to do the same when people criticize thee, though I admit it is a weakness and I ought not to do so. But in thy case I am the more tempted as I so am convinced that the criticisms are undeserved that it doesn't seem worth arguing, as one always argues partly to convince oneself.

I wonder whether thee will ever get over the disagreeable impression my last letter must have produced. I felt it was foul when I was writing it, but I couldn't stop myself and I was so self-satisfied that I couldn't have written anything better. Thee knows however that, whatever I may write in such a mood, whenever I am really myself I do not merely love thee as devotedly as a human being can, but also revere thee morally so that any criticism of mine seems like a sacrilege; for at bottom I am a weak vacillating wretch and have always derived what strength I had from others and now derive mine (such as it is) solely from thee. Only I despise myself for having obtruded myself on thee and saddled thee with such a burden. I feel tonight as if I were like Phillimore[2] coming to be made good, a kind of being I

---

1. To Pembroke Lodge. It is hard to imagine it was as pleasant as Alys reported in her letter of 23 April, but doubtless Alys's assessment was relative and Granny was on her best behaviour.
2. Robert Phillimore (1871–1919), the son of Sir Walter Phillimore, a rich Liberal Law Lord. In February 1894 he had proposed to Alys and been rejected. He was now pursuing 'Lion' Fitzpatrick (see letter 21) whom he married in 1895. Russell's dislike of him was not merely that of a rival suitor (see *Autobiography*, vol. II, pp. 212–13).

loathe and despise from the bottom of my heart. Forgive all this folly: it is genuine contrition whatever it may seem.

Wednesday Evening. I am going home for the day on Sunday as my people wish me to see the Dr Anderson mentioned in my uncle's letter. I shall leave there at 7.42 in the evening, in time to catch the last train back here. Will thee be in town and if so shall I come for Sunday night to Grosvenor Road? I would leave at my usual early hour next morning. It would in no way interfere with my work as I should be at it by 11 and could easily get my daily 6 hours done after that. I might even work in the train on the way up! – The memorandum I meant was the one I sent thee before, from my uncle.

It would be nice if we could meet on Sunday but I don't allow myself to think it possible. Thee would find me *very* serious, ridiculously so, I dare say.

But I shall be half afraid of meeting thee again I am so terribly ashamed of myself. I have almost forgotten why now, but the feeling remains.

I am still working hard and have succeeded in keeping most of my thoughts on shop perhaps that is why my other thoughts are so foolish. Forgive this foolish letter and all my other follies if thee can –

Fare thee well my dearest. Whatever else may be foolish in me I am thine heart and soul in that I am wise.

Thine devotedly
Bertie

Despite the fears his family was instilling in him, Russell continued to work for his Moral Science Tripos, which was now drawing very close.

[33]

Trinity College
16 May 1894. 9.15 p.m.

My Darling Alys

Thy letter *is* delightful, though I try to be sorry thee was unhappy at our parting yesterday, but find this effort is too much for me. It means all the more joy when we are together. It *was* a heavenly two days! The most heavenly we have ever had. The day at Friday's Hill was even nicer than the days at Fountainebleau. It certainly is a pity in some ways that we shan't be able to live in the country, but I dare say we shall be able to leave London pretty often for a day or two, and for months in the summer, and that way we shall get the advantages of the country without its drawbacks. There's a platitudinous sentiment platitudinously expressed!

I am very glad thee liked my letter to my Aunt Maude.[1] Now my people are completely absorbed in my Aunt Gertrude's having had a daughter: both are hitherto going on well, and the event will put them in such a good humour that if they do hear of the *Wild Duck* it won't make so much impression as before.

I have done a little work since I came back, but I didn't mean to do much. I had a final interview with Stout today, who made me promise to come and tell him how I had done after the exam, though I told him I was going down immediately. He has taken quite an affection for me apparently, as I have for him, though as McTaggart says, he is an acquired taste. I am going to the sea tomorrow with Moore, who also has a Tripos (the Classical) beginning on Monday. We mean to walk 15 miles a day till Sat. on which day I have to be back to dine at the Lodge; but I dare say we shan't walk quite so far really. I feel sure that our whole talk will consist in my trying to persuade him that the phrase 'unconscious will' is meaningless, which doubtless seems to thee a very frivolous topic as indeed it does to me.

Dickinson and I have each got 12 copies of Carpenter's *Woman*[2] which we are distributing; it is not so striking as *Sex Love*, but seeing he had to avoid repeating himself, it seems to me about as good as possible.

I find I shall have to be here Saturday to Monday June 2–4 and some two days in the following week, the latter to look after Aunt Elliot;[3] after that I shall be finally done with the place. It is true our time is mostly spent in partings, but we *will* have a grand long time together in the summer! It is a mercy I don't mind inconsistencies; I used to, when I was a good deal

---

1. Rumours had reached Aunt Maude about the engagement and Russell had written to inform her of the situation, but also to tell her to deny the rumours until the engagement was formally announced. The rumours arose from the fact that Alys and Bertie had been seen together early in May at a performance of Ibsen's *Wild Duck* in London. Bertie and Alys were worried that news of this outing might reach Pembroke Lodge.
2. Edward Carpenter (1844–1929), a poet, writer, socialist, and moral reformer, often called 'the English Tolstoy'. He studied at Cambridge but resigned his Fellowship on religious grounds. He practised 'the simplification of life' on a small farm near Sheffield while working in the University Extension movement. Openly homosexual, he advocated the reform of sexual relations in a number of pamphlets, including *Sex Love* (1894) and *Woman* (1894). Dickinson was a friend and spoke warmly of him in his *Autobiography* (pp. 156–7).
3. Probably either Harriette Emily Elliot, the younger daughter of Granny's uncle Charles Gilbert Elliot, or Granny's younger sister, Charlotte Mary Elliot.

younger, but I found long ago that there was no wisdom except in abandoning consistency, which I have since found very comforting and convenient doctrine!

I was not sleepy yesterday till evening, but I went to bed early and had a very long sleep. Our last meeting was so perfect that it has made everything seem a bore up here, but fortunately it is not for long.

I expect the sea will make my brain very fit. If thee will write to me on Saturday morning, I will write again on Sunday, and I shall hope for thy promised letters every day during the Tripos! I too love thee continually more and more, though my love is no longer agitating as it used to be. It seems to have got too far below the surface and too much a constant part of me for that. I *shall* be glad when Wednesday comes!

Fare thee well my Beloved Alys
> Ever thine
>> Bertie

On 31 May, a week after the end of Russell's examinations, his engagement was announced. This led to a rather tense series of meetings over the next few days between Alys and her mother and various members of Russell's family. Russell was safely immune from all this in Cambridge waiting for his Tripos result and making plans for the future. His plans were still rather ambiguous, and remained so for some time. As the next letter shows, he had still not firmly decided to try for a Trinity College Fellowship (for which a star of distinction in the Tripos would stand him in good stead). He intended that at least part of his time would be devoted to practical political activity, and was evidently unprepared to work so hard for a Fellowship that it would preclude this.

[34]

Trinity College
3 June 1894. 12.30 p.m.

My darling Alys

I hope thee is having an amusing day in the country and that Zangwill's new humour is as scintillating as usual. Nobody up here reads the papers, so that still only the Society know about us. The Society I think are all delighted, as far as I can judge, though Marsh says it takes people's breath away to be told: such an event is so rare and unthought of in their world. They are all amused at the light it throws on my paper last term:[1] they had

1. 'Lövberg or Hedda', on the admission of women to the Apostles. See letter 25 above.

thought it a work of colossal imagination and find it nothing but a piece of description.

I was very glad, as it turned out, that they had Mr Bennet for me to write on,[1] as Sidgwick and two other angels[2] turned up and the other subjects were too intimate to read about before an old man like Sidgwick. As it was, he was invaluable; he spoke excellently, making a very subtle and ingenious distinction between wit and humour, and illustrating his points by good stories, none of which any of us, even those who knew him best, had heard him tell before. He went away before we divided, but left his vote at my disposal, as we had on the whole agreed in the discussion. Moore, as one might have expected, attacked Sidgwick's view and set up a still more subtle one of his own; but I think Sidgwick's was more true. People seemed on the whole to agree with most of what I said, and fortunately they laughed at all the things I had said were laughable (except the Male of the Same Species, which I left out).

I enclose a pile of letters.[3] I have accepted Lady Stanley's invitation for Thursday, so I suppose thee needn't call with thy mother till after that.

I am going to lunch in half an hour with Moore and his two sisters, whose acquaintance it will be very interesting to make. Couldn't thee come Friday for the day? I believe it would be better than Saturday to Monday. I have been invited to the Marshalls[4] Sunday evening at 9, to meet the examiners; so of course I must go. And a great deal of the rest of the time I *ought* to be talking to Ward and Stout and Mackenzie,[5] at least if I do well. If I get a star, it would mean, I believe, that I should be certain of a fellowship if I worked, even without stopping up here, and it would be rather a question as to how much work it would require which would I suppose decide whether or not I should go in for one. This sort of point would require a good deal of discussion with the dons. However I probably shan't get a star, and that will greatly simplify the problem.

If thee could come Friday and Friday night and we could go up to the picnic together Saturday, it would be a good deal more convenient, as I

1. Russell's paper on Mr Bennet (in *Pride and Prejudice*) is lost.
2. 'Angels' was the society term for members who no longer regularly attended meetings.
3. Presumably letters of congratulations on their engagement.
4. Alfred Marshall (1842–1924), the father of neoclassical economics. He was Professor of Political Economy at Cambridge. At this time economics was still included among the Moral Sciences at Cambridge.
5. John Stuart Mackenzie (1860–1935), a philosopher educated at Glasgow and Cambridge and at this time a Fellow of Trinity College. He went on to become Professor of Logic and Philosophy at Cardiff.

should be forced to be busy almost all Sunday, what with my final packing to do too.

I am sorry this letter is so dull but my brain is in a whirl with answering all the enclosed, and I can think of nothing. I hope the days till Thursday won't take too long in passing. I will write again tomorrow morning.

Thine ever

Bertie

Russell's First (with the star of distinction) in the Moral Science Tripos was announced on 8 June, and he decided as a result to pursue a Fellowship. This required him to submit a dissertation in the summer of 1895. Such dissertations were quite commonly rejected the first time round, in which case a revised version would have to be submitted the following year. In keeping with his plans to do at least some political work, Russell considered writing on political economy. With this in mind, he had visited Alfred Marshall on 5 June to get a reading list. But, although he was still toying with the idea much later in the year, this plan took second place to the idea of writing a dissertation on the philosophy of non-Euclidean geometry. This topic was arrived at on 10 June in discussion with James Ward, with whom Russell discussed his performance in the Tripos and his prospects for a Fellowship.

These plans are announced in the next letter, where also we have the first reference to Alfred North Whitehead (1861–1947), who later became famous as the co-author with Russell of *Principia Mathematica* (1910–13) and, after that, as one of the century's most important metaphysicians. Whitehead at this time had shown little overt interest in philosophy and was working exclusively on mathematics. He was a Fellow of Trinity but was little known outside the University. His first major independent work, *A Treatise on Universal Algebra*, which greatly excited Russell when it appeared, was still four years in the future. Whitehead had already played a significant role in Russell's undergraduate career before Russell went to discuss the mathematical literature on non-Euclidean geometry with him on 10 June. Russell had attended his lectures as a mathematics student and Whitehead had been instrumental in getting Russell the scholarship with which he entered Cambridge and in getting him elected to the Apostles (see Lowe, *Whitehead*, vol. I, pp. 222–4).

Fixing on a topic for his Fellowship dissertation was almost Russell's last task in Cambridge. Writing the dissertation did not require residence there (although he would return several times for visits), and he was still planning to spend some time in Berlin studying economics. On 11 June he packed and left the University which, for the previous four years, had been to him in many ways a more satisfactory home than Pembroke Lodge. His next home, significantly enough, was to be Friday's Hill, where he would start work on his dissertation.

[35]

Trinity College
10 June 1894

My Darling Alys

It *is* a pity we couldn't celebrate the anniversary of the Temperance Demonstration[1] as we had planned long ago; but I have been too busy to think of it till now. I arrived just at the end of the meeting last night[2] in time for the talk. I heard it had been dull except that Moore had refuted McTaggart on some point or other. McTaggart gave me double congratulations, but I am sure in his heart the one balanced the other instead of increasing it. I got a host of letters some of which I enclose and all of which I have answered. Please return them all to Pembroke Lodge as my people will want to see them. Zangwill arrived all right and was very amusing, so that Sanger and Marsh were much charmed with him. He remarked that we were much more theoretical than the dons he is staying with: they discuss eels instead of ideals (ideels he pronounces it); and much more in the same strain. He said he liked thee better than any other young lady he knew; from him, this may probably be taken as true. He stayed nearly 3 hours so I suppose he enjoyed himself.

This afternoon I went to the Ward's; he was out at first so I discussed German and Russian literature with Mrs Ward, who is a splendid person in every way. He then arrived and took me up to his study and discussed matters. He said my Essay paper was the best; that he had never seen two better Essays done in three hours; so I told him the stroke of luck I had with one of them and he laughed and said 'you didn't tell the Examiners that'. But he still seemed to think it a good paper and said my having done well in Essays augured well for the Fellowships. He said I was much more likely than not to get one, and that that was not only his opinion as someone (he didn't say who) had remarked that I was presumably safe for a Fellowship. I *ought* apparently to get it two years from September, but it *may* take a year more. We discussed a lot of possible subjects and finally seemed to fix on the Epistemological Bearings of Metageometry, which sounds well at any rate. I then went on, at Ward's recommendation, to a somewhat younger member of the Society, named Whitehead, another Trinity don, who has worked at this subject from the mathematical side, and he instructed me in the Bibliography of the subject. I may write on the meaning and validity of the

---

1. On 9 June 1893 Russell had attended a temperance demonstration with Alys.
2. The weekly Apostles' meeting.

differential calculus instead, but I think that would be harder and less exciting. In either case I shall be able to utilize both my Triposes, and so, I hope, make my dissertation unintelligible to all my examiners, in which case I shall be safe. Ward seemed to think I should be able to do a certain amount of Economics as well, and that it wouldn't matter being away, indeed that Germany would be quite a good plan. I shall have to go in first September year [*sic*] which may interfere with our wedding tour I fear. This is sad, but I suppose unavoidable.

This evening I went to the Marshalls and had a long talk with Maud Joachim who was very pleasant, though she has been ploughed in her Tripos.

I have accepted my cousin Maggie Elliot's[1] invitation to tea on Tuesday as my Grandmother is very fond of her, and it will be very easy for thee to win her heart. It will be quite easy to go to the Matthews's too I imagine. She is dull rather, and the daughter of the late Dean of Bristol, very old-fashioned and kind-hearted. Relations are all a nuisance but they needn't pester us long.

All my ideas are disjointed and dull. I hope thee is well again. I live in hopes of Tuesday. Fare thee well Dearest.

Thine devotedly

Bertie

Once Russell's Tripos was over, Granny lost no time in launching her new campaign against the marriage in earnest. By now written evidence was available from the Pearsall Smith family doctor, and it seems that Russell was summoned to Pembroke Lodge to be told about the closeted skeletons of both families. The most impressive exhibit on the Russell side was mad Uncle Willy, locked away in a lunatic asylum, about whom the family had rarely hitherto spoken. There was also Aunt Agatha, whose insane delusions had caused her engagement to be broken off; and there was the fact (or the supposed fact) that Russell's father had suffered from epilepsy. Pickings were slimmer on the Pearsall Smith side, but, in addition to Uncle Horace, the manic-depressive, rumours had reached Granny's ears that Alys's father was mad as well. (There was some irony in the distress this caused Hannah and her family, for the source of the rumours was certainly Hannah herself, who for years had mocked and exaggerated the foibles and eccentricities of her husband, whom

1. Margaret Elliot (1828–1901), a distant cousin of Granny, was the elder daughter of Gilbert Elliot, who had been Dean of Bristol Cathedral. The visit took place on 12 June 1894. For Russell's later, rather jaundiced recollections of it, see his Journal for 15 March 1903 (*Papers*, vol. XII, p. 21). The Matthews cannot be identified.

she despised.) The inference to be drawn from these dark facts, according to Anderson and a succession of physicians instructed by him, was that any children which might result from the marriage would very probably be mad.

Granny's scheme revealed the extremes to which she was prepared to go to get her way and the extent to which she was prepared to sacrifice her grandson in the process. It also revealed a manipulative shrewdness in dealing with the young which is rather unexpected in a woman of nearly eighty. She obviously realized that the values by which she set such store – considerations of class and family name, of the inexpediency of the marriage for Russell's expected political career, and of the deference of the young to the wishes of their elders – were not likely to cut much ice with Bertie and Alys, who, rather self-consciously, saw themselves as modern, pioneering, and indifferent to the values of the fading Victorian world. But, as Granny evidently realized, these very characteristics ensured that they could not be indifferent to what were supposed to be the findings of the new and fashionable 'science' of eugenics.

Granny proved skilful in using the new weapon and Russell found it difficult to resist medical authority. The result was one of the most difficult periods of his life. Torn between his love for Alys and his genuine affection for Granny and respect for the people at Pembroke Lodge, he came to fear for his own sanity. In a secret diary he kept at this time, he wrote desperately of the 'hopeless and unalleviated' tragedies 'which have made up the lives of most of my family' and of the 'gloom which hangs like a fate over P[embroke] L[odge] ... taking all joy even out of Alys's love'. 'I am haunted', he wrote, 'by the fear of the family ghost, which seems to seize on me with clammy invisible hands to avenge my desertion of its tradition of gloom' (*Papers*, vol. i, pp. 65–6). It was a period during which Russell had recurrent nightmares of being murdered, and both the nightmares and the fears they fed upon continued to trouble him for the rest of his life (*Autobiography*, vol. i, p. 85). In the end, he overcame his family's opposition and the happiness of his marriage gradually restored his stability. But for many years he avoided deep emotion and lived what he described, in a famous phrase, as 'a life of intellect tempered by flippancy' (ibid., p. 86).

The first step in the process of combating Granny's new campaign was to get a second medical opinion, one uninfluenced by Granny's instructions. For this purpose Bertie and Alys consulted Dr Daniel Hack Tuke (1827–95), a specialist in mental health who had treated Russell's Uncle William. Alys went to see him, in Cavendish Square, on 19 June and evidently got a more optimistic assessment of the situation than Dr Anderson had been instructed to give. However, she did not tell Tuke about Uncle Horace. In the next letter Russell urges her to do so and to get Tuke's opinion in writing. Alys wrote to Tuke on 19 June and Tuke replied on 21 June affirming, though perhaps more guardedly than they would have wished, that he saw no harm in their marriage. The strain, by this time, was evidently beginning to tell on them both.

[36]

Pembroke Lodge
19 June 1894

My Darling

I have nothing to say, not having seen my doctor; but it is a satisfaction to write. I am *very* much happier tonight, but I shall not feel *quite* happy till thee has told him about thy uncle and got his opinion in writing. Also I am too tired to feel much of any sort of feeling. I hope thee will not make more social engagements than are necessary next week as after such a time a little rest would be beneficial. I have to go to Cambridge on Monday for the day and to a garden-party on Saturday afternoon June 30, with my grandmother; but I shall be able to come to Haslemere that evening after it is over.

My uncle is here tonight and I told him we were referring the matter to Dr Hack Tuke and he seemed to think that a thoroughly satisfactory plan. I told him more or less what he had said, but also that it was not final. He knew him by reputation, so he was then better pleased.

I am more than ever convinced of the impossibility of living without thee, having made the utmost efforts to imagine such a life and found it impossible. And for thee too, I believe it would be *very* hard. I cannot think we can in future have a much severer trial than this, and I am amazed how well we have stood it. But a few more days of it would have certainly knocked us both up.

I hope thee got thy speeches prepared and did not break down after thy meetings.

Goodnight my beloved, thee *is* my life and soul, and life without thee is meaningless to me. God bless thee and preserve me from being the cause of many more such sorrows for thee, my darling.

Thine more utterly than ever before

Bertie

Faced with the challenge from Dr Tuke, Pembroke Lodge acted swiftly to re-establish Dr Anderson's authority.

[37]

44 Grosvenor Road
Wednesday [20 June 1894]. 5.00 p.m.

Dearest Alys

It is necessary for my peace of mind as well as my people's that Dr Anderson should see Dr Tuke. Unless thee objects I shall therefore ask him to go tomorrow morning as soon as he has seen me; at least if thy letter from Dr Tuke reaches me in time. Nothing new has turned up but my people are very solemn. It seems everyone has been telling them thy father is crazy or at any rate queer, and as the Drs in America have not contradicted it categorically they of course believe it. I however am still content with what thee told me yesterday.

Thine,
     Bertie

I have taken the Guicciardini.[1]

Without Tuke's opinion in writing, Russell was in a weak position for his interview with Anderson on 21 June at which Anderson duly maintained that, if they got married, they ought not to have children. Russell mentions this meeting in his *Autobiography*:

> After receiving this verdict in the house of the family doctor at Richmond, Alys and I walked up and down Richmond Green discussing it. I was for breaking off the engagement, as I believed what the doctors said and greatly desired children. Alys said she had no great wish for children, and would prefer to marry, while avoiding a family. After about half an hour's discussion, I came round to her point of view. We therefore announced that we intended to marry, but to have no children. Birth control was viewed in those days with the sort of horror which it now inspires only in Roman Catholics. My people and the family doctor tore their hair. The family doctor solemnly assured me that, as a result of his medical experience, he knew the use of contraceptives to be almost invariably gravely injurious to health. My people hinted that it was the use of contraceptives which had made my father epileptic. A thick atmosphere of sighs, tears, groans, and morbid horror was produced, in which it was scarcely possible to breathe. (*Autobiography*, vol. I, p. 84)

1. In all probability a reference to the *Storia d'Italia* by the Florentine historian and diplomat, Francesco Guicciardini (1483–1540).

The ensuing week must have been grim indeed. It is not directly recorded in the letters, however, either because the letters were destroyed or, more likely, because Alys and Bertie met frequently during the week to discuss the situation. Later correspondence makes clear that Russell told Dr Anderson of their decision to use contraceptives and that Anderson told Russell's family. Anderson joined with Pembroke Lodge in a chorus of medical and moral disapproval.

Granny evidently felt the need to separate them and, to this end, packed a reluctant Russell off for two weeks on a walking tour of North Wales with Eddie Marsh. On 2 July a tired and depressed Russell tried to put a good face on things prior to his departure. (The postscript refers to Russell's bicycle pump, which Alys succeeded in having mended.)

[38]

Pembroke Lodge
2 July 1894

My darling Alys

Nothing whatever has happened so I have nothing to tell thee. Fortunately Mrs Trotter is still here, so there has been no opportunity for confidential talk: but my grandmother seems in good health and spirits, so I suppose she thinks it is all right, and perhaps even imagines my good spirits come from a newly-acquired good conscience.

Tansley[1] never turned up, and I was bored to death till dinner-time, and mad at having wasted so much time. I hope thee caught the 4.10, otherwise thee too must have wasted a lot of time.

I am very sleepy, but otherwise in good spirits; I believe I shall even manage to enjoy Wales if the weather is fine.

What a heavenly two days it was! I am sure now that nothing short of death can succeed in separating us, and *quite* sure we are doing right. It seems to me now as if fate had descended upon us in full force in the form of heredity, and we had worsted it, and henceforward should be dependent on ourselves, and not on outside influences, for our happiness. But all this is rubbish.

I hope thee was not too much bored on the journey home, in spite of my having forgotten to buy thee a trashy novel. Goodbye dearest. A fortnight hence I hope and believe the bad novel will come to its natural conclusion

---

1. Arthur George Tansley, a Cambridge friend. (See letter 5.)

of 'and so they lived happily ever afterwards', not only people in *bad* novels do.

   Thine devotedly
     Bertie

By the way if thee wants to use my machine, thee must buy a new syringe as mine is out of order. I will pay for it when I come back.

The separation gave Pembroke Lodge another chance to work on Alys alone, as they had done while Bertie was in Rome. Russell had not been gone long when it became clear that Dr Anderson wanted to see Alys on her own. And it seemed possible that Granny might write to her. Alys viewed both prospects with alarm and looked to Russell to prevent them. As the next two letters show, he found this harder to do than might have been expected.

[39]

Prince Llewelyn Hotel
Beddgelert, North Wales
6 July 1894

My Darling Alys
   I put off my letter till today because the only post is in the evening, and now I am glad I did, as I have thy letter to answer. I am very sorry thee is worried: I thought like me, thee only minded interviews and didn't care what people wrote. I am pretty sure my grandmother will not write to thee, as without telling her so point blank, I made her understand thee wouldn't be affected in thy conduct by her opinion. But the Dr may write to thee. It is impossible for me to have no more dealings with Dr A as, having consulted him in the first instance, mere politeness demands that I should at least tell him the final result. I admit it is hateful for thee to have these people discussing our plans, and from my grandmother's letter this morning I gather she considers it certain to be off.[1] I am going to write *to my aunt* today[2] and tell her brutally I have *no* thought of breaking it off and that if they hint to any body that it's likely to be, we will marry at once. I also think of writing rather curtly to Dr A to ask him to say to me what he says behind my back,

1. Granny's letter was extraordinarily shrewd and shows exactly why Russell was having so much difficulty in escaping her control. It is printed in the Appendix.
2. Aunt Agatha was much easier for Russell to cope with and he directed much of his anger at her rather than at Granny.

about dangers etc.; to tell him I have medical opinion to back me,[1] and to beg him to give up stirring up my people. Also to ask him to write to *me* not to *thee*. But I shall not do this till I hear from thee again, as I think thee might not approve.

If they do write to thee, thee may answer any way that gives thee pleasure as thy acts will be so grave an offence that words would hardly aggravate it.

I wish too I had told them not to write; but it is almost impossible to do so, as thee would know if thee heard them talking of it. I think thee ought not to be made so very miserable by letters from people who, whatever they may have been to me, are really nothing to thee. Do try to regard their actions with indifference, so long as they don't affect our relations.

We have had glorious weather and I have really enjoyed our walks and bathes. If thy face was like greasy Joan's, mine is like Marion's from sunburn;[2] a perfectly disgusting spectacle! I am glad thee doesn't see me. We walked 21 or 22 miles yesterday, to places called Tremadoc and Pwllhelli. We felt great pleasure in walking about a village whose name begins with Pwl. They were both by the sea and we bathed in it and lay in the sun on the rocks to dry, and felt like gods. Today we are going to have a slack day and only walk about 10 miles and sleep here. Then I think we shall go to Caernarvon and Anglesea, and then to Wicklow.

I do hope thy next letter will be happier. I also hope thy swelling did not reduce thee to the English Miss,[3] I don't think thee could stand not talking, from habit. Poor Maud Levitt![4]

Goodbye my darling. Don't let thy spirits droop whatever my people do. Thee knows they have no power over me, which is all that would really matter.

Thine most devotedly
Bertie

1. By now they had been driven to get a second opinion on the likely effects of contraception. For this they consulted a Dr Philpot. Philpot was a friend of Alys's, though understandably they did not inform Pembroke Lodge of this fact.
2. While Greasy Joan is easy to identify – she 'keels the pot' at the end of *Love's Labour's Lost* – 'Marion' seems not to be a literary allusion. It is possible she was a servant at Friday's Hill, or one of the girls from Alys's club.
3. Alys's jaw was swollen, the result of an infected tooth as it turned out. The Pearsall Smiths were planning a trip to Henley that day and Alys had said that, on account of the swelling, she feared she would have to go as an English 'Miss' and not talk at all.
4. Maud Levitt cannot be identified except for the fact that she held absurd views about marriage which she shared with a Mr Little. Matters were not running smoothly, however, for, while she was determined to see him, he was unwilling to see her. She had taken pains to arrange things so that a meeting at Friday's Hill was inevitable.

[40]

Beddgelert
6 July 1894. 7 p.m.

Dearest Alys,

Thee was cheated of one day's letter so I will write two today to make up, especially as this morning's was rather unsatisfactory. I am afraid thee was rather unwell when thee wrote, which I hope was partly the cause of thy unhappiness. It is difficult for me to be firmer than I am with my people, as I feel that however they may worry thee, thee after all gets thy way and they don't, so that even thy temporary unhappiness hardly outweighs my grandmother's misery in my mind; and I *know* her conscience will be easier, however foolish such a conscience may seem to thee, if she has been allowed to try *everything* which seems to her a possible means of separating us. That is why I didn't put a veto on the Dr's writing to thee, for I was sure he was only doing it out of deference to her wishes, and I knew it couldn't be a *very* serious worry to thee, since we are so near the end of what they can do to us. And I still think we were right in telling them, for I had rather have them blame us for what we *are* doing than for a sin which we would never think of committing. Thee sees, being fond of my grandmother, I cannot so put her aside as thee would wish. As I said this morning, I must write to the Dr or see him once more, out of mere courtesy, but it seems to me that if he writes to thee, thee would do well not to answer him at all. As for my grandmother, I am *very* sorry she should have been able to annoy thee so much, but whatever she does I cannot bring myself to be angry with her except momentarily, for it is really a foolish and misguided conscience which dictates even her most unpleasant acts, such as what she said to thee before Paris. Since the real victory must be on our side we can surely have patience with them for a short time: and when we are married they will be powerless, particularly as this will separate us from them so completely. I have been thinking about them all day, but these banalities are the only result. Their letters ought not to make thee completely miserable, as thee says they will, since they cannot really touch us. I am sorry to have brought thee into such a nest of worries, and I suppose, having been used to my people all my life, I don't quite realize how disagreeable they are to thee; but I *must* make things as easy as possible for my grandmother, however much that may cost thee. Don't go and see her however. All that is necessary is that she should feel that *she* has done her utmost. Excuse this moralizing letter. Thee knows I would have spared thee anything I felt I could rightly spare thee; and the other three, whom I don't care a straw about, are involved with my grandmother unfortunately. I have been rather troubled all day thinking about thee and them, and consequently very anxious to be with thee again; but all *shall* be well by Sunday week. Goodbye my Darling. I *do* hope thy next letter will be cheerful.

Thine devotedly
Bertie

Dr Anderson wrote the dreaded letter to Alys on 5 July. In it he attacked their decision on moral as well as medical grounds, and asked Alys to see him on her own. Alys was furious at his impertinence and wrote him a very firm letter refusing to see him. She complained to Russell that Anderson was conspiring with his family and urged Bertie once more not to consult him again.

[41]

The Castle Hotel, Bangor
8 July 1894

My Darling Alys

I have now got two letters of thine to answer, but to the last and Dr A's there doesn't seem much to say. Thy answer to him seems to me all right, but I don't know why thee should have been so furious, since he had professionally a certain right to tell thee what he believed would be the effect on me, and probably thought *I* could only be restrained by dangers to thee, not to me. I wish thee had written to Dr Tuke, as I should like to have his opinion, whatever it may be, before writing to Dr A myself. After Dr A's letter I don't *think* my grandmother is likely to write. But it *is* a little hard on thee to be told nobody objects to thy engagement![1]

I daresay it would be better to wait till next year before marriage, but it must depend on my people's conduct. If they go on trying to break it off, and seem likely to use talk to outsiders as a means, we shall *have* to marry. Does thee think we *could* go to Boston with Lady Henry without causing scandal? If so I should simply *love* to go. I should like to consult my Aunt Maude.

I am *very* glad thee has read Mill's *Autobiography* at last. It is at the bottom of

1. Maud Levitt (see above, letter 39), absorbed in her own problems with Mr Little, had said she envied Alys because no one was objecting to her engagement.

a great deal in me. I am particularly glad thee should understand better what I feel about religion, as there has always been rather a want of comprehension in both of us on that head. I feel as if I understood thy religion in a sort of cruel intellectual way, but I cannot, or at least hitherto could not, *feel* sympathy with it.

I am glad thee enjoyed thy party, and the gipsy incident sounds very amusing.[1] Poor Maud Levitt! Thee makes me abhor Mr Little by telling of his good spirits.

Yesterday we walked to Bettws-y-Coed and came on here by train, and today we are going across to Beaumaris and back again to Caernarvon. It is not very hot hereabouts as there are both sea and hills to cool it. I took some Viriolia for my complexion, but it gets pretty bad all the same.[2] I am glad I am interesting to talk to! I hope soon thee will be happy even when it is not too d——d hot to think.

We are much interested in Meredith,[3] but each of his sentences is like a meat-fill[4] for compressed thought. He really is thoughtful. The whole of the thought in Carpenter's two pamphlets is put into two pithy sentences of the book we are reading. And his psychology is really marvellous.

I read yesterday an admirable article of Karl Pearson's on Socialism and Natural Selection in the *Fortnightly*;[5] do read it. It says a host of things which have always seemed to me true, though I never saw them said before. (That's why I think it good!) The whole thing comes from the misleading metaphor of the *struggle* for existence. I remember saying something similar to thee at Reigate when thee was learning to ride a bicycle.

I will give thee *The Egoist* and we will read it together. Do write to Dr Tuke. Only a week tomorrow now! The time on the whole does not pass

1. Alys had had her fortune told by a gypsy.
2. Russell's remarks about his sunburn on 6 July had led Alys to bemoan the fact that he had forgotten to take his cucumber lotion with him.
3. George Meredith (1828–1909), the poet and novelist, then held in high regard by Russell and his Cambridge friends. Meredith's evolutionary naturalism, his hatred of sentimentality and egotism, and his belief in the intellectual equality of women would make him a congenial author for Russell. Alys had been trying to read him but had been put off by the obscurities of his style, though she promised to read *The Egoist*, his most celebrated novel, if Russell gave her a copy. Russell was reading *One of Our Conquerors* (1891).
4. Probably the filling of a meat pie. *The Oxford English Dictionary* does not recognize the word.
5. Karl Pearson, 'Socialism and Natural Selection', *Fortnightly Review*, 1 July 1894, pp. 1–21, an account of the muddles involved in using natural selection as an argument against socialism. Benjamin Kidd's *Social Evolution* (1894) is his main target.

very slowly; especially when thee is happy! But of *course* thee must always say when thee isn't. Goodbye dearest Alys

Thine devotedly

Bertie

Russell returned from Wales on 15 July. After a brief visit to Pembroke Lodge, where he found a short note from Aunt Agatha saying that Granny had been too ill to be shown his letters from Wales, he went on to stay at Friday's Hill. Alys had prepared a study there in which he could work, and for the next month he worked, in relative calm, at his Fellowship dissertation on geometry. 'My people', he recalled, 'wrote almost daily letters to me about "the life you are leading", but it was clear to me that they would drive me into insanity if I let them, and that I was getting mental health from Alys' (*Autobiography*, vol. I, p. 86).

Though it was clear by now that the marriage would not be abandoned through fear of heredity, Granny was still not prepared to give up the fight. Her latest plan was for a six-month separation – negotiated down to four months and, finally, to three. Alys, reasonably enough, was against any separation, arguing that they had already been separated several times and that Russell's family ought now to concede defeat. Russell himself had hitherto firmly resisted any demand for a separation. But Granny's hand was strengthened now by a major (and possibly even genuine) deterioration in her health. The doctors feared cancer, brought on, they implied, by anxiety at Russell's behaviour, and now only to be stayed by the peace of mind which would result from his acceding to her demands for a separation. As a result, Russell felt obliged to make one more concession to his grandmother. Worried by news from Pembroke Lodge about Granny's failing health, he called there for a night on the way to visit his Uncle Lyulph Stanley at Penrhos, near Holyhead.

[42]

Pembroke Lodge
17 August 1894

My Darling

While the Dr is with my grandmother I may as well begin a letter to thee. So far I have had no blame, at least no direct blame, from my people, but I am terribly affected by my grandmother's illness. Dr Gardiner[1] is afraid (but this is *quite* private) that it has caused some incurable internal complication, I don't know what, and he is calling in a specialist on that subject to see if he is right. If he is, though she may live many years, she will never recover

1. A partner in Dr Anderson's practice.

her former active habits, but still be constantly laid up and will be liable, I fear, to pain and acute illness at times. I am just going to see Dr Gardiner, when I hope he will tell me all.

When I arrived I saw my aunt, who told me with sighs and broken sentences, and hints of what it would be better I shouldn't know, of what there might be to bear, etc. She tried to weep, but is really of course in the best of spirits – it gives her an opportunity for indulging in the precise kind of spiteful sentimentality she loves. Best of all, she has 'given up' Scotland (which she hates) because she 'can't bear' to leave my Grandmother at such a time.[1] I am convinced it was only in order to say so that she ever formed the scheme of going away, for though it would no doubt be good for her, she cannot make the exertion of moving and forming a decision.

Then I went to my Grandmother, and found her on the sofa in her sitting-room. We embraced in silence for some time and then I looked at her sadly with tears in my eyes and she said 'Well I'm worse than you thought I was'; not with an air of triumph, but of mild reproof for my heartlessness in having felt so little anxiety. She besought me to consent to an absence; she says everybody who comes thinks it strange I should not be here when she is so ill, and that both thee and I are suffering in reputation in consequence. She gave repeated assurances (which I didn't need) of her absolute unselfishness in urging my home-duties; she really does care only about my moral welfare, which she feels to be imperilled by such neglect. And she wishes very much that we could both have some time apart to think over our conduct; poor woman she still thinks if we deliberated we should act differently. She besought me to do this one thing entirely on my own account without consulting thee; be a man, she said, and insist on it. She thought to rouse me by taunts of unmanliness, but to these I was utterly deaf. I said for the moment I didn't feel a separation to be right, and anyway neither of us ever took a decision without the other's approval but I could not answer her quite decidedly in the negative till I had seen the Dr and consulted with thee.

10.30 p.m. I have had a fairly long interview with Dr Gardiner, a bluff hearty straightforward young Scotchman, whom I have always greatly liked. What

1. Plans had been afoot for some time to find Agatha an alternative place to live. Scotland was evidently one possibility. A more alarming proposal was that she should move in with Bertie and Alys after their marriage! Pembroke Lodge did not belong to the Russells, but to the Queen. She had granted the use of it to Lord John for his lifetime and, on his death, had granted the same privilege to his widow. There was, of course, no expectation that the privilege would be transferred to Lady Agatha on Granny's death.

he fears, and what I am afraid amounts almost to a certainty, is something of the nature of cancer. He sets the outside limits of her life at 18 months or 2 years, and says she may die much sooner, and of course may die of something else first. It seems there has always been a tendency to cancer, and perfect peace of mind is apparently a preventive. But now that it exists, he says peace of mind is only indirectly useful, as its opposite lowers general vitality and so facilitates the growth of the malignant organism. I told him what my Grandmother had been asking of me, and explained to him the effect which living at home has on me. He saw this, and therefore urged me to travel for 4 or 6 months, as he was sure (as alas I am too) that it would greatly diminish my grandmother's unhappiness. He urged that she has not long to wait for any happiness that may still be in store for her, whereas we have. He urged also that it would be good for her health, so that in what he called his own interest he couldn't help urging it. Finally he said he must lay aside the Dr and make a personal appeal as her friend; and he thought that would be the more generous course. He was very tactful and didn't blame anybody for anything. I said I couldn't make such a decision without some deliberation and in that he thought me right.

I fear I shall have to do it, unless thee can find some good reason against it which I haven't thought of. I shall hear at Penrhos the result of the consultation with the expert.[1] Think it over and tell me what thee thinks. I am too much affected by pity for my grandmother to think calmly – I have not yet felt unhappy at the prospect, as I have not yet made up my mind whether it is right, and shall not till thee has thought it over. But if we do decide that way, let the parting have been today: I couldn't bear the wrench nearly so easily if we met again, and this morning would be so divine a thing to look back upon all the time: far better than a stormy and passionate parting.

All this misfortune, present and prospective, cannot make me unhappy tonight, when I have my mind so full of our sudden and wonderful conquest of purity and love.[2] I hope tomorrow I shall feel differently and not think a parting right – at any rate I want thy deliberate judgment. Perhaps thee

1. The expert, a Dr Veith, found the situation 'less grave' than those at Pembroke Lodge had feared – as even Aunt Agatha had to admit when she wrote to Russell with the news on 22 August.
2. This incident is referred to a number of times by both Russell and Alys. The conquest of purity and love had occurred before Russell left Friday's Hill that day, when he had kissed Alys's breasts. To their mutual relief, they found that this physical expression of their love did not compromise its purity. The incident helped allay their fears that they would drift into mere sensuality – a remote danger, one would have thought, for such a very prim young couple.

might consult Logan and thy mother, since they will be biased opposite ways and thee may pick out the truth better then. But don't mention medical details, at least to thy mother. Goodnight dearest – I am divinely happy in spite of everything, for I believe nothing now can rob us of our perfect purity and joy in each other.

In the train   9.15 a.m. [18 August 1894]

Nothing fresh has happened to tell thee of. I was so sleepy that I slept like a log and therefore had very little time to think things over. But I feel this morning as if I simply *could not* bear to be 4 months away from thee. My mind shies at the thought so that I cannot imagine quite what it would be like but I know it would be all but unendurable. On the other hand I fear my Grandmother's ghost when she is dead if we don't do anything for her sake. Poor woman she has been unspeakably gentle and kind this time: her spirit is quite broken. But oh I do hope and pray thee may think a separation unnecessary.

Don't give way to the horror of the thought and let that make thee feel it inevitable, as thee is apt to do. Our heavenly quiet September that I was so looking forward to I cannot give it up – and yet better that than have my Grandmother on my conscience all my life. Tell me honestly thy deliberate thoughts on the subject. I don't think clearly today. Goodbye my soul and life

    Thine in every thought
      Bertie

[43]

In the train to Holyhead
18 August 1894. 5 p.m.

My Dearest

I may as well begin a letter now having nothing else to do. I don't know what to say – I am absurdly unhappy, far more so than the circumstances warrant. I am seized with profound discouragement at these endless complications and worries – the supply seems inexhaustible. If thee writes that we ought to be separated I shall make one last appeal to my Grandmother's mercy, which may touch her though I don't for a moment suppose it will change her wishes. – In talk I cannot tell her how dependent we are on each other because she is too unsympathetic, but in a letter I think I could.

My unhappiness is increased by a racking headache and by the fact that I have no dress shoes with me and didn't see my luggage put into the train and that it is perpetually stopping where it shouldn't. – All these add to my sense that the world is too difficult for me to grapple with though they are ludicrous in themselves. – But it will be vile to have to face the Stanleys' nagging and contempt for all of them.

I cannot believe it was only yesterday we were so happy. I was at Grosvenor Rd this morning looking for shoes, and again on the West Departure Platform at Euston, and both brought back to me the unutterable horror of last time and I have been living in dreariness since. It is absurd to be so cast down but I feel as if worry would never cease – especially after I remember how I thought there would be no more after my Tripos! I don't see how I could bear 4 months away from thee – I am miserable now and should be all the time, and I hate everybody not connected with thee and should not be at all in a mood to see the world but only to sit alone and brood – however unmanly such feelings may be!

Penrhos 10.30 p.m.

When I arrived my luggage had been left behind and I had to face the jibes of the family. This was however a comic misadventure which got me out of the tragic vein. I shan't feel tragic again till sleep has restored my faculties.

Nobody is here except Algernon[1] and Miss Davies (Crompton's aunt), so it is dull but unalarming. We discussed Cooperation at dinner – Miss Davies stood up for it, but the rest of us laughed at it.[2] (I secretly from the point of view of Socialism, though I managed to keep this dark.) We were divided into just the same parties on the subject of the Master of Trinity,[3] and finally my Grandmother settled she must be regaining her health because she was able again to speak evil of people. (She had never lost her health except in her imagination.)

It is a deadly bore here, but I shall work and read *Princess Casamassima*,[4] which interests me much – and it pleases me it should begin with a description of Millbank, because the neighbourhood interests me![5] I have nothing more

1. Russell's Uncle Algernon, Lady Stanley's third son, the papal chamberlain who had shown Russell round Rome.
2. The cooperative movement developed powerfully at the end of the nineteenth century both in the form of producer cooperatives, in which the workers capitalized the enterprise and shared in its profits, and in consumer cooperatives, in which consumers were members and received a dividend from the profits. Emily Llewelyn Davies's niece, Margaret, was the founder of the Women's Co-operative Guild.
3. Henry Montagu Butler (1833–1918).
4. By Henry James.
5. Millbank, on the Thames embankment, is a continuation of Grosvenor Road where the Pearsall Smiths lived in London.

to say tonight – all my faculties, even that of feeling, being completely exhausted – so goodnight.

August 19 8.50 a.m. I have just got thy letter and it is heavenly – I am so glad to have at least one perfectly peaceful and happy letter from thee. – I feel less than ever as if I could bear four months away from thee. Now that we are separated my love is not at all calmer than it used to be; though it is as pure as in the Bô-Tree.[1] – Thank God we have that divine morning to unite us always. I am sorry this is such a querulous letter – my poor grandmother rather upset me and made it impossible for me to feel otherwise.

I will enclose the sort of letter I thought of sending as an appeal to my Grandmother in case thee thinks we ought to separate which I pray thee won't. If thee honestly doesn't, my grandmother's ghost won't haunt me. It really would be misery the whole time.

Now I must go to breakfast so goodbye my joy – I would give anything for one moment with thee now –

    Thine in every thought,
      Bertie

Forgive me, I fear I may have made thy duty harder for thee by my querulousness, but I simply couldn't help it.

The Stanleys, as both Russell and his brother agreed in their autobiographies, were much heartier companions than the Russells. The cheerful atmosphere at Penrhos and a bit of sympathy from Aunt Maude improved Russell's spirits.

1. Robert Pearsall Smith had had an elaborate tree-house constructed at Friday's Hill, largely as a refuge from his wife, who was unable to climb up into it. He called it 'The Bô-Tree house', not because it was in a Bô-Tree, but because it was under such a tree that the Buddha found enlightenment. Robert, who was much attracted to Buddhism at this time, went there often to 'contemplate'. He did so in comfort, for the Bô-Tree house was equipped with windows, chairs, and even a sofa. It was there that Alys and Bertie had discovered the purity of their love the previous Friday. In a letter of 24 August Russell described that occasion as 'the happiest morning of my life'.

[44]

Penrhos
23 August 1894

My Darling Alys

I am glad thee is beginning to grow cheerful again, and I hope my last few letters will have made thee more so. I have done all that seemed to me right to avert a separation (for, as thee says, *I* have the data for deciding, and now that I have had time to think my mind is clear about it), and I hope by tomorrow or Sunday to know whether my efforts have been successful, though I don't for a moment think they will have been. I believe I *could* stand the three months without serious harm, partly if I could spend a good deal of them with Mariechen, who is no effort to live up to – and if my Grandmother insists on asking it, it will be necessary to make the effort for my own conscience' sake. If however she herself lets me off, my conscience will be quite clear. For the moment I am very happy, but I remember that during our former months the 1st week was always easy, and it got gradually worse as time went on, so I am not confident about the future – I enclose a note from my Aunt; what a bitter disappointment it obviously is to her not to be able to rub it in more!¹ – Now I am going to write of cheerful things.

The conversation here is great fun, and since my mind has been freer I have enjoyed it very much. My Grandmother is so pleased with me that when I came down to dinner the other day she said 'I wish you could be reduplicated' and when I said 'Why Grandmama?' she answered 'Because I should like to have another like you.' Such a compliment from her means a great deal.

There is a lady here, a Mrs Erskine (some sort of cousin I believe) who is the greatest Tory I ever met. Seeing an advertisement of some book she said 'We don't need any more books on labour and property, there are quite enough already. Besides, there will soon be no more property.' She is rather old and has seen something of slums and of decayed aristocrats, so she gives herself great airs of superior knowledge. – She says perpetually 'It is not theories I'm giving you, but only what I *know*.' She said to me 'You know, most people only know one side; *I* know something of two or three. Now, for instance, you strike me as a very wise young man, *but* you don't know much.' She thought poor mild little Miss Davies (who is almost too timid to say anything, and is barely a Unionist) a very aggressive and obnoxious

---

1. Aunt Agatha reported that Dr Veith was not as alarmed about Granny's health as the other doctors had been.

Radical. This impression was strengthened by an amusing slip of the tongue. Yesterday at breakfast we had been talking of Tom Mann and John Burns and such people,[1] and my Aunt Maude began telling of an employer who was very rich and sweated his men atrociously and went round all day preaching philanthropy. 'Ah! then he's a gentleman' chimed in Miss Davies, meaning only in wealth, as opposed to the labour leaders. The great question of late has been whether there are *any* points of manners in which we might learn from our inferiors: it was finally agreed they are more patient. I thought of 'keeping company',[2] but held my tongue. My Grandmother is great fun – she was talking of a Mausoleum they have at Castle Howard[3] at dinner last night. First they discussed a long time whether it could be consecrated or not – no one knew, till at last my Uncle Algernon began authoritatively 'Well you all seem very ignorant of the laws of your church: I know, – but I'm not going to tell you.' And not another word could be got from him. Then my Grandmother went on 'You know, only a part of me's going to be buried: my brain is left to the College of Surgeons: you know they only have brains of paupers and criminals as a rule, and they have never had the brain of a clever woman.' *Mrs Erskine* 'But how if it should turn out to be just like the other brains?' *Mrs —* (a young shy lady, full of information, sitting next me and seeing her chance): 'I read in a paper the other day that there is no appreciable difference between the brain of a Papuan and that of an educated European.' *I* 'What paper did you read it in?' *Mrs —* 'I don't remember.' *My Grandmother* (overhearing) (she was on my other side) 'No I should think you *wouldn't* remember.' *I* 'I should think it may have been true of the man who wrote that article.' *My Grandmother* 'Ah I'm glad you agree with me.' *I* 'Yes *I* agree with you, Grandmama.' *She* 'Well I shouldn't at all like to be buried in that Mausoleum – the part of me that is to be buried.' *Algernon* 'Oh don't you flatter yourself – *you*'d never be admitted into the family tomb of the Howards.' At this we laughed, and my Grandmother grew hurt and said 'It's very unkind of you all to laugh at the thought

1. Tom Mann (1856–1941) and John Burns (1858–1943) were trade-union leaders who played an important role in extending unionism among unskilled workers during the last years of the nineteenth century. Both had been active in the great dock strike of 1889.
2. In a letter several months before, Alys had commented on seeing a servant girl and her boyfriend 'keeping company' together and had regretted that class propriety made it impossible for Bertie and her to be together so easily.
3. The home of Rosalind Howard, Lady Carlisle, another of Russell's aunts. The house appears as 'Brideshead' in the television production of *Brideshead Revisited*.

of my burial', at which we laughed the more, and Algernon poked more fun at her.

In the evenings I played chess with Ld Stanley[1] till he went, then whist, which I like very much. I have hitherto been successful in both, and so increased the Stanleys respect for me: they all *worship* success: it is their only god.

I have got a lot of fun out of them by letting it be discovered (only in answer to their questions) that I'm a Socialist. They all have the vaguest ideas (derived from Marcella) as to what a Socialist is, and I have great fun drawing them out and mildly correcting them.

Yesterday evening, during a pause in the whist, my Grandmother asked me what they do at Pembroke Lodge in the evenings, and I said 'They sit round and think they'll talk'. She seemed impressed with the liveliness my answer depicted. I also told her how they are always expecting me to get cancer from smoking; this is the sort of timidity that annoys her most, so it was a good thing to tell her.

I'll tell thee more of the conversation as it occurs. I stay here till Monday night or Tuesday morning – then I go to the Burdetts for two or three nights.[2] What I do after that depends on whether we separate; that will have been a fortnight anyway. Perhaps if I look ill I shall go home, to try and soften their hearts. If not, I shall go to Germany to Mariechen. Goodbye my dearest: I feel sure now that all will be well in any case. No real harm can come to us and our love.

Thine devotedly
Bertie

Russell called at Pembroke Lodge before going on to visit the Burdetts. He found his grandmother much improved – she had been out for a drive and cancer was no longer feared. Russell further improved the situation by falsely giving Granny to understand that he and Alys would not sleep together after their marriage. Granny felt this arrangement preferable to the use of contraception, which she considered more dangerous than having children. 'Now that I know she is going to die soon I mind less giving her hopes not likely to be fulfilled,' Russell said with unconvincing heartlessness.

1. Henry, third Baron Stanley of Alderley. He was a Muslim.
2. The family of Sir Francis Burdett (1813–92). During Russell's childhood they had lived in Richmond and Burdett's youngest daughter, Maud, was one of Russell's few playmates. On this occasion Russell was going to visit them at their country home, Ramsbury Manor in Wiltshire.

The comparative harmony of this visit, however, did not mean that the separation was no longer insisted upon. The one concession was that Russell was to be allowed to spend the time abroad, since the objection to that had been that it would look bad if Russell were abroad when his grandmother was seriously ill. They no doubt thought, as well, that Russell's going abroad would remove him more completely from Alys's malign influence.

The next day Russell travelled on to the Burdetts. He spent his time urging Maud to go to Newnham College, against the opposition of her sister, Maie, and her mother. Despite a determined and somewhat hectoring campaign from Russell, Maud stayed at home and looked after her mother. To Russell she epitomized the wasted lives of women bound by Victorian propriety. Ironically, in this case Russell was able to see quite clearly that Maud's affection for her mother was being used by her family to prevent her going to Cambridge, but he couldn't see that his own affection for his grandmother was being similarly manipulated.

[45]

Ramsbury Manor, Wiltshire
Wednesday evening, 29 August 1894

My Darling Alys

I got thy second letter this morning after I had written mine to thee: the servant for some reason didn't bring it to me, though both came by the same post.

Certainly, I think the school-board would be an admirable thing for thee,[1] I believe thee could exercise thy faculties splendidly in that, it would be work which I should enjoy having thee do too. It *is* nice in many ways not to be going to have children for I should have hated to have thee idle, and I don't think it would be at all good for thee.

I'm glad thee is quite determined not to stay in England when we're married, as anything would be better than that.[2] Thee may send as many

1. Alys had suggested that she should stand for the London School Board in the elections to be held on 15 December. Beatrice Webb was involved in this idea. The School Board elections were held simultaneously with the London local-government elections, in which Beatrice was standing as a Radical. As an alien, Alys was not entitled to stand, but once married to Russell this objection would be overcome. In the event, she stood (though for the Westminster Vestry in the local-government elections rather than for the School Board), having married on 13 December, just in time to be a candidate. All the Radical candidates, however, were defeated.
2. Not surprisingly, Alys was preoccupied with getting Russell out of the clutches of his family. Nowhere in England seemed safe from them – hence the plans to live abroad.

documents as thee likes to Edith Thomas:[1] in fact I sympathize so much with her psychological interest that I think the more thee sends the better.

I have been having a tremendously interesting time here from a psychological point of view; I have been urging Maud to revolt, as thee will gather from the enclosed to Miss Young, her former governess, now schoolmistress at Wimbledon, a thoroughly advanced and thoughtful woman.[2] There are great difficulties in the way, and I'm *very* doubtful whether Maud will ever overcome her false conscience, but I've been working hard all day to influence her, so that after an interval of general society she fairly shook herself and said the idea of Newnham which I had been preaching had given her quite a new sense of freedom already. Her home is *perfectly deadly*, poor thing; she says her sister Maie would really be as much against her as anybody, although she says every now and then 'How hard it must be for you living at home', it seems her sympathy is quite impractical and theoretical, and combines itself with a hot preaching of home duties, which comes ungraciously from one lately and painfully emancipated by the unsatisfactory method of marriage. Maie's husband, Mr Byron, it seems, would also be dead against her; and *'pour comble de malheur'* she has a genuine affection for her mother, and still more for the memory of her father, whose dying wish it was that she should stick by her mother. Also it seems her mother is jealous of her affection for Miss Young, so that Maud can never see her without a struggle at home. On the other hand, Maud has £350 in her own right, and has a friend in Miss Young, able to give her not only a respectable dwelling but also the coaching she requires for Newnham. Her home and neighbours are really more unutterable than anybody could have imagined possible, except from a material point of view (the house is an extremely nice one of the Restoration, and the park and neighbourhood are full of the finest beeches I have ever seen; the place is close to Savernake forest).

Her mother has scores of objectionable phrases: if you say 'Coffee is very nice after dinner', the only style of remark possible to such a woman, she answers, with the air of a person making a great concession, 'Well, perhaps you're right'. Whenever she delivers an opinion she prefaces it with 'Well you know, *honestly*, I think', etc.

1. Edith Thomas (née Carpenter) had been a college friend of Mariechen's. She married Alys's cousin, Bond Thomas, the brother of the redoubtable Carey Thomas of Bryn Mawr. Alys was keeping her informed of the battle of the marriage and, doubtless to avoid disbelief, sought Russell's permission to provide documentary evidence in the form of copies of letters.
2. Russell enclosed a copy of a letter he'd written to Miss Young asking her to allow Maud to stay with her while she coached for the Newnham entrance examinations.

Maud was impressed (rather foolishly it seems to me) by my knowledge of Maie, because I said she liked me, thinking me a funny fellow, and that I had noticed she always laughed rather more at my jokes than she would if someone else made them, because she expected *me* to say amusing things. It is quite true that she, for some reason, stimulates my humour to a much higher level than is normal to it.

I have taken great trouble with Maud, warning her against diffidence and false conscience, and against all the sundry appeals individually that her people can make to her, and using any of my own experience, that seemed relevant, to back up what I said. Poor Maud has a very hard life of it here, and I would do a great deal to get her away from so pernicious a place; where she is withering up and growing morbid and wasting her faculties. When we are married we shall be able to be useful to such unfortunates. I am going to get up early to walk with her before breakfast, so Goodnight Dearest; I love thee more and more, but calmly and purely, thanks to our wonderful discovery.

8.30 a.m.

Please send me here a telegram yes or no on the enclosed *here* [*sic*]. I have had no time to think yet but am blindly averse to it because aristocratic and from my people. I think I should enjoy the actual time, only it might have disastrous consequences. I have had no time to think but what it has taken me to dress. I stay here at least till [the] day after tomorrow. I will telegraph my plans after that.

> Thine in haste
> > Bertie

The matter on which Russell sought Alys's advice in the hasty addition to his letter of 29 August was an important one. He had received an offer from Lord Dufferin, the British Ambassador to France, to work for three months as an honorary attaché at the British Embassy in Paris. The offer had been engineered by Russell's family, with which Dufferin had long-standing ties: he had begun his diplomatic career as Lord John Russell's attaché at an abortive conference in Vienna intended to negotiate an end to the Crimean War.

Russell was initially averse to accepting the offer because he had no interest in diplomatic work and because he feared it would extend his separation from Alys. Without waiting for Alys's telegram, he wrote to Aunt Agatha virtually turning the offer down. Alys's telegram, however, which arrived late the next afternoon, advised him to accept Dufferin's offer. While Russell's family at Pembroke Lodge saw the position in Paris as an opportunity to remove Bertie from Alys's influence, Alys saw it as an opportunity to remove him from the influence of Pembroke Lodge. For once, therefore, the demands made on him from both sides coincided. Dutifully, despite his strong personal dislike of the idea, he immediately decided to accept. He was adamant, however, that the position in Paris would not be used as an excuse to extend the separation beyond the agreed three months. His hope now was to marry as soon as possible after the separation ended on 17 November and he was understandably anxious to discover when his work at the embassy would end. In the event, it did not extend the separation, though it did delay the marriage into December.

The separation often took its toll on their good humour. Although the postal service was excellent by modern standards, their practice of writing several times a day made it inevitable that their letters regularly crossed and this in turn made it easy for them to misjudge each other's moods. A case in point occurred early in September when Russell tried to emphasize how much accepting Lord Dufferin's offer ran against his own inclinations. He feared that his family would try to press him into a career in the diplomatic service or some other field that would yield immediate success. His own desire was to work 'quietly and unobtrusively, in a way which ... is very unlikely to bring me the slightest fame or success till I'm 50 at least' (3 September; the letter is printed in Russell's *Autobiography*, vol. i, pp. 99–101). This would involve forgoing much experience of the world which, otherwise, he would find very tempting and conflicted with the picture Alys treasured of their married life, in which they would form a partnership working together for social reform – very much like the Webbs. But what probably offended Alys most in his letter was his suggestion that she might not support him in his resolve to do theoretical work:

> Once for all, God Almighty has made me a theorist, not a practical man.... *Do* be stern and consistent in accepting this view of myself, as otherwise (if I have to fight thee as well as my relations and the world) I shall certainly miss what I *hope* it lies in me to do. (*Autobiography*, vol. i, p. 100)

The subsequent history of philosophy bears out the wisdom of Russell's remarks. Moreover, Russell's fears that Alys might not support him were not entirely groundless – she had, after all, been very keen to involve him in the practical work of social reform and had tried, on several previous occasions, to send him out into the world in quest of 'experience'. None the less, Alys cannot have been pleased to find herself lumped together, even hypothetically, with Russell's relations.

Russell wrote again later the same day apologizing for his earlier letter – he felt he had exaggerated. But he was in low spirits that day – he said he was bored and had lost faith in himself – and the letter of apology was weak and added its own points of friction: he preferred Bradley's metaphysics to Alys's religion, and he preferred her working on the school board to her temperance work with its 'religious wash'.

Alys replied fiercely to both letters, predicting damningly that he would end up like Herbert Spencer. If she had to choose between the school board and temperance work, she said she would choose temperance work. Her mood was made fiercer by the fact that she had caught a cold which she was treating with eucalyptus and homoeopathic medicines – the latter, she said, were not intended to cure it, but to annoy Bertie. Two days later Russell's mood has passed and he replied good-humouredly.

[46]

Pembroke Lodge
5 September 1894. 10.30 p.m.

Dearest Alys

To begin with business, in case of my forgetting it again, I suppose thee ought to write to Miss Morris, explaining (I suppose) that thee knows her situation and is not shocked. I am afraid she will not do credit to thy taste when she is elected, but if she becomes a Countess thee will be justified more or less![1]

I am glad of thy cross letter, as it makes me think perhaps thee really exists, which of late has seemed to me very unlikely. I have lost the power of visualizing thee, which I only keep a few days after parting, and the photos I have bear no resemblance to thee, and I have seen none of thy belongings (I *do* hope I shall find thy mother tomorrow),[2] and lofty sentiments do not seem to have any point of contact with present reality, which is mainly boredom; but a person who has a cold and is cross and says I shall grow like Herbert Spencer (*Dieu m'en garde!*) seems possible and human in my present frame of mind. But I hate to think of thy smelling Eucalyptus, because my aunt spends half her life in an atmosphere of it, and I have such a devouring hatred for her that it makes me detest any association with that smell: in Rome (when I hated her *far* less than now) the Eucalyptus trees used to turn me nearly sick. I hope when we are married thee will find some other equally effective cure for colds. Homoeopathic medicines don't annoy me if thee

1. Frank had written to Alys to ask her to propose Miss Morris, his 'hypothetical fiancée', for membership of the Pioneer Club.
2. He was to visit their house in Grosvenor Road to pick up some belongings.

takes them *only* with that end, though it *would* make me rage and storm if I thought thee believed in them.

So thee has failed in every point to be irritating; in fact I am positively glad thee should have wished to be, because it makes me feel freer in abusing thee if thee repays me in my own coin than if thee played the injured saint or were grieved and said nothing, or meek and accepted it. Thee needn't mind writing letters in a different mood from mine: what I chiefly want from thy letters is to know thy mood just as it is, and the irrelevant matter amuses me, though there is usually nothing interesting to be said about it, so that I take no notice of it in my letters. – The two tracts I sent thee are both great fun, so I would read them if I were thee.

Thy plan of a cottage by the sea is *too* heavenly, only let it be in France, because there we shall be more irresponsible and unattainable. We could get one in a remote place for next to nothing, and be in heaven all the time we staid [*sic*] there. We'll begin next summer. The idea is too heavenly for words, and has always been my ideal of bliss; only until lately I had a notion thee hated the sea, so I never proposed it. I don't know why I thought so, except that I have a tremendous romantic passion for it, and thee has always seemed to me quite devoid of passions of that kind. – 'Ich liebe das Meer wie meine Seele' as Heine says.[1] It satisfies all my love of boundlessness and change and vast regularity, and has an extraordinary exhilarating and yet calming effect on all my thought and feelings.

See how horribly easily I grow sentimental just now! It is because all my life is in the past and the future, so that there is nothing real and unsentimental to think of.

I hope thee realizes, when I write blue letters to thee, that by the time I have written them the mood which produced them is past: all my unhappy moods only require expression to make them vanish; the happy ones, fortunately, are intensified by it.

If thee would like to do me a real kindness and give me some pleasant hours, thee would mention some special points in the Bradley[2] on which

---

1. 'I love the sea as my soul': Heinrich Heine, 'Geschrieben auf der Insel Norderney', *Reisebilder*, II (*Sämtliche Schriften*, Munich, Carl Hanser Verlag, 1969, vol. II, p. 224).
2. Alys was now reading Bradley, but probably *Ethical Studies* (1876) and some current articles in *Mind*. Alys did not ask for any points to be elucidated and Russell never wrote the notes he suggested. This was not the only such offer. The previous year he had written a little essay for Alys on Green's *Prolegomena to Ethics* (*Papers*, vol. I, pp. 208–11) and a few weeks later he wrote an elucidatory paper on free-will for Mariechen. There is much evidence, apart from his enormous output, that Russell enjoyed the process of writing. He was a natural writer, who, at this time, was in search of topics.

thee wants elucidation, and I would write notes on them for thee. I don't
for a moment imagine thee takes enough interest in him to care about them
when they are written, only it would give me something pleasant to do and
to think about. In short writing is at any time a complete distraction to me,
and if thee can suggest any other subjects on which thee would like me to
write essays or anything, whether for style or thought, for thee or for Logan,
it would be a real boon to me and a help in getting through the time of our
separation – particularly if I thought thee was going to read the result.

I will take back with pleasure what I said about Mrs Sidney Webb: I only
said it because I had never heard her mentioned by any economist as a person
of note: but then I haven't seen any since their joint book came out.[1]

I am staying on here because I find I can stand it, and therefore I think I
owe it to my Grandmother. However I shall probably get off by Friday
morning, that is if I can see the Foreign Office people tomorrow. In Paris I
shan't have much time to be bored, as there will be too much novelty about
everything. If thee knows of any Bohemians who are going to be in Paris
any time, I hope I shall be able to see them – a little of it would be so
refreshing after stiff English aristocrats.

My Darling I can't write any more irrelevant stuff I am overcome with a
sudden spasm of longing for thee – would I could kiss thee just once and see
thy eyes again. I feel as if I should never see thee more never have relish in
the fairy power of unreflecting love[2] – damn it will it ever be unreflecting
again? I feel again as in June so infinitely wearied, as if I should never have
the spring and elasticity to feel as I felt in Fontainebleau. I don't believe in
anything now – I believe in thee but I grow despondent sometimes. – But
all this is folly – Don't bother to write and sympathize: better laugh at me –
it's all folly – Oh for a moment to drink life from thee! Pardon my weakness
I don't want to make things harder for thee and I wish I had more faith and
fortitude – Now I will go and post this – the night air will *do me* good –
God bless thee – thee is life and strength to me

    Thine
      Bertie

1. Russell had said that Beatrice Webb could never hope to be more than a shadow of
her husband, Sidney – a judgement that is certainly perverse in the light of their
subsequent history. In this he was likely to have been influenced by the extraordinary
view his mother recorded in her diary, that Beatrice was frivolous (*Autobiography*, vol.
I, p. 16). Alys detected a slight against women and wrote in Beatrice's defence, saying
that Beatrice was the thinker of the two, a judgement which Russell echoed in his
Autobiography (vol. I, p. 95). The Webbs' joint book, the first of many, was *The History
of Trade Unionism* (1894).
2. Keats, 'When I have fears that I may cease to be'.

Russell left for Paris on Monday, 10 September, writing to Alys from Victoria Station on the way over and again from his hotel as soon as he arrived. The letters continued twice, and sometimes three times, a day. The generally leisurely way of life at the embassy gave him plenty of time to think about his love and about sexual relations in general. He was already developing the views for which he became famous, and occasionally notorious, much later on. This is especially clear in the views he expressed in the next letter on sex education, which changed little over the next seventy-five years. Even his ambition of running a coeducational school, in which information about sex would be imparted without moral prejudice as a normal part of the curriculum, was realized when he founded Beacon Hill School with his second wife, Dora, in the 1920s. None the less, despite what they described as their perfect sympathy for one another and despite the magical Friday morning in the Bô-tree house in August, they found it by no means easy to write about the physical side of their relationship. Russell's suggestion that they exchange sexual reminiscences was no doubt in part an attempt to broach this delicate subject. The reminiscences were written and mailed but have not survived – the pages on which they were written were removed from the letters and destroyed. It seems highly unlikely that they contained anything very scandalous.

The next letter opens with Russell's first impressions of the people at the embassy (whom he liked no more than he expected).

[47]

Hôtel du Prince de Galles,
Rue d'Anjou, Paris
Wednesday, 12 September 1894. 11.20 p.m.

My Darling Alys

I have been dining with Lord Terence,[1] whose acquaintance I made today, at the Restaurant Laurent, which I understand to be very swell, and that has made me too late for this evening's post – however I think thee ought to get this by the first post on Friday all the same. I have been bored to death all the time, as the talk was entirely sporting – about drag-hunts at Constantinople and pig-sticking in India – but at last Lord Terence got on the subject of my cousin Herbrand,[2] the present Duke, and said he had been very intimate with him at Simla, and that he (Herbrand) was a very silent person, but a very good friend when you knew him – so I *said* silence was

1. Lord Dufferin's second son, Terence John Temple (1866–1918). In 1894 he was Third Secretary at the Paris embassy. He had married an American, Florence Davis, in 1893.
2. Herbrand Arthur, eleventh Duke of Bedford (1858–1940).

a family trait (having been necessarily silent all through the sporting talk) and *hoped* he would infer the other was also in the family. Although he married an American, I don't like him – he wears loud cheque [*sic*] suits and has an accent which is a queer mixture of American twang and cockney – he is an awful snob, and brags of his doings in the sporting line, in various outlandish countries where one can't verify his stories. If I have to do much dining with the other Attachés I *shall* hate the place – and it seems highly probable I shall have to, as I'm dining with Phipps[1] on Saturday.

To come to pleasanter subjects: I have read Carpenter on *Marriage*, and it seems to me fairly good talk, but too indefinite – in *Woman* there were several practical reforms proposed, but here, even on the subject of divorce, nothing at all definite is said. He entirely omits (except for one brief allusion) the subject of children – perhaps he will write a separate pamphlet on that. I feel that *the* thing I have learnt this year is that any improvement in the condition of the great mass of women is only possible through Socialism, and it is this discovery which has made me a Socialist. Of course I know so little about the subject as yet that I may be mistaken, but I should love to go into it thoroughly, historically, economically, deductively – every way it can be gone into. In fact it is from realizing this connection of the Woman Question with Economics that I have become keen on social questions, which I never was before, believing nothing possible except by a gradual raising of the moral tone of the community, which always struck me as a very dull and uninteresting doctrine. But, from a more individual point of view, I am convinced a really happy marriage is seldom possible unless the man is pure-minded, and *that* he can never be as long as the only women with whom he can be intimate before marriage are prostitutes, and as long as everything sexual is to him associated primarily with them. I am sure the great thing is co-education, and great freedom of intercourse, with perfect knowledge of sexual matters, throughout the period of puberty – if the mystery were removed, half the morbid lust which belongs to that period would be removed with it. It is untold what anguish, what moral struggles, what dread and what despair I might have been saved at that time by a few words from any pure minded elder. Instead of which, I was left to learn what I could from the smutty talk of immoral companions – oh it is scandalous, what suffering and wrong-doing I might have been spared by ten minutes candid instruction. And the same holds of most boys who have in them the power

1. Sir Edmund Constantine Henry Phipps (1840–1911), Minister Plenipotentiary at the British Embassy in Paris until late in 1894 when he was posted to Brazil.

of strong and pure feeling on sex-matters. At that time I grew gradually accustomed to the absolutely incessant foul talk of my companions, until I could laugh at it, and even repeat it if necessary – but now I am grown again almost morbidly sensitive to the minutest impurity of thought, word or deed: I know now the tremendous importance of purity of thought and the beauty of a reverent view of sex: and the opposite shocks me more and more every day, till the society of all men except my personal friends is become nauseous to me, and even of most women, because they think sex is shocking, which is only the other face of impurity – if their minds were pure, and they could think sanely and holily about it, they couldn't imagine it shocking. (I'm afraid this applies to thee as thee *was*, not as thee *is*.) I wish we were going to have children, if only to give them a sensible education in matters of sex – I should almost like to start a co-education school for the purpose of applying my theories (and everybody's who thinks about it, I suppose) only nobody would come to it. – I feel more inclined, if thee would like it equally well, to send the history of my knowledge of sex up to the time of my fancy for Fitz's[1] sister, only if I did, most of it would have to remain between thee and me.

I enclose my letter to Lord Dufferin. I had some difficulty in saying what I had to say politely, but I *think* I succeeded – thee may give it to Logan as an instance of the advantages of rewriting!

Today they gave me no work – nothing, in fact, but about 5 minutes instruction from Lord Terence. However I was not bored – part of the time I listened to their work, part of the time we talked, and part of the time I read the French papers. In the afternoon I went a long walk along the river, as far as the Jardin des Plantes, and bought a catalogue of the Louvre pictures on my way home. I arrived at last at the part of the river where thee and I used to walk, which was filled with associations, pleasant today, though on many days they would have been painful – but today I was in a very exalted mood, feeling as if I could be happy my life-long merely in the thought that thee existed, and as if I could transform my love in a purely spiritual affection like Dante's for Beatrice – of course I couldn't really, but I felt today as if I could. However, every time I meet a happy couple I feel a pang, I feel the

---

1. Edward Arthur FitzGerald (1871–1931) was Russell's special friend at the crammers in Southgate where he prepared for his entrance to Cambridge. They had a serious falling out, however, apparently over Fitz's treatment of his mother. See Russell's *Autobiography*, vol. I, pp. 43–4, and *Papers*, vol. I, pp. 60–61. His sister, Caroline (1866–1911), became a translator of Italian literary works. Russell's 'fancy' for her occurred in 1889 when he went to Paris with the FitzGerald family. In that year, however, she married Lord Edmond Fitzmaurice.

longing for the touch of thy hand, of thy lips, for the lovely look of thy eyes – and I feel how insufficient a purely spiritual love without physical companionship is for a person who is not devoid of human feelings. But if I can keep myself from hating my companions here, I shall not feel discouraged – on the contrary, as the memory of physical sensations fades (and such memories always fade very quickly) my love becomes more and more purely spiritual, so that I need thy actual presence less, and if thy letters are satisfactory, I can even be quite happy in the thought of thy love. I think that is why last autumn and the early times have been so much in my mind lately, because then also there were no physical sensations involved or even (on my side) thought of. Even the time on Oct. 6 when we held hands a moment, it was to me *purely* the symbol of a spiritual union, and quite free from the slightest physical feeling, though this was no longer the case the second time.

Dearest we *have* a divinely beautiful life before us – of that I am quite certain. I shall not have anything to teach thee, though love will teach us both many things. When I see how we have both improved in our relations to each other, how physical feelings have not weakened the spiritual love, but only made it deeper and stronger, until it has imbued them with its own beauty, so that the two are welded into a pure and perfect whole, I feel *absolute* confidence in our power to make each other happy, and to adapt ourselves to each other in every way that may be necessary. I am more and more convinced every day that we are ideally suited to bring about the best in each other, and *therefore* to be always divinely happy together. Goodnight my Life.

Thine in every fibre.
    Bertie

Despite Russell's repeated claim that, with the separation, his obligations to his grandmother were satisfied, she was still able to cause a good deal of anguish by her continuing efforts to prevent the marriage. A letter from her which is now lost provoked the following *cri de cœur*, which Russell added to a letter written earlier the same day describing his meetings with a number of friends and acquaintances among expatriate artists living in Paris. The earlier part of the letter is omitted.

[48]

[Paris]
18 September 1894. 5 p.m.

My Darling Alys

I must write now because I am seized with a mood in which I simply *must* get at thee somehow. I am very unhappy – all my patience has given out. I had a very disagreeable letter from my Grandmother which depressed me a great deal – it doesn't give me a bad conscience! I really believe I have done with that – but I am sorry that all my sacrifices to her should be in vain – that she isn't a *little* grateful to me for turning what might have been the 3 happiest months of my life into the 3 most miserable since I left Southgate, simply and solely to please her. Do write me a very nice letter – I do need something to keep me from morbid misery. Oh my Darling it is hard to live without thee – I feel so utterly and terribly alone – I have no friends here even, in fact I almost feel as if I had no friend anywhere but thee. Thee and I, merely in the way of friendship, are so all in all to each other, besides our love – at least thee is all in all to me – thee sums up all beautiful human relations to me, not only that of love.

Oh I do long for thee – it is so difficult to go on with ordinary tasks and meeting people I hate when I am absorbed in craving for thee in every fibre. It is horrible to forget what thee looks like, to forget almost the sound of thy voice – I have only names and words to assure me of thy existence and they are so cold and unreal. I have spasms of pain which are so extreme they make me cry out sometimes. Forgive me I *do* not want to be bothering thee and making it worse for thee, but I *can't* be happy – I have tried *so* hard. Thee has spoilt me for everybody else – they all seem so cold and hard and indifferent. I hope this mood will pass soon. Now I must be off to the Embassy again. Oh Dearest when shall we be together again? It seems as if it would never come.

Later. I have been to the Embassy where there was almost nothing for me to do, and have had some tea to cheer me up, so now I feel quite in good spirits again. A large part of my mood was mere physical weariness.

I am going to dine with Costelloe and Dr Bull[1] tonight – he is in Paris about 2 days, and came to look me up at the Embassy this morning. It might have been very nice seeing him, but somehow it wasn't. I enclose also a letter

1. Frank Costelloe, of course, was Mariechen's husband. George Joseph Bull (1848–1911) was an eminent Canadian ophthalmologist then working in Paris at the Sorbonne. Russell enjoyed talking metaphysics with Frank, while Bull, it seems, was completely bored.

from Marsh, which has amused me greatly – though his French mathematical impropriety is quite unintelligible to me.[1] My Grandmother says her letters are for me alone, but I have told her so often that we have no secrets from each other that I have no compunction in sending them on. Please return her letter though when thee has read it.

I only said 'for thee alone' because the sort of reminiscences I had thought of writing before would have been for Logan too if he had cared for them, and would have made some sort of literary effort as well, vain as that would have been. Perhaps I will write them yet.

I will write again tomorrow morning, but probably only a short letter as I've written now.

I am anxious to see just as many people of thy friends and acquaintances as possible, both because they are pleasant, and because they occupy my thoughts and take me away from the aristocrats. I am of a mood to like them all, even Conder,[2] whom I should loathe at any other time. No one in that set is the least philosophical however – I wonder now at Logan's being so *much* so – it must be due to Oxford.

Goodnight Dearest.

Thine heart and soul
Bertie

Russell's frustration with the separation continued to grow, and soon all things Parisian began to grate upon him. His own sexual frustration and his conventional English view that Paris was a centre of vice and decadence did not make the city easy for him to live in. Even a second metaphysical discussion with Costelloe proved less enjoyable than the first. Russell was well aware in what low esteem Costelloe was held at Friday's Hill, and he may well have wished to counteract the impression given in an earlier letter that they were getting on well together.

1. The letter is printed in Russell's *Autobiography*, vol. i, pp. 109–11, though the supposedly unintelligible mathematical impropriety is omitted.
2. Charles Conder (1868–1909), the Australian painter. A friend of Whistler, Rothenstein, and Toulouse-Lautrec, he lived a 'dissolute life' in Paris in the 1890s according to Alan McCulloch (*Encyclopedia of Australian Art*, p. 136).

[49]

Prince de Galles
Thursday, 20 September 1894

My Darling Alys

Thy letter is very interesting, and I am very glad to have thy reminiscences. But how easy everything was to thee! I didn't want to sentimentalize in what I wrote thee, but in the struggles of those times I really went through the most terrible trials; half-believing in conventional morality (wholly, by instinct), but strongly drawn away from it both by desire and reason; and keeping *everything* to myself, and having an idle solitary life to lead – the awful thing was the suddenness of the whole new complication, with no one to give me advice. My uncle was restrained by mere craven fear, or 'delicacy' as my Grandmother calls it. But my case, as to the way I got my knowledge, was very typical – only that it came to me a little later than to most, because I saw less of other boys. I always had a strong instinctive horror of vice, and when I went to Southgate this became intensified, and I set to work to eradicate impure thoughts, which I had before not seen any harm in. But the process *was* hard: it is barely ended yet.

I hate this place – I have been walking about at night, and the endless rows of prostitutes with their painted lips and coarse 'allure' get on my nerves and depress me terribly. The French man too is an unutterable beast: I suffer a physical pang every time I come across any coarseness even of word or feeling, and this, instead of getting less as years go by, gets greater and greater. It makes me despair of the world and the sex-question to see people so destitute of the rudiments of right feeling as they are here – they haven't enough of it to make them hypocrites even. I get to loathe the prettiness of everything, the pleasure-seeking air of the whole town. I should almost love to plunge into some ancient monastery and take any number of vows, to get away from the oppressive sinning of this place. I love to get over to the other side, where things are comparatively poor and ugly and genuine, and where vice does not wear such a loathsome luxurious air as here.

I spent about 2 hours last night walking the streets with Costelloe – first we talked about Darwinism, and he was so unscientific I nearly lost my temper with him, and said rude things several times. I had a headache which made his loud voice reverberate all through my brain as if it had been a gong, and yet he would keep dinning endless arguments into me, always voluble and clever, but always wilfully misunderstanding my point, and always assuming himself perfectly competent to pronounce on points requiring a thorough knowledge of Mathematics, Biology, and Geology all combined.

His mind is theological and legal, not scientific or philosophical. Even his philosophy is held in a theological sort of way, by authority, and because he fancies it supports Catholicism. I can well understand poor Mariechen being nearly ready to murder him – I got to loathe him last night.

Finally, being afraid of myself if we talked longer about Darwinism, I began on prostitutes. On this subject he told me many interesting legal experiences[1] but though he is the soul of morality himself his views shocked me – I think they were rather those of the Catholic Church – his objections to vice seemed almost wholly religious, and he plainly had never thought of it from the larger social point of view, or from that of women – though he did reiterate dozens of times that 'society rests on the family'. I am in a terribly nervous state, because the noises in the street wake me up so early – as well as for other reasons! It is almost impossible to me to keep sane-minded over here – the whole tone of the place is so antipathetic to me, and my most vehement hatreds are so continually aroused. – I ought to have been a woman brought up on the pedestal theory: facts are sometimes almost too much for me. I have no appetite or digestion, and I can't do a scrap of thinking. But I shall acclimatize myself to the place in time, and then it will be better.

I have read a lot of Galton,[2] which interests me vastly and is frightfully good – it is the best distraction I know of, not having a type-writer![3]

It never occurred to me Louise[4] was like thy mother – but now thee suggests it I can see it. It is true, when I first saw her I couldn't think why thee had said she was beautiful – but I soon came to think her so – and I'm sure her character is nicer than Kate's. I certainly thought (though they're so muddled up it's hard to tell) that Sturgess[5] preferred Louise, though I should hardly have said he was much in love with either – but perhaps my standard is too high.

I went exactly the same walk again yesterday, by the Villa des Dames and

1. Costelloe was a barrister.
2. Francis Galton's *Hereditary Genius*.
3. Alys was learning how to type and had sent him one typed letter.
4. Louise Kinsella, one of three sisters from Boston with whom Logan was friendly. The other two were Frances (usually known as 'Joe') and Kate. They were the daughters of Thomas Kinsella, an Irish-American congressman. They shared a flat on the Left Bank and were well known in the artists' community there, modelling on occasion for Whistler.
5. Jonathan Sturges, a would-be poet. Alys was curious whether Sturges was in love with Kate or Louise. Although he failed as a poet, Sturges had some success as a translator of Maupassant. Russell counted his friendship with Sturges, which lasted until Sturges died, as the one thing of permanent value that he derived from his stay in Paris (although he continued to misspell his name for some time) (*Autobiography*, vol. I, p. 87).

Logan's place – and I got back more successfully into that time, so that I felt moderately happy for the time. As a rule, lately, I have been feeling very miserable, chiefly because I'm not in good health I think. I shall be a perfect scarecrow by Nov. 17 if I go on at this rate! But I shall soon get used to the life and then my health will be all right again – I move into lodgings over the Embassy tomorrow. Do write me nice letters (thee always does!); I live for nothing else, and grow daily more dependent on them – they give me about a quarter of an hour's happiness a day. I don't feel now as if Nov. 17 were getting a bit nearer – it seems again as if a catastrophe would happen before that. I am sure our affairs have been set in the tragic vein hitherto, and artistic appropriateness requires they should end so! – I got a nice letter from Lion:[1] a great tribute to us, it seemed to me. O my Darling I do long for thee and I feel as if there were no one else in the world I ought to see – Goodbye my Beloved –
　　Thine devotedly
　　Bertie

Not many of Russell's early letters to his friends have survived, but three that he wrote from Paris to C. P. Sanger have. The one included here deals largely with his Fellowship work. The view he expresses in it, that a constant measure of curvature is a priori necessary (i.e. that real space must be of uniform curvature), is central to his first philosophical book, *An Essay on the Foundations of Geometry* (1897). His views on Euclidean geometry, however, had changed by 1897. In the *Essay*, he holds that it is (most likely) an empirical truth, whereas in the letter he adopts, rather surprisingly, a position which seems quite close to the conventionalism of the French mathematician, Henri Poincaré, according to which we choose Euclidean geometry over the alternatives because it is more convenient. (In 1899 he argued against conventionalism in a well-known exchange of papers with Poincaré. See *Papers*, vol. II, pp. 390–415.)

He also uses the letter to pump Sanger for information both about Euclid's congruence conditions for solids (a central issue for his proof of the necessity of constant curvature) and about income tax. Sanger had started the practice with his 'three connundrums [*sic*]', three detailed questions for Russell on French politics.

1. 'Lion' Fitzpatrick (see letter 21).

[50]

British Embassy
29 September 1894

Dear Sanger

I was very glad of your letter, but much alarmed at your three connundrums. I hope in time to be able to give some sort of answer to them, but as yet I have only had to copy dispatches and cypher and decypher telegrams, from which one doesn't learn much. However when people come back to Paris I shall see something of French politicians, and then I hope to find out something. I have an introduction to M. Ribot,[1] who used to be foreign minister – you might give me a brief account of the prominent facts about him, which you probably know by heart; also to a man whose prominent interest is the Income Tax, which he wants to introduce in France.[2] If you could send me some pamphlet on it or tell me how to get it up before seeing him, I should be deeply grateful.

Now for a connundrum on shop: You I believe possess a complete Euclid – would you mind telling me if in Bk XI or elsewhere there is any comparison of volumes, and if so, whether this is effected by Congruence and super-position and the axiom about it (axiom 8 or 10 I think)? I don't know of any other way of establishing Geometrical Equality, but in I.4 it is always said to involve the 3rd Dimension, and in this case its use for solids which involves the 4th. I see no alternative to congruence but the Identity of Indiscernibles, which is not very geometrical. Do tell me how e.g. it is proved that two cubes, each of a unit side, are equal. I am quite in a fix. Tell me also if you know of any other way of establishing Geometrical Equality besides Congruence. To me it seems to have no meaning except possible Congruence.

I think I may be able towards the end of Oct., to come over a Saturday to Monday – if so I will write a paper. If Trotter still wants a paper for the Moral Sciences club, I would *perhaps* write him one on Space and Geometry, which perhaps you would read. But only if he is still badly in want of a paper. My present view is that Euclid has the same superiority over Metageometry[4] that Kepler has over Epicycles – both seem possible ways of

1. Alexandre Ribot (1842–1923), a Republican deputy. He was Minister of Foreign Affairs from 1890 to 1893.
2. Probably Jacques Cavaignac, a Republican deputy (see letter 61).
3. W. H. Trotter, the secretary of the Cambridge Moral Sciences Club. Sanger read the the paper Russell proposed on 9 November 1894.
4. Non-Euclidean geometry. Russell contrasts Kepler's heliocentric model of the solar

accounting for the given sensations, but the former in each case is the simpler. Constant measure of curvature on the contrary is I think an a priori necessity of thought, in the sense that its denial involves philosophic absurdities such as absolute position.

I'm more contented now than I was – I get a certain amount of my own work done, and I ride a bicycle, which is a great score. I've made the acquaintance of Whistler,[1] having an introduction to him from the Pearsall Smiths, which is also a score. And later on, when there are more people in Paris, I dare say I shall have a comparatively good time. But I've seldom been more lonely and dreary than my 1st fortnight here – away from everything and everybody I cared for.

Yours fraternally,
Bertrand Russell

Russell's perhaps unexpected susceptibility to the extremes of nineteenth-century romanticism is exhibited in the following excited letter written immediately after a performance of Wagner's *Die Walküre* at the Paris Opera. It is less surprising, especially given his mood of irritation with all things French, that he should have preferred German romanticism to French. He had originally told Alys that he would write to her, on the mid-point of their separation, during the intermissions in the opera. In the event, this did not prove feasible.

Remarks toward the end of Russell's letter have often been quoted in isolation to illustrate Russell's patronizing attitude to Alys. That element can't entirely be denied, though the context considerably dilutes it. Russell's complaints about Alys's priggery had produced a good-humoured apology from her. But she had expressed the fear, which would recur, that she was not intelligent enough for him. He was hardly in a position convincingly to deny that he was unusually intelligent, least of all to Alys who both admired and was attracted to his intellect. Even at this stage in his career he had a truly formidable reputation for brilliance. (Harold Joachim, the Oxford philosopher, had told Alys about this time that he was pleased Russell couldn't read Greek because, in all other respects, he was far too clever.) Russell's reply, ironically and at times cynically stated, was intended to be reassuring and seems to have been received as such, for Alys did not complain in her reply. Nor

system with the Ptolemaic model in which the earth is at the centre of the solar system and the other bodies revolve around it. The apparent, occasional backwards motion of the planets in their orbits was explained on the Ptolemaic model by the addition of epicycles, but needed no such *ad hoc* device on the Keplerian model.

1. The American painter. Russell had called on him the previous day. Logan knew him quite well.

should it be forgotten that Russell's remarks come in a letter of uncharacteristic megalomania in the aftermath of *Die Walküre*. An older, or perhaps a more confident, lover might have evaded the issue more adeptly – the letter was, as Russell admits, 'conceited' and 'egotistical'.

[51]

1–2 October 1894
midnight

My Beloved Alys

It was impossible to write between the Acts, but I will celebrate the moment of passing the middle of our separation by a midnight letter. I am back from the Opera – and naturally in no mood for bed. For some reason I was bored throughout the first act, but after that the fire gradually entered my veins and now I have got the fever, and shall not be content till I've seen all the lot many times. It has given me a wonderful exhilaration and feeling of omnipotence which is perfectly divine while it lasts – the sort of omni-potence in which everyone shares because all wish the same thing – the sort mankind *will* have some day.

The French words were excruciatingly banal, but at every note I felt the massive German and worshipped him – I wish I had been born a German – it was glorious to get something so un-French – they seem mere ingenious pigmies beside anything really big of the Teutonic Titanic sort. Even the absurdities – the thunder and lightning (which were worthy of Sir Augustus Druriolanus)[1] – are big and invigorating after the stifling finniky [*sic*] appro-priateness of everything French. I can understand Sanger's remark about incest which he once made in the Society à propos of Wagner – though personally it would never have occurred to me to think of it as incest. Also it gives me a feeling for the way Carpenter begins his pamphlet on *Woman* – the Valkyrie are a fine apotheosis of the great primitive woman such as Walt [Whitman] loves to praise and such as drawing-rooms destroy. It strikes me all these remarks are incoherent but it is midnight and my ideas are not in a coherent state.

I wonder why music gives one such a sense of power – it is discouraging to reflect soberly that after all the world doesn't lie at one's feet to be remodelled according to one's own will, as it seems to do tonight. I feel like

---

1. The nickname of Augustus Harris, the manager of Drury Lane, who was well known for staging spectacular melodramas.

Caliban's conception of Trinculo,[1] and about as unlike what I really am – worse luck! Power is a glorious passion. I am sure if I had been in the place of Christ in the Temptation I should have yielded when the Devil showed me all the cities of the Earth – and yet no – to bow down to the Devil would have spoilt it – even a little independent power would be better than that of a slave. But it *must* be fine to feel oneself one of the men who really turn the currents of events or of thought – banal as such an observation may be.

I suppose all men love mastery in some form or other – I love the most subtle and absolute, the mastery over people's wishes and thoughts and hopes, not merely over their outward acts. I feel utterly unmoral tonight – the whole realm of moral and immoral seems to have vanished, and left only the great and the small, and the wish to be of the former. The practical point of all which is to work hard and think hard and come as near greatness as possible. Music is a grand stimulant.

It is odd that until this year I never was ambitious since boyhood, but now the boyish passion has come back. I think it is due to the exhilaration of love and the stimulating effect of it on all my faculties and the wish to have as much as possible to lay at thy feet. If it lasts it will be an immeasurable help to my work.

I'm too egotistic to mind thy not having more than the very fair share of brains thee has – provided thee is sympathetic it will always be enough – and thee has somehow managed to get most of thy opinions those that clever people have, which is the great point. I do believe that our marriage will be the best thing possible for me in every way.

If I hadn't met thee or thee hadn't cared for me, and I had been left to myself and my people, it might have been years before I got into the right sort of work – and as I said just now thy love is wonderfully stimulating. If thee had more brains thee wouldn't care so much about mine and then I shouldn't be so much stimulated. I'm very conceited tonight but that is part of the exhilaration of the music. I feel like chanting a paean tonight – life seems so big and free and fine and so full of things to do. The thought of thee to share in them and care about them is just what completes it and makes the whole thing glorious instead of merely Satanic. I used to wonder at Keats's sonnet 'When I have fears that I may cease to be' because he puts Love and Fame together and Fame seemed such rubbish in comparison – and so it would be if one had to choose one or the other – but where love is already, Fame does seem to grow to be almost as great – it reinforces love and makes it greater and finer.

1. Trinculo, a jester, is mistaken by Caliban for a powerful spirit (*The Tempest*, II, ii).

It has been occurring to me however that if ambition grows upon me I shall become more and more egotistic, and I'm in danger of growing unsympathetic. I have always more or less of a fear that some day thee will find a sort of intellectual unsympathy about me – a sort of dry pedantry which may creep over me and make me think everything human ought to give way to work. But I hope we shall manage to do work in which each will be useful to the other. However I feel that if thee were strongly to take up anything I thought illogical or foolish I might be very disagreeable – it is well to realize the danger so as to guard against it.

This is an odd scrambling letter. I got thine before going to the Opera and will answer it tomorrow morning when I'm sober again – and probably I shall pay for tonight's elation by a racking headache, but it is worth it, to get new ideas. I don't know how I ever got on without thee – but for thee I should have been very miserable tonight. I should have been just as strongly stirred, and then have been baffled by the overpowering feeling of the nothingness and uselessness of everything – it makes the whole difference to be able to refer everything to thee.

Goodnight my Beloved – this is a grand celebration to me of the passage to the 2nd half of our time, and tonight I can feel happy in the thought of thee though thee is not by. Thee is the world to me – thee is Life and Hope and everything. Goodnight my Strength and my Joy.

> Thine to the depths,
> Bertie

The halfway mark in their separation led Russell to further reminiscences about their relationship. Alys's mood of a few letters earlier had dissipated. She wrote a charming letter from her bed in which she announced she was planning to write on socialism and the woman question, a topic on which Russell offered rather advanced opinions in the following letter. He obviously explained his views on eugenic social policy to Alys's sister, Mariechen, when they were together in Paris the following month, for she wrote to Berenson:

> Berty's idea is to have the state provide 'procreation tickets' of a certain colour, and to have heavy fines for those who dare to have children with those whose ticket doesn't correspond – thus eliminating disease. The congenial ones could marry all the same, even if their tickets weren't right, but must use checks. . . .
> They are both against marriage, in the present sense, altogether. Alys has a little penny pamphlet containing pictures and prices of half a dozen varieties of check, all safe and harmless, from one shilling to 2/6. . . . Shall I send thee

one? ... Among his friends, Alys says, these questions are hotly discussed. ...
At one of their Cambridge meetings, one of Bertie's friends read a paper
on the following subject, 'Is it wise to cohabit with a woman one loves
psychologically?' (B. Strachey and J. Samuels, *Mary Berenson*, p. 60)

Russell, like many others at the time, was much concerned about 'the future of the
race' – a problem brought forcibly to his mind by the medical opinion that he and
Alys were unfit to have children. His interest in it had been intensified by his recent
reading of Galton (who coined the term 'eugenics'). The opinion was widely held,
and Russell seems to have shared it, that reproductive rates were higher among the
lower classes than among the upper and that this would result in the survival of the
unfittest by sheer weight of numbers. The naïve transition from alleged sociological
data to Darwinist conclusions is unsupported, and it is strange, from a logical point
of view, that Russell didn't see this, since he had agreed with Pearson in rejecting
an equally naïve and unsupported transition from Darwinist data to sociological
conclusions in favour of *laissez-faire*.

[52]

British Embassy
Tuesday morning, 2 October 1894

My dearest Alys

Since it has such a good effect on thy headache and spirits, and makes thee
write such lovely letters, I think thee had better stay in bed the rest of the
time!

Today I shall begin counting days to come, not days past. I'm sure unless
anything unexpected turns up the time will fly now for me. I've got back
into something of the mood I had last Autumn, when my feelings were very
Platonic and I was very happy in the thought of thee without needing to be
constantly with thee. If I'd been sure of thee then it would have been quite
easy to be happy without seeing thee – it was getting out of the *habit* of
being together which was so painful this time – now that I have a full-
fledged set of new habits which leave no loop-hole for possibility of other
things, it is much more bearable to be separated.

It was this day last year, at Prayers at Pembroke Lodge, that I got thy
letter from Cardiff, beginning 'When I got your letter I realized that the
person I was afraid of *was* myself' and going on to say how thee liked to
hear me say I loved thee (at some length), and how I oughtn't to say it (very
briefly). Naturally then I felt I could easily overcome thy scruples, and felt
far less sure of our not drifting into love-making. I *never* thought the sort of

friendship thee proposed would *satisfy* me, but I thought thee was more strait-laced, and I knew that whatever restrictions thee imposed I could respect, for any length of time. But of course when I found the restrictions were irksome to thee as well as to me, I determined to have done with them. For a moment I saw how likely it was we should drift into love-making, and that and thy avowal of pleasure in my love (which is next door to love itself) made that Cardiff letter one of the pleasantest I ever had. – I know all the relevant part of it by heart, or nearly so. – But I shied at the vision of future love-making, because I wished it to come, but wished to *think* it wouldn't come – and I easily sophisticated myself into the belief that it wouldn't – but almost always from misjudging thee not me. I knew pretty well my feelings wouldn't long be Platonic, as thee might have gathered at Cambridge, but felt sure I could repress them as long as thee wished me to – as I did.

I am very glad thee is going to write on Socialism and the Woman Question.[1] I know nothing about it except Pearson's obvious argument: – In any race that survives, the vast majority of women must be mothers – women's disabilities come from helplessness during maternity – maternity is work for Society though not for any individual, i.e., no individual gets economic profit out of it – therefore Society ought to pay for child-bearing, and there is no other way of securing economic independence to the mass of women. This doesn't land one in downright Collectivism, which I don't think I do believe in, but in a lot of Socialistic legislation. Thee might observe incidentally that if the State paid for child-bearing it might and ought to require a medical certificate that the parents were such as to give a reasonable chance of a healthy child – this would afford a very good inducement to some sort of care for the race, and gradually as public opinion became educated by the law, it might react on the law and make that more stringent, until one got to some state of things in which there would be a little genuine care for the race, instead of the present haphazard higgledy-piggledy ways. I shall be very much interested to see thy draught and thy final paper – thee knows much more about it than I do, in fact most of my ideas on it I have got through thee, though I have no doubt given them a more statistical and biological turn than they have in thy mind.

I have not much headache today, and still feel rather godlike – my letter last night seems to me on reading it over less drunken than I thought it. I

1. Alys's paper was intended for her 'Development Society'. She intended to take her ideas from Pearson, Carpenter and *Darwinism and Politics* by the Hegelian Fabian, D. G. Ritchie. The paper was never written.

lay awake ever so long with a certain interval ringing in my ears which I finally discovered to be the minor fifth[1] – it dominated my whole idea of the opera and seemed to be always recurring. Now I must end this long letter. I shan't write again till tomorrow. Goodbye Dearest – don't be ill and keep in good spirits. I'm glad Mariechen cheers thee up.

Thine devotedly

Bertie

P.S. I'm *sure* thy father will forget to bring the letters from town.

Advanced theoretical views on marriage did not make it easier for either of them to discuss their own physical relationship. Whatever their views about birth control and eugenics, in their personal attitudes to sex they both conformed to what are now conventionally thought of as the Victorian stereotypes. Alys was nervous about the sex act itself and thought she would not enjoy it. She hoped that intercourse would be infrequent and would not take place immediately after they were married. Russell, by contrast, was eager to have the experience as soon as possible and thought he would like it rather frequently. He was anxious, however, that Alys should not be offended by his enthusiasm. Once they were married, however, the problem resolved itself. Although they found 'a certain amount of difficulty' in their first attempts at sexual intercourse, they found the difficulties 'merely comic' and they were soon overcome. In the event, it seems to have been Russell who found he didn't like sex too frequently, since he recalls a time three weeks after their marriage when, 'under the influence of sexual fatigue', he disliked Alys and wondered why he had married her. But this feeling, too, soon passed (*Autobiography*, vol. I, p. 124).

At all events, Russell's priggery as regards the *discussion* of birth control could hardly be outdone.

---

1. It is not clear what Russell means by this – the diminished fifth, the most natural suggestion, is not very prominent in *Die Walküre*. He may have misidentified the interval or had in mind some more complicated structure based on the fifth.

[53]

British Embassy
Thursday, 4 October 1894. 2 p.m.

My Beloved Alys

Thy two letters and thy journal[1] have given me great pleasure, and I'm glad thee was not too humble to have a *little* fling at my folly. Another time if I write like that thee'd better just ignore it.

I'm glad thee is coming round to the views I had in our discussion of July 23, because I think as we've had to alter our plans it is very important for our happiness that thee should feel a thoroughly good conscience,[2] and unless desire were mutual, there *could* be no satisfaction of it to me, and though it probably wouldn't die, I shouldn't be able to get the minutest pleasure out of anything which was not a pleasure to thee. In everything of that sort I feel thy feelings almost as if they were mine – physical contact seems to make our minds merge too, and I get a sort of thought-reading feeling, so that nothing not perfectly mutual *can* be anything but disgusting. I believe seriously that that is why physical contact is such a help to sympathy – like professional thought-readers, who hold one's hand or one's forehead, we feel each other's instinctive small movements and so on, and get to feel each other's feelings by their means.

I hardly like to discuss the question now, because I'm sorry to say my thoughts have had a tendency to impurity lately – for physiological reasons the more sensual pleasures are far easier to imagine, so that long absence makes them apt to come into the mind – but it will be all right as soon as we're together again, and the state of transient feelings like that doesn't affect my opinions – I don't venture to form opinions on such subjects except at the times when I know I am quite free from all sensual desire. But I'm sure thy former views came from the notion that there was never any desire on the woman's part, which is utterly untrue; I have never been able to see any harm in moderate intercourse, where it is perfectly mutual and *quite* subordinate (which in people so un-sensual as ourselves it will be very easy to make it – even if we ever found ourselves drifting it would be very easy to pull up, and we should be all the more secure from the experience and knowledge of danger, as we have already found in minor things).

1. Alys had sent Russell the book in which she kept her journal as he had requested in his letter of 28 September. They both made entries in it. See *Papers*, vol. I, pp. 41–2.
2. Alys had at one time thought that sexual intercourse apart from procreation was immoral.

I don't like thy little book on 'True Morality'[1] – it is coarse and crude – his 'of course' in enunciating the Greatest-Happiness principle shocks my mind trained in ethical controversy – but setting squeamishness aside I've no doubt it is a book which might be useful to uneducated people. It is lovely the way he quotes among his authorities for Neo-Malthusianism,[2] The Lord God – unfortunately quotations from that individual can never be verified in the original but only in some one else's quotation – a method which accurate scholars do not approve!

But I have an instinctive dislike of the whole subject of Neo-Malthusianism. I've no objection to the practice, but the discussion of it fixes the attention so *very* much on the actual process that it is very hard not to grow coarse in thinking about it.

However, on the whole, when I compare my feelings now with those in June or July, I see that I'm much happier in my conscience, and really glad we're not going to have children (except when I think what a heavenly mother thee'd make) – it will leave thee to me so much more. I was always jealous of the children in anticipation, though that was a selfish feeling – but I used to see in advance how thee'd feel a duty to be always with them, but never a duty to be with me, because thee'd fancy I could look after myself (I can't a bit). That was in the old days though, when thee used to talk of getting bored. Besides it will be a great relief not to have the anxiety involved in thy having children – knowing of the death of thy namesake, Uncle Rollo's 1st wife, I have got it on the brain, and the anxiety, lasting so long, would have almost worn me out.

Does thee remember the wood at Versailles? I dreamed the other day that we were married and at Pembroke Lodge, and thee had a child, almost painlessly – and my Grandmother was vexed at the way thee got off lightly in all life's troubles – she thinks it shows a shallow nature not to suffer as much as possible. I heard her telling Sinclair, her maid, and Sinclair protesting against such an unkind feeling. All my Grandmother said was: First a sigh, then '*She* always gets off easily in all the troubles of life – (another sigh) *some* fortunate people are made that way' – and I said to myself that I always knew thee was a splendid animal, and I was proud of thy being so efficient. I'm afraid this view may shock thee – but I always worship physical health and strength. I suppose because I have seen so much of the bad effects of its opposite in my family.

1. Perhaps the 'penny pamphlet' on checks that Mariechen had referred to in her letter to Berenson. If so, Russell had evidently disowned it.
2. i.e. birth control.

I'm very glad my people have converted thee to Social Utility instead of Personal Holiness.[1] I'm sure the change is practically important, though in theory one reconciles the two. But when one sees the Personal Holiness theory logically worked out and applied, as with them, one cannot help seeing how unlivable it is, and how it drives them into asylums or epileptic fits.

I enjoyed part of my dinner[2] last night very much, because there was a singer, a Miss Butt,[3] who seemed to think herself very famous, and had a perfectly divine voice. – I sat between her and my vulgar hostess at dinner, and quite fell in love with her. – She was over 6 foot, very tall and dark – a regular tragedy queen, a magnificent woman – also a person of much penetration in the way of character, though her own was of the simple artistic kind, that does what it feels like doing. Her voice would have done better in an Opera House – it was too massive for a drawing room – but it was glorious and made me hate all the vulgar Americans who heard it.

There were Miss Jay Gould[4] and her brother – everybody of course tried to ingratiate himself with her, but I found her deadly dull, as well as frightfully plain – my hostess said to me at dinner, to my *intense* annoyance: You're not engaged are you? I weighed for an instant the consequences of a lie – the certainty that it would be discovered, the consequent endurance not only of the disgrace of a lie, but of the supposition that I was ashamed of my engagement, which my dear relations would be sure to spread about – and I settled these consequences were too serious to be incurred merely to spare a squeamish taste, so I said 'I am'. She replied she had thought there must be something up, because I was the only one who didn't seem to care to please Miss Gould – vulgar woman – she asked me thy name, which I told her, as well as thy nationality, she being American. For a moment she thought I was making fun of her, and I've regretted ever since that I didn't give simply Smith as thy name, as that would have persuaded her I was making up the whole thing, and have spared me her saying later 'Come and let me introduce you to Miss Grant, she's a sister of the Countess of Essex, and when I tell you that you'll know she's an American girl, just like *your*

1. By reaction to their practice!
2. It had been arranged by Dodson, a colleague at the embassy, and 'an awful American woman' to whom Russell had been introduced at the Opera.
3. Clara Butt (1872–1936). She was very famous, or at least became so. She had made her first concert and stage appearances in 1892.
4. The daughter of the American financier and railway magnate, Jay Gould (1836–92).

girl' – vile woman! Her dresses are so low she looks like Potiphar's wife[1] in the pictures.

Then there was a vile little parson (English) with a retreating forehead who talked in a squeaky little voice which suggested machinery; and there was an English schoolboy, and a collection of vulgar Americans. The dinner was very swell, and I was flabbergasted by what seemed to me to be ices right in the middle – but Dodson tells me they were not ices, though they were iced, and that that is the very swellest thing. I hope this description is vivid. I have taken no pains with it, but on reading it over it strikes me as good, from a literary point of view, for an amateur, except Miss Butt, whose character I have only told, not shown by quotations – There's conceit! Tell me what thee thinks of it.

I am *so* glad to have the Journal, but I think I shall send it back soon, as I shouldn't write anything in it. When I've written to thee there's nothing left to write. But it is lovely to have the heavenly times we've had together in the Book – they all come so vividly before me as I read. I only wish I'd gone on keeping the Journal till I gave it to thee – some chronicle of this time last year would have been very nice. But it is sad to see how many entries there are since Aug. 17 of thy having cried thyself to sleep, looked at my photo and felt sad and depressed and wept, and so on.

Thee is too sympathetic – for when my letters are not depressed thee is happy, comparatively – which is an additional reason for my keeping up my spirits. I believe 3/4 of thy love is due to my dependence on thee and not to any more valuable quality! I really *am* utterly dependent – whether I'm sad or happy, everything has reference only to thee – when I think of the time when we're married and can be always together and the world cannot any longer come between us, I grow dizzy with the heavenliness of the thought, and I feel a thrill all over as at splendid music. I feel as if the joy would almost kill me. We've been happy together before, but it will be quite a new joy, far better than it ever has been, when we can feel that we *do* belong inseparably to each other, that there is no more danger of separation or worry. – It will be such a relief that I believe I shall weep as we start on our wedding-journey. Every now and then I'm seized with tremendous longing to be able to stroke thy hair, or put my hands on thy shoulders and read thy

1. Potiphar's wife attempted to seduce Joseph, who fled from her advances unwisely leaving his coat behind – thereby supplying her with evidence for her claim that he had attempted to seduce her, on which charge his master, Potiphar, had him thrown into prison (Genesis 39). It's not clear which pictures Russell had in mind, but they can well be imagined.

eyes, or put my arm round thy neck – it is terrible when I feel the wish, it is so powerful – I daren't think much of such things.

I think most of last year about this time – it will be a year tomorrow since the day which I always regard as the really decisive one – it was that day that made it a really serious thing, and after that I would no longer have told my Grandmother it was *quite* as likely as not never to come to marriage. And that was the day thee wrote me the letter which of all the lot has given me most pleasure – thee told me thee would have done what thee thought wrong because thy 'feelings would have made' thee; – that was delightful – and then thee was thankful, and so was I – God knows how thankful – that 'it was not that' – and thee ended 'Goodbye dear Bertie – I must say it once, for I believe in Him – God bless thee'. I haven't got the letter out, but I know it by heart. And I felt so mad to think thee was going to America, and would be busy with prosaic things, and reflect where thee was drifting to, and perhaps return well primed with fortitude against all wiles! But fortunately the 6-months' question came up – but for that we might long have remained mere friends – on thy side!

I *was* happy in those days – there was a simplicity and single-mindedness about my happiness which is lost now, though I *am* so much happier really – but I suppose I shall never *really* quite get over June and my people's preachings, and besides now I'm always a little afraid of impurity in my thoughts – that will settle itself when we're married, but in the meantime I'm anxious every now and then, though not seriously. If I made thee unhappy, it would only be through me, for at the most I could *never* find pleasure in what was distasteful to thee – such a thing is inconceivable – only I might be unhappy at its *being* distasteful to thee – but I'm really *quite* sure of myself, and fears are only morbid really.

This is an absurdly long letter. I am too glad to work, because I was up late and early with the Embassy work, so there is no reason why I should stop, except that finally it grows absurd to go on. I am much interested about Logan and Miss Sellars.[1]

Goodbye my Life. Do write Saturday afternoon or I'm left 36 hours without a letter. Thine most devotedly

Bertie

---

1. There was apparently an abortive courtship between Logan and a Miss Sellars. According to Alys, it consisted, on Logan's part, of his putting on his best clothes, picking some flowers and wandering aimlessly about waiting.

Nervousness was not the only reason Alys wished to postpone sexual intercourse for some time after they married. She felt that it was imprudent to rely solely on contraceptives and that, to be safe, they should only have intercourse two weeks after her period – a dangerous error. By her calculations, this meant that they should wait for two or three weeks after they were married, that is, until the first week of January. This was not a delay which Russell could accept with equanimity. Sex immediately after marriage was, he thought, necessary to keep his mind from impure thoughts.

[54]

British Embassy
Friday, 26 October 1894. 10 p.m.

My Darling Alys

When I said I wouldn't write tonight I had forgotten it was Friday, or I wouldn't have said so. Thy letter tonight is lovely and I'm *very* much relieved that my letter didn't worry thee at all. What I feel now is that until we have had one experience of coition the thought will be fearfully exciting to me if we sleep together – I feel as if it would keep me from sleeping and keep my mind far more on that one subject than it should be – chiefly out of desire for the knowledge of the ultimate experience. When we are together my thoughts turn less to physical things than when we are separated, and it may be it will be better then; but during these last months I have felt as if the excitement would be too much for me almost, until it had happened once. After that, I feel sure restraint would be easy. I agree that we ought in general to choose the times when conception is least likely, but I imagine checks are pretty safe now, from what Dr Philpot said, and in one departure there would not be an appreciable risk. The fact is that all this loneliness and depression has a good deal lessened my self-control for the moment, but when we are married and away it will soon come back.

As to frequency, I am sure it ought not to be great, but beyond that it is entirely a question for our joint experience to decide, and on which I don't think we can decide now. I too try to distract myself, by repeating poetry and in other ways, from exciting physical thoughts, but I seldom succeed. – I feel as if after this long time in which every moment almost is a concentrated effort of self-control (except when I'm writing to thee or reading thy letters) I should want for once to have a little holiday from it, and if only for 24 hours break loose from it and just live. But if thee feels it would be disagreeable to thee until we have been some weeks married, of course it will be *so* heavenly to be together that it will really be easy to wait – much easier probably than it seems now.

I have had a lovely time with my two visits to real human beings,[1] but now I am home again I feel as if perhaps it were almost a mistake to intersperse any pleasures – I shall never get to bed tonight, as I'm fearfully excited. I will write all about my visits tomorrow; I have just come back and found thy letter and like thee I can't write about irrelevant things. I *have* got impure things for the moment rather on the brain, as I know for a certainty from dreams – I remember telling thee once that happiness and a full active life were necessary to me in that respect – in old days when I was unhappy I was perpetually haunted by impure imaginings, like the early Christian hermits I put in my paper last February.[2] I feel sure it will be well when we're together, but for the moment all troublesome thoughts are too strong for me – my will is wasted in carrying on my daily life, and there is none left for other needs. – As a matter of fact I've been very happy all day and this is mere reaction. – I can hardly ever recall the mood of our last days now – the thought of thy breasts produces only an intense sexual excitement, and none of the divine calm of that time – of course calm is impossible when we're apart, but those divine feelings will come back when we're together again.

I remember when my feelings first began to be no longer Platonic, the thought of kissing used to torment me when I was away, and then when we met I forgot all about it, because the emotion took its place.

I don't believe we shall find coition such an absolutely different thing from previous physical things, and I believe experience in the one can more or less be extended to the other – but I dare say not. Except for that one little point, I agree with thee *entirely* – and even on *that* point I shall agree if thee continues to feel as thee does, for all depends on how thee feels.

I grow the more impatient that I still *know* how I felt those last days, but I cannot feel it any longer – it is like Shelley's 'divine Feelings that died in youth's brief morn',[3] and till we meet they are a closed book to me – worse luck! All calm and peaceful feelings are grown unintelligible to me now, as they were before I knew thee – joy again to my imagination is wild and passionate excitement – but all will be well in 3 weeks, from tomorrow morning. Till then there is nothing for it but grim endurance.

1. He had been to see Clara Butt and two American friends, Edith and Bryson Burroughs. In his letter next day, he asked Alys to try to find out if Butt was 'as famous as she says'. 'Perhaps she sings under a pseudonym,' he added.
2. 'Lövberg or Hedda', *Papers*, vol. I, p. 85.
3. 'The Magnetic Lady', III, 1. 7.

I have more than ever perfect confidence that all will be well, in spite of my present thoughts – thee is so splendid about it. I never hoped for such a wonderful development. I too, for thy sake, I am sure, can do *anything*.

Goodnight My Beloved My Life and Joy and Strength. I am nothing without thee and I feel the need of thee every hour and every minute. All I hope for and all I ought to be depends on thee.

Thine thine thine
    Bertie

Russell had been planning for some time to take a weekend away from the embassy in order to return to Cambridge. One purpose of the Cambridge visit was to discuss his plan to do two Fellowship dissertations; another was to read his paper 'Cleopatra or Maggie Tulliver' (*Papers*, vol. I, pp. 92–8) to the Apostles. He arranged to leave for England on Friday, 2 November, and return to the embassy the following Monday. In keeping the terms of their separation, he was not allowed to see Alys during the visit.

Meanwhile, Alys informed him of another development. Her sister, Mary, was planning to visit Paris in order to catalogue pictures in the Louvre while Berenson was away in America. Alys was entirely in favour of her visiting Russell while she was there, hoping that it would cheer him up. But she expressed a fear that Mary might compromise herself if they saw too much of each other. Since Mary's relationship with Berenson was no secret, Russell thought this improbable. Mariechen was hoping to stay near the embassy, and Alys thought it a pity she couldn't stay with Bertie. In the event, she stayed in the same hotel and they shared a sitting-room. Russell dined with Mariechen on the Sunday, as he suggested in the next letter, and they travelled to Paris together.

[55]

Paris
Sunday, 28 October 1894. 3 p.m.

My Beloved Alys,

Thy letters on Friday were *not* horrid, quite the reverse – and if they had been, I should have known it was only because you were ill. (Odd I should have written *you*: it was because I was thinking of the awful Friday, when Marsh came round to inquire about thy pretended illness, and I was imagining his words.) But certainly thy letter this morning was nicer – it *is* good news about Mariechen – it has made me quite happy all day. Now that the worst time is over, I have grown ashamed of having so foolishly given way to depression – it occurs to me that anyone with a really strong will would not have done so. But it is a blessing that 'things at the worst are ready to amend'[1] – my loneliness is so much amended that I can feel quite happy. My visit to Edith and Bryson had a wonderful effect – I was beginning to despair of goodness and feel the whole world sordid and vile, and myself along with it. The inspiration even enabled me to get on with my paper on Space, and write several fairly good pages, embodying an entirely original and very bold idea,[2] which I got during the month at Friday's Hill one day when thee was in town. It is *so* bold that it almost terrifies me. I shall be interested to see what they think of it at Cambridge.

This afternoon my thoughts are oppressed by my letters to my Grandmother and Aunt – I have sent thee the drafts.[3] My courage all but failed me at the last moment, but I put it through and have now sent off the letters. My aunt at least will see them. The one to her is stronger than it would have been but for my Grandmother's illness, because I think that will keep her from worrying my Grandmother too much about it. They will never give the promise I ask, so we will either go together and not leave each other alone, or else not go at all. It is terrible how it still excites me to write such letters – my hand shakes and my heart beats wildly and my knees tremble – it is really absurd, and I can't make out why the excitement should be so intense.

I have not written to the Davies's yet and I don't know if they're in town. Couldn't I dine with Mariechen, unless thee's going to be at 44 and she's going to dine there. Graham[4] comes back on Nov. 1 so from that evening onwards my address will be Hotel Vouillemont, Rue Boissy d'Anglas, which is close to the Embassy. I don't think Mariechen need be afraid of 'compromising' herself – under the circumstances that would be difficult. I remember before Margo's engagement was announced her sister Lady Ribblesdale came down to Richmond one Sunday with Asquith, and the only remark made by a lot of Londoners who were there was that that

---

1. Longfellow: 'Things have been mended that were worse, / And the worse, the nearer they are to mend' (*Tales of a Wayside Inn*, 'The Baron of St Castline', ll. 264–5).
2. This was the paper on 'Geometrical Axioms' which Sanger read to the Moral Sciences Club in Russell's absence. It, and the very bold idea, are lost.
3. Bertie and Alys had been summoned to an audience at Pembroke Lodge at the end of their separation. Alys had refused to go alone and Bertie had written demanding that they promise not to be unpleasant to her if she did.
4. R. W. Graham, an attaché at the embassy. Russell had occupied his lodgings while he had been away. Russell was not allowed to take his weekend in Cambridge until Graham had returned to the embassy.

proved Asquith and Margo really were engaged.[1] But I'm glad I shall be in a Hotel; that will leave me more independence. I shall have a sitting-room, where I can give Mariechen tea. I see nothing of the Embassy people now except during the work and at déjeuner: not even at déjeuner if there is any reason for me to go elsewhere. I lunched again yesterday with Col. and Mrs Talbot[2] – she's pleasant, and a friend of my Aunt Agatha as I told thee before. I *think* she liked me though I'm not sure.

It is lovely to think I shall have no more solitude after Friday. I will write and ask Edith and Bryson to dine with me at a Café on Wednesday or Thursday. Where shall I take them and what does thee suppose they could be induced to eat? Even Foyot's would I fear be too smart for Edith.

I remember well thy request at Reigate[3] – I was rather shocked by it, because it seemed to me just as unfair as the present law. If we *had* had children I believe I should have been just as fond of them as thee, after they ceased to be babies, and almost better able to enter into their feelings. There's conceit! But they would have been an awful trial, for they'd have been sure not to be satisfactory

It is lovely to have thee say I satisfy all thy needs now – I only hope there will never come a time when thee will feel the need of children. I can scarcely dare to hope thee will always find me enough to satisfy thy need of loving. But I am sure I shall never cease to cling to thee and depend upon thee for all my happiness.

I can't get on with this letter for thinking the same old thoughts about thee – how absolutely I love thee and am absorbed in thee and how thee is all my Life and Strength. No other thoughts will come as I have nothing more to write. I am glad thee liked the bit from 'Epipsychidion':[4] it *is* a perfect expression of the inexpressible isn't it? Fare thee well my best-Beloved my dearest Joy.

  Thine absolutely and eternally,
   Bertie

1. 'Margo' was Margot Tennant, the sixth daughter of Sir Charles Tennant, a Scottish industrialist. She married Herbert Asquith, then Home Secretary later to be Prime Minister, in 1894. Her sister, Charlotte, had married the fourth Baron Ribblesdale, Lord John Russell's stepson, in 1877.
2. Col. Reginald Talbot, the Military Attaché at the embassy.
3. At the time when they still expected to have children, Alys had asked Russell to sign an agreement waiving legal rights in their offspring.
4. Russell had quoted lines 560–72 in his letter of 25 October. The passage begins: 'And we will talk, until thought's melody / Become too sweet for utterance'.

With his trip to Cambridge getting close, Russell was in a more cheerful mood and was able to work with some enthusiasm on geometry.

[56]

Paris
Monday, 29 October 1894. 9 p.m.

My Beloved

Thy letter is *too* heavenly – thee has indeed written 'something to help and calm' me. It is *divine* to have thee call me thy great inspiration – nothing thee *could* call me would give me such exquisite joy. May I be not too unworthy of the name! It brings back pure feelings to think how thee trusts me. I have really felt much calmer in the physical way ever since I wrote, partly from having expressed myself and partly from seeing Edith and Bryson – the things I see have a terrible effect on my imagination, for good or ill. I am sure the heavenly calm of our last days will come back soon, but just at first there will be a wild unbearable joy which must seize on any and every expression possible. After being a long time unhappy, the revulsion makes *calm* joy at first impossible.

Thee needn't worry about my impatience – Mariechen will be a good outlet for it, and will make it much less and much more endurable than if I had to keep it bottled up. – I believe I shall be like Mariechen's account of women, to some extent; I don't believe the purely *physical* pleasure of copulation could last long with me, though I can imagine the psychological enjoyment doing so. It seems to me sometimes as if I had *no* physical pleasures to speak of – even my tea and tobacco I care about only for their mental effects, and I have observed lately that the *taste* of both is rather *un*pleasant to me than otherwise – I remember the dentist giving me sal volatile, and I liked it just as well as tea, because it had the same effects. And so with other things that seem physical – it is not really the actual sensation as a rule that I care about. So I feel sure of myself as soon as it has grown normal and natural for us to be together. But I'm *very* glad thee can sympathize with my feeling of wanting just simply to *live*, without restraint, if only for a day – it comes of repression, but it is not so bad now as last October, when I felt it more strongly, and thee was shocked at it. I shall never again feel so wildly anxious just to *live* as then, when this pent-up impatience of years was gradually expressing itself and getting satisfied. But I *am* relieved that thee is not shocked now, and I haven't the *slightest* anxiety now about the future. I *am* thankful, more than I can say, that thee is so sympathetic. – I am honestly and *entirely* glad that thee is feeling so calm and happy, which is a pretty good proof that I am more or less so too. Dearest, it will be divine to be together again and see those eyes and kiss those lips that I love so well.

I shudder to think of thy 5 hours' wait at Southampton, but thee ought to produce a magnificent abstract in that time![1] Thee must send it to me as soon as possible. I have a savage desire to pull it to pieces, and I shall be quite cross if it's not full of fallacies. But I expect it will be very good, and certainly *much* better than anything I could have done on the subject.

I am psychologically gratified and amused at thy picking out the two practical points in my paper[2] for praise: to me its value lay in the theoretical emphasizing of desire and analysis of virtue, and in the statement of the difficulty about transcending the Self in Ethics. I think they won't like it at Cambridge – they'll think it too moral and edifying.

I have finished my paper on Space, to my great relief: it seems to me much too hard to be understood when read aloud, and the crux of the argument, the psychological part, has been treated much too sketchily, for want of the necessary knowledge: but there seems to me to be a good deal of good reasoning and solid thinking in it. When I'd finished it, I gave a sigh of relief, smoked a pipe, and felt like God on the 7th day, when he 'saw that it was good'. Excuse the blasphemy! I can well understand his blessing the 7th day and hallowing it. I am thinking of showing the paper to Ward, because it differs so much from most of the books that I'm alarmed, and feel as if I must be on the wrong tack. But my interest in the subject (which dates from 10 years back, when I began Euclid with my brother)[3] has revived, and I feel impelled to set the matter at rest in my own mind. I will take Ward's suggestion of writing 2 dissertations, at any rate at my 2nd shot[4] – I shall be able to do much more work than on only one, because my mind won't go

1. Alys had been to Southampton to meet Evelyn Nordhoff, an old college friend of Mary's. The boat had been delayed by storms. Alys and Russell had taken to exchanging abstracts of the books they were reading. Russell had sent Alys an abstract of Sigwart's *Logik*, and was now abstracting Adolph Wagner's *Grundlegung der politischen Oekonomie* (in two volumes, 1892–4) and part of Mill's *Principles of Political Economy*. Alys was abstracting the Webbs' history of trade unionism.
2. 'Cleopatra or Maggie Tulliver', *Papers*, vol. I, pp. 92–8. Russell read the paper to the Apostles on 3 November.
3. Russell had received his first lessons in Euclid from his brother at the age of eleven. It was, he said, 'one of the great events of my life, as dazzling as first love'. Bertie's delight was, however, marred by the fact that the axioms couldn't be proved. (See *Autobiography*, vol. I, p. 36.)
4. Fellowships were rarely awarded on the first attempt. Russell evidently expected to have to submit his dissertation(s) twice, although, in the event, he gained the Fellowship with only one dissertation on the first attempt.

at more than a certain rate on any particular subject; though I was greatly flattered by what Ward said about my working fast, which is odd, as I'm an extraordinarily slow reader, and take ages to follow a new train of reasoning. I have also finished the part of Mill I meant to read,[1] so till I go to Cambridge I shall go on with Wagner – after that, Mariechen will I hope afford a pleasant occupation for my spare time.

I will write again tomorrow morning. Fare thee well my beloved. 18 days more to our happiness. It *will* be happiness!

Thine heart and soul

> *Bertie*

It had by now been decided that Evelyn Nordhoff, the friend newly arrived from America, should be present when Bertie had dinner with Mariechen in London. Alys had asked Mary to give Bertie a kiss from her.

[57]

Paris
Tuesday, 30 October 1894. 10 p.m.

My Darling,

Thy letter has only just come – half an hour ago the Concierge assured me there was no hope of it now, and I had retired upstairs disconsolate to read over old letters as the best substitute. But as I was thus engaged, he came rushing up with thy letter. I believe, good people, that they have guessed what source so many letters in the same hand must come from, and being French they are sympathetic.

I don't quite know *why* I care so much what other people think – it's an instinct, which I suppose goes with a vivid imagining of their thoughts – but I can't *bear* the thought of people I have to meet every day desecrating our relation and tearing it to shreds behind my back. Despising people is no good with me – or rather hating them isn't. It is an absolutely insurmountable instinct with me to wish the people I habitually associate with to think well of me and of what I think well of – I spent years thinking it both foolish and immoral and trying to cure it, but quite in vain. They won't be surprised

---

1. *Principles of Political Economy*, bk III.

at my not having spoken of it[1] – most men don't speak to each other of such things and my telling Lord Dufferin was sufficient proof to the contrary. I don't care what people think whom I don't have to associate with, but I haven't the power of putting myself on a pinnacle and condemning my associates as fools – in feeling that is: intellectually, that is my habitual attitude.

I don't agree at all about children[2] – thy argument is the same in principle as my Grandmother's – she has suffered so much for me that I ought to suffer for her and she ought to have rights over me – suffering gives no rights, and that is what makes it so intolerable. But luckily the point doesn't have to be argued – it *is* a mercy we're not to have children, we shouldn't have agreed about a single point as regards their education – and I should have been *very* stubborn, and so would thee probably, because in that line thee'd have no respect for my judgment.

How strange thee should write about Mariechen giving me a kiss from thee – I had thought about it as a thing which was impossible, but would be *delightful* if it *could* happen, and I shall not think it an indecent exhibition of emotion to a *sister* – how should I? The thought of it is strangely pleasant.

I don't understand a bit why writing to my people should be so fearfully disturbing – it belongs to that same instinct of *longing* to live at peace with everybody – every year it becomes more intolerable to me to have strained or unsympathetic relations with anyone. And partly it is the *horror* of my Grandmother's pain, which is extraordinarily great in me.

I must protest against thy saying I should have loved our children only because they were thine – there'd have been 1,000 other reasons – because they were mine, and children, and helpless, and because they'd probably have been *nice* children, and fond of both of us – but *very* largely from mere parental instinct.

I am very glad Mariechen will dine with me Sunday – the train leaves 8.30 p.m. from Victoria and if she wouldn't mind it would suit me best to dine at the station probably – but I don't know the trains up from Cambridge yet. I shan't mind Evelyn Nordhoff for so short a time especially as thy account of her has made me anxious to see her. It will make me very shy to

1. 'They' were the people at the embassy; 'it' was Russell's engagement. Russell was only now summoning up the courage to tell them about it, although he had told Lord Dufferin when he accepted the position as his ground for desiring only a short appointment. Alys had called him a goose for not telling them when he arrived.
2. Alys had continued to argue that, since only mothers suffered childbirth, the children should be theirs 'absolutely'.

kiss Mariechen but I shall try and imagine it is thee for the moment – though that will be rather difficult.

I am glad thee agrees about developing my manner – I'm certainly right.[1] Sensitiveness has grown almost to mania with me since I have been here, and has been the source of half my miseries. Knowing now what ideal sympathy is, anything less is rasping and painful and almost unendurable, so that absolute solitude becomes almost my ideal of bliss. I am almost sure now that if we had separated in June this tendency would have developed till my mind was nearly or quite unhinged – which is a very cheering thought.

I am charmed at the children's description of me[2] – they could hardly pay me a greater compliment, the more so as it is sincere. Children have a tremendous effect in putting me in good spirits, because it is so easy to give them pleasure, and there is honestly no greater joy to me than to feel that *I* am giving people pleasure – an egotistic, though not a selfish feeling.

I am oddly excited – somehow the queer thought of transmitting a kiss by Mariechen requires analysis, it is so complex and confused. I shall certainly never look depressed when we're married, except sometimes the days I hear from my people. As long as my Grandmother lives, her pain will give me a certain amount of sympathetic pain – when she's dead, all will be well, thanks to this separation – otherwise I should have felt like a murderer.

I shall post this tonight, to Grosvenor Rd, and I want thee to tell me if it comes tomorrow night or not. My former letters never did, but that may have been because I didn't post them at a Bureau.

The days still pass, thanks to thy letters – this time 3 days hence I shall be on my way to dear England. I've grown passionately patriotic – the sound of the French in the streets makes me shudder, and I *hate* Frenchmen with the sort of hatred Hedda had for Tesman[3] – all their ways annoy me, and their mere presence is acute pain. I am full of mad and foolish impulses due to repression – but in 3 more days I shall begin to have an outlet, and it will grow better as the time of our meeting draws near which will prevent my going quite mad. If the time had been 6 months I dare say I *should* have done something foolish during some part of it.

1. Alys had hoped that Bertie's stay in Paris might improve his shy and reserved manner. Russell had said that it had had quite the contrary effect.
2. These were Mary's children, Ray and Karin Costelloe, respectively seven and five years old. They continued to live with their father at 40 Grosvenor Road, though their grandmother took a great interest in their upbringing. Mary used to return from Italy each summer to be with them. They had said that Russell was always smiling or laughing.
3. In Ibsen's play, *Hedda Gabler*.

I have been pretty cheerful all day, and am never really unhappy now. This is a silly letter – I'm a bundle of nerves now-a-days, but it's late and thee mustn't imagine this to be my usual mood. Fare thee well my dearest Life. 17 days more – will they ever pass?

Thine eternally and entirely and absolutely

Bertie

Russell's visit to Cambridge was a decided success. His paper on the passions, the best he had so far read to the Apostles, got a good reception. On Sunday he had discussed his work on geometry with Amos and Sanger, who were encouraging about his 'new and very bold idea'. His friends seemed more delightful even than he had remembered them. On the train, as he left Cambridge on Sunday afternoon to have dinner in London with Mariechen, he wrote Alys an account of the weekend in a very cheerful and optimistic mood (see *Autobiography*, vol. I, pp. 107–8).

His buoyant mood survived his arrival in Paris, where life was made much more agreeable by Mariechen's company and by the thought that his separation from Alys now had only two more weeks to run. Alys, however, was by no means so happy: she was more anxious than Russell about the consummation of their marriage and was now facing the appalling prospect of a solo visit to Pembroke Lodge. More important, she had felt particularly excluded by the fact that she had not been able to see Bertie on his visit while so many of her friends and relatives had.

Russell's letters after his return to Paris were relentlessly upbeat. With an exuberance and conviviality he had rarely exhibited before, he detailed his conversations and outings with Mariechen and the pleasure he took in her company. Alys became miserably jealous, though Russell didn't realize it for some time. Alys, in fact, tried to hide it and Russell, his conscience clear (for it was Alys, after all, who had thrust Mariechen upon him), failed to read signs of her distress between the lines of her letters. Certainly, in his own letters – for example, in the condescending tone of the next letter – he was less sensitive to her feelings than previously.

Tensions between Alys and her sister went deep and pre-dated Russell's friendship with Mariechen. Alys no doubt already felt she was the slighted younger sister, for she came from a family in which the eldest daughter was habitually (and more or less overtly) favoured over her siblings. Moreover, Alys deeply disapproved of Mary's leaving her husband and children for Berenson and of her uninhibited behaviour since. These animosities were mostly concealed by Alys's habitual efforts not to think ill (and especially not to speak ill) of people and, no doubt, by genuine sisterly affection as well, but they could not entirely be denied.

Russell, who shared Alys's moral criticisms of Mariechen, seems at first to have been puzzled that he found her so agreeable. This led him to wonder whether Alys had been fair to her. A more serious point of friction between Bertie and Alys, however, arose from Mariechen's intellectual criticisms of Alys. Alys was generally inclined to belittle her own intelligence. Just before Russell's trip to Cambridge, Mariechen had complained to Alys that her modesty in this respect was a cover for laziness; that she was much more capable intellectually than she gave herself credit for, but that she used lack of intelligence as an excuse for not thinking for herself. Alys reported all this to Bertie, who, she said, had already made similar criticisms. She thought the criticisms quite just and vowed to change. Such sisterly criticism delivered at Friday's Hill was one thing. It was another when Mariechen turned up in Paris and repeated the criticism to Bertie. And it was still another when she encouraged him to think of his forthcoming marriage as an opportunity for intellectual cooperation with Alys much like her own collaboration with Berenson. This was a hope to which Russell, if he had ever had it, had hitherto not dared to give utterance. But now Mariechen, who surely knew Alys as well as anyone, made it seem tantalizingly possible, if only Alys could be persuaded to think more highly of her own intelligence. Russell could hardly fail to be attracted by the idea of working together with Alys on philosophy and social theory – he handling theoretical matters and she historical and factual ones.

Alys also had hopes of a marriage centred around joint work, but her model was the Webbs (by whom she was at this time much influenced). The work she envisaged was practical and political rather than theoretical – at least as much a life of committees, elections, pamphleteering, and behind-the-scenes persuasion as of writing and research. The Webbs, however, were not a role model that appealed very much to Russell. He had little interest in such work and recognized that his own best talents lay in a different direction. In this, his resolve had been strengthened by the unequivocal advice of his Cambridge friends to concentrate on the theoretical work at which he was best. Alys, for her part, recognized that, in the sort of collaboration Mary proposed and Bertie was now advocating, she would end up as little more than Bertie's research assistant. But the most hurtful thing for Alys about Bertie's friendship with Mariechen and the plans they were confabulating together in Paris was that they evoked a bitter sense of her own inadequacy. Perhaps, she thought, Bertie needed a more vivacious and intelligent wife. She wrote poignantly in her diary just after receiving the next letter: 'I am so afraid I shall not be able to make B. happy, I am so dull' (B. Strachey, *Remarkable Relations*, p. 142). In the end, it was this that led her to send Russell a sharp rebuke and an indictment of Mary. For the time being, however, she held her peace.

[58]

[British Embassy] Paris
Monday, 5 November 1894. 12.15 p.m

My dearest Alys

I'm dropping from sleep but I ought not to go quite off in the Chancery here so I'll begin a letter to thee. I slept very little on the journey, half an hour at most, but have had about an hour's sleep since. Mariechen continues to be charming – we are established in rooms pretty near each other and are going to use my sitting-room as common property – we began by break-fasting there this morning and hanging up Mariechen's genuine old master in place of a vile thing which was native there. She seems anxious to be 'stimulated', and as I love to stimulate it works very well. She continually says *lovely* things about us which make her very pleasant to be with. She is rejoicing at her escape from family life, and from an atmosphere where she is disapproved of – they are feelings I can sympathize with though I shouldn't have thought your family would give them strongly. She *said* there was only one person she cared for enough to tell lies to save her pain and that was thy mother. She feels I suppose that she has a right to conduct her life her own way and I can well imagine so easy-going a person seeing very little harm in such proceedings. However I am biased by her being so agreeable and such a perfect companion for my present mood – I've no doubt really that all thee says is just, only I don't *feel* it, and I'm sure it's a good plan to behave as if one approved even if one doesn't. Thee must tell me some time, when its disagreeableness is less recent, all about the negotiations which have led to that result about her and the children and the wedding.[1]

She has produced her Nietzsche and I have produced my Germans too, and I foresee we shall have a battle royal on the Psychologist's Fallacy.[2] She has been repeating what she said to thee about thy modesty and laziness, with assurances that thee is really quite capable intellectually if thee chose. Of course one doesn't imagine thee would do any brilliant original thinking, but thee might form part of the indispensable intelligent audience, which involves a lot of exertion and severe thinking, in order to get good taste in thoughts. And then thee will be able to criticize my thoughts, instead of laughing at the good ones and admiring those that are really commonplace.

1. Frank Costelloe was refusing to allow the children to be seen in public with Mary. This entailed, in particular, that either Mary or the children, but not both, could attend Bertie and Alys's wedding.
2. The fallacy of reading into a mind (or life) being studied what is true of one's own.

This is a very conceited remark: it is due to Mariechen's flattery. I will finish later.

Later – I have had no more time so this must go to the post. Fare thee well Dearest. I hope thee is in better spirits now that I'm well away again. 11 more days doesn't seem so fearfully long now – and it *will* be *divine* when it is over!

 Thine eternally and devotedly

  Bertie

Mariechen was not the only relative of Alys's in Paris. One of her cousins, Helen Thomas, Carey Thomas's youngest sister, was also there with her close friend, Lucy Donnelly. They had both graduated from Bryn Mawr, and Lucy was now enrolled at the Sorbonne. Despite his initial misgivings about Lucy, Russell became close friends with them both. Although both were shy, Lucy was the more reserved and bookish of the two. After a second meeting Russell thought they were 'almost too good to be interesting' (to Alys, 10 November 1894).

Helen at first found Russell conceited, opinionated and quick to generalize (J. T. Flexner, *An American Saga*, p. 292), but Russell liked her almost immediately: 'She was gentle and kind, and had very lovely red hair. I was very fond of her for a number of years, culminating in 1900. Once or twice I asked her to kiss me, but she refused' (*Autobiography*, vol. I, p. 132). In an unpublished note, he admitted that he 'fell more or less in love with Helen, but she kept our relations rigidly correct'. Many years later he told her flatteringly that she had taught him all he knew of unrequited love. In 1903, after an unsatisfying period teaching English at Bryn Mawr, Helen married Simon Flexner, who later became the director of the Rockefeller Institute for Medical Research.

While Russell's affection for Helen did not end with her marriage, his friendship with Lucy, who was devastated by Helen's marriage, grew stronger as he tried to help her through the crisis. Russell found Lucy 'less vivid and less interesting' than Helen (holograph note in Russell Archives), but none the less wrote her many of his best letters.

Since his letter the previous day, one important development had occurred: Granny had sued for peace (or so Russell thought). Curiously, she had not approached Bertie directly, but had written to Lord Dufferin who summoned Bertie to hear the news. (Russell's apprehension at the summons was due to his fear there might be some impropriety in his being in Paris with Mariechen: he had already consulted officials at the embassy on the matter.) As previously, Russell was unduly optimistic about his grandmother's change of heart. In fact, in sending Alys a copy of his response to his grandmother he added cannily at the bottom:

I don't feel *sure* she meant as much as all this, but it is obviously my cue to take it she meant as much as possible: it would be so very ungraceful to crawl down and explain, after all my gratitude, that it wasn't deserved.

Maybe Granny now accepted the wedding as inevitable, but, even if she did, it did not stop her from causing small unpleasantnesses right up to the day of the marriage. If it was a capitulation, it was not a very gracious one.

[59]

Hôtel Vouillemont
Tuesday evening, 6 November 1894

My Dearest Alys

I can't imagine why thee didn't get a letter last night – these posts are altogether beyond me. I gave the letter to the man at Dieppe, and saw him put it in the box, which he said left at noon, and I thought it couldn't help reaching thee last night. However it wasn't a very interesting one, being written a sentence at a time – every effort to write brought on sea-sickness which could only be cured by stopping. It is only since this separation I have been susceptible to that ailment!

Mariechen and I went to see Miss Thomas, and her friend whose name I've forgotten, in a pension in the Avenue de Friedland. I like her very much, and so did Mariechen – she is pretty and pleasant, but her efforts to conceal her deafness are rather painful. She and I talked about Anglo-Saxon, and I questioned her about her work – she seemed sick of German Scholarship, and anxious for something more human. Her friend I cared less about – she wore a pince-nez and had a character typified by it. Mariechen is making mercenary plans of practising for her guide-book in showing them pictures at the Louvre.

Then we dined near the Rond Point, and came home and smoked and read Nietzsche, whose confusions I succeeded in pointing out to Mariechen. She seems genuinely interested in Metaphysics and is always getting me to talk about it, which I enjoy very much. She is also always saying charming things about thee and thy possibilities, but I'm never sure to what extent her views spring from the desire to please. She says if thee comes to have a juster and more confident view of thy brains thee will give up most practical work and take to thinking with me – which of course would be charming, but I don't agree with her in thinking it probable. She's always saying what a charming time we shall have – I think poor dear she has little twinges of envying us our possibility of happiness and freedom. I *hope* to induce her to stay on beyond the time when I come back after the great 17th – she makes the time pass so easily.

Wednesday evening. Only 10 days now! Less really. I am glad of thy letter this morning – it seems nice and cheerful again. (At this point I was interrupted by Mariechen coming to breakfast.)

Later in the Chancery. On coming here I found a request from Lord Dufferin to see me. I had a momentary twinge of conscience and wondered what he would say – but to my surprise and relief it was – what *does* thee think? – proposals of peace from my Grandmother, which shyness, I suppose, had led her to make through him. I was never more surprised and delighted in my life, but the worst of it is that it makes me think perhaps we *ought* to go there Saturday to Monday after all – our joy in being together, and after a long day *tête-à-tête* (for we wouldn't go till evening) *might* make it *endurable* – and she has apparently written a charming letter to Lord Dufferin, saying at first she had been nervous on the score of my youth and so on, but had now grown to view the matter differently – and apparently she showered adjectives of praise upon thee – Lord Dufferin wrote back to say *most* young men preferred Gaiety Girls, and she might be 'thankful it is a woman we can all respect and like'. This is the way my Grandmother *should* have taken it! He congratulated me, and was, as always, perfectly charming, though he seemed to have some difficulty in choosing his words – I think however that was put on, because he thought it proper to touch on so delicate a matter in that way.[1] I heard from my Grandmother this morning, and her letter was kind and peaceful. I fancy she has persuaded herself we shall not follow our wicked plan after all, and as she can't live long enough to be surprised at thy childlessness I see no reason to undeceive her. We can tell her we shall learn from experience of married life, and that she may trust us to come to the wisest and best decision.

Really it is wonderful how effective this separation has been. Of course she will be sad at our being abroad while she is dying, but all such things will be small compared to past things. It is very nice that she should speak so highly of thee to him – I believe she will prevent anybody from speaking ill of *thee* to her knowledge, and will attribute all thy aberrations to thy mother, which matters less. Lord Dufferin remarked that when Howard came there would be 5 American ladies at the Embassy and would be 6 if

1. Maybe it wasn't put on. There are stories, though they seem scarcely credible, that Lord Dufferin would hesitate for *days* in choosing the right word in a telegram!

thee had been coming. So I'm well in the fashion. Write and say what thee thinks of going Saturday to Monday to my people – I wish we could cut it down to Sunday to Monday – half our time wasted after so long *does* seem hard. Perhaps as they are humbled now they would be thankful for small mercies, and we could content them with less. I *loathe* the idea so utterly that I can't think of it fairly. Tell me *all* thee thinks as soon as thee has thought it because my people asked me to answer at once, and I must wait for an answer to this letter. Of course it would be only natural to go there as they ask us and are proposing peace – but it *would* be *vile*.

I have had a more cheerful letter from Maud Burdett which I will send thee when I've answered it – she's thinking of Newnham again. I hope she may get there after all – I *should* feel proud and happy if she did.

I feel in *very* good spirits at the thought of my Grandmother's capitulation – it seems as if the last barrier to our final happiness were removed. – Fare thee well Dearest. I *am* glad we have had this separation – we shall be the happier all the rest of our lives I do believe now. I am much more glad it is all but over. Oh for that moment of heavenly joy!

Thine ever most devotedly,
Bertie

Despite the distress she recorded in her diary, Alys replied encouragingly to Russell's letter of 5 November: 'I am *so* glad thee has got M. to make the time pass for thee, Dearest. Thee may fall in love with her all thee likes, but I *shall* be mad if she converts thee to Nietzsche' (B. Strachey, *Remarkable Relations*, p 142) Whatever the other dangers, Russell was in no danger of being converted to Nietzsche.

[60]

[Hôtel Vouillemont]
Thursday, 8 November 1894

My Dearest Alys

I don't know why thee didn't get a letter Tuesday night – I gave it to the hotel people and I suppose they muddled it. I like to think of the white cat again[1] – it is so like this time last year. I am glad thee is enjoying thy German lessons, and I hope they will prove profitable!

Mariechen and I went to *Carmen* last night, which was charming – some of the music (most of which I knew, though I'd never seen the Opera) is delicious, only it has disagreeable associations with Fitz, who used to be

1. Alys's pet. She had mentioned it in her letter.

always humming bits of it. We are to have a Wagner orgy soon, and Mariechen has been pouring forth her soul on the subject in a most delightful way. She is so nice and emotional that she fits my present mood to perfection. But I can't succeed in falling in love with her, because every now and then one hits on a hard rock of stony selfishness beneath her silken exterior, which gives one a sort of shock and pang of surprise. However she is very interesting, and her talk is full of psychological profit. I am quite convinced that her relations with Obrist[1] and Berenson are almost purely mercenary, indeed the mercenary nature of her affections is one of the things that shock me about her – but at any rate they will keep her from forgetting herself with *any* man.

How *could* thee fancy she would convert me to Nietzsche? My metaphysical conscience is the most immutable thing about me. I couldn't admire an amateur philosopher even if thee made it a condition of marriage, I believe. On the contrary *I* have led her to exclaim of her own accord, 'Why that's rather silly, or commonplace, or not worth saying, isn't it?' several times, and have shown her why certain questions mustn't be asked e.g. Why seek truth? because the answer, if true, involves that one didn't set the question honestly but *was* covertly seeking truth in setting it – and if false, then equally we were not honest in seeking the answer.

She makes me expound metaphysics popularly, and seems to get the ideas pretty well, though of necessity somewhat crudely. It is very natural to be only stimulated by young men – I find myself similarly able to talk much better to young women, though I don't often get new ideas from them – they only make my own mind work faster and express itself better. Besides she is right that many more men care about thought or accuracy for its own sake than women. She has a historical passion, which has made me wish very much that thee had it too – thee has quite enough brains to be a good collector of historical material, and it would make a grand way of cooperating – otherwise I shall have to do it myself, which will not improve my work but will be necessary. A collection of material for the history of the position and ideal of women for instance would be vastly important and interesting, no discussion of the woman question can be complete without it, and its absence is the chief drawback to Mill's *Subjection*.[2] There is so far as I know nothing of the sort in existence, books such as Bebel[3] are contemptible from that point of view.

1. Hermann Obrist, a German sculptor with whom Mariechen was having an affair.
2. J. S. Mill's *The Subjection of Women* (1869).
3. Ferdinand August Bebel's *Woman* (1883), which Russell had read the previous June.

Mariechen's expression about 'nabbing a gent' I got from Crist. [*sic*] Howard,[1] whose mother when she was ransacking his desk during his illness found a letter from an actress saying she was going to be married but that needn't make any difference – and when I asked him whether it were an actor he said 'No she's nabbed a gent'. This story is not for publication but I couldn't resist telling Mariechen because such things amuse her so much.

Mariechen had a Jewish friend to tea yesterday who is a director of the Louvre or something similar. I was interested and bored with their shop, but afterwards we got on to heresies and mystics, which he seemed to know a lot about and which I have a passion for, so I was interested and quite liked him, though he had the Jew's money-grabbing instinct, and cared about art only as a profession.

Did I ever tell thee I heard in the Chancery that poor Lady Edmond[2] is suing for divorce on the ground of nullity of marriage? I always regretted her marriage so I couldn't help feeling a sort of joy to think she should get rid of him and start afresh – it seemed from the first to have a blighting effect on her – but the cause is strange and makes me wonder much. I could never make up my mind whether she was in love, or married from ambition, or both but this persuades me it must have been ambition as he has been a failure – though of course she may have once liked him and got disgusted since.

Thee must write me every minute detail of thy visit to Pembroke Lodge on Sunday – this is just the crisis where if they choose they can still obtain forgiveness – and I hope and pray they will. Lord Dufferin's words yesterday have taken a real weight off my mind and made me feel altogether more buoyant. I *am* glad we made the three-months' sacrifice.

Doesn't thee think, if she asks about our plans, it will be better to tell her gently but firmly, as I was suggesting, that experience alone can decide our course and it is useless discussing it now? That will leave her hope, and keep her from worrying us.

I am writing this during luncheon at the Hôtel Vouillemont waiting for Mariechen. I get so much time spent in talk now with her that I seize odd moments for writing.

Later, in the Chancery. I must stop this letter and begin copying – then I'm

1. Howard was the colleague at the embassy mentioned in the previous letter.
2. Lady Edmond Fitzmaurice (formerly Caroline FitzGerald; 1866–1911), the sister of Russell's friend Fitz. She had married Lord Fitzmaurice, a Liberal politician and historian, in 1889. The marriage was annulled in 1894. Russell himself had been attracted to her just before her marriage (see letter 47).

going to pick up Mariechen at the Louvre and walk to Notre Dame to make use of the delicious weather. It is lovely to have the days go by – they go so quickly now – to feel how soon we shall be married and away and able to begin really to live. Goodbye Dearest – only 8 more days after today. Thine absolutely, heart and soul.

   Bertie

Alys, as might have been expected, objected to Russell's plans for her to do historical research. As in previous exchanges on the topic, Russell stuck by his decision to do theoretical work himself. But this time he did not entirely give up hope of converting Alys to it, for Alys, too, had regretted that they would not have work in common. In her letter of 9 November Alys had said, rather soberingly, that she was not as optimistic about their marriage as Mariechen was because she was not intelligent enough and their interests were very different. Russell, however, still failed to read the danger signs and continued his efforts to win Alys round.

[61]

British Embassy
Thursday, 15 November 1894. 2.30 p.m.

My Darling Alys,

   I got thy 2 letters together this morning, for what reason I don't know, but it didn't matter, as I was too sleepy last night to take an interest in anything but bed. I went to bed soon after nine, and spent 11 hours there. I feel exactly as thee does about our meeting – much less excited than when I came to England 2 weeks ago – but feeling my spirits rise every day like a thermometer in the sun, till by this time they are quite buoyant. I *was* glad of the photos – one of them, in which thee is sitting with the white cat, I like *very* much – though it makes thee look rather like the patient Griselda.[1] But I am so glad to have something to call thee up to me just before we meet. I have already spent hours looking at thee in the picture, and kissing it at intervals. The other, in spite of my letter sticking out of the pocket, I don't like: thy mouth has an ugly leer and thy eyes a sly disagreeable look, and thee looks altogether inferior.

   Mariechen was glad to have those and the children, and carried them off with her to Munich by the Orient Express last night. I went to the station with her and saw her luxurious sleeping compartment all to herself. She felt very swell travelling in such style. We bade each other a very affectionate

---

1. The heroine of the last story in Boccaccio's *Decameron*.

farewell, and I felt very grateful to her for having made what would have been a very hard time pass very pleasantly. (4 very's in one sentence! Not bad.)

Don't be afraid I'm going to try and make thee into an abstract thinker, which thee isn't by nature. I was only thinking that thee probably knows thyself less than I know myself, because of thy foolish modesty, which has hitherto prevented thy undertaking anything which presented the slightest difficulty to thee – and that if thee ever got a taste of the joy of thinking (which with thy love of brains couldn't fail to be pretty great) thee might get to prefer those practical questions which require most thought, and to wish to have some hours every day for bookwork of a historical or economic kind. In this way we could cooperate without so far as I can see violating thy nature – rather I think thy present life unduly starves thy intellect – thee is a case of passion resisted from laziness, as I said in my paper.[1] I did intend at first to live a practical life more or less, and thought in *that* way we should cooperate – but I am quite sure now that a practical life would ruin *me*. Whereas I half think that the sort of life I was suggesting might be positively *better* for *thy* development than thy present life, in which others' standards are low and thee probably gets a good deal of undeserved praise and no use for such brains as thee has.

I have just come from déjeuner with a M. and Mme Cavaignac,[2] whom M. d'Estournelles[3] had given me a letter to – he is a deputy, apparently very radical and apparently much interested in finance. He was glad I was a Gladstonian and glad I liked Harcourt's Radical Budget.[4] There were 2 other Deputies, and 3 daughters of the house, more or less in the pigtail stage. The youngest looked and smiled, as if she had seen through me like Ray and Karin,[5] but I don't know how she should have, in the midst of my solemnity.

1. See 'Cleopatra or Maggie Tulliver', *Papers*, vol. i, p. 96.
2. Jacques Godefroy Cavaignac (1853–1905), Republican deputy for Saint-Calais. He had been the Minister for the Navy and the Colonies, and in 1895 became Minister for War. He sat on the budget commission for many years and had made several proposals to introduce progressive taxation.
3. Paul-Henri-Benjamin Balluet d'Estournelles de Constant (1852–1924), a French diplomat who had been ambassador to London. He became a left-wing deputy in 1895 and worked to improve Anglo-French relations and reduce armaments. He won the Nobel Peace Prize in 1909.
4. Sir William Harcourt (1827–1904), Chancellor of the Exchequer 1892–5 in Gladstone's Liberal administration and under Gladstone's successor, Lord Rosebery. In his budget of 1894, which was enacted despite opposition by both Gladstone and Rosebery, he took the radical step of introducing death duties.
5. Ray and Karin were Mariechen's children (see letter 57).

The wife was of the order of intelligence that tells you with an important air that in *her* nursery the use of the left hand is as much taught as that of the right.

They were discussing Madagascar most of the time.[1] I liked my host and thought him clever – the other 2 seemed to me 2nd rate. The whole lot were atrociously dressed. It was interesting to see and hear them, but there is not much to tell about them. They could hardly believe I went in for no form of athletics. Of course my hostess had known a lot of my relations, especially Ampthill[2] (whom *all* foreigners know) and Lord Arthur.[3] They questioned me about Cambridge and other matters. To my surprise I was shy at first, from feeling that I didn't thoroughly understand their standards of politeness – but I soon got over it, and held forth in answer to questions in the most approved form.

I will write again tonight – the last of this interminable series thank Heaven! Oh the joy of being together again – it *will* be too much for us almost.

Thine most devotedly,
  Bertie

Alys had been away at a temperance conference at Birmingham, returning home on 14 November. From the conference she wrote fairly cheerful letters, giving lively accounts of what must have been fairly dull proceedings, and resolutely maintaining her intention to continue with such work. Despite the amusement with which she writes of some of the absurdities of the conference, it is clear she felt at home and useful there. But on her return home she found a letter from Russell which, she said, was so condescending and superior that she tore it up. 'Thy letters', she complained, 'have all been utterly unsympathetic since Mariechen has been there. . . . Thee knows how utterly unsympathetic she has always been to anything I have really cared about, and since her last week at home I have had such a loathing of her morals and conduct that I can hardly think of her without shuddering.' About practical work, she put her foot down firmly: 'I feel I can't [give it up] and still be

1. The British and French had contended for control of Madagascar through most of the nineteenth century. In 1890 Britain had recognized it as a French protectorate, but the French were still considering how to assert their authority on the island. In January 1895 they invaded.
2. Odo Russell, first Lord Ampthill, a nephew of Lord John Russell. He was a diplomat and had been British ambassador in Rome and Berlin.
3. Lord Arthur Russell (1825–92), one of Russell's uncles. Russell describes him as 'a man of wide culture, a Hegelian philosopher, M.P. for Tavistock, a Liberal, but not . . . a Radical' (*The Amberley Papers*, vol. II, p. 449).

myself ... all thee has written brings back all my old fears and doubts about our ultimate congeniality' (B. Strachey, *Remarkable Relations*, p. 143).

A long view of their marriage shows the wisdom of this last remark, but little in the next few years would support it. They decided each to do their own type of work, with occasional collaborations when Russell undertook more practical work than was usual for him at this time (e.g. when Alys contributed a chapter to Russell's first book, *German Social Democracy*). For seven or eight years the policy worked well and resulted in a happy and unusually productive marriage.

For the moment, the best Russell could do to head off disaster was to send an abject apology written in the large, erratic handwriting he reserved for distraught letters.

[62]

Hôtel Vouillemont
Thursday night, 15 November 1894

My Beloved, My Dearest Alys

I can't tell thee how ashamed and miserable thy letter has made me – Oh how shall I forgive myself? I can't think how I could have been such a *fool* as to write in an unsympathetic way. It is true Mariechen kept drawing pictures which seized on my imagination and I foolishly gave way to them. Oh forgive me Dearest. I had a sort of lurking feeling my letters were somehow not what they should be but somehow since thee didn't say so I went on thinking all was well. Thank God we are to meet so soon, or else this would have been unendurable. I know now I think of it how unsympathetic Mariechen has alway been about thy work, but she had such a plausible air and seemed so well [*sic*] only to be anxious for thy happiness and welfare. I believe she was too, in a superior, truly sisterly way. I must have written very lightly for I have no recollection of the things I said to make thee miserable – I wrote another that day which I hope was less bad. Oh dear I don't know how to forgive myself. I *have* been blind and brutal. But oh I *will* make it up when we meet if anything can. But it will never quite be the same now I have shewn such weakness and such a want of sympathy and perception. I feel like a brute to have been so happy over thy picture when I might have thought how my words had affected thee. I can't get on with this letter I am too utterly miserable and can't think of any words at all but just feel a sort of dumb shame throbbing inside of me. My Darling why didn't thee say sooner that I was making thee unhappy before it came to this pass? Blind fool that I have been. Thy letters seemed unusually cheerful, or else mine wouldn't have been – except just the first ones after my journey to Cambridge. I don't know *how* this next day will *ever* pass – I feel as if I *must* come instantly to ask thy forgiveness, and yet I cannot. Oh I feel as if thee would never be able to trust me again to be sympathetic and a help instead of a drag on thy work – I feel as if I must have poisoned the prospect of Germany for thee. I have often told thee I was weak, but never shewn it before towards thee – now thee will believe it only too thoroughly. If we were not going to meet so soon, this would be almost the blackest moment of my life. Will thee ever feel the same trust in me again? I cannot do anything but write to thee, and yet my thoughts can't find words. Well thee will be spared answering this letter and going through a formal forgiveness. When we meet I will persuade thee I *can* still be sympathetic. Oh that I could gaze in thy eyes and pour out my love and penitence infinitely without the need of lifeless words.

I only hope writing that letter made thee happier – thee surely *must* have known Dearest that all was well at bottom, however idiotically I might write at the moment? It seems sad this should be the last of my letters during our separation – but all *shall* be well when we meet – as well as it can be when I have given thee just cause for contempt.

I feel a brute to think how happy I've been all day, looking at thy picture with the cat and kissing it and thinking how soon we should meet, and how I had got rid of all those feelings I'd had a while ago and felt confident in the purity of my love. And all the time thee has been miserable and crying, and trying to keep a cheerful face before the world. It is too horrible. Well I hope at least this letter will make thee a little happier for the last night before we meet. I wish I could do something to make thee cheerful sooner – I would telegraph only that one can't say such things that way.

Once more, forgive me my Beloved. I shall be miserable till I can see thee and make thee feel my love. If only we had been together, this could never have happened – I *should* have seen then in time not to make thee miserable. Oh my Life, thy happiness *is* my dearest wish and I can never forgive myself for having made thee so wretched and unhappy.

Thine eternally in every wish,
    Bertie

The crisis was a sour note for the separation to end on. But even though it was the worst crisis of the separation, it should not be overemphasized. Alys had followed the letter quoted from above, written in the early evening of 14 November, with a somewhat apologetic one written at midnight – though she stuck to her guns about practical work. And Russell reported that when they met on 17 November it took him only ten minutes to make his peace (*Autobiography*, vol. I, p. 87). Their four days together at the end of the separation seem to have been perfectly harmonious, despite the fact that they had to spend half their time at Pembroke Lodge. Alys's first letter after the separation expressed amazement that she could have felt so doubtful and distressed only a week before; and Russell, in his first letter on returning to Paris, said that the four days had been the most perfect time they had so far spent together.

Russell returned to the embassy on 20 November for another ten days. By this time their correspondence had to some extent run out of steam. They both wrote as frequently as before, but emotionally they were merely marking time until their wedding. None the less, Russell could still be interesting and amusing about his friends and relations; and Granny's reactions to the wedding arrangements could still provide occasional points of difficulty.

[63]

Hôtel Vouillemont
Monday, 26 November 1894. 10 a.m.

My Darling,

The London posts have prevented my having any letter since yesterday morning, but I hope for two tonight, and will write again, a short letter, this evening, unless some unforeseen circumstance prevents me. However I got a nice letter from Mariechen this morning – she is coming back tomorrow or next day, but is going on to Havre in a few hours to meet B.B.[1] as she calls him, so I shan't see much of her, except probably Thursday night.

I got through all I had to do yesterday without being *quite* dead. – Helen Thomas and Miss Donnelly and I lunched at Duval and then went to L'Amoureux's[2] which was rather disappointing – I'm told it is usually much better – the only completely satisfactory thing was a Beethoven Violin Concerto, exquisitely played. There was an intolerably vulgar thing by Saint-Saëns, applauded out of patriotism – it confirmed my hatred of the French by its tawdry chique [*sic*].

I walked back with them to the corner of the Rue du Bac, and then went to Whistler's – Mrs was ill, but Whistler was very polite and pleasant, and I felt a purely snobbish pleasure in meeting the great Mallarmé, whose talk, unlike his books, was lucidity itself, and in the most exquisite French. There

1. Bernhard Berenson.
2. Charles Lamoureux (1834–99), French violinist and conductor. They were attending one of the regular Concerts Lamoureux at the Paris Opera.

was also an American sculptor McMonnies[1] or some such name, who, I am told, is very successful, and whose appearance seemed designed to imitate Whistler's. The Robinsons[2] were there, but on the whole I had little pleasure there except from snobbery and the thought of bragging about Mallarmé in future.

Then I went on to Mme Cavaignac, whom I had lunched with 10 days ago – I found her alone and we talked of political corruption, French and English,[3] and of kindred subjects. She is a pleasant honest sort of woman, with more moral sense than one might expect.

When I got home, there was just time to dress before going out with Graham to dinner and the play. I talked a great deal, to relieve the deadly boredom of his society; but he was shocked at half the things I said. I make a fresh effort with each of them, thinking: now *this* one *will* be human if I show him that I am – but every time it fails, and I have to retire into my shell – except with Harford, who had a sense of humour, and with whom I used to get on very well, though I couldn't admire him morally.

I have nothing to say, not having a letter to answer – I am bored, but happy. It *will* be a joy to be back though our meetings after Saturday are sure to be rather unsatisfying – till the great 13th,[4] if it ever comes!

Fare thee well dearest: in 5 days we shall have done with letters, joyful thought!

Thine most devotedly,
    Bertie

Alys and Hannah had visited Pembroke Lodge on the 24th to discuss the wedding arrangements. The meeting had not been a success. Granny had taken Hannah aside, while Aunt Agatha dealt with Alys. The two of them had objected to all the arrangements for the wedding – partly to vex the Pearsall Smiths and partly because Maude Stanley had approved of them. Chief among the objections was the major

1. Frederick MacMonnies (1863–1937), an American sculptor then quite well known in Paris. At this time he was associated with Whistler with whom he opened an *atelier* in 1898.
2. 'Joe' Kinsella (see letter 49) and her husband, a former sailor. Sturges had described Robinson as the most Rabelaisian man he had ever met.
3. An interesting topic in view of the fact that the previous year Lord Dufferin had been accused of bribing French officials to oppose the Franco-Russian Alliance. Shortly afterwards the documents on which the accusation was based were shown to be forgeries.
4. The marriage had been set for 13 December. The original plan had been to hold it on the 14th, but Pembroke Lodge had objected on the ground that the 14th was the anniversary of Prince Albert's death!

issue of whether Bertie should be identified as 'The Honourable' on the wedding invitations: Aunt Maude thought protocol demanded that he should, Lady Russell thought that to do so was vulgar. Alys's family sought advice widely and kept the title. Hannah's motives may well have been mischievous, but the rebuke she provoked from Granny was extraordinary:

Of course where different people give different advice, you were obliged to reject that of the persons whom you might think least competent to give it, or least concerned in the matter, which *last* you could hardly think of us. You need not have feared, as Americans, that you would be thought to pay too little deference to titles – the invariable charge is the other way. (B. Strachey, *Remarkable Relations*, p. 145)

Bertie made it clear that he didn't give two hoots about whether 'The Honourable' stayed or went, and generally was less than fully committed to the Pearsall Smith side of these disputes. In the next letter, as Barbara Strachey writes, there is 'an indication of his later irritation with Alys for her "excessive" devotion to Hannah' (*Remarkable Relations*, p. 144). He evidently had little interest in the plans for the wedding itself and had some regrets that he had agreed to a Quaker ceremony. The ominous reappearance of his large erratic handwriting indicates that he was more disturbed by the new friction between Alys's family and his own than is conveyed by his words. But after the contretemps at the end of the separation he was on his best behaviour, especially when Mariechen made a brief reappearance in Paris.

[64]

Hôtel Vouillemont
Monday, 26 November 1894. 12 midnight
My Beloved Alys

Sturgess has been here again since tea-time, and now I am so tired that I mustn't write a long letter that I should like to. Thy two letters were a great joy – I read them once while Sturgess was ordering dinner, but was not able to read them again till this moment. It was brutal of my people to annoy thy mother – they think her almost inhuman, I believe, and incapable of really suffering from what they say. When we meet, thee must tell me as much as thee can of what they said.

I too am frantically impatient – that is why I sit over the fire and smoke – any other occupation takes my thoughts away from the one absorbing topic – and requires a resolution and energy I haven't got. – But I am *very* happy all the same, because the goal of impatience is so near. I'm glad of the

Vestry business[1] and of everything which will estrange us from all damned aristocrats. For that reason I should have been almost glad of a Registry Office, though I quite see that would have been going too far – but I do *loathe* all this business from the very bottom of my soul – I have tried to conquer the feeling but it only grows and grows as the time comes nearer. However it will soon be over. But it is so hateful to make the sacredest thing in life a prey to vulgarity, and, to my views, to lies also. It is the same to me as it would be to a religious person to have to parade the streets as a sandwich-man with 'I [do not] believe in God and a future life' printed on the boards. This however is a morbid and foolish feeling which I shall probably get rid of as soon as we are together again. I *shall* be glad when Saturday morning comes.

I believe I ought to spend my first Sunday at home. I could go a walk in the afternoon for about 2½ hours and if thee were to come down to Richmond station we might spend most of that time together – but as we are so soon leaving my people for good I think I ought to give them at least my first day entirely. However we can settle on Saturday.

I had already written to Mariechen telling her I had found out about Evelyn[2] – I couldn't well have kept it from her as she would have been sure to talk of the matter again, and I don't see how it will do any harm. Mariechen was perpetually comparing me to B.B. which one cannot but regard as a compliment from her, whatever he may really be. She talks of thy having fallen into my hands as though thee didn't exist as a separate independent person at all. She was so insinuating that I was barely conscious of the lurking insult at first – she thinks like her thee will take the colour of any man without the least individuality of thy own, which I am happy to say is not the case. I used to keep insisting to her that thee had influenced me as much as I had thee, but when she asked me to say how, I found it hard to specify – it has been a more subtle and less palpable influence, but not a whit less real. I also kept telling her that most of what she regarded as my good practical sense was learnt from thee, but she wouldn't believe me.

1. The Vestries were the old form of local government in London. Alys's plan to stand in the elections on 15 December depended upon her being married by then. Russell's relations, including this time Aunt Maude, had been horrified that they should bring the marriage forward on account of the elections. It is possible that their objection to having the marriage on the 14th had less to do with Prince Albert's anniversary than with their hopes of thwarting Alys's political career, to which they were implacably opposed.
2. Evelyn Nordhoff had confided to Alys that she was in love with a much older married man in America, and that both of them had been made acutely miserable by Evelyn's coming to England. Alys had passed the news on to Bertie.

I have no opinion at all about poor Evelyn's affairs till I can see thee and discuss the question – it seems to be a hopeless impasse by what thee says. But I can well believe that her strength may be unequal to the strain, and that if she resists the primary impulse, others, more mad, may spring out of it, sooner or later.

I don't know what to say about Sanderson – my impulse is *no*, but I don't care really. I forgot among my friends A. G. Tansley, 167 Adelaide Rd, N.W., the first of them whom I told about thee.

Logan's letter is amusing – tell him I am quite prepared with an extempore prayer – From all Quaker Weddings Good Lord deliver us, it shall begin. – Marsh *is quite* right about the nameless grace.[2] I always thought him a youth of excellent taste! But seriously this time of self-control and self-repression has made me more of a man – that and the time in June have diminished my youthfulness enormously, more than years of ordinary life – I feel ever so much older than Sturgess, who hadn't the elementary art of keeping his troubles to himself or veiling wounds to his vanity. – I have begun again to think it is Louise[3] – I had only assumed it was Kate from what I had been told and at Vétheuil I thought it was Louise. Here he has never spoken of them singly – but I will write all he said tomorrow. Now I must take this to the Bureau at the Madeleine to post, and then I shall have earned my bed which I am very ready for.

Fare thee well my Life – I live in the hopes of our heavenly times together, away from all bothers and all irrelevant people – it will be more divine than I can allow myself to think of!

Thine in every thought.

Bertie

---

1. The perplexing problem of whether Russell's former guardian, T. J. Cobden-Sanderson, should be invited to the wedding. He was an atheist but, despite the fact that the Russells had taken him to court to gain control of Bertie's upbringing, the objection to his being invited came from the Pearsall Smiths.
2. Eddie Marsh had sent Alys a letter saying that he thought Bertie had acquired a 'nameless grace' in Paris.
3. i.e. that Sturges was in love with Louise, rather than Kate, Kinsella.

3. 'A LIFE OF INTELLECT TEMPERED BY FLIPPANCY'

===

(1895–1901)

The two weeks following Russell's return from Paris were largely taken up with preparations for the marriage. Alys and Bertie were together for most of the time, except for the weekend before the marriage when Russell went to Cambridge to hear G. E. Moore read a paper, appropriately enough on lust, to the Apostles. The wedding took place on Thursday, 13 December, at the Friends' Meeting House in Westminster. Although Fra͏ˑ and some of Russell's Stanley relatives attended, Rollo, Agatha, and Granny pointedly stayed away.

For their honeymoon, Alys and Bertie went to The Hague for three weeks and then travelled on to Berlin, where Bertie enrolled as a student at the University and attended lectures on economics. In Berlin they got to know some of the members of the Social Democrat Party, then the most powerful Marxist party in Europe. Sir Edward Malet, the British Ambassador in Berlin, was a relative of Russell's, but their welcome at the embassy was cut short when it became known that they were attending socialist meetings. It is pleasant to record that on this occasion Granny sided completely with Bertie and Alys. 'The issue', Russell explains, 'was a public one, and on all public political issues, both she and my Aunt Agatha could always be relied upon not to be illiberal' (*Autobiography*, vol. I, p. 125).

Russell and Alys left Berlin in March 1895 to travel through Italy, staying with Mariechen at Fiesole and then travelling down the Adriatic coast. Russell remembered this as 'one of the happiest times of my life. Italy and spring and first love all together should suffice to make the gloomiest person happy' (ibid.). On returning to England he settled down to work:

> With my first marriage, I entered upon a period of great happiness and fruitful work. Having no emotional troubles, all my energy went in intellectual directions. Throughout the first years of my marriage, I read widely, both in mathematics and in philosophy. I achieved a certain amount of original work, and laid the foundations for other work later. I travelled abroad, and in my spare time I did a great deal of solid reading, chiefly history. ... This was intellectually the most fruitful period of my life, and I owe a debt of gratitude to my first wife for having made it possible. (ibid., p. 126)

In Berlin he had made ambitious intellectual plans, but the first task to be accomplished on his return home was to complete his Fellowship dissertation on the philosophy of geometry. For the summer of 1895 they lived at Friday's Hill with Alys's family and it was there that the dissertation, Russell's first piece of serious original work, was written. The next three letters concern various stages of this work. The first was written when Russell had returned to Cambridge to discuss his work and look up books.

[65]

Trinity College
29 May 1895. 12.15 a.m.

Dearest Alys,

So far all goes well, though I've not got much work done yet – absolutely none, in fact, except an infinite amount of shoppy talk. I missed my train to Cambridge, owing to the Derby, so I was $\frac{3}{4}$ hour later getting here. But I managed to get one book out of Trinity Library before it closed – the rest were not in it. I lunched with Wedgwood,[1] and saw his and Amos's Tripos papers. I'm glad I'm not in this year, as they're much harder than mine were. I argued about the presuppositions of my dissertation with Amos, who thought my position crude, being himself immersed in Hegel. Marsh and I dined with Moore, and I had a lot more argument with him about Lotze,[2] whom Moore's been reading with Sanger – also about philosophy in general. Then I walked about King's Fellows' Garden in the moonlight with Dickinson, which was very jolly. We had more shop, and agreed that McTaggart was the only man we knew to whom a belief in immortality would be a real consolation for the death of a friend. We then went to see McTaggart himself and found him cheerful, although he is examining for the Tripos – an example of the real consolation he derives from religion.[3] So I've had loads of shop and Society, both pleasant.

Moore, whom I asked for as long as he could stay, said he could come for about a week from June 15. I hope thee won't mind having him so long.[4]

1. Ralph Lewis Wedgwood, a Moral Science student and member of the Apostles. He was the heir to the Wedgwood pottery fortune, but became a very successful railway administrator.
2. Rudolph Hermann Lotze (1817–81), a German idealist philosopher who was very influential in the latter part of the nineteenth century.
3. Russell uses the word 'religion' loosely to cover McTaggart's idealist philosophy. McTaggart was an atheist, but Russell always sensed a religious side to his adherence to idealism.
4. Alys and Moore did not get on well. It was probably not coincidental that she was away from home for most of Moore's visit.

Now I'm sleepy, and must go to bed – I wish I were with thee. I shall certainly stay till Thursday.

Thine devotedly,

Bertie

This is a fearfully dull letter, but I've talked so much I have no thoughts left.

Alys's work for temperance and women's suffrage often took her away from home. On one such occasion, Russell reported the Oxford philosopher Harold Joachim's reaction to parts of his dissertation as it neared completion. Joachim, who was Rollo Russell's brother-in-law, lived near Friday's Hill.

[66]

Friday's Hill

5 August 1895 9.30 a.m

My Darling Alys

I'm not sure if this will reach thee, but I'll write on the chance.

I'm getting on very well so far, and have enjoyed Harold and Dr Bull. Poor Harold had to read some of my dissertation, and seemed impressed, in parts, with the argument – altogether, it seems not to be utter nonsense, as I feared it might be. Dr Bull was very interesting about optics, and I did him a trick with my eyes which I have had since childhood, which he had never seen or heard of before, so he was charmed.[1]

Now I hope for a good morning's work, though I don't know what to write. I'm sorry to have been so often grumpy and discontented lately, but it will be all right when my dissertation's finished. – I hope thee's having a good time. Fare thee well, Dearest Girl.

Thine most devotedly,

Bertie

P.S. Costelloe has taken the children to town, probably till Thursday morning, and certainly till Wednesday evening. I've written to my grandmother and heard from my aunt.

1. Dr Bull was the ophthalmologist Russell had met in Paris with Frank Costelloe (letter 48). It is not known what trick Russell could do with his eyes.

Russell submitted his dissertation in August. A Trinity Prize Fellowship, however, required not merely a dissertation but a further set of examinations as well. These were held at the beginning of October, just before the results of the Fellowship competition were announced. During the examinations, Russell (surveying the competition) thought his chances of Fellowship were good. But later, when he discussed his dissertation with his examiners, Ward and Whitehead, his hopes sank. Neither, it seemed, had much sympathy with his position. He wrote rather disconsolately of his meetings with them to Alys the day before the results were announced.

[67]

Trinity College
9 October 1895. 3 p.m.

My Darling Alys,

Although I have already written once today, I must write again after thy lovely letter just received. (I have no blotting paper, so this must remain.)[1] Thy letter cheered me after a rather depressing talk I have just had with Whitehead. He says he and Ward (who are both ultra-empiricists)[2] disagreed with almost every view I advocated; Ward also found my metaphysics and Psychology rather thin – like my chances, I thought when Whitehead told me. So I don't think I shall be elected tomorrow, and I suspect I am not much good at Philosophy: but they will talk more freely after tomorrow. As it was, he wouldn't say a word directly as to my merits or demerits, but only criticized definite points. He said however that Ward and Sidgwick were more dissatisfied than he was: so I drew the blackest inference. The only thing he said that was pleasant was that certain parts, more or less as they stood, were well worth publishing. – Adieu to sweet dreams! though of course in my inmost soul I tell myself Ward doesn't really appreciate it duly. But this I would utter to no soul but thee! I hope to see Ward after tea and get a talk with him about it.

I'm glad thee liked the young man, and I hope Auntie Lill[3] will offer thee some consolation at the last. *Auf Morgen früh*. I *long* to see thee again, Dearest Old Lady.

Thine ever
Bertie

1. This follows a large ink-blot.
2. It is strange that Russell should think of either Ward or Whitehead as ultra-empiricists. It indicates, however, how far from empiricism his early work was.
3. Elizabeth Smith (1825–1913), an aunt of Alys's on her father's side of the family.

Alys travelled up to Cambridge on the 10th for the announcement of the Fellowship results. Russell by this time was so pessimistic that he did not attend the announcement and his friends had to come to tell him he had been elected, as had his friend Sanger and two others out of the twelve who had competed. Whitehead's wife later chided Whitehead for criticizing Russell so severely on the 9th, but Whitehead defended himself by saying that it was the last time he would be able to criticize Russell as a pupil (*Portraits from Memory*, p. 95). Russell's Fellowship ran for six years, involved virtually no duties (not even residence in Cambridge was required), and carried a small stipend. The money was not important to Russell (he gave the stipend away to the newly founded London School of Economics), but the recognition of his philosophical abilities was — it enabled him to devote himself with a clear conscience to purely academic work.

Russell's earliest philosophical work was done within the roughly Hegelian tradition which then dominated British philosophy. Russell himself was less influenced by Hegel than by the Oxford philosopher F. H. Bradley, the most important of the British neo-Hegelians. Something of Russell's admiration for Bradley is revealed in the next letter, written when Russell was visiting Harold Joachim at Bradley's college, Merton.

[68]

Merton College
22 October 1895. 10 a.m.

My Dearest Alys

Here I am established in Harold's rooms: he is re-writing lectures on Plato, and so I am free to write. I am almost sorry I came here, instead of enduring the woes of furnishing: it is so sad to be away from thee again. But it is nice to see Harold and Oxford and the typical young don, of whom I met seven copies in Hall last night. They struck me as uninteresting, but I dare say they would have improved on acquaintance. Bradley, alas, is not up, but I must come again some time and meet him. All Harold tells me of him sounds most delightful: one trait particularly pleased me: it seems the greatest sign of friendship he can give anyone is to take them to see his dog's grave in the garden. There are those who would not sit down among the angels, he says in his book[1], if their dog were not admitted with them; and Harold's story completes this saying.

I have seen the great man's name over his door (which is just opposite Harold's), and felt the true emotion of a hero-worshipper. It seems he got a second in his schools, and had the greatest difficulty in getting any college

1. *Appearance and Reality* (1893), ch. xxvi, p. 509n.

to give him a fellowship. Even now, Harold says, Andrew Lang[1] patronizes him: 'Oh, has he gone on with Philosophy? I'm glad to hear he's been doing well.' Contemptible puppy!

Harold has charming rooms, like those in Logan's 'Broken Journey'[2] – but the life seems calculated to dry him up, even more than it would at Cambridge. In hall, apparently, no one may talk shop, or indeed anything but frivolity: his days are spent in lecturing to fools, whom he catches out in copying passages out of books when they are supposed to do papers of their own; and the other dons seem hardly to be his intimate friends. I don't think fools ought to be allowed to do philosophy, as they cannot understand it, and it gives them no sort of training.

I shall come up to town early tomorrow, and wait for thee – and am quite absurdly impatient to be back with thee again, and shall be delighted to get abroad on a second honeymoon.

Fare thee well, Dearest: I am looking forward to a letter tomorrow morning, and to thee in the evening.

Thine most devotedly,
    Bertie

The second honeymoon Russell referred to was a return visit to Berlin in November and December 1895, this time for a serious study of the German Social Democrat movement. From Berlin Russell wrote a letter of political commentary to his grandmother – though she could not be expected to sympathize with the socialist and revolutionary programme of the Social Democrats, she could be relied upon to share Russell's anger at the German government's attempts to suppress them.

[69]

Hotel Windsor [Berlin]
2 December 1895

Dearest Granny

We have just got your nice long letter of Berlin reminiscences:[3] we have been having skating the last few days, in lovely sunny frost – it has been sunny almost ever since we came – but today it is snowing hard, and the fine weather and skating seem to be at an end.

1. The writer and folklorist, also a Fellow at Merton.
2. A story in Logan's first book, *The Youth of Parnassus* (1895), a collection of stories about Oxford.
3. The letter has not survived, but Russell's grandmother was in Berlin while her father was British Ambassador there from 1832 to 1834.

We know no Prussian officers, and I must say, I am glad we don't. Whenever I think of any particular evil in Germany, I always find, however remote it may seem, that it really springs from militarism and Alsace-Lorraine.[1] I doubt if any historical crime has been more severely punished. But I have got such a hatred of the German Army from it, that I could hardly bring myself to be polite even to an individual officer, though of course individuals are not to blame. The odd thing is, that even the most cultivated and intelligent opponents of Social Democracy think its internationalism frightfully wicked. We were introduced to a delightful and most gentlemanly man, Professor Sering,[2] but he said as a young man he had been hindered from joining them by the contempt they cast on the glories of the Franco-Prussian war – it never seemed to occur to him that these glories were in reality a bitter shame and disgrace.

I wonder if you have seen in the English papers that the whole organization of the Social Democrats has been declared illegal and dissolved? It has existed exactly in its present form for five years, but the police, in consequence of their raid the other day, have suddenly discovered it to be illegal.[3] Such measures are petty and irritating, but are not likely to do the party any harm, rather the reverse.

They have imprisoned for three months a most admirable young man, Dr Foerster,[4] editor of the *Journal of Ethical Culture*, and not a Social Democrat, because he blamed the Emperor for calling the Social Democrats a rabble rout unworthy of the name of Germans. – We are too full of fury about everything to have any other thought.

I hope all goes well at Pembroke Lodge.

Your loving grandson

Bertrand Russell

1. Alsace-Lorraine was territory ceded by France to Germany at the end of the Franco-Prussian war of 1870–71.
2. Probably Max Sering (1857–1934), an agrarian economist and professor at the University of Berlin.
3. The German Social Democrat Party had been outlawed in 1878 under the so-called 'Exceptional Law'. This law had been allowed to lapse in 1890. On 29 November 1895, after a month of almost daily political trials of leading Social Democrats, the police banned most of the organizations associated with the Social Democrats in Berlin, raiding offices and private homes in their search for evidence. New legislation was not invoked. Instead the police reactivated the repressive Coalition Laws that most German states had enacted after the failure of the 1848 revolutions.
4. Friedrich Wilhelm Foerster, a teacher and pacifist. He had been convicted on 29 November for an article published in his weekly, *Ethische Kultur*.

On his return to Britain early in the new year, Russell began writing a series of lectures on German Social Democracy for the London School of Economics. These were delivered in February and March 1896 and became the basis for his first book, *German Social Democracy* (1896).

The Russells' domestic situation changed in April 1896 when they took possession of The Millhangar, a tiny workman's cottage in Fernhurst close to Friday's Hill, to which they added two extra bedrooms and a study for Bertie. The house remained small, even after the additions. Helen Thomas gave the following account of it to a friend when she visited the following year:

> [I]t is the most charming and at the same time the most absurd of habitations. Imagine a tiny cottage in an adorable old garden, full of fancifully shaped box trees and sweet quaint flowers and at the back an orchard. The new part of the house, Bertie's study, is skilfully hidden from the front so that there is nothing to show the ownership of civilized beings. The inside however is extremely sophisticated, and, I noticed to my no small amusement, Bertie, although he pretends to think nothing at all of his family ... has hung his walls with pictures of the Dukes of Bedford, the Stanleys of Alderney and so forth. (Letter of 23 July 1897)

The next letter was written from London where Bertie had gone to check references for *German Social Democracy*. The American trip that Russell refers to was to Pennsylvania to see Alys's relatives. While there he gave a series of lectures, based on his dissertation, at Bryn Mawr (Alys's old college) and at the Johns Hopkins University.

[70]

British Museum
9 September 1896. 2.30 p.m.

Dearest Alys

I had no time to write before leaving this morning, and now I must write quickly, as I wish to get my references finished today. I got thy letter this morning with great pleasure – it is quite forlorn without thee.

Santayana[1] came up with Logan and me, and I got with difficulty into the

---

1. George Santayana (1863–1952), the American philosopher and man of letters. Russell's brother had met and become friends with him in America in 1885. Russell later said, 'I admired him as much as I disagreed with him' (*Autobiography*, vol. I, p. 211).

School of Economics, by appealing to a suspicious old lady and shewing her the proofs I had to correct. Now I am pursuing the same business here. Tomorrow I shall go shopping in the morning and lunch with Miss Fairchild:[1] Logan will be there and probably Sturges. I am glad to be going to see her again: I have hardly ever liked anyone so much on such a short acquaintance.

Santayana is really a nice person, genuinely cultivated through and through: Logan liked him very much, and so did I. His drawbacks are laziness and a tendency to aesthetic sentimentality. By the way, he says he is just bringing out a little book on Aesthetics[2] which we must buy when we get to America.

I shall go back to Friday's Hill tomorrow, and come up again Sunday evening. – I am too much distracted by this place to have anything more to write, except that I am glad thy people are not too bourgeois, and that thee caught the 12.10. I shall certainly come to Wallington[3] by the earlier train on Monday. Fare thee well, Dearest. I miss thee fearfully, but have no new words.

Thine
    Bertie

German Social Democracy was published in December 1896, by which time Bertie and Alys were in America. They sailed on 3 October, returning to England on 23 December 1896. Before leaving Russell had sent his second book, *An Essay on the Foundations of Geometry*, to the publishers. This was a revised version of his Fellowship dissertation; it was also the first instalment of a projected philosophical encyclopedia of the sciences. Russell had conceived the idea of a dialectical system of the sciences, rather in the manner of Hegel, in which an analysis of each science would reveal contradictions to be eliminated by a transition to another, more complete, science. By the time the *Essay* was published, in the middle of 1897, Russell

1. Probably Sally Fairchild, although in his *Autobiography* Russell says he first met her later in the year in Boston. He describes her as 'an aristocratic Bostonian of somewhat diminished fortunes ... not strikingly beautiful, but her movements were the most graceful that I have ever seen' (*Autobiography*, vol. I, p. 135). In a letter written the previous day Russell described her extraordinary demonstration of the relaxation exercises she taught. She was, apparently, extremely flirtatious, though Russell seems to have been relatively immune to her attentions until she visited Friday's Hill in the summer of 1899 (see B. Strachey, *Remarkable Relations*, p. 155).
2. *The Sense of Beauty* (1896), based on lectures Santayana had given at Harvard from 1892 to 1895.
3. A station near Croydon on the way from Haslemere to London.

was already hard at work on the next instalment, a study of the foundations of physics.

Over the next few years, Russell's philosophical work became closely intertwined with G. E. Moore's. Russell had an enormous respect for Moore's intellect from their first meeting in 1893 when Moore was still a freshman: 'For some years', Russell wrote after their first meeting, 'he fulfilled my ideal of genius. He was in those days beautiful and slim, with a look almost of inspiration, and with an intellect as deeply passionate as Spinoza's. He had a kind of exquisite purity' (*Autobiography*, vol. I, p. 64). Moore had been admitted to the Apostles in February 1894 and his first contribution to their discussions had elicited from Russell some rather embarrassing hyperbole when he described the scene to Alys on 18 February (see Paul Levy, *Moore*, p. 125).

They were none the less very different personalities. Unlike Russell, Moore was not witty, nor even a good conversationalist. Though influential in the Apostles, his influence was due almost entirely to the passionate sincerity with which he tried to get clear about philosophical issues. His puzzlement was intense, palpable, and contagious and his mature philosophical writings convey very much the same impression. Like his conversation, his writings moved slowly and are marked by endless attention to detail and frequent repetition as he tried to express exactly what was intended.

Russell, by contrast, wrote quickly and aimed for an extreme compression in everything he wrote, rarely bothering to repeat a point or even to make explicit all the steps in his argument. In discussion likewise Russell was amazingly fast. Discussions between the two of them, therefore, were curious affairs, as Leonard Woolf noted (*Sowing*, p. 134). While Moore searched haltingly for the sentence which would express the, ever elusive, exact meaning that he wanted to convey, Russell would leap at breakneck speed bewilderingly from premiss to conclusion.

It seems clear now that, although Russell was for several years enchanted by Moore's personality, Moore almost from the first was apt to be irritated by Russell's. Moore's earnest scepticism concealed a good deal of diffidence, and he was easily distressed by Russell's sometimes aggressive self-confidence. Moreover, Moore sometimes felt Russell's debating skills gave him a victory that his arguments, based on premises which in Moore's opinion had not been sufficiently examined and clarified, did not warrant. Moore's correspondence reveals more of this than does Russell's. None the less, Russell's letters from 1897 on occasionally reveal hints of Moore's irritation.

Moore had started out as a classics student. It was on Russell's advice that, after getting a first in part one of the Classical Tripos, he turned to Moral Sciences. In 1896 he got a first in part two of the Moral Sciences tripos and a second in part two of the Classical Tripos. In 1897 he had written a Fellowship dissertation, ostensibly on Kant's ethics but in fact having a much wider range, but it was rejected by the examiners in October. Russell wrote him a letter of condolence and encouragement from Venice where he and Alys were holidaying. The holiday and Venice combined to put Russell in an uncharacteristically relaxed and indolent mood.

[71]

Palazzo Capello
Rio Marin, Venice
19 October 1897

My dear Moore

I am sorry to see from *Nature* — the only English paper I get — that you did not, apparently, get your Fellowship at this shot. However, as Fletcher[1] and Lawrence[2] were both at their last chance, I suppose they could not be passed by. I am much surprised about Fletcher, though I had heard vague rumours of his having done well since his Tripos. The important thing for you, however, is what people say of your chances for next year, and whether they commended your dissertation. Please write and tell me all such facts as may be told concerning the examiners' opinions. From what you told me of not having nearly finished your work, I infer it will be longer and better next year; this, taken in conjunction with the bequest falling in, must make you nearly certain for next time.

I have received E. T. Dixon's work:[4] it is 40 pp. close print, and rather a

---

1. Walter Morley Fletcher (1873–1933). He had completed part two of the Natural Science Tripos in 1895 and went on to a distinguished career in medicine.
2. Frederick William Lawrence (1871–1961), the fourth Wrangler in the Mathematics Tripos of 1894. He later changed his name to Pethick-Lawrence and became a Labour peer. He was gaoled for conspiracy in 1912 on account of his activities for the women's suffrage movement and was active in the Union of Democratic Control during the First World War.
3. A bequest to Trinity College made the competition for Fellowships less severe in 1898.
4. Proofs for E. T. Dixon's 'A Paper on the Foundation of Projective Geometry'. These were circulated before the paper was discussed at a meeting of the Aristotelian Society on 13 December 1897. Dixon published the paper as a book the following year. In it, he took issue with many of Russell's claims in *An Essay on the Foundations of Geometry*, though he was primarily concerned to develop his own account of projective geometry. Despite Russell and Moore's disdain, Dixon's work was not wholly without merit. Although ten years Russell's senior, Edward Thomas Dixon (1862–1935) had interrupted a military career to study mathematics at Cambridge (ranking seventeenth Wrangler in

constructive theory than a criticism. He refers me constantly to his own work for an expression in plain English of the doctrines which I have wrapped up in the unintelligible jargon of Idealism. He seems to feel personally offended by all philosophers, from Kant downwards, who are too profound for him to understand. Poor man!

It is perfectly divine here in Venice: I wish you could be here a while and forget the problems of Ethics in sensuous joys. The place is like Heaven, too good for morality. One has only to float lazily through the warm days and nights, and allow every sense to be perpetually steeped in the best things the world can offer it. I know no place, not Florence or Rome even, so poetic and so satisfying. We live in a palace with a huge hall, longer than any of our College halls, out of which the rooms open. It has also a garden, which is rare in Venice, and the most charming furniture. It is described in Henry James's *Aspern Papers*, which takes place in this house. We inhabit the first floor, and above us lives a renegade ex-priest, whose father is a Scotch Calvinist, and addresses him, when they have to correspond, as 'Sir'. Thus we live in Heaven from day to day, and do without philosophy, morality, or the consolations of religion. Tell George Trevy[1] we are so lost that even the suffering millions don't trouble us.

The above is my address till Nov. 19. Please write to me as soon as possible about your affairs.

Yours ever fraternally,
    Bertrand Russell

Russell's *Essay on the Foundations of Geometry* had been published in May 1897. One of its claims to originality was that it argued for the philosophical importance of projective geometry, a topic until then generally ignored by philosophers. It was received rather indifferently in Britain – E. T. Dixon's interest in it was an exception. In France, however, the *Essay* was received with some enthusiasm, as the brief notice Russell quotes from the *Revue de métaphysique* illustrates. Over the next few years various French journals published several long articles on Russell's geometrical work, and a French translation of the *Essay* was published in 1901.

Russell's Tripos of 1893). After a brief period of mathematical activity, he returned to military life and served in the Boer War.
1. G. M. Trevelyan, the historian. See letter 22.

[72]

The Millhangar
29 November 1897. 5 p.m.

My dearest Alys,

I got thy letter when I came in from my walk this afternoon and it was a consolation to hear from thee. I am glad thee caught thy train, which I had some fears of, and I hope thee reached the station before the rain got heavy. I was drenched, and had to change: the wind was so strong that after having my umbrella blown inside out, I had to shut it up. I am charmed to think of thy getting to town Wednesday night, and as thee is going to be there I will certainly come to Grosvenor Rd before going to Cobden Sanderson's, even if I come by the 4.15: at least, provided I should find thee there to go to Hammersmith with.

I have heard from Moore, and he will come on the 14th. He says he has only read the beginning of Dixon's paper, 'in which he seems to show himself a pretty good specimen of a fool'. I alas! have now read it through, and shall have to read most of it again. It is 'as dull as dog-pie'. Altogether I have at present no enthusiasm for work, and no plan of campaign; but I suppose it will come. The *Revue de Métaphysique*, which arrived this morning, has a brief preliminary notice, in which, after a short abstract, it expresses itself very properly: 'Ce résumé succinct ne peut donner une idée de l'érudition scientifique de l'auteur, de la clarté et de la rigueur de ses raisonnements, de l'unité systématique de sa doctrine; mais peut-être fait-il pressentir l'importance et l'intérêt de cet ouvrage magistrale ... '!¹

I am very sorry about Bonté, and I will probably write to her. What a foolish and tiresome complication about her mother.² There is a letter here for Grace³ from Baltimore, forwarded from the Capello;⁴ but as I don't

1. 'This brief summary can give no idea of the scientific learning of the author, of the clarity and rigour of his reasoning, of the systematic unity of his doctrine; but perhaps it will show the importance and interest of this masterly work.'
2. Bonté was Maurice Amos's sister. She was studying to become a doctor, a plan not approved of by her mother who was fanatically religious. Russell reports in his *Autobiography* (vol. I, p. 141) that 'a few weeks before her final examination her mother developed the habit of waking her up in the night to pray for her'. Russell and Alys sent her money to enable her to live away from home.
3. Grace Thomas Worthington, a cousin of Alys's. Her marriage had broken up a few years before and she had moved with her three children, but without any money, to England. At this time she was working in an antique shop Logan owned in Pimlico and often travelled to Italy looking for *objets d'art* to buy. Russell paid for the education of her eldest son, Val.
4. Where Russell and Alys had been staying in Venice. See the previous letter.

know her address I am keeping it. I will bring it to town with me and thee can re-direct it.

Sturges seems a trifle less seedy today, and we have had a lot of good talk, about Logan, Trevy, the Universe etc. I had a charming walk this afternoon in beautiful weather, along the top of Henley Hill. I got to some delightful places, where I must bring thee some day, as they are not beyond thy range.

I miss thee more than usual, and Sturges, amusing as he is, by no means takes thy place! Fare thee well, Dearest.

Thine ever devotedly
   Bertie

[73]

The Millhangar
30 November 1897

Dearest Alys

How unnecessary of me to brag about my reviews, when others keep thee informed! I wish one could always tell when creditable things would leak out without one's having to boast of them.

I have just received Dixon's book on Geometry, which I felt bound to look at before Dec. 13. It looks uncommonly dull, and his preface is terribly conceited.[1]

I wrote this morning to Bonté and to Moore – neither of them very amusing letters. It is almost impossible to do much work with Sturges in the room, as we infallibly begin to talk. I hope to get really to work on Friday. Sturges prefers the 4.15, so I shall come by it, and make efforts to work in the morning.

Last night we read the Bible, and sat up till midnight. Sturges, who is primed, picked out all the indecent passages in Genesis, which are certainly pretty strong. He also read the death of Jacob, which is one of the most splendid pagan primitive things I know of. Today we got on to the *Woman's Bible*,[2] which I found he had never seen before. We have also hammered at Catholicism again. Sturges, though he has more interest, has no more power

1. It is hard to know exactly what Russell had received. The Preface to the published book is dated 'January 1898' and refers to the discussion at the Aristotelian on 13 December. (Dixon complained that the discussion had been mainly on epistemology rather than mathematics – for which Russell and Moore must have been largely responsible.) Maybe Russell had been given page proofs and the Preface was later changed.
2. *The Woman's Bible* was an attack on Christian attitudes to women by the militant American feminist, Elizabeth Cady Stanton (1815–1902). It created so much controversy

than Logan to think out a philosophical argument or expose a fallacious contention.

I am just about, thee will rejoice to hear, to write to my grandmother – though I don't know what the hell to say to her.

I well remember Grimsby in the time when we were engaged: all the places thee went during that time have a peculiar halo, from my sense that they were blessed, in thy presence, above all other places on earth.

Thine devotedly

Bertie

The brief notice which appeared in the *Revue de métaphysique* at the end of 1897 was a good augury of things to come. As 1898 began Russell must have been able to look back with some satisfaction on the three years since his marriage. Though still only twenty-five he had two books to his credit and at least the beginnings of an international reputation. In 1898, however, his confident progress through his Hegelian encyclopedia of the sciences came to a halt, and his book on the philosophy of physics was left unfinished. Problems arose which could not be solved within the confines of the neo-Hegelian philosophy then prevalent.

It was the break with neo-Hegelianism, which came in the middle of 1898, that linked Russell's work with Moore's. Russell later described the break as the one real revolution in his philosophical career (*My Philosophical Development*, p. 11). His attack on neo-Hegelianism was brilliant, and he eventually carried the philosophical mainstream with him. The first version of the new philosophy, due jointly to Russell and Moore, was a form of Platonic realism, in which propositions were treated as complex subsistent entities comprised entirely of terms which either existed or subsisted. (The distinction between existence and subsistence which Russell insisted on is far from clear, but Russell himself gives as comprehensible an account of what he meant by it as any I have seen in letter 137.) The central task of philosophy, in Russell's new view, was the analysis of propositions in the naïvely literal sense of identifying their constituent terms. Not surprisingly, this became known as 'analytic philosophy', a term which has since become much more elastic but is still used to describe much of the philosophy done in Britain and the United States. This first form of analytic philosophy, which can be called analytic realism, appeared in unpublished writings by both Moore and Russell from the middle of 1898 on. Moore got into print first, with an article in *Mind* in 1899. Russell published his

when it appeared in 1894 that the National American Woman's Suffrage Association, of which Stanton had been the president for over twenty years, publicly disowned it.

own version in *The Principles of Mathematics* (1903), a book he'd been working on under different titles since the summer of 1898.

Russell, on many occasions, acknowledged that his own contributions to the development of this new philosophy were indebted to discussions with Moore. The next letter contains a tantalizing glimpse of perhaps the first of these discussions, when Russell read a paper which led to a long discussion with Moore about the meaning of 'existence'. However, the glimpse remains tantalizing because, apart from the letter, no other trace of Russell's paper remains.

[74]

Trinity College
Saturday, 12 March 1898

Dearest Alys

Many thanks for Bonté's letter, which I return. It is nice of her to enjoy our society so much – but I can't guess what she means by my moral failings! I have none.

I do hope thy toothache got better yesterday, and that the dentist did it good. My dentist, whom I had to visit twice yesterday, tore up my gums so that eating is still a pain – and then had the impudence to tell me it was good for the gums and stimulated the circulation! All the circulation I was aware of went into his basin!

I read my paper last night, to an audience of about 10 people. 'That owl' Masterman[1] was there, and two Scotchmen. As for the rest, they left most of the discussion to Moore, and he and I soon lapsed into a duologue, which emptied the room of all but one Scotchman. No one could understand what we were saying, and he was the only man who thought he could. Moore told me afterwards, by way of a friendly goodnight, that I too hadn't perceived what we were arguing about. All the same I got him into several nasty holes, which he was unable to get out of. It was the old question, whether existence means anything or not. Though you mightn't think it, you can knock philosophy into a cocked hat if you can prove that existence has a meaning.

I hope thee is all right in town, and not bad with toothache. I must be off

---

1. Charles Frederick Gurney Masterman (1873–1927). He had graduated from the Natural Science Tripos in 1895 and took part two of the Moral Science Tripos the following year. He obtained a fellowship in 1900 and went on to become a Liberal MP and one of the architects of the National Insurance Act of 1911.

to the Labs now – for the last time *this* year, thank Heaven![1] Fare thee well
Dearest
   Thine devotedly
     Bertie

Though Russell and Alys were able to live off unearned income they were by no
means wealthy, and lived a rather spartan existence by middle-class standards of the
time. They had only one or two servants neither of whom lived in the house. (Alys
usually employed an unmarried mother who otherwise would have had difficulty
finding employment.) By contrast, the Whiteheads had eight, four of whom lived
in. The strict economy which the Russells practised in their own lives makes their
generosity to friends and acquaintances the more remarkable. In the next letter
Logan rather casually becomes the beneficiary of a £100 loan, leaving Russell with
just £80 in the bank. Logan was a frequent recipient of such loans but so too was
his mother and any number of Alys's other relatives, none of whom seems to have
found it easy to live within even quite generous means. Later on Russell helped
support the Whiteheads for many years. In addition, there was a steady stream of
Alys's charity cases, most of whom required much smaller amounts. Russell's
principles were non-egalitarian: some people, he supposed, needed more money
than others; since he needed less than he had, he saw nothing odd in giving to
people richer than himself. The largest sums, however, he donated to institutions:
Cambridge University, Newnham College and the London School of Economics
all received substantial gifts.

[75]

The Millhangar
30 March 1898

My dearest Alys
   It is too bad thee is away now, just as the spring has come. It is warm and
sunny and every way delightful here – except for thy being gone.
   I did a vast amount of work, however, owing to thy absence. I found no
time to write to Mariechen, and I thought I would wait till I had thy answer
to the letter I sent thee from her. Costelloe is a beast.[2]

1. In order to acquire some direct experience of experimental physics, Russell had been
going to the Cavendish Laboratory in Cambridge where he had performed a number of
routine experiments of the sort commonly given to undergraduates as exercises. He did
not, however, find the experience very profitable.
2. It is not clear what his current sins were.

Logan came to lunch, and employed his time so profitably that he went away £100 richer than he came! I did not remember how much we had meant to lend him, but as he wanted it at once and I had heard it was in the Bank, I gave him what he believed it to be. My Pass Book has come this morning, and I am suprised to see that we were not overdrawn. Now, after paying Logan, we have about £80 balance left.

Last night we read Gibbon as usual; and when I got home I read two of the *Contes Cruels*.[1] The first I liked immensely; the second, which concerned a broken-hearted widower who feels presences and sees ghosts, though it made me feel very unhappy, and superstitious too (as it was late at night), did not seem to me nearly as good as the first. I always hate the quasi-supernatural in modern stories – people don't do it with conviction. However, I went to bed very creepy, and wondering whether thee had been killed in a railway accident. I always find myself liable to foolish fears when thee is away, if I read any exciting story.

I hope all goes well with thee, and that the B.W.'s are not too B—.[2] I really miss thee terribly, Dearest.

Thine devotedly,

Bertie

Alys's work took her away from the Millhangar more frequently than did Russell's. On such occasions, Russell was left at home with Logan whose limitations, already hinted at in earlier letters, began increasingly to irk Russell.

[76]

The Millhangar
31 March 1898

My dearest Alys,

I got thy letter yesterday just as I was starting out on my bicycle, and it was a charming letter. We *did* have a *perfect* week, one of the very nicest we have ever had I think.

Yesterday Bertram Elliot[3] came down to see High Buildings,[4] so Logan

1. Poetic and macabre stories by Villiers de l'Isle Adam.
2. Probably a reference to the British Women's Temperance Association (BWTA).
3. Probably Bertram Charles Elliot (1867–1933), one of Russell's relatives on Granny's side of the family.
4. A house near Fernhurst that Logan had rented in 1897 and in which he lived for most of the next nine years. It seems that Bertram Elliot was considering subletting from him.

didn't come to lunch. They seem to have got on very well, and arranged things to their mutual satisfaction. It was a heavenly warm spring day, and the country was looking its best; which was fortunate for letting.

In the evening we read another chapter of Gibbon. At dinner we talked about the desire to be a great man, and Logan confessed, in an unusual moment of serious frankness, that like the painter Hadyn[1] he often 'spends a miserable morning comparing himself to' whoever is really great in literature. He has the passion to be absolutely first rate, and says other people's good work makes him miserable. I haven't got the passion myself, and was surprised to find he had it. It is an unfortunate one for him, as he will obviously not get it satisfied.

I wish it were Saturday, and thee were coming back today! It is sad when thee is gone, but I console myself by doing a great deal more work than usual. Fare thee well, thee Dearest.

Thine devotedly,
  Bertie

By the middle of 1898 Russell was writing a book on the philosophy of pure mathematics, 'An Analysis of Mathematical Reasoning', a precursor of *The Principles of Mathematics* which he published in 1903. Although the new book was largely from the point of view of analytic realism, he had not yet completely abandoned neo-Hegelianism. The book was a curious amalgam of both lines of thought; not surprisingly, it was never published. As far as mathematics was concerned, it owed a good deal to Whitehead's *Universal Algebra* which Russell read with great excitement when it appeared in March 1898. But philosophically the main influence was G. E. Moore. The work progressed rapidly, though not without difficulty – it was the first work for which Russell's training at Cambridge had in no way prepared him.

During its composition Russell returned to Cambridge for discussions with Moore and Whitehead. Unfortunately, he does not report the content of his discussions in the letters he wrote on this occasion.

1. The English historical painter Benjamin Robert Haydon (1786–1846). His ambition exceeded his conceit, though both were considerable, and his journals record many such melancholy reflections as the one Russell cites. Cf. *The Autobiography and Memoirs of Benjamin Robert Haydon*, edited by Tom Taylor (London, 1926).

[77]

Trinity College
10 May 1898

My dearest Alys

I have been feeling ashamed all day of the foolish things I said after breakfast, and since my mood has changed I can scarcely imagine having felt as I did. In any case I am determined to go to the concert on Tuesday, and make a vigorous effort to be less fussy if possible. I am particularly sorry to have depressed thee, which was quite uncalled for. I hope however, that the press of business soon made thee forget all about it.

Rollings[1] was late for the train at Liverpool Street: I saw a porter with my bag vainly pursuing the train as it went out. However, the bag came on by the next train, and was delivered here: so I had no inconvenience.

I have had a most agreeable day here, talking mainly to Moore, who seemed on the whole inclined to assent to what I had to say. I lunched with George Trevy, who inveighed against the Papists: from McTaggart and Dickinson it appears the Papists will probably be beaten by a narrow majority.[2] Trevy and I started on a bicycle ride, but his tire punctured, so I went on by myself. On the way home, I met Mrs Whitehead (senior and junior) driving, but as I was going 18 miles an hour, I couldn't stop in time to talk to them. I haven't yet seen Whitehead, but I hope to see him tomorrow morning. In hall I sat between McTaggart and Bevan[3] so I had a good time. McTaggart is going to start for New Zealand a fortnight earlier than he had intended, so we shan't see him again after this time.[4]

I have an uneasy sense of having looked up trains for thee to get from Ireland, on the assumption thee was coming on a weekday instead of a Sunday. If so, they are all wrong: at least from Bletchley to here.

I enjoy being here again immensely, and expect to get my ideas considerably polished up: I have already had one error pointed out by Moore,

---

1. Probably one of the Pearsall Smiths' servants.
2. There was to be a vote in the University on according 'quasi-college' status to a Roman Catholic lodging-house. The anti-Papists, among whom McTaggart and Dickinson were prominent, won by a large majority. (Cf. Dickinson, *McTaggart*, pp. 39–40.)
3. Anthony Ashley Bevan (1859–1933), Professor of Arabic at Cambridge from 1893 to 1933. He was an important Arabist and got on well with Russell.
4. On an earlier visit to New Zealand McTaggart had fallen in love. He was now returning there to get married; he left on 12 June. His trip was important to Russell because Trinity College asked Russell to give in his absence the course of lectures on Leibniz normally given by McTaggart. Russell gave the lectures from January to March 1899; they became the basis for his *Critical Exposition of the Philosophy of Leibniz* (1900).

which fortunately, is very easy to set right. But I shall be immensely glad to see thee again, especially as I want to be less disagreeable than I was this morning. I shan't expect to have long letters from thee, as thee must be terribly busy: but I shall be delighted if thee does have time for letters. It seems like the old times when we were engaged, and I was always writing letters from here apologizing for my bad behaviour. Fare thee well dearest Alys.

Thine most devotedly,
  Bertie

In 1897 Russell had published a review of *De l'infini mathématique* by the French philosopher Louis Couturat (1868–1914). Although the review was rather critical, Couturat wrote to Russell thanking him for it and also commenting favourably on Russell's *Essay on the Foundations of Geometry*. In his *Autobiography* Russell said that he had 'dreamed of receiving letters of praise from unknown foreigners, but this was the first time it had happened to me' (vol. i, p. 133). Couturat's letter started a long and important philosophical correspondence, conducted on both sides in French. Couturat played an important part in getting Russell's work known in France: he wrote extensively on it himself, and through his association with the *Revue de métaphysique* helped get reviews by others published. He also encouraged Russell to reply to his critics and helped arrange for a French translation of Russell's *Essay*.

Most of Russell's letters to Couturat are too technical to be included here, but in the next letter Russell undertakes to write a reply to Couturat's review of the *Essay* which had just been published in the *Revue de métaphysique*. In his book Russell had argued that the question of whether space was Euclidean was an empirical matter. Couturat, in his review, had argued that it was a priori. Russell defended his original claim in his reply to Couturat (see *Papers*, vol. ii, pp. 325–38).

Russell did not always find it so easy to defend his early position. In his letter, he announces the major changes in his philosophical position, and tells Couturat of 'An Analysis of Mathematical Reasoning'. The antinomy of the point and the circle of definitions, which he mentions, were two of the contradictions generated by his Hegelian treatment of geometry in the *Essay*. Like his allegiance to Kant, they persisted despite the beginnings of analytic realism, but not for long: they were gone by the end of the year.

[78]

[To Louis Couturat]   The Millhangar
                                                        3 June 1898
Sir,

Your review, which I received three or four days ago, gave me very great pleasure. Not only the flattering remarks, but also the fairness of your criticisms, gave me the keenest satisfaction. I have been thinking of how to respond to your objections, and I have found that several of them seemed to me so sound that I have nothing to reply to them. Nevertheless, I shall say what I can about the empirical nature of the Euclidean axioms, and I will send it to you in about three weeks – which will be early enough for the July issue, won't it? I think there will be about 4,000 words in my response which would make about 10 pages in the *Review*. If you think this would be too long, I could shorten it – however I would have difficulty saying more briefly all that seems important. You will see that on a number of main points, I present arguments against my former opinion. To be frank, I have changed much in my philosophy since I wrote my book and I no longer have many opinions of whose truth I am certain. This scepticism makes it difficult for me to defend any opinion as sharply as I did in my book. To support my position, I have availed myself of a few results – which in any case are all found in Kant – which I have thought to obtain recently in asking myself the question of the *Prolegomena*, 'Wie ist reine Mathematik möglich?'[1] I am preparing a work of which this question could be the title, and the results will be, I think, purely Kantian for the most part.

There are one or two questions that I will not discuss in my reply, which will concern itself exclusively with the empirical nature of the Euclidean axioms. The first relates to the antinomy of the point. What constitutes the antinomy is that, not only are two points different, but they differ by a completely special difference, different from the difference between two other points, and that this difference is what constitutes distance.[2] This difference must, therefore, be the difference between two positions, and yet two positions, in themselves, have only a material difference. The difficulty does not depend entirely on a Leibnizian theory of identity.[3] As for the circle

1. The first part of Kant's *Prolegomena to Any Future Metaphysics* (1783) was devoted to the question 'How is pure mathematics possible?'
2. Much material on these rather intricate matters can be found in *Collected Papers*, vol. II.
3. The identity of indiscernibles, i.e. the doctrine that no two distinct things are exactly alike. Couturat had supposed that the antinomy of the point arose because Russell had assumed the identity of indiscernibles.

of definitions, these are definitions in the philosophical sense, that is to say, definitions which give what truly constitutes the defined object, and not merely some verbal definition.

Let me thank you most heartily for your review and please accept my warm good wishes.

Bertrand Russell

While Russell worked on 'An Analysis of Mathematical Reasoning', Moore had been preparing his own version of analytic realism in the form of his second fellowship dissertation. It was submitted in the summer of 1898 and this time Moore was successful, though the outcome was closer than expected, as Russell reported from Cambridge when he heard the details.

[79]

Trinity College
15 November 1898

My dearest Alys

I arrived here safe and sound last night, though Providence did all in its powers to hinder me. I very nearly missed my train at Liverpool Street, and as soon as it had started it plunged into the densest fog I have ever seen, which made us $\frac{3}{4}$ hour late arriving. I was in the train with a parson, who began by assuring me railways were a wonderful thing, but ended by abject terror of an accident, particularly as we were just next the engine.

It is charming here: I have seen Whitehead and Moore. Mrs Whitehead seems to expect the catastrophe this week or next:[1] Whitehead seems in good spirits, however, and says she has been in better health than they expected. It seems very doubtful, therefore, whether they will want us to lunch on Saturday. There seems a chance of Raleigh[2] reading a paper to the Society on Saturday, in which case I should be greatly tempted to stay up: but I am not sure whether it could be managed.

Moore seems to have had a very close shave for his Fellowship: Ward thought him too sceptical, said he reminded one of Hume and Bradley, and therefore (!) had better give up philosophy. Ward admitted his arguments to be unanswerable, but said, if such points were raised, the poor philosophers

1. Eric Alfred Whitehead, their third child, was born on 27 November 1898.
2. Walter Alexander Raleigh (1861–1922), critic and essayist. He had graduated in 1885 from Cambridge where he had been an influential member of the Apostles. In 1898 he was Professor of English Literature at Liverpool University College.

would never get anywhere. Bosanquet,[1] who was referee, said much the same, but betrayed, according to Moore, a crass ignorance of the subject, even of its literature. I am confirmed in all I have ever thought: for this is the impression which a really first-rate young man ought to make on men of 50. Whitehead also takes this view. But it is awful; to think he might have failed to get his Fellowship.

I hope thee found thy box and is having all the fun thee hoped. How is Port–u–gal?[2] Fare thee well Dearest.

Thine devotedly,
    Bertie

It was on this visit to Cambridge that Russell actually got to see Moore's dissertation for the first time. He seems to have taken a copy away with him, for in the next letter he offers some comments on it. Russell and Moore's new philosophy made its first public appearance in October when Moore had read 'The Nature of Judgment' to the Cambridge Moral Sciences Club. He read the same paper in December to the Aristotelian Society and published it the following year in *Mind*: an important, but at the time not widely noted, event in the history of philosophy.

At this time Russell was preparing for his lectures on Leibniz at Cambridge, while Moore was lecturing on Kant's ethics at the London School of Ethics and on social philosophy at the Passmore Edwards Settlement. Moore in fact gave two different courses of lectures at the LSE (London School of Ethics) – both ostensibly on Kant, though only the second actually discussed him: the first was entirely taken up with Moore's own views on ethics.

[80]

The Millhangar
1 December 1898

Dear Moore

I shall come up on Dec. 10th, as Ward is reading then.[3] I shall not be up for the College Meeting,[4] as I should have to leave the night before. As for

1. Bernard Bosanquet (1848–1923), a well-known neo-Hegelian philosopher. Although he shared many opinions with Bradley, with whom he is often associated, he was a good deal less sceptical.
2. The meaning of this private joke is lost. There is no reason to suppose it had anything to do with Portugal. Alys, it seems, was at home at the Millhangar.
3. James Ward was to read a paper to the Apostles.
4. The general meeting of Trinity College which all Trinity Fellows were entitled to attend, with a right to vote on college business.

Commem., I never come to feasts. I am glad to hear you are lecturing on Kant again next term. I don't know when my Leibnitz lectures will be, as Rouse Ball,[1] with his usual idiocy, had got up a printed list in which they came at the same time as Ward's, and it has been my painful duty to write and tell him he's an ass.

It is not very unwise to write about the Society on a p.c.: none but porters would read it, and none but the initiates would understand it. However, it is perhaps better to avoid it.

I have read your dissertation – it appears to me to be on the level of the best philosophy I know. When I see you, I should like to discuss some difficulties which occur in working out your theory of Logic. I believe that propositions are distinguished from mere concepts, not by their complexity only, but by always containing one specific concept, i.e. the copula '*is*'. That is, there must be, between the concepts of a proposition, one special type of relation, not merely some relation. 'The wise man' is not a proposition, as Leibnitz says.[2] Moreover, you need the distinction of subject and predicate: in all existential propositions, e.g., existence is predicate, not subject. 'Existence is a concept', is not existential. You will have to say that '*is*' denotes an unsymmetrical relation. This will allow concepts which only *have* predicates and never *are* predicates – i.e. things – and will make everything except the very foundations perfectly orthodox.

I cannot conceive an answer to your arguments for the priority of the concept and truth to existence – the few comments of Ward and Bosanquet (especially one about the judgment of similarity) show a gross misapprehension of your meaning.

Yours fraternally,
   Bertrand Russell

Russell delivered his lectures on Leibniz at Trinity during Lent Term 1899. They became the basis for a book, *A Critical Exposition of the Philosophy of Leibniz* (1900), which became a classic, dominating Leibniz scholarship for decades. It is still worth reading today. In it Russell not only offered an impressive new interpretation of Leibniz's philosophical work but presented an account of some of his own philosophical ideas.

1. W. W. Rouse Ball (1861–1925), a Trinity mathematician.
2. G. W. Leibniz, *Nouveaux essais sur l'entendement humain*, bk IV, ch. 5, sect. 1.

[81]

The Old Granary[1]
Silver Street, Cambridge
8 March 1899

Dearest Alys

I posted thy pamphlets at 4.30 – fourteen of them, as some had corrections in MS. I hope they will arrive in time.

My lecture went off successfully – the parson, I hope, not too much shocked.[2] Hardy[3] came to lunch, and said Whitehead's lectures had grown even more unintelligible since his illness. We went a walk, after which I took the step of giving the typed copy of Lecture III to Ward. I begged him, in the usual terms, to give me a perfectly frank opinion on it, which he promised to do next term.[4] He is worried by his Gifford lectures – says he could say the whole thing now much better in half the space.[5] So I provided the required encouraging remarks, hoping to get something similar from him next term! He feels that Leibniz was a scoundrel, that he plagiarized shamelessly – and I must say, since I have been reading Spinoza lately, I have come to think so too.[6]

I went out to the Whiteheads, where I found Mrs W. recovered. She

1. While Russell gave his lectures in Cambridge, he and Alys rented the Old Granary. The building, which stands right on the edge of the River Cam, had been built as a granary during the Napoleonic blockades and converted into a house in 1895. It was owned by Sir George Darwin, the son of the naturalist, who let it to Arthur Clough, the son of the poet, who sublet it for a brief period to the Russells. The house is now part of Darwin College. Its interesting history is described by M. E. Keynes in *A House by the River* (1976).
2. Earlier correspondence suggests that this remark concerned Russell's argument that Leibniz's God couldn't know anything. (Cf. Russell, *Leibniz*, pp. 14–15.)
3. The mathematician, G. H. Hardy (1877–1947). He had been fourth Wrangler in the Mathematics Tripos of 1898 and went on to a Trinity Fellowship in 1900. He eventually became Sadlerian Professor of Pure Mathematics at Cambridge. At the height of his powers he was (by his own no doubt accurate evaluation) the fifth best pure mathematician in the world.
4. Ward is thanked for his comments in the Preface to Russell's book on Leibniz.
5. Ward gave two series of Gifford lectures. The first, to which this refers, was published in 1899 under the title *Naturalism and Agnosticism*.
6. In his book Russell makes no secret of his disapproval of Leibniz's character – though he does not accuse him of plagiarism. It is not surprising that, in Russell's estimation, Leibniz should have suffered by comparison with Spinoza, who was a touchstone of moral integrity for Russell.

has been to Grantchester[1] twice and lost her temper with Mrs Gwatkin[2] once. Miss Hardcastle was there of course and Stotesbury[3] was at Ward's.

Fare well. Success to thy oratory.

Thine devotedly

    Bertie

I haven't answered either of the invitations.

For two or three years at the end of the century Russell eagerly sought Moore's opinion on all philosophical matters. On the postcard which follows, he inquires about the progress of Moore's review of *An Essay on the Foundations of Geometry*. The review (published in the July 1899 issue of *Mind*) was very critical of Russell's neo-Hegelianism, though Russell himself agreed with the criticisms by the time they were published (see the letter to Couturat which follows).

Moore, from the start, had been much more forthright than Russell in attacking neo-Hegelianism. His scepticism, deplored by the examiners of his dissertation, was most useful in demolishing the old philosophy. But Russell, after he had abandoned the idea of a dialectical encyclopedia of the sciences, still wanted to construct a philosophical system on a comparably vast scale. Moore's scepticism, however, was not as useful in constructing the new philosophy as it had been in demolishing the old.

[82]

[To G. E. Moore]   The Millhangar
                                                   18 May 1899

I wonder whether you got my review done in time. Do let me have a p.c. to know. Poincaré has 27 pp. on me in the May *Revue de métaphysique*,[4] not complimentary, but on the whole able, though his philosophy is hopeless.

1. In 1898 the Whiteheads had bought the Mill House there and lived there most of the time. During term, however, they often rented accommodation in Cambridge.
2. The wife of Henry Melville Gwatkin (1844–1916), Dixie Professor of Ecclesiastical History at Cambridge.
3. Probably Herbert Stotesbury, an American student at Trinity.
4. Henri Poincaré, 'Des fondements de la géométrie: à propos d'un livre de M. Russell', *Revue de métaphysique* (May 1899). Russell replied later in the year with 'The Axioms of Geometry' (*Papers*, vol. II, pp. 394–415). Poincaré (1854–1912) was an eminent French mathematician and philosopher of science with an astonishingly diverse range of achievements in both areas. As a philosopher of science he was a conventionalist, a doctrine with some similarities to Kant's philosophy which Russell had lately rejected.

I have done no work since I saw you, and found out nothing further about Being. Have you?

B.R.

Moore, it seems, had not found out anything more about Being, and Russell's own efforts were blocked. He had now abandoned 'An Analysis of Mathematical Reasoning', had started and abandoned two other books on the foundations of mathematics, and finally had started on a new book to be called 'The Principles of Mathematics', but he was still not at all clear how to proceed. In fact, the next major breakthrough was to occur at the International Congress of Philosophy, held in Paris in July 1900. Couturat was one of the organizers and in June 1899 he invited Russell to give a paper.

In his reply to Couturat Russell offers brief opinions on some other British philosophers he thought worth inviting. He also mentions his reply to Poincaré's review of the *Essay*. Again, it was Couturat who had urged him to reply. The 'new theories' he mentions consist in a new axiomatization of projective geometry. Poincaré had savaged Russell's previous account of the foundations of projective geometry and Russell, in ignorance of previous work in the field, now set about a rigorous axiomatization, the first he had attempted of any theory.

[83]

[To Louis Couturat]   Friday's Hill
                                                                         2 July 1899

Dear Sir,

I thank you most cordially for the gracious invitation to the Congress of 1900. I shall be very pleased to attend it. As to giving a paper myself, I wouldn't like to reply definitely at present. I would like to do one, but at the moment I don't know on what subject; it may even happen that I won't have any results worth presenting. Please let me know a date by which you need a definite reply, and I will try to decide. I suppose we would be reading in French?

I don't know many men in England who are interested in the logic of science. It is a very neglected subject over here. I recommend Professor *James Ward* (Professor of Logic at Cambridge: his address is: 6 Selwyn Gardens). He has published nothing other than the article 'Psychology' in the *Encyclopaedia Britannica*; but he is very well informed about everything to do with the logic of the sciences. My friend *G. E. Moore* (Trinity College, Cambridge) is, in my opinion, the most subtle in pure logic. You will see (if you read

Mind) his review of my book in the present number. Although he is not a mathematician, I agree with nearly all his criticisms, which are rather severe.

Dr *Robert Latta*[1] (University of St Andrews, Scotland) is knowledgeable about history, in particular of the invention of the infinitesimal calculus – though, not being a mathematician, he does not know exactly what it is that was invented. In metaphysics, you no doubt have the name of McTaggart.

I have made an outline of my reply to M. Poincaré. Will you allow me to present some new theories, independent developments, though related to the questions raised by M. Poincaré? It would need the addition of a little mathematics, but not much. In that case the article would be about 35 pages. I will send it only when my book is published.[2]

Please accept my best wishes.

Bertrand Russell

The Boer War had broken out in October 1899 when, after much provocation, the Boer republics, the Transvaal and the Orange Free State, invaded British territory, Cape Colony and Natal. The Boers quickly put British forces to flight and laid siege to the towns of Ladysmith, Kimberley, and Mafeking. Russell, at first, did not take it very seriously, assuming (like most in England) that the Boers would soon be defeated. The arrival of massive British reinforcements, however, did not prevent a spectacular series of British defeats in the so-called 'black week' of 11–16 December 1899. At this point, Russell (again like most in England) became seriously alarmed. The British defeats had pushed philosophy out of his mind when writing to Couturat on 18 December. In those days Russell was favourably disposed to imperialism and he hoped anxiously for a British victory – 'through stupid and instinctive patriotism, but also for deeper reasons', as he had told Couturat in that letter. As might be expected, Couturat was by no means so distressed at British embarrassments in southern Africa, and Russell in the next letter attempted to explain the British point of view.

1. Latta (1865–1932) held the Chair of Moral Philosophy at St Andrews only briefly before moving on to Aberdeen. In 1898 he had edited a selection of Leibniz's philosophical writings and it was presumably through his work on Leibniz that he became interested in the history of the calculus.
2. The French translation of the *Essay*. In the event, there was a delay with the translation and the paper was published first.

[84]

[To Louis Couturat]   West Lodge
                                          Downing College, Cambridge[1]
                                                        16 January 1900
Dear Sir

At last I am sending you the proofs [of] pp. 17–48.[2] I kept them because there were some references which I wanted to verify, and it had to wait until I was in Cambridge. I have found almost nothing to correct.

As for what you said about our war, I understand very well how such views are held on the continent.[3] To begin with, I too thought that the war was very unjust. But I have changed my mind and I must tell you my reasons frankly. I had thought, initially, that the Boers were not a very formidable enemy, and that they would never dare start a war; that they only desired independence, and that they were not at all dangerous. So I found the war terribly unjust. But our disasters have shown that this was not true. It has become clear that they were waiting for the moment (which may be coming) at which we will find ourselves at war with Russia in order to attack us, in order to stir up a rebellion in the Cape, and in order to overthrow our whole empire there, an empire nearly as great as that in India. We knew they were hostile and ambitious, and our government knew, what I did not realize, that it would be impossible to defend our possessions in Africa if we went to war with India. Perhaps you did not know that they have declared the annexation of all the English territory that they have occupied so far, and that they have declared that they will not make peace without the accession of territory. Thus, for us, it is a war of defence, and if we finish by annexing the Transvaal, it will be solely because it is the only way of protecting ourselves, and of destroying militarism in South Africa. They have an army of 100,000 hardened men, and if we are not successful, we will have in Africa all the miseries of European militarism. If we had waited any longer, we would certainly have lost our empire. Imagine for yourself a hostile army of that size right in the middle of France, waiting for difficulties overseas, and you will understand what the English inhabitants of our Africa feel.

(Please pass this on to M. Cadenet,[4] who writes to me in the same terms that you did.)

1. This was the Cambridge address of the legal historian, Professor F. W. Maitland. He left Cambridge for Madeira each winter for the sake of his health. On this occasion the Russells rented his house while he was away.
2. Proofs of the French translation of *An Essay on the Foundations of Geometry*.
3. In France and Germany there was a good deal of sympathy with the Boers.
4. The translator of *An Essay on the Foundations of Geometry*.

Please accept my best wishes for the New Year and give my regards to Mme Couturat,

Bertrand Russell

Russell's efforts in the philosophy of mathematics at this time were little more successful than the efforts of the British armies in South Africa. The initial advances that analytic realism had brought in 1898 had run out and Russell was looking for some new method by means of which to proceed. By now Moore's leadership had failed. Mathematics, logic, and even metaphysics were far from Moore's main interests in ethics. But even in ethics Moore's work proceeded at a snail's pace. There is evidence that in 1899–1900 Moore went through a period of depression. Its causes are not clear and Moore almost certainly never took Russell into his confidence about it. None the less, Russell seems to have realized that something was wrong and he became quite concerned about his friend's moodiness and failure to get on with his work. The next letter indicates just how touchy Moore had become.

[85]

[Cambridge][1]
18 January 1900

My dearest Alys

I am very glad thy Y's[2] did so well, and that thy health is keeping up. I hear that the poor Whiteheads are getting deeper and deeper in ill luck. Evelyn has caught Influenza too. Walker had tried to get a nurse, but failed. However, he hoped to get one today. I shall go out there this afternoon to inquire, and see if anything is to be done.

Moore has been having Influenza too, but is practically well. He and I went to tea with Smythe[3] yesterday, and he began to fill a pipe before tea. Smythe urged him to wait till after tea, and I, in a joking manner, seized his pipe and pouch, leaving him without means of smoking. Whereupon he got up silently and walked out, with a very black face. I have not seen him since. I hope it was only Influenza made him so foolish. I found Smythe just as worried about his idleness as I had been, so we had a long talk about him, but found no method of inducing him to reform.

1. Russell used the Millhangar stationery but was certainly at Cambridge.
2. The Youth Branch of the British Women's Temperance Association, of which Alys was organizer.
3. Probably Austin Edward Arthur Watt Smyth (1877–1949), an Apostle and former classics student who was friendly with Moore.

I will ask Smythe about tea on Sunday when I next see him. He will be delighted, I am sure.

This morning it appears that we had no news because nothing happened to Buller. I hope he will soon do something. I am astonished to see that some of the Boers were found bathing![1]

It will be nice to see thee tomorrow.

Thine ever devotedly

Bertie

Russell's defence of British imperialism cut little ice with Couturat, who accused him of believing that might is right. Russell replied hotly in the next letter.

In the meantime Russell and Couturat had discovered that they had something else in common, for Couturat, like Russell, was working on Leibniz. The book which resulted, however, *La Logique de Leibniz* (Paris, 1901), was more narrowly focused than Russell's. Russell had by now definitely decided to give a paper at the Paris Congress in July.

[86]

[To Louis Couturat]   Friday's Hill
                                                                        5 May 1900
Dear Sir

It is very curious that, without knowing it, we have come to agree on the subject of Leibniz. In my case, my book is rather an outline of his entire philosophy than a monograph on one part of it. None the less, it is the *Logic* which has interested me the most, and it is because I saw that the rest of the system was grounded in the logic that I wrote the book. I will send it to you when it is published, i.e. probably in the autumn. I will also be very curious to see your book.

I want very much to know what is the greatest length which will be

---

1. Sir Redvers Buller (1839–1908) was in charge of the British army attempting to relieve Ladysmith. His first efforts to do so resulted in a major defeat at Colenso, the culmination of 'black week'. After this, Buller's army licked its wounds for some time while even more reinforcements arrived. After a long period of inaction, the advance on Ladysmith was resumed on 10 January. *The Times* of London on 18 January reported that an advanced force from Buller's army under Lord Dundonald had seized Springfield Bridge on the Little Tugela River. The Boers, some of whom were bathing in the river, were caught by surprise – as was Dundonald's commanding officer, who had ordered him not to advance.

allowed for my paper at the Congress:[1] I see that I have chosen a topic that cannot be treated briefly, largely because my arguments depend in part upon a new logic (*vide* Moore, 'The Nature of Judgment', *Mind*, April 1899). If I put my arguments too briefly, they will not appear convincing. – I will translate the paper into French myself, but I will be very grateful to you if you would be willing to correct any mistakes found in it.

As for the war, I am not going to respond at length, for it seems to me that discussions in which there is no chance of changing one another's opinions serve no purpose, and have a tendency to become more or less irritating. But I will respond on two points, (1) my actual opinions on the subject of political philosophy (2) how I have changed my opinions about the war.

(1) I do not know how you could believe that I would espouse a doctrine so banal or so stupid as the right of the stronger. It seems to me that one can refute that doctrine by formal logic, unless one believes in God, for then it is a result of Providence. I beg you to re-read my last letter,[2] and you will see that it points to quite a different principle. Moreover, did I not say that I regretted the fall of Napoleon, which would not be possible if I believed that might makes right. I see that you have not understood my last letter at all, so I will restate my doctrines in other words.

(α) In theoretical ethics I am not a Kantian at all, but (as in logic) more of a Platonist than anything modern. But I believe that it is impossible to apply theoretical ethics to politics, or even to private life, for the circumstances are so complicated that one would not know how to do the necessary reasoning. It is necessary, therefore, to appeal directly to common sense for *middle axioms*.

(β) There are two main objects which, it seems to me, a statesman ought to have in view in external affairs: (a) to preserve and safeguard the peace (b) to spread civilized government. (It is clear that you do not know the facts about the government of Negroes in our colonies: as for alcohol, we enact very severe laws and the Negroes do not have the opportunity for abusing it when our government is established among them.) I deduce from (a) that one ought, as far as possible, to seek scientific borders. Human nature will always be the same, and people will always love to fight: it is left, therefore, to the statesman to make war as difficult as possible. For that, one should

1. 'L'Idée d'ordre et la position absolue dans l'espace et le temps', *Congrès international de philosophie, logique, et histoire des sciences* (Paris, 1901), vol. III, pp. 241–77.
2. A letter of 24 March 1900 mainly taken up with Russell's comments on a philosophical manuscript Couturat had sent him.

have frontiers at the coast, or in inaccessible mountains. I deduce also that the fewer states there are, the fewer the borders and the less militarism. I despise patriotism, and I do not find that patriotism in small states is an absolute reason for their preservation, except in Europe, where their sub-jugation is impossible. That it is the small states which ought to disappear results very simply from the fact that one cannot conquer large states. Nevertheless if the small states are content not to interfere in international affairs (like Switzerland for example), they do no harm. But Poland in the past did a lot of harm, and I approve its partition.

(b) If you had read anthropology books, you would know what a truly savage country is, and what are the benefits which result from civilized government. I wish that every part of the world were governed by a European race – it doesn't matter which, to begin the argument. Now, the stronger a nation, the less fear it has of insurrections by the savages – therefore the strongest, *caeteris paribus*, are the best colonists. But it is only within these very narrow limits that I am on the side of the strongest. And I find that the principles which apply in Europe, where the nations are now well-defined, are very different at present from those which must be applied elsewhere.

On all these principles I have not changed my opinion for several years.

(2) What you find irritating is very simply explained. For a long time I have been convinced that the annexation of the Transvaal was necessary for the peace and prosperity of Africa. But I believed that the Transvaal was so weak that annexation could be achieved by diplomacy, and that one had only to wait for a favourable time. Therefore I blamed Chamberlain for having sought by war what I thought could have been attained later without war.[1] But when I saw the strength of the Transvaal, I realized that we could never have repeated the annexation of 1877[2] without a war, and that if we had waited, we could not have been victorious. Many of my reasons for preferring the English government to that of the Boers are to be found in the quotation I am sending you from an American bishop who knows South Africa very well.[3]

1. Joseph Chamberlain (1836–1914), as secretary of state for the colonies, had been provocatively anti-Boer and enthusiastically welcomed the war when the Boers attacked.
2. In 1877 Britain had annexed the Transvaal on the pretext of protecting its white inhabitants from tribal insurrections. Once this danger passed, however, the Boers started an insurrection of their own against the British, who were defeated at the Battle of Majuba (1881). Thereafter the Transvaal accepted an ill-defined British suzerainty which gave Britain plenty of scope for further meddling in the country's affairs.
3. Russell enclosed a press cutting giving the views of Bishop Hartzell of the American Methodist Mission in Africa. Hartzell supported the British side on three grounds: that

It is only on this matter that I have changed my opinion, and not on the principles. I still hold that patriotism is bad: is it not the patriotism of the Transvaal which has led it to fight, instead of submitting peaceably? You appear to believe that patriotism is bad for us, but good for our enemies. As for myself, I hold that patriotism ought to have no influence on either side.

I differ from you on the nature of political principles. I hold that they are ends which one ought to have in view – you, with Kant, that they are maxims of conduct. I will give you in another letter, if you want, a short history of my political opinions – because I began with the same opinions you have at present.

Please excuse this long reply, and accept my warm esteem.

Bertrand Russell

It is hard to overestimate the importance of the International Philosophy Congress in Paris for Russell's work. It was there that he discovered the means for developing a new philosophy of mathematics:

The Congress was a turning point in my intellectual life, because I there met Peano. I already knew him by name and had seen some of his work, but had not taken the trouble to master his notation. In discussions at the Congress I observed that he was always more precise than anyone else, and that he invariably got the better of any argument on which he embarked. As the days went by, I decided that this must be owing to his mathematical logic. I therefore got him to give me all his works, and as soon as the Congress was over I retired to Fernhurst to study quietly every word written by him and his disciples. It became clear to me that his notation afforded an instrument of logical analysis such as I had been seeking for years, and that by studying him I was acquiring a new and powerful technique for the work that I had long wanted to do. (*Autobiography*, vol. I, p. 144)

Giuseppe Peano (1858–1932) was an Italian mathematician and logician with achievements in diverse fields of mathematics, but now best known among logicians for his five postulates for the axiomatization of arithmetic and the logical notation which so impressed Russell. As Russell put it later, his methods 'extended the region of

the English 'stood for' liberty and progress, the Boers for stagnation and conservatism; that British rule would enhance the position of the blacks; and that British rule would be good even for the Boers who, without it, would remain 'narrow, superstitious and ignorant'.

mathematical precision backwards towards regions which had been given over to philosophical disagreement' ('My Mental Development', p. 11).

Alys attended the congress with Russell and gave a paper on women's education. Whitehead also went with his wife. After the congress the four of them went on a brief holiday together. Russell reported to Moore about the congress as soon as he got back home.

[87]

Friday's Hill
16 August 1900

Dear Moore

It is a long time since I have had any proofs from you:[1] if, as I suspect, you have left Cambridge, shall I send you the Gerhardt?

We got back from abroad last night, after a most successful time. The Congress was admirable, and there was much first-rate discussion of mathematical philosophy. I am persuaded that Peano and his school are the best people of the present time in that line.

Have you ever considered the meaning of *any*? I find it to be the fundamental problem for mathematical philosophy. E.g. 'Any number is less by one than another number'. Here *any number* cannot be a new concept, distinct from the particular numbers, for only these fulfil the above proposition. But can *any number* be an infinite disjunction? And if so, what is the ground of the proposition? The problem is the general one as to what is meant by any member of a defined class. I have tried many theories without success.[2]

I found that Whitehead has a great reputation: all the foreigners who knew Mathematics had read and admired his book, and were delighted to meet him.

Yours ever
Bertrand Russell

P.S. We should be delighted to have a visit from you any time in September.

1. Moore was reading the proofs of Russell's *Leibniz*. His classical training came in useful in checking Russell's Latin translations. Hence Russell's offer to send him Gerhardt's multilingual edition of Leibniz's works.
2. This problem was not one of those to be solved by the study of Peano, and it remained unsolved for some time. The account Russell offers in *The Principles of Mathematics* is hopeless. The solution was to be found in the work of Frege, which Russell did not read until later.

In the course of his research on Leibniz, Couturat had travelled to Hanover to study Leibniz manuscripts in the Königlichen Bibliothek. He was richly rewarded and the manuscripts became the basis for a second book, *Opuscules et fragments inédits de Leibniz* (1903), as Russell suggested in the next letter. At this time Russell's enthusiasm for Peano was at its height. 'By the end of August', Russell wrote, 'I had become completely familiar with all the work of his school. I spent September in extending his methods to the logic of relations. It seems to me in retrospect that, through that month, every day was warm and sunny.... The time was one of intellectual intoxication.... For years I had been endeavouring to analyse the fundamental notions of mathematics.... Suddenly, in the space of a few weeks, I discovered what appeared to be definitive answers to the problems which had baffled me for years' (*Autobiography*, vol. I, pp. 144–5).

[88]

High Buildings,[1] Haslemere
18 September 1900

Dear Sir

I was happy to receive your souvenir of Hanover, and I was pleased to hear that your stay had been profitable. Why not publish all the Leibniz MSS., since it seems that there still remains something of importance.

I promised to read the original English of the paper I read at the Congress to the Aristotelian Society in January. We usually publish the papers which are read there, but I have told them that I had no right to publish it. Do you know if there would be any objections to the English publication? It is not, moreover, a literal translation. I would like to publish it in England if I may, but I know that I need permission of the editor of the proceedings of the Congress.[2]

The Congress seemed to me an enormous success. For my part, I learned a great deal, and I met many scholars who interest me; the papers seemed to me to be for the most part of great importance. I heartily congratulate you, you and your friends from the *Revue de métaphysique*, for having organized such a useful and enjoyable conference.

I have begun to study the works of Peano and his disciples: I am considering

1. The Russells were staying with Logan.
2. The French editors had no objection and the English version of Russell's paper was published in *Mind* (1901).

doing an article for *Mind*, similar to the one you did for the *Revue*.[1] I very much admire what Peano has done for Arithmetic and Pieri[2] for projective geometry: the formulaire[3] also seems to me a great and beautiful enterprise, that I would like to see advanced.

Please give my regards to Mme Couturat and tell her that we count on seeing you and Mme Couturat in Cambridge during the winter.

With best wishes,
    Bertrand Russell

Russell never published the paradox he explains in the next letter about no number being very large. It is now known as 'Wang's paradox', though the logician, Hao Wang, to whom it is credited didn't publish it either. (See Michael Dummett, *Truth and Other Enigmas*, London, 1978, ch. 15.)

[89]

Friday's Hill
23 October 1900

My dearest Alys

I hope thee reached thy destination safely, despite the sins of the southern railways. I wonder what Miss Farnell[4] has had to say to thee. I have had no opportunity to telegraph to thee, having neither broken my leg nor eloped.

I went a charming ride yesterday down to the end of our valley and over the hill to Trotton: the weather was lovely, and though the ride was rather long, I had plenty of time for work. I am just beginning to get a glimmering of the nature of numbers: and in consequence of a letter I wrote to the Secretary of the Aristotelian, Moore is booked to read on Identity,[5] so I shall

1. Russell wrote the article, 'Recent Italian Work on the Foundations of Mathematics', but it remained unpublished. Couturat's article, 'La Logique mathématique de M. Peano', had been published in the *Revue de métaphysique* in 1899.
2. Mario Pieri, 'I principii della geometria di posizione, composti in sistema logico deduttivo', *Memorie dell'accademia reale di Torino* (1898). Having tried to axiomatize projective geometry himself, Russell was in a good position to appreciate Pieri's work.
3. Peano's *Formulario matematico*, a project announced in 1892 for a compendium of all the known theorems in mathematics to be stated and proved using Peano's logic.
4. Ida Farnell was apparently headmistress of St Michael's Hall, a girls' boarding-school at Brighton. Alys was staying there and reported to Bertie that Ida had told her 'all her affairs'.
5. The paper was read on 25 February 1901 and published in the Aristotelian Society's *Proceedings*. It seems likely that Russell was trying to prod Moore into print.

get to know something about the number *one*. I am very glad Moore is to read, and I consider I have done a good work. I can now prove that no number is very large. For 1 is certainly not so, and if any number you like to take is not very large no more is the one next after it: and so no number is very large because they can never begin being so.

I miss thee very much, but I am so relieved at the absence of the innocent and pure young lady whose sweet feminine influence we have been under-going,[1] that that makes up for the present. Give my kindest regards to the Bishops' wives.

Thine ever devotedly,
   Bertie

In 'A Fifty-Six Year Friendship', an account of his friendship with the classicist Gilbert Murray (1866–1957), Russell wrote that he had got to know Murray in 1901 when he was staying in Cambridge. In fact, as the following letter shows, he was already friendly with Murray the previous year. It was not surprising that they had met. Murray had married Mary Howard, the daughter of Rosalind Howard, Lady Carlisle. Lady Carlisle was Russell's aunt (see letter 44), a radical Liberal, a social reformer, and the president of the British Women's Temperance Association. More-over, in the summer of 1899 the Murrays had moved to a house in the village of Churt not far from Haslemere. Murray had that year resigned as Professor of Greek at Glasgow and, supported by his wife's wealth and a small pension, was devoting himself to the translations of Greek drama for which he is now best known, as well as other literary projects (including a scholarly edition of Euripedes which he had started at Glasgow). He very quickly became one of Russell's closest friends.

[90]

Friday's Hill
5 December 1900

My dearest Alys

   As the weather kept fine, I went over to Churt after all and I was amply rewarded by a most delightful time with Murray. He really is both as able and as charming as any man I know: I came near to falling in love with him. The youngest Howard girl – Audrey I think her name is[2] – was there, but

1. It is not clear who this was, but possibly 'Lion' Fitzpatrick (see letter 21) who after her marriage became, according to Russell, 'profoundly cynical, and amazingly obscene in her conversation' (*Autobiography*, vol. II, p. 213).
2. Aurea Howard, Lady Carlisle's youngest daughter.

not yet out apparently: so she uttered not a word, and disappeared as soon as lunch was over. She is just like all her brothers (except Morpeth)[1] to look at. Murray and I talked of everything in heaven and earth. His children[2] seem very intelligent: they followed our conversation, and asked explanations of what they didn't understand. One of them is a master of repartee. Murray said to him 'Come along little pig' and the child replied 'All right, big one'. Murray said he heard we had had the arch fiend Haldane[3] staying with us, to which I replied that he had shown no signs of being 'inly racked'.[4] He rode back as far as the Huts with me, and said that he and Mary would like to come and see us after Xmas for a night.

When I got home I accomplished a large amount of work, and as I did not feel fit in the morning I lost no time in going.

May all prosperity attend thy meetings and thy digestion!

 Thine devotedly,

  Bertie

At the end of the nineteenth century a rather bizarre controversy broke out as to when the new century actually began. Uninstructed common sense had it begin with 1900, but a sizeable body of opinion held that the year 0 should not be counted and thus that the hundred years were not up until 1901 began. Russell subscribed to the latter view and accordingly gave his reflections on the turn of the century in the following letter.

Its recipient was Helen Thomas, the youngest of Alys's Thomas cousins, of whom the oldest was the redoubtable Carey Thomas of Bryn Mawr. He had met Helen Thomas in Paris in 1894 (see letter 59) and they had kept in touch during the early years of his marriage through Helen's letters to Alys. The following letter, prompted by her thanks for a copy of his recently published *Philosophy of Leibniz* which Alys had sent, appears to be the first that he wrote directly to her.

At the time it was written Helen was teaching English literature at Bryn Mawr, though she was very unhappy there and hoped to leave to devote herself to writing full time.

1. Charles James Stanley Howard, Viscount Morpeth (1867–1957), the eldest son of the ninth Earl of Carlisle.
2. At this time Murray had three: Rosalind (b. 1890), Denis (b. 1892) and Agnes (b. 1894).
3. R. B. Haldane (1856–1928), a Liberal Imperialist politician and lawyer with interests in neo-Hegelian philosophy as well. He was a friend of the Webbs, with whom he worked to found the London School of Economics.
4. Satan is 'inly rackt' while replying to Jesus in *Paradise Regained*, bk III, l. 203.

[91]

Friday's Hill
31 December 1900

My dear Helen

I am glad to hear that my *Leibniz* reached you safely, and I could wish that, like the game of Spellicans,[1] it afforded amusement at the same time that it conveyed instruction. But I consider your government very benighted to charge duty on a work so admirably calculated to improve its citizens. You may tell it, if you meet it, that no amount of protection will enable America to produce its philosophy at home.

I have been meaning to write to you for a long time, but I have been so hard at work writing philosophy that I have had no leisure of mind for other forms of composition. I was very sorry to hear that your operation has been more troublesome than was expected:[2] you must have found the whole thing disagreeable and a great waste of time. It is very exciting that you have actually sent in your story: I shall be very anxious to hear whether the Irish Faust gets successfully born.[3] You will be amused to hear that I have undertaken, for filthy lucre, to write a popular article on recent advances in mathematics for the *International Monthly*,[4] an American (but) most contemptible periodical. It will probably appear in April or May. I think of beginning with the remark 'In this capricious world, nothing is more capricious than posthumous fame', from which I shall go on to point out that all recent advances are due to Zeno, who was pre-Socratic. That ought to irritate your up-to-date compatriots!

I have had only two reviews of my *Leibniz*: one said that Leibniz was in touch with modern thought, the other that he was not. I hardly know which remark to think the more inane. How I hate allusions to this age! Thank goodness a new age will begin in six hours.

I have been endeavouring to think of a good resolution to make, but my

1. A game in which the object is to pull small sticks – spillikins, or spellicans – out of a pile without disturbing the others. It is not clear why Russell should have thought it instructive.
2. An operation on her ears. Helen was deaf and suffered all her life from severe earaches.
3. These seem to have been two distinct works. The first was a story she had sent to the *Atlantic*, which rejected it. The 'Irish Faust' seems to have been a more substantial and more troublesome work about 'Michael Farnell and Faust and Marguerite' (see James Thomas Flexner, *An American Saga*, p. 311).
4. 'Recent Work on the Principles of Mathematics', *The International Monthly* (July 1901), pp. 83–101. The opening remark Russell suggests below does occur in the article, but not at the beginning.

conscience is in such a thoroughly comfortable state that I have hitherto failed. In October I invented a new subject, which turned out to be all mathematics, for the first time treated in its essence. Since then I have written 200,000 words,[1] and I think they are all better than any I had written before. So I have no good resolutions to make, unless I could resolve that you should come over next summer. It will be *very* sad if you are unable to do so. I never pass Green Hill[2] without wishing you were there: and I often make the same wish without passing Green Hill.

I hope you and Lucy[3] are not overworking and that she is recovering from the effects of our brilliant conversation! Please assure her, from me, that Russians talk languages well, that human nature is the same all the world over, and how small the world is. It may have a soothing effect.

Grace[4] is here, and is a charming visitor: and in spite of my child–hating properties, I find her children also very agreeable. Mrs Berenson (if you know who that is) is now safely married, both by church and state.[5] The religious marriage greatly amused me. With all possible good wishes,

Yours affectionately

Bertrand Russell

The final months of 1900 had been a time of unparalleled progress for Russell. The 200,000 words he had written at that time were indeed better than any he had written previously. Peano's mathematical logic was a marvellously sharp instrument for work in philosophy. While Peano had used his logic in formulating mathematical proofs and in axiomatizing mathematical theories with a much greater degree of rigour than had previously been possible, he had neither applied the logic in philosophy nor drawn philosophical consequences from its application in mathematics. Russell did both and, in doing so, produced a revolution in philosophy and

1. The first draft of *The Principles of Mathematics*.
2. A hill behind High Buildings, Logan's home near Fernhurst.
3. Lucy Donnelly (see letter 59).
4. Grace Worthington, Helen's sister (see letter 72). She had three children: Val, Mary, and Harold. Russell, in fact, as other letters show, rather enjoyed the company of children and regretted that he had none of his own.
5. Mariechen had married Berenson after her first husband, Frank Costelloe, had died of cancer in 1899 at the age of forty-four. There were two ceremonies: a civil marriage took place on 27 December 1900, followed by a Catholic ceremony in a chapel in the grounds of Berenson's villa, I Tatti. The irony of the Catholic ceremony was that Hannah and her entourage had grabbed the children, Ray and Karin, within an hour of Frank's death in order to return them to Mary's charge and prevent their having the Catholic education that Frank had stipulated in his will. Helen had little time for Mariechen.

in the techniques that philosophers use. His work on the philosophy of mathematics over the next ten or fifteen years was rigorous, subtle, and precise to a degree previously unknown in British philosophy. Among his contemporaries, only the work of Frege (a mathematician, still unknown to Russell and working in virtual isolation in Jena) was comparable.

It is not easy to explain in a generally comprehensible way why Peano's work was so important for Russell. Couturat, however, had remained sceptical of the new techniques and in the next letter Russell tried to win him over. By this time, Russell had already made a significant contribution to Peano's programme. In his attempts over the previous couple of years to identify the fundamental concepts of mathematics, Russell had come to the conclusion that relations must be among them. He had found, however, that previous philosophical theories of relations were hopelessly inadequate and, moreover, that Peano offered no formal treatment of relations in his logic. Russell remedied this in a paper, the first of his many contributions to mathematical logic, 'Sur la logique des relations avec des applications à la théorie des séries', published in 1902 in Peano's journal *Rivista di matematica*.

In the letter Russell explains both the advantages of Peano's notation and the use he was making of it in dealing with Cantor's theory of the infinite. The paragraph on Cantor is of particular importance because it shows Russell working toward his discovery in May 1901 of what is now known as 'Russell's paradox'. Indeed, in the letter he states one of the other famous antinomies of set theory, the paradox of the largest cardinal, though he does not yet see it as a paradox. In the logic of relations Russell had defined cardinal numbers in terms of classes: the number n was the class of all n-membered classes. (The definition appears circular, but is not because it is possible to define what is meant by an 'n-membered class' without appealing to numbers.) Since, for every term, there is a class containing just that term as member, it seems evident that the class of all classes must be the largest possible class and hence must define the largest possible cardinal number.

However, Cantor had proven that for every class, C, the class of all subclasses of C has more members than does C itself. A class S is a subclass of C when every member of S is a member of C. For example, if the class C has three members $\{a, b, c\}$, it has the following subclasses: $\{a\}, \{b\}, \{c\}, \{a, b\}, \{a, c\}, \{b, c\}, \{a, b, c\}$, and $\{\ \}$ (the class which has no members at all, and is a subclass of every class). Cantor proved that there are always more of these subclasses than there are members of the original class C. This is evident enough when C has a finite number of members, but Cantor proved that it held for infinite classes as well. The class of all subclasses of C is now known as the power-set of C, and Cantor's theorem is called the power-set theorem.

Using Russell's notation '*class*' from the next letter to represent the class of all classes, it follows from Cantor's theorem that *class* has fewer members than its power-set and thus that there must be a cardinal number larger than that defined by *class*. The paradox is complete, since all the members of the power-set of *class* are classes, and therefore are members of *class* itself. It appears, therefore, that *class* has both more and fewer members than its power-set. As he explains in the letter, however, Russell at this stage thought that Cantor's proof of the power-set theorem was faulty.

Two paragraphs from the letter have been omitted. They are not more technical than those included, but they are less interesting. One deals with the definition of real numbers and the other is a contribution to a discussion Russell was having about geometry with the French philosopher Georges Lechalas.

Couturat was very much involved with propaganda on behalf of an international language and had tried to get Russell's support. Russell did not object, but obviously took the idea far less seriously than Couturat.

[92]

[To Louis Couturat]   Friday's Hill
                                                       17 January 1901

Dear Sir

I was pleased to receive your article about the congress,[1] which I found excellent. What you said in the P.S. and what you write to me, effectively reply to what I wrote to you about the international language. A logical analysis of ideas does not give a language which could be spoken in the streets. But I would reply, in the first place, that the convenience of travellers does not appear to me to be a very important end, and secondly, that one may travel without inconvenience in countries where one doesn't know a word of the language: I have done it myself several times. But I agree that we must have an international language for science, since the Germans and the Russians have unfortunately stopped writing in French, like dear Leibniz. And it is this which suggested to me the observation about Peano, since, so far as mathematics is concerned, his symbolism strikes me as sufficient from this point of view.

As concerns the value of his symbolism, I do not completely agree with you. I find, on the contrary, that it is excellent as symbolism, and I find that it is above all Peano's symbolism which has enabled the Italians to do such good work in mathematical logic. In all problems of that kind, I now entirely

1. 'Les Mathématiques au Congrès de philosophie', *L'Enseignement mathématique* (1900), pp. 394–410. The postscript Russell refers to in the next line is an addendum to this paper about international languages.

use this algorithm which I have completed by an algebra of relations different from that of Peirce and Schröder.[1] I have found (1) that logical analysis is made very much easier; (2) that fallacies become much rarer; (3) that formulae and proofs become a thousand times more easy to understand. When I read Cantor, for example, I always translate him into Peanoesque formulae, although before the Congress I had not read a word of that school. And from the point of view of formal logic, I think that we have insisted much too much on equations, which have hardly any importance, and that we were wrong to ignore the distinction between ε and $\supset$ – in my opinion, an indispensable distinction for the theory of the infinite, and even for all of what is called mathematics. I have even succeeded in making new discoveries in the field of pure mathematics, something which I never succeeded in doing with the old methods. For these reasons I find Peano's symbolism immensely superior to all its precursors.

I agree with Burali-Forti that it is false to affirm for order types:[2] $a = b$ $\cup a < b \cup a > b$. What is more, I suspect that one cannot affirm the same thing for the cardinal numbers. Cantor's arguments on the subject are not conclusive. I will be very grateful if you would send me the article by Burali-Forti, which I have not seen.[3]

Concerning the class of classes, if you admit a contradiction in this concept, infinity will remain forever contradictory, and your works as well as Cantor's have not resolved the philosophical problem. For there is a concept *class* and there are classes. Therefore, *class* is a class. Now it is proven (and this is essential to Cantor's theory) that all classes have a cardinal number. Thus, there is a number of classes, that is, a number of the class *class*. But it does not result in any contradiction, since the proof which Cantor gives that:[4]

$$\alpha \, \varepsilon \, Nc. \supset . \, 2^{\alpha} > \alpha$$

1. Charles Sanders Peirce (1839–1914), American logician and philosopher, and Ernst Schröder (1841–1902), German logician and mathematician. Both developed logics of relations which were based on the work of George Boole (1815–64). They differed from Russell's Peanoesque theory in several respects, e.g. in not distinguishing between class-inclusion and class-membership (represented in Russell's system by $\supset$ and ε respectively). Russell remarks on the importance of this distinction below.
2. The formula states the so-called 'trichotomy law' in Peano's notation: for arbitrary order-types, a and b, either a is identical with b or a is less than b or a is greater than b. Cantor had stated the law for cardinal numbers but had not been able to prove it. Not surprisingly, the difficult cases concerned infinite order-types and cardinals. Russell, following Peano, uses the sign '$\cup$' for disjunction rather than '$\vee$' which is now standard.
3. 'Una questione sui numeri transfiniti', *Rendiconti del circolo matematico di Palermo* (1897).
4. The formula essentially gives Cantor's power-set theorem in Peano's notation, where α is the cardinal number of the class and 2^{α} the cardinal number of its power-set.

presupposes that there is at least one class contained in a given class u (whose number is α) which is not itself a member of u, that is, one has:[1]

$$\exists\, \mathrm{Cls} \cap v\; 3\, (v \;\supset\; u\,.\,v \sim \varepsilon\, u)$$

If we put $u = \mathrm{Cls}$, this becomes false. Thus the proof doesn't hold.

· · · · · · · · · · · · · · · · · · · ·

We very much regret that you are not able to visit Cambridge, but we hope to have the pleasure of returning your hospitality on another occasion.

What do you think of current politics in France? I hope that M. Waldeck Rousseau will be successful in his fight with Rome, but that is a formidable opponent.[2] I'm always against the church. Though I prefer Christianity to the other religions, I cordially dislike it. Why are you ashamed of the amnesty? Wasn't it necessary?

My wife joins me in sending our best wishes.

Bertrand Russell

Our address until the 1st of May will be West Lodge, Downing College, Cambridge.

1. The formula which follows translates Russell's previous sentence into Peanoese. The point of the remark which follows the formula is that if u is the class of all classes then every class that is 'contained' in it (i.e. every subclass of it) is also a member of it. Before the month was out Russell would realize that the paradox was not so easily avoided.

2. Through much of 1899 the French Republic had been in a state of turmoil centred around the Dreyfus affair. In 1894 Alfred Dreyfus, a hitherto obscure Jewish officer in the French War Ministry, had been gaoled for treason. The evidence was unconvincing and it subsequently came to light that key documents had been forged. The case polarized French political opinion: intellectuals, anti-clericals, republicans, liberals and the left supported Dreyfus, while conservatives, anti-republicans, nationalists, Roman Catholics and anti-Semites were opposed. In June 1899 Dreyfus was granted a retrial, an event which led to much agitation and disorder on the part of the anti-Dreyfusards. The disorder brought Pierre Waldeck-Rousseau (1846–1904) to power to form a 'government of republican defence' intended to save the Republic from right-wing subversion. Anti-clericalism, designed to restrict the political power of religious orders, formed a key part of his strategy. Meanwhile, in September 1899, the court which retried the Dreyfus case persisted in finding him guilty despite the absence of evidence (though extenuating circumstances were now admitted and his sentence was commuted). The government, however, pardoned him and, in December, announced an amnesty for all those involved, thereby ensuring that those responsible for the original miscarriage of justice would go unpunished. The intention of the amnesty was to close the case, but the Dreyfusards were not satisfied and the affair dragged on until Dreyfus was finally rehabilitated in 1906.

4. NEW CRISES

(1901–2)

The address Russell gave Couturat in the postscript to the previous letter was that of the historian, F. W. Maitland. For a second winter the Russells had rented Maitland's home while he was away. This time, however, they shared the house with the Whiteheads. It was convenient for Russell, who was giving lectures at Cambridge on mathematical logic; and the Whiteheads, Evelyn especially, welcomed an escape from the relative rural isolation of Grantchester. But above all it was useful for Russell's and Whitehead's mathematical work. Russell had persuaded Whitehead of the value of Peano's symbolism and this opened the way to one of the most extraordinary collaborations in the history of philosophy. Both were planning second volumes on the basic principles of mathematics: Whitehead for his *Universal Algebra* and Russell for his still unfinished *Principles of Mathematics*. They had not yet, in 1901, decided to abandon these plans and collaborate on a joint sequel, *Principia Mathematica* — it is not, in fact, clear when this decision was made — but the winter months of 1900–1901 saw the very beginnings of their joint work.

Given his intellectual successes at the end of the previous year, the new techniques of mathematical logic and the support he was now receiving from Whitehead, Russell no doubt faced the new century optimistically. Optimism, however, was quickly dashed. For, with the new year, came a series of three crises which turned Russell's emotional and intellectual life upside down. The first was a mystical experience in February. Three months later, he discovered a fundamental inconsistency (now known as Russell's paradox) in his treatment of mathematics. Finally, over the course of the following year, his feelings towards Alys changed, as a result of which his marriage began a long-drawn-out and painful dissolution.

The first crisis occurred on 10 February 1901. Alys and Bertie had gone to Newnham College to hear Gilbert Murray read part of his new translation of Euripides' tragedy *Hippolytus*. In the play, Phaedra falls in love with her stepson, Hippolytus. Though she resists the passion for as long as possible, she eventually declares her love, only to have it rejected by Hippolytus. She commits suicide, though not before writing to her husband, Theseus, accusing Hippolytus of trying to rape her. (Murray's reading ended at Phaedra's suicide.)

After the reading the Russells returned to Downing College where they found Evelyn Whitehead in the middle of what appeared to be a dangerous and acutely painful angina attack. Now it seems unlikely that Evelyn Whitehead in fact suffered from angina: despite what Alfred referred to as frequent 'bad heart attacks' she survived for another sixty years – outliving all of them except the redoubtable Bertie. It seems, instead, that she suffered from a psychosomatic disorder, pseudo-angina, which duplicated the symptoms of real angina but was not physically based. The danger was therefore illusory, but the pain was real enough, and so was the anxiety caused by the repeated attacks. Russell, apparently, never realized the truth about her condition.

Russell had seen the attacks before but either this one was especially severe or Russell was made more susceptible to it by the emotions engendered by the *Hippolytus*. At all events, this attack had a profound effect upon him:

> Suddenly the ground seemed to give way beneath me, and I found myself in quite another region. Within five minutes I went through some such reflections as the following: the loneliness of the human soul is unendurable; nothing can penetrate it except the highest intensity of the sort of love that religious teachers have preached; whatever does not spring from this motive is harmful, or at best useless; ... that in human relations one should penetrate to the core of loneliness in each person and speak to that. ... (*Autobiography*, vol. I, p. 146)

The last time Russell's emotions had been unleashed in this way was in the terrible summer of 1894, when he felt his grandmother's efforts to prevent his marriage had driven him to the brink of insanity. Since then, to preserve his sanity, he had thought it necessary to avoid deep emotions. For six years of marriage his emotional life had been 'calm and superficial' and he had been content, he said, with 'flippant cleverness'. Moved now by poetry and pain, things changed dramatically in those five minutes:

> I had become a completely different person. For a time, a sort of mystic illumination possessed me. ... Having been an Imperialist, I became ... a pro-Boer and a Pacifist. Having for years cared only for exactness and analysis, I found myself filled with semi-mystical feelings about beauty, with an interest in children, and with a desire almost as profound as that of the Buddha to find some philosophy which should make human life endurable. (*Autobiography*, vol. I, p. 146)

The *Hippolytus* itself was not incidental to this transformation. Nietzsche in *The Birth of Tragedy* had elaborated two principles of Greek culture: the Apollonian and the Dionysiac. The former represented reason, harmony, order, and structure; the latter madness, ecstasy, drunkenness and fertility. These ideas caught on among Cambridge classicists. Both Gilbert Murray and another of Russell's friends, the Cambridge classical archaeologist, Jane Harrison, had been influenced by it. Harrison had studied Nietzsche directly; Murray was influenced both by her and by the Cambridge anthropologist, J. G. Frazer's study of Dionysian religion in the first volume of *The Golden Bough* (a work which Russell had read the previous year and read again in April 1901). Though Murray was not himself at Cambridge he became associated with this group and came, as a result, to view the classical Olympian religion as a thin veil of rationality thrown over older, deeper and more savage Dionysian cults. The main theme of Murray's translation of the *Hippolytus* is that the darker side of human nature, represented by Dionysus, cannot safely be ignored.

Such a play had a direct message to a man who had tried to live by 'flippant cleverness' and one which was driven home by Evelyn Whitehead's plight. But Russell exaggerated the superficiality of the previous six years, as he probably exaggerated the drama of Evelyn Whitehead's illness. Like Evelyn herself, he was prone to heighten such episodes, though doubtless unintentionally. Two days later, Alys had to go to Manchester for her temperance work and Russell wrote to her the following subdued and reflective letter.

[93]

Downing College
12 February 1901 8.45 p.m.

My dearest Alys

All goes well so far, in spite of thy absence. Evelyn achieved the journey to the drawing-room, though she naturally felt rather dizzy. Two Miss Shuckburghs[1] came, one to play with the children, the other to talk to Evelyn. She sends thee a message to the effect that she ate her dinner, though she felt very gross in having special dishes. She really seems to be getting much better, and the dizziness is only natural. We played Milligan[2] before dinner, which seemed to give her great pleasure.

The day before yesterday seems to me such a remote epoch that it might be two months ago: I have to assure myself solemnly that it is not. Since the time of our engagement, I have felt nothing so poignantly as the last two days.

I hope all goes well with thee. I am forwarding only one halfpenny

1. The daughters of Evelyn Shuckburgh, a classicist at Cambridge and Fellow and Librarian at Emmanuel College. He was a close friend of Alfred's. The Shuckburghs lived in Grantchester and it had been their suggestion that the Whiteheads take the Mill House there.
2. It is not clear what game this was. It is not included in any list of contemporary pastimes that I have seen.

envelope and a note from Mrs Holunden [?], which I have not answered.
Fare thee well Dearest I long for thee to be back.
Thine ever devotedly
    Bertie

On her return from Manchester, Alys took over the running of the Whitehead household. The two families stayed together for six weeks at Downing College and then Alys and Bertie moved in with the Whiteheads when they returned to the Mill House in Grantchester. The stay with the Whiteheads was not a happy period for Alys, though she confided her feelings about it to no one. Her family assumed her depression was due to the physical exertion of running the Whitehead household with its three small children and invalid mother. Despite the numerous Whitehead servants – augmented now by a nanny for the children and a nurse for Evelyn – it is likely Alys took on more of the day-to-day business of the household than was necessary: at one point she complained to her mother that she was doing the nanny's work for her. But this seems not to be the whole story. It is quite likely that Alys felt all the fuss about Evelyn was excessive. Her family took a much brusquer attitude to equally dramatic illnesses and even to genuinely dangerous ones. Though Alys was more sympathetic than her mother in these matters, she was none the less influenced by Hannah and may well have seen through some of Evelyn's ongoing melodrama, for there is little doubt that Evelyn was playing her illness for all it was worth. If Alys did see through Evelyn, she had little chance in convincing Bertie, who by now had conceived of Evelyn as a figure of 'intense tragedy and pain' (as he put it ten years later to Ottoline Morrell) and the inspiration for his mystical insight into the tragedy of the human condition. His emotions had been deeply stirred, though by a figure who now seems more theatrical than tragic, and they were not going to be dispelled by a little common sense.

Russell's relations with Evelyn have been the subject of much speculation. Rumours of an affair were probably exaggerated; Russell certainly never admitted to one. Yet after his mystical experience in February it is clear that he came to feel love for Evelyn; she evidently stirred his emotions in a way that no other woman apart from Alys had. His feelings, no doubt, were not entirely asexual, but there is no reason to suppose that they received any physical expression. Russell himself might not even have recognized that he was in love with Evelyn until afterwards, for in a sense he was more in love with his new mystic vision, which she embodied, than with Evelyn herself. His fascination with Evelyn after the mystical experience is not in the least surprising. The emotions he had denied since 1894 had suddenly escaped from his control and required something in his life to which he could direct them. Since Evelyn's apparent angina attack had been the occasion for their escape, it was natural that her misery and loneliness should become their focus. Evelyn herself was far from averse to this process of mythologization; indeed she was quite anxious to appear fascinating.

Alys no doubt felt excluded as Bertie's intimacy with Evelyn developed; it also fed her feelings of insecurity, never far from the surface, reviving the fears she had felt before her marriage that maybe she was too dull and that Bertie needed a more interesting wife. There is little evidence, however, that Russell's feelings for Alys diminished in the immediate aftermath of his mystical experience. Indeed, it was also quite natural that he should try again to make Alys the focus of his emotions as he had in 1894. In the end, this attempt failed; by the end of the year Alys had in effect conceded that she could no longer give what Bertie now wanted from her. Maybe she was too tired and depressed to set up a new relationship at the highly charged emotional level Russell now wanted. Maybe she saw through Evelyn too well to take her seriously; both Evelyn and Alfred came to dislike her. Maybe, as Russell later suggested, she was too close to her mother and her mother's virtues, both of which Bertie had come to hate. Or perhaps, not sharing Russell's tragic sense of human loneliness, she was incapable of the sort of emotional intimacy he now yearned for and could not understand what it was that had become so important to him. (One senses something impersonal and even slightly glacial in Alys's good nature, a personality created more by duty than by feeling.) Whatever the reasons, the gap in their marriage which opened up in the year after Bertie's mystical experience proved impossible to bridge.

Alys and Bertie returned to the Millhangar in May: Alys tired and depressed by her stay with the Whiteheads; Russell simmering with inchoate and barely contained emotions. In July he was back at Grantchester again, this time planning a six-week Mediterranean cruise for the four of them.

[94]

The Mill House
10 July 1901

My dearest Alys

I have just got thy letter. It is a relief that BB[1] is staying at King's. I will arrange all about lunch.

I miss thee too very much, in spite of the pleasure of seeing Evelyn. I was so pleased to find her well that I forgot all about my grievances. Mary

1. Bernhard Berenson was in England with Mary and his mother visiting Mary's relations.

Beeton[1] is, as might be expected, in great trouble: no one knows whether the worst has happened. It is vexing that she is coming while I am here, but it makes me the more glad that I came early. I made Evelyn promise to send her away a week before we sail; she had meant to keep her to the last.

Yesterday we went to Madingly wood with the Rickshaw:[2] Evelyn had a headache, but today she is very well. I am enjoying being here very much indeed; but I am feeling very slack, as I lay awake most of the night remembering bad times, as I always do when I first come back here.

Today we go to tea with Dickinson in King's Fellows' Garden. Fare thee well Dearest. Thine devotedly,

Bertie

[95]

The Mill House
13 July 1901

My dearest Alys

Miss Beeton, good lady, is ill, and cannot come till Monday: this has filled our hearts with joy.

Evelyn and I had an exceedingly frank talk last night on the subject of Alfred. She saw all that we felt about him when she was ill, in a way that was really uncanny. But at that time, as she confessed, she was too much inclined to think herself neglected by him to argue with us. However, I was able to say last night whatever was necessary to her happiness, as I have felt somewhat differently since I observed him not telling Forsyth[3] of her last bad attack – also since I have got back my usual feeling of the importance of work, which I lost in the winter. She was much relieved to have talked it out, and though I did not express my whole mind, I completely avoided lying to her. She is really extremely well, and in very good spirits: there are no crises, Alfred's work goes on gloriously, and all is merry as a marriage bell.

I have just got thy most amusing letter, of which I will read bits to Evelyn.

---

1. The daughter of Henry Beeton, a wealthy friend of the Whiteheads. It is not known what trouble she was in.
2. The Rickshaw was a two-wheeled conveyance for Evelyn which attached to Alfred's bicycle.
3. Andrew Russell Forsyth (1858–1942), a Trinity mathematician and one of the closest of Whitehead's Cambridge friends.

I have also got my article in the *International Monthly*,[1] but not yet the cheque. That however will probably follow.

I hope to see thee again, but I am very happy here. Evelyn is more lovable than ever, and I quite like Alfred again.

Thine ever devotedly,

Bertie

[96]

Mill House
14 July 1901

My dearest Alys

It was a great pleasure to hear from thee by the first post this morning. I am glad thee is happy and amused that thee enjoys the adulation.

Nothing very new has happened here. Mary Beeton has finally decided to come this afternoon. At present Forsyth is in the drawing room, having come to lunch; hence the paper.[2] Dickinson comes to supper, but otherwise no gaieties are anticipated. All goes well: Evelyn was tired last night, but slept like a top. We have had more talk about Alfred. She has cured herself of the feeling of being neglected, but knows all we felt. I am much relieved at the removal of a secret, and so, it appears, is she.

Now it is luncheon time and I have nothing more to say.

Thine longing to see thee,

Bertie

The nature of Bertie's tête-à-têtes with Evelyn can only be conjectured, but it is possible that it was on this occasion that they discussed ways of saving Alfred from a nervous breakdown. In his *Autobiography* (vol. I, p. 150), Russell reported that behind Whitehead's calm exterior there were 'impulses which were scarcely sane' which he resisted with 'more self-control than a human being could be expected to stand'; that Whitehead was prone to complete silences lasting several days; and that he used to scare Evelyn and the servants 'by mutterings in which he addressed injurious objurgations to himself'. Though Russell came to think that Evelyn exaggerated the danger ('for she tended to be melodramatic in her outlook'), she spoke to him of Alfred 'with the utmost frankness, and I found myself in an alliance with her to keep him sane'.

1. 'Recent Work on the Principles of Mathematics', *The International Monthly* (July 1901), pp. 83–101.
2. It was not the usual Mill House letterhead.

Whitehead's biographer, Victor Lowe, suggests that it was on this occasion that Evelyn confided to Russell their financial difficulties and Russell agreed to help without letting Alfred know (Lowe, *Whitehead*, vol. i, pp. 243–5). But there is no clear evidence of this and it seems possible that Russell's financial help came later, although Lowe seems quite confident that additions to the Mill House in 1902 were paid for by Russell's money (p. 246).

The Mediterranean cruise, intended mainly to help Evelyn recuperate, went off almost as planned. They left Southampton on 17 August and returned on 29 September – except for Alys who left for home one week before the others. Letters written at the time they set out make it clear that Alys expected to return at the same time as the others and there is no indication of what may have happened to change her plans. It is certainly possible to read a significance into this event that it might not have possessed. But in view of subsequent events, it is tempting to suppose that Alys and the Whiteheads (especially Evelyn) had got on each other's nerves. It is true that Alys's letters to Nathaniel Wedd from the Mediterranean gave no sign of any trouble, but then she would hardly have confided in Wedd (or anyone else for that matter) whatever the problem. At all events, in view of what was about to happen, her unexpected departure was ominous.

They returned to England just in time for Alfred and Bertie to resume their teaching at Cambridge. In November Bertie joined the Whiteheads at the Mill House, Alys following a few days later. The Mill House again unleashed Russell's emotions and produced a remarkably affectionate letter to Alys. In it his love is clearly changed, but seems unabated.

[97]

The Mill House
6 November 1901

My Darling Alys

In spite of the fog, I managed to get here by 2.20, and to get across town in a bus. The weather here was dreadful, and Evelyn did not get out. I found her very seedy, and this morning she was too tired to see me till lunch. But since she has been out in the Rickshaw, she is much better; and some chrysanthemums which Bond[1] brought have quite completed her cure.

My lecture yesterday was very successful: Johnson[2] had prepared a con-

1. Possibly Alys's cousin, Bond Thomas, or perhaps a servant.
2. William Ernest Johnson (1858–1931), a Cambridge logician. His work, though in many respects original, lay in the older tradition of logic and was overshadowed by the rise of mathematical logic as developed by Russell and others.

undrum which he thought I should not be able to answer; but he only displayed his own failure to understand Peano's innovations.

There are no letters for thee, so far as I can discover. Harriet[1] has been having trouble with the dentist, which has greatly occupied her.

Coming back to the fog and Evelyn's illness gave me very much of a feeling that our honeymoon was over; still the accumulated happiness has so far pulled me through very successfully. Dearest, thee does give me more happiness than I can say – all the happiness I have, in fact. Thee is the only person I know well and yet really and thoroughly admire. I love the absolute certainty that all thy thoughts will be magnanimous and free from all pettiness. Since last winter I have known that life without thee would not be possible. It is alarming to be so absolutely dependent, but so it is.

I am fairly longing to see thee again. Separations grow more and more unendurable. I feel as though I could spend my life making love to thee, and never work any more.

Thine ever devotedly,
Bertie

With hindsight it is easy to see a note of desperation in this letter. In October 1894, stimulated by hearing Wagner at the Paris Opera, he had written to Alys that such strong emotions no longer disturbed him, as they would have once, because he could refer them to her. His letter of 6 November was an attempt (almost the last that has been recorded) to refer the new emotions unleashed by his mystical experience to Alys. He seemed confident of success, but when a few days later Alys arrived at the Mill House, things did not go well. Her depression intensified and on a bicycle ride to Newmarket her reserve broke and she expressed her misery for the first time. Bertie advised her to see a doctor, but she refused, fearing that the doctor would recommend a separation. There was still no sign on Russell's part that his affection for her had diminished. If it had, neither of them was prepared to admit it. The outburst on the way to Newmarket led to efforts to put things right. When the Cambridge term ended, Alys and Bertie spent three weeks holidaying in Nice on their own. But Alys's depression was contagious, and Bertie's year-end letter to Helen Thomas was unrelievedly gloomy.

1. The maid at Friday's Hill.

[98]

Friday's Hill
30 December 1901

My dear Helen

It was a great pleasure to hear from you, but I cannot tell you how sorry I am to hear that your recovery is so slow. It is terrible to be cut off from all activity of mind and body, especially when, as in your case, the instinct for activity remains.[1] I suppose that everything is being done to make you better, but you must be growing fearfully depressed and impatient. I do not know of any consolation to offer – except hope, which is an insult when offered by people who do not share the trouble. Since I wrote to you this time last year, the greatest part of my thoughts has been occupied almost continuously with the subject of illness; Mrs Whitehead's condition has remained a cause of anxiety. The mood in which I wrote to you last was very transient; the next day I went back to Cambridge in frost and fog, and found no cause of happiness awaiting me. Some sorrows can only be met by patience, and the reflection that life is both short and unimportant. This is a consolation not open to the Christians, and it is one which gives us a real advantage over them.

The world of mathematics, which you condemn, is really a beautiful world; it has nothing to do with life and death and human sordidness, but is eternal, cold and passionless. To me, pure mathematics is one of the highest forms of art; it has a sublimity quite special to itself, and an immense dignity derived from the fact that its world is exempt from change and time. I am quite serious in this. The only difficulty is that none but mathematicians can enter this enchanted region, and they hardly ever have a sense of beauty. And mathematics is the only thing we know of that is capable of perfection; in thinking about it we become Gods. This alone is enough to put it on a pinnacle above all other studies. If you will contrast the dignity of (say) *Samson Agonistes* with Shelley's 'I fall upon the grass, I die, I faint, I fail'[2] etc., you can conceive of mathematics as standing to Milton as Milton does to Shelley. I have come to feel a certain shame in thinking of transient things, and to regard a year spent, as this year has been, in human sympathy, as

1. Helen was in hospital more or less completely immobilized with sciatica.
2. 'Oh lift me from the grass! / I die! I faint! I fail!', 'The Indian Serenade', ll. 17–18. It is significant that Russell should choose Milton's *Samson Agonistes* for a comparison. Many of the themes of Milton's tragedy – resignation in the face of fate, moral regeneration from despair, and a life's purpose which entails the destruction of the life – are frequent themes of Russell's more personal writings of the next few years.

something weak and slightly contemptible. But the life of pure reason remains a remote aspiration, which (fortunately, you probably think) I do not find myself attaining.

Alys and I, finding ourselves rather tired by the term's labours, went to the South of France for three weeks. We saw Avignon, Arles, and Nîmes, and moralized duly about the Popes and the Romans, the flight of time and the fall of empires. We have been home a few days, and I am working hard to get my lectures in order for next term. But I doubt whether anybody will come, now that they know what to expect! We have been reading the Gramont Memoirs,[1] the most amusing, delightful, and improper book that I have ever read. Do get it at once, unless you know it already. It tells all the details of all the intrigues in Charles the Second's court. Scandal is like things of beauty, its loveliness increases; I much prefer it two centuries old.

We have been hearing from Grace about Miss Garrett[2] and the Xmas dinner — the whole business is delicious. I wonder whether the dinner disagreed with the family as much as they did with each other — I hope not!

I am sorry this letter is not more amusing. The wind is howling, and it has been raining for 10 days, the house is empty, as Alys has gone to town, so that everything inclines to melancholy. But melancholy is on the whole a pleasant mood: 'cheerly, cheerly, she loves me dearly, and ah! she is so constant and so kind'.[3]

I hope the New Year will bring you luck, and that your next letter will give better news.

Yours affectionately,
Bertrand Russell

The gloom that had settled on Russell's personal life had not yet spread to his work. Early in the new year Russell sent Couturat details of his course on mathematical logic at Cambridge, the lectures Russell had mentioned to Helen Thomas in the previous letter. Russell's letter to Couturat contains two important announcements: The first is a clear statement of Russell's intention to show that the whole of

1. *Mémoires de la vie du Comte de Grammont* (1713). The Comte de Gramont (1621–1707), a Huguenot émigré, dictated his memoirs to Anthony Hamilton. It's not clear whether Russell read the original French, which is a prose masterpiece, or the English translation, which is indifferent despite the help of Walter Scott.
2. Mary Garrett was a rich friend of Carey Thomas's. She was a guest for Christmas dinner at Helen's home, a prospect which Helen's family had not looked forward to. But their reasons, which Grace evidently explained to the Russells, have not been explained to us.
3. Keats, *Endymion*, bk IV, ll. 176–9.

mathematics could be deduced from purely logical principles using Peano's techniques. This doctrine, known as logicism, became the core of Russell's mature philosophy of mathematics. In the letter, Russell indicates that a good deal of progress had been made on the project. None the less, it was not until *Principia Mathematica*, published in three massive volumes in 1910–13, that a definitive statement of results was achieved – and even then, the task was unfinished, for a fourth volume on geometry was never completed.

The task was immense. However, it was not delayed so long by simple size alone, but by the fact that in May 1901 Russell had discovered that the contradictions he had discussed in his letter to Couturat the previous year (letter 92) were not so easily avoided as he had then thought. In particular, he had discovered a new contradiction which indicated that something fundamental was wrong with the logical principles upon which the logicist deduction of mathematics was based. This discovery was undoubtedly a blow, but Russell did not immediately realize how serious a one. 'Throughout the latter half of 1901', Russell wrote, 'I supposed the solution would be easy' and that 'probably there was some trivial error in the reasoning' (*Autobiography*, vol. I, p. 147). There was, however, no error in the reasoning, and the attempt to find a satisfactory solution led Russell to undertake a reappraisal of the entire foundations of logic, perhaps the most comprehensive and profound reappraisal the subject had received since Aristotle.

The other announcement in the letter was that this work was now going forward in collaboration with Whitehead and that the book which resulted would be a joint work.

A paragraph dealing with further criticisms of Russell's work on space by the French philosopher Georges Lechalas has been omitted.

[99]

[To Louis Couturat]   Friday's Hill
                                                       7 January 1902

Dear Sir,
    I am writing you to ask for some information about the *Inédits de Leibniz* that you are going to publish. Your book[1] was sent to me to be reviewed for *Mind* but I think that if the *Inédits* are going to appear soon I will do

---

1. Louis Couturat, *La Logique de Leibniz d'après des documents inédits* (1901). The reference to Couturat's '*Inédits de Leibniz*' refers to his *Opuscules et fragments inédits de Leibniz*, which did not appear until 1903. Russell's review of the former, along with Cassirer's *Leibniz' System in seinen wissenschaftlichen Grundlagen*, appeared in *Mind* (1903). He reviewed the *Inédits* in *Mind* (1904).

better to wait, since it would be better to discuss your book and the *Inédits* at the same time.

.   .   .   .

For the moment, mathematics is occupying me completely. In my course at Cambridge, I began with 22 Pp[1] of general logic (such as the syllogism)[2] and I deduced from them all of pure mathematics, including Cantor[3] and geometry, without any new Pp. or primitive concepts. All of this will appear in the book that I plan to publish with Whitehead. We could even deduce rational mechanics. Naturally the axioms are replaced by definitions; this process is the only one that would be valid for non-Euclidean geometry.[4] We would have to create the same for non-Newtonian mechanics.

I return in a week to Mill House, Grantchester, Cambridge, in order to finish my course.

I send my best wishes for you and Mme Couturat.

Bertrand Russell

Bertie and Alys returned to the Mill House as planned. Their trip to France the previous month had done little to lift Alys's depression and the return to Grantchester did much to worsen it. For a while they continued to drift apart. In January 1902 Russell made another attempt to bridge their solitudes, but by then hope was virtually dead. He recorded the event in his journal, almost a year after it happened, in the lachrymose style he adopted for such things over the next few years:

I am haunted by the memory of a day in January of this year. I walked alone through the woods. . . . Alys was ill at home; anguish lay behind, sorrow and

1. Primitive propositions, i.e. axioms. Twenty axioms for mathematics, no doubt very similar to the ones used in his lectures, are stated informally in *The Principles of Mathematics*, ch. 2.
2. That is, the proposition that if p implies q and q implies r, then p implies r.
3. That is, Cantor's transfinite arithmetic.
4. Axioms were basic unprovable propositions whose truth was assumed in the deductive system. Definitions, by contrast, were not assumed to be true since they did not presuppose the existence of the item defined. Since the various geometries, Euclidean and non-Euclidean, required different and mutually incompatible axioms, it was not possible to axiomatize them all within a single consistent system. Russell's way around this problem was to employ definitions instead of axioms for the various types of geometry. The analogous treatment of mechanics, which Russell mentions next, was never undertaken in detail, but see Whitehead's 'On Mathematical Concepts of the Material World', *Philosophical Transactions of the Royal Society* (1905).

difficulty ahead. It seemed as though winter would never end, and dimly I felt
that the springs of other years were gone for ever. But out of the snow two
pale untimely primroses raised their struggling heads, giving an earnest of
better times to come, when the sun would be warm, the air mild, and
sadness merely a poetic memory. Surely, I thought, with the flowers and the
nightingales joy too will return, again love will gladden our hearts, and discord
will be forgotten. Joy is not dead ... soon, soon, our sorrows will be over, and
she will recover the buoyant happiness that used to brighten every moment. I
took the two primroses from their bed of snow, and offered them to her as a
little token of love. Both of us were touched, deeply touched, and for a moment
hope whispered honeyed words; but in our hearts we knew they were lies, we
knew that spring was gone and youth was dead, we knew that never again
would the sun shine for us as he had shone. . . . The pathos of her life lived
in my imagination in that moment, and I longed, with an infinite tenderness,
to revivify my dying love. Almost I succeeded; but it was too late. (*Papers*,
vol. XII, p. 14)

Russell's rather self-conscious attempts at poetic elevation – themselves a symptom
of his emotional turmoil – tend to obscure what must have been a genuinely poignant
incident.

In Russell's *Autobiography* there is no attempt to explain these events; there is just
the surprisingly matter-of-fact description of the famous bicycle ride on which he
realized that he no longer loved Alys:

I went out bicycling one afternoon, and suddenly, as I was riding along a
country road, I realized that I no longer loved Alys. I had had no idea until
this moment that my love for her was even lessening. (*Autobiography*, vol. I,
p. 147)

Russell makes no other reference to the fateful bicycle ride. But we know it must
have taken place early in February 1902, for, ten years later, Russell told Ottoline
Morrell that he realized he no longer cared for Alys on 'almost the very same day'
that Ottoline married Philip Morrell. Ottoline's marriage was on 8 February 1902.
The bicycle ride, however, did not bring Russell's marriage to a speedy end. Russell
did not immediately tell Alys of what had happened, though 'of course she perceived
that something was amiss' (ibid., p. 148), and they continued to live together until
1911 and were not divorced until 1921.

Since their marriage Bertie had become the emotional centre of Alys's life –
notwithstanding her initial scepticism, her work, her demands for independence,
and the claims of her mother. The realization that he no longer loved her was

devastating – even when it was merely the perception that 'something was amiss'. In fact, Alys's perception that something was amiss seems to have gone back at least to the previous summer, but it seems not to have been until Bertie told her so in as many words, probably in June 1902, that she could bring herself to recognize that his love was dead.

Through the early months of 1902 their relationship deteriorated, until, in April, Alys was forced to seek medical help. It is not clear what precipitated this crisis: she may have had some kind of breakdown, or it may have been simply the failure of her long depression to lift. She may even have threatened suicide – Russell mentions such threats (*Autobiography*, vol. i, p. 151), but they seem to belong to a later period. Little firm information is available about their married life in the first months of 1902. Neither of them found it possible to confide in others: Russell's references to the period are the ones already cited; and Alys's diary, always intermittently kept, breaks off in July 1901 for six years. There are no letters between them until mid-April 1902, and the ones which were written then largely avoid the main issues.

Alys sought help for her depression from a friend, a Dr Boyle, who ran an establishment in Brighton specializing in rest cures. (Helen Thomas had already been a patient there.) Alys went there in mid-April intending to stay four weeks, though, in the end, she stayed much longer. The rest cure now seems an improbable expedient, more likely to promote ill-health than cure it. (Charlotte Perkins Gilman's story, 'The Yellow Wallpaper' (1892), is a chilling account of the horrors of the turn-of-the-century rest cure, in a form rather less severe than the one Alys went through.) Alys was confined to bed for most of the time (even after six weeks she was allowed to be up for only six hours a day); she was not allowed to see close friends or family who might disturb her; her activities were limited to reading and a small amount of letter-writing. Bertie's letters to her were restricted to a single sheet each day. These he dutifully wrote, offering as much affection as he could. It is hard to say whether, at this stage, his frequently repeated hopes for an improvement in their relationship were genuinely felt or disingenuous kindnesses designed to assist in her cure: quite possibly both. At all events, these daily letters, even making allowances for the length restrictions imposed by Dr Boyle, are a pale shadow of the daily letters which passed between them eight years earlier. For her part, Alys in her replies tried to put as cheerful a face on things as she could, pretending, and no doubt also in part genuinely believing, that things might return to normal once her cure was effected.

The first letter Russell sent after Alys began her cure is printed from a photocopy supplied by Camellia Investments who own the original, since the Russell Archives' copy of the letter is incomplete. Russell, himself in hardly better shape, took his own kind of cure, in a cycling holiday in Wiltshire.

[100]

County Family Hotel
Salisbury
15 April 1902

My Dearest

Thy postcard came this morning, it was some comfort. The parting was very difficult: I hardly know how we both got through it. As for me, the incidents of the ride distracted me. When I got here I was in that mood of acquiescence that physical fatigue gives. I was in bed $9\frac{1}{2}$ hours and slept between 6 and 7 of them. Today it is pouring, and I am waiting here in hopes of its clearing up. But it hardly looks as if it would.

The coast from the downs into Salisbury is one of the best I know: I did a mile in $2\frac{1}{4}$ minutes. – If the weather gets no better, I shall go by train to Marlborough. It is so wet that even with my waterproof cape I could not have gone. Fortunately, I had planned rather a short ride for today, so if it clears I can do it all after lunch. This is an excellent Hotel: even the black coffee is delicious.

Did thee see a joke in Parliament last night? A member remarked 'Sir, I represent a very dense population.' Mr Swift McNeill:[1] 'Natural Selection!'

Dearest, do try to keep up thy spirits and thy hopes. Four weeks seems an eternity, but it will be over some day, and then I do trust everything will be very different. If we could once begin an emendation, it would rapidly get better and better. Goodbye my Darling. Take care of thyself, and try not to be too unhappy.

Thine ever devotedly
  Bertie

[101]

The Mill House
20 April 1902

My Dearest

I am glad thee feels a little more cheerful, and it is nice to think that by now thee is away from the Pandemonium of little Darlings. I hope thee will keep thy spirits up in town, and that the Rest Cure will do thee real good. I am rested today, having had a good night. Grantchester suits me very well,

1. John Gordon Swift MacNeill (1849–1926), an Irish Nationalist member.

except when I have to watch its effect on thee.[1] But the fact is that I arrived here in a state just as collapsed as thine. On my tour, it was the utmost I could accomplish not to cry in public. But now I begin to feel more master of myself. I must not get so tired again if I can help it. But I feel sure that after Brighton thee will feel like a different person.

Jack[2] was here yesterday and was very witty. I said I should like to write sermons to parsons, and he said 'You might call them proud talks to mean people'. Other good things too he said, but Evelyn was disgusted with him for being so fat.

It is delicious weather, and we have the nightingale and cuckoo, the garden too is lovely. Everything is extraordinarily peaceful for this household, and Alfred is charming.

Goodbye Dearest. Let me know what Dr Boyle thinks of thee.

Thine ever devotedly,

Bertie

In view of his own exhaustion, it is surprising that in the next letter Russell announces his intention to finish what he describes as 'the big book'. This was not the collaborative effort with Whitehead that Russell had announced to Couturat at the beginning of the year, but *The Principles of Mathematics*, a book Russell had been working towards since 1893. *The Principles* was intended to be a two-volume work, and it was the first volume, a philosophical preliminary to the main task, which he intended to complete in 1902. The second volume, the planned joint work with Whitehead, was to contain a detailed proof of logicism by providing a rigorous and comprehensive derivation of mathematical results from logical principles. In the end it expanded beyond the confines of a single volume and became *Principia Mathematica*. Russell was obviously anxious to bring the philosophical preliminaries to completion quickly in order to be free to work on the mathematical proofs with Whitehead. But that he should attempt it while Alys was in Brighton probably indicates that he was finding it easier to work when she was not around – certainly, after her return, he often went away to work.

1. Alys had said that she didn't think the Whiteheads' company at Grantchester suited Bertie any better than it suited her.
2. Probably 'Jack' McTaggart.

[102]

The Mill House
30 April 1902

My Dearest

It is a comfort to be allowed to write and receive letters again daily.[1] Post-cards are simply impossible to me. I am very glad thee is not worrying about plans, as worries would keep thee from getting better as soon as thee might. But do be guided by the Dr's advice; for I am quite certain thee is not a good judge thyself of what is good for thee. I am not the least surprised myself at her ordering thee three months' rest. I am sure thee needs as much as that.

I slept seven hours last night – the best night I have had for a very long time – so I feel a good deal fitter today. I have decided that as my big book does not need very much more work to be finished, I must screw myself up to get it done while we are separated, as that will leave me freer to devote myself to thee, and will make me feel that it doesn't matter if I do get a bit tired. I cannot, in the time and in my present condition, finish it in style, but I can patch up something that will do for publication.

I am glad the massage was pleasant. I stay with Crompton[2] for Monday night, and I have decided to go back to Friday's Hill on Tuesday and only come back here on the Saturday: I am hoping to accomplish some work. Jane[3] comes to Friday's Hill for Whitsuntide, I am glad to say. I saw Mrs Shuck[burgh] yesterday: she is going to give a ball and garden party!

Thine ever devotedly
Bertie

The most important matter alluded to in the next letter is Alys's feelings of desertion. Bertie had long wanted her to seek medical advice about her depression, but she had always resisted it because she feared a doctor would recommend a separation from Bertie. Bertie had not pressed it because he feared that Alys would think the separation was what he wanted.

1. For a short period Bertie and Alys had been allowed to correspond only by postcards.
2. Crompton Llewelyn Davies (see letter 13).
3. Jane Ellen Harrison (1851–1928), a classical archaeologist and Fellow of Newnham College, Cambridge. Despite (or perhaps because of) her reputation as a formidable bluestocking, Bertie and Alys were her close friends.

[103]

Mill House
11 May 1902

My Dearest

I am very glad of thy letter yesterday, as it seems more nearly normal than anything for months past. I have been very well aware that thee thought I no longer cared for thee. But for that, I should have *insisted* on a separation in January, as it was obvious thee ought not to be here. As it was, I was almost distracted by the conflict between thy morbid feelings and the obvious fact that thee ought to go away. It *is* a comfort that thee is really better now.

Helen's[1] letter is very nice and affectionate. I *do* hope Kathleen will be available to go to Switzerland with thee.[2] She would be the ideal person. I think thee cares for affection from others more than thee realizes; I utterly disagree with Helen about people's not wanting affection.

I have not yet seen Evelyn today. When I do I will read the description.[3] I think it is exactly like me!

I am in rather a dull mood my head exclusively full of work still, and no feelings of any sort left in it. Otherwise I should have liked to write a more worthy answer to thy nice letter. But the Nature of the Variable dominates my thoughts, and must be decided today or tomorrow at an internal oecumenical Council.

Thine ever devotedly
Bertie

1. Helen Thomas.
2. Alys had plans to go to Switzerland after the rest cure, if she could find a suitable companion. The choice of companion was discussed inconclusively in a number of letters. Alys at this time was also contemplating a different plan, namely to go to Donegal to stay with Kathleen, who is otherwise unidentified (rather oddly, for someone close enough to be considered as a companion). In the end, Alys went to Switzerland with Beatrice Webb.
3. The description, which Alys had enclosed with her letter, was from a letter of Horace Walpole to Sir Horace Mann (27 May 1776) about Walpole's friend John Chute. Alys transcribed the following extract: 'His impatience seemed to proceed from his vast sense, not from his temper: he saw everything so clearly and immediately, that he could not bear a momentary contradiction from folly or defective reasoning. Sudden contempt broke out, particularly on politics. ... His truth, integrity, honour, spirit and abhorence of all dirt, confirmed his contempt; ... His possession of the quintessence of argument reduced it at once into axioms, and the clearness of his ideas struck out flashes of the brightest wit' (Walpole's *Letters*, ed. Paget Toynbee, vol. IX, pp. 367–8). Alys thought it an excellent description of Bertie and told him to ask Evelyn whether she agreed.

Even when exhausted Russell still had a prodigious capacity for work. Two weeks had been sufficient for him to write Part I of *The Principles of Mathematics*. For the remainder of the book he had drafts that were in need of rewriting, a task which he expected to accomplish quickly. As things turned out, however, less rewriting was needed than he'd anticipated and the book came to a rapid conclusion the following week – rather than in the two months he predicts in the next letter.

[104]

Friday's Hill
16 May 1902

My Dearest

I am very sorry thee is having another attack of depression. Thy letter of Wednesday is very nice in being so affectionate, but it is depressing in other ways. I have given up thinking of a fixed date when the separation will be over, and I am not surprised at the Dr's postponing Switzerland. My plans are not very settled. I mean to go back to Cambridge on Tuesday and stay a week or a fortnight: I work hard there now, and *never* sit out chatting in the garden.[1] But I find myself feeling rather lonely when the Webbs are my only society,[2] and I prefer to be where there are plenty of people to see.

I expect to have my book quite finished in another two months, if only I can keep fit and go on working hard. It will not give me any feeling of elation, merely a kind of tired relief as at the end of a very long dusty railway journey. The book will be full of imperfections, and will raise innumerable questions that I don't know how to answer. There is a great deal of good thinking in it, but the final product is not a work of art, as I had hoped it would be. I shall send it to the Press at once, as the load will not be off my mind until I cannot make further corrections.

I had two splendid nights at Bournemouth,[3] but last night again was not so good: between 5 and 6 hours. However, I am really rested now, and feel quite equal to doing my work. The worst time was just after the separation began, when I had no longer a motive for keeping up.

1. Alys had asked whether he was going to do so.
2. The Webbs were staying at Friday's Hill. They had originally intended to stay nine weeks, but ended up staying only a little over five. The purpose of the visit is not known: Sidney seems to have been frequently away in London and Bertie was often away visiting the Whiteheads.
3. It is not clear why he went to Bournemouth.

I prefer to know, if thee doesn't mind, how thee is from day to day.[1]

I believe now in what Dr Boyle says about the fat and the thin: certainly I have a quite extraordinary power of recuperation as soon as I can get sleep. Yet it *was* hard to guess that my nerves were stronger than thine.

I have no definite plans; I mean to go backwards and forwards between here and Cambridge, working in both places; until this separation is over.

When is thee going to get that £100? If thee will send me one large cheque when thee does, I will pay the bills. I have just managed to get on with cash, as I spend more at Grantchester.

Thine ever devotedly

Bertie

[105]

The Mill House
22 May 1902

My Dearest

No letter from thee, owing no doubt to the move into the country.[2] I am forging ahead with my book, and shall very soon reach the point where I shall have only more or less mechanical work to do – if only I can keep on a little longer. But I do get tired over work. I have learnt to pull myself together and make efforts which formerly I should have thought impossible; but I suppose there are limits to the process. I should like to put as a dedication to my book: 'To Moloch this Altar is dedicated by a Sacred Victim'. But I fear the mathematical public might be puzzled.

Yesterday Evelyn was out to lunch and tea. I had lunch with the children and tea with Alfred; except for a short ride, I worked all day. Nothing of interest occurred and I have had no thoughts except concerning matter and motion, which I am now working at.

Take care of thyself and be happy.

Thine devotedly

Bertie

1. Alys had suggested that she not write of her condition each day for fear of distracting him from his work.
2. On account of renovations at Brighton, Alys was moved inland to Burgess Hill on the Sussex Downs.

[106]

The Mill House
24 May 1902

My Dearest

Thee will be surprised and amused, after all my talk of two months, to hear that I finished my book yesterday. I found that a pile of old MS, which I had expected to have to re-write, required only a few additions and corrections, so I arrived at a sudden termination. I have never known or even imagined such a relief as I have been feeling. The weather suddenly turned warm, and I sat by myself in the garden. For the first time for ever so long, I saw that spring was beautiful: I have had no eyes for anything of late. Wedd[1] came out, and I enjoyed a long talk with him. He asked after thee, as he always does, with great solicitude. Although I contemplated two months, I feel now as if another day would have ended me. It is extraordinary how one collapses when one has been going on nerves: there are few feelings more complete or more delicious. Last night I slept well, which I had not done for some time. And today, with thy cheery letter, I feel happier than any time since April 14.

I am glad thee likes the country, and thee too must be feeling the comfort of having summer at last.

I have not had time to read Lucy's[2] letter to Evelyn: she is very full of social engagements, and I have been full of work. So that I have scarcely seen her of late. I wrote yesterday to R. T. Wright,[3] my aunt, and Lucy. Also at last I began to read Mrs Carlyle's letters.[4] It was very kind of thee to send such charming picture postcards to the children.

1. Nathaniel Wedd.
2. Lucy Donnelly.
3. Robert Thomas Wright (1846–1931), the secretary of the Syndics of the Cambridge University Press, to whom Russell sent the manuscript of The Principles of Mathematics.
4. This casual reference to Jane Carlyle's letters is of more significance than it seems. Alys had read the three volumes of Froude's edition at the beginning of her rest cure and had sent them on to Bertie to read. The Carlyles' marriage was unhappy and marked by virtually continuous ill-health on Jane's part, chronicled almost daily in her letters. Froude, in his edition of the letters, makes it clear that he held Thomas responsible for Jane's misery. He had, Froude implied, tyrannized over his wife, starved her of affection, and made her life a misery by his moods and petulance. It is plausible to think that Alys, who had great difficulty in speaking directly about her own marital problems, was trying to do so indirectly through Jane Carlyle's letters: she had told Bertie that she could hardly stand Carlyle after reading his wife's letters. There is no evidence, however, that Bertie took the hint.

I *hope* my book will be out in October with luck.
Thine most affectionately,
    Bertrand Russell[1]

Hard on the heels of Russell's announcement that he had finished *The Principles of Mathematics* came an announcement from Alys that Dr Boyle would allow Russell to visit her. Although Russell anticipated a full day's visit, he was allowed to see her only on Saturday afternoon. At this time there seems to have been optimism on both sides that the worst was behind them, and that regular weekly visits would thereafter be permitted.

[107]

The Mill House
2 June 1902

My Dearest
    Yes, if Dr Boyle permits it, I can come at the end of the week perfectly well, Saturday or Sunday. I am very much rested these last few days and could quite manage a short trip. I do not gather how long is permitted; but I suppose a day and two nights is the outside limit? Will Dr Boyle put me up, or shall I stay in a hotel? It will be a wonderful event to meet again after this long, long time of separation. I have been very busy all day with engagements in Cambridge and have not had a moment since thy letter came till now! We can discuss plans indefinitely when we meet, and get all sorts of things settled.[2] I do hope it will be a real help to thee, and that thee will feel things more natural and simple afterwards.
    How wonderful it is to have peace![3] The joy of it made me dizzy, and I could not help weeping for sheer relief. And now the news that we are to meet so soon is almost overwhelming.
    Thine ever devotedly
        Bertie

1. That Russell should have signed himself thus might seem ominous. But, given his distracted state of mind on finishing his book, one must beware of reading too much into it. Alys teasingly took him to task for it and Russell duly apologized, saying that it was pure absent-mindedness. They, at any rate, saw less in the slip than post-Freudians might be inclined to.
2. The plans included what Alys was to do once her rest cure came to an end. In particular, the details of her recuperative trip abroad had still to be settled and a companion for her found. They also had to settle on longer-term living arrangements, ones which would keep Alys away from the Whiteheads and Bertie away from Alys's mother, Hannah.
3. The Treaty of Vereeniging, finally ending the Boer War, was signed on 31 May 1902.

Beatrice Webb, who was still at Friday's Hill while Bertie was away at Grantchester, had by now volunteered to accompany Alys to Switzerland.

[108]

The Mill House
4 June 1902

My dear Beatrice

It is very kind of you to suggest going abroad with Alys, and I wish she would agree, but I fear that it is very unlikely. I am thankful to say I am at last to be permitted to see her for the inside of a day on Sunday, so I hope she is really getting better. When we meet, we shall of course talk over plans and get everything more or less settled, I hope.

I come home on this day week, the 11th, and then I shall not be away again till after you go, except probably a couple of days at Pembroke Lodge with my Aunt Agatha at some convenient time.[1] I am very much flattered that you should be looking forward to getting me back, but it is superfluous to be jealous of Mrs Whitehead! The May Term here is a perpetual round of social functions, occupying all the time of any woman who does not want to be out of everything; but I have been in no mood for garden parties, and Balls and such nonsenses. I often go into College to lunch and tea and dinner, and sit late in Fellows' Garden, watching the fading twilight through the willows. Since I finished my book, I have devoted myself to what you would call mental hygiene, with good results so far. Beyond reading a mathematical MS of Whitehead's,[2] I have done no work for the last fortnight, but have spent my whole days out of doors basking in the return of summer. – I am glad that your regimen leads to 5 hours a day.[3]

It will be pleasant to see Mackinder[4] when he comes.

---

1. Though Granny had died in 1898 – an event unremarked in Russell's surviving correspondence except for some business letters relating to her will – Aunt Agatha had continued in residence by royal favour, but she was now preparing for a move to Hindhead, where her brother, Rollo, still lived.
2. Possibly the manuscript for 'On Cardinal Numbers', *American Journal of Mathematics* (1902). In this case, however, Russell did more than merely read it, for he is credited as the author of section III, 'On Finite and Infinite Cardinal Numbers'.
3. Beatrice Webb frequently adopted regimens, usually in diet, for the sake of her health. This, however, seems to have been a regimen of five hours' work each day.
4. Halford J. Mackinder (1861–1947), reader in Geography at Oxford. He became the director of the London School of Economics in 1903. In her diaries Beatrice Webb

The Press here are so full of exam papers just now that they have not begun my book yet. But I have had interviews to arrange everything, and probably in a few days they will get on. Miss Whetham, your niece's sister-in-law,[1] has been staying here for a Ball in the Village. She is an agreeable person, but not wildly exciting.

Love to Sidney,

Yours ever,

Bertrand Russell

Please tell Harriet not to forward any books that came for me.

The meeting with Alys took place as planned, but it was not a success. This seems hardly surprising: a single afternoon gave little time to re-establish a relationship after such a fraught separation. The separation itself had done little to help. Alys found that Bertie had changed while she had been away (she did not say in what ways) and that it was difficult for her to adjust to his new attitudes – again, not surprisingly given the brevity of the meeting. During the meeting Alys broke down and cried, an event that alarmed and depressed Russell. But his offhand letter about indifferent topics when he returned to Cambridge could have done little to help. Indeed, the tone of his letters to Alys changes quite sharply after the meeting; as he admitted in his journal a year later, he was 'writing cold letters ... in the deliberate hope of destroying her affection' (*Papers*, vol. xii, p. 22).

[109]

Trinity College
8 June 1902

My Dearest

It was very nice to see thee again, and I hope that next time thee will be better, for thee is not well yet by any means, alas!

I found all three Davies's at Barton Street. Crompton and Theodore were agreeable as they always are. This morning I got into the crush of people

reported that Bertie thought him 'brutal', though she would only go as far as 'coarse-grained' herself (*Diaries*, vol. ii, p. 252).

1. The sister of William Dampier-Whetham (1867–1952) who had married a daughter of Lawrencina Potter, Beatrice's eldest sister.

waiting to see the King go to St Paul's,[1] which nearly made me miss my train, but I managed to get round in time.

I had a pleasant lunch with the Darwins:[2] Jane[3] was there. She cannot believe people are ever mistaken about their motives, which amused Mrs Darwin and me.

There is no news, so goodbye.

　　Thine ever devotedly,
　　　　Bertie

[110]

Trinity College
9 June 1902

My Dearest

Thy letter found me all right this morning and I was very glad to know that thy tears had not been wholly for unhappiness. It is difficult to write much about myself, as I do not know when I am away from thee what things will be suitable to thy mood. I agree that it will be better not to come next Saturday, as we have made a beginning now for thee to get better on, and it would not do to have thee upset emotionally too often. I was not too tired out by any means; when it is only one day, one can rest after it, so that no harm is done.

Jane goes to Switzerland almost at once, so I can make thy going later a reason for not going with her.

I had a pleasant evening with Trevy: Halévy[4] is up staying with McTaggart, and they came round after Hall. McTaggart thought the pain of the good no more vexing than that of the wicked – he is a true Utilitarian.

I shall have plenty of cash for wages.[5] My morning has been spent talking shop with Moore and paying bills. Now I am going back to Moore's to

1. Preparations were under way for the coronation of Edward VII planned for 26 June.
2. The family of Frank Darwin (1848–1925), Charles Darwin's son and biographer and himself a noted naturalist. He taught botany at Cambridge.
3. Jane Harrison (see letter 102).
4. The French historian Élie Halévy (1871–1937). Halévy had already published a history of the tradition of philosophic radicalism that Russell's parents had been part of, and he was now engaged in a massive work on British history in the nineteenth century that he never lived to complete.
5. The Russells seem to have been rather hard up at this time, their capital depleted though by no means exhausted. Money is referred to in a number of letters; on this occasion it is servants' wages that have to be paid.

lunch. I hope thee will have enjoyed seeing the Sidney Buxtons.[1] This pen is atrocious.

Thine ever devotedly
Bertie

While writing these bleak and indifferent letters to Alys, Russell turned to other correspondents to express himself. The results often were not intimate, but efforts to express a philosophy of life which would do justice both to the philosophical position he had adopted since 1898 and to the mystical insight about human pain and loneliness he had experienced the previous year. A frequent recipient of such letters was Helen Thomas, who was treated to the following extraordinary essay on romanticism, as Russell struggled to gain control over the emotions that had been unleashed in his mystical experience. The letter also makes clear Russell's divergence from the system of values emphasized in Moore's *Principia Ethica*, published the following year, and re-emphasized subsequently by the Bloomsbury Group.

[111]

[Trinity College]
10 June 1902

Dear Helen

Thanks for your letter, and for your compliments. As for the 'splendid stoicism of my sentiments', you will feel less enthusiasm when you have put them in practice for a time. What one believes to the point of action soon loses its halo.

You say that Lucy regards me as a 'great romantic'. This is a rare opportunity for combining egotism with one of the great themes, so I shall treat you to an Essay, to which I shall expect a refutation in the shape of quotations from the best authorities.

Romanticism, it seems to me, is the creed of passion, the belief that the good consists in overmastering emotion, of whatever kind, the stronger the better. Hence, it is led to dwell specially upon the strongest emotions – love, hatred, rage, jealousy – with one exception: No romanticist praises fear, though this is certainly as strong as any emotion can be. The reason is that the romanticist loves emotion as an assertion of personality, of individual force, while fear expresses the exact antithesis to this, the slavery of the individual to the world. The world, in the view of romanticism, is primarily

1. Probably a branch of the Buxton family that had supported Robert and Hannah's first Evangelical forays in England.

material for the development of the individual – thus Kant is the parent of the romantic movement, and Nietzsche is its child. Its antithesis is not classicism, but Buddhism, quietism, the doctrine of submission to fate; and the hope of annihilation or absorption as the reward of virtue. This is, of course, more akin to romanticism than classicism is; but that is the nature of antitheses.

The worship of passion has, I confess, a great instinctive attraction for me, but to my reason it is utterly abhorrent. As well might one hold – as I sometimes think Wagner does – that the purpose of music is to make as much noise as possible. It is not the quantity but the quality of emotions that is important; and those that have the finest quality are often, like the best effects in literature, delicate and fugitive and evanescent, while hatred, rage and jealousy are utterly to be eschewed. 'To burn always with a hard, gem-like flame'[1] is not the purpose of life, in spite of the modern Athenians, who find the vices of antiquity more congenial than its virtues.[2] There are three classes of emotions, those that are beautiful, those that are hideous, and those that are beautiful to the possessor and hideous to every one else. The true Byronic creed glorifies the third class, and in this it is utterly mistaken.

But the fundamental error of romanticism lies in the fact, which it shares with Christianity, that it places the end of each man's life within himself – personal holiness, or personal excellence of some kind, is what is to be achieved. Leaving quite aside the whole daily mechanism of life, which must absorb most people's activity, this theory misconceives radically the purposes which should be aimed at by those who are free to choose their ends. And it is here, I think, that classicism is infinitely more in the right. There are great impersonal things – beauty and truth – which quite surpass in grandeur the attainments of those who struggle after fine feelings. Mathematics, as a form of art, is the very quintessential type of the classical spirit, cold, inhuman, and sublime. But the reflection that such beauty is cold and inhuman is already romanticism – it gives a shiver of feeling in which Self has its share. The true classical spirit loses itself in devotion to beauty, and forgets its relation to man. Human or inhuman, beauty is a source of simple and direct joy, and is not contrasted with the lot of man, but rejoiced in for its own sake. For my part, I can rarely attain to this point, and the emotion, when attained, appears to have a certain thinness as compared with the great reflections on human destiny. But I believe this to result solely from too

1. Walter Pater's characterization of success in life in *The Renaissance* (1873).
2. Perhaps a reference to then current views on the importance of the Dionysiac principle in Greek culture.

great interest in Self and its circumstances, and to be wholly of the nature of a weakness.

So Lucy's remark, however true of my instincts, is not true of my reason; but as it is instinct that usually talks and writes, the voice of reason is comparatively feeble.

I am sorry to hear you have been having a horrid time. Your 'theoretic life', in which you forget Lucy's existence, amuses me; but I don't wonder she finds it the very reverse of amusing.

I saw Alys on Saturday for the first time; she is still secluded from every one she knows well, but I was allowed the inside of a day with her. I found her less well than I had hoped, and I am still very much worried about her. But I hope Switzerland may set her up.

Affectionately yours

Bertrand Russell

With *The Principles of Mathematics* in press Russell began belatedly to study closely the works of the German logician and mathematician, Gottlob Frege (1848–1925). He had known of Frege for several years but had been frustrated in his attempts to understand his works by the idiosyncratic symbolism in which they were written. He had, in fact, little reason to think that Frege, then almost completely unknown, would turn out to be any better than innumerable other writers on mathematics and logic whose works he had read. However, in 1901 he read a review of Frege by Peano who accused him of 'unnecessary subtlety'. This led Russell to read him: 'As Peano was the most subtle logician I had at that time come across, I felt that Frege must be remarkable' (*Portraits from Memory*, p. 22).

Even so it was not until the summer of 1902 that Russell began a serious study of Frege. He found that many of the views put forward in *The Principles of Mathematics* had been anticipated by Frege – who, for example, had conceived the idea of deriving arithmetic from logic and had anticipated Russell's definition of number – while in some respects (e.g. his logical treatment of words like 'some' and 'all') Frege's work was already in advance of Russell's. Russell mentioned Frege to Couturat on 25 June 1902:

Do you know Frege, *Grundgesetze der Arithmetik*? It's a very difficult book, but I have finally succeeded in understanding it, and I found many things in it which I believed I had invented.

Although *The Principles of Mathematics* was already with the publisher, Russell resolved to add an appendix to it dealing with Frege's work.

Russell also discovered that Frege's logical system gave rise to the same contradiction that he had discovered in his own logic in May 1901. This contradiction,
now known as Russell's paradox, arose from the apparently common-sensical
assumption that any property whatever can define a class. If we consider the property
of being a class which is not a member of itself, it seems to be a property possessed
by many classes, e.g. the class of teapots is a class and not a teapot and therefore not
a member of the class of teapots. But if we consider whether this property defines
a class, the class of classes which are not members of themselves, we arrive at the
Russell paradox. Russell himself explains the paradox simply enough:

> [T]he classes that are not members of themselves . . ., it seemed, must form a
> class. I asked myself whether this class is a member of itself or not. If it is a
> member of itself, it must possess the defining property of the class, which is to
> be not a member of itself. If it is not a member of itself, it must not possess
> the defining property of the class, and must therefore be a member of itself.
> Thus each alternative leads to its opposite and there is a contradiction. (*My
> Philosophical Development*, p. 76)

The paradox is similar to the one concerning the greatest cardinal which Russell
had discussed in his letter to Couturat in January 1901, though at that time Russell
had mistakenly thought that there was a mistake in the proof. He thought the same
about his own paradox for some time, though he was sure enough about it in May
1902 to include it in *The Principles of Mathematics*, together with some cautious hints
as to how it might be resolved. While the book was in press he added a further
appendix to deal with it, though he was still not satisfied.

The solution of the paradox was absolutely crucial to the success of logicism, for
mathematics should not be derived from a logic which gave rise to contradictions.
Yet it proved extraordinarily difficult to devise a logic which would be both adequate
to mathematics and free of the paradox. In fact Russell spent much of the next six
years trying to do so. Moreover the problem is still alive in contemporary discussions
of the foundations of mathematics, for most logicians do not like the solution Russell
eventually adopted. This was the so-called ramified theory of types which eliminated
the paradoxes but at the cost of a logic of stupendous (and largely redundant)
complexity and the addition of special axioms of a highly problematic nature that
even Russell disliked.

Russell seems to have said little about his paradox in the year after its discovery,
but on finding that it could be derived in Frege's logical system he decided to write
to Frege about it. This, his first letter to Frege, has become famous. It was written
in German and is here printed in a translation by Beverly Woodward (which Russell
approved) which was first published in J. van Heijenoort (ed.), *From Frege to Gödel:*

A Source Book in Mathematical Logic, 1879–1931 (Harvard University Press, 1967). Frege replied promptly; on 25 June Russell reported to Alys:

> I have heard from Frege, a most candid letter: he says that my conundrum makes not only his Arithmetic, but all possible Arithmetics totter.

It was, indeed, a crushing problem for Frege to be faced with at the very time when he thought his life's work was essentially complete. Sixty years later, in giving van Heijenoort permission to publish the letter, Russell wrote of Frege's response:

> As I think about acts of integrity and grace, I realise that there is nothing in my experience to compare with Frege's dedication to truth. His entire life's work was on the verge of completion, ... his second volume [of the *Grundgesetze*] was about to be published, and upon finding that his fundamental assumption was in error, he responded with intellectual pleasure clearly submerging any feelings of personal disappointment.

It is worth saying something similar on Russell's behalf. He had spent five years working in almost complete isolation on the *Principles* only to find, when it had gone to press, that much of what was best and most original in it had been anticipated by Frege. Yet, even in his private correspondence, he never gave so much as a hint of any concern about his loss of priority, but only his delight at having found a thinker with similar ideas. It required an integrity beyond the call of duty to add to the *Principles* an appendix drawing attention to Frege's work and generally to do what he could to make it better known. It was, after all, Russell who made Frege's work known to philosophers, who had hitherto entirely ignored it. It is galling, therefore, that it is sometimes suggested that when Russell wrote the *Principles* he knew more of Frege's work than he admitted to and had made use of this knowledge in writing it. There is not the slightest justification for this accusation.

A postscript to the letter, giving the paradox in Peano's notation, has been omitted from the letter. It can be found in van Heijenoort's collection, where Frege's reply is also published.

[112]

[To Gottlob Frege]

Friday's Hill
16 June 1902

Dear Colleague
For a year and a half I have been acquainted with your *Grundgesetze der*

Arithmetik, but it is only now that I have been able to find the time for the thorough study I intended to make of your work. I find myself in complete agreement with you in all essentials, particularly when you reject any psychological element in logic and when you place a high value upon an ideography [*Begriffsschrift*] for the foundations of mathematics and of formal logic, which, incidentally, can hardly be distinguished. With regard to many particular questions, I find in your work discussions, distinctions, and definitions that one seeks in vain in the works of other logicians. Especially so far as function is concerned (§9 of your *Begriffsschrift*), I have been led on my own to views that are the same even in details. There is just one point where I have encountered a difficulty. You state (p. 17) that a function, too, can act as the indeterminate element. This I formerly believed, but now this view seems doubtful to me because of the following contradiction. Let w be the predicate: to be a predicate which cannot be predicated of itself. Can w be predicated of itself? From each answer its opposite follows. Therefore we must conclude that w is not a predicate. Likewise there is no class (as a totality) of those classes which, each taken as a totality, do not belong to themselves. From this I conclude that under certain circumstances a definable collection does not form a totality.

I am on the point of finishing a book on the principles of mathematics and in it I should like to discuss your work very thoroughly. I already have your books or shall buy them soon, but I should be very grateful to you if you could send me reprints of your articles in various periodicals. In case this should be impossible, however, I will obtain them from a library.

The exact treatment of logic in fundamental questions, where symbols fail, has remained very much behind; in your works I find the best I know of our time, and therefore I have permitted myself to express my deep respect to you. It is very regrettable that you have not come to publish the second volume of your *Grundgesetze*;[1] I hope that this will still be done.

Very respectfully yours,
Bertrand Russell

1. The first volume had appeared in 1893; the second was in press as Russell wrote. Russell's paradox required that an appendix be hastily added to the second volume. It began: 'Hardly anything more unfortunate can befall a scientific writer than to have one of the foundations of his edifice shaken after the work is finished. This was the position I was placed in by a letter of Mr Bertrand Russell, just when the printing of this volume was nearing its completion.'

Russell's second visit to see Alys in Brighton took place two weeks after the first; this time they were together only two and a half hours. Russell afterwards declared himself satisfied with the improvement in her health, but his letters (both to Alys and others) throughout the second half of 1902 invariably speak of Alys's improving health. Since no cumulative gain was ever reported, Alys's recuperation seems to be like one of the infinite series Russell was studying in mathematics. In fact, Alys was not getting better (though whether her health was to blame is debatable). From the time of Russell's first visit to Brighton a painful disparity appears in their correspondence between Russell's brief, offhand letters and Alys's much more affectionate ones.

It seems clear that Russell had already realized that their relationship could not return to what it had been before February 1901 (or else he had decided that he did not want it to). Alys, on her return from Brighton, was presented with a *fait accompli* to which she found the greatest difficulty adjusting. Her love, slower than Russell's to kindle, took much longer to burn out. Her letters over the next few years make painful reading as she struggles, often pathetically and always unsuccessfully, to regain Russell's affection or at least to prevent his becoming further alienated from her.

And yet, despite the *fait accompli*, they seem to have decided from the beginning that they would not divorce or even separate. With hindsight this seems clearly the wrong decision: both of them were acutely miserable for years as a result of it. It is not easy to see what their motives were. Respect for conventional propriety is unlikely as a reason: neither of them had much of it and, though divorce was then still difficult and often scandalous, there were ways of effecting a legal separation which need be neither. Alys, it seems, hoped for a long time that Russell's love would return. We know, also, that at some stage she threatened suicide if Russell left her. Russell himself may well have felt it his duty to stay for the sake of her health; it was not an obligation he found easy to bear.

Given the fact that they were not going to separate, a number of decisions had to be made for the future. The most important of these concerned where they were going to live. Russell found it quite impossible to continue in close proximity to Alys's family at Friday's Hill. Alys, likewise, found it impossible to spend part of each year with the Whiteheads. In June 1902 two plans were under discussion: the first was to move just the other side of Haslemere to Churt where Gilbert Murray lived. The other was to live in London, the 'London plan' mentioned in the next letter. Alys favoured Churt and Russell London. On either plan, it was clear that they would spend much time apart, since Russell's collaboration with Whitehead would inevitably take him frequently to Cambridge and Grantchester.

More immediately, Alys was to return to Friday's Hill from Brighton on 28 June for two days before leaving for three weeks in Switzerland with Beatrice Webb.

Meanwhile, Berenson, Mariechen and other friends and relations had joined Bertie and the Webbs to await Alys at Friday's Hill – not very much to Bertie's pleasure: the Webbs got on his nerves and the others, with the exception of Berenson, made him feel, he said, like an alien to the human race.

[113]

Friday's Hill
24 June 1902

My dearest Alys

I do not want to insist absolutely upon the London plan, and as thee says we can leave it unsettled until thy return from abroad. But I am not in the slightest degree convinced by anything in thy letter. I will let all arguments be, though, until thee gets home from Switzerland.

It is a comfort that the Dr allows thee to come on Saturday. I will see that Voller[1] meets thee.

It is nice to hear of thy going out so much: Brighton seems to be full of social life! – This warmth is perfectly delightful, but it makes the virtue of sitting indoors working a very difficult one. Yesterday I allowed myself to go out at 7.30, just to see the sunset; otherwise I have not fallen yet.

Today the invasion of Friday's Hill begins, and I shall retire into my room. I am sorry to be seeing no more of Mrs Webb, though her prompt energetic executive ways get on my nerves, and I have to make great efforts not to be aware of her table manners.

Thine devotedly,
    Bertie

On Alys's return from Switzerland, she and Bertie, following neither the Churt plan nor the London plan, rented Little Buckland, a farm house near Broadway in Worcestershire for the remainder of the summer. 'There', Russell wrote in his journal the following year, 'I felt that Mrs Webb had gone over to the other side, and I quarrelled with her' (*Papers*, vol. XII, p. 23). Indeed, she had: 'Altogether I am inclined to think that the *mental* hygiene of the husband is more at fault than that of the wife!' she wrote to Sidney at the beginning of the Swiss trip in her prompt, energetic, executive way (*Letters*, vol. II, p. 152).

Yet Beatrice Webb probably understood what was going on more clearly than anyone. Before leaving for Switzerland she wrote in her diary:

1. A servant at Friday's Hill.

It would be a sin and a shame if these two should become separated. . . . [T]hey have both erred in sacrificing themselves and each other to an altogether mistaken sense of obligation to other people. It is quite clear to me that Bertrand is going through some kind of tragedy of feeling. . . . (*Diary*, vol. II, p. 252)

She followed this with an excellent character-sketch of Bertie, making essentially the same points as those in the passage Alys had culled from Horace Walpole (letter 103), but using them to create a rather less agreeable picture:

Bertrand Russell's nature is pathetic in its subtle absoluteness: faith in an absolute logic, absolute ethic, absolute beauty, and all of the most refined and rarefied type. His abstract and revolutionary methods of thought and the uncompromising way in which he applies these frightens me for his future and the future of those who love him or whom he loves. Compromise, mitigation, mixed motive, phases of health of body and mind, qualified statements, uncertain feelings, all seem unknown to him. A proposition must be either true or false, a character good or bad, a person loving or unloving, truth speaking or lying. And this last year he has grown up quite suddenly from an intellectual boy into a masterful man struggling painfully with his own nature and rival notions of duty and obligation. His hatred of giving pain and his self-centred will, I think, will save him from the disaster of doing what he would feel afterwards to have been wrong. (*Diary*, vol. II, pp. 252–3)

Unfortunately, Bertie's sense of duty was not always very helpful as far as Alys was concerned. He wrote in his journal: 'I realized [at Little Buckland] that Alys's love must not be killed, and that her virtue must be my care, probably for ever; and day by day the inspiration left me, and the long task claimed me. But still, often, I said cruel things that stabbed her, and I felt dimly that only what gives pleasure is wrong, but what gives pain is always either right or at least pardonable' (*Papers*, vol. XII, p. 23). It is hard to see what could provide a rationale for these bizarre reflections. Evidently Russell had convinced himself that Alys was in need of moral reformation – his journal contains several references to her insincerity, for example – a task which he felt it his duty to undertake. It seems not to have occurred to him that much that he complained of in Alys, especially the insincerity, was in part the result of his own attitude toward her, and that, even if the need for reform were real, he had ceased to be the person to bring it about. In a longer retrospect, he admitted in his *Autobiography* that 'in . . . revulsion I went too far, and forgot the very great virtues she did in fact possess', 'my self-righteousness at that time seems to me in retrospect repulsive' (vol. I, p. 148).

From Little Buckland the Russells moved to London, taking a six-month lease on 14 Cheyne Walk in Chelsea. Alys moved in early in September while Russell went back to Cambridge to work with Whitehead. In fact, his days were spent at Grantchester, but he spent the nights at Trinity College since the ceiling of the bedroom he had at the Mill House had fallen in.

[114]

Trinity College
14 September 1902

My dear Alys

I found thy letter of Friday when I got out to the Mill House yesterday morning, and I am hoping to find one of yesterday today. I have ordered *Tristan et Iseult*.[1] Yes, I am quite fit and cheerful, though the associations of College, of these rooms especially, are so strong with recent pain that an effort of will is required to shake them off. I believe, however, and I am sure thee would be better if thee could believe, that by deliberate courage it is possible to be happy in a kind of way whatever one's circumstances may be, and even to sympathize with the sorrows of others without losing the dignity of an internal serenity. But it is a hard doctrine, of which I have only very lately learned the truth; perhaps thee will find it too hard. What it requires is resignation, the feeling Christians express by 'Thy will be done', a feeling on which W. James has plenty to say.[2] To me, this feeling has become part of my habitual consciousness; I hope earnestly that it may in time become part of thine.

Alfred and I got through a lot of work yesterday. Beeton[3] came down in his motor-car, and took Evelyn and the children (except poor Tiny)[4] and me for a drive. It was as exhilarating as a sea-voyage, the swift wind destroying all possibility of thought, and I felt almost ready to sell my soul for such a narcotic.

Poor Hatty Johnson! She has quite broken down in health – the honey-

1. The famous adaptation by Joseph Bédier (1900). It was to be lent to Evelyn. Two days later Russell described it to Helen Thomas as 'exquisite, tender, beautiful' but 'strangely free from ... thought of any kind'.
2. In *The Varieties of Religious Experience* (1902).
3. The Whiteheads' wealthy friend Henry Beeton was an early motoring enthusiast. Alfred Whitehead wrote a poem in the style of Swinburne in praise of Beeton's motoring trips.
4. The Whiteheads' daughter, Jessie, then eight, who had recently had an adenoid operation.

moon was too much for her.[1] Is it not the cruellest thing thee ever heard of? I cannot bear to think of it.

I shall be glad to hear news of thy visit to Pembroke Lodge;[2] also how thee is getting on with Cheyne Walk.

Thine ever affectionately,

Bertie

Alys, not surprisingly, reacted angrily to Russell's recommending resignation. It was hard enough, she wrote, to resign herself to what she referred to as her disease and to the fact that he no longer loved her. It was harder still to accept, as he had told her at Little Buckland, that their whole marriage had been harmful to him. But she could not accept his condescending advice. She urged him in future to write only of superficial things to her.

There was also the tricky question of how she was to renew contact with the Whiteheads. Evelyn had suggested a visit to Cheyne Walk to see her, but Alys thought she could not stand a tête-à-tête with Evelyn, and suggested instead that she visit the Mill House herself. This, rather surprisingly, was greeted warmly by Bertie and the Whiteheads, though it clashed with Bertie's plans to visit Cheyne Walk to see the house. In the end Alys decided not to go.

[115]

The Mill House
17 September 1902

My dear Alys

Thy coming here will not interfere at all with my work, and I should be really glad if thee would come. But I think I will come to thee this Saturday to Monday, and thee could then come here the following Saturday to Monday. I told Alfred and Evelyn thee was hoping to come, and they were both quite delighted. Alfred is a very different person from what he was last winter, and will be, thee will find, really agreeable now. Evelyn, as thee knows, is exceedingly anxious to see thee, and would rather have thee here than make the journey to town. But she is *quite* unemotional now-a-days, witty and amusing, but not at all likely to upset thee. So thee need not fear coming. The new bedroom has such a beautiful view of meadow and wood

1. The surviving correspondence does not reveal who Hatty Johnson was.
2. Alys was planning to bicycle there for tea on Sunday, 14 September, for a last visit before Aunt Agatha moved out.

that I hope thee might really enjoy it. I should like, however, to see the new house, and thy account of my study sounds most attractive; so I will come next Saturday, and thee can come here the following one. Saturday to Monday is best, because the railway fare is less.

I am very sorry my letter upset thee and I will do my best to do nothing unnecessary to hurt thee.

The work goes on faster than I had expected, so I can easily spare two days. – If, however, Saturday week is impossible for thee, come here some earlier time, as they are anxious to have thee and it would be a pity to seem unfriendly.

The Shuck[burgh]s dine here tonight, and I dine with them tomorrow.

Thine ever devotedly
    Bertie

Russell planned to stay at the Mill House until early in October, when the Cambridge term started. Whitehead, it seemed, insisted on this for the sake of their work. But Alys's unhappiness forced Russell to leave early, as he tells Gilbert Murray.

[116]

14 Cheyne Walk
Chelsea, s.w.
29 September 1902

Dear Gilbert
    Thanks for your letter of a fortnight ago. I have been back at Friday's Hill for some days since then, but Alys was rather low at the time, and I did not like to leave her for so long as it takes to get to Churt. Besides, I thought it probable that you were too much occupied for visitors. I had been going to stay longer at Cambridge, in hopes of getting on with the work I am doing with Whitehead, but I found Alys was not really well enough, so I came back much sooner than I had intended. Since we came here, she has been very much better, and I hope Town will be a great success. I managed to get over to the Roberts's,[1] and enjoyed greatly seeing them, though to my shame I blundered into the rudeness of talking against politics – which is only one side of what I think on the subject.

1. Probably the family of Charles Roberts, a Liberal politician who had married Mary Murray's sister, Cecilia.

No, your spelling of *Berenson* is not right![1] They are leaving Friday's Hill probably at the end of this week.

I hardly dare to expect that you will be able to come and see us here any time soon, but if you are in town, remember what a great pleasure it would be to have a talk with you. This house is charming, and has a delightful view of the river and Battersea Park. At night, from my study, I see Orion rise and Saturn set, so I have most of the pleasures of the country. Though town is a very new departure, I expect to find it interesting, and on the whole not a waste of time.

Don't bother to write to us if you are busy; but if you have time, it will be a pleasure to hear from you, and I shall be glad to hear about Mary's health.

There is a spare room here in case you ever spend a night in town.

Yours ever

Bertrand Russell

If Alys rebuffed his advice of resignation in the face of sorrow, Russell was still prepared to tender it elsewhere, for example to Helen Thomas. Still unable to explain the particular nature of his troubles, he confined himself to vague and often wordy generalities about life, and virtue, and suffering. The philosophy of life he was fashioning for himself was a rather fragile stoicism which received one of its more robust public statements the following year in his famous essay, 'The Free Man's Worship'. Like many lonely people, he cultivated a rather self-conscious sensitivity to the troubles of others, in this case Helen's persistent ill-health and her despair over her life at Bryn Mawr.

[117]

14 Cheyne Walk
14 October 1902

My dear Helen

Many thanks for your letter. It is a comfort to me that you should write frankly to me of your sorrows, and I like to think that I may be useful to you in the way of encouragement; for I know that I have not always been so. You must not think that I prefer it when you write upon more irrelevant topics; indeed the very opposite is the truth: troubles and difficulties and the need of strenuous effort have made me feel more at home in a sombre

1. Murray had spelt it 'Behrensen'.

than in a gay world, and the more serious sides of life almost alone interest me now. You may reckon upon my keeping *absolutely* private anything you may wish not to have repeated; and if the expression to me of the experience which you feel that you will some day have to give to the world would be any comfort, I beg that you will not feel restrained by any scruples.

I know very well the feeling towards the young which you express, and also the complete death of private desires. It is well to learn the art of filling one's life with desires that have no reference to Self: they are more useful, less liable to lead to tragedy, and in their own nature more full of dignity and beauty. The large charity which is born of suffering is especially to be prized; and there ought to go with it an insight into people's possibilities of good, that we may inspire them to nobility by the faith that they are capable of it. We are all like lost children, crying in the night for home and love; let us be gentle with those who have not strength to bear their solitude, and let us regard our strength, not with pride, but with the feeling of a sacred duty to those still more unfortunate ones who have it not. The great gift that comes through sorrow nobly borne is wisdom, and from wisdom comes at last serenity, the peace which passeth all understanding. This peace, if we live rightly, will not be refused us at the last.

I am ashamed to say I have never read Marcus Aurelius,[1] but I am sure I should agree with you. Spinoza is a person of whom people foolishly say similar things. People seem not to know how much baffled emotion is required for austerity, how it is always the narrow door by which hunted men escape the clutches of despair. Austerity is not needed by those who do not have to struggle with all but overwhelming passions: it is the reply of the strong to the outward victory of Fate.

This place is singularly beautiful. Alone at night in my study at the top of the house, I see far below me the busy world hurrying east and west, and I feel infinitely remote from their little hopes and fears. But beyond, borne on the flowing tide of the river, the sea-gulls utter their melancholy cry, full of the infinite sadness of the sea; above, Orion and the Pleiades shine undisturbed. They are my true comrades, they speak a language that I understand, and with them I find a home: rest and peace are with the calm strength of Nature.

1. Helen, apparently like everyone else in Russell's circle of friends, was reading William James's *Varieties of Religious Experience*. She was annoyed by James's criticism of the 'coldness' of Marcus Aurelius, whose *Meditations* are a readable summary of Stoic philosophy.

Alys was not at all well until about a week ago, but now she is very much better, and I earnestly hope the improvement may last. In spite of her illness, I try to do a little work, and still more to keep alive my interests: I have been reading a good deal lately. But it is difficult, and the tax on one's energies is very great. However, if she remains better, all will be well.

Aunt Agatha has given up Pembroke Lodge. I paid her a last visit there, and it was inexpressibly sad to see the last of the old garden which I have loved almost more than if it had been a human being, to think of profane hands making it new and smart, destroying the beautiful memories of the Past which live in every part of it, and thinking nothing of all the joys and sorrows which seemed its inalienable property.

Write again whenever you can find time. Love to Lucy, though she owes me a letter; but I know she is too busy to write.

Yours affectionately,

Bertrand Russell

For Christmas Alys and Bertie visited the Berensons in Florence. They invited Gilbert Murray, but he declined, citing several weighty reasons. The Murrays' marriage was suffering its own difficulties at this time. Mary, in particular, found domestic life rather stressful. Raising children, even with the help of nurses and governesses, was a chore and a worry. She also found the household at Churt hard to manage, despite the large number of servants they employed. The help on which she depended for these household duties was provided, since Gilbert had given up his lucrative professorship at Glasgow, by the largesse of her mother. But this had its costs as well, for Lady Carlisle, a demanding and domineering woman at the best of times, used it as an excuse to interfere in her daughter's domestic arrangements. Mary, it seems, was obsessed with the health of her various charges, discovering illnesses that were undetectable to others. Gilbert, who must be counted among the charges, obliged by a continual and lifelong invalidism, generating enough mysterious symptoms to tax even Mary's diagnostic imagination.

The final straw for Mary was the birth of her fourth child, Basil, in June 1902, after which she had a breakdown. After this, she was often away in Italy or Switzerland for the sake of her health, leaving Gilbert to look after the house and the children. Gilbert seems to have taken a genuine delight in the closeness to the children that this gave him. But he seems to have felt some strain in having to become the healthy partner in the marriage. It is pleasant to record that both Mary and Gilbert, and their marriage, survived these troubles: they died within a year of each other in the mid-1950s.

[118]

14 Cheyne Walk
16 December 1902

Dear Gilbert

If I had allowed myself to dwell upon the thought of your coming with us, I should be disappointed; as it is, I see that your grounds are strong, and that it is quite impossible. I am very sorry indeed for some of your reasons, though I cannot say they surprise me. The one about the Ram is obviously of great weight![1]

I am grieved that you should be suffering from depression – it is a curse that seems to afflict all who try to live a life of the mind. The world is so full of causes of depression that one cannot always be oblivious of them all. I have been making myself a shrine, during the last 8 months, where I worship the things of beauty that I have known; and I have learnt to live in this worship even when I am outwardly occupied with things that formerly would have been unendurable to me. A private world, a world of pure contemplation, is a wonderful refuge; but it is very necessary to preserve it from pollution. Strange, the isolation in which we all live; what we call friendship is really the discovery of an isolation like our own, a secret worship of the same gods. Tonight I dined out: on one side sat a woman I did not know, shy, rather stiff, speaking so low that I could hardly hear her, whom I knew by her smile and her face to be a person I could have given a great affection to;[2] and almost the whole time I was compelled to listen to my other neighbour, a hard, vulgar, pushing adventuress,[3] who boasted of knowing Sir Francis Jeune,[4] and of his passion for indecent novels, and then assured me he was not as cynical as I was. One has to learn to make the most of the shadows that pass silently by the mouth of the cave. What a description Plato's is of the philosopher's life[5] – that he learns to know and love the sun, and then returns voluntarily to the subterranean twilight. Since I have lived here, the symbol of life has been to me the long trail of light on the river

1. Murray had given as one of his reasons that the engineers were coming to disembowel the Ram and give it a new soul. One suspects it may have been a water pump.
2. Lady Hermione Blackwood (1869–1960), daughter of the Marquess of Dufferin.
3. Géneviève Sherman, who married Henry Jeyes, an editor at the *Standard* in 1901. Russell gave an amusing account of his conversation with her in his journal (*Papers*, vol. XII, p. 16).
4. Francis Henry Jeune (1843–1905), a friend of Frank Russell's and a famous divorce-court judge.
5. In *The Republic*, bk VII.

from invisible barges that float past in the foggy night. But they ought to be beautiful ships!

Your first criticism on the Carlyle paper is quite obviously right; the other I do not wholly agree with.[1] I am glad you think the statement fair.

This letter does not seem quite the thing to cure your depression; but I doubt whether the conventional view is right, that when one is unhappy one wants cheerfulness. At least I have not found it so altogether.

Do write to me when you can do so without neglecting duties. My address will be I Tatti, Settignano, Florence.

Yours ever

Bertrand Russell

1. The Carlyles' famous house on Cheyne Row was just around the corner from the Russells' home on Cheyne Walk. It was preserved as a shrine to the Carlyles' memory and Murray had visited it with Russell the previous Saturday, 13 December. They had disagreed about the Carlyles, for Murray disapproved of both of them, and Russell had written out his views in a paper which he sent to Murray. The paper is now lost, which is unfortunate in view of the fact that Alys had seen in the Carlyles' troubled marriage some similarity to her own. What has survived are Murray's two criticisms which are intriguing enough. The first was stylistic: that Russell had used phrases like the 'peace of death', 'the healing hand of death' and 'death, her only friend' too frequently of Jane Carlyle. The second was that Russell had said that Thomas Carlyle had only understood his wife once she was dead. Murray, on the other hand, believed that Carlyle only understood the people he studied for his books and that once his wife was dead he began to study her for the same purpose. (It was Thomas Carlyle who prepared the collection of Jane's letters which Froude subsequently re-edited for publication.)

5. 'THE LONG TASK OF THOUGHT'

(1903–11)

The Christmas visit to the Berensons at I Tatti left Russell with ambiguous feelings. He was impressed by the beauty of the place – although the Berensons had not yet converted it fully into the sumptuous residence it finally became – but, as he explained to Gilbert Murray, 'the business of existing beautifully . . . always slightly shocks my Puritan soul' (*Autobiography*, vol. I, p. 162). Despite this difference of values, Russell and Berenson had got on well together. While at I Tatti Russell started to write 'The Free Man's Worship', the best of all his attempts to express the stoicism with which he felt an indifferent and meaningless universe should be confronted. He finished the essay after his return to England and wrote to Berenson about it in February.

[119]

14 Cheyne Walk
28 February 1903

Dear B.B.

After much labour, I have abandoned, at any rate for the present, the hope of writing anything of a purely imaginative kind. The intellectual habit is too imperious with me, and I cannot get it out of my instincts. So I finished the Essay I began when I was at I Tatti; it is very short, and very inferior to what it should be; but I do not expect to achieve anything better. I am convinced the Essay is the proper style for me; it is indeed the only one I can believe in while I am doing it, and all my other attempts have been utter failures, palpably so even to me. And in my heart, the whole business about Art is external to me – I believe it with my intellect, but in feeling I am a good British Philistine.

I hear you are better; I hope that is really the case.[1] My mind is very full of pleasant memories of the time at I Tatti, of cypresses and pines and views, and still more of our talks. I shall be curious to hear how you get on with

1. Berenson's health had broken down early in 1903, the result of overwork on his massive study of some three thousand drawings by the Florentine painters. As a result he had had to put off a trip to the USA planned for the spring.

Gilbert Murray.[1] I have a very great and warm affection for him, but I never expect my friends to like each other.

Alys, on the whole, has been much better lately; her factory experience gave her new interests, and was altogether most beneficial.[2]

I read the other day Sabatier's St Francis;[3] what a perfectly delightful Saint! But Sabatier seemed to me odious, patronizing, rhetorical and indecent; he is perpetually assuring one, concerning the most admirable things, that they are not so foolish as one would think; and then he is so ridiculously Protestant.

Please return my Essay when you have done with it. I do not expect any parts of it to please you except those you have already seen.

Yours ever
     Bertrand Russell

Early in the new year Russell had received news from Helen Thomas of her engagement to the American scientist Simon Flexner (1863–1946). Flexner had already made a name for himself as a bacteriologist: he had isolated the dysentery bacillus in 1900 and in 1907 he developed a serum for spinal meningitis. He was Professor of Pathology at the University of Pennsylvania, but in February 1903 it was announced that he would join the newly created Rockefeller Institute for Medical Research in New York City as director of laboratories. He played an important part in organizing the Institute, eventually becoming its director in 1920 and making it the pre-eminent centre for viral-disease research. Russell already knew of Flexner when he received Helen's news and subsequently spoke highly of him as a scientist.

The prospect of Helen's marriage and her moving to New York threw her friend, Lucy Donnelly, into virtual nervous collapse. Lucy and Helen had been inseparable since their student days and Lucy cherished hopes that they would always live together. It took considerable tact and patience on Helen and Simon's part to extricate Helen from the relationship. Bertie tried to console Lucy with letters and in the autumn she went to stay with the Russells in London.

There may also have been some embarrassment on Helen's part, at the time of

1. Murray was in Florence to study Euripides manuscripts at the Laurentian Library and, at Russell's urging, stayed for a while with the Berensons. Though Murray complained to his wife of 'this over-brilliant, exotic society here', he seems to have got on well with Berenson himself – at least for a while. See D. Wilson, Gilbert Murray (Oxford, 1987), pp. 99–102.
2. To improve her knowledge of working-class conditions Alys had disguised herself as a working girl in order to work for four days in a rope factory. She wrote an interesting account of her experiences, 'Four Days in a Factory', Contemporary Review (July 1903).
3. Paul Sabatier, Life of St Francis of Assisi (London, 1894).

her marriage, on account of Russell's romantic interest in her in 1900, which she to some extent reciprocated. This was, at any rate, an aspect of her past which she felt obliged to confess to Flexner, who seems not to have been unduly perturbed by it. For this, and other reasons, Russell's correspondence with her became more intermittent for the next few years and lost some of its former intimacy.

[120]

Churt, Farnham[1]
13 May 1903

My dear Helen

Like you in your last letter, I am writing now because I am too exhausted for work; so you must pardon dullness. All that you write about yourself is most interesting to me. It is one of the most extraordinary experiences in life to find oneself seized by one of the great emotions that unite one with the life of nature; and when the emotion is one that has come to you, the experience is full of joy, which is not so in other cases. You need not feel guilty towards Lucy. Women's friendships always have the possibility in them of being interfered with by marriage; but marriage is too desirable a thing to be foregone because of the pain it may involve. And besides, suffering which is not complicated by anybody's wrong-doing is by no means one of the greatest of evils; it is even a thing which one would rather not have been without. Still, it is hateful to be the cause of pain.

As to repaying confidence with confidence, surely I do so already: I write no franker letters than those I write to you. There is a comfort in saying out what one feels, without stopping to ask oneself if this feeling is foolish; and if one only mentions one's very sage and dignified thoughts, the effect is a person quite unlike the real one.

My book[2] is out at last. It seems to me a foolish book, and I am ashamed to think that I have spent the best part of six years upon it. Now that it is done, I can allow myself to believe that it was not worth doing – an odd luxury! But the effort of keeping up one's belief in the value of anything except human happiness is to me very great; and though it is painful to think my whole life a mistake, it is less trouble than to think the opposite.

In spite of these thoughts, I have to work at a second volume, which has

1. The Russells, having tried 'the London plan' (see letter 113) the previous winter, were now trying the Churt plan for the summer. In October they returned to London once more.
2. *The Principles of Mathematics*, published in May 1903.

been filling all my time and energy of late; when once that is done, perhaps I may be able to shake off the burden for a while.

As for the lay sermons,[1] I have hitherto written only two: doubtless they will be published in time. If I see you before that happens, I will give them to you in MS; if not, I will send you them with pleasure when the time comes. At present, I am so weary that *everything* seems to me futile; and in that mood I cannot write. But I suppose some day I shall begin to think some things less bad than others again.

Give my regards to Lucy, and write again when you can find time. Alys keeps better, and is full of activities again.

Yours affectionately,
    Bertrand Russell

Alys's renewed activities are reflected in the next letter, as are Bertie's continuing labours with mathematical logic. Their marriage had not improved over the year since Alys's rest cure, but there had been a serious attempt to work out long-term living arrangements which both sides would find bearable. Russell has been cast in a rather brutal light for his treatment of Alys over the next few years. There is certainly an indictment to answer based on Alys's evident misery and on Russell's own self-recriminations in his 'Journal'. But there is another side to the story. Russell certainly was no happier than Alys. He seems to have stayed with her out of a (possibly misguided) sense of duty occasioned by the very real fear that she would commit suicide if he left. And, in staying, he seems to have made very great efforts to do what he considered (again, possibly wrongly) to be the right thing.

The best insight into the state of his marriage in 1903 comes from the daily letters that Lucy Donnelly wrote to Helen Flexner while she was staying with the Russells during the autumn. The letters are a depressing and intimate chronicle of the daily functioning of a marriage that had failed. Lucy found Russell a changed man, he had lost his 'brilliant hardness' and 'disconcerting manner'. She found him now 'very sympathetic', though the sympathy was learned and didn't always work. After his mystical experience of 1901, Russell was making determined, though not always successful, efforts to remodel his personality; it was his capacity for sympathy rather than for brilliance that he now cared for most. Bertie's sympathy did little to lift Alys's depression. Lucy records his efforts to be kind to Alys and occasions –

1. In his previous letter to Helen Thomas, Russell had announced that in the intervals of his mathematical work he had taken to writing lay sermons in an attempt to find some consolation for his despair. The phrase 'lay sermons' is not to be taken too seriously – it derives from a book of that title that Russell's brother had published in 1902, while in gaol for bigamy. The two sermons Russell refers to are lost.

sometimes, tragically, the very same occasion – when his actions reduced her to tears. Alys did not welcome the role of invalid into which she had been cast in 1902 and in which she was now confined by Bertie's sympathy. There was no tradition of invalidism in her family, unlike Bertie's which was rife with it. Indeed, the matriarchs of the Pearsall Smith family treated invalids with something like contempt, and Alys's cherished sense of self-possession would have suffered when she found herself in this role.

But her self-regard suffered also in other ways. Russell's mystical experience in 1901 had persuaded him that human life was suffused with an unbearable loneliness which could only be alleviated by deeper and more intimate and emotionally charged relations with other people. But, from Alys, this insistence upon emotion and intimacy demanded something that was not hers to give. She was emotionally, perhaps, rather a cold woman; her relations with others were marked by benevolence rather than affection. These traits, not surprisingly, became more pronounced as her marriage deteriorated. A crippling sense of inadequacy fell upon her. Such feelings had swept her occasionally during their courtship, but now they had come to stay. They were exacerbated by the fact that Bertie could evidently find in others the sort of emotional rapport he could no longer find in her. Although the emotional rapport he found was often with women, the relationships which resulted were genuinely platonic. Undoubtedly an element of sexual attraction was present in some of them, and an element of sexual jealousy in Alys's reaction to them. But Russell said that he did not have sexual relations with any other woman until 1911 and there is not the slightest evidence to suggest that this was not the truth. The sexual aspects of Russell's friendships at this time were pretty thoroughly sublimated. But the distress they caused Alys was none the less real for all that. The fear she had expressed before their marriage seemed to her to have come horrifyingly true: Bertie, she thought, really did need a more intelligent, interesting and passionate wife.

Lucy found the new Russell wallowing in introspection and as insistent as the Ancient Mariner in confiding his miseries to her. Alys, by contrast, avoided introspection by a continuous round of meetings, committees, and speeches. Alys's resumption of her public life, while it had its uses as a distraction from misery and as a help to her battered self-confidence, imposed strains of its own, and she cannot have found it easy, in these circumstances, to keep up the gruelling round of good works to which she subjected herself. But, while Bertie waxed eloquent, and at times even mawkish, about the state of his emotions, Alys kept her feelings to herself and nothing she wrote at the time indicates the success or failure of good works as an opiate.

Logic was Bertie's opiate. The writing of *Principia Mathematica* is the constant background to all his letters written over the next few years. In scope and rigour it was a work unparalleled in the history of logic and it was all the more difficult because the contradiction which he described to Frege (in letter 112) had made it necessary to reconsider the most fundamental concepts. Had logical matters already been settled the derivation of mathematical results would have been an enormous but relatively mechanical task. The contradiction, however, made it necessary to reconsider everything from scratch. Moreover, since nothing of the kind had been attempted before, Russell and Whitehead had to forge the tools they needed for the task as they went about it. (The copy-editing alone of a manuscript which when completed ran to an estimated 6,000 pages, mostly of symbols, would have been a mind-numbing labour.) Even Frege had attempted nothing on this scale. Such work must have been an effective opiate for the hours Russell spent on it, for it could hardly have been done at all except by a mind that was totally absorbed in it.

[121]

Trinity College
26 May 1903

Dearest Alys

I am anxious to hear how thee got on at thy meeting last night, and whether thee succeeded in going through with thy speech. It must have been a trying occasion and I expect thee is very tired.

Yesterday I lunched with Dickinson, which was most agreeable. We sat in King's Fellows' Garden, and enjoyed the beauty of the world. I came back to tea with him, and then had a second tea at Mrs Ward's.[1]

Evelyn seems very well. Alfred has worked like a horse since he got my letter, and has done a lot of things that have to be considered: we have to adopt a joint policy before we can go on with the writing out of our book, and that demands discussion. We began at once yesterday, the instant he had had his tea.

I saw Moore in the evening, and discussed whether there was any difference between knowing Arithmetic and knowing one's grandmother; he thinks not. Tomorrow I lunch again with Dickinson to meet young Keynes,[2] the admirable youth who stole my book from his father. I think of asking him to pay us a visit, if I like him, as from all I hear he is a person I ought to know and talk to.

Now I must settle down to examining Alfred's notation.

Thine Affectionately

Bertie

1. Mary Ward, the wife of the philosopher, James Ward, Russell's former tutor.
2. The economist, John Maynard Keynes (1883–1946), then a mathematics student at King's College, Cambridge. His father, John Neville Keynes, was a Cambridge logician, and the book stolen was Russell's *Principles of Mathematics*.

Politics provided Russell with another distraction. For the next year Russell was much occupied with the tariff-reform controversy that had broken out in England. Since the 1850s free trade had been economic orthodoxy in Britain and was widely credited with the country's prosperity during the middle years of the nineteenth century. By the end of the century, however, faltering exports and the adoption of protection by Britain's main economic rivals, Germany and America, had called the orthodoxy into question. In May 1903 Joseph Chamberlain, the Colonial Secretary in Balfour's Conservative government, had broken with his party to advocate the so-called 'imperial preference', a system of tariff reform which would offer preferential duties within the British empire while imposing protective duties against goods imported from outside. Chamberlain appealed over the heads of his Cabinet colleagues directly to the electorate. In September he resigned from the Cabinet and undertook a major speaking tour to promote tariff reform. As a result, the Tories split on the issue, some following Chamberlain, others adopting a more moderate protectionist package known as 'retaliation'. The Liberals remained true to free trade.

Russell was ardently in favour of free trade. In July 1903 he was evidently so exercised by tariff reform that G. F. Stout thought he might abandon philosophy and enter politics. This opinion was passed on to Russell by Élie Halévy, the French historian with whom Russell had become friendly (see letter 110). Russell, however, was in no hurry to enter the public debate, feeling quite confident that Chamberlain's proposals would be rejected. Halévy, a very well-informed observer of the British scene, was less certain both that Chamberlain would be defeated and that it would be a good thing if he were. These differences led to an exchange of political views.

[122]

Churt, Farnham
19 July 1903

Dear Halévy

I am very sorry indeed, and so is my wife, not have seen you and Madame Halévy while you were in England. What you report concerning my book is most pleasing;[1] for my part, I am very dissatisfied with it, and it only remains to hope that Vol. II, in which Whitehead and I are collaborating, will contain fewer errors and fewer unsolved difficulties.

No, Stout's expectation of my going into politics in no way surprises me, though I do not intend doing so. I was brought up in the instinctive and unquestioned belief that politics was the only possible career: throughout

1. Halévy's letter is lost, so it is not known what good things were reported of *The Principles of Mathematics*.

my undergraduate time, I fully expected to go into Parliament; it was only when I got my Fellowship that I decided to stick to academic work. And since then, at intervals, especially at times of crisis, I have thought seriously of standing as a candidate. But at present my Vol. II absorbs me; I must get that done before my mind is free; and when it is done, I shall be too old and too inelastic to acquire the habits of a practical life. So politics are really out of the question. But the idiocy and blackguard cowardice of the Liberal leaders does often nearly drive me mad; and if I really thought Chamberlain had a chance, I don't know what I should do. As it is, I feel no serious doubts of his being badly beaten: the big loaf and the little loaf is such a good election cry.[1]

My wife, I am sorry to say, is not yet quite well, though she is much better.

I don't know your address, so I am sending this to Paris. I hope you will find Ireland interesting. It is a beautiful country, and the people delightful; and *you* would not feel responsible for the ruin and desolation that one sees everywhere.

Yours sincerely
B. Russell

In September Alys and Bertie took a week's holiday in Normandy with the Webbs; it turned out to be a rare interlude of domestic harmony. On their return, they continued their holiday (this time without the Webbs) with a tour of the Lake District, ending up at Naworth Castle, Lord and Lady Carlisle's other stately home, near Carlisle. From there Bertie wrote separate letters to Gilbert and Mary Murray, recently reunited after one of Mary's rest cures (see letter 118).

[123]

Naworth Castle, Carlisle
26 September 1903

My dear Gilbert
Here we are established in your ancestral home–in–law. The beauty of the place is beyond what I had expected and gives me great delight, especially

---

1. Chamberlain's opponents raised the cry that his duties would increase the price of food, a potent electoral consideration in British politics ever since the repeal of the Corn Laws in 1846.

after six weeks of hotels. Lord Carlisle is not yet here, but my Aunt Rosalind[1] is most gracious, and I feel her charm. As for the discomfort, I have not had to feel it, but Alys is going to be set to making Temperance speeches and doing her public duty.[2] I like the atmosphere of work, and the way the tourists are allowed everywhere. Altogether, I am enjoying the visit.

Alys has been quite well for a long time – the Normandy plan was most successful. I hope she will not relapse when we get back to town. As for me I have not been doing or thinking anything at all – exercise and an out-door life make my brain stop working, which is comfortable but unprofitable. In Normandy I read the Report of the Mosely Commission,[3] a most interesting document, on which one could hang many discussions as to the end of society. It seems indisputable that the American working classes are far happier and a good deal more intelligent than ours, and that this result has been obtained by devoting all the best brains of the country to the question of how to increase output. This suggests, as many other things do, an antagonism between the democratic ideal of a happy community and all the other things one cares for. Theoretically, one ought to be able first to secure the happy community, and then the other things, but practically, when a nation is prosperous, it seems to sit and stew in its own happiness, until it might as well be sunk beneath the sea. It seems to me that the philanthropist and the historian pursue opposite ideals; most of the things that make good history contain the kind of beauty that belongs to tragedy.[4] I don't know what to think, except that I feel sure your Hedonism is pig-philosophy.

We had a visit from the Webbs in Normandy and I minded them more than usual. They have a competent way of sizing up a Cathedral, and pronouncing on it with an air of authority and an evident feeling that the LCC[5] would have done it better. They take all the colour out of life and make everything one cares for turn to dust and ashes.

---

1. Rosalind Howard, Lady Carlisle, Russell's aunt and Gilbert Murray's mother-in-law.
2. Lady Carlisle was president of the British Women's Temperance Association.
3. In 1902 Sir Alfred Mosely (1855–1917) had financed a deputation of employers and trades unionists to visit the USA to study American industrial practices. Their report, published in 1903, offered conflicting advice, but generally favoured better worker education, improved working conditions, new attitudes by employers to their workers, more advertising, and more labour-saving machinery. The *Economist* approved the generally optimistic tone of the report, which concluded that Britain's industrial eclipse by America was by no means inevitable.
4. Russell offers further reflections on this theme in his essay 'On History' (*Papers*, vol. XII, pp. 76–82), written earlier in 1903.
5. London County Council.

Since then we have been in the Lakes with Miss Harrison, who was most agreeable. Mrs Frank Darwin's[1] death was a good deal of grief to her. She was a most delightful woman, for whom I had a strong affection. She had had heart disease so many years that everyone had given up thinking of her as likely to die, and at the end it was a great shock. Miss Harrison has a curious antipathy to moral sentiments, which causes always a more or less latent antagonism between her and me, and makes my liking for her less than my respect and admiration. She says she likes or dislikes people chiefly according to their behaviour to her, which is very feminine and rather a pity; but I am sure it is not wholly true.

It is a long time since I have seen you. I hope you will be in town. We get there (I believe) on the 1st – 13 Cheyne Walk. Alys heard from Mary that we might hope to see her in town soon, but I didn't gather whether you were coming too. The rest cure, it appeared, had done some good, if not much.

Give Mary my best wishes, and write when you can. We are here till Wednesday.

Yours ever

Bertrand Russell

[124]

Naworth Castle
Sunday, 26 September 1903

My dear Mary

Cecilia[2] tells me today is the end of your exile, so I want to send you my good wishes. I hope the burden of daily tasks will not oppress you as much as it did, and that you will really enjoy being home, which must be a comfort to you. I suppose we are all more apt to see the good in other people's lives than to sympathize with the evil; but it seems to me that children, in spite of all the anxieties and labours they cause, are the greatest tie to life that one can have, and give a constant visible motive for one's Ego which seems easier and more natural than any other. Don't you think what is true about Christian Science is that one ought rather to control one's emotions than one's acts. I used to think I could always act rightly by self-control, and so

---

1. Frank Darwin's wife, Ellen, had died on 1 September at the age of forty-seven. She had been a close friend of Jane Harrison's, a fellow eccentric.
2. Cecilia Howard (1869–1947), one of Lady Carlisle's daughters.

needn't mind what I felt. But that leads to a conflict which is horribly tiring, whereas if one can once get the appropriate conditions, one can act rightly with no mental fatigue, or only the unavoidable minimum.

Alys was perfectly well the whole time we were travelling, which was a great comfort. I am enjoying my visit here very much: I get on excellently with your mother, who is most kind to me.

It will be very nice to have a visit from you in town – we are both looking forward to it. Give my love to everybody, and tell Miss Bomfield I arrived here with a punctured tyre and my machine yelling for want of oil – this will give her pleasure.[1]

Yours ever,

B. Russell

Halévy had replied to Russell's letter of 19 July with a thoughtful defence of protection. The letter went unanswered for some time, prompting Halévy to write again in case he had offended Russell. Russell's reply is very characteristic in the emphasis it places on internationalism and morality in politics.

[125]

13 Cheyne Walk
3 November 1903

My dear Halévy

I am most truly sorry to have been so remiss about answering your last letter, but how could you suppose it could offend me? The fact is I have been meaning to answer it every day, and hardly any day has passed without my thinking of it. But it needed a careful answer, and my holiday came to an end soon after I got it; so that I have had difficulty in finding the leisure of mind for an answer. However, I will now do my best.

I do not deny the theory of List[2] and of most non-English economists, that protection is necessary for building up manufactures where none exist: I do not admit it, but I know too little to deny it. But we in England are not now in that position; and Germany and the United States are not in that

1. It is not known who Miss Bomfield was nor why she should take pleasure in Russell's squeaky bike.
2. Georg Friedrich List (1789–1846), the Austrian economist. He advocated tariff protection to stimulate national economic development, notably in his most important book, *The National System of Political Economy* (1841).

position. As for purely historical arguments, they cannot be applied before '46, because, where all nations were Protectionist, the Method of Difference is impossible.[1] Since then we have vastly increased our prosperity, though other nations have also done so. All the stories of our decline are statistically false: our present prosperity is quite unexampled in Europe, by every conceivable test.

As for money, I would observe (a) that foreign trade is hardly at all conducted by money, (b) that a postal order is not money,[2] (c) that with the system of bills of exchange all but a very small portion of international trade really *is* barter.

As to trading with protectionist or free trade countries, yes, I think the argument for Free Trade in England is equally strong whatever the fiscal policy of other nations. Further I gravely doubt whether we should benefit if other countries adopted Free Trade. For when one foreign nation protects a commodity which we import from another foreign nation, the duty lowers the price of that commodity in England; if France and Germany did not protect corn, the price of corn in England would be much higher than it is.

I believe that it must make a profound difference to a nation whether it is agricultural or manufacturing; but I think it impossible to decide which is preferable, for one suits the body and the other trains the mind. Also the conditions in this respect differ in different nations. In Australia the agricultural population is celibate: this seems to me a good reason for protecting manufactures. In Russia, there is hope that manufacturing may cause revolution – again an excellent reason. But in England I can see no shadow of a reason, whether economic or uneconomic.

I sympathize fully with all internationalism; and my *enthusiasm* for Free Trade is derived from this, not from economics. But what makes the case of Free Trade different from the abolition of armaments is that in many nations it suits national interests as well as the interests of the world. If we in England abolished our navy, we should be annihilated, like the Italians at the end of the 15th century;[3] and nothing would be done for internationalism. If you abolished your army, you would suffer similarly. The point is that Free Trade can be safely adopted by one nation though others avoid it: this does

1. The method of difference is one of Mill's methods of inductive inference. In the case in hand, to show that protection caused prosperity one would have to compare the prosperity of two countries alike except that one was protectionist and the other not.
2. In his letter Halévy had argued that if one were owed £1 one would rather receive cash payment (e.g. a postal order) than a live pig worth the same amount.
3. At the end of the fifteenth century Italy, after a period of unparalleled prosperity, fell victim to aggression by France, Spain and Austria.

not apply to disarmament. And as regards England, coal, cotton, and shipping would (I believe) be ruined by Protection; yet Free Trade in England is also in the interest of the world.

As for Free Trade being demonstrable yet not adopted, I reply with Leibniz: If Geometry were as much bound up with human passions as Ethics is, it would be equally controversial.[1] People are unable to see arguments when they are subject to passions – in this case, hatred of the foreigner, and the hope of a prize in the lottery.

Chamberlain is very strong, but it seems he will not win the next election, chiefly because of education, which has roused the nation far more [than] the Fiscal Issue.[2] If he lives,[3] I fear he will win the next election but one; but I hope not. I feel the issue chiefly moral, and that morally England is on trial.

Forgive my delay, and if it happens again please believe it is only due to work.

Yours very sincerely,
Bertrand Russell

Russell's comments about *The Principles of Mathematics* in his letters seem absurdly modest. The book was undoubtedly a work of genius; in some ways, the greatest thing he ever wrote. Radically new in its philosophical approach, written on a vast scale but with an attention to detail that was unmatched in previous British philosophy, and densely packed with argument, it offered not merely a new philosophy of mathematics but a new way of doing philosophy. Yet Russell had set himself impossibly high standards and his disappointment in the book was genuine. None the less the book's publication had made Russell a hard philosopher to ignore and, for those used to the older way of doing things, a harder one to understand.

Perhaps the first clear sign Russell received of his new eminence as a philosopher was a letter from F. H. Bradley (1846–1924), the most distinguished philosopher then working in Britain. Bradley was the leader of the British neo-Hegelians, the school against which Russell and Moore had reacted, and he had a reputation as a ferocious philosophical polemicist. But his letter to Russell about the *Principles*, rather unexpectedly, lacked any trace of his usual acerbity; it was even admiring. That he was not converted goes without saying and he enclosed some pages of

1. G. W. Leibniz, *New Essays on Human Understanding*, bk I, ch. II, sect. 12.
2. The Tories' Education Act of 1902 had extended public funding from the rates to church schools. This had made it extremely unpopular with nonconformists, many of whom refused to pay their rates as a result.
3. Joseph Chamberlain was sixty-seven. He still had another ten years to live, but his political career was ended in 1906 when he was paralysed by a stroke.

criticism of Part I of the book – blaming ill-health for preventing him from proceeding further with his reading. But his criticisms were unfailingly respectful and often surprisingly diffident. He was worried, in particular, that his inability to follow Russell's survey of symbolic logic in Chapter 2 of the *Principles* had impaired his ability to understand the rest of the work. Altogether, it was a handsome letter for Bradley to write to a philosophical opponent.

Bradley had once been Russell's philosophical hero, and Russell, though often contemptuous of other Hegelians, always retained his respect for Bradley. Their philosophical positions, however, had become so far apart that their subsequent exchanges were less interesting than might have been expected. Arguing from radically different premisses each tended to miss the other's point. Russell was clearly delighted by Bradley's letter about the *Principles* and replied modestly, but with evident pride – though his postscript suggests, perhaps, that he was not anxious to enter into an extended debate with Bradley.

[126]

14 Cheyne Walk
11 February 1904

Dear Mr Bradley

In spite of your saying I am not to answer your letter, I am venturing to send an indication of the sort of reply which I should make to the criticisms which you have been kind enough to send me. In the book, on the whole, I avoided fundamental questions; as I say in the Preface, my premisses are simply assumed. But I hope some day, when the second volume of my present work is finished, to attempt something on the more purely philosophical side of Logic. Hitherto I have been hoping Moore would do this better than I could but I believe he contemplates going into more purely metaphysical questions.

In regard to my second Chapter, I was in a difficulty. Strictly and logically, it is hardly necessary to master it; but so many of my views are really suggested by Symbolic Logic that I believe, practically, not only it but the second volume are almost indispensable.

I am most grateful to you for letting me know how the book has struck you.

I am,
      Yours truly,
         Bertrand Russell

Please do not trouble to read my notes if you are busy with other things.

Russell's confidence that Chamberlain's tariff-reform proposals would find no favour with the electorate had been dashed by the results of three by-elections in December in which tariff-reform supporters did unexpectedly well. It would hardly be an exaggeration to say that it was one of those occasions on which Russell felt that European civilization was in danger. Free trade was a central plank of his family's liberalism, from the political heroes of his grandfather's heyday in the 1830s and '40s to the thorough political training his grandmother had given him. Free trade, according to this Whig credo, led to progress and prosperity at home and to peace abroad.

With this family tradition behind him, it is not surprising that Russell felt more was required of him than merely private opposition. In January, therefore, he launched into a public campaign against tariff reform on behalf of the Free Trade Union. From January to March 1904 he gave many (maybe as many as twenty-two) public lectures mainly in London in support of free trade – including a series of six at the New Reform Club – as well as writing a number of articles and letters to the editor on the subject. (His publications on the subject are reprinted in *Papers*, vol. XII, pp. 181–235.)

Such an expenditure of energy and thought was a useful distraction from his domestic unhappiness and the gruelling struggle with *Principia Mathematica* which went on mainly in the summers when Whitehead was free from teaching. Moreover, the free-trade campaign achieved encouraging results. Fresh by-elections in January and February brought Liberal victories and reversed the trend of support for Chamberlain. After the campaign was over Russell wrote in his diary: 'What I liked was the cooperation with such a large part of the nation in an object which I believed to be very important. The relations with other people engaged in the same work were very agreeable to me' (*Papers*, vol. XII, p. 27). Political work had its drawbacks, however. Though Russell was by now much more self-confident than when he lectured on German Social Democracy in 1896, he was not yet an easy public speaker and he found public life tiresome. In a letter to Gilbert Murray towards the end of his campaign he seemed quite downcast and was looking forward to a holiday.

[127]

14 Cheyne Walk
17 February 1904

Dear Gilbert
    I find that I shall be able to get away for a holiday any time after March 20. In case we could manage to be together, it would be delightful to me –

I am open to all parts of the earth's surface from which one can return within a month. Do you think, however, if you and Bradley[1] were planning going away together, that it would be disagreeable to him to have an addition? Especially me, whom he scarcely knows? Tell me *quite* frankly what you think, as I could easily make other plans.

The state of politics is most delightful; people seem to be looking on Protection as quite dead since Herts.[2]

Nothing of interest has happened to me lately. I feel old and rather weary; the odd process of becoming (subjectively) a personage is taking place in me; I begin to feel weighty and think pompous official thoughts on matters which the British public conceives to be important. It is a disgusting transformation, like the Prince who was turned into a frog; and it binds up one's heart in bands of iron as it did the Prince's man.[3] It makes all the things of real importance seem remote and dries up one's springs of feeling strangely. I feel myself one of those absurd old gentlemen I used to wonder at, who, one knew, had thought and felt in their youth, and had acquired the respect of Society because of what they had been and because they had ceased to be so. I am glad to think I needn't bother with politics much longer. It is a most deadening occupation.

I have just finished *Martin Chuzzlewit*, being a convert to Dickens. His *America*[4] delighted me. Let me know about the holiday when you can. Love to everybody. I am longing to be near Barford[5] again.

Yours ever

Bertrand Russell

1. Andrew Cecil Bradley (1851–1935), the Shakespeare scholar and brother of the philosopher, F. H. Bradley. He had been Professor of English Literature at Glasgow while Murray was there and now was Professor of Poetry at Oxford. Bradley and Murray had been close friends since their time at Glasgow. They shared a passion for golf – a game in which Russell, so far as I know, evinced no interest.
2. In February the Liberals won St Albans, Hertfordshire, from the Tories by a narrow majority.
3. In the Grimms' fairy tale, 'The Frog-King'. When the prince is turned into a frog, his servant's heart is bound with iron lest it should burst with grief.
4. *American Notes* (1843), Dickens's relatively diplomatic record of a trip to America. In *Martin Chuzzlewit*, written about the same time, he took his revenge on the country, sending his hero there to be mortified by its provincialism and mediocrity. Dickens was one of Murray's favourite novelists, a fact he had avowed to the Berensons when he stayed at I Tatti in 1903. As a result, Mary Berenson told Alys, 'a fearful gulf opened, a dark chasm between our spirits' (Wilson, *Gilbert Murray*, p. 101). The Berensons and Logan all hated Dickens.
5. The Murrays' house in Churt.

Russell didn't go on holiday with Murray and A. C. Bradley. Instead he went on a walking holiday in Cornwall, accompanied for part of the time by Desmond MacCarthy (1877–1952), the literary critic. MacCarthy's easygoing personality, in many ways the opposite of Russell's, made him a restful companion. Russell enjoyed himself with MacCarthy, but found the time spent alone useful for sorting out his emotions.

With the spring the Russells moved again to the country, this time renting Ivy Lodge at Tilford, near Farnham and just north of Churt. In April, however, Russell returned to Cambridge to work with Whitehead during the university vacation. The work concerned the analysis of descriptions, expressed in English by phrases of the form 'the so-and-so'. A satisfactory analysis of descriptions was essential to the attempt to derive mathematics from logic but, although Russell was well pleased with the work done in April, the final solution did not emerge for another year, when it was discovered by Russell on his own.

On 9 April he wrote to Alys about the work:

We had a great day of work, morning, afternoon and evening. Even after lunch we still worked. Much of the time we sat discussing whether the present King of France is bald – it is astonishing what intricate and remote considerations can be brought to bear on this interesting question. We finally decided that he isn't, although he has no hair of his own. Experienced people will infer that he wears a wig, but this would be a mistake.

The question of whether the present King of France is bald is one of the examples Russell used when he published his final theory of descriptions in 'On Denoting' (*Mind*, 1905). It is now one of the most famous examples in classical logic.

There was even hope, a few days later, that the analysis of descriptions would solve the Russell paradox, which was still the main problem on the agenda:

Alfred and I had a happy hour yesterday, when we thought the present King of France had solved the Contradiction; but it turned out finally that the royal intellect was not quite up to that standard. However, we made a distinct advance. (Letter to Alys, 14 April)

The solution of the paradox, however, needed more heroic measures, though Russell in his *Autobiography* (vol. I, p. 152) says that the theory of descriptions was the first step towards it. Historians of philosophy have not been able to agree on how the two were connected.

[128]

Trinity College
11 April 1904

Dearest Alys

I got thy letter written on Saturday after I had posted my p.c. of this morning. I am interested by all the news it contains, and very glad that Fan Wilson had the 10s. to make life tolerable for the moment.[1] I have long meant to read George Fox's journal – it must be most interesting.[2]

I saw the Wards today – she seemed far from well. She is thinking of going to France for the late summer while he goes to St Louis as an exhibit.[3] He thinks it very doubtful whether Moore will get his fellowship.[4]

I then went on to the Verralls,[5] where I found Gilbert just arrived. Verrall, though he looked horribly ill, was in splendid form – I have never heard him wittier. His theme was the quarrels of Assyriologists.

The weather today was beautiful, and the backs are full of spring. I read Alfred's recent work, which is very good. He has been most active for some time past; I only wish my parts of the book got on equally fast.

Thee tells me nothing of thy spirits. I wish I could think they were in good order.

Thine affectionately
   Bertie

In August Russell visited his aunt, Lady Carlisle, at Castle Howard. A large number of family members, including the Murrays, were there and relations among them were not always harmonious. Writing to Lucy Donnelly on 15 August Russell had said of his aunt (*Autobiography*, vol. I, p. 174):

1. She received the money from the Sesame Club, a charity with which Alys was involved.
2. Alys was reading the journals of George Fox (1624–91), the founder of the Quakers.
3. James Ward visited the USA in the summer of 1904. He gave a public lecture at the International Congress of Arts and Sciences held in St Louis in connection with the International Exposition being held there. Later he taught for a term at Berkeley.
4. For the previous six years Moore had had a Prize Fellowship from Trinity (the same sort of fellowship that Russell had won with *An Essay on the Foundations of Geometry*). This was now coming to an end and Moore had applied for a Research Fellowship to continue at Cambridge. This application was about to be decided and Moore, as Ward expected, was not successful.
5. Arthur Woollgar Verrall (1851–1912), a Trinity classics don. A brilliant lecturer and a witty conversationalist, he subsequently became the first professor of English literature at Cambridge.

Lady Carlisle conducts conversations in a way which makes it a game of skill played for high stakes. It is always argument, in which, with consummate art, she ignores relevancy and changes the issue until she has the advantage, and then she charges down and scatters the enemy like chaff before the wind.

Russell, despite the family tensions which were at times serious, enjoyed matching wits with her.

Alys did not accompany Russell this time. There seems to have been a serious falling out between her and Lady Carlisle on the previous visit.

[129]

Castle Howard
17 August 1904

Dearest Alys

Thy letter of Monday came this morning. I am very glad thee has so much time to thyself, and I hope some of it thee uses for resting; also I am glad the girls are such a good set.[1] It must be encouraging to see that they do really improve.

Oliver and Muriel[2] went away on Monday for a few days, which made the atmosphere much less tense. The differences over politics and religion, before that, often demanded careful steering.

We had a long discussion over the relative merits of Girton and Newnham, Dorothy loftily patriotic, and her mother agreeing out of respect for my grandmother.[3] Ultimately the issue narrowed itself down to the merits of Miss Harrison, on which subject I delivered a harangue in favour of the love

1. Alys was, once more, looking after a group of factory girls. Russell had inquired about them in his previous letter.
2. Lady Carlisle's son and his wife. Oliver Howard (1875–1908) had just returned from Nigeria, where he had been an administrator. Russell described him as 'smart, thin, delicate, conventional, with a soft manner concealing an oriental cruelty and power of fury'. Russell preferred Muriel, who was equally conventional but had 'real good nature' (letter to Lucy Donnelly, 15 August 1904). Russell's references to Oliver's temper were likely not exaggerated. Elsewhere he described an occasion during his stay when Oliver, goaded by his mother's teasing, seized a bread-knife to attack her.
3. Dorothy Howard (1881–1968), Lady Carlisle's third daughter. She went to Girton College, Cambridge, which Russell's maternal grandmother, Lady Stanley, had helped to found in 1869. Russell was more closely involved with Newnham, the other women's college at Cambridge, where Jane Harrison was a don.

of learning, which Lady Carlisle has mildly chaffed me about since. The arguments are perpetually forming new alliances as the issue changes: it is more like Italian States in the Renaissance than anything else. Yesterday at dinner we got into a series of reckless opposed generalizations on men and women: Jones[1] advanced the paradox that women were not all alike, but we agreed that this position did not deserve serious consideration. We also argue about the education of children, the Boer War, and every other imaginable subject. It is of course a pure game, with no attempt to get at the truth; Lady C. is wonderfully skilful, and I enjoy her victories and my own almost equally. There is so large an audience that their suffrages always suffice to adjudge the victory.

I like Jones more and more – he is I think most admirable.

    Thine affectionately,
      Bertie

Lucy Donnelly's stay with the Russells the previous autumn had formed the basis for a deep friendship with Bertie. She had not adjusted easily to her return to the USA, especially since her friend Helen was now married and expecting a baby. Moreover, inspired no doubt by Bertie's moralizing, she found herself troubled by the problems and moral failings of those around her. She had complained of her sister's frivolity and been urged, in reply, to attempt a reform. The efforts had not been a success. Again she had been worried about the relationship between a painter and a country girl she knew. Russell waxed indignant about the behaviour of the painter who, one suspects, wanted to paint the country girl in the nude. Again, Lucy's efforts to warn the country girl or to dissuade the painter were not successful. (In this case, at least, things seem to have ended happily. Two years later, Lucy told Russell that the couple were setting sail for the artistic life in Italy. One assumes, also, that time – all too quickly – cured Lucy's sister of frivolity.)

Since his mystical experience in 1901 Russell had become quite assiduous in trying to solve other people's problems; he wrote in his diary that it had become his 'chief consolation' (Papers, vol. XII, p. 25). But Alys seems to have resented it. She thought that Russell had become unstable since the mystical experience and warned their friends against taking his advice (Papers, vol. XII, pp. 24–6). Although Russell said that in 1904 he had achieved a *modus vivendi* with Alys, it is not difficult to see traces

1. Leifchild Stratten Leif-Jones (1862–1939), first Baron Rhayader, was Lady Carlisle's private secretary. In a letter of 15 August 1904 to Lucy Donnelly Russell described him as 'an infinitely lovable man; he does everything for everybody, has sunk his own career, his own desires, the hope of a private life of any personal kind: and all [Lady Carlisle's] family take him as a matter of course'.

of paranoia emerging on both sides. Russell's efforts to solve his friends' problems did not mean that he was able to solve his own.

Moreover, Russell's incipient career as an agony aunt sometimes posed its own moral dilemmas, the abstract structure of which he explained to Lucy in the next letter. The occasion for the perplexity was quite specific and is not fully explained within the letter. In the course of his work for the Free Trade Union Russell had come to know Ivy Pretious (1881–1958), who then worked as the Union's secretary. She was twenty-five at the time and was being courted rather assiduously by Reginald McKenna, a banker and politician – the 'blackguard' Russell mentions in the letter. Russell thought her in grave danger from McKenna's advances and took it upon himself to rescue her. In the course of doing so they became very friendly, to the point where some of Russell's friends feared that Bertie, having driven off McKenna, would ruin her reputation himself by too close an association. George and Janet Trevelyan, who knew of Russell's own marital problems, resolved that Janet should warn him of the dangers and advise him not to see Ivy Pretious again nor to write to her for some time. (Evelyn Whitehead offered the same advice.) Though there is every reason to think that Russell's relationship with Ivy was entirely platonic, both Janet Trevelyan and Evelyn Whitehead were tearful that his friendship would lead Ivy to fall in love with him. Alys knew Ivy and of her friendship with Bertie and seems to have been upset by it, though she always denied that she was. Russell took the Trevelyans' advice and stuck by it, despite several letters from Ivy imploring him to see her. Everything ended well when Ivy married Charles Tennyson, the poet's son, in 1909. Further details of her relationship with Russell can be found in the autobiography of her son, Hallam Tennyson, *The Haunted Mind* (1978). Janet Trevelyan's warning evidently disturbed Russell and led to the complex moral reasoning which follows.

[130]

Ivy Lodge
Tilford, Farnham
19 September 1904

Dear Lucy

Your letter of September 2 was very pleasant to get. You are quite right to give the freshness of your mind to work, but indeed your letters do not suffer by your doing so. I think the evening is the real time for letter-writing – one's mind is only then free from its daily preoccupations. I am glad you are having an easier time at last, for indeed your first weeks in

America must have been very bad. You seem to me to have behaved absolutely rightly about your sister: one ought beforehand to give people the benefit of the doubt, but [it] is a sheer waste of force to go on if they do not respond, for then one may be sure that, if they are not hopeless, they are at any rate not amenable to oneself.

Everything that you have to say about Helen is deeply interesting to me, and I feel more than I can say for you and her and Simon.[1] I do not know enough to give any advice, and I am quite sure that your own affection will lead you right. I believe the only thing is patience, and less attempt to give principles when sympathy is desired than one would make if there were no physical cause of irritation. It is quite likely that what she feels is only an exaggeration of things that she has felt off and on for a long time; but one's retrospects are always very much coloured by one's present mood. Memory selects what fits in with the emotion of the moment, so that what were really the thoughts of a moment, dead almost before they were born, appear as the realizations of things always present but unacknowledged. I think one cannot insist very much on the unreality of people's troubles under such circumstances – one must be gentler than one would otherwise be. But of course the great difficulty is to know whether, in any degree, perfect sincerity should be sacrificed to kindness. This must depend entirely on the particular case, and one cannot make any rule.

I know very well, and like very warmly, a woman[2] who, under similar circumstances, became perfectly ungovernable and uncontrolled, and nearly drove her husband to suicide. But afterwards she pulled herself together, and recovered her usual degree of submission to circumstances. And this, I am sure, is very common. Any trouble is endurable if it has a definite end, and this one, I am convinced, will end completely.

Do let me know if any further developments occur in the situation of the country-girl and the artist. I am now and have been for some time horribly anxious about a girl[3] for whom, though I see her very seldom, I have a great deal of affection, though not, I think, a bit more than she deserves. She is in the gravest danger from a man who is simply a blackguard, but who has a great influence over her by means of his ability and strength of will. There is nothing I can do, except to exhort her on the rare occasions when

1. Lucy's letter has not survived so it is not clear what the difficulty was, although it is known that Helen was upset by her pregnancy.
2. Dora Sanger, the wife of Russell's friend C. P. Sanger. Sanger had married Dora Pease in July 1900. According to Russell, she was apt to be spiteful, but nothing can be discovered of the particular episode Russell seems to have in mind here.
3. Ivy Pretious.

the opportunity occurs. I only know what I know because I guessed her circumstances and got her to confess, and she will not let me speak to him. Such cases make me long to be a woman – one could do so much more. Almost the hardest moral problem that has ever faced me is this: I have very little chance of success unless, in the course of exhortations, I allow her to feel that I take a good deal of interest in her: yet, if I do, she is sure to think I take more than I do, and I run the risk of a harm almost as great as the one I am trying to prevent. It is most despairing, and at first it quite tired me out. I am so beset by moral problems that I hardly know how to go on from day to day, and I feel less able to give advice than to ask it. By the end of my holiday,[1] I was so worn out that I doubted if I could get any work done, and I began to fear that my mind would lose its keenness. So I thought I would take a little holiday from moral preoccupations, and act more on impulse, as most other people seem to do. I ceased almost at once to feel tired, I got very much interested in my work, and did very good work indeed with the liveliest enjoyment. But now things have occurred which have pulled me up short,[2] and shown, what I really knew quite well, that it does not do for me to get out of the habit of meticulous self-examination. As soon as I do so, I begin to live in a superficial way, liking the society of people whom I do not at bottom approve of, and giving them the impression that I like them when really I do not. When you see Miss Minturn,[3] I am sure you will find that she thinks I like her very much. Another difficulty is this: I have a good deal of charity in feeling, but absolutely none in opinion: that is to say, I try to think of people exactly as they are, and not better. The result is that there are people whom I like a good deal although I think they have faults which less critical people could not acknowledge to belong to anyone they liked. If I let such people see that I like them, I deceive them, because they cannot suppose that I think them capable of bad actions; if I let them know what I think, apart from pain, I may make them more prone to act in the way I fear. On the whole, a friendly relation seems to be impossible between a person who has a love of truth and a person who hasn't; yet that seems hard, since the love of truth is very rare. All these problems, as you will guess, arise chiefly in my relations to women. Sometimes I feel as though I ought not to know any women well; but the difficulty is that I get intimate

1. The walking holiday with Desmond MacCarthy.
2. The warnings from Janet Trevelyan and Evelyn Whitehead who, Russell said in a note added to the letter, 'combined to scold me as a philanderer'.
3. Mildred Minturn (1875–1922), a former Bryn Mawr student who was a friend of Lucy's. Russell had met her when he visited Bryn Mawr in 1896.

very quickly, and that, at least in some cases, I seem able to do good; there is also a purely selfish difficulty, which of course ought not to weigh with one, but I fear it does. And sometimes it makes me behave weakly: above all I shrink from inflicting pain, or from disappointing expectations. I never take many wrong steps, but sometimes one is enough to do a great deal of harm. Of course all such problems can be avoided by not undertaking difficult tasks which are not obviously one's business; but I shrink from that way out, though it is perhaps the right one. If you have any advice to give, give it to me and I shall be grateful. Do not think only of people I can thoroughly respect, like yourself; think of (say) Bonté Amos,[1] in great difficulties, needing help, a little fatuous, but unable to accept help unless believing it accompanied with respect and liking.

Fortunately, it has suddenly become convenient for Theodore,[2] whose plans were upset, to go to Brittany for a walking-tour with me, so I shall get away for a whole fortnight from all kinds of difficulties. It is very agreeable to look forward to: I shall get the refreshment that I got in Cornwall in the spring.

I do agree most intensely with what you say about order and system. But yet I sometimes feel that I have neglected impulse too much: I become too much of a schoolmaster and a prig, and am incapable of some very good things which more impulsive people have.

It is very interesting, the way you care for good prose: it is the way one ought to care about the thing that makes the value of one's work. It is in that way that I value certainty and system, which are, in the end, what most of my life is devoted to.

It would be great fun to do characters in the manner of La Bruyère,[3] but, though I am much flattered by your appreciation of my descriptions, I do not believe myself capable of anything sustained and deliberate.

This letter is full of Self: you will of course understand that it is very private. About the girl I mentioned, please don't answer except in general

1. The sister of Russell's friend, Maurice Amos. See letter 72.
2. Theodore Llewelyn Davies. It is not known what plans of his were upset.
3. Jean de La Bruyère (1645–96), French writer and a misanthropic moralist. His best-known work, *Caractères de Théophraste traduit du grec, avec les caractères ou les mœurs de ce siècle* (1688), included a series of brilliantly written, though embittered and deeply misanthropic, character sketches of French social types (often based on individuals), in the manner of the Greek philosopher, Theophrastus. The descriptions by Russell which Lucy Donnelly had admired occurred in his letter to her of 15 August from Castle Howard. It is published in his *Autobiography*, vol. i, pp. 173–4.

terms. Life is sometimes oppressively difficult, and it is a relief to write out one's doubts and perplexities.

My very best wishes to Helen.

Yours affectionately

Bertrand Russell

Although the Russell Archives contain a large number of letters from Whitehead concerning the writing of *Principia Mathematica*, there are only three extant letters from Russell to Whitehead. One contained a lengthy abstract of a book on projective geometry; another gave long, detailed reflections on how to incorporate some material on the theory of types into the text of *Principia*; the third is printed below. It was a letter Russell sent enclosing a logic manuscript called 'On Functions'. Whitehead left instructions that all his personal papers be destroyed after his death and his wishes seem to have been very effectively complied with. The following letter survived only because Whitehead returned it to Russell still attached to the manuscript. Though highly technical, it gives an impression of the work that passed between them week after week as *Principia* alternately progressed and stalled.

[131]

Ivy Lodge,
Tilford, Farnham
27 October 1904

My dear Alfred

I send you herewith a somewhat rambling MS, containing a mixture of rhetoric and aspiration. In my own feelings, it embodies a distinct advance: I have begun to feel the Contradiction to be obvious and just what we might have expected; also the functionality (or the reverse) of this or that complex begins to seem obvious on inspection, except in very marginal cases.

The bare bones of the matter are these

(a) $\varphi'\hat{x}$ is not a constituent of $\varphi'x$; hence
(b) $\varphi'x$ is not a function of φ and x; hence
(c) $x \varepsilon u$ is not a function of x and u, and $\hat{x}\varepsilon u^1$ is not a function of u.

The point is really that there are two senses of *function*, namely

(1) a complex of which x is to be a constituent;
(2) a dependent variable whose value is determinate when the value of x is determinate.[2]

1. Underneath this Whitehead has written: '$\hat{x}(x \varepsilon u)$'.
2. This is not indefinable, being of the form $t'f.'x$; or generally $F'(\hat{z}\varepsilon f'x)$. There are no doubt other forms, but each in turn is definable. [Russell's footnote.]

In $(\varphi) \cdot f'(x, \varphi'x, \varphi'\hat{z})$ the values of φ concerned must be such that x is a *constituent* of $\varphi'x$, i.e. *function* has the first of the above two meanings.

I wonder whether you could find a proof of any of the prop[osition]s in XLVI of my MS?[1] I do not despair of their being demonstrated, but I have failed to prove any of them in spite of many efforts.

All well here,

Yours affectionately,

B. Russell

The collapse of Chamberlain's tariff-reform campaign and the split it produced in the Tory Party dramatically changed the political situation in England. Russell's expectation that a minority Liberal government would be returned at the next election gave way to hopes that the Liberals would win outright. He was not overly optimistic, however, about what such a government would achieve, for he retained his low opinion of the Liberal leaders. In December 1905 Balfour's Conservatives resigned and the Liberals won the ensuing general election (January 1906) by a landslide. The Liberal government, which lasted into the First World War, achieved more than Russell expected, but in many respects (notably on women's suffrage and Ireland) much less than he hoped.

Halévy was less optimistic than Russell about the longer-term prospects for the British Liberal Party, which he thought would be eclipsed either by a radical anti-militarist, anti-imperialist party or, more likely, by the Conservative Party's adopting a 'German state socialist programme'. On the more limited issue of tariffs he asked Russell whether he thought that in ten to fifteen years, despite the defeat of Chamberlain's campaign, Britain would not adopt some form of protection rather for the sake of its own economy than to strengthen the empire. But if it did that, he said, surely Russell did not believe that there could be an imperial federation without preferential duties. (The idea of a federation of Britain's self-governing colonies was often talked about following the federations of Canada and Australia and expectations, now that the Boer War had ended, that South Africa would federate too.) Russell replied with the following detailed assessment of the British political scene.

1. i.e. the manuscript 'On Functions' which Russell enclosed with his letter.

[132]

4 Ralston St, s.w.
10 March 1905

Dear Halévy

Yes, I thought your book very impartial, and accurate in everything I knew about.[1]

As for the political future in England, I know nothing. But I will say what I can about your two questions.

1. Chiefly owing to the unpopularity of food-taxation,[2] the Tory party seems likely to suffer a débâcle as complete as that of 1880.[3] This happens in spite of the immense prestige with which Chamberlain started, and of the complete absence of ability on the Liberal side. I think the result of the next election on the Tory party will be to make protectionists cautious and free-traders bold, so that at the election after that protection will occupy the kind of place in the Tory programme that Home Rule occupied in the Liberal programme of 1900.[4] I think protection of manufactures alone could have been carried if Chamberlain had taken it up originally; but now, for a long time to come, Liberals will be able to persuade working-men that any protective measure really means food-taxation sooner or later. Thus Tory candidates, who after all chiefly desire to be elected, will tend to repudiate protection for a generation. It is not likely that at the end of that time there will be only one able statesman, and he a protectionist. We have also, more or less permanently, some important forces on our side: (a) Protestantism and anti-clericalism (stronger than you perhaps realize); (b) Labour: immensely strong just at present, on account of the judicial decisions against Trade

---

1. Halévy had sent Russell a copy of his book *L'Angleterre et son empire* (Paris, 1905).
2. Chamberlain had started his tariff campaign by advocating general import duties, including duties on food. But when duties on food proved unpopular he started to advocate duties on manufactured goods only. The impression that protection would bring food duties was, none the less, not easy to dispel. Food duties had been hated in Britain ever since the Corn Laws were repealed in 1846 in the wake of the Irish potato famine, when duties restricted food supplies to the benefit of corn merchants.
3. When Gladstone won a sweeping victory in the general election.
4. Irish Home Rule was a cross that the Liberal Party had borne ever since Gladstone had moved his first Home Rule bill in 1886. The Liberal Party split over the issue, the bill was defeated, and the Tories dominated British politics for the next twenty years. The failure of Gladstone's second attempt to pass Home Rule in 1893 led the Liberals to treat the issue with great caution.

Unions;[1] Land Reform, particularly Taxation of Land Values, a measure which the Liberals advocate, which is immensely popular, and (in my opinion) thoroughly sound economically.[2] I think it likely that success will attract able young men to the Liberals, as it has already attracted Winston Churchill;[3] that the Tories will come back at the next election but one, in a position analogous to that of the Liberals in 1892;[4] and that until they drop protection they will be too weak to carry out any measures of importance. Even Balfour's policy has been much discredited by the rise in the price of sugar, which is popularly attributed to the Brussels Convention.[5] Thus for the present I expect the Liberals to come in on a policy of favouring Trade Unions and Land Reforms; they will make fools of themselves, but will improve by practice; and 10 years hence, the Tories will probably not have a monopoly of ability.

2. I don't think federation without preferential duties is inconceivable. It would be on the Continent, but in England people dislike a scheme merely on the ground that it is coherent. The English nation seems to me to have three fundamental antipathies: (a) Catholicism, inherited from the 17th

1. It had been assumed that legislation in the 1870s had protected trade unions against liability for losses caused to employers as a result of strikes. In 1904, however, the courts ruled in favour of the Taff Vale Railway in a dispute with its workers over such losses. After this all political parties agreed that new legislation was needed to give the unions the protection they had been assumed to have since the 1870s. This was achieved by the Liberals early in their term with the Trade Disputes Act (1906).

2. Russell had long been an advocate of land taxes as proposed, e.g., by Henry George in *Progress and Poverty* (1879). In 1892 he had joined the English League for the Taxation of Land Values, of which Crompton Llewelyn Davies was the secretary. The League's proposal was to tax the value of land rather than buildings, with a view to shifting the burden of taxation on to the landlords. Radicals and New Liberals took up the cause as a means of financing social reforms, and land-tax reforms were included in Lloyd George's famous budget of 1909 (a fact which Russell put down to Crompton's influence). Russell himself preferred more radical measures, including the outright nationalization of land (*Autobiography*, vol. I, p. 46), but doubtless supported the taxation of land values as the strongest measure that had any prospects of getting through Parliament.

3. Churchill had left the Tory Party and joined the Liberals in 1904, mainly over the free-trade issue. He was, however, also in favour of land taxes.

4. When Gladstone, committed to the divisive policy of Home Rule, had formed his fourth and last ministry without an overall majority in the House.

5. The Brussels Convention (1902) applied Balfour's policy of 'retaliation' to sugar by imposing heavy duties on subsidized sugar. The measure, undertaken on account of Britain's sugar-producing colonies, which were being hurt by European sugar subsidies and wooed by US offers of a preferential tariff, had few domestic economic benefits (beet sugar was not produced in significant quantities in Britain, while British consumers benefited from the dumping practised by France and Germany).

century, (b) food-taxation, derived, as Balfour said, from the period 1815–46, still remembered by old men, (c) Little Englandism, acquired during Gladstone's government of 1880.[1] If the rejections of (b) and (c) are hard to reconcile, the electorate will insist on a compromise which seems to avoid both; and will reject any scheme involving either. And preferences without food-taxation are impossible. Of course preferences are also disliked as a sacrifice of autonomy, which people always find hateful. What I expect is merely a gradual development of Colonial Conferences;[2] perhaps a permanent Board composed of Agents General under the presidency of the Colonial Secretary. I expect the Cabinet to follow the advice of this Board, as far as possible, in matters affecting the Colonies; but I should be surprised at any formal constitutional step towards federation.

My private feelings are against any influence of the Colonies on our affairs. I think our Colonists are more crude, ignorant, blatant and self-assertive than we are; e.g. if we had followed the advice of Canada we should have had war with the U.S. over the Alaska Boundary[3] – an inconceivable disaster, so much so that the War Office has ceased to include defence of the Canadian frontier among the contingencies it professes to provide against. I think also that the Colonial Labour Parties, especially that of Australia, are infinitely inferior to ours, in that they have no love of liberty, and no idealism of outlook; they could not produce a man like John Burns.[4] Still, I fear they will influence us; it is to be hoped we may influence them in return.

1. 'Little Englandism' was used to describe British foreign policy under Gladstone, especially during his second ministry of 1880–85. The policy was intended to avoid colonial expansion and secure peace. It became deeply unpopular when General Gordon, charged with extricating an Anglo-Egyptian force from the Sudan in the face of an uprising, disobeyed orders and fought the rebels, gambling that London would be forced to send a relief force. One was sent, but arrived too late to save Gordon, who became yet another quixotic British war hero, while Gladstone and his Little England policy were vilified.
2. In the absence of any definite scheme for imperial federation, the leaders of the self-governing colonies had met in London at a series of Colonial Conferences (1887, 1894, 1897, 1902) to discuss imperial policy.
3. The dispute was over the boundary of the Alaska panhandle. It was submitted in 1903 to an international commission which decided very largely in America's favour. It was hardly the triumph of internationalism Russell suggests. President Roosevelt began a long tradition of American respect for international law by assuring Congress that he would accept only a favourable verdict from the commission. The British delegate, Lord Alverstone, for his part also began a long tradition by voting with the Americans.
4. John Burns (1858–1943), British labour leader and trades unionist. (See letter 44.) He became president of the Local Government Board when the Liberals took office in 1906.

I will write again if this answer is not full, or if you raise objections to it in any point.

Yours sincerely

Bertrand Russell

Since 1902 the Russells had had no permanent home, but moved frequently from one rented place to another. In 1903 Lucy Donnelly had commented to Helen Flexner on the uncared-for and unlived-in appearance of the Russells' home in Cheyne Walk, and there is no reason to suppose the other places they lived in at this time were any better. For the last two years, however, they had been making plans to change this. They had had a house designed for them by H. M. Fletcher, a relative of the Llewelyn Davieses and in 1904 had bought land on which to build it at Bagley Wood, just south of Oxford. They moved in during the spring of 1905 and it remained their permanent address until 1910. (The house is described in *Country Life* (1924) and *Homes and Gardens* (1924–5).)

Given the state of their marriage, it may seem odd that they were planning a new house. But they had no plans to separate and the move gave them a chance to make a fresh start. Bertie no doubt also thought it desirable to establish home away from Alys's mother, whom he had long since come to detest. Their married life had been mostly spent in close proximity to her and he likely thought that more distance would improve things. If so, he was sorely disappointed, for a year after they moved Hannah – by now confined to a wheelchair, but no less disagreeable to Bertie – gave up Friday's Hill and moved with Logan to Court Place on the Thames at Iffley, just across the river from Bagley Wood.

[133]

Chelsea
10 April 1905
11 p.m.

My dear Lucy

Many thanks for your letter. How can you say most men would not have patience with it? I cannot think so ill of them as to suppose they set no value on friendship; and for my part, I always get a very real happiness from your confidence.

Your letter was brought me in bed this morning, and as I read I felt it almost uncanny, it expressed so exactly the mood I have been living in lately.

It acted as a tonic, for it set me trying to think of antidotes, instead of simply indulging in depression as I had been doing. But although I have thought about it in all the intervals of my day, I have found very little that seems worth saying. I believe that when all one's usual moral devices fail, without any special and abnormal outside cause, it is generally a sign of fatigue, showing the need of a holiday, or at least of a less fatiguing daily life. It is unheroic to treat things physically when one feels them morally, but I believe often what is needed is a holiday if possible, or, if not, a tonic or more sleep or more exercise, or some simple remedy of that kind. I know, in my own case, my ordinary daily existence, even when I am not working, is exceedingly tiring, and I get periodically into a frame of mind from which I escape by a walking-tour. I think when one has a great deal of work to do and little possibility of holidays, it is important to avoid everything tiring that can be avoided; but if one's enjoyments are tiring, one has to strike a balance, since minor enjoyments are almost indispensable if one has to put up with a life which in its main lines is not what one would wish. This whole question has been occupying my thoughts a great deal lately, as I have felt that, if I am not to fail in my main work, I must somehow diminish the wear and tear from other causes. Whether you can hit upon any way of doing so in your life, I don't know; but if not, the only thing to do is to live through the bad days in the hope that they will pass, and that the zest will return. A minor plan, which I have found of some use, is to keep a few specially delightful things for the bad days: letters that one values, poems that have associations, memories one usually avoids. Also it is a good plan to relax one's rules, to read amusing novels, or do anything innocent that one's unavoidable duties leave time for. I have gradually come to admit, what is most humiliating to my pride, that more than a certain degree of strain is insupportable in the long run, and ruinous to one's efficiency. Of course if one could wholly kill the desire for happiness, many things would cease to be tiring, and one's power of work would be greatly increased. But though I have laboured hard to produce this result, I have not yet succeeded; and probably it is scarcely possible to succeed completely. I feel all this is very weak and unsatisfactory; but if I knew anything better, I should not myself be struggling with just such troubles as you describe. Life is so much longer than one realized in youth, and heroic efforts leave such years of weariness to be endured. But it is a comfort to remember the Temple of Death at the end of the dusty road, where the long task of thought is ended, and the partings and solitudes of this life oppress us no longer.

I am sorry for what you tell me about Helen's health; I do hope she will not again be seriously ill. All that you say on the question of Simon's silence strikes me as most wise. I am sorry the President worries you on the subject.[1]

Alys has been very tired and very depressed lately. Certainly London is bad for her; I think for several years at least we are not likely to take a house in town again. We shall both have to make a new start at Oxford; perhaps new surroundings and new people will make it easier to do so.

Tomorrow the *Trojan Women* is to be acted,[2] and we are going to it. The next day we both leave town, she for Oxford, I for a walking-tour with Bob Trevelyan in Somersetshire and Gloucestershire. I am looking forward to seeing Wells, which everybody says is beautiful. I shall be settled in Oxford by about the 24th, and then I shall get back to work, which for a time will solve all my problems for me.

I wonder whether you have realized how satisfactory the course of English politics has been. Chamberlain has fallen lower and lower in popular estimation, Balfour is discredited, and protection, for the present, is dead. One of Balfour's ministers having resigned, he filled his place solely by the consideration of where a by-election would be safe; yet the Liberals were victorious, and the new minister is left without a seat in the house.[3] Things have changed wonderfully in the last 15 months. Whenever the election comes, there is every reason to think the Liberals will have a sweeping majority.

What you say about my attempts at writing is most pleasant, as your appreciation always is. But at present I have neither the energy nor the faith for anything beyond my own work, in which I am helped by many years of habit.

Please write again when you can. You know how I value your letters and your friendship and your sympathy.

Yours affectionately,
    Bertrand Russell

Russell had been shaken by Janet Trevelyan's warnings about his friendship with Ivy Pretious. He had kept to his undertaking not to see her again, and his cor-

---

1. Helen was suffering from an unspecified illness, but from Lucy's letter to Russell it seems to have been Lucy who was keeping silent about it to Simon for fear of worrying him. The President is presumably Carey Thomas, the President of Bryn Mawr, but it is not clear from Lucy's letter how she had been worrying anyone. Russell's information may have come from Lucy's letters to Alys.
2. Another Euripides translation by Gilbert Murray. It was performed at the Royal Court eight times between 11 and 28 April 1905. The production was not a success.
3. Ailwyn Fellowes had resigned as Junior Lord of the Treasury. His replacement, Gerald Loder, stood for election in Brighton but was defeated by the Liberals on 5 April 1905.

respondence with her had been intermittent. The Trevelyans' fears that she would fall in love with him evidently had some foundation, for she wrote several times imploring him to meet her. Though Russell was fond of her, he felt obliged to say 'no' as tactfully as he could.

[134]

Lower Copse, Bagley Wood
6 July 1905

My Dear Ivy

Thank you for your letter; it is kind of you to want to know about me. But I am very sorry to say I do not think I ought to come and see you, although Janet has no objection. I didn't mean to give the impression that it was because I had promised her that I thought I ought not to come, but because my judgment went with what she said: Yes, of course there is no change in spirit; only a realization of things I was too much inclined to forget. One reason, which alone now seems to me sufficient, is that my wife is so much less unhappy than in town; and however much one may feel her feelings unreasonable, I still hardly feel justified in giving her so much pain unless it is for some very important and definite purpose. In town I was angry, and that clouded my judgment; I was in fact much more angry than my manner showed. But I do think the duty of common humanity does not cease because the victim protests that it is a base injury to think that she finds the torture unpleasant.

I may be over-sensitive, but I suffered a shame both outward and inward which I do not want to suffer again. All this will diminish with time. What I think myself is that it would be best I should see you first under Janet's auspices, if she thinks fit, after she and George have come back to town.

I suppose Miss Sheepshanks[1] told you I was overworked, because I spoke of a long skirt, in a fit of absent-mindedness, when I meant a short one. I am not a bit more so than I always am after I have been working some time, so you may feel quite easy in your mind about me. My life is easiest when I am at work.

1. Mary Sheepshanks (1872–1958), a graduate of Newnham College. She was in love with Theodore Llewelyn Davies, though he was not in love with her. She had met Russell as an undergraduate and they remained in touch through the Llewelyn Davieses and through various political causes they had in common, including women's suffrage and land-tax reform.

I did very wrong to let my friendship become anything you would miss, since in any case I should have seen very little of you. I have only been to town once since April.

I shall be away next Monday to Tuesday week, so don't write here during that time.

This letter is not easy to write; but I am certain I should have done wrong to write otherwise.

Yours always
   Bertrand Russell

Russell's relations with the Llewelyn Davieses were tragically changed in July 1905 when Theodore, with whom Russell had been on a walking holiday only the previous September, drowned while bathing in a pool near his parents' home. Theodore and Crompton had been especially close. They lived together in a small house on Barton Street, near Westminster Abbey, and they both loved the same woman, Meg Booth, the daughter of Charles Booth who investigated social conditions among the London poor. Meg, however, loved only Crompton – though she rejected him when he proposed to her after Theodore's death. Theodore's death devastated his family, but none more so than Crompton, whom Russell tried hard to comfort. In his *Autobiography* Russell wrote:

> Crompton, who loved his brother above everyone, suffered almost unendurably. I spent the weeks after Theodore's death with him, but it was difficult to find anything to say. The sight of his unhappiness was agonizing. Ever since, the sound of Westminster chimes has brought back to me the nights I lay awake in misery at this time. . . . Gradually Crompton recovered, but not fully until his marriage. After that, for no reason that I could understand, I saw nothing of him for many years. . . . I think that I had become so much associated with his suffering after Theodore's death, that for a long time he found my presence painful. (Vol. I, p. 58; see also the letters from Crompton, ibid., pp. 195–6)

As a result of Theodore's death Russell became the confidant of Mary Sheepshanks (mentioned in the previous letter), whose love of Theodore had gone unrecognized. There are desolate letters from her in the Russell Archives in which she says that Russell is the only person she can confide in: 'You are almost the only person who has been to see me or written to me' (see S. Oldfield, *Spinsters of This Parish*, London, 1984, p. 140).

After staying with Crompton at Barton Street, Russell went with him in August to Normandy. From there he wrote to Crompton's sister, Margaret.

[135]

Hôtel des Bains
Asnelle, Calvados
Saturday, 12 August 1905

Dear Margaret

Crompton is very well indeed here, quite wonderfully better than he was in town. He eats well and sleeps well (we share a room, but I have slept too soundly myself to know very much beyond that he goes to sleep at once when he gets to bed, and is not disturbed by my undressing; for the rest he says he sleeps soundly). He enjoys the sands and playing about with the children, who are friendly and jolly. He joins in conversation with every appearance of real interest. Altogether I am very well satisfied about him.

The life here is very idle; we stroll along the coast, or sit on the sands, sometimes talking, sometimes reading. The place is a paradise for children, of whom there are great numbers. For my taste it is too much sea-side, but I think Crompton really prefers that to greater solitude.

I feel I did not nearly succeed in telling you how very great the loss has been to me, nor how much I wish to be of any possible use to those to whom the loss is greatest. But I think you knew without my saying it.

Yours very sincerely,
Bertrand Russell

Russell's correspondence with Helen Flexner had been interrupted by her marriage, her ill-health, and by her pregnancy and the depression which came after it. The flow of letters never entirely ceased, however, and in 1906 it resumed much of its former warmth as Helen's life returned to something like an even keel.

[136]

Bagley Wood
15 March 1906

My dear Helen

Many thanks for your nice letter; I had been wondering when I should hear from you, but I was not surprised, as I heard you had not been well, and had had worries with servants etc. I am much amused by your account of the Bengal tiger.[1] Think of Welch being already so sophisticated as to enjoy sham terrors! What a product of civilization and security! The younger generation come on fast – I expect he has already seen through as many delusions as we had when we were twenty, and by the time he is 10 will settle down to cultivate his garden, like Candide. The younger generation already give me an occasional *frisson*, just such as I used to give my elders: their frankness and fearlessness and intolerance of sentiment and humbug leave me panting in the rear. I am glad it is so; but for them I should have thought I had achieved what in them takes my breath away. But as regards Welch, though no doubt he already possesses all wisdom, he is no doubt still 'provokingly close', like the baby Shelley interrogated on Magdalen Bridge.[2]

I am very glad to hear you have begun on a novel which will take years:[3] it will be a companion and a solace and a sedative to worries. There is nothing like a book for giving continuity. It is a pity Simon is overworked, and I hope he will be careful. But everybody who works at all is overworked, except me. I was surprised and pleased by what you report of my reputation at Harvard[4] – I knew I was read by Royce[5] and a young man named Huntington,[6] but I did not know any one else read me. I can't help thinking

---

1. Her son, Welch, was fascinated by the roars of a Bengal tiger in the zoo.
2. Shelley once asked a woman with a baby whom he met on Magdalen Bridge, Oxford, whether the baby could tell him anything about pre-existence. When told that the baby could not speak, Shelley insisted that it could not have 'forgotten entirely the use of speech in so short a time'. When neither woman nor child could be persuaded Shelley said to his companions: 'How provokingly close are those new-born babes! But it is not the less certain, notwithstanding the cunning attempts to conceal the truth, that all knowledge is reminiscence.' (See Thomas Jefferson Hogg, *Life of Percy Bysshe Shelley*, 1858, vol. I, pp. 239–41.)
3. She sent him a draft in 1908. It was never published.
4. Helen had reported that a Harvard psychologist who was a friend of Simon's had said that the philosophers at Harvard were very much interested in Russell's work and that he was quoted there more than any other living philosopher. Russell, with pardonable self-interest, came to regard the Harvard philosophy department as the best in the world.
5. Josiah Royce (1855–1916), Professor of Philosophy at Harvard. Although an Idealist, Royce supported Russell's work on mathematical logic. In particular, he agreed with Russell's claims in *The Principles of Mathematics* that order and relations were fundamental concepts. Russell had been told that his work had been praised by Royce in an address to the 1904 International Congress of Arts and Sciences in St Louis which Ward had attended.
6. E. V. Huntington (1874–1952), American logician and mathematician. He had already published a number of papers in logic, including a major article on transfinite arithmetic (*Annals of Mathematics*, 1905), which mentioned Russell's work. He spent almost all of his career at Harvard.

the report must have made the most of things. It is funny and pleasant how, after one has published a book, one's reputation gradually grows without needing any fresh publications for a long time.

My work all last year went extraordinarily well,[1] and I expect for the next four or five years to have a very pleasant time of it, until the book which Whitehead and I are doing jointly is finished. That will be a monument of industry which few books will surpass, though I says it as shouldn't; unfortunately it will require almost equal industry in the reader, so we do not expect a public of more than half a dozen.[2]

It is disappointing that you and Simon cannot come to England this summer, but we are looking forward to seeing Lucy. What you tell me about her is very interesting.

Give my respect to Welch, and my kind regards to Simon. Write again when you can; I shall be interested in everything concerning yourself and your affairs and your reflections.

Yours affectionately

Bertrand Russell

Russell's efforts to comfort Crompton after Theodore's death had brought him closer to the entire Llewelyn Davies family. In particular, a friendship sprang up between him and Margaret Llewelyn Davies (1861–1944). She was the only daughter among the seven children of John and Mary Llewelyn Davies. Russell had met her as an undergraduate when she visited Crompton at Cambridge, but he had not seen her again until Theodore's death. By 1906 she was the mainstay of the Women's Co-operative Guild, which she ran from an office in her father's rectory in Kirkby Lonsdale in Westmorland. She was also very active in the women's suffrage movement and Russell's direct involvement in the cause over the next few years owed much to her persuasions.

Their early letters, however, discuss broader topics. Russell had sent her a copy of his essay 'The Study of Mathematics' (written in 1902 but not published till 1907), a popular account of his mathematical Platonism as well as a homily on the value

1. The theory of descriptions which Russell published in his famous paper 'On Denoting' (*Mind*, 1905) was a major breakthrough, one of his most important contributions to philosophy. It gave Russell a new method for the treatment of philosophical problems, one which he (and many others) applied to different issues time and again in the following years.
2. Russell was right about the demands the book would make of its readers, and probably not far wrong about the number of readers. He said much later that he knew of only six people who had read the whole book (*My Philosophical Development*, p. 86).

of studying mathematics (see *Papers*, vol. XII, pp. 85–93). In sending it he had some misgivings: 'I am not quite sure but what it is a little indecent, a little lacking in reticence about things better suggested than said' (letter of 27 February). Margaret, however, replied encouragingly and Russell responded with an elegantly concise summary of his philosophy of mathematics.

[137]

Bagley Wood
26 March 1906

Dear Margaret

Thank you very much for your letter, and particularly for the poem, which is beautiful.[1] (I return it herewith.) I had hoped Crompton would have been here yesterday, but as Harry[2] came to town Crompton telegraphed that he couldn't come. I haven't seen him now for a good while, as I have not been away from here since I came back after we were abroad.

I am very glad you like my paper about mathematics. I did not mean that the objects of mathematical or other abstract thoughts *exist* outside us, still less that there is any universal or divine mind whose ideas we are reproducing when we think. What I meant to say was that the object of any abstract thought is not a thought, either of the thinker or of any one else, and does not *exist* at all, though it *is* something. Thus in mathematics a new theorem is a *discovery* in the sense that the discoverer for the first time apprehends the fact discovered, which fact has a timeless *being*, not *existence*; but it is a *creation* in the sense that the only thing that *exists* in the whole matter is the *knowledge*, not what is known, and the knowledge is created by the mathematician. All this I am afraid must seem like foolish subtlety, but I don't know how to explain myself otherwise. The main point is that the things that actually exist or have existed or will exist are only some among the things one can think of; but whatever one can think of must be something, and must be other than the thought of it. And mathematical objects are all of them among the things that don't exist. Nobody can point to a place where (say) the 5th proposition of Euclid is to be seen growing in a pot.

I don't think as ill of Santayana as you do, but I think the volume on Society is the worst, except perhaps the one on Art. The last, on Science, is

1. The poem cannot be identified. It was one of Theodore's favourites and may actually have been written by him. Margaret described it as a 'Waldstille' (literally: forest silence).
2. Probably Harry Llewelyn Davies (1866–1939), Margaret's younger brother. Possibly, Harry Fletcher, a friend of Theodore's and the Russells' architect.

the best, I think; and the first has very good things in it. But it is true he is artificial: I have been wondering if he is the truly civilized man, and suspecting it is only the northern barbarian in me that is outraged and infuriated by him. I have been reviewing his last volume in the *Speaker*; I suppose it will be out in a week or two.[1]

Nothing whatever has been occurring to me. I have sat here working, anxious in a depressing passive way about Forsyth and the Whiteheads.[2] But all that seems better now. Forsyth is mending fast, and so are Tiny and Goo. Forsyth is professor of pure mathematics, and has been a close friend of Alfred's ever since his undergraduate days. It must have been a very severe strain both for Alfred and for Evelyn. I have not seen them since it began.

Our wood is lovely, when it isn't under snow. It has been almost as cold as the sunny south, but Bagley Wood is full of spring flowers, and we walk in it with a sense of achievement, after all the labour of getting permission.

Everything of Theodore's is interesting to me, and I like to think of the joy in nature that made him love that poem.

Yours ever,
Bertrand Russell

Would you mind returning my mathematics paper when you have done with it? There is no hurry about it.

In the spring Russell went by himself to Clovelly, just west of Bideford on the Devonshire coast, for two months' intensive work on *Principia*. The reason for this was that at long last he seemed to have a solution to the paradox he had discovered in 1901. This was what he called the substitutional theory of classes and relations. Since the new theory was part of the foundation of *Principia*, the whole work had to be developed on the new basis. Over the next few months he wrote many hundreds of pages of manuscript based on the substitutional theory. On 10 May he left Clovelly to read a paper on the theory to the London Mathematical Society, returning to Clovelly a few days later and staying there until 5 June.

1. The philosopher, George Santayana, an old friend of Russell's brother (see letter 70), had just published *The Life of Reason* (1905–6) in five volumes: *Reason in Common Sense*, *Reason in Society*, *Reason in Religion*, *Reason in Art*, and *Reason in Science*. Russell's review appeared in the *Speaker* (7 April 1906). Margaret had found *The Life of Reason* artificial.
2. A. R. Forsyth, the Cambridge mathematician (see letter 95). He was seriously ill for some months in 1906. The Whiteheads' children Jessie ('Tiny') and Eric ('Goo') were also ill at the same time. (See V. Lowe, *Whitehead*, vol. I, p. 315.)

[138]

Providence House,
Clovelly, nr Bideford
22 April 1906

Dear Margaret

The delay about my paper didn't in the least matter – I only wanted to have it back some time. I have no others to send you, but if I had I should not want the 'better behaviour' you promise.

I am here immersed in work, seeing absolutely no one, and getting through a great deal. I have been for some time getting into the state of 'book-fever', and I suppose I shall get worse and worse for the next few years, till the thing is finished. As long as I have nothing to distract me, I enjoy being immersed in the book. And this place is very beautiful – I have delightful walks. But I am half shocked to find how well, for a time, I can do without human society.

I wonder how the deputation to C.B.[1] will go off. It seemed to me the Government made unmitigated fools of themselves over the Trades Disputes Bill,[2] but I was very glad they yielded to the Labour Party.

I don't think I shall become 'civilized' in Santayana's sense, as I don't wish to. I find his temperament very repulsive.

Do write when you have time. In this solitude, a letter would be specially grateful.

Yours ever,
    B. Russell

I should not feel it in the least a bother to answer any other questions I can answer about the mathematics paper.

From Clovelly he wrote an unusually untechnical letter to Louis Couturat about his work.

1. Henry Campbell-Bannerman (1836–1908), the new Liberal Prime Minister. On 19 May he received a joint deputation from the National Union of Women's Suffrage Societies and the more militant Women's Social and Political Union. See Halévy's *History of the English People in the Nineteenth Century*, vol. VI, p. 519, for an account of the meeting.
2. See letter 132. The Liberals had wavered on the key question of non-liability, though in the end the unions received the protection they had been promised.

[139]

[To Louis Couturat]   Providence House
                                                                    Clovelly
                                                              15 May 1906

Dear Sir,

I was very glad to receive a letter from you again, but I'm sorry to learn that you are tired by your course. Don't be afraid to talk in your course about things that I have passed on to you; in the first place, as you say, it will not lead to indiscretions, and then, even if it did, that would upset me very little.[1] I have retired here alone for nearly two months, in order to get through my work a little faster than usual. I still believe that my solution to the contradictions is good, but it seems to me that it needs to be extended to propositions, that is to say that the latter, like classes and relations, cannot replace ordinary entities.[2] To say, for example, that the principle of excluded middle is not red, would be to utter a nonsense, and not a truth. I will follow your advice in replying to M. Poincaré.[3] For this reason, I will not reply quickly, because I would like to get into order what I have to say about the solution of the contradictions. As regards Peano, I am completely of your opinion.[4] I intend to compare my reform to the exclusion of infinitesimals

1. Couturat was conducting a course on mathematical logic and was concerned that Russell might think he was plagiarizing ideas Russell had passed on to him in correspondence. Russell was admirably untouchy about such matters.
2. The extension of the substitutional theory to propositions was no easy matter, and, in fact, when Russell made the extension the contradiction reappeared in a new form. The discovery of the contradiction in the substitutional theory caused Russell to withdraw from publication, after it had been set in type, the paper he had read to the London Mathematical Society on 10 May. It caused him also to return to the theory of types, first suggested in *The Principles of Mathematics* but very much elaborated for *Principia Mathematica*, as a solution to the paradoxes. None the less the line of thought about propositions expressed in this letter to Couturat still appears in *Principia.*
3. Poincaré had published a general attack on mathematical logic, 'Les Mathématiques et la logique' (*Revue de métaphysique et de morale*, May 1906), paying special attention to Russell's article 'Some Difficulties in the Theory of Transfinite Numbers and Order Types' in the *Proceedings of the London Mathematical Society* (March 1906). Russell wrote a long rejoinder, 'Les Paradoxes de la logique' (*Revue de métaphysique et de morale*, September 1906). Russell's original English version, 'On "Insolubilia" and Their Solution by Symbolic Logic', was published in *Essays in Analysis* (1974). The dispute, in which many other logicians including Couturat played a part, had a significant influence in the development of the philosophy of mathematics, in that it helped to lay out the early demarcation lines between the three main philosophies of mathematics: logicism, formalism, and intuitionism.
4. Poincaré acknowledged some of Peano's achievements but denied that Peano's math-

from the differential calculus, which has not, however, ruined the work of Leibniz.[1]

I learn with great regret that you and Mme Couturat will not be coming to visit us this year. I hope that you will next year.

With my best wishes to you and Mme Couturat

Bertrand Russell

In June 1906 a second tragedy struck the Llewelyn Davieses. Margaret's brother, Arthur, a lawyer, was found to have cancer of the jaw. A minor operation in May for what was thought to be an abscessed tooth revealed the disease and in June he underwent a massive operation to remove his cheek bone and half of his upper jaw. Extreme as the operation was, it was not a success, and by September it was clear that the cancer had spread and could no longer be treated. Margaret found herself face to face with death once again and wrote despairingly to Bertie about the need for a deep submission to a mysterious fate – 'one gropes for light and help somewhere'. Russell offered what consolation he could in the next letter.

The other issue it deals with was the question of tactics in the campaign for women's suffrage. In 1905 Emmeline Pankhurst and her daughters, Christabel and Sylvia, had founded the Women's Social and Political Union, a militant organization aiming to secure women's suffrage by direct action, unlike the other groups which used only legal means. Liberal political rallies were among the early targets of the suffragettes, as the radicals came to be called to distinguish them from the moderate suffragists. Russell could not agree with their support of the Tories. But they did attract a lot of attention for the cause and that, Russell conceded, was all to the good.

[140]

Trinity College
3 November 1906

Dear Margaret

Thank you very much for your letter – I am grateful to you for it. The sense of a mystery and a hidden meaning and purpose is overwhelming in face of the fear of death, and sometimes I can't believe it is an illusion. But I think really it is only the difficulty of believing that anything important

---

ematical logic was one of them or had played any part in the others. Russell and (by now) Couturat thought that Peano's logic was his crowning achievement. Couturat had asked Russell to include a defence of Peano in his reply to Poincaré.

1. See *Essays in Analysis*, pp. 192–3.

can happen without being willed, so that one is compelled to think of material forces as working towards some intended end. But when I think there are no mysteries, I feel that that may be a very shallow view. In any case, I am not anxious any one should share it, because it seems to make things more utterly painful and baffling. And so I grow almost afraid to speak of great things, because it seems as if all I can truly say were better unsaid.

It is great relief that the anxiety is less now. I see Arthur has an article in this month's *Independent*,[1] which I haven't yet had time to read. It *is* a good thing he is able to work.

I am very much divided in my mind about the 'Suffragettes'. At first I thought they were making a mistake, but now they do seem to have really helped on public opinion. I think the prudent are glad to be able to be in favour of woman suffrage, and yet acquire an air of moderation by repudiating the extremists. And certainly everybody has been set discussing the subject.

I have come over here to attend a Newnham Council meeting[2] and to read a paper on Truth – the latter I successfully accomplished last night.[3] Work is still prospering with me, though judging from previous experience I shall probably soon get into another quagmire. Alys has been very much absorbed lately by the Bedford College Headship; I gather, however, that Acland really decides. Man proposes. Acland disposes.[4]

Do write again when you have time. I do hope everything is going well.

Yours affectionately,

Bertrand Russell

1. 'A Defence of the Trades Disputes Act', *The Independent Review* (November 1906).
2. Russell served on the Newnham College Council, the College's governing body, for ten years from 1901 to 1911. He played an active part in its affairs and missed only five of its meetings in ten years. See S. Turcon, 'Russell at Newnham', *Russell* (Winter 1987–8).
3. 'On the Nature of Truth', *Proceedings of the Aristotelian Society* (1907).
4. Bedford College was in those days a women's college in London. In 1906 the Principal, Ethel Hurlblatt, resigned to become warden of a college at McGill University in Montreal. She was replaced in 1907 by Margaret Tuke, who held the position until 1929. Sir Arthur Dyke Acland (1847–1926), a leading Liberal education spokesman, was the chairman of the College Council from 1903 to 1913. It is not known what role Alys Russell played in Tuke's appointment. Possibly she was a member of the selection committee.

The renewal of Russell's friendship with Helen Flexner was achieved, in part, through Lucy Donnelly's help. In the next letter to Lucy, written on the same day as the previous one to Margaret Llewelyn Davies, Russell reflects on his relationship with Helen.

[141]

[Trinity College]¹
3 November 1906

My dear Lucy

Thank you very much for your letter; I was very glad to hear, and to find out why you had waited so long before writing. But *please* don't, another time, write letters and tear them up without sending them – it is really quite unkind.

Helen's letter to me was very simple, not going into things at all, but glad of the removal of misunderstandings. I am grateful to you for having managed things so well, and I do not see that there is anything further you need do in the matter – you seem to have been completely successful. I should say Helen is quite right to take everything simply, since she can; my feelings are not very simple, and are not likely to become so, but there is no reason why I should obtend any complication there may be in them. So much of what I feel concerning her is centred in myself, and has nothing to do with anything she is in herself. Partly I have a sentimental memory of her as a part of youth: but the Helen whom I view in that way is dead and buried, and quite unconnected with the present person. Partly I feel towards her as a Thebaid hermit towards Woman; this is the obverse of the sentimental feeling. Partly I associate her in my mind with merited humiliations incurred through Grace's² kind offices. Then again she is on the one hand your friend, on the other hand a Thomas. Through the mist of so many associations, it is quite hard to pierce to Helen herself. If I saw her, of course the real present person would become alive to me; otherwise, it is hard. I don't know why

1. The letter is written on Bagley Wood letterhead.
2. Grace Worthington (see letter 72). She was Helen's sister. It is not clear what the humiliations were or why they were merited. Very likely they had to do with Russell's 'falling in love' with Helen in 1900 (see letter 59). Even by the extreme standards of the Thomas family, Grace was an excessive campaigner on behalf of the purity of women against the bestiality of men. In 1903 she had warned Lucy Donnelly, during Lucy's stay at Cheyne Walk, against Russell's malign influence, though Russell was never attracted to Lucy. It seems altogether likely she should have been even more protective of her sister to whom he was.

I should write all this to you, except simply for the relief of being frank on a subject which I generally have to be silent about. Apart from associations, my present feeling towards Helen is quite simple and wholly friendly.

I am delighted indeed that you have got over the habit of worrying. I wish I were able to profit by maxims as you are: I can administer sage advice persuasively, because it has to be so *very* persuasive before I take it myself. I don't worry much over the greater ills of life, but I worry over occasions when I have made a fool of myself.

The mathematical student you spoke of (I can't remember her name)[1] has not yet turned up. Do you know when she is likely to come?

I had heard absolutely nothing of the Hodders' affairs, and am much interested as to the outcome.[2] Mrs Hodder's happiness probably comes from love of excitement: I have seen the same kind of thing in my brother.

Mildred's marriage[3] seems to me quite all right for her – whether for him, I can't judge. Not that I suppose they will be specially happy – marriages seldom are – nor yet that I think her desperately in love with him. But I don't think she would ever be very much in love, and as she is sure to be very jealous, he perhaps won't know the difference. I fancy he is a thoroughly nice man, and I think for her it was essential to marry, or else she would have gone to the bad in a few years in some way or other. I don't believe desire to be rid of her people had much to do with it.

These remarks are of course quite private, and are largely conjectural.

1. Marion Reilly (1879–1928). She was a Bryn Mawr student, and became dean of the College in 1907. She came to Cambridge to study logic with Russell.
2. Alfred Hodder (1866–1907). Russell had met him in 1896 when he was Professor of English at Bryn Mawr. He must have been impressive since Russell, despite his suspicion of English professors, described him as 'a very brilliant young man' (*Autobiography*, vol. I, p. 131). His love life, however, constitutes his main claim to fame. He brought with him to Bryn Mawr a woman who was thought to be his wife, although he seems to have told a number of people that he was not really married to her. Despite her presence at Bryn Mawr he had a number of affairs including, most remarkably, one with Carey Thomas's companion, Mary Gwinn, who fell in love with him, much to Thomas's displeasure. In 1898 Hodder and Gwinn left for New York. It was some years before they could marry, since he had to disentangle himself from the woman who may or may not have been his wife and Gwinn had to secure the approval of her rich mother. But these difficulties were at last overcome and they married in 1904. Hodder died in 1907 'worn out by riotous living' according to Russell (*Autobiography*, vol. I, p. 132). His affair with Gwinn formed the basis for one of Gertrude Stein's early short stories, 'Fernhurst' (1905).
3. In October 1906 Mildred Minturn (see letter 130), then living in Paris, had married Arthur Hugh Scott, the head of a French boarding-school. They continued to live in France until 1912 when they moved to England.

Mildred was unusually nice during her visit to us the other day; so it has had the usual good effects.

If you ever feel inclined to write what you didn't say during the summer, you may feel confident that, whatever it is, it won't make any awkwardness. I know you much too well for that.

My work has been prospering very well indeed. I am at Cambridge today to attend a Newnham Council: last night I read a paper on 'the nature of truth', in which I proved that Harold Joachim[1] thinks Bishop Stubbs was hanged for murder.[2] The great event here has been the reform of the Mathematical Tripos, including abolition of the Senior Wrangler, which we carried by a narrow majority.[3] The thing has been proposed periodically for the last 30 years or so, and I was overjoyed at its being carried.

MacCarthy[4] and John Shuckburgh[5] are married, and Keynes[6] is in the India office. Otherwise my friends are as they were. As for me, I have done nothing but work since we came back from Ireland, which, as you suspect, seems so long ago I can hardly remember it.

1. Harold Henry Joachim (1868–1938), the idealist philosopher at Merton College, Oxford (see letter 68). In his book *The Nature of Truth* (Oxford, 1906) he defended the coherence theory of truth advocated by the Idealists against the views of Russell and Moore. Russell counter-attacked in a number of papers written at this time.
2. This joke can be found in Russell's paper, *Proceedings of the Aristotelian Society* (1907), p. 32. William Stubbs (1825–1901) was Bishop of Chester and Professor of Modern History at Oxford.
3. The final examinations at Cambridge were called Triposes. The Mathematical Tripos was one of the oldest in the University. The system as Russell went through it in 1893 was highly competitive: all the students were ranked in strict order of merit, the student who came top being called the 'Senior Wrangler'. The old system overvalued computational speed and exam techniques acquired through years of practice at Tripos questions. Students were not encouraged to learn anything of current research, nor to develop any kind of insight into, or feeling for, mathematics. The abolition of the order of merit, and with it the position of Senior Wrangler, was an essential preliminary to changes in the curriculum. Russell and many of the younger dons had long wanted such a reform, but, though the system had often been tinkered with, the radical step of abolishing the order of merit had been blocked hitherto by the opposition of the older mathematics dons.
4. Russell's friend, the literary critic Desmond MacCarthy (1877–1952), married Mary ('Molly') Warre Cornish (1882–1953) in July 1906.
5. John Evelyn Shuckburgh (1877–1953), the eldest son of Evelyn Shuckburgh (see letter 93). He had married Lilian Violet Peskett in 1906.
6. John Maynard Keynes (see letter 121). Having graduated from Cambridge (in mathematics and moral sciences) Keynes had started work at the India Office in October 1906. He stayed there for two years.

Do write again soon. Are you anxious I should burn your letter, or was it merely an expression of modesty? I would rather not burn it.

Yours affectionately

Bertrand Russell

The next letter indicates how busy Russell was on this trip to Cambridge. It also records an important step in Beatrice Webb's evolution as a feminist. But the most important allusion in it is the reference at the end to 'the lump'. Alys had recently discovered a lump in her breast. She consulted Dr Boyle, who had supervised her rest cure, about it and was told it was not dangerous. None the less, over the next few months it continued to grow, and Alys, in her misery, began to hope that it was cancer. In June 1907 she consulted another doctor, who also assured her it was not dangerous. That month there is a heart-wrenching entry in her diary, the first since her marriage began to collapse:

Now my blissful hope of six months is destroyed – even the chance of death I do so long to leave Bertie free to live with a woman who ... does not bore him desperately and get on his nerves as I do. .... Little duties keep me going from day to day. But they don't satisfy the awful craving hunger for Bertie's love. .... If only I could die – it's such a simple solution. (B. Strachey, *Remarkable Relations*, p. 222)

The lump was definitely not cancerous, though it continued to grow, and two years later began to cause her pain. In late April 1909 she had an operation to remove it. It seems unlikely Bertie ever knew her hopes and fears concerning it; she confided them only to her diary in two unbearably sad entries.

[142]

[Trinity College]¹
7 November 1906
Tuesday

Dearest Alys

Thy letter of yesterday reached me before dinner. Mrs Fawcett said Beatrice Webb had come around to the suffrage, and sent her a long screed in explanation, which Mrs Fawcett forwarded to the *Times*, as it was too

1. Written on Bagley Wood letterhead.

'philosophical' for her comprehension.[1] I suppose Beatrice has discovered that women eat less than men.

Yesterday Alfred arrived in College about 10, and I worked with him some time; then did some business, e.g. boot-buying; lunched with the Verralls,[2] Council meeting,[3] General Meeting afterwards (where I met Miss Silcox,[4] Miss Strachey,[5] Mrs Wedd,[6] and others), went to Miss Harrison's[7] afterwards for an hour, then to W. E. Johnson's[8] to talk shop; then got McTaggart to talk shop to me while I dressed; then to the Wards[9] (Mrs Fawcett, Miss Kennedy,[10] Cornford,[11] Pa & Ma

1. Rather surprisingly, Beatrice Webb in 1889 had made public her opposition to women's suffrage. Although she had soon seen the error of her ways, she had never recanted publicly. In 1906, as the campaign for women's suffrage grew in intensity, she did so at the request of the veteran suffragist, Millicent Fawcett (1847–1929), in the letter Russell refers to. It was published in The Times (6 November 1906) and reprinted with some words of explanation by Beatrice Webb in her autobiography, Our Partnership (London, 1948), pp. 360–63. Millicent Fawcett, one of the founders of Newnham College and a prominent Cambridge figure, had been president of the moderate National Union of Women's Suffrage Societies since 1897. Russell's next sentence is probably a sarcastic reference to Beatrice Webb's eccentric diet fads.
2. A. W. Verrall, the Cambridge classicist (see letter 128), and his wife, Margaret (1858–1916), who also wrote on classical culture.
3. See previous letter. The General Meeting of Newnham College which followed was the meeting of all members of the College entitled to vote on college matters. The Council was a smaller executive body whose decisions were subject to approval at the General Meeting.
4. Lucy Silcox, a friend of Russell's who was headmistress of St Felix School, Southwold. Russell described her in an unpublished note as 'one of my dearest friends for very many years'. Her letters to him are in the Archives, but the whereabouts of his to her are unknown.
5. Joan Pernel Strachey (1876–1951), the seventh of the Strachey children (Lytton was the eleventh). Almost all her academic life was spent at Newnham: she studied languages there, 1895–9, and became a don at the College in 1905.
6. Rachel Evelyn White had married Nathaniel Wedd (see letter 23) in 1906. She was a classics lecturer at Newnham.
7. Jane Harrison (see letter 102).
8. W. E. Johnson, the Cambridge logician (see letter 97).
9. James Ward, Russell's former teacher, and his wife, Mary.
10. Either Marion or Julia Kennedy, the daughters of B. H. Kennedy, the Professor of Greek at Cambridge. Both daughters and their father were connected with Newnham College and all three were active in the campaign to allow women to take Cambridge degrees. (Despite the existence of the two women's colleges, the University still did not officially grant degrees to women.)
11. Francis Macdonald Cornford (1874–1943), Fellow of Trinity College and lecturer in classics. He became Laurence Professor of Ancient Philosophy in 1931.

Keynes,[1] the Batesons[2]); then back to Cornford's room, where there was a crowd of undergraduates with whom I talked more shop. So on the whole I filled my day pretty full.

I am glad Dr Boyle was satisfied about the lump.

I shall be home for lunch tomorrow.

Thine affectionately

Bertie

Although an organized campaign for women's suffrage had existed since the middle of the nineteenth century, by 1906 the activities of the suffragettes brought the issue to the centre of public attention and, with the election of the Liberals, the cause seemed to be on the verge of some degree of success. There were problems, however: the enfranchisement of women was very controversial and the Liberal government itself was split on the issue. Moreover, the House of Lords had a solid Tory majority and the Tory leader, Balfour, was using it to reject any measure (such as women's suffrage) on which the Liberals would be unlikely to win an election.

Like free trade, women's suffrage was a cause that appealed deeply to Russell's liberalism. His secular godfather, John Stuart Mill, had been among the most prominent protagonists of the cause in the middle of the nineteenth century and a major inspiration to Millicent Fawcett and the National Union of Women's Suffrage Societies (NUWSS), the leading moderate suffrage organization. Russell's parents had campaigned for it, and Russell himself felt it a matter of elementary justice whose time was long overdue. In 1907, as in 1904, he was drawn again into a political campaign.

Russell had written two papers on women's suffrage in 1906 (see *Papers*, vol. xii, pp. 246–65) but had not published them. His first public move was to join the council of the NUWSS late in 1906. The following February he was elected to its Executive Committee. He took the work of the NUWSS very seriously: giving both time to the meetings of the executive and money to the cause. Russell was attracted to the NUWSS rather than the Pankhursts' Women's Social and Political Union, partly because he feared a backlash against the tactics of the suffragettes and partly because the Pankhursts, having despaired of getting what they wanted from the Liberals, had turned to the Conservatives – a change of allegiance which would have been unthinkable for Russell whatever tactical grounds might have commended it. Alys, coming from a different radical tradition and with no strong links to the

1. John Neville Keynes (see letter 121) and his wife, Florence; the parents of John Maynard Keynes, the economist.
2. William Bateson (1861–1926), the naturalist, and his wife, Beatrice. Bateson was a Fellow of St John's College and became Professor of Biology in 1908.

Liberals, was more prepared, it seems, to throw her lot in with the militants. Russell told Lucy Donnelly on 4 February 1907 that he was having difficulty keeping her out of prison.

The suffrage movement was divided not only between the suffragettes and suffragists, but between those who wanted to enfranchise women on the same terms as men and those who wanted universal adult suffrage. Since no more than 60 per cent of men were entitled to vote, the former policy was far from democratic and served to entrench class privilege even more deeply in the franchise. The more limited measure was supported by the NUWSS, which had its origins in the middle of the nineteenth century when adult suffrage was not politically feasible. Russell himself was in no doubt about the desirability of universal adult suffrage. None the less, he thought for some time that a limited enfranchisement of women would stand a better chance politically, in view of the power of the House of Lords, and that more radical demands might prevent any reform being made.

He discussed these matters, and others related to the suffrage, in a number of letters to Margaret Llewelyn Davies.

[143]

Bagley Wood
2 April 1907

My dear Margaret

I was glad indeed to hear from you – it was ages since I had heard either from you or from Crompton. What you tell me of Arthur seems much better than one could well have hoped.[1]

I wish I had known when you were at Barton Street,[2] I would have come to see you. Do let me know next time, as I am very often in town. Crompton has been, hasn't he, going to Berkhamsted[3] most nights? I haven't seen him for a very long time. I hope he is keeping well.

I wish I could get to Kirkby[4] this Easter, but I can't well manage it. I am going to Devonshire to walk with North,[5] which I shall enjoy – he is as much a companion as if he were really grown up. After that I want to see a

1. It had been clear from the beginning of the year that Arthur was dying. By now he was confined to his bed and unable to speak, but he could still communicate by written messages and was bearing the disease stoically. He died on 18 April.
2. Crompton's home in London.
3. Where Arthur and his family lived, just outside London. Margaret was staying there, helping to look after her brother.
4. Kirkby Lonsdale, Westmorland, where Margaret lived with her father.
5. Thomas North Whitehead (b. 1891), Alfred Whitehead's eldest son.

good deal of Alys's cousin Val Worthington,[1] who is just at the end of his school time, and is going up to Christchurch next October. I expect to be quite free from Thursday 2nd to Thursday 9th, and if you are either in London or at Kirkby during any part of that week, do let me know if I could see you at either place.

I have been a good deal exercised about Suffrage things too – I can't make up my mind about the best policy. Some points seem clear: (1) that we shan't get anything out of this government, and that any plan aimed specially at the present Parliament is useless. (2) That the main thing is to have a great body of people really anxious for the Suffrage in some form – if they differ as between adult and the restricted plan, that doesn't seem to me to matter much, provided they remain friendly. But beyond that I feel in a fog. All my sympathies are with Adult Suffrage: women who merely want to be among the oppressors rather than among the oppressed don't seem to me worthy of much sympathy. But it seems plain that Adult Suffrage can only be got after a tremendous agitation, extending over many years; and not then unless a large majority of women can be brought really to desire it. I think Liberals would pass an Adult if it was practicable, since it comes within the formula.[2] On the National Union [of Women's Suffrage Societies], which is largely undemocratic, I have tried putting the case for Adult, and what they say is that if such a Bill were brought in, it would be altered to Manhood Suffrage in Committee. But that could of course be prevented if the demand was sufficiently vigorous. An undemocratic suffragist seems to me in an odd position – I can't think what arguments there are for such a view. And it seems plain that only the general democratic arguments have any chance of success; unless, what I fear, the Tories take up the limited suffrage and carry it. As for the W.S.P.U. I think their election policy is very mistaken,[3] and they, surely, are asking for a limited Bill just as much as the old stagers. But I like their enthusiasm and energy.

1. See letter 72.
2. The Liberals were more reluctant to pass a limited enfranchisement of women, which would have strengthened the Conservative Party's electoral base, than to pass adult suffrage, which would have enfranchised classes more likely to vote Liberal. Campbell-Bannerman had told Parliament on 8 March that he was 'in favour of the general principle of the inclusion of women', though he opposed the particular franchise bill before the Commons which (he claimed) would have enfranchised only a small number of well-to-do single women. It was probably to a more precise undertaking along these lines that Russell referred when he spoke of 'the formula'.
3. They opposed all Liberal candidates, even those in favour of women's suffrage, on the ground that, since the Liberals would not give women the vote, the government would

The Whiteheads are leaving the Mill House in a few days.[1] They have an interregnum before getting into their new house – part of it they will spend with his mother in London. I was there the other day – the last time at Grantchester. Alfred and the children were very flourishing. All the family are glad of the move, which I believe will be an excellent thing.

I am in need of a holiday, tired and depressed, constantly trying to forget troubles it is useless to remember, and not succeeding very well. I wish very much indeed to see you again, and I do hope you will let me know how and when it can be managed. Generally, I try to live on the surface of things, because that seems best; but the ache for something more real is sometimes overpowering.

Yours affectionately,
Bertrand Russell

In 1907 a by-election was called in Wimbledon, the result of the retirement of the Unionist incumbent. It was 'the safest Conservative seat in the whole of Greater London', according to Henry Pelling (*Social Geography of British Elections: 1885–1910*, London, 1967, p. 67) and the Tories chose as their new candidate, Henry Chaplin (1841–1923), 'the quintessential Tory squire', according to Russell's editors (*Papers*, vol. xii, p. 266). Against such a man in such a seat the Liberals decided it would be pointless to field a candidate. The NUWSS, however, decided that good publicity could be gained if a candidate stood on a women's suffrage ticket. At the beginning of May they asked Russell to stand.

[144]

82 Prince of Wales Mansions
Battersea Park
1 May 1907

Dear Margaret
Probably I shall not be able to come to K[irkby] L[onsdale] after all, as it is nearly settled that I am to stand against Chaplin at Wimbledon in the interest of Woman's Suffrage. It is horribly annoying, but I try to regard it as a joke. It may come to nothing, but it will be settled tomorrow morning.

---

have to be defeated. The Pankhursts came to be more and more closely associated with the Tories.
1. The Whiteheads moved from Grantchester in April 1907 to a house on Cranmer Road in Cambridge.

If I don't write again, you will know I am standing. The idea was not mooted till this afternoon so it is rather sudden.

Yours affectionately,

Bertrand Russell

Don't mention it in case it comes to nothing.

Russell had no hope of winning the by-election, indeed he stood as a candidate only because he was sure to be defeated – he needed to finish *Principia* before he could think of a political career. He was the first person to stand for election on a women's suffrage ticket and that in itself generated a good deal of publicity. Russell worked hard on his campaign. Contemporary feminists will not be surprised to learn that he recalled in his *Autobiography* that the popular opposition he suffered as a pacifist in the First World War 'was not comparable to that which the suffragists met in 1907' (vol. I, p. 153). On election day, 14 May, he gathered a respectable number of votes for a Liberal in such a constituency but was defeated by a resounding 7,000 votes. Apart from women's suffrage he stood on a straight Liberal platform, though the Liberal Party itself gave him no official recognition. Sylvia Pankhurst in her book *The Suffragette* (London, 1911) wrote, rather unfairly: 'That Mr Bertrand Russell cared very much more for Liberalism than he did for Women's Votes was at once apparent' (p. 170). Her remark, of course, reflects the party politics of the Pankhursts, but it could be argued that the NUWSS would have made better propaganda for the suffrage issue if they had fielded a candidate (if one could be found) who agreed with Chaplin on all issues except women's suffrage. Three weeks after the election Russell sent an account of his adventures to Helen Flexner.

[145]

Bagley Wood
9 June 1907

My dear Helen

Many thanks for your kind letter about my brief excursion into politics. It was a funny time – partly horrid, partly amusing. The first meeting was the worst – a huge hall absolutely packed, about half violently hostile, and come only to make a row, whistling, cat-calling, getting up free fights, pretending to have fits, and getting carried out – everything imaginable to make speaking inaudible. The papers averred that rats were let loose, and the myth grew – I never saw them, and no one I asked did, until at last I found a man who said two had been let loose at the very end, and he had seen one dead. I was nervous before the meeting, being quite unaccustomed to speaking; but of course the opposition roused one's fighting instincts, and I shouted at them for about half an hour in a mainly futile struggle to get heard. Then Alys tried, and after listening a moment they started again. After a number of others had failed, it came to the turn of my cousin St George Fox Pitt,[1] the Buddhist, who was Liberal Candidate there at the General Election. He is a fatuous person, and advanced with a smile, as much as to say 'I'll show how it's done'. He began 'Now I want to tell you a story about Mr Chaplin'. More yells. And in a few moments he had to sit down. But he remained as self-satisfied as before. At our next meeting they tried pepper, and hit Alys with an egg as we were going away. But after that they were quite well-behaved. St George, as you may remember, is the person who wanted to marry Sally Fairchild, and failed because he wouldn't back her up in a row she had with his mother.

I don't quite understand why you say Women's Suffrage involves the perfectibility of the human race. I hope not, as I don't believe this last.

The Murrays are back. They both loved America, and cannot speak too highly of the kind way they were received.[2] They both spoke particularly warmly of you and Simon, in spite of the discussion on vivisection! I am glad Lucy had them to dinner – they enjoyed it, and it must have been a pleasure to her. I hope she is not too utterly worn out with her College work, and will get rested this summer.

I am back at work, trying to forget public affairs. Miss Reilly[3] from Bryn Mawr has just come here from Cambridge, and I am looking forward to talking shop with her during the next fortnight. This place is full of beauty at this time of year – when are you coming over to see it?

Please remember me to Simon, and give him my best wishes for his success in all his undertakings.

Yours affectionately,
Bertrand Russell

1. St George Lane Fox Pitt, the son of General Lane-Fox Pitt-Rivers and Russell's aunt, Alice Stanley, Lady Avebury. According to Russell he invented the electric light and went bankrupt fighting the Edison Company for the patent. He eventually married a sister of Lord Alfred Douglas.
2. In April Gilbert Murray had given a series of six lectures on the Greek epic at Harvard. While in the USA he and Mary Murray visited Bryn Mawr and the Flexners in New York.
3. See letter 141.

After the excitement of the by-election Russell returned to work on *Principia*, which had reached a crucial stage. His attempt to extend the substitutional theory to propositions had revealed another paradox, which led to his abandoning the theory. In its place he adopted a much more elaborate version of the theory of types, which he had originally published in an appendix in *The Principles of Mathematics*.

The solution of the paradoxes by means of the theory of types removed the main obstacle which prevented the completion of *Principia*. As Russell put it, 'it only remained to write the book out' (*Autobiography*, vol. i, p. 152). The task was still immense and the bulk of it fell to Russell because Whitehead's teaching duties left him insufficient time. Although Whitehead had his teaching, Russell still had his administrative duties on the Newnham Council (and occasionally at Trinity) and his much more demanding duties in the women's suffrage movement. Russell, however, seems not to have been bothered by these claims on his time: 'I live an odd double life between mathematics and suffrage,' he told Lucy Donnelly on 18 March 1908, 'the two worlds are so very distinct. On the whole I find I can do more than if I stuck to one of them – each is rather a rest from the other.' In fact, for some time Russell found himself working longer hours on the book than previously.

[146]

Bagley Wood
Xmas Day 1907

My dear Ivy
Thank you very much for your nice letter and card. They both say nice things. – You were *most* unlucky about Montana, but I hope you are having an enjoyable Christmas. I would send you wishes for the New Year, except that you know, without my telling you, how much I desire all good fortune for you.

I would have stayed longer at Janet's if I could have, but I had already been there over an hour, and I had other quite imperative things to do. I don't think I would have gone home with you; at least I think it would have been a mistake if I had. But it was rather vexing to have only such a very short glimpse of you, though it was better than nothing. I was sorry to hear that the FTU [Free Trade Union] are inclined to treat you badly, but I hope you will continue to be a match for them. What you told me about Whiteley[1] and only supporting Liberals shocked me much from a public point of view – it is just the sort of thing to turn the Labour men into enemies.

I am sorry you are overworked – I suppose everybody is. Certainly I am.

1. Ivy Pretious's letters have not survived and it is impossible to identify Whiteley.

A book to write becomes as bad a taskmaster as an office. I work 9 or 10 hours most days, so that the rest of the day I am in a mere lethargy. Today, in honour of our Saviour, I have only done 7½ hours. But I get a great deal of pleasure out of my work, and it is far the most satisfactory thing in my life, so I can't complain of it. Only tonight I am tired and therefore discouraged, and I wish everything was different, beginning with myself. But that is foolish, so goodbye, Ivy dear —

Yours always

B.

In April 1908 Russell's work on *Principia* was interrupted by the fourth International Congress of Mathematicians held at Rome. These conferences were held every four years, until the First World War interrupted them. It was at the second, in 1900, in Paris that Russell had first discovered Peano's work, which had formed the basis for his own contributions to the philosophy of mathematics. Russell's position in the mathematical world at the Congress of 1908 was very different from what it had been in 1900. None the less, he did not give a paper at the Congress nor is his participation in any discussions recorded in the Congress *Proceedings*, despite the presence of philosophical opponents like Poincaré and Brouwer to provoke him. (The record of discussions in the *Proceedings*, however, is very incomplete.) On the other hand, he did have a number of informal discussions outside the Congress meetings, as the next two letters show.

[147]

Hotel Minerva, Roma
6 April 1908

Dearest Alys

Thy letter duly reached me this morning – it took a good deal longer than I did. It is a pity thee was just unable to get to Charing Cross. The crossing was all right, though a Frenchwoman near me was sick all over her clothes, which she attributed to the cold, while her husband advised her not to waste her handkerchief on it, but to wait for Boulogne and borrow a towel.

The Congress here is a very grand affair – there are an amazing number of mathematicians. Last night we had a party at the University, where the Rector made a speech; this morning we had the opening session in the

Capitol, and the King himself was present. The George Darwins,[1] as was to be expected, were on the platform beside him. The Minister of Education and various bigwigs made speeches, and at last we got to business. They run special motor busses [*sic*] for us, and admit us to most sights gratis. We meet in the Palazzo Corsini.[2] Yesterday I did the statues in the Capitol, the Forum, and St Peter's; today the Congress took all the time. Most of the mathematical bigwigs are here. I have had some pleasant talk with Peano. Poincaré is staying in the same hotel.[3] The hotel is grander than I should have chosen, but I haven't the energy to move. Forsyth read a paper this afternoon, but many people were having tea at the time and therefore missed it.[4] Tomorrow we begin at 9. I leave here Sunday morning.

Uncle Rollo is seriously ill.[5]

Thine affectionately,

Bertie

[148]

Rome
11 April 1908

Dearest Alys

Thanks for letters. It is very discouraging about Abingdon and the Licensing Bill.[6] If I were at home it would depress me; here it seems remote.

I have had an interesting time, though nothing like so profitable as 1900. I find the Germans most polite; I am even being contended for by rival factions each of which wishes to start a new learned journal for which they

1. Sir George Howard Darwin (1845–1912), Charles Darwin's second son and Plumian Professor of Astronomy at Cambridge. He lived at Newnham Grange, next to the Old Granary where the Russells had lived in 1899 (see letter 81). He was a member of the international committee responsible for organizing the Congress.
2. An eighteenth-century palace in which the art collection of the Galleria Nazionale was housed.
3. Given Russell's ongoing dispute with Poincaré about the importance of formal logic, one might have expected the Congress to provide an opportunity for them to exchange views. But Poincaré fell ill during the conference and was unable to take part.
4. A. R. Forsyth (see letter 95) gave one of the plenary lectures of the Congress, 'On the Present Condition of Partial Differential Equations of the Second Order as Regards Formal Integration'.
5. He had blood poisoning, which remained undiagnosed for so long that one of his legs had to be amputated.
6. An extremely complicated piece of legislation designed to reduce the number of public houses over a fourteen-year period, which the Lords had rejected. Abingdon was Montagu Arthur Bertie, seventh Earl of Abingdon, a Tory peer.

want my support. On the whole, however, they are a cliquey set, and find it hard to realize the existence of foreigners. Peano and his school are very cordial. Pieri some years ago published a criticism of some of my views;[1] in the course of an animated argument in the streets, I convinced him, and he admitted unreservedly that he had been mistaken, which was nice of him. The French are the least friendly – they have all been put off by Couturat's dogmatism.

Yesterday I made friends with a Russian, Itelson,[2] who lives in Berlin because he found that if he stayed in Russia any longer he would be sent to Siberia, which would put an end to his pursuit of logic. He began in a most unpromising way, by complaining that Couturat had bagged from him without due acknowledgement the word 'logistic'.[3] But later on he improved. He is very poor, and lives in an apartment without any servant; yet he makes it a rule to give to every beggar who comes to his door, and says they are almost all genuine. He says also that he has 'eine noble Passion' for old books, of which he has collected a fine library. I gave him a good dinner, which I imagine he had not had for a long time. As long as he kept off questions of priority, he was charming.

Today I gave lunch to Miss Collier[4] and Miss Meyer,[5] after which we went a drive in the Campagna. Tomorrow morning I depart, reaching Naples 3.45, leaving there 7.20, and arriving at Palermo about 7 in the morning.[6] – Thee needn't forward letters on business or obviously of no importance.

I feel disinclined to go to Sevenoaks, unless there is some real reason why the Scotts should not come to us.[7] When I get home, I shall want to get to work.

1. Mario Pieri, an Italian logician and geometer and a member of Peano's group. Russell is probably referring to his article 'Sopra una definizione aritmetica degli irrazionali', *Del bollettino dell' accademice gioenia di scienze naturali* (1906).
2. Gregorius Itelson (1852–1926). He seems to have been an entirely independent scholar, never holding an academic post.
3. Both were anticipated by Leibniz, who used the term 'logistica' for his proposed calculus of reasoning. The term in its modern use, to refer to mathematical logic, was put into circulation independently by Couturat, Lalande and Itelson at the third International Congress of Mathematicians at Heidelberg in 1904. It is impossible to verify Itelson's priority claim, since Itelson seems not to have published anything.
4. Presumably the daughter of A. B. Collier, a Cambridge mathematician who was attending the conference.
5. Margaret Theodora Meyer, a mathematics lecturer at Cambridge.
6. After the conference Russell took a holiday with George Trevelyan, retracing Garibaldi's route from Marsala to Palermo.
7. Possibly Arthur Hugh and Mildred Minturn Scott (see letters 130 and 141), who may have been visiting Britain.

I find there is a philosophical congress in Heidelberg in September, beginning the lst, but I don't suppose I shall go.

Fancy Val being late for the boat-race,[1] like the Kinsellas! However, he would have seen the defeat of his side.

It is infinitely beautiful here – the views yesterday were quite wonderful. I have learnt at last to care for sculpture! I learnt in the Vatican yesterday.

Sorry I forgot to tell thee the Suffrage procession was not till June.[2] Good luck to thee. I flourish greatly.

Thine affectionately,
 Bertie

One important indication of Russell's changed status in the intellectual world was his election as a Fellow of the Royal Society. His election took place on 21 May, a characteristically busy day divided between mathematics and suffrage, which he described to Ivy Pretious. The letter also gives an idea of his progress to date on the writing of *Principia*. (The background to his election to the Royal Society is described in an article by I. Grattan-Guinness in *Russell*, 1975.)

[149]

Bagley Wood
25 May 1908

My dear Ivy

Thank you for your letter of the 20th. I am very glad to know all the things you tell me. He's a queer fish – he must be quite destitute of sense.[3] I dare say George's[4] 'short letter' was not 'sweet', but it is not exactly the behaviour of a gentleman to vent his anger on you. You are very wise to go to balls and do everything, instead of sitting at home and moping – the great thing is to be always occupied.

I don't think it would be a good plan for me to come a walk with you

1. The Oxford–Cambridge boat race. Val by this time was a student at Christ Church, Oxford. Cambridge won in 1908. For the Kinsellas see letter 49.
2. Although there were very many suffrage processions at this time, Russell is probably referring to the massive rally at Hyde Park on 21 June. *The Times* estimated that up to half a million people were there.
3. The 'queer fish' was probably a young barrister, the ninth son of Lord Napier, whom Ivy was expecting to marry. He was now having second thoughts about it.
4. Possibly George Trevelyan, who may have intervened once more in Ivy's romantic difficulties and written to Napier.

when you are with Gemma Creighton.[1] My rule is to work after tea, and to break through it would be very marked. I don't suppose you would wish to come here to tea on Sunday with Gemma? We could get a few minutes talk by my taking you round the garden. But I dare say you would rather not come here.

I am frightfully busy. On average days I do 9 or 10 hours' work at my book – on other days I have various jobs. For instance on Thursday, after doing $1\frac{1}{2}$ hours at my book I had to go to London. In the train up and down I read the proofs of the French translation of my book on Leibniz[2] practically the whole time. In London I had a Women's Suffrage Committee,[3] (it was the day after Asquith's remarks on the subject)[4] and then I had to go to the Royal Society to be admitted as a Fellow. I got home at 8, and after dinner I had to write an article and several letters on Women's Suffrage,[5] and a critical letter to Graham Wallas about a book of his I have been reading in MS.[6] After that I went to bed.

I have written about 2,000 pages of the MS of my book since last September; there will be about 6,000 or 8,000 altogether. I have no time to think about anything, which is very pleasant. And it is comforting to have a big continuous job on hand.

My wife is at home again and is practically well.

Write again soon giving me all the news you can of yourself and your feelings and your health. It is a fine thing to have as much courage as you have in facing life.

Yours always,
    Bertrand Russell

1. The daughter of Mandell and Louise Creighton. Mandell Creighton (1843–1901) was an ecclesiastical historian who became bishop of London; his wife also wrote on history.
2. Translated by J. and R. Ray (Paris, 1908).
3. A meeting of the executive of the National Union of Women's Suffrage Societies (NUWSS).
4. Asquith had made a statement to a group of Liberal MPs on women's suffrage. It is explained more fully in connection with the next letter, but it produced a crisis in Russell's relations with the NUWSS and the flurry of writing on the topic that Russell goes on to describe.
5. The article is probably 'Liberalism and Women's Suffrage', *Contemporary Review* (July 1908) (*Papers*, vol. XII, pp. 279–84), although it is possible that he wrote another article now lost. The letters are lost but their subject-matter can be gauged from the article and the letters printed below. Presumably one of the letters was to Millicent Fawcett. Letter 150 is Russell's response to her reply.
6. Graham Wallas, *The Future of English Education in Light of the Past* (London, 1908). A copy of Russell's letter is in the Russell Archives.

In April 1908 Henry Campbell-Bannerman had resigned as Prime Minister through ill-health and was replaced by Herbert Asquith, a known opponent of women's suffrage. Asquith's succession to the leadership had long been expected and, in evident anticipation of his ascent to power, Russell had been to see him at the end of January as part of an NUWSS deputation led by Millicent Fawcett. The chances for women's suffrage, however, were not seriously weakened now that the Prime Minister was an anti-suffragist. Even under Campbell-Bannerman it had been unlikely that the Liberal government would take the risk of including women's suffrage in its programme, and private member's bills on such a topic had little chance of passing into law. In February 1908 a private member's bill had passed its second reading with a majority of 179 but had been referred to a Committee of the whole House, thereby killing it.

Numbers of Liberal MPs, however, supported the reform and on 20 May Asquith told a group of Liberal supporters of women's suffrage that the government would put forward an Electoral Reform bill which could then be amended to include women on a private member's motion. (This was the statement that Russell referred to in the previous letter.) The resulting bill would have the support of the government and would be likely to pass the Commons. The only condition of government support for the measure was that it should significantly widen the franchise for both sexes, since any measure which extended the vote to women but kept the existing property qualifications would favour the Conservatives electorally.

Most feminists were apt to be suspicious of Asquith's statement as a mere political ploy. After all, he had still not committed the government to women's suffrage. Moreover, even if he was as good as his word and a suitably amended reform bill passed the Commons, its chances of becoming law were still slim, for any such measure would almost certainly be rejected by the Lords. In view of this, many feminists thought there was little to be gained from the Liberals. Russell, however, thought that Asquith's statement should be welcomed and tried to persuade the suffragists not to oppose the government. He was desperately anxious to keep the Liberals in power until the Lords rejected some issue that the government could take to the country. Then, it was to be hoped, the Liberals could curtail the Lords' power, making a more radical Liberal programme possible. Russell, in short, was concerned not merely with women's suffrage but with the entire Liberal programme. His allies on the NUWSS, and still more so the militants in the WSPU, were concerned with the suffrage issue only. The preservation of the Liberals was not on their agenda.

Shortly after Asquith's statement (presumably on the evening of the 21st, after the executive meeting of the NUWSS in London), he wrote to Millicent Fawcett to try to convince her not to oppose Asquith. He also stated his opinions publicly in a letter in the suffrage journal, *Women's Franchise* (28 May) (*Papers*, vol. XII, p. 276). Mrs Fawcett replied saying that she thought Asquith's statement was a 'trick of official liberalism' and that Asquith was prepared to countenance an adult suffrage amendment, rather than the limited enfranchisement of women on the same terms as men, merely because he was certain that the wider measure would be rejected by the Lords – who might pass a limited enfranchisement of women because it would favour the Tories. Russell replied in the following letter.

[150]

Bagley Wood
26 May 1908

Dear Mrs Fawcett

I fear you must think me a person very easily taken in, but I cannot help feeling that Asquith's concession is more important than you apparently think it. It is evident, is it not, that, barring improbable accidents, Women's Suffrage must be carried in the present House of Commons as part of a Government Bill, though a part not proposed by the Government. I had supposed hitherto that our object in pressing for a Government Bill rather than a private Member's Bill was that private Member's Bills never get through all their stages. But this by no means applies to a private Member's Amendment to a Government Bill, which, if carried when first proposed, has exactly the same chance as if it were proposed by the Government. So far as I can see, the only obstacle to our securing Women's Suffrage in this Parliament is the House of Lords. That, I admit, is a great obstacle, but I should have supposed that was a reason for objecting to the House of Lords rather than to Asquith. As to Asquith's personal opinion, and his motives for the concession, I cannot see how they concern us. As for the 'Adult Suffrage trap', it has surely been clear for some time that this House would never pass the limited Bill. Therefore I should have supposed that friends of Women's Suffrage would have to resign themselves to a somewhat wider measure. – I do not of course know what you know about the tricks of official Liberalism; but surely no Prime Minister has hitherto made any promise on the subject to a body of members?

Yours very truly
Bertrand Russell

The next day Russell wrote about the situation in more detail, and with more evident exasperation, to Margaret Llewelyn Davies. With her he did not have to argue the virtues of adult suffrage; as a socialist she was in favour of it. But she had no more sympathy with the Liberals than Fawcett did, and she remained unpersuaded by Russell. At this time she was promoting the idea of an umbrella organization to unite the various contending factions in the suffrage movement. Russell was not optimistic about its chances.

[151]

Bagley Wood
27 May 1908

Dear Margaret

Thanks for your letter and enclosures. I haven't yet had time to read the latter, but I am full of things to say about the situation. Let us see if we can agree about the facts over which we have no influence.

(1) The Liberals won't look at the Limited Bill.

(2) The House of Lords won't look at the other; therefore:

(3) The only chance of W.S. [women's suffrage] actually becoming *law* is to hope that the Conservatives will take up the Limited Bill after they have done with the Tariff; unless

(4) such an agitation can be got up during the next 12 months as shall frighten the Lords, which seems unlikely.

As to the course of events in this Parliament, I suppose that if Asquith remains where he is, a private member will move the inclusion of qualified women and wives of qualified men (or something of the sort); this will probably be carried (I should say certainly but for the S.&.P.U.,[1] who seem to me to be doing everything likely to defeat W.S. in this House); it will then become part of a Government measure, just as much as if the Government had proposed it.

This being so, I don't quite see what we should gain, except a sense of triumph, by having the Government take it up to start with. By the time the Bill has been defended by Liberals in the Lords, and thrown out by Conservatives, the Government will be thoroughly committed to W.S. for the future; and the Lords are even more likely to throw out W.S. if it comes officially from the Government, which they hate, than if it comes from the members. I see no objection to agitating for the Government to incorporate W.S. in their Reform Bill, because one must agitate for something definite. Otherwise, I don't see much to be gained. It seems now fairly certain that a Government Bill will be sent up to the Lords containing W.S., and we can't

1. The militant Women's Social and Political Union. As the militant campaign gathered steam Russell became more and more convinced it would alienate public opinion and scare the government away from reform.

get more. What we can do, and are doing, is so to discredit the Government as to make the Lords more likely to reject the Bill. The reason we always pressed for a Government Bill was that other Bills don't go through all their stages, but that doesn't apply here.

As to the united effort you talk of, I fear it is out of the question. Mrs Fawcett is in a temper, and says Asquith is trying to lead us off into the 'Adult Suffrage trap' (in a letter to me); she hates 'democratic lines', though most of the N.U. disagree with her about this, except as a matter of tactics. I find a rooted objection to marriage as a qualification, on grounds of 'principle' which don't appeal to me, but I think the objection worth paying attention to if the enfranchisement of wives can be brought about by some other plan; or perhaps it would be worth while, for the sake of form, to enable husbands also to qualify on their wives' qualifications.

To continue about Union: the W.S.P.U. won't join, because it would involve admitting that there are other Societies, and it would not be worth so great a sacrifice as that to obtain the vote. Our people won't join because they feel that this measure won't pass, and they don't want to be saddled with advocacy of Adult. (I think they make a mistake, and shall continually do what I can to get them towards Adult, unless I have to leave them, which is possible.)[1] Lady Carlisle will do nothing further against her Party;[2] Miss Ashton[3] I can't answer for either way – I don't know her present frame of mind. I have been in a state of excitement and irritation ever since Asquith's pronouncement, because all the women who want the vote seem to me to be taking it in the way least likely to lead to success. The difficulty is that, as Asquith has obviously yielded to pressure, if he gets no reward he will feel it not worth having yielded, and if members get the same hostility from the W.S.P.U. they will feel there is no use in being in favour of Suffrage. It is surely a paradox that those who are prepared to take a course which will lead to women's enfranchisement before the next Election should be in every possible way weakened and discredited in favour of those who, if they dare, will defeat the measure (in the Lords). It makes me really believe in a mental difference between men and women; because I think any man would think such a course insane. Contrast Redmond's conduct in a similar

1. In fact Russell did resign from the NUWSS the following year.
2. Lady Carlisle had publicly welcomed Asquith's statement. Margaret Llewelyn Davies had said that she thought this was more dangerous to the cause than the Pankhursts' opposition.
3. Margaret Ashton, Manchester's first woman councillor. She had started as a Liberal, but in 1908, after the failure of the Liberals to introduce women's suffrage, she stood as an Independent.

situation.[1] I am lying awake at nights worrying over it – it seems to me so suicidal. And Mrs Fawcett's attitude equally vexes me. I think long advocacy of a reform almost always destroys judgment; I always remember that the Abolitionists were among Lincoln's most bitter enemies.[2] Do write again soon, I want to hear fully all you think.

　　Yours affectionately,
　　Bertrand Russell

At last, in October 1909, the enormous labour of *Principia Mathematica* was done. There was, of course, still the work of seeing it through the press and some material at the end had still to be written. Indeed, the book was never finished, for there was to be a fourth volume dealing with geometry, which never appeared. This was to be Whitehead's work and what must have been an extensive set of manuscript materials relating to it was destroyed after his death. None the less, on 19 October 1909 the main manuscript – some 4,500 pages – went to the publishers, Cambridge University Press, and Russell, not surprisingly, was left in a rather peculiar mood as he explains to Lucy Donnelly.

[152]

Bagley Wood
18 October 1909

My dear Lucy

　　Since your letter came I have been too busy to write until now, but now I have time to write, having arrived at a great moment: tomorrow I go to Cambridge, taking with me the MS of the book for the printers. There is a certain amount at the end that is not yet finished, but over 4,000 pages are ready, and the rest can be finished easily.[3] I have been working like a black to get the last bits of revision done in time for my visit to Cambridge

1. John Redmond, the leader of the Irish Nationalists in the House of Commons. Irish Home Rule depended for its success on Asquith's eventual victory over the Lords. Redmond therefore refrained from any action which might cause the Liberals to lose power. The analogy between the two cases, however, was inexact in two respects. First, the Liberals were far more strongly committed to Home Rule than they were to women's suffrage, as Llewelyn Davies pointed out in her reply. Second, the Lords were far more implacably opposed to Home Rule than they were to women's suffrage – a limited suffrage bill could well have passed the Lords.
2. Although Abraham Lincoln was responsible for abolishing slavery in the United States, he was a somewhat reluctant abolitionist. A group of abolitionists in his own party, the Radical Republicans, opposed him in the election of 1864.
3. Russell may have had in mind the projected fourth volume on geometry, since in a later letter he says another 1,000 pages of manuscript had still to be written.

tomorrow, and now the MS is packed in two large crates, and now I feel more or less as people feel at the death of an ill-tempered invalid whom they have nursed and hated for years. It is amusing to think how much time and trouble has been spent on small points in obscure corners of the book, which possibly no human being will ever discover. Owing, I imagine, to the near prospect of taking the MS to the Press, I have been lately in a state of strange and unusual excitement, very loud and bristling and argumentative. The political situation also is extraordinarily exciting: more is at stake than at any time that I can remember, and the issue quite impossible to foresee.[1]

The suffrage question, as usual, bristles with difficulties. Margaret Davies has started a 'People's Suffrage Federation' whose aim is Adult Suffrage, and after some hesitation I have decided to join it.[2] It is having a very great success, but is regarded with grave suspicion by most ardent suffragists, and I am having a difficult time with Mrs Fawcett & Co. However, Mrs Fawcett is having a more difficult time with me: she misbehaved again the other day by going directly contrary to the decision of the Committee, and several of us banded together to tell her what we thought of her conduct; the major part of the plain-speaking fell to my lot. That was at Cardiff, where we had our quarterly council meeting; besides denouncing Mrs F., I was myself denounced on three several counts by different people, among them Margery Strachey,[3] who reproached me sadly and fiercely for talking against Mrs F.

1. In April 1909 Lloyd George had introduced his famous budget, making income taxes and death duties sharply more progressive and introducing for the first time a land values tax, all based on the now quaint principle of making the rich help pay for the functioning of the country which supports them. The budget had not yet been approved by the Commons, though it was certain to be passed there. The main issue was whether the Lords would take the unprecedented step of rejecting it. Since the Lords had systematically thwarted the Liberals' legislative programme, Lloyd George and other radicals in the Liberal Party (notably Churchill) hoped that they would, for it was a popular budget on which the Liberals could be expected to win an election and thereafter curtail the power of the Lords permanently.

Fainter hearts among the Liberals, notably those of Asquith and Grey, had hoped to avoid confrontation, but, in the storm Lloyd George and Churchill had whipped up, they had come, by the time Russell wrote, to recognize that a fight with the Lords was inevitable. Nine days before Russell's letter Lloyd George had made a particularly ferocious speech against the Lords at Newcastle upon Tyne which considerably raised the political temperature.

2. After some further hesitation he resigned from the executive of the NUWSS on 25 November 1909. In January 1910 he became a member of the executive of the PSF. Margaret Davies was one of the secretaries of the organization.

3. Marjorie Strachey (1882–1964), Lytton's sister. She was a schoolteacher, and wrote novels and history books as well as being active in the suffrage movement.

I have besides, recently written a long article for the *Revue de Métaphysique et de Morale*,[1] and a short article for a Suffrage handbook that Margaret Davies is getting out.[2] So you will see I have been pretty busy, and the result is that I have grown very egotistical.

I was much interested by all you wrote about Helen. She wrote to me some time back, and now I shall write to her soon. I am glad she is happier.

It seems to me you are quite right not to use your influence with your sister against your brother-in-law. I should suppose, from what you tell me, that it is to be hoped she will not go back to him; but it does not follow that one ought to try to keep her from going back. As you say, harm is very apt to come of interference in intimate relations. I should gather that you have been doing exactly right all through. I fear the business is likely to be a burden on you for a long time to come.

When Alys decided against America (or rather when Karin did) I gave up Cambridge after a little hesitation.[3] (I go tomorrow for a few nights only.) It was a disappointment to me: it would have suited my work, and I was looking forward to seeing people there.

It is odd how much emotion has got connected with this book I have been at so long. I have made a mess of my private life – I have not lived up to my ideals, and I have failed to get or give happiness. And as a natural result, I have tended to grow cynical about private relations and personal happiness – whether my own or other people's. So all my idealism has become concentrated on my work, which is the one thing in which I have not disappointed myself, and in which I have made none of the compromises that

---

1. 'La Théorie des types logiques', *Revue de métaphysique et de morale* (May 1910). The article was used also as part of the Introduction to *Principia*.
2. No such 'handbook' can be identified. It is possible that the article Russell wrote for it was published instead (or also) as 'Should Suffragists Welcome the People's Suffrage Federation?' in *Common Cause* (9 December 1909), the journal of the NUWSS. (See *Papers*, vol. XII, pp. 291–3.)
3. The exact nature of the plans Russell refers to can only be conjectured. Karin Costelloe, Mary Berenson's daughter, had recently returned from a year at Bryn Mawr to study for her examinations in philosophy at Newnham in 1910. It seems that there had been a plan for her to stay longer in the USA and for Alys, who was much more closely involved in looking after Karin than Mary was, to return to the USA to be with her. Karin had very serious ear trouble and was deeply depressed by the deafness which had resulted from it, and she might well have been thought to need a parental figure to be with her so far from home. Mary had gone over with her in 1908 but had come back earlier in 1909. Bertie meanwhile had been offered a lectureship at Cambridge (England) to coincide with the end of *Principia*, but had evidently decided to turn it down. Presumably he would have moved to Cambridge while Alys was in the USA.

destroy faith. It is a mark of failure when one's religion becomes concentrated on impersonal things – it is monkish essentially. But so it is; and therefore year by year work has become a more essential outlet to my rage for perfection.

I am very glad Bryn Mawr has shown due appreciation of you[1] – it would be very ungrateful if it did not. I am also more glad than I can say that you feel you have found 'peace of mind and heart'. I suppose peace is a thing I shall never find – some demon within keeps me always restless. I have felt it at moments, but it has been when sheer fatigue has momentarily destroyed feeling. At such moments I have sometimes made up a philosophy to suit – but that was humbug, like all general philosophies of life.

Please don't wait a long time before writing again. The things you only imagine telling me remain unknown to me until you commit them to the actual material post, and you must not forget that I care very much to get your letters and to know what is happening to you and what you are feeling.

Forgive the tone of this letter – it is due to rather more work than usual, and would have been quite different if I had waited a week before writing it.

Yours affectionately
Bertrand Russell

In 1909 the suffragettes embarked upon a new and much more militant campaign. Excluded from Liberal meetings, they took to breaking the windows of the meeting-halls and of government buildings, and to (usually symbolic) attacks on policemen and politicians. The most serious incidents had occurred at one of Asquith's meetings on 17 September when suffragettes had climbed on to the roof of the hall and thrown slates down on police and Asquith's car as he arrived. Later, as he returned to London, a lump of metal was thrown at his train. A month later a suffragette attacked Winston Churchill with a whip as he arrived by train in Bristol. The government, primed by a police report that two suffragettes were training with revolvers, feared an attempt would be made to assassinate Asquith.

Russell was very strongly opposed to the new tactics, especially since they came at a time when the Liberal Party was preparing to take on the Lords and needed all the support it could get. He let out his anger in a letter to Lucy Donnelly.

1. Donnelly had recently been promoted to assistant professor of English at Bryn Mawr. She had previously been a lecturer.

[153]

Bagley Wood
17 November 1909

My dear Lucy

Many thanks for your letter. I am sorry indeed that your personal news is not better. I know well the state of mind in which one overworks from restlessness – it has been my state of mind lately. I am sorry too about Helen. As one grows older, some degree of separation from friends (I mean mental separation) seems unavoidable unless one has a common life. The interests of one's life play such an increasing part in absorbing one's thoughts as one grows older. And there is an increasing temptation to live on the surface when everything real is full of pain.

The business of getting printed hangs fire. The Press funks the expense (which will be great) and wants us to get a grant from the Royal Society. That, if it can be managed, will take time.[1] I don't think now there is any chance of the book being published by 1912, so I shall have to put off America till 1913 or 1914.[2]

I am interested in your impressions of Mrs Pankhurst,[3] whom I have never met. She must be a powerful and striking person. In judging her, or at least her cause, you should however remember that none of the S.&P.U. have any respect for truth. I will give you a small recent instance. Mrs Brailsford, Lady Constance Lytton, and several women of no social position were recently imprisoned. They all adopted the hunger strike, and Mrs Brailsford and Lady Constance were let out on medical grounds, because they had heart disease. It was of course said that they had been let out for snobbish reasons, and Mrs Brailsford stated, both publicly and privately, that it was 'almost the first she had heard of her heart being bad.' Now I happen to know some of her most intimate friends, who told me years ago that her life was in constant danger from heart disease, and told me recently that she has to spend a large part of her life on the sofa.[4] I think an absurd fuss has been made

1. In the end Russell and Whitehead received a subsidy of £200 from the Royal Society but still had to contribute £50 each themselves to make good the Press's expected loss.
2. Harvard University was making determined efforts to get Russell to visit.
3. Emmeline Pankhurst (1858–1928), the leader of the WSPU.
4. Jane Brailsford, the wife of the Liberal journalist H. N. Brailsford, Lady Constance Lytton (1869–1923), and a number of other suffragettes were gaoled for one month following disturbances at Lloyd George's budget speech in Newcastle upon Tyne on 8 October. Suffragettes commonly went on hunger strike when in prison and the government, at this time, commonly force-fed them. Constance Lytton did have several heart attacks and, in 1912, an incapacitating stroke. The claim that they had been released for snobbish reasons was published in *Votes for Women* (22 October 1909).

about forcible feeding. It had been constantly resorted to for ordinary criminals without anybody's objecting to it. The women to whom it has been applied have committed serious acts of violence, such as throwing large stones at Asquith, hurling heavy bits of iron from roofs on to the crowds, and other things calculated to kill innocent people. If the Government lets them out when they starve, all criminals will adopt the hunger strike, and the criminal law is at an end. It is not as if these women had committed purely technical offences, like the earlier ones; they have endangered lives, and everybody expects that they will soon resort to assassination. There can now be no doubt that they are very seriously injuring the cause of Women's Suffrage, and that their persistence is due to pride and unwillingness to confess an error.

The last straw which led me to join the People's Suffrage Federation was that the popularity of the Budget made it not unlikely that the Liberals would return to power at the General Election. The Liberals won't look at the Limited Bill, and can't carry Adult Suffrage till the country is willing to have it. Therefore it becomes imperative to create a demand for Adult Suffrage. Even if the Liberals do not come back, the chief objection to the Limited Bill is that it would lead to Adult Suffrage; it is therefore necessary, even to the passing of the Limited Bill, that people should not greatly dread Adult Suffrage. I do not for a moment expect Adult Suffrage to be carried at a blow, but I think until it has ceased to be a bogey, people will not carry any measure of women's enfranchisement. And Adult Suffrage is what I really believe in. It is not women as women that I want enfranchised, but women as human beings. And even *poor* women are human beings. Mrs Fawcett's position is that although the vote should be independent of sex, it should not be independent of property. I have no sympathy with this view.

I gather from your letter to Alys that you, like every one else, know all about the Wells–Reeves scandal.[1] It is a bad business. I knew about it when

---

1. H. G. Wells's affair with a young Fabian, Amber Reeves, had exercised the Fabians throughout the autumn of 1909. In April 1909, when he learnt that Reeves was pregnant, Wells had left his wife and gone with Reeves to France. He was unable to settle there, however, and had returned to Britain with Reeves at the end of the summer. Neither Reeves nor Wells made much attempt to conceal the affair and the Fabians, fearing a public scandal, made strenuous efforts to get Wells to renounce Reeves. The public scandal broke when Wells published *Ann Veronica* in October 1909: the main character was modelled on Reeves and the book enraged the guardians of public morality who wanted it banned. At last, after the harm was done, Wells agreed not to see Reeves for two years.

you were with us, but I then hoped it could be kept quiet. Amber Reeves, however, told everyone, regarding it as a feather in her cap. I expected it before it happened, and blame myself for not having done more to prevent it. But I knew neither of them well, and disliked both, so it was difficult, and I held my tongue, from dislike of suggesting scandal. Wells is an unmitigated cad and scoundrel. In *Ann Veronica*, though the hero is not up to much, he is better than his prototype. All the young people who had taken to preaching free love under Wells's influence are disgusted, and are getting married in Church, with the veil and all the rest of it.

I am very anxious about the General Election. The Budget, as you know, proposes heavy licence duties on public houses. The brewers told Lord Lansdowne[1] they would not contribute to Tory party funds, or help in the election, unless the Budget was thrown out. This would have meant disaster to the Tories. So Lord Lansdowne gave notice that the Lords would reject the Budget, and the very next day the brewers announced a reduction in the price of beer. I fear the great heart of the people will find this bait irresistible. At first the Tories made the mistake of attacking the Land Clauses of the Budget, which are popular; but since they have taken to beer, they have improved their position day by day. However, there is still a good chance of our being victorious.

Alys urged me to stick to the Cambridge plan,[2] and told people I was doing so, but I gave it up, after a short hesitation, when she decided not to go to America. Write again soon. It is a great pleasure to me to hear from you and to know your news.

Yours affectionately,

Bertrand Russell

On 30 November the House of Lords took the momentous step of rejecting Lloyd George's budget by an overwhelming majority. The House of Commons replied on 2 December by declaring that the Lords' action was in breach of the constitution. The Commons was dissolved on 15 December and a general election called for January.

1. Henry Charles, fifth Marquess of Lansdowne (1845–1927), the Unionist leader in the Lords.
2. I.e. Russell's plan to lecture at Cambridge (see previous letter).

[154]

Bagley Wood
13 December 1909

My dear Helen

Your nice letter gave me very great pleasure, and I have been meaning to write every day since I got it. You say, however, that I am a sinner in supposing you capable of abandoning your devotion to Lucy. I don't know why you say this, unless because, as a general question, I do not agree with you and Shelley that 'to divide is not to take away',[1] and I doubt if Mary Shelley would have agreed. An outward separation, with keen separate interests, does in time make some inward separation even in the most faithful; but I don't think that comes to more than you admit.

I only dimly remember attacking Creighton's[2] view that a person is the sum of his relations. I don't know why I objected then, but I should object now that it leaves out the impersonal things – love of truth or beauty or freedom or what not – which are the source of all that is best in our relations, and the motive powers in all lives that count.

We are all here immersed in politics. A crisis is upon us such as we have not had since 1832,[3] and it looks as if the nation would do right. I find excitement and hope keep me perfectly happy; I have chucked my work till after the General Election, and am throwing myself into politics, speaking and canvassing. I have just been, for the last time till after the election, talking as a pure suffragist, to Ray's 'League of Young Suffragists';[4] now I am just going off to canvass in North London slums for Dickinson,[5] who brought in a Suffrage Bill in 1907, and now belongs to the People's Suffrage Federation.

1. 'True Love in this differs from gold and clay, / That to divide is not to take away.' Shelley, *Epipsychidion*, ll. 160–61.
2. Mandell Creighton, Bishop of London (see letter 149). The origin of his remark is not clear. Helen had reported it to Russell some years earlier.
3. When Russell's grandfather, Lord John Russell, steered the first electoral Reform Bill through Parliament.
4. Ray Costelloe was very much involved in the suffrage movement. She subsequently wrote a history of the movement, *The Cause* (1928), and a biography of Mrs Fawcett (1931). The League of Young Suffragists was probably a Cambridge group. On 2 December she told her family that she had had interesting discussions on the suffrage with 'Uncle Bertie': 'I *think* I agree with his views. One cannot be sure, for he puts things too clearly' (B. Strachey, *Remarkable Relations*, p. 249).
5. Willoughby Hyett Dickinson (1844–1928), a Liberal backbencher. His bill had proposed to enfranchise women on the same terms as men. He had hoped to include wives of electors as well, but had failed to get support for this from the suffragists.

Tomorrow I have to go to Cambridge to make some arrangements with the Press about my book, which I have almost forgotten about in the excitement of politics; but in the evening I shall be canvassing again. After Xmas I shall be working for Philip Morrell,[1] whose constituency is in our neighbourhood. Alys is on strike because she is dissatisfied with the Government about Suffrage, so she will only do Suffrage work in the election. I think it well some people should take this line, but I cannot take it myself in such a tremendous crisis. Land Values, Free Trade, Home Rule are all first-rate issues which I care about greatly, but they are all overshadowed by the House of Lords and the constitutional question.

I am very glad indeed that your boy's ears are healed.[2]

I was present in the House of Lords at the end, when they rejected the Budget. It was a great moment.

Yours affectionately

Bertrand Russell

The general election on which so much depended was held in January 1910. Russell, at the height of the election campaign, wrote excitedly to Lucy Donnelly about the political turmoil.

[155]

Bagley Wood
2 January 1910

My dear Lucy

I have hoped for some time to hear from you, but meanwhile I have to thank you for your present to us of the Giles.[3] The Chinese poems are interesting: often very artistic, with a peculiar quaint quality; the only thing that is disappointing about them is that they are not more unlike our poetry

1. Philip Edward Morrell (1871–1943), a lawyer and Liberal MP. He was a close friend of Logan Pearsall Smith. In 1906 he had been elected for South Oxfordshire. He lost this seat in January 1910 but was returned for Burnley in December 1910, a seat he held until he retired from politics in 1918. Although the Russells did not live in Morrell's constituency, Russell preferred to canvass for Morrell as he thought his own MP dishonest (see next letter). Morrell, ironically enough, came from a prominent Oxfordshire brewing family with strong links to the Conservatives. They virtually disowned him when he stood as a Liberal in Oxfordshire.
2. Helen's eldest son, William, had had ear trouble earlier in the year.
3. H. A. Giles, *Chinese Poetry in English Verse* (London, 1898).

in sentiment. I am amused to find the 18th century indulging the same kind of sceptical rationalism as prevailed in Europe at that time.

This letter is really Alys's. She tells me to say she is too busy to write this week, so I am writing for her. She is organizing Suffrage work in our constituency (N. Berks) and in Oxford. Tomorrow (as a result of her organizing) Wicksteed[1] and I and six other Liberals of standing in the constituency go on a deputation to our member to tell him what to think about Suffrage, and to be informed that he thinks it. I fear, however, we shan't get much out of him. I am doing nothing for him because he is shifty and supported the brewers last year. Alys is getting signatures to the voters' petition for Suffrage, which is going astonishingly well.[2] A large majority, so far, have been willing to sign; working men have volunteered to take the petition to their pals and get them to sign. I am amazed.

I am working for Philip Morrell, whose campaign has only just begun. I have spoken for him in Newnham, Sandford and Littlemore: at Littlemore poor Logan took the chair. I didn't know there were so many people in those villages. Practically all the men and many of the women turned up: only one Tory, apparently, exists in the three, and he is at Sandford. Tomorrow I speak with Morrell at a big meeting at Henley. On spare nights I shall canvass for him. I have already canvassed in North St Pancras (for Dickinson,[3] a Suffrage champion) and in Oxford. I am very optimistic indeed; I think the Tories will have at most 200 members in the new Parliament; but I think most Liberals are less hopeful.[4] I base my views chiefly on the reports of meetings; the Tories can hardly hold a public meeting because of the opposition, whereas Liberal meetings everywhere succeed. It is chiefly the prospect of food taxes that alarms the working man. There is immense interest in the election everywhere – I don't think the country has ever been so excited. The issues are tremendous: first, the constitutional question – the power of the House of Lords is to be either immensely increased or almost destroyed; second, Free Trade and Protection, which alone made the last election the most important I could remember; third, the Land Taxes, embodying a principle I have cared for ever since I began to know economics, and capable, I believe, of transforming the lives of working people; fourth, Home Rule, which convulsed the country for

1. Philip Henry Wicksteed (1844–1927), a Unitarian minister and university extension lecturer.
2. The NUWSS had decided to use the election to gather signatures from voters for a petition to Parliament in favour of women's suffrage.
3. See letter 154.
4. In the event the Liberals' majority was much reduced: the Tories had 273 seats.

10 years, but now is almost unnoticed. The power of the brewers, which is the worst influence in our politics, is also involved; and I think Suffrage stands a chance if the Liberals are returned, whereas it certainly has no chance from the Tories.

Every part of the country blazes with Tory posters representing men out of work owing to foreign competition, with wife and children weeping. Unemployment is the chief basis of the Tory appeal to the working man; their other support is beer. Our strong cards, besides cheap food, are Old Age Pensions[1] and the popularity of the proposed Land Taxes; also the idiocy of the Peers, who are on the stump, and make fools of themselves everywhere. All the brains and all the oratory are on our side; all the money is on theirs. Almost everybody who is neither a nonconformist nor a working man is going to vote Tory, even those who voted Liberal last time. But the Liberal enthusiasm is much greater than four years ago. Lloyd George is worshipped as Gladstone was, and Winston has shown himself capable of speeches which put close economic reasoning in a form that anybody can understand. The Tories rashly boasted that they would win Lancashire by a whirlwind campaign, but before they got going, Winston addressed 40,000 Lancashire men in a week, and showed that they would be ruined by Protection, and now the Tories daren't show their faces anywhere near Manchester. The Liberal appeal has been very full of argument and solid instruction, and so far as I can discover that is what people are wanting — they seem to resent appeals to their emotions. It is all very interesting, and I can think of nothing else.

I have resigned from the National Union Executive, because I wanted a free hand to support Liberals. I am now on the Executive of the People's Suffrage Federation, and as my book no longer occupies my whole energies, I hope to do a lot of work for Adult Suffrage when the election is over.

Write soon. I am anxious for news of you. What prospect is there of your coming over next summer? I wish to goodness you were coming.

Yours affectionately,

Bertrand Russell

The next letter shows Russell in an unfamiliar role as uncle and teacher. Russell had not done any regular teaching since he had lectured in mathematical logic at Cambridge in 1902. But he had taken a keen, though occasional, interest in the

---

1. The Liberals had introduced old-age pensions in 1908, an expensive, but popular, social reform which was to be paid for by the new taxes included in Lloyd George's budget.

education of the young people he knew. Perhaps his most sustained effort was with his niece, Karin Costelloe, who was studying philosophy at Newnham. Of his two nieces, Ray, the eldest, was the family favourite; but Russell had a soft spot for Karin. Karin had suffered from the obvious (and sometimes shocking) favouritism shown Ray and had suffered further from the social isolation into which she had been thrown by her deafness. Both Bertie and Alys seem to have made special efforts to help her, and in Bertie's case this consisted in tutoring her in philosophy. She had a definite talent in philosophy and went on to write a dissertation on Bergson, on whom she eventually published a book. Russell disagreed vehemently with her views about Bergson, but admired her ability and the verve with which she defended herself against his criticisms. In June 1910 she got a First in part one of her Tripos and Russell wrote to congratulate her.

[156]

Bagley Wood
17 June 1910

My dear Karin

I am overjoyed to hear you have got a First. Considering how little time you had for working at the subject, it is a remarkable feat. Keynes père told me some time back that your work for him was up to First-Class standard, but sagely observed that he knew nothing about your other work, and succeeded in giving me the impression that he hardly expected you to get a First. You may reckon that you have a real aptitude for philosophy, and I expect Part II will suit you even better than Part I.

I have been feeling more or less as if I was being examined myself, and am relieved at having satisfied the examiners – probably, however, in virtue of your prudent disagreements.

Your affectionate uncle
Bertrand Russell

Russell's lack of formal teaching experience made his career as a philosopher somewhat unusual, though less unusual then than it would be now. Like others at the time, he could afford to live off inherited wealth and while *Principia Mathematica* was being written he avoided teaching as an unnecessary drain on his time and energy. By 1910 not only was his part of *Principia* essentially finished but his capital was almost exhausted. As a result in May 1910 he accepted an offer from Trinity College for a five-year lectureship in Logic and the Principles of Mathematics. The job required him to give twenty-four lectures per term and to live in Cambridge during term time. There were, moreover, personal reasons for his return to Trinity, not all of which are explained in the next letter to Helen Flexner.

Living with Alys at Bagley Wood had not been a success. In 1903 he had written of Alys in his Journal: 'When she is not present, I am sorry for her; but when I see and hear her, I become all nerves, and can think of nothing but the wish to escape' (*Papers*, vol. xii, p. 24). When Alys had visited Cambridge a few months earlier she had been terribly unhappy because, Russell explained, 'being pressed and pressed as to why I wouldn't live in Cambridge, I had had to tell her ... that she got on my nerves when she was with Cambridge people' (ibid., p. 17). Nothing seems to have changed in these respects in the intervening seven years, except that by 1910 it was clear that Alys would not follow him to Cambridge. The job at Trinity, with its residence requirements, offered an escape route from domestic life at Bagley Wood. In October 1910, Russell moved into rooms in college and Bagley Wood was put up for sale – though, when they found no buyers, they decided to let it. Alys moved to a rented cottage in Fernhurst, although she did join him in Cambridge for a while in the new year when they took lodgings in town. This arrangement was not a success.

By the end of 1910, the country was facing another election campaign, this time over reform of the House of Lords. The government wanted to restrict the Lords' power to veto legislation; the Lords vetoed the legislation to limit their veto. The Liberals took the issue to the country with the understanding that, if they were returned and the Reform Bill was still rejected by the Lords, the King would create enough Liberal peers to ensure its passage. A list was drawn up of several hundred people, including Russell, who would be given peerages if need arose. In the end the Lords gave way and passed the Reform Bill after the Liberals won the election in January 1911.

[157]

Trinity College
15 November 1910

My dear Helen

I was very glad indeed to get your letter, indeed the oftener you write the better pleased I shall be. You asked me to make allowances, but I saw no need. You will have to subject me to severer tests in order to discover whether I have improved in that respect. Speaking seriously, I do believe I have grown far less ready to condemn, and far more ready to realize other people's feelings and points of view. I believe it was only once that you had reason to complain of my uncharitableness, and then I was in a very abnormal frame of mind. So I would ask you to be less sceptical as regards my improvement in charity, though this has gone, as it usually does, with deterioration in other ways.

I am glad you speak of the 'certain prospect' of our meeting; does that mean that you feel fairly sure you will come with Simon when he comes? It is over ten years since you stayed with us in Downing;[1] how well I remember it! I shall enjoy showing you Cambridge again. I do not know yet where our house will be, but my rooms will probably be the ones I am in now, in the Cloisters, which perhaps you remember. I have all my work-books here, and intend always to do my work in College. Then Alys can have as many drawing-room meetings as she likes without my being disturbed. At Oxford it was always rather upsetting when she had 50 or 60 ladies to tea. I enjoy living in College very much – for a long time I have been starved for talk on things connected with my work, and here I get my fill of it. Also it is pleasant to live in a society which values the sort of work I do. Gratified vanity is always a great part of one's pleasure in other people's company. I find teaching extraordinarily pleasant; I have about a dozen people to deal with, most of them very able, and I enjoy the chance of telling them what I feel sure it is important they should know. So altogether I am finding life more agreeable than I have done for many years.

My little book of collected essays,[2] which I told the publishers to send to you, has, I hope, reached you. The first volume of the big book that Whitehead and I have been engaged on for the last 10 years is going to appear in a few weeks, and the second and third vols. will appear as fast as they can be printed. This will be a great event in my life. Doing the book has been a continuous dead heave, involving constantly the maximum effort of which one was capable. Now I intend to take life easily for some time. But I still have a few bits of the end of the book to write; also I have to do a paper for the Aristotelian Society,[3] and a shop-assistants' guide to philosophy in 50,000 words of one syllable.[4] Moreover the Xmas vacation, which would be the natural time for doing such things, will probably be taken up with electioneering – canvassing all day, and speaking at night. So I can't begin taking things easy just yet.

You invite me to rejoice in Carey's faults.[5] I have been doing my best

1. Downing College, Cambridge. See letter 84.
2. *Philosophical Essays* (London, 1910).
3. 'Knowledge by Acquaintance and Knowledge by Description', *Proceedings of the Aristotelian Society*, (1911); read to the Society 6 March 1911.
4. *The Problems of Philosophy* (London, 1912). Russell had been asked to write this for the Home University Library, of which Gilbert Murray was one of the editors.
5. Carey Thomas's faults were her supreme confidence in her own abilities. They were

since I got your letter, but some practice is still required to make me perfect.

I am very glad indeed to hear that Lucy is so well. I hope she will not get run down again this winter. It was a great pleasure seeing her.

What you tell me about Simon's work is very interesting. Please thank him from me for 'The Contribution of Experimental to Human Poliomyelitis',[1] which I am glad to have, though I can't pretend I have read it. But such gruesome visions of children's illnesses as you tell me of are a severe price to pay for one's husband's eminence.

I remember writing a paean to you on the last day of last century, very nearly 10 years ago, when I had just finished the most successful bout of work I have ever had, and got the ideas I have been working out ever since. My mood now is similar. I wish you were here – you really would find me quite pleasant, I believe, and not at all inclined to be offensively critical. Write again soon, and tell me of all that interests and concerns you. I always like to hear it, even if I have no comment to make when I answer your letters. Goodbye.

Ever yours affectionately
 Bertrand Russell

to be rejoiced in, Helen had suggested, because they enabled her to be more effective in developing Bryn Mawr.

1. *Journal of the American Medical Association* (1910).

6. NEW LOVE

====

(1911–14)

Russell's canvassing for Philip Morrell in the January election of 1910 changed his life in ways that couldn't have been anticipated. As a result of it, he got to know Morrell's wife, Ottoline. 'I discovered', he wrote, 'that she was extraordinarily kind to all sorts of people, and that she was very much in earnest about public life' (*Autobiography*, vol. I, p. 202). After Philip lost his seat in January, Russell did not see much of the Morrells for the remainder of 1910. But in March 1911 Russell was invited to give three lectures in Paris, including one at the Sorbonne. It was convenient for him to spend the night in London on the way over and he asked the Morrells if they could put him up.

On the night Russell came to stay Philip had to be away at Burnley, his new constituency, and after the other dinner guests had departed Bertie found himself alone with Ottoline:

> During dinner we made conversation about Burnley, and politics, and the sins of the Government. After dinner the conversation gradually became more intimate. Making timid approaches, I found them to my surprise not repulsed. It had not, until this moment, occurred to me that Ottoline was a woman who would allow me to make love to her, but gradually, as the evening progressed, the desire to make love to her became more and more insistent. At last it conquered, and I found to my amazement that I loved her deeply, and that she returned my feeling. . . . For external and accidental reasons, I did not have full relations with Ottoline that evening, but we agreed to become lovers as soon as possible. . . . It was already late when we first kissed, and after that, though we stayed up till four in the morning, the conversation was intermittent. (*Autobiography*, vol. I, p. 203)

Ottoline was less bowled over by the events than Bertie. 'My imagination was swept away', she wrote, 'but not my heart, although it was very much moved and upset. . . . No woman is dead to the flattering influence of a great man's passion. . . . I was indeed partly overcome, carried away and elated by this new experience; but underneath there lay a cold, horrible feeling of discomfort that I was not being true, and that the intoxication of his own feelings blinded him from seeing that I was not equally in love with him; to tell him this was more than I had courage to do' (*Memoirs*, vol. II, pp. 267–8).

The next morning, Russell, no doubt tired but certainly excited, went on, not immediately to Paris, as he says in his *Autobiography*, but to a round of appointments in London and thence to Paris to deliver his lectures. It was the beginning of a long and, in Russell's case, passionate love affair. It also produced a correspondence of epic proportions, which began in the train to Paris.

[158]

In the train
Tuesday [21 March 1911]

My dearest

My heart is so full that I hardly know where to begin. The world is so changed these last 48 hours that I am still bewildered. My thoughts won't come away from you – I don't hear what people say. All yesterday evening Bob Trevy babbled on; every now and then I woke up and wondered who he was talking about just then. Fortunately *yes* and *quite so* and *ah indeed* were enough for him. I see your face always, though as a rule I can't imagine anybody's face. I love you very dearly now and I know that every time I see you I shall love you more. I long to be with you in beautiful places, where your own beauty and the beauty you create everywhere will be in harmony with other things.

Before I really knew you, I began to wish to, because of what I saw you were making of Philip; then I remember a day when you came to Bagley Wood and we had a talk on the way to the river; that was for me the beginning – since then I have never consciously lost an opportunity. But only dim instinct knew what was happening – my conscious knowledge was fugitive. I wish it had not been. But now I know I have what I longed for. Only it is altogether extraordinary to me that you should love me – I feel myself so rugged and ruthless, and so removed from the whole aesthetic side of life – a sort of logic machine warranted to destroy any ideal that is not very robust. My own ideals can endure my own criticism and thrive on it; yours, I believe, can also. But most people's can't. People think me cynical, but that is superficial. The bottom feeling is one of affection for almost everybody. I could often wish to be more ruthless in feeling – it would simplify life.

I don't really know you yet. You must help me to. I want to know every bit, absolutely.

In Paris I shall have to try to collect my wits. It won't do to be thinking of you while the philosophers are making objections to my views. But I fear the whole thing will seem less important than it did before.

Friday night I dine and sleep with my brother, 57 Gordon Square. He is likable in some ways, but in others not. I will come Saturday about 10.30. I have to catch a 2.40 to Haslemere. We stay at Fernhurst for the Vacation, and I have undertaken to coach Karin for her Tripos.

Goodbye my Dearest, I grudge the hours till I am with you again. With all my love,

B.

Lady Ottoline Violet Anne Morrell (1873–1938) was at this time only at the beginning of her career as a society hostess. She was the fifth child and only daughter of Lieutenant-General Arthur Bentinck, who had died when she was four. When she was six her half-brother succeeded a distant relative as the sixth Duke of Portland and she and her mother moved to Welbeck Abbey, the Portland family seat in Nottinghamshire. Her life there was lonely. Her brothers, all older than she, were away much of the time and ignored her when they were not. She was brought up to be the wife of an aristocrat and her education was limited to what was thought necessary for this role, that is, to virtually nothing at all. There is a picture of her at the age of sixteen looking like a stuffy, rather plump, Victorian princess. But thereafter she developed admirably and in ways it would have been hard to anticipate.

Her transformation began in adolescence when she became interested in religion. Initially inspired by Thomas à Kempis's *The Imitation of Christ* (a book that had once been important to Russell), the later development of Morrell's religiosity was inspired by an Anglican nun, Mother Julian, whom she met around 1894 and who became her spiritual mentor. Religious differences were occasionally a source of friction in her relations with Russell. But Russell would also have taken Ottoline's religious beliefs, like her political interests, as evidence of a deeper side to her nature, a side not perhaps readily apparent to those who saw her only as a hostess. Without that aspect to her life, Russell might have found it difficult to take her seriously.

After a desultory period of travels abroad and two attempts to study at university (one at St Andrews, the other at Oxford), she finally escaped the fate her family intended for her by marrying Philip Morrell on 8 February 1902. Philip Morrell (1871–1943) was then a young London solicitor who found both his work and the life associated with it unsatisfying. Shortly after their marriage, under the persuasions of the Webbs, he entered Liberal Party politics. This appealed to Ottoline's social conscience, which was one permanent legacy of her adolescent religiousness. It also made for an irrevocable break with their families, both of which had strong Tory connections. In the Liberal landslide of 1906 Philip was elected as the member for South Oxfordshire and the Morrells moved to a larger house in London, 44 Bedford

Square. There in 1906 she gave birth to twins, a boy and a girl. The boy died a few days later, but the girl survived and was christened Julian, after Mother Julian.

The life of an MP was certainly busier and more exciting than that of a solicitor, but still all was not well. Though the Morrells began with high hopes of radical Liberal reform, they did not find the Liberal Party politicians with whom they spent much of their time either sympathetic or interesting. Ottoline remembered an occasion when Philip cried out in despair: 'We must make some friends. We haven't any friends' (*Memoirs*, vol. I, p. 132). It was a decisive moment. Ottoline took upon herself the task of acquiring friends and began to build a circle of artists, writers, and intellectuals, thus beginning her career as one of the great twentieth-century hostesses.

The differences between Ottoline Morrell and Russell are striking and a serious love affair between the two of them might seem improbable. In fact, however, the passion owed much to the differences, for neither Russell nor Morrell were satisfied with the way their lives had turned out and each sought in the other things that were missing from their own life. For example, Ottoline's aesthetic sense, which was highly developed in the visual arts, was very important to Russell, who felt himself to be unusually deficient in visual sense. In recalling his night at Bedford Square, the first thing he remarked on was the beauty with which the house was decorated with its pale grey walls and yellow taffeta curtains. 'Ottoline had very exquisite, though rather startling taste,' he wrote (*Autobiography*, vol. I, p. 203). In matters of taste, Ottoline was far removed from Alys's Quaker austerity. Indeed, in all respects, Ottoline was a marked contrast to Alys.

Undoubtedly Ottoline's exoticism appealed to Russell, while her genuine concern about social conditions and even her religiosity would have helped convince him that on the deep issues of public and private life they had some point of contact. There were similarities in their backgrounds too. Both had suffered lonely childhoods. Both were aristocrats who had rejected their class. As they approached their forties they perhaps realized that they had burnt their bridges and there was no way back to the world they had been born into, nor yet any effortless adjustment to the upper-middle-class world they had chosen to enter. Russell commented that they were 'both a little alien to the world in which we chose to live' (*Autobiography*, vol. I, p. 205).

Still more important for Russell in 1911 was Ottoline's passion for intimacy. Since his mystical experience in 1901 Russell had been anxious to pour out his soul to whoever might understand it. With women he had been most successful in this when they were safely on the other side of the Atlantic, for he was still restrained by a restrictive social code on sexual relations and even more so by his own puritanism. Ottoline, considerably more daring in these matters than Russell at this time, was able to overcome his scruples, and her kindness (which he had observed during the election campaigns of the previous year) encouraged his initial 'timid advances'.

Her affair with Russell was not Ottoline's first. A year or two after her marriage she had had an affair with John Cramb, a rather courtly and pedantic history professor at Queen's College, London. A few years later, going to the opposite extreme, she had become romantically involved with Augustus John, and then with Henry Lamb, a younger artist in John's retinue. Finally, about the time her affair with Russell began, she had become entangled with Roger Fry, who had fallen in love with her. She seems to have regarded Cramb as a mentor who could fill some of the gaps in her education. John's bohemianism and artistic inspiration also offered something for which she felt a need. But with Lamb and Fry the situation seems to have been reversed. She was ten years older than Lamb and she thought him in need of her support and protection. Fry also, though considerably older, was going through a difficult time. His wife had recently been confined to a mental hospital, and Ottoline offered sympathy and understanding. There was, in many of her relationships with men, an element of pastoral care. There was certainly a pastoral aspect to her relationship with Russell. She recalled him telling her at a dinner before their affair began, 'There is always a tragedy in everyone's life, if one knows them well enough to find it out' (*Memoirs*, vol. I, p. 193). It was the first time she realized how unhappy he was. She was interested in other people's tragedies, and did her best to help.

Russell also offered an intellect much more capacious and daring than Cramb's, with something of John's inspiration and sense of purpose though without John's disquieting waywardness in everyday life. The previous year, after a visit to Bagley Wood, she wrote in her diary: 'Bertrand Russell is most fascinating. I don't think I have ever met anyone more attractive, but very alarming, so quick and clear-sighted, and supremely intellectual' (*Memoirs*, vol. I, p. 183). She had noted that he had 'an intense, piercing, convincing quality' (ibid., p. 193). But whether she was quite prepared for the intensity with which he fell in love with her is doubtful. As with many of her affairs, the entanglement came easily, the disentanglement was much more difficult.

She certainly did not anticipate that Bertie would immediately conceive the idea that she should separate from Philip and he from Alys. Ottoline had no intention of leaving Philip or her daughter, as she made plain to Bertie when he returned from Paris and in the 'little note' Russell mentions in the next letter. And yet, in the little note she made it seem as if her resolve could be overcome with just a little more persuasion. The only alternative Bertie could see was a complete break with Ottoline. After seeing Ottoline again in London, he went on to Fernhurst to see Alys, resolved to tell her what had happened and to effect a complete break with her, whether or not the relationship with Ottoline would continue. From Fernhurst he wrote Ottoline the first of many fretful letters.

[159]

Van Bridge, Fernhurst
Saturday night [25 March 1911]

My Dearest

It was good of you to give me your little note this afternoon. I know you are not killing our love – but love dies in the end if it is not nourished, and if we have to part it will die. I don't know quite why I have to ask for all or nothing, but I know I am right. I feel that if you refuse all, I shall be terribly tempted to accept less, but it would be wrong – I should be somehow degraded by it, and that would degrade our love. In time I suppose I shall know why this is so – now I only know it is so. I shall tell Alys on Monday – I can't tell her while she has our visitors on her hands. I have written to tell the Whiteheads, and the letter will go by the same post as this. I should be very glad if you were to see them during this time of waiting. They are my best friends – they have known all my intimate concerns, or all that could be told, and they have helped me in all difficulties. Dora Sanger's remark about Mrs Whitehead is wholly unfounded. Dora always speaks ill of women – I have heard her speak ill of you, in days before I knew you at all well.

The first few hours after I left you I felt confident you would decide as I wish; now I think you won't. I am so tired that I have no feeling left except utter weariness. Your will is very strong, and it is hard work to battle against it. I know you are not deficient in courage, indeed your courage is splendid. But there is one sort of courage which consists in choosing one's own happiness on those rare occasions when it is right to do. Only generous people have any occasion for this sort of courage. There have been many things in my life which I should have wished to tell you, but that I am not at liberty to do so; they would have illustrated why I am so certain of what I think right. But Dearest I honour you the more for your self-sacrifice; and formerly I should have been more ready to think it right.

I ought to go to bed, but I can't stop writing to you. It is horrible here – poor Alys gets on my nerves to such an extent that I don't know how to bear it another moment. I always find her very trying after an absence, but this time naturally it is particularly bad. However, I have talked and laughed the whole time, so that inobservant people would have supposed I had not an anxiety or a trouble in the world. Karin and Ray are both here. I don't much like Ray – I think she is exactly like Alys – kind, hard-working, insincere and treacherous. Karin is quite different. I have undertaken to coach her this Vacation in things I don't know properly myself, so that I shall have to work hard to get them up. I have also undertaken to finish by July a popular book on philosophy, which I have not yet begun. Heaven knows how I shall manage, but I must do it as I have signed the contract.

Dearest I feel sure you will decide against me, and that it will be the wrong decision. If I were less tired I should be more hopeful, but just now I merely feel that life is one long irony, in which the good things come in glimpses that only make common life harder. I cannot understand the wish for a future life – it is the chief consolation that in the grave there is rest. Goodbye, Goodbye,

B.

The following Monday, Russell told Alys. Alys reacted with fury and threatened a divorce, citing Ottoline. This was something Russell had to avoid at all costs, and he told her he would commit suicide rather than have Ottoline involved in a public scandal. 'I meant this', he wrote, 'and she saw that I did. Thereupon her rage became unbearable' (*Autobiography*, vol. I, p. 204). Russell's account, however, telescopes together the events of a three-week period, for he implies that at the end of their arguments this weekend he rode away on his bicycle and did not see Alys again 'till 1950, when we met as friendly acquaintances' (ibid.). In fact his relations with Alys were not so speedily terminated, for he was back at Fernhurst the following weekend trying to negotiate some permanent arrangement for their separation, and these visits continued for some time after that.

Bertie had expected that Ottoline would break the news to Philip as soon as he returned from Burnley. Indeed she told him that she had done so and that Philip had merely expressed the wish that his marriage to her continue as before. In her *Memoirs* she told a similar story, although there she records that Philip had said that if she wanted to leave him she must do so (*Memoirs*, vol. II, p. 267). However, in this case Philip for once had the last word. After Ottoline's death Philip prepared her *Memoirs* for publication and took the opportunity to add his own footnotes. In one of them he pointed out that Ottoline had not told him that Bertie was in love with her, but merely that he was very unhappy with his wife and had asked for Ottoline's 'sympathy and support' (ibid., p. 267n). What Philip didn't know was that she had told Bertie that she and Philip were now merely friends. The fact that Ottoline had told Bertie that she did not love Philip and had not told Philip that she did love Bertie (though she told Bertie that she had) explains a good deal of Russell's bewilderment in the next letter.

[160]

In the train
Tuesday afternoon
[28 March 1911]

My Dearest Dearest

Your letter is very persuasive – I have been very much to blame, and going all against my code, in making it a conflict of wills. I must come back to reason – but it is hard. What you ask me to accept is very difficult – and it is curious that you do not know how difficult. Curious also that after being told Philip should wish to go on in the same terms as hitherto. The situation is one I have not known of before in any case I have ever heard of, and it takes time to understand. The thing I find really unintelligible is why, things being as they are, you attach so much importance to continuing to sleep with him. If I understood that, things might be better. Would you not feel it if I continued to sleep with Alys? But I am quite willing to believe I ought not to mind. The question is whether I can learn not to mind without my love being chilled, and whether, further, I can believe that you do right. All I ask is that he should not share your room. Try to make me understand why it is important he should. Till I do, I shall be liable to a sudden chill which would be horrible to us both. You need not be afraid I shall break suddenly or violently. But when I am with you it is so hard to think. And I might agree to what would be beyond my strength. Of course, I shall not be degraded by anything my reason acquiesces in. But what you propose seems to me, so far, somehow unclean. I have not myself avoided acts which were really bad, which have filled me with a shame that drove me to the verge of suicide. But I will not let shame come between you and me, and I must understand to acquiesce. Till I understand, I shall not have that mental union with you which is necessary to love. That is why I should be degraded. It is all very difficult. I am very willing to be convinced I am wrong, but I must be able to think of it without feeling the chill it gives me now. I can see with my intellect the point of view from which what you wish is noble and right, and I dare say I should have advocated just such a course, in another case. But it is not as yet what I feel.

The enclosed telegram suddenly summoned me to 17 Carlyle Square Chelsea,[1] where I shall be tonight and tomorrow morning. But I would

1. The Whiteheads' new home in London. Whitehead had resigned from Cambridge in 1910, and moved to London, where he eventually obtained a professorship at University College. The telegram was presumably in response to Russell's letter to them from Fernhurst.

rather not see you tomorrow – I must think more first – a few days more at any rate. How could you suppose Mrs Whitehead could put me against you? In the first place no human being could, and in the second place she would not wish to. She has written a line quite approving of it, and whatever you may think, she does like and admire you. I must necessarily see a lot of Whitehead until the printing of our joint book is finished, which will be another year or 18 months. We have worked together since 1900, and before that he was first my teacher and then a very helpful critic. I owe a very great deal to him and have a strong affection for him. But I do not ask you to do anything you would rather not do. Only it seems rather a pity.

I cannot write as I should wish while things are as they are. I feel that there must be no conflict before I can write otherwise. I fear it is my nature that is poor. I will try to conquer it. If I can, I dare say all may be well. But it is dangerous to try to force one's instincts by the use of reason – it leads to insincerity, and ultimately the instincts rebel and there is tragedy. But oh I am hungry for you. Such happiness so near, and such a slender obstacle. My belief, based on what you have told me, is that he would not mind separate rooms. Could you not try to find out if it is so? Oh Ottoline I do long to take and give. We shall have to try whether things can be managed your way, if you are obdurate. But I cannot answer for the result.

I shall return to Fernhurst tomorrow afternoon. It is impossible for us to meet there. But I can come anywhere. Goodbye, Goodbye,

B.

Over Philip and her family life, Ottoline was not prepared to make concessions. But at the same time she did not want to end her affair with Bertie. She did go and see Mrs Whitehead, as Russell had urged, though the results were not what Russell had hoped for. Ottoline left an account of the meeting. Though she couldn't remember much of what Evelyn Whitehead said, except that Bertie was not 'faithful or constant', she did remember 'the discomfort of sitting in a strange elaborate little drawing-room, talking to a strange elaborate lady, who looked on me with suppressed mistrust and jealousy' (*Memoirs*, vol. II, p. 269). Immediately after the meeting, however, Ottoline wrote to Bertie to say she now saw that they must break it off, but she begged for one last meeting to say goodbye.

[161]

17 Carlyle Square
[29 March 1911]

You are right, my heart, we must end everything but what we can treasure in our own thoughts. I shall be glad to see you once more, tomorrow morning, here, as soon after breakfast as you can. There is no bitterness and no hatred in my heart, and no rebellion – it must be so. All that has been is good, and remains – your love remains to purify me. I am glad of what has been – deep in the depths I am happier than before it happened, in spite of the pain. Do not fear that I shall doubt the strength of your love – there are things one must put before love, if one is to be worthy of love. You will live in my heart with the things that make religion, and redeem the world in spite of the terror and the pain. O my love, I bless you for what you are, for your love and for your strength. You shed a light upon this world for me, and that nothing can take away. Goodbye goodbye goodbye.

This 'fatal meeting', as Philip Morrell described it in one of his footnotes, did not go as planned. The account Ottoline gives in her *Memoirs* begins to diverge further from that suggested by her letters to Bertie – though the latter are not necessarily to be believed just because they are closer to the events. Russell evidently begged her not to break it off and, convinced of the efficacy of persuasion in these, as in other, matters, pressed his case with all the considerable eloquence and zeal at his command. According to her *Memoirs*, Ottoline was taken aback: 'He was like a Savanarola, exacting from me my life, my time and my whole devotion' (vol. II, p. 269). But she did accede, at least partially, to his exactions and the letter for him she took with her to the meeting makes it clear that this decision was not unpremeditated. It seems clear that, while she was reluctant to get as deeply involved as Bertie wished, she was equally reluctant to break with him entirely. The encouraging tone of her letter cannot be explained by her not having the courage to tell him that she didn't love him as much as he loved her; nor by the other explanation, both patronizing and compassionate, in her *Memoirs*: 'How could I allow him to return to the dreary life that he had risen from? It seemed that I could not refuse to take upon me the burden of this fine and valuable life' (vol. II, p. 268). Whatever her motives, the meeting and her letter left Bertie in transports of joy.

[162]

17 Carlyle Square
[30 March 1911]

Dearest my whole soul is flooded with joy – your radiance shines before me, and I feel still your arms about me and your kiss on my lips. You have become to me something holy; my touch will be gentle because I reverence you. Our love shall be always sacred, and I will give you a devotion worthy even of you. You have released in me imprisoned voices that sing the beauty of the world – all the poetry that grows dumb in the years of sorrow has begun to speak to me again.

Later (I was interrupted.) I would not for the world not have had the dear letter you gave me when you went away today. But indeed I do not deserve what you give me. All that is good in me comes of reverence, but where I find no occasion for reverence I sink below what you will ever know – at least I have done so in the past. I too thought you self-sufficing – that is why no thought of love came to me sooner. I did not know I loved you till I heard myself telling you so – for one instant I thought 'Good God what have I said?' and then I knew it was the truth. My heart spoke before my brain knew – and then love swept me on in a great flood and lifted me to the heights. It is strange to have been so sure so quickly, but I knew at once that I could give you *everything* that my nature is capable of. It still seems to me strange that you should love me.

Dearest, I will accept whatever of your time you feel you can rightly give, and I will not ask for more. The inward union is so deep and real that today I feel as if nothing else really mattered – but of course it will be harder when the days have gone by and your voice and face are less vivid to me. I must have your picture – otherwise the image of you will not remain clear in my mind.

Today is such a contrast to yesterday – I had quite made up my mind that we must part. Even if we had parted, you would have given me a deep peace which would have survived all the pain. As it is, I have that and happiness as well.

I have gone back to reading poetry which I had not read for many years. I suppose there is no poet you don't possess, or I would give him to you. I want to give you something, but I feel you have everything. I have been ascetic and starved my love of beauty, because I could not live otherwise the life I had to live. Now all that is over. I cannot write more tonight. Goodbye, my heart. I am yours, yours utterly.

B.

Don't address here after tomorrow morning. I go back to Fernhurst early Saturday, and come back Monday to Wednesday. Tuesday we have an Adult Suffrage Conference with some MPs at the House.[1] If you think there is any likelihood of my meeting Philip I suppose I had better stay away.

After the crucial Thursday morning meeting with Ottoline, Bertie returned to Fernhurst to try once more to make arrangements with Alys for a separation. On Sunday, 2 April, he reported to Ottoline from Fernhurst:

> Alys has been speaking in a most harrowing way, and has made me for a moment full of the thought of her pain. But I am sure, really, that she will be happier when she has given up the struggle to make some sort of life with me – otherwise I could not ask her to give it up. I mind her pain more than the pain of people I like better – it is like the pain of a wounded animal. At times I have thought I ought never to have told her I no longer cared for her, yet I feel that a life of active and constant hypocrisy would have been impossible and wrong. But giving pain deliberately is very terrible.

Once back in London Bertie took stock of the situation with Alys and addressed the pressing problem of how he and Ottoline were to meet in London without attracting the suspicions of their friends. Ottoline had suggested a meeting at Kew Gardens or Putney Heath. While in London he also looked for a book of poems to buy for her, but he was having difficulty finding any which came up to the exalted standards of his love.

[163]

More's Garden
Cheyne Walk[2]
Monday night [3 April 1911]

My Darling,
    It was a joy to get your letter tonight. I get so hungry for you, and I was troubled by the time at Fernhurst. The whole atmosphere jarred, and Alys

1. Presumably the aim was to muster support for an adult-suffrage amendment to the Conciliation bill then before Parliament. This was a private member's bill, so-called because it had been proposed by an all-party Conciliation Committee designed to resolve the suffrage issue.
2. Russell wrote against the address: 'This is where I sleep. Address 17 Carlyle Square.' More's Garden was a block of flats on the Embankment. The Murrays had a flat there and Russell may have been borrowing a room of it from them.

was very difficult. At present she is behaving well, but I doubt whether she will permanently. I am afraid that if a serious scandal is to be avoided, it may be necessary for me to remain on terms with her. She has written to Mrs Whitehead demanding sympathy and an interview. After that has happened I shall know better what to expect, as she is likely to let out more truth than she would to me. I proposed to halve our joint income, but she refused with indignation to touch a penny of my money. This looks like trouble. Meanwhile she agrees to retire for 3 months, and I agree not to decide finally as to keeping up appearances until that time is over. Without telling me, she wrote to resign all her committees. Altogether there may be much difficulty.

As to Wednesday – I have had no opportunity yet of asking Mrs Whitehead, but before I had read your letter she was saying we could meet occasionally at Carlyle Square, but not often, because she doesn't want her servants to know, or her son – he is very perceptive, and if he saw you he would guess at once. So I hardly like to ask her as I know she wouldn't wish to refuse. I think it is better to avoid places like Kensington Gardens, where we should meet all our friends. The only plan I can think of is to meet at some underground station exit, and take a cab to some out of the way place like Putney Heath where we could walk if it was fine.[1] This doesn't seem a very excellent plan, but I don't see anything better. If possible, I ought to get away by the 6.40 from Waterloo, but I should not do so if you were free longer, as it is not imperative. If you can't think of any better scheme, I would suggest Walham Green, which you can reach in about 15 minutes from Charing Cross Underground. But I should like almost any other plan better if you could think of one.

I have been thinking and thinking about what to give you, till I got as complicated as a character in Henry James. I would rather it was something we both like than something you haven't got – also I would rather give you a small book that one could easily have with one out of doors, also I find the bindings that shopkeepers think beautiful are almost always hideous. Then I thought over all the lyrics I like. Shakespeare's songs are sometimes absolutely perfect, especially 'Hark Hark the lark'.[2] But his Sonnets – though I almost lived on them at one time – came, in the end, to seem lacking in idealism. I felt, at last, a certain trail of the common sense that made him a successful man of business. There are exceptions, of course – especially 'That

1. Ottoline scouted the idea of meeting at a railway station and suggested instead either his room in More's Garden or an art gallery near by.
2. *Cymbeline*, II, iii.

time of year thou mayst in me behold'[1] – still, somehow, he is too finite. Matthew Arnold, at one time, I found exactly what I wanted, and 'Dover Beach' still expresses my feeling, but it does not express yours.[2] And the schoolmaster and pedant in him grows tiresome at last. Finally it seems to me that Shelley and a few things in Blake were what fitted best. Shelley has been ever since I was a boy the poet I have loved best – I seldom read him because I know him so well, but he is constantly in my thoughts. A few things in Blake are wonderful – 'Tiger, Tiger', and 'The Sunflower', and 'The Garden of Love'. 'The Pebble and the Clod' is in the nature of a sermon, but it is one I need.[3] Today, though I foraged as long as I could, I got nothing, but I will make a beginning – only a beginning – by Wednesday. I am so glad about *Deirdre*[4] – nothing in literature seems to me to fit so well with what I have been feeling.

I am glad about Lamb – you must be the chief barrier between him and degradation.[5] I am fond of his brother, though he is not commendable and often shocks me.[6] But sincerity makes most things bearable.

Yes, Dearest, we do seem strangely near in thought and feeling – more so than I could have believed we could be. I have the sense that you will always understand me, though I know I am difficult, because things affect me in strange ways. I believe and hope that I shall always understand you – there does seem something fundamental that makes it possible. You fill my world – I find I am constantly not hearing what is said to me because my thoughts are with you, and I can't bring them to what is happening. Beloved, you do make me feel your love – I feel it with me every moment – I feel it keeping me to the best, making the vision live and peace grow in my soul. It has been a troubled and tortured soul – I have sought truth before all, and have

---

1. Sonnet LXXIII.
2. A reference to their religious differences. Matthew Arnold's 'Dover Beach' is about the loss of religious faith.
3. 'Love seeketh not itself to please' is the song of the clod, while the pebble sings: 'Love seeketh only self to please,/ To bind another to its delight'. All the Blake poems Russell mentions are in the *Songs of Experience* (1794).
4. J. M. Synge's one-act play *Deirdre of the Sorrows* (1910), based on the tragic Celtic love story in the Ulster cycle. Both Ottoline and Bertie liked the play. Ottoline had told him she had just bought a copy.
5. Poor Henry Lamb was still in love with Ottoline. Ottoline had assured Bertie she was going to pack him off, though she still felt obliged to help him. The situation did not change dramatically – it was a long-standing tale of mutual irritation and reconciliation.
6. Walter Lamb, formerly a classics student at Cambridge. In 1913 he became Secretary of the Royal Academy and thereby the source of much amusement in Bloomsbury. Lytton Strachey nicknamed him 'The Corporal'.

been willing to let anything go to the wall rather than that – it has made me sometimes hard, sometimes reckless, but now it seems easy to make the other good things fit with truth. O Dearest, your love is absolute happiness to me, but it is more than happiness – it purifies all my thoughts, it stills the intolerable home-sickness of the exile, it revives the worship of beauty that I set out to kill in order to endure my life. I wonder if you ever read the thing I wrote about why I love Mathematics[1] – you would be able to understand all but a few sentences of it, and it would tell you how I tried to live. But mathematics is a cold and unresponsive love in the end; and it is hard to generate all one's force from within. Now I must stop – it is nearly two o'clock. Goodbye, goodbye. Your letter was a perfect joy. O Dearest I do hunger to be with you. I could not have believed I could love so absolutely. My heart, my soul, goodbye.

    B.

The problem of finding a satisfactory meeting place was solved for the time being by Ottoline's going on holiday to Studland in Dorset. Philip would be with her for part of the time, but Bertie would be able to visit when Philip's parliamentary duties required him to be in London. Bertie was eagerly looking forward to it. It would be their first chance to have sex and to spend much time alone together. In her *Memoirs* Ottoline said she found the prospect of Bertie's arrival oppressive: 'I was not able to feel the same anticipation he did. It is miserable to be expected to give more than one has; one becomes obsessed with one's own bankrupt condition' (vol. II, p. 272). This was not, however, the impression she conveyed to Bertie in a number of long and very affectionate letters from Studland.

At this time their relationship seemed to have stabilized and Bertie addressed himself to outstanding points of difficulty. One was Ottoline's fear that she was not intellectual enough for him. Another was Bertie's desire to have children. The latter issue was emotionally complicated for both of them, even ignoring the fact that they were not married. Bertie had always wanted children and, since attempts to have one with Alys (after fears of hereditary insanity had been laid to rest) had come to nothing, he may well have doubted whether he was fertile. Ottoline had not wanted to have children and felt herself lacking in maternal instinct. She tried to do her best for Julian, without ever feeling that her best was very good. The death of her son so soon after his birth made her feelings even more difficult to cope with. On top of this, two years after she had given birth she had to have an operation

1. 'The Study of Mathematics' had been recently republished in *Philosophical Essays* (1910). Russell had sent her a copy.

which prevented her from having any more children, though whether she knew this for sure in 1911 is unclear. Her reply to Russell's suggestion about a child was equivocal. She appeared flattered that Bertie wanted to have a child with her, though she feared the birth would be very painful. She did indicate that she might not be able to have one, but did not suggest that it was impossible. But at all events, it could not be rushed into: they would have to give it more thought.

[164]

Fernhurst
Thursday morning [13 April 1911]

My Dearest Dearest,

Your beautiful letters have just come. I am so sorry to have troubled you with my depression – it is gone, but it was real. I am not really ashamed of having written it out, because it is what I should have wished you to do with me, so that I was following the Golden Rule. But you may always know absolutely for certain that my depression would go if I were with you. And don't ever fancy it could have anything to do with being disappointed in you: I could not possibly be disappointed in you. You are far more wonderful than I knew or supposed, and I love you quite infinitely more than I did at first. You seem to think I must want you to be 'clever', but I never thought you that, if that is any comfort to you. My judgment of people's brains has nothing to do with my liking or disliking them. On the purely intellectual side, I have scarcely any companionship because intellectual work is not easily shared, though I have the rare good fortune of sharing mine with Whitehead. But that is not what I want from you, and I am not disappointed at not getting it. My world is full of 'clever' people – most of them so clever that they have seen the folly of everything I value. *Serious* people are not 'clever' inside. If they seem so, it is only a mask. What matters is how one feels about the things that are important. And your way of feeling is much better than mine, and just what I should wish mine to be. But if I ever did feel differently, of course I should tell you, because without truth-speaking and the knowledge that there will be truth-speaking, nothing worth having can be preserved.

Yes, Dearest, we must never again let a chance go by.[1] You must certainly come to see me in Cambridge. I long to be able to feel your presence in my rooms – the once that you were there last term is not enough to count. And

---

1. The chance of a meeting: Ottoline had regretted that so many opportunities had already been missed.

I want you to know all about how I spend my life. But as a rule it will be better for me to come to London. I will see about getting a little house in Chelsea as soon as I can. But it may take some time, because it must be cheap and I won't have it squalid.

I should like to see you with your hair in two plaits and looking very wild.[1] Oh how happy we shall be when I come – I shall feel like a boy fresh from school for the holidays, and almost unable to seem sensible.

Yes it is often difficult to know the real value of one's emotions, but chiefly when they have little value. I never had one instant's doubt of the value of my love for you. I don't know how or why, but from the first it was clear to me that it was great and real and deep. The reason I was sure so quickly was that without my knowledge love had been growing and growing and suddenly it blossomed. I am very blind to feelings I don't expect. And then at once it appeared how much more wonderful you were than I had ever known – and your answering love was so unbelievably beautiful. But in moments of depression it happens to me to think that nothing in life is as long as life. I long for the continuity that comes with children – but that is a useless thought. Would it matter if you had a child? Although I should loathe its not being ostensibly mine, still it would be on the whole a joy. – Am I to make friends with Julian? I could readily love her very much, and if I did she would probably like me. But if she talked of me to Philip, it would be enough to drive him mad; so that I think perhaps I had better not make her notice me.

Breakfast has been ready for ages, and I can not get up. Goodbye my Dearest. Think of me as very happy, and wearing out the hours by long long walks spent in thinking of you. My loved one, I long for you. I long for complete union.

Goodbye, Goodbye,

B.

Russell was to arrive at Studland on 18 April, the Tuesday after Easter. But, just before Easter, a new and totally unexpected blow fell. An appointment with his dentist revealed something wrong with his mouth which the dentist thought was cancer. A specialist was recommended but turned out to be away on holiday and Russell had to wait three weeks for an appointment. 'When the dentist told me,' Russell wrote, 'my first reaction was to congratulate the Deity on having got me

1. Ottoline had told him that in the country she was wearing her hair down in two plaits.

after all just as happiness seemed in sight' (*Autobiography*, vol. I, p. 204). He did not tell Ottoline of his fears, and went to Studland as planned and with undiminished enthusiasm. When he finally got his appointment with the specialist it turned out that nothing serious was wrong.

The cancer scare did not mar his time with Ottoline. 'The three days and nights that I spent at Studland', Russell wrote, 'remain in my memory as among the few moments when life seemed all it might be, but hardly ever is' (*Autobiography*, vol. I, p. 204). Ottoline in her *Memoirs* was more equivocal:

> I could not easily get over my feeling of shyness and strangeness with him; but by degrees it wore off, and I was able to be more natural and easy. Still his passionate intensity made me feel constrained. I felt uplifted that this remarkable man should carry me up with him into worlds of thought I had not dreamt of. (*Memoirs*, vol. II, p. 273)

She was not strongly attracted to him physically, and thought he lacked 'charm and gentleness and sympathy'. But Ottoline's account in her *Memoirs* is a good deal cooler than the letters she wrote to him at the time.

Bertie had no such reservations. Ecstatic letters flowed back to Studland, beginning on the train just after he'd left her. He stayed the night in London and then travelled on to Cambridge, where a new term was beginning. Cambridge, which two terms earlier had seemed a liberation when it was an escape from Alys, now began to irritate him slightly. It separated him from his love and cramped his romanticism.

[165]

Trinity College
Saturday evening [22 April 1911]

My Dearest Dearest

Your lovely letter reached me here almost immediately after I arrived, when I was still opening my other letters. It was a joy to have it. No, I hardly feel yet that we are parted, and I go about with such a sense of happiness that I can hardly contain it. Everybody here meets me with something that they consider a tale of woe – from a threatening of consumption to sea-sickness in the Channel – and I feel quite out of it, having no woes to produce.[1] One man I met was cheerful – Professor Hobson[2]

1. Ottoline had still not been told about the cancer scare.
2. Ernest William Hobson (1856–1933), Sadleirian Professor of Mathematics at Cambridge. His more famous brother was John Atkinson Hobson (1858–1940), an important economist who never held an academic position.

(brother of the economist), who is not lecturing this term, the first time for 32 years. What a life!

I have been struggling with the material world, finding my room without a carpet through some error, and having to search out where the carpet was – buying food etc., unpacking, and generally altering the position of matter in space – a form of activity I dislike, because it achieves nothing important. I have been cunning, and have arranged, with the full concurrence of the authorities, to give only two lectures a week, supplemented by individual teaching. The result is that I shall be able to come to London sometimes without having to put off a lecture. This is very desirable.

The only odd letter I received this morning was from an American named Henderson, the Professor of Pure Mathematics in the University of North Carolina (which apparently exists), and the author of a life of Shaw which he has sent me.[1] He is tall and lank, and appeared late at my first lecture, saying 'Please Sir, I'm from North Carolina'. I don't think he learnt much.

When you come, or sooner if you like, I can give you various unsuccessful attempts at writing, mixed up with private reflections, that I made nine years ago.[2] You will see just how they fail, and why I had to give it up. The only point of your reading them would be to see how they fail.

I have refused today an invitation from the Astronomer Royal of Ireland to go to Dublin and lecture for a term. I told him my duties here unfortunately forbade my going – but I reflected that even duties may sometimes be convenient.

Your pen is delightful – I am using it now. I wish it would write your thoughts for me, but it is sadly subservient, and expresses itself just as if it had never been yours.

This place is very much where the civilized half of me belongs. I love the courts and the willows, and my own rooms, and the feeling that the things of the intellect are respected here. But the other half of me is restive under the restraint and the artificiality and the absence of anything like real life; and the timidity of mind and body that dons suffer from always seems to me rather pitiful – they never view life as an adventure, except when they are really immoral. The quiet courts, shut in and allowing no horizon, really

---

1. Archibald Henderson (1877–1963) was a research student at Cambridge 1910–11. His *G. B. Shaw: His Life and Works* (1911) was the first of several books he wrote on Shaw. He wrote voluminously also on American history and literature, but little on mathematics.
2. Some at least of these pieces survived among Ottoline's papers. They are published in *Papers*, vol. XII, pp. 35–55.

suit them. It is a pity – a little adventurousness would improve their work enormously.

Now Dearest I must stop for the present – I will finish my letter later, after dinner.

Later. Una Birch has sent me her book on Secret Societies and the French Revolution,[1] parts of which I have read in the form of separate articles. I never can quite make out why she is not more interesting. Her feelings are strong and genuine, and her mind is very fair. But the trail of the *Spectator* or rather the *Edinburgh Review* is over all her thoughts, so that they are never vivid or illuminating. I think that although she feels strongly about her own affairs, she does not feel strongly about historical things, and she has very little imagination – that must be the reason.

I have been talking at dinner and since with McTaggart, but without getting much of interest out of him. I rather resent the hold that this place and work (which belongs with the place) have on me; habit is so strong that work gets hold of me even more than it need.

Have you seen that there is a thing by Mrs Whitehead in this week's *Nation?*[2] She has been expecting it for some time, but it was delayed. It seemed to me to have great merit.

Dearest, you have given me greater happiness than I had ever known or imagined. All the world is filled with splendour by the thought of you. After I had stopped writing to you this afternoon, I went out to see the sunset and hear the birds – everything seemed a thousand times more beautiful than other springs – the daffodils and young lime leaves and thrushes and the sky and the meadows – it all seemed transfigured. Darling, I am so glad you found you could speak to me of things that have been important in your life – all about the boy that died, and all you have felt and not felt about Julian – I was very glad you cared to speak of it. You need never mind speaking of Philip whenever you wish to. Dearest, your love seems to me absolutely perfect – I cannot imagine a more perfect love. I can still feel your arms and your kiss and see your beauty and hear your voice. Absence is not difficult till I have lost that – as yet I can live over again every moment of the three days. Now goodbye my Beloved. My love is increased a thousandfold, by the three days, by knowing you more completely, and by the

---

1. Una Constance Birch, later Dame Una Pope-Hennessy (1876–1949), the author of several books on history, travel, and literature. Her *Secret Societies and the French Revolution* was published in 1911.
2. A sentimental short story, 'Suspense', published in the *Nation* on 22 April 1911. It described the thoughts of a husband as his wife lay dying.

utter joy of our perfect union. Goodbye my Ottoline. I am yours in every thought.

B.

Their next meeting was in London on 1 May, when Bertie took Ottoline around the parts of London in which he had grown up. The next day he had to hurry back to Cambridge very early to have breakfast with his brother. Bertie seemed to relish such breathless schedules, especially in the cause of love; but Ottoline, though she had returned to London several days before, found them tiring. She seems often to have been on edge during their meetings in London, perhaps fearing that their secret would be discovered. No doubt also Bertie's nostalgic journey back to Richmond Park encouraged a more reflective mood. At all events, the mood of this meeting, though still satisfactory, was rather different from that which had prevailed at Studland. The meeting produced the usual letter from Russell written on the train as he rushed back to Cambridge.

[166]

In the train
Tuesday 5.33 a.m.
[2 May 1911]

My Darling
    You know exactly how long this letter will be, because you know how much paper I have with me.[1] But I will write as small as I can. I suppose it was the combination of your fatigue and my visit to the Whiteheads that made us so solemn yesterday – but I think it is when we are solemn that I know most completely how much I love you and how deeply. I know then that in any crisis or misfortune we should be drawn closer together. I got on with Alys very well until the Boer War. I felt the Boer War so much that I could not think of anything else, and Alys was jealous of it. She was a foreigner, and in any case couldn't understand feeling so much about anything that didn't touch one personally. Although the war was not what actually produced the rupture, it was the real cause. At the beginning of the war I was an imperialist more or less. In the middle of it, for other reasons, I had a sudden 'conversion', a change of heart, which brought with it a love of humanity and a horror of force, and incidentally made me a pro-Boer. Alys was puzzled, and disliked it – I remember one day when we were talking

1. It was written on Ottoline's notepaper with her Bedford Square letterhead. There were two sheets, doubtless provided for the purpose, and Bertie filled them completely.

with other people she said casually that she wouldn't like to have a child like me. I felt she was opposing what was best in me, and also that she did not care for me much, which was true until she found she had lost me.

All this is a parenthesis to say why I am glad that we are sometimes solemn together. You and I are I suppose both fundamentally people to whom things are easily tragic, and it would be a pity if our happiness made us forget that. So many things seem possible when one is light-hearted that don't turn out to be possible. Darling, don't worry about my work – except the little book for the series,[1] I have very little creative work that I ought to do for years to come, in fact I had been wondering how I should keep myself off writing till I had lain fallow for a bit. And one can't worry about what may happen years ahead. As for the book for the series, I have more or less promised to go with North Whitehead alone to Lockeridge[2] for a fortnight at the beginning of July – I shall get it nearly finished in that time. What remains I can do in August if you go abroad then. So that is all right. Dearest, nothing really matters so long as we do not have a crime on our consciences – that seems to me the only thing that could ever divide us – *because* we should feel alike about it.

When I spoke yesterday about having found out what pleased you, and then not saying it, I was thinking of all the things that make religion to me. They are very real, but it is a crime against religion to use it to make you love me, so I feel I can only talk about it when the impulse is straight and clean. Fortunately, with you, it often is. It is an unspeakable joy getting to know you better. I know now just how your face will look with different thoughts. I love it when it is very serious – but your laughter too – it is exquisitely delightful. Darling, I am filled full of a song of joy for having found you – I could not have thought the world contained you, and now I feel I have been searching for you all these years. Only at times it seemed a fruitless search and one gave up hope. I have an irritating variety of moods, but I see that you fit them all – except the hard intellectual mood, which essentially wants no one. I don't really believe that in the long run I fit you as well as you fit me. Still, you saw a fair amount of me in an ordinary way, and you seem to have liked it. I think what you would hate about me is the insincere person whom I keep for clever people I dislike, or for companies where I don't wish to be too real. But as long as present circumstances continue you won't see that person – and perhaps he'll die a natural death. I wonder whether you would dislike the person who denounces. I remember

1. *The Problems of Philosophy.*
2. Near Marlborough. The Whiteheads had a country cottage there. For unknown reasons, these plans were changed and Russell and North went to the Malverns instead.

Mary Murray was so shocked because a young lady whom we knew very slightly, but who seemed quite nice, got engaged and brought her fiancé to Bagley Wood to tea, and I became persuaded he was a rank humbug – she was a methodist and he became one to please her – and I attacked him and argued and showed him up, without any invention. The engagement was broken off soon afterwards, and I am sure it would have been disastrous if it hadn't been. Still, my conduct was questionable. How nice it must be to be insincere, and able to alter to suit. But as you say, we do change each other – but it is by bringing out the best, by giving one the courage of the good one would hardly allow to grow. Dearest it is wonderful how you do that for me – and all the asperity and bitterness I am capable of and all the tendencies to cynicism you melt and destroy.

I rather enjoyed getting up early. I got nearly 5 hours of absolutely sound sleep, and was amused to see the City *really* empty, not merely as it is on a Sunday. As far as I could see there was only one other passenger at Liverpool Street. By the time my brother comes to breakfast, if he does, my day will be far advanced.

It was rather queer yesterday going with you to places where I had been in childhood, places where I remembered going on sunny days with my grandmother. She would have liked you very much, as soon as she had got over thinking you too smart – she had a passion for dowdiness. You would have liked her, I think, because she was deeply religious and utterly unworldly. She was very full of anxious morality, and you might have felt her stuffy. Like all virtuous people of her time, she was insincere in thought when sincerity would have been shocking – she never, for instance, knew that she hated my brother. My attempts at truth always distressed her, and I soon learnt to keep them to myself. But I owe a great deal to her. Politically, she was perfectly generous and absolutely fearless; in private, she thought the only thing that mattered was a good heart, and she was genuinely utterly indifferent to all the things of the world. She opposed my marriage bitterly, and it produced a certain coolness during her last years. When she was dead I felt remorse, but on looking back I don't think I was *much* to blame.

But, Dearest, the only thing I really want to write about is our love. I have not before felt nearly as much love as I did yesterday. It was partly that made me so solemn. It was so great a thing one couldn't be otherwise than solemn. It is absorbing me more and more completely – I could almost wish I were not a mathematician because you are not. I grudge every thought I cannot share with you. I want to give myself utterly and wholly to you. But I also want to be worth giving. I feel that a lifetime is too short for all the things we have to say to each other. When we kiss, it is more joy than I can bear almost – it seems curiously little physical, but as though our souls kissed. And then at moments when I look at you, you seem wonderful and great and far-away, and I can hardly believe I have dared to kiss you. Without your touch, I can almost feel as if I had dreamed it all, and we were still on formal terms. And then it comes over me that we know each other's souls, and it seems strange and almost like a traveller's tale.

It is strange. I rejoice almost more that you have found an occasion to give love than I do that I have received it. It would have been too terrible if your power of love had been wasted. There is so much, so much, in my love that is just the love of what is beautiful and good, with no thought of any relation to Self. It is partly that makes me shy sometimes – I feel almost ashamed to ask that you should have any relation to me – it seems like asking the sun to shine for one's own private benefit. However, mercifully you are less impartial than the sun, and do not shine also upon the just.

Now we are nearly at Cambridge and I must stop. Goodbye my heart. You are my life and my joy, and apart from you I no longer have any life that counts. I love you – but that word falls far short of what I mean. All religion and life and thought seem to meet in my love – it is all my being.

    Your
      B.

If you see Mrs Whitehead, don't treat her as very ill unless she tells you. She always tries to appear less ill than she is, and it is important she should.

Waiting for Russell in Cambridge was news from Alys that her mother had died from the effects of a stroke a few days before. He wrote to Ottoline about it in a letter otherwise filled with an ironical account of the vicissitudes of Cambridge life.

[167]

Trinity College
Tuesday evening [2 May 1911]

My Dearest
    I dare say you will have heard by this time that Mrs Smith died yesterday. I found a telegram and a letter from Alys waiting for me when I arrived.

Later. I was interrupted at this point, and now I have your letter with Logan's. I wired to Alys to say I would come to Iffley[1] unless she wished otherwise,

---

1. Where Alys's mother had lived with Logan.

but she sent the enclosed reply, so I am here. I sent word I would not dine out, as it seemed more proper. I believe Mrs Smith improved greatly her last years – I only saw her about twice a year latterly. But when she was more vigorous she was terrible. I have never seen Logan so upset as he was by her heartlessness at her husband's funeral. His last wish was that £5 should be given to the gardener, but she refused point blank, and the rest of us had to make up the sum – not a large one after all.

My brother did not come to breakfast, but at 9 o'clock chests of books from Bagley Wood began coming, and men like Jybus in the Arabian Nights kept bringing more and more, and spreading them on the floor till there was no room to move. So I went out into the town and bought a bookcase and began feverishly putting them in. The floor is still littered with them, but some order begins to appear. I am choosing out those I am keeping – the rest will go to Alys. Alys will be as well off as I am now, which solves all difficulties as to money. It is a comfort, for I could not help sympathizing with her in her refusal to take money from me now, and yet if she didn't it was intolerable.

In the afternoon I had to go to Newnham to give help to my Danish lady Miss Lehmann[1] who comes to my lectures and is a bit puzzled. I somehow missed her for a long time, which resulted in my having a talk with Miss Harrison meanwhile.

The very high parson who lives above me, and is said to confess undergraduates, came in and offered to help with my books. I was much touched, but refused. Everybody I meet greets me with the question 'why were you not at the meeting?' and each time it is a different meeting. Really the intellectual life here is something dreadful.

I have just had a long interruption from the senior tutor, who tells me the Council would like my rooms for A. E. Housman[2] (the Shropshire Lad) but wished I would say I should not mind moving. However, I should mind, so I said so, and the Council will discuss the whole matter again. There is something curiously petty about life in a community. We all enjoy small advantages which others covet, and there is a tendency to petty spite, just because it is often people's duty to be unpleasant. I think all forms of communism develop the competitive instinct in bad ways. This is a paradox, but true.

1. She was, presumably, a Newnham student, but can't otherwise be identified.
2. A. E. Housman (1859–1936) the poet, best known for his early collection of poems, *A Shropshire Lad* (1896), was also a Fellow of Trinity and the Professor of Latin at Cambridge.

Tomorrow morning a Scotch pupil named Laird[1] is coming to argue with me. He is very superior, and more apt to impart instruction than to receive it. But apart from his Scotchness he is all right.

My floor is still littered with books, which makes me uncomfortable. I can't bear a piggery – it absorbs all my thoughts. The first interruption I had in writing this letter was from my Russian, Chrouschoff, who is clever but slack, and now thinks he has a bad heart and can't work, though his Tripos comes in a few weeks.[2] He began a tale of woe, and I had to laugh at him just as much as I thought he could stand. He is a little afraid of me, which is as well. Then I had a visit from the Secretary of the 'Heretics',[3] the body my brother was talking to last night – an energetic person who reads everything, and has something wildly intelligent to say about everything, but has no real brains and no quality at all, though he is nice and as good as gold. I talked to him about Shaw's play,[4] and he burst out against Amber Reeves[5] – he is a Fabian, and feels the nuisance she has been. I tried to deflect his anger on to Wells, not wholly successfully. It is a funny world here – so unreal, and yet not unimportant. But all the topics are unreal. The other night I went to see Bevan, the Professor of Arabic,[6] whom I like and who likes me. We talked about the Gnostics, St John's Gospel, Revelations, Apocalypses generally – all kinds of remote things; and not one word of reality did either of us breathe.

Darling I don't think you very dumb – I know your thoughts now often when you don't speak, and feelings come out without words. Dearest, my spirit is very far from being pure gold, though I think when I am with you it *is* pure gold – but that is because of what you are. Yes, I do feel what you do when we kiss – a merging of all our being. It is utterly untrue that you are small compared to me – you *must not* think it. It is only that I have a gift

1. John Laird (1887–1946). He had quite a distinguished career as a philosopher, ending up as Regius Professor of Moral Philosophy at Aberdeen. In 1910–11 Russell regarded him as the most promising student in his class.
2. His fears may have been genuine, for his name does not appear on the Tripos list published later that year.
3. Charles Kay Ogden (1889–1957), a linguist with diverse intellectual interests and accomplishments, then a classics student at Cambridge. He went on to edit the *Cambridge Magazine* (1912–23) but is best known as the originator of Basic English, to which he devoted most of his efforts after 1927. The Heretics were a Cambridge society for the discussion of religious topics.
4. Probably *Fanny's First Play*, which had opened at the Adelphi in London two weeks earlier.
5. See letter 153.
6. See letter 77.

of words, which sometimes I am half ashamed of. It has sometimes abandoned me these last weeks – it did when I had just left Studland. I should be sorry if nothing could make me dumb.

My Dearest, I am already hungering for you – other things seem so trivial, and other people have no quality. One seems to see all round them so easily. And rest and peace are with you – I had not imagined there was such peace this side of the grave. I have longed for peace, and been driven on and on by my inward demon – always seeking, never finding – till now at last the demon turns out to have been a guardian angel, because he has led me to you, and now I have found what I sought through all the years of weariness and struggle. Peace is the inmost heart of my love – passion is not, though it is necessary to the peace. I am thankful that my soul has remained pure and kept its fiery worship of the good through the years, because now I can give it all to you – every bit of good that I have preserved is something added to the strength and beauty of my love, and something to help in knowing your soul and loving it.

Dearest this must be posted or you won't get it by the first post. I love you I love you I love you. There is nothing else – Goodnight.

Your D.

At Cambridge on Thursday evenings Russell had got into the practice of holding an 'open house', when friends and acquaintances could drop by for conversation. Russell's 'Thursday evenings', as he called them, attracted a varying group of students and dons. He describes one in the next letter.

The letter was written just before Ottoline left for Paris to see Henry Lamb, over the objections of Philip. Bertie had no idea that the purpose of her trip was to see Lamb.

[168]

Trinity College
12 May 1911

My Darling

It seems a pity to waste all this good note-paper,[1] and I can't write to anybody else on it, so I am reduced to writing to you. I am thinking of you getting ready to go to Paris – you ought to have a very pleasant journey

1. The notepaper had Ottoline's Bedford Square letterhead.

today. I had quite a crowd last night – Oliver Strachey,[1] McTaggart, Shove,[2] Lamb,[3] young Birrell[4] again, and a host of people. They are difficult to manage. They sit round in a vast circle and wait for me to start topics. One young man who didn't know the rest came in to talk about Adult Suffrage business, and while I talked aside to him the rest preserved a dead silence, unable to think of anything to say without me to stir them up. McTaggart always goes to sleep, and can't be got to speak unless one attacks him fiercely, when he suddenly becomes witty. Karin says the only nice thing about young Birrell is his conceit – I rather think that is true.

Mrs Webb has been getting up Indian things with a view to her visit there, and has become an ardent nationalist – almost as fierce as Keir Hardie.[5] She really is generous-minded.

I have just been invaded by a woman I didn't know from Eve, who turned out to be Mrs George Haven Putnam, the publisher's wife,[6] a college friend of Alys's, whom Alys had never got me to meet, because when they were both girls Mrs Putnam denounced her for much the same things which I in the end found trying. (I heard this in a round-about way.) Mrs Putnam is staying with Frank Darwin, and was trying to find out where Alys is.

My Dearest, all this was only to fill up the time 'till the post came, with

---

1. One of Lytton's brothers, Oliver Strachey (1874–1960), had been sent down from Oxford without a degree and taken a job with the Indian railways. In India he got married (and divorced) and corresponded with Russell about philosophy. He returned to England in 1911 and met Ray Costelloe while visiting the Russells at Fernhurst in March. They got married at Cambridge on 31 May.
2. Gerald Frank Shove (1887–1947), an economist. He was then a student at King's College, taking part two of the Economics Tripos. He subsequently became a lecturer in economics at Cambridge.
3. Probably C. M. Lamb, a moral sciences student at Caius College. His father was Sir Horace Lamb FRS, a Cambridge-trained mathematician then the Professor of Mathematics at Manchester.
4. Francis Frederick Locker Birrell (1889–1935), journalist and drama critic, the son of Augustine Birrell, the essayist and politician. He was a student at King's College and became closely linked with the Bloomsbury Group.
5. In June 1911 the Webbs left on a world trip, spending most of their time in Asia. They did not return until May 1912. Norman Mackenzie, the editor of the Webbs' letters, says that their travels made them more hostile to imperialism and more sympathetic to the politics of Keir Hardie's Independent Labour Party (*Letters of Sydney and Beatrice Webb*, vol. II, p. 371), but Russell's letter suggests the change came slightly earlier. Keir Hardie, like Russell, had been a staunch anti-imperialist since the Boer War. Russell had broken with the Webbs' discussion group, 'The Coefficients', on the issue in 1903.
6. Emily Smith, the Dean of Barnard College, had married G. H. Putnam, the publisher, in 1899.

your dear letter. It wasn't a 'bald horrid letter' at all – it was so like you, as your letters always are. Some of the dons keep the beauty of the place fresh[1] – Dickinson does, and that is one of the reasons I have liked him so much. – I am interested about the poor blind woman – what a terrible existence.[2] I always wonder how people live without either happiness or work. I am glad you sent tulips to Mrs Whitehead – she has a passionate love of flowers.

It is odd to think of you in Paris. I have been remembering queer times when I have been in Paris. The first time was 1889, when I went with my enemy-friend Fitzgerald[3] and his people – it was the first time I had been abroad since I was two, and a great excitement. But I was tormented by shyness. The next time was in April 1894, when Alys and her people were there and I joined them on the way back from Rome – I was engaged then, and it was a time of delicious enjoyment. Then I was three months at the Embassy as honorary attaché in the autumn of the same year – my grand-mother so hated my engagement that she begged me to go away for a time, in hopes that I should get over the infatuation; so she got Lord Dufferin to offer me this as a reason for going, and to please her I went, and married as soon as the time was up. I loathed that time and the Embassy and everything to do with it. It was then I made friends with Sturges, whom I met first at the Kinsellas.[4] I also, oddly enough, made great friends with Mrs Berenson, and made the acquaintance of Berenson, whom I disliked: he began by telling me Alys was a snob, which though true was not exactly tactful, and was rather a case of pot and kettle. The next time of importance that I was in Paris was in 1900, when Alys and I and the Whiteheads went over for a philosophical congress. I was immensely struck by the Italian Logician Peano, who in all discussions seemed better than any one else; so I read his works which revolutionized my work, and started me on my present lines. I persuaded Whitehead to think equally well of Peano and that was the beginning of our formal cooperation. All through the autumn of 1900, I worked like one inspired – every day new worlds opened before me, and I saw clearly things which had been in a dim mist before. Intellectually, it was the supreme time of my life, and my work since has been mainly developing what I saw in outline then. So in the end my impressions of Paris are rather a jumble; but the strongest of them is the three months at the Embassy.

1. Ottoline, in her letter (the first of three that day), had commiserated with him about the stale Cambridge dons.
2. A childhood friend of Ottoline's whom she had been to see. The woman lived alone and miserably, and generally was very disagreeable to visitors.
3. See letter 47.
4. See letter 49 for Sturges and the Kinsella sisters.

Now I must post this, my Beloved. It is a dreadful long time till next Wednesday – luckily for me I shall be so busy that I shall hardly have time to think, except in the way that I always think of you whatever I am doing. My Dearest, when we have been together I am filled so full of joy that I don't feel your absence at first – it is only gradually that the hunger for you becomes hard to cope with. For some time, I feel your presence – I can almost imagine you are kissing me still. But what I do long for is time to share everything – books and thoughts and all – I hate having our daily lives so separate in their interests and occupations. But that can't well be helped – and my work would always remain separate for the most part. – Goodbye my life – I long to be with you – you are my all. Goodbye – my whole soul goes out to you.

    Your

    B.

Ottoline returned from Paris on 17 May, pursued by adoring letters from Lamb, and faced almost immediately two crises in her unusually tangled affairs. The first was occasioned by a visit from Roger Fry who accused her of spreading rumours that he was in love with her. What was surprising about this accusation was that Fry was (or, rather, had been) in love with her, and had told her so himself. But Fry had now contracted a much more serious passion for the painter Vanessa Bell and was worried lest it be cut short by word of his earlier attraction to Ottoline getting back to Vanessa via the notorious gossips of the Bloomsbury Group. Fry, rather unreasonably, was furious and Ottoline was deeply hurt and broke down in tears at the end of their meeting.

A few days after this scene, Ottoline had another visit, no more pleasant, this time from Logan. The separation arrangements Alys and Bertie had made in March were intended to last for only three months, after which the situation would be reviewed and a permanent resolution sought. The third month was now upon them and Logan, in a comprehensive round of visitations, came to negotiate on his sister's behalf. Alys still insisted that if there were to be a divorce Ottoline would be cited. Writing to Ottoline on 25 May, after Logan's visit, Bertie described his earlier discussions with Alys at Fernhurst:

> Alys, of course, wants to ruin you. When she said she wanted freedom, I tried to put your side, and even asked her if she would be equally willing to use sham evidence not involving you – but that had no attractions; if you were not brought in, she saw no point in a divorce.

Logan had several meetings with both Ottoline and Philip around this time. He denounced Bertie to Ottoline and Ottoline to Philip and said that unless the affair ended he would not be able to see them again. The climax came on 28 May when Philip and Ottoline had gone to stay with their friend Ethel Sands, the American painter, at her home, Newington, in Oxfordshire. Logan turned up and continued his denunciations to Sands. That evening Ottoline summed up her thoughts in her journal:

> What a frenzied time it has been. Bertie's meteor coming flashing into my life I suppose has upset all these meaner stars. He is wonderful, rare and important, and is worth, I think, the loss of much else. Philip is angelic, and sticks by me in a supreme way, which draws me more and more to him. . . . He *is* generous.
>
> Roger does not stand the test and has gone after Vanessa, and cannot be courageous, so shelters himself behind excuses. Logan loses his head like an old maid and says he cannot come any longer to my house. . . .
>
> [W]e decided that Logan's friendship . . . must be given up, and Ethel's displeasure brushed aside, and that I must stand by Bertie who at that time seemed really to need me, and was quite determined to leave Alys whether I remained his friend or no. (*Memoirs*, vol. II, pp. 275–6)

It was a courageous decision.

Meanwhile, Bertie, staying with the Whiteheads in London, aware of the meetings taking place that day but not of their outcome, wrote a noble letter to Ottoline, offering to relinquish his love to save her from further distress and to remove the threat to her marriage and reputation.

[169]

17 Carlyle Square
Sunday night
[28 May 1911]

My Dearest Life,

Sunday in London is a dreadful day, with no letters coming in. By going to the main South-Western Post Office, I managed to post a letter which I hope will reach you by the first post tomorrow, and I hope I shall get a letter from you then too. I have had endless painful talk with the Whiteheads, both of them, till I am sick of the whole sordid coil. I am tired and my head is aching. I told them I had offered Alys bogus evidence if she wanted a divorce, and they thought the offer ought to be repeated – that it would probably not be accepted, but Logan would then be against anything else. I could not say anything definite, because of course even that would in fact involve you more or less, and you might feel it better to break. It wouldn't of course matter to me, because none of my friends would believe it. For my part, I think it an excellent plan. Alys has a right to be free if she wishes it, and if she rejects that offer it shows that she only wants to ruin you, which she couldn't admit even to herself. I shall hear tomorrow afternoon what Alys and Logan have said. Apparently they are likely to tell all their family. And that will make it harder for them to do nothing.

The Whiteheads were out this evening so I went to dine with the Sangers. He went off early to go to a play, and I was left with Dora. She didn't say anything spiteful, and was rather nice, but not interesting.

Dearest, if you feel you ought to break with me now while there is time, don't mind saying so. The danger – and it is very real I think – is that Alys will do something sudden in an access of rage, which she would no doubt regret all the rest of her life – but half an hour's madness would be enough. If you feel it right to break now, I shall acquiesce. And it would not necessarily be for ever. But I would rather you decided in my absence and I would rather not see you again after you decided – it would be too great a tax upon one's strength. I do not feel that you are safe unless you break with me. I think it probable all will go well, but not certain.

The plan of a bogus case has one *great* advantage, that if she accepts it her power is at an end – she can do nothing further ever. That makes me favour it, as well as other reasons. It is *intolerable* being in her power, and until there is a divorce that will continue. You needn't imagine you would be accepting a sacrifice on my part. The relief of being really free from her would entirely outweigh the apparent disgrace, which in any case would not affect my friends. And as far as I am concerned, there is only one thing of real importance, which is to find a way of not losing you and yet not ruining you. Things like reputation and so on are the merest dross – even from the point of view of work and general usefulness they are of less importance, because now if I had to face life without you I should find it very hard to keep the energy necessary for work. Things go round and round in my head till I feel mad, and just wish it was all ended somehow, no matter how. If only one could fight them – it is doing nothing that is so trying.

The Whiteheads always depress me – I dare say I shall be thoroughly cheerful again when I get away. But I must say they have more reason this time than usual. The uncertainty is terribly trying.

I am reckoning on arriving at Henley at 4.46 on Tuesday, if that is not too early for you, and you are not afraid of my coming. It is hopeless to try to tell how I long for you. If you want me to come later, or not to come, please wire tomorrow to Carlyle Square. Dearest all this horror is making me love you more and more. But you mustn't feel you are *bound* to me in any way – if you think it right to break, you must. But O my heart, life would be a parched desert without you. I would do my best, for your sake – but it would be so empty that it would be hard to achieve much of a life.

This is a foolish letter to send you and perhaps I am mad. But I can't write anything else. Anything else would be untrue to what I am feeling. But don't be afraid I shall be in a state of depression on Tuesday – while I am with you I shall forget the future and be utterly happy. Only now I *must* think of it, because things *must* be thought out and decided. Forgive this rigmarole. Now I must go to bed. Goodnight my soul. I feel like some foolish child at sea, who has risen on the crest of the wave till he thought he could reach a star, and now finds there is another descent to be gone down and the star is as inaccessible as ever. But *reasonably* I still think it will be all right.

Your loving
   B.

Part of the reason Russell was finding the Whiteheads depressing was that they had been pointing out to him some of the likely consequences if his affair with Ottoline became known. It would have ended his career at Cambridge. Whitehead had witnessed at close hand the vindictive respectability of the Cambridge establishment when his friend A. R. Forsyth had eloped with a married woman. Forsyth felt obliged to resign his Trinity Fellowship. Whitehead urged the Trinity Council not to accept the resignation, but to no avail, and, in a very uncharacteristic display of anger, Whitehead walked out of the meeting. Trinity's treatment of Forsyth was one of Whitehead's reasons for leaving Cambridge himself. He handed in his own resignation two months after Forsyth's was accepted. Already, on the Whiteheads' advice, Russell had decided to resign his position on the Newnham College governing body as a precaution in case news of the affair got out. But the more serious prospect was that he might have to leave Cambridge altogether. He had no doubts that Ottoline was worth the sacrifice, but it was a sacrifice that would hurt deeply. 'I find I should be rather sorry to be hounded out of this place,' he had told her on 26 May. 'It is more nearly a home to me than any other place.' Moreover, the danger of a public scandal was very real, for there was now talk that Alys and Logan would hire a private detective to watch Bertie.

With a flood of depressed letters from Bertie, Ottoline wondered whether he wanted to break with her and whether she was worth the trouble she was causing him. In particular, she worried in case his work would be ruined, either because she was too much of a distraction or because he might have to leave Cambridge on account of her. She put all these concerns to him in a letter he received the morning after Logan's visit to Newington, at the same time making it clear that she didn't want to end their relationship. She asked him to be ruthlessly honest in his reply. Bertie responded with a detailed analysis of his priorities.

[170]

17 Carlyle Square
Monday morning [29 May 1911]

My Dearest Life,

It was a comfort to get a letter from you again after the Sunday blank. But I am *very* sorry my letters gave you the impression that they did. You must be very tired to have got that impression. As for things like being watched they don't worry me as much as mud on my collar would – they rather amuse me, and they relieve the moral tension by making things frankly a contest. And as for worry and anxiety, you don't know how preferable they are to blank misery. I really rather enjoy storms and anxieties, only I don't find it easy to bear the thought of parting from you. If they involved *anything* short of that, I should find them pleasant. I am sometimes dumb about love, but those are not the times when I feel least – I don't quite know what makes me dumb – I want your letters more at these times than at any others. Now I will make up an exact statement, and please keep it in mind however dumb I may be, because it is at all times true.

1. I want to keep you and I want not to ruin your life. I want both equally – I can't honestly say that I want one more than the other, though I should *choose* rightly if the choice were necessary. Compared to these two, all other things in life are trivial to me. Don't doubt this.

2. I want to accomplish, during my life, a good deal more work in philosophy, of which I already have the idea in germ. But I am no longer quite young, and I have spent a great deal of energy on the big book now printing, so that it will be uncertain whether I shall have enough energy left for another big job. I can however do a good deal in any case.

3. I want to write general things on religion and morals and popular philosophy. I could do this even if I were discredited, because I could publish anonymously. I can imagine a sermon on Strife, on the lines of what I wrote to you about the river[1] – and innumerable things of that sort.

---

1. This may well be a reference to an earlier letter in which he had compared the tranquillity of the Thames to human life, 'a vast purposeless chaotic struggle' (27 May).

4. I like teaching, but that is inessential.[1]

I have put these four in order of importance, the most important first.

There are certain things you must clearly realize. First: *Whatever* may be involved in our holding to each other, the harm to me will be less than if we parted. I believe seriously that the spring of life would be broken in me if we parted now. I have been very active, and have no longer the inexhaustible energy of youth – to begin all over again would not be easy. What I should do would be to settle down to try and write the sort of religious things we have talked of – if I succeeded, I should pull through; but I fear hatred of Alys would prevent me from succeeding. Already, whenever I am not on the watch, my imagination is busy concocting letters to her which would be calculated to make her life unbearable, and would probably succeed. They flash before me in a moment before I know what I am doing. I thoroughly realize that this is base, and I am trying to cope with it. Of course if she settles down there will be no difficulty.

As far as I am concerned, everything is simple. Both my happiness and my work are bound up with you, whatever may be the cost of our keeping to each other. As for you, I think you may be forced to choose between Philip and me, if the Smiths persist. I believe then it would be for your good to sacrifice me, and I should do my best both at the time and afterwards to make that course not too painful to you. But if you think it would not be me whom you would sacrifice, I should be glad to know it. Of course but for the conventions you could remain friends with P. whatever happened. I feel there is no conflict between P. and me – we both want your good. I could now, if he wished it, talk with him just as dispassionately as if I were in no way involved.

Dearest, you may really count on me always to tell you the exact truth, even if it would hurt cruelly. That is why I wrote what I did about Cambridge[2] – I had no further thought except that I had said something rather different and felt I must correct it. But you must *know once for all* that life holds nothing for me that compares with you for one instant – my good, which you wish, is *you*. If I have you, there are other goods that may be added; if I don't have you, there are no other goods. You must not doubt this when I don't say it. It is this fundamental point from which everything else starts. But I shall not fail in truth. At all times I care for it greatly, and where I love, I care for it most. You shall have always the cold steel that has

1. This fourth point was squeezed in as an afterthought.
2. In the letter of 26 May, in which he had explained how much Cambridge meant to him.

been tempered in the fire. The knowledge of the hurt to you, if I ever had anything painful to say, would make it more cold – but you would know what passion could alone produce it.

O my heart I ache for you. I feel as if I could hardly live through the joy of your kiss tomorrow. I have never imagined such love. I have had the feeling too that I ought to keep it back from you, so as not to interfere with your freedom – but I can't do it. Only you *know* I want you to decide freely and calmly and as *you* think right. But you must not imagine that worries or public disgrace or *anything* could weigh on my side as *anything* compared to you. That you must remember once for all. O my life, I long for tomorrow as I never longed before. With you there is life and joy and peace and all good things – away from you there is turmoil and anguish and blank despair if we must part. Goodbye my Light and my Life.

Your

B.

Logan had taken to Newington a set of conditions to be met if Alys were not to seek a divorce. The most important of these was that Bertie and Ottoline should never spend a night together. There was an implied blackmail here, that if the conditions were not adhered to Alys would seek a divorce citing Ottoline (hence the prospect of the private detective). Although these conditions were accepted, Alys was reluctant to admit that the separation was to be permanent: she still hoped that Bertie's love might return. Early in June Bertie received a letter from her which indicated that she still thought of the separation as temporary. Bertie was alarmed and the Whiteheads, presumably at his request, embarked upon yet another round of diplomatic activity to persuade her that the separation really was permanent. In this they were at last successful as Bertie reported in the next letter.

[171]

Trinity College
Tuesday evening [6 June 1911]

My Darling

I don't know if this will arrive before me, but I want to say I have just had a few minutes to talk with Mrs Whitehead, who has been with Alys, and is quite clear that there is not the slightest ground for anxiety any longer. She saw the letters Alys wrote about our separation and says they were excellent letters. She says Alys is in a very good mood, and determined to put it through in the best way. She was very emphatic about there being *no* need for anxiety now. The only thing she seemed to think important was that you should avoid even the slightest word, so as not to vex Logan. She saw the letter Alys wrote to Mrs Berenson, and says it was a very good letter – it said she wished never to discuss it with Mrs Berenson.

I do really think we may dismiss all fear from our minds now. When once that line has been taken with other people, it is really impossible for Alys to go back on it. Besides, there is no reason why she should grow *more* upset than she has been – on the contrary she will get used to being away from me and will come to prefer it, and then she won't feel any vindictive impulses.

Darling I long for tomorrow. I am hoping for a telegram but none has come yet. I am hungry for your arms and your kiss, my Dearest, my Ottoline.

Your loving
B.

Russell spent the first half of July with North Whitehead at Upper Wyche, near Great Malvern in Worcestershire. There he hoped to finish writing *The Problems of Philosophy*, the popular book that he referred to as his 'shilling shocker'. He had started it only the previous month and the contract called for its completion in July. However, the writing did not go smoothly at Upper Wyche. Russell was kept from his work by walks and discussions with North and further delayed by the arrival of proofs in French for one of the lectures he had given in Paris in March and by yet more proofs for *Principia Mathematica*. The proof-reading of 'the big book', as he called it, took an inordinate amount of his time until 1913 when the last volume appeared.

While Bertie was in the Malverns, Ottoline had moved for the summer to Peppard, the country cottage she and Philip owned near Henley-on-Thames. She always found the social demands of city life tiring and must have felt especially pleased to get away this summer. Later in July Bertie was going to take lodgings for a month at Ipsden, a village near by, from which he could easily visit her.

At the end of his first week at Upper Wyche, Bertie had to return briefly to London for a dinner of the Aristotelian Society, his first official function as the Society's president for 1911–12. On the way he took in an afternoon visit to Peppard, where he met Henry Lamb, now returned from France. (Ottoline had instructed him beforehand to be nice to Lamb.) Russell seemed a bit depressed about the meeting afterwards, but his letter of that evening brought renewed protestations of love from Ottoline who explained that her lassitude was due to a headache and her menstrual period, and she assured him she didn't think he was a 'solemn prig'.

[172]

My Darling

I won't post this till I come back tonight,[1] but I will begin it now. It was delicious in the woods at Peppard. I think it was a better place than any we have been in yet. Only the time was so short that even I could not imagine it was for ever, as I usually manage to do. I felt too that you were very tired. Please don't give another thought to my wish for children. From the first moment, you told me not to expect them, so I hadn't set my heart on your having a child. It is in every way more convenient that it should not happen, and it is by no means vital to me.

I was sorry I was tiresome about Roger. When I talk about anything of that sort, I am apt not to talk naturally, but as a moralist; because I am so apt to muddle things that I have lost confidence in my natural way of feeling. It seems to me that your way of feeling is extraordinarily like mine, only I am doubtful if that way is successful in practice.

Yes, I am horribly afraid of acting impulsively on things that are not genuine – at least I have been – at present I have no temptations of that sort. Dearest, I have a feeling that whatever either of us may think ill of in ourselves is really an added bond, because the likeness is so great. I see that you have more courage, more reticence, more power of suffering without complaining. On the other hand I have a rather more active desire to get at the exact truth. But more and more I am struck with amazement at our agreement in instincts. At first I could not quite believe it – I know that love plays one tricks, and I feared it might be less complete than it seemed. Now I have no such feeling. I know that if your love cools some day – I shall so well understand it that I shall feel no bitterness; and I feel it would be the same with you. And I am quite sure that whatever happens a very deep devotion will remain on both sides, because we respond with our best to each other's best.

It is funny, I am not at all afraid of my serious faults with you, but I am always afraid of your finding me a solemn prig. I know that is what I am at bottom, however I may try to disguise it.

The dear little heart with your hair will be an unspeakable joy to me – it

---

1. That is, back to his hotel room from the Aristotelian Society dinner.

was dear of you.[1] You needn't be afraid of being sentimental – I am at least as sentimental as you are.

Dearest Love, it is time for me to dress. I will finish this letter when I come home. I am rather tired from travelling and a very long walk yesterday. I do long to be established at Ipsden and see you daily almost. It will be too wonderful. When I see you with other people, I still feel odd – I can't believe the last months have really happened, and I go back to the time before in my mind. It would be natural to me to call you Lady Ottoline – I feel quite like a casual visitor.

Julian was *too* funny, she wouldn't begin her tea, she said 'I shall wait till Mummy comes, she *is* my mother you know.' She told me she had learnt one of the Blakes by heart. I asked her to repeat it, but she fetched a book and gave it me to read – she was very shy about it. I love her very much.

Midnight. The dinner was mildly amusing. Bosanquet in the chair,[2] Wildon Carr, Secretary and host;[3] Balfour,[4] McTaggart, Schiller,[5] Caldecott (a half-witted parson),[6] Hill (Vice-Chancellor of London University),[7] old Benn whom you may have met in Florence,[8] two people I didn't know, Nunn[9] (a teacher of philosophy in London and more or less a disciple of mine), Moore, Benecke (an aged habitué of the Aristotelian Society),[10] Self, Sorley (Professor of Ethics at Cambridge, dull, pompous, hypocritical and stupid

1. She had given him a locket containing a strand of her hair.
2. Bernard Bosanquet (1848–1923), the neo-Hegelian philosopher.
3. Herbert Wildon Carr (1857–1931). As a broker on the London Stock Exchange he had earned enough money to retire and devote himself to philosophy. He served as secretary of the Aristotelian Society for many years and in 1918 became Professor of Philosophy at London.
4. Arthur James Balfour (1848–1930), a politician and amateur philosopher. He had been Prime Minister until the Liberal landslide of 1905.
5. Ferdinand Canning Scott Schiller (1864–1937), the leading advocate of Pragmatism in Britain.
6. Rev. Alfred Caldecott (1851–1936), the Professor of Mental and Moral Philosophy at King's College, London. He wrote mainly on religious matters.
7. Micaiah John Muller Hill (1856–1929), Professor of Pure Mathematics at London (1884–1923) and Vice-Chancellor of the University 1909–10.
8. Alfred William Benn (1843–1916), a historian of philosophy and a member of the Society for the Promotion of Hellenic Studies. He had lived abroad, in Italy and Switzerland, since 1866.
9. Thomas Percy Nunn (1871–1944), a Realist philosopher, he became Professor of Education at London in 1913.
10. E. C. Benecke. He was very active for many years in the Aristotelian Society, chairing meetings and taking part in discussions but not reading a paper himself.

and Scotch),[1] and so back to Carr. (These are in order left to right.) Schiller used his chance to advertise pragmatism with Balfour, who was elaborately unassuming and professionally charming. McTaggart also got his innings, and looked as pleased as a cat when you scratch it. When we got to business, Balfour was quite useful in a mild way. But he is hateful. He makes such an impression of not caring about anything worth caring for. I can believe, though, that he is affectionate and kind; it is the lack of ideas that is so repulsive.

Moore walked back to Paddington with me, and came up to my room and sat there till the last train to Richmond – this made me miss the midnight post. Moore was very nice – he is much more friendly with me than he used to be. He had been to Iffley[2] and had encouraged Karin to write philosophy, which he says she is very doubtful about. He says the examiners had no doubt about giving her a distinction – that he thought her better than my Scotchman Laird, but the other examiners thought her less good.[3]

I got on very well with Sorley and quite enjoyed talking to him, in spite of his being all I have described. I find nowadays I like almost everybody – Balfour and Caldecott were the only people I didn't like tonight. Moore burst out to me against Schiller, and I admit all there is against him, yet I can't dislike him. Liking most people makes life amazingly easy. I wish you could get your nerves rested, so as not to be irritated by people – it makes life so much less tiring. I hope very much that living more in the country will do it for you.

Goodnight my Darling. It *was* a joy being with you today. I will write in the train, to reach you by 1st post the day after tomorrow. I *shall* be thankful when this time at Malvern is over. I enjoyed the journey up – I really am glad sometimes to be there with other people, it brings out things that wouldn't come out otherwise. Lamb was really angelic – I don't feel as if he disliked me, though one would suppose he must.

Goodbye my Beloved.

Your

B.

1. William Ritchie Sorley (1855–1935). He had succeeded Sidgwick as Knightbridge Professor of Moral Philosophy in 1900 and held the chair until 1933.
2. Where Logan still lived.
3. Both Karin Costelloe and Laird had got Firsts with Distinction in their Moral Science examinations the previous month.

Russell, of course, still didn't know the truth about Ottoline's relations with Lamb. Now that the two men had met, this situation had become a little awkward since Bertie might now learn the truth from Lamb rather than from Ottoline. Ottoline tried, very indirectly, to broach the matter in a letter to Bertie in which she ventured that the love she and Bertie had for each other was not selfish and would not exclude 'affection and love' for other people and that it might even be a good thing if others were included. Bertie took this to mean that she would not object if he became intimate with another woman. He rejected this suggestion resolutely – remembering, no doubt, the embarrassment over Ivy Pretious some years before. Nor was he any more encouraging about the converse suggestion, that he would not mind if she became intimate with another man. His response did not encourage any further confidences about Lamb.

Russell wrote his reply from the home of his old friend 'Lion' Phillimore (see letter 21), where he spent the weekend after his stay at Upper Wyche. 'Lion' and the depression occasioned by Ottoline's letter brought on a pang of remorse about his treatment of Alys.

[173]

Battler's Green, Watford, Herts.
Sunday night [16 July 1911]

My Dearest Love

For some reason, I hardly know what, I have suffered all day from rather acute depression. It is connected with your letter, but I find it hard to disentangle. First, you must not wish me to make friendships with women. Mrs Whitehead I have a friendship with which I would not lose for a great deal – indeed could not lose. Lucy Silcox I know well and like greatly; but she is not really important to me. Believe me, I *know* I am right in saying it is better I should avoid intimacy with other women. You will make a grave mistake if you go against this knowledge. Secondly, I have been troubled all day by a hypothetical jealousy. You were probably thinking *you* would not stand in *my* way, but this was a mistaken feeling – it is not the way of salvation for me. But I can't help feeling that you also think *I* ought not to stand in *your* way in some hypothetical future. I hope I shouldn't. But my nature is not large enough to avoid jealousy. You speak of 'affection and love'. I don't know if you were speaking exactly. If you gave love to anyone else, though I could acquiesce and remain a devoted friend, and not in any way alter my *opinion* of you, I should not continue to give love. Altogether, you would have a first-class tragedy on your hands. If I gave love myself to someone else, it would be most deeply unfortunate for me – morally I should suffer, and there would be a profound inward damage which would lead to spiritual ruin. All this is ungenerous and not as good as it might be, but I know it is true. It is quite immeasurably more important to my welfare that I should maintain my exclusive love for you than that I should have a child by someone else. If this is not clear to you we must talk of it; you must know it fully. You have great powers of making people enlarge their instincts, but it is impossible to do more than a certain amount.

Lion has talked more about you. She said she was amused to see such a devoted couple as you and Philip, that you and he went about with your arms round each other and that you called him 'Philip Darling'. So evidently she will not readily suspect anything. She evidently liked you *very* much.

I *long* to be with you – I think then my devils will leave me. For the present everything seems black. I don't know what has come over me. I am very tired. Lion, whom at first I liked very much, has got on my nerves again; I see her good qualities and like them, but am troubled by her making it so hard to speak sincerely to her. Marie Tempest,[1] who is taking this house, came to tea – I disliked her – she seemed hard and shallow. Being with Lion, whom I have known since before I got engaged to Alys, has vividly recalled to me the early days of my love for Alys, when she was young and happy and blooming, and full of simple un-self-distrustful kindness. Now she is broken, tortured, twisted, with no self-confidence, no hope, no purpose. It is all my doing. And so many years have gone, with their fresh hopes, their certainties and simplicities and innocences – and I feel old, and courage and faith seem to leave me. Please don't tax my instincts more than is necessary. Life has troubled and complicated them, and I long for simplicity; I want a rest from battling with them. I am feeling again what I have almost not felt these four months, the infinite unendurable weariness of inward mental strife – the feeling of the doomed Titan wearily upholding a world which is ready to slip from his shoulders into chaos. All this is largely the result of having been working again; I find myself tired out, and on the physical side quite dead; but thinking goes on and on, all the more. Darling, you will have to bear with me in depressions. They are not mainly personal; impersonal things are always ready to depress me, but personal happiness holds them at bay except at times. I do not believe the world to be good, I do not believe the universe has a purpose, I think what we value is passing and powerless. And I feel my task of thought just as if it were an order from a

1. The stage name of Mary Susan Tempest (1866–1942), an actress who started her career playing in musical comedies but switched to dramatic roles later. In 1911 she became a theatrical manager.

superior power − something which *must* be done, without reasoning about it or caring to know why; and I know that it involves the utmost of my powers, a stretching and goading of my intellect which is curiously painful.

O my Beloved, my soul turns to you out of this strange incomprehensible pain − I know that with you there is peace and rest and joy. I long to lay my head on your breast and feel your soothing touch and know that even during life there is peace, and not only when the brain has ceased to flog my weary thoughts. You *are* the goddess who raises the storms and then gives healing and comfort to the shipwrecked sailors.

I wonder whether you know and understand the odd sense of dedication that I have towards Philosophy. It has nothing to do with reason, or with any deliberate judgment that Philosophy is important. It is merely what I *have* to do. I often hate the task, but I cannot escape it − and of course at bottom I don't wish to.

I have written myself out of the blue devils now, and I hardly know what it was all about. The real root was I think an instinctive conviction that you will get tired of me, due to fatigue and to feeling myself a poor creature − with just a few tunes that come over and over again like a musical box. And the moment anything troubles me about you, it opens the floodgates to all the sorrows of mankind. Living without any religious beliefs is not easy. Darling my love to you is rather terrible really − it is so absorbing and so necessary to my life. And I dread your feeling oppressed by it, and feeling that it is a prison. It shan't be a prison to you my Dearest if I can help it. Goodnight.

Your

B.

Russell's correspondence with other friends had suffered since his affair with Ottoline began. His attention was focused on Ottoline so completely that this was inevitable to some degree. Moreover, the fact that he couldn't tell most of his friends about Ottoline made his letters even more remote from the main themes of his life. In the case of those who were also Alys's friends there was the additional difficulty of telling them of the separation. His correspondence with Helen Flexner and Lucy Donnelly, in particular, suffered in this way as the next two letters show. Russell told Ottoline around this time that, in the past, he had often felt rather noble in appearing to be cheerful when in fact he was deeply unhappy. But now he had to appear miserable when in fact he was happy and this, he felt, was base − but unavoidable given the situation.

[174]

Trinity College
24 July 1911

My dear Helen

Very many thanks for your interesting letter. I don't remember what I said about free will. My view is (a) that determinism is not *proved* (b) that it is very much more probable than the contrary (c) that I feel convinced there is some way of making the whole puzzle clear, and that no one has yet got to the bottom of it. It seems to me that the notions of 'dependence', 'determination' etc. are not so clear as most people think, and perhaps, when made clear, do not warrant some of the uses they are put to.[1] I do *not* believe in a soul which has an origin and destiny separate from the body.

Yes, Manichaeanism[2] is very attractive. But like Christianity it views the world too much under moral categories. Good and evil are alike human: the outer world is neither. I agree with you in feeling fury at the idea of a God of love who created such a world as this. But I think the intellectually essential error, the anthropomorphizing of the outer world, is committed by Manichaeanism also.

I find that religion and the religious attitude to life occupy a very great deal of my thoughts. I am glad to hear your view of life has simplified. I find year by year I grow simpler. I think all the *important* truths are simple. I should immensely like to hear more of your 'spiritual adventure'.[3] You are certainly right in counting upon my sympathy. There is nothing simulated by it, nor should I ever simulate an interest I did not feel.

Thank you very much for your kind words about Alys and me. There has been much pain, spread over a long time. Now one turns one's thoughts resolutely to the future. For my part, I find so much work that I wish to do that I have no difficulty in avoiding vain regrets over what is inevitable.

I have been interrupted, or would have written more. Now I must stop as I am very busy – pupils, a popular book on philosophy to write, proofs,

---

1. Russell worked on these and related themes the following year for a paper, 'On the Notion of Cause', which he gave to the Aristotelian Society on 4 November 1912 (published in the Society's *Proceedings*, 1913).
2. The view that good and evil are forces of equal power in the world.
3. Helen said she had been going through some sobering experiences which had changed her life and turned her toward a more religious view of the world. She had come to find Manichaeanism attractive. She did not offer any details.

etc. Please remember me to Simon and give my love to Lucy.
    Yours affectionately
      Bertrand Russell

[175]

Ipsden
20 August 1911

My dear Lucy

I am very sorry indeed that you feel I have vanished from your world. Believe me, you have not vanished from my thoughts by any means. It is true, of course, that my separation from Alys makes you hear less of me, and will lead to my seeing less of you when you come to England; still I shall hope to manage to see a good deal of you when you do come. I did not realize you had never been in Cambridge – it is odd. Cambridge is more like home to me than any other place. I have known it 21 years, most of the people I know with similar pursuits live there, and many of the most important events of my life have happened to me there. You must imagine me in a fairly large room, looking out on a Renaissance cloistered court, with Wren's library at one end and the Elizabethan College Hall at the other. My room contains many books, but only one picture (the picture of my mother that used to be at Bagley Wood), and the little Spinoza and Leibniz. In the main it is rather severe. For the moment, there is no one at Cambridge, and I have taken lodgings between the Thames and the Chilterns, in a region I got to know bicycling from Oxford – very beautiful, a mixture of corn-fields and beech-woods climbing the hill-sides. Towards the end of September I go back to Cambridge. Meanwhile I am very busy; I have just finished my book for the Middle West,[1] which I will send you when it is out. I have already started another little book;[2] I have proofs constantly, a presidential address for the Aristotelian Society[3] to write, Trinity Fellowship Dissertations to read, etc. My main plan in the way of work is to write a big book on Theory of Knowledge, but I don't want to embark on that for a good while[4] – I want to read a good deal first. Lately, I have been reading a lot of Plato (in English!); he is extraordinarily good.

1. *The Problems of Philosophy.*
2. 'Prisons' (see next letter).
3. 'On the Relations of Universals and Particulars', *Proceedings of the Aristotelian Society* (1913). Read to the Society on 30 October 1911.
4. He started it in 1913, but it was never finished. The 350-page manuscript is published as *Papers*, vol. VII.

It is very good news about Helen. I am *so* glad you and she no longer have any friction. One's life is terribly the poorer when one's comrades of many years fail one in any way.

All you tell me of Seal Harbour and of the children interests me greatly.[1]

Our politics have been exciting, and until lately very exhilarating.[2] But just now we are in the midst of a railway strike.[3] Traffic is not so much upset as might be expected, but there is great bitterness; the Government has been very unsympathetic to the men, and has probably lost much ground in consequence.

I am not going abroad. Now that I am at Cambridge I find it hard to do much writing in term-time, so I must stick at it in Vacations. My duties at Cambridge are distracting, not tiring, so I have very little need of a holiday. But I am only working a very moderate amount. The heat, for a long time, has been greater than I have ever known it in England – I like Italy in August, but the heat here has been too great for me.

I am happier than I have been for many years. The cessation of daily friction has set free a great deal of energy which I put now into thinking, and I feel prepared to embark upon new big tasks as I did not before. I fear Alys still minds, but I can't help thinking in the long run it will be for her happiness too. For many years past she has been bitterly miserable, and the only issue for us both was to face it and begin a new way of life.

Please give my love to Helen. Write again sooner than before, please, and don't think of me as if I no longer existed.

Yours affectionately

Bertrand Russell

By the time he wrote to Lucy Donnelly, Russell was coming to the end of his month's stay at Ipsden. While there he spent the mornings writing and then bicycled to see Ottoline at Peppard six miles away, 'arriving about noon, and leaving about

1. Lucy Donnelly was staying at Seal Harbor, Maine, with Helen Flexner and her children.
2. On 10 August, after a long fight with the Commons, the House of Lords reluctantly passed the Liberals' bill to restrict its powers, rather than have the King create enough Liberal peers to ensure the bill's passage. Russell had hopes that a more radical political agenda would now be possible for the Liberals.
3. Among much other industrial unrest, a national railway strike had started on 18 August in support of demands for better pay and conditions. There was even the prospect of a general strike at the beginning of August. Asquith, not surprisingly, was bolder in standing up to the workers than he had been in standing up to the Lords. Churchill, as Home Secretary, called out the troops to keep the trains running.

midnight' (*Autobiography*, vol. I, p. 206). This naturally reduced their correspondence, though there were still letters written on Russell's occasional forays to London or Cambridge, and there were even some written from Ipsden itself.

The summer, as he had told Lucy Donnelly, was very hot and Ottoline and Bertie took their lunch out in the woods, returning late for tea. Ottoline described their excursions:

> It was one of those marvellous summers ... when day after day the weather was hot and cloudless. Bertie ... came over every day to see me. So we grew more and more accustomed to each other, and more intimate.
>
> The beauty of his mind, the pure fire of his soul began to affect me and attract me ...; his unattractive body seemed to disappear, while our spirits united in a single flame, as if his soul penetrated mine. We took tea into the woods, and read such things as Plato and Spinoza and Shelley, and talked of life, politics and things to come....
>
> It was exhausting but delightful for me to have my mind kept in strict order, driven on to the end of a subject, through tangled bushes and swamps, till it reached open ground. . . . Bertie would ... urge me on ... telling me that I was not being honest, and that I must face the truth. (*Memoirs*, vol. II, pp. 278–9)

These tutorials in the woods often included a discussion of Russell's own work. At Ipsden he finished writing *The Problems of Philosophy* and he took the chapters to Peppard as they were done to read to her. He also started to write a book on religion called 'Prisons' which was very different from his previous work. Russell's attitude to religion at this stage of his life was not so straightforward as has often been supposed. While he continued to reject organized religions and all their doctrines, he thought that there was something of value in a religious feeling or attitude towards the world. In this he felt he had some common ground with Ottoline, who was by no means a doctrinally correct believer. The attempt to develop this idea of a non-doctrinal religion in 'Prisons' was one plan they had for common intellectual work.

The writing of 'Prisons' was well advanced by the time Russell left Ipsden on 23 August and the book eventually ran to at least 129 typed pages. Both copies of the typescript have been lost, but what survives by way of drafts and outlines can be found in *Papers*, vol. XII, pp. 97–122. In the end nothing much came of Russell's attempts to develop a non-doctrinal religion, but he returned to the topic several times under Ottoline's influence – most famously in his essay 'Mysticism and Logic' (1914).

The main difficulty during the summer at Peppard was Ottoline's nearly continuous bad health. She had severe headaches almost daily and her eyes were giving her trouble. Her biographer says she was close to a nervous and physical breakdown at this time (Darroch, *Ottoline*, p. 104). When life in the country failed to restore her health she decided to take a cure in Marienbad. She left on 27 August, as Russell wrote her a farewell letter.

[176]

c/o Miss Morris
Basset Manor, Checkendon, Reading[1]
Sunday night. 26–7 August 1911

My Beloved

I can never hope to tell you all that this time has been to me. It has been the birth of a new life – in happiness, in thought, in feeling and insight and power. My life has reached its completion in every way, through you. All that I have been blindly groping after I now possess. I had dimly imagined such a love as ours, but I had never thought I could come to know it. I know now that together we can achieve great things which we could not achieve apart. You not only fill me with your thoughts, but you give me such an incentive as I have never had – the wish to express you and to give you your use to the world. I feel no doubt of being able to accomplish it, if nothing unpredictable interferes, even if what has been written is inadequate. The whole world is changed to me – it is larger, freer, more infinite; what was obscure is clear, but there are endless horizons beyond, where as yet I see only possibilities. You spoke of your always pressing on – you will find me quite as eager and as little inclined to rest in what is done. I had always thought of happiness as apt to produce the effect you described in Oliver Strachey.[2] But our happiness is just the opposite – it opens mind and heart more and more.

Julian evidently minded your going a good deal, but wouldn't let anything appear. I stayed a little while, she showed me the Japanese house, and I took her a little way on my bicycle. She wanted Nurse to read to her, not me.

1. Russell had taken new lodgings, not far from Henley, until 8 September. Opposite the address he wrote: 'I stay at *Grosvenor Hotel* in London, as I start from Victoria.' On earlier trips to London he had stayed at the Paddington Hotel; from his new location, however, he would now arrive in the city at Victoria Station and chose a new hotel convenient to it.
2. Oliver Strachey, Ray Costelloe's new husband, was not noted for a strong sense of direction. Having given up his job in India, he decided not to take another one, but to live off Ray's money while they wrote a history of India together. Nothing came of this enterprise, though they did at length produce a joint book, *Keigwin's Rebellion* (1916).

Did Nurse tell you she said 'Daddie's gone and Mummie's going – it's a queer world.'[1]

Since then I have finished my chapter – 17 pages, which is my longest day's work so far.[2] I haven't begun to miss you yet, I feel you with me so fully, and the work is almost like talking to you. I hardly believe I shan't see you tomorrow – it has come to seem so natural to see you every day. But it won't be long till I see you again. I do hope Marienbad will do you good. Your headaches and bad eyes have been the only thing that was not happiness – except Socrates!

My Darling, I love you with all my heart and mind and soul – every bit of me is yours, absolutely. Goodnight my heart. I wish I could close your dear eyes with kisses four.[3]

  Your
   B.

Ottoline's stay at Marienbad was to be a long one, and on 9 September Russell went out to join her for a few days. Though he stayed in a different hotel, he appeared so often at Ottoline's that the manager ('a typical Prussian', according to Ottoline) banned him. On the 13th Bertie set out back to England to take up lodgings once more in Ipsden, Ottoline rather rashly seeing him off at the station. She said his departure was 'rather a relief' to her for she minded 'being looked on as an abandoned woman' (*Memoirs*, vol. II, p. 279). Shortly after Bertie had left, Philip arrived and the hotel manager told him about his wife's persistent English visitor. Philip merely said he was glad to hear it.

[177]

[Ipsden]
Saturday afternoon
[16 September 1911]

My Darling Darling

Your two letters of Wednesday and Thursday were both brought to me when I was called this morning. They were more joy to me than I can say – every word of them. I feel I have written miserable letters, but it is very hard to write during a long journey – the thoughts belonging to the journey seem

---

1. Philip was away in London; Ottoline was going to Marienbad.
2. This was to be part of 'Prisons'.
3. Keats's 'La Belle Dame Sans Merci', stanza viii: 'And there I shut her wild wild eyes/ With kisses four.'

to numb one. Darling I am glad my flowers came. I ordered them in the morning while we were packing. Yes I was surprised to see you at the station – the fat boy saw you first. I was very very much touched by your coming – it was very dear of you. But of course I was conscious of the fat wretch and his thoughts and I felt I ought to have more prudence on your behalf. I was very vexed with myself for not being more astute the evening before.

Yes I should certainly have been cross if you had thanked me for coming – it would have been too absurd. All the thanks, if there were to be any, would have been the other way, as you ran all the risk. – Darling I was quite as dumb as you were at the end. The end was different from what I had expected; I had not known it would be so impossible to say what one was feeling. And when I am with you I can't really believe I shall ever not be, it seems so natural and inevitable to be together. – You are not nearly so dumb to me as you think, because I almost always know what you are feeling.

I don't now ever feel that your other ties war against me, and I don't believe I should whatever happened. At first I had the desire for utter and complete absorption on both sides, which made me dread the thought of my having to go back to work as well as your ties. Now I find everything else that we both have to do an added bond. But that could hardly have happened if we hadn't had long times together, so that I can feel you with me in spirit even when you are absent in the body.

Young Isaacs[1] again asked me if I was doing a cure, so I too mentioned my friend. But I didn't say his name, which is Oliver Mansfield. I knew him first at the crammer's. Then he went out to India, and was doing brilliantly, but unfortunately lost his health, had to throw up his position, and is now clerk to a County Council.

I have enjoyed the big sponge and still more the hair wash because it smells like your head.

I *am* sorry your eyes have begun hurting again. I believe you ought to live on the East Coast when you are in England – it is hideous but dry. However anything is better than the Thames Valley.

Yes our talks were much more like communings – there was so *much* more

---

1. This was definitely Sir Rufus Isaacs (1861–1935), then the British Attorney-General, who was also taking the waters at Marienbad, though why Russell referred to him as 'young' is not known. Nothing is known about Mansfield beyond what Russell reports here. Presumably he, too, was at Marienbad and Russell pretended to be visiting him. The 'crammer's' was the school which prepared Russell for his Cambridge entrance examinations (1888–9).

than was said – each word seemed to have such a world behind it. I loved talking to you about my work – it was strangely intoxicating.

Thank you for letting me see the letter about Mother Julian.[1] It would *never* have entered my head to think you sentimental about her – indeed I am sure I should have felt as you do if I had known her. I wish very much indeed that I had.

I am writing by the river near South Stoke, where I shall post this. It is heavenly autumn weather – hot sun and cold wind – they say there was a frost this morning. I arrived for dinner – found mountains of proofs, Broad's dissertation,[2] and endless letters – one from Carr[3] of the Aristotelian Society, asking me to have the annual meeting the last Monday in October, to suit the everlasting Bergson,[4] who would then be present; one from Stout,[5] asking my opinion of a communication of a man in Cracow, who applies symbolic logic to time-relations, and wants his work published in *Mind*;[6] and one from Ivy Pretious[7] (which I will send when I have answered it) begging me not to avoid her. The letter caused me some perplexity, but I think I must call in London some time – I have really no right not to, but I should have been glad not to have to renew acquaintance, as the need for philanthropy is past. I shall be glad to hear your opinion after I have sent you her letter. – After dinner I wrote mountains of letters and began reading Broad. This morning I spent on proofs, and got through about half. Owing to Bergson I shall have to begin my Aristotelian paper[8] while I am here, but I have the energy of 20 steam-engines, just now, and can plough through my work at a great rate. Broad is just as I expected. Maurice Amos[9] comes

1. While in Marienbad Ottoline had heard that her mentor, Mother Julian, had died.
2. The Fellowship dissertation of Charlie Dunbar Broad (1887–1971), formerly a Trinity student now teaching at the University of St Andrews. He returned to Cambridge in 1923 and succeeded Sorley to the Knightbridge Chair of Moral Philosophy in 1933. The dissertation was later published as Broad's first book, *Perception, Physics, and Reality* (1914).
3. H. Wildon Carr (see letter 172). Russell, as president of the Society, had to give a paper at the annual meeting.
4. Henri Bergson (1859–1941), the French philosopher, then a professor at the Collège de France. In 1911, following the publication of his *L'Évolution créatrice* (1907; English translation 1911), he was something of a cult figure. Russell, who had met Bergson during his visit to Paris in March, had a great deal to do with him during his visit to England in 1911.
5. Russell's former teacher, now editor of *Mind*. (See letter 25.)
6. Presumably Russell did not think well of the article, for it was not published in *Mind*.
7. See letter 130.
8. 'On the Relations of Universals and Particulars', read to the Aristotelian Society on 30 October 1911 and published in their *Proceedings* the following year.
9. An old friend, see letter 9.

to me in Cambridge the week-end of Oct. 15. I shall not go to my Aunt Agatha as she has gone to the Isle of Wight; I go to my Uncle Rollo Sept. 29 (address Steep, Petersfield) and next day to Cambridge. I don't know yet about the Whiteheads.

Darling I can't manage to be sorry that you missed me. I don't know how I should have endured it if I had had nothing to do and had had to stay passive in the same place. As it is, I feel the work I have to do must be done, and I should not be worthy of your love if I were idle. My imagination is empty for the moment because I put it all into 'Prisons', and I feel the need of hard dry reasoning – it has a kind of tonic bracing effect. It is a kind of homage to the unimportance of the individual.

Goodbye my Beloved. I feel you with me in spirit every moment – whatever I am doing, I am conscious of your love and of what you are – it envelops me like the sunshine. Goodbye my Joy my Ottoline. Do keep well.

 Your utterly devoted

  B.

Russell spent the rest of September at Ipsden, returning to Cambridge at the end of the month in time for the beginning of term on 10 October. His time was taken up with various philosophical tasks including writing his Aristotelian Society paper on universals and particulars and reading a great deal of Bergson in preparation for meeting the great man in October. This year he was an examiner for the Trinity Fellowship competition, which entailed reading the examination papers of all the candidates in addition to reporting on Broad's dissertation which was in his special area of expertise. Though he performed all these tasks, and many others, with exemplary dispatch, he was really marking time until Ottoline's return. Tasks like the Aristotelian paper occupied him only a couple of days and, without a major task to deal with, he filled his time voraciously reading novels.

Ottoline left Marienbad towards the end of September, but instead of coming home straight away, took a leisurely tour through Europe, visiting Prague, Vienna, Munich and Paris, while Bertie awaited her arrival with as much patience as he could muster.

[178]

Trinity College
Monday afternoon
[16 October 1911]

My Darling Darling

Two dear letters have come from you, one written in the train and on arriving, and one yesterday – they are such a joy. *Of course* I understand that you can't come for long at first. It was stupid of me not to have thought of it. If you get home Friday night I will come up Sat. morning (as early as you think worth while) and engage a sitting room at the hotel at the top of Tottenham Court Rd (new, the Grafton I think). You can then ask for me simply. That will be nicer than Bedford Square – if you think it a good plan. We can do the same Monday. Tuesday I can stay the night in town. Oh dear I do long for you. It is awful – I didn't get to sleep till after 3 last night – as soon as I stopped reading I got wide awake thinking of you – as the time grows short one's patience oozes out.

I am interested about the Lausanne Dr.[1] I hope you will go back at Xmas or sooner and really get good from him He sounds thorough.

I have had a blow: Alys and Logan are coming to Chelsea after Xmas, so I must give up that neighbourhood.[2] Where shall I go? I might go to Kensington, or to Gray's Inn (which would be nearer you). If you have views, do let me know at once, as I want to settle on a place.

This morning I went to hear Moore lecture[3] – he was extraordinarily good – very clear, caring passionately about the subject, obviously feeling it quite overwhelmingly important to get at the truth, thinking so hard that whenever he came to a stop he was panting – only just enough aware of his audience to keep him talking, otherwise absorbed in his topics. He had a good class – 20 people. My first lecture is 5.30 today. Maurice[4] and I lunched with the Fletchers[5] and I came away early in order to find your letter and have time to answer it before the post goes. He is nice and I am very fond

1. This was a Dr Combe, a specialist in neuralgia.
2. Russell was still looking for a flat in London at which they could meet without fear of discovery. Towards the end of October he finally took one in Russell Chambers, Bury Street, in Bloomsbury near the British Museum.
3. Moore had returned to Cambridge as a lecturer in 1911. Owing to the wide range of subjects included among the Moral Sciences at Cambridge and the teaching needs of the University, Moore's lectures were (rather surprisingly) on psychology.
4. Maurice Amos.
5. Walter Morley Fletcher (1873–1933), a physiologist then lecturer in natural sciences at Trinity, and his wife, Mary.

of him, but I shall be glad when he goes. His talk is incessant, and he
interferes with work – besides I have to see so many people that it gets a
burden.

I am very very much interested in what you write about God. I think,
like most believers, you greatly overestimate what your belief in God does
for you – I know I did when I believed. You would find quite as much
infinity in the world without him. I have realized that hitherto you are quite
unshaken, because your belief is not based on reason and therefore can't be
attacked by reason. If I could make you feel that unbelief is nobler I should
begin to have hope. – Yes, Lucy Silcox is a Christian. You would like her
very much. I wish you knew her – can't you get Miss Stawell[1] to bring her?
But intellectually she doesn't count. I mean her reasoning power is *nil*. I
think if she knew you even a little she would guess the truth. Personally I
shouldn't mind, and should even be glad if she knew; but it is a point to be
taken into consideration.

Tolstoy is wonderful[2] – he helped to keep me awake. I can't read of people
renouncing the world without a feeling that that is right. Intellectual things
seem thin and inhuman – besides, they are aristocratic, only the few can get
the good of them. I often long to be simple and good, never say a clever
thing again, never bother about subtle points, but give up my life to love of
my neighbour. This is really a temptation – but it is Satan in an angelic form.
I feel so intimately every twist and turn in Tolstoy's struggles after simplicity –
and all his troubles with his wife and friends. I can't feel for one moment
that he would have done better to go on writing novels. It all excites me –
his renunciation attracts me with the same kind of power as one might feel
with ordinary gross temptations. I often think I shall end by something of
that kind. The intellectual life is hardly enough to make one a decent citizen.

I gather from the *Daily News* that it was a mistake about Miss Malecka.[3]
I haven't heard again from Mrs Murray. I told her I thought she ought to
believe the Consul.

Darling Love it is bitterly disappointing about your headaches – I mind

1. Melian Stawell, a classicist at Newnham.
2. Russell was reading the second volume of Aylmer Maude's biography (1908–10).
3. Miss Malecka was an Englishwoman, a friend of Melian Stawell's, who was being
held in Warsaw by the Russian government on a charge of revolutionary treason. The
Daily News reported on 16 October that bail had been refused, though the British Consul
in St Petersburg said it had been set for £2,000. Russell's friend C. P. Sanger had
guaranteed the whole sum himself and then set up a fund to raise the money. On 24
October the money reached St Petersburg and Malecka was freed and returned home.
It is not known how Mary Murray was involved.

very much, but I shall hope your Lausanne man will do wonders. My Beloved, your letters are such a joy – I hardly know which I singled out to like – they are wonderful – but it was one in answer to one of mine about your being depressed in Vienna.

O my heart I love you I love you. I long for you my Ottoline, more than you can imagine – Goodbye my Dearest Life.

Yours

B.

[179]

Trinity College
Wednesday evening
18 October 1911

My Beloved

Your dear dear letter of yesterday reached me when I got home – I *was* glad of it. You will see that at last my things have arrived from Goring[1] and I can't resist writing to you at once on your writing-block. I love using things you have given me, especially for writing to you. I am feeling very happy tonight, really believing I shall see you soon, and somehow having a sense of your presence more than I have had lately. You might have thought such severe criticism of 'Prisons'[2] would have depressed me, but it has only stimulated me.

I got home at 4.30. I had just read your letter and made my tea when Ogden (Secretary of Heretics) came to say Chesterton[3] is speaking the night of my P.S.F.[4] meeting – this raised a lot of complicated problems, which we were in the middle of when an unknown German appeared, speaking very little English but refusing to speak German. He turned out to be a man who had learnt engineering at Charlottenburg, but during his course had acquired, by himself, a passion for the philosophy of mathematics, and has now come to Cambridge on purpose to hear me. This took till 5.15; in the next few minutes I settled my business with Ogden, and then went off to

1. Goring is a village near Ipsden (Russell had sometimes posted his letters from there), but why his things were there (rather than at Ipsden) is not known – probably it was the nearest railway station.
2. The Whiteheads had been shown 'Prisons'. Alfred had not managed to get through much of it but Evelyn had read it all and not liked it. On 18 October, Russell had reported that she found it dull: 'the most severe criticism there is', he said.
3. G. K. Chesterton (1874–1936), the writer.
4. The People's Suffrage Federation (see letter 152).

my lecture, where I found my German duly established. I lectured very well, owing to excitement and insufficient preparation. I am much interested by my German, and shall hope to see a lot of him. Ogden has undertaken to do P.S.F. work for me, which is a *very* great relief.

I am sending back some books you lent me, also Crashaw.[1] I do wish you would tell me of some books you would like to have. I will give you anything in philosophy that you would care for. Spinoza first. Descartes' *Meditations* you might like. Do you possess Berkeley? Do let me know what you would like, not only in philosophy.

Thanks for the information about Gray's Inn. I will look for rooms, tomorrow if possible. But I don't want to be *too* near Marsh.[2] You could come there very easily – you might be going to consult your lawyer.

Tomorrow it will be 7 months since the world began. A lot has happened in the time – it seems much longer. My Darling, it is incredible how you have changed my life – it is all so much easier – before, I was always struggling and always falling short, and so filled with inward discords. Now it is utterly different. I feel I have so much to give to every one – and I don't have any longer the restless longing to give that made me give too much and to the wrong people.

Now I must stop – Goodnight my Darling. Very soon I shall hold you in my arms and our souls will meet in a long long kiss. The joy you give me is infinite and divine and above all words. Goodbye my heart.

Your B.

The 'unknown German' who turned up just before Russell's lecture was in fact the Austrian, Ludwig Wittgenstein (1889–1951), the most famous of Russell's students by a considerable margin. It is significant that Russell should have found him noteworthy even on so brief an acquaintance. The next day, Wittgenstein was already making his presence felt at Russell's lectures – 'he came back with me after my lecture', Russell reported on 19 October, 'and argued till dinner-time – obstinate and perverse, but I think not stupid'. In Wittgenstein Russell found the sort of student he'd dreamed of teaching and the two men quickly formed an intense intellectual friendship which transcended the teacher–student relationship. Russell's work had an important formative influence on Wittgenstein's philosophy; but the influence was mutual – Wittgenstein's criticism forced Russell to develop new lines of thought and abandon some old ones.

1. Probably the *Poems* of the English religious poet Richard Crashaw (1612/13–49).
2. Eddie Marsh (see letter 22).

Wittgenstein was noteworthy enough to be included in Russell's survey of the beginning of term in his next letter to Lucy Donnelly.

[180]

London
28 October 1911

My dear Lucy

It was a great pleasure to get your letter a few days ago, and to have news of you again. You must have had a trying time in Brooklyn.[1] There is something much better than flattery in being useful. After all, wisdom teaches one only to worry over what is within one's own power, and therefore one can hope to have a mind at peace when one is useful but not otherwise. And apart from the self-centred wish to spend one's time well, the love of humanity in general becomes a pain if one is not being useful to some part of humanity.

I am glad you feel me less lost now. My rooms are close to the Trinity Library, which you tell me you remember.

Tonight I am in London, having come up to meet Bergson at dinner. He is giving lectures in London which are reported in the daily newspapers – all England has gone mad about him for some reason. It was an amusing dinner. Our host was Wildon Carr, a humble stockbroker who happens to be secretary of the Aristotelian Society – a man rather like the host in one of Peacock's novels, but milder.[2] He had Bergson on his right and Shaw on his left. I sat between Bergson and Younghusband[3] (the Thibet man), who cares much more about philosophy than about soldiering. I had heard of him from McTaggart, but had never met him before – I liked him very much indeed – simple, sincere, and massive. The only other guests you should know about were Zangwill[4] and Wallas.[5] Bergson's philosophy, though it shows constructive imagination, seems to me wholly devoid of argument and quite gratuitous; he never thinks about fundamentals, but just

1. She had been there to nurse her mother through an illness.
2. The hosts in Thomas Love Peacock's satirical conversational novels usually serve merely to facilitate the talk of their guests. Carr must have been mild indeed to be milder than Peacock's hosts.
3. Sir Francis Younghusband (1863–1942), soldier, traveller and diplomat. In 1903 he had led a British army into Tibet to force the country to serve as a British trade route to China.
4. See letter 30.
5. See letter 25.

invents pretty fairy-tales. Personally, he is urbane, gentle, rather feeble physically, with an extraordinarily clever mouth, suggesting the adjective 'fin'[1] (I don't know any English equivalent). He is too set to be able to understand or answer objections to his views. Shaw made an amusing speech explaining how glad he was that Bergson had adopted his (Shaw's) views,[2] and expounding how Bergson thought we came to have eyes.[3] B. said it wasn't quite that way, but Shaw set him right, and said B. evidently didn't understand his own philosophy. Everybody congratulated themselves and each other on their possession of freedom and on their escape from the barren scientific dogmas of the sixties.[4] I still believe in these dogmas, so I felt out of it. When people laughed during Shaw's speech he said 'I don't mean to make a comic speech, and I don't know why you laugh, unless because religion is such an essentially laughable subject.' They seemed to me like naughty children when they think (mistakenly) that the governess is away – boasting of their power over matter, when matter might kill them at any moment. Younghusband, who held his tongue, was about for the first time after four months' illness consequent on being run over by a motor-car.

I am interested to hear I have admirers in Columbia – the American Realists[5] take very largely the same view of the nature of things as I do, and seem to be the dominant school among the younger men. I have at my lectures two Germans, one of them an engineer (or nearly one) from Charlottenburg, who came to the conclusion he would like to know about the foundations of his subject, and therefore threw up everything and came to

1. 'Fine', 'delicate', 'subtle' are possible translations.
2. There is a good deal of similarity between the vitalism of Bergson's *L'Évolution créatrice* (1907) and Shaw's notion that evolution proceeds purposefully through the exercise of will which he expressed in *Man and Superman* (1901–3) and later plays such as *Back to Methuselah* (1922).
3. In *L'Évolution créatrice*, Bergson had argued that Darwinian natural selection could not explain the evolution of complex organs such as the eye. In its place, he posited 'un élan original de la vie' (an original impetus of life) which operated throughout the universe and which was responsible for the evolutionary process.
4. Nineteenth-century scientific materialism had its heyday in Britain in the 1860s. T. H. Huxley's *Man's Place in Nature* (1863) was a key work. (See J. A. Passmore, *100 Years of Philosophy*, ch. 2, for a survey of themes and influences.) Bergson's philosophy was hostile to the claims of mechanistic science, in particular to scientific determinism.
5. A group of American philosophers – E. B. Holt, W. T. Marvin, W. P. Montague, R. B. Perry, W. B. Pitkin and E. G. Spaulding (often called 'The Six Realists') – who in varying degrees espoused the views of Russell and Moore in reaction to idealism. The group formed in 1909 and published a manifesto ('The Program and First Platform of Six Realists', *Journal of Philosophy*) in 1910. Of the six, Montague and Pitkin were at Columbia University, New York.

Cambridge. I have also a Maltese who had studied for years to become a Jesuit, and had already taken the first vows. But they told him he must accept the scholastic philosophy, and he wouldn't. So now he comes to me, and will doubtless soon be an atheist. I have an uncomfortable presentiment that when that happens his morals will go to pieces, but there is nothing to be done.

I can still see in my mind's eye the beauty of Bryn Mawr in autumn. Our autumn too has been very lovely.

Comparative literature be damned.[1] When will Americans learn that intelligent people are only repelled by an easy familiarity with great names, without the knowledge and feeling that should go with it. Great men are to be approached reverently, when one's mood permits a vivid realization of their greatness. The other is a sort of lust, like sexual relations without love.

I am much interested by what you say about Helen. It would be an excellent plan if she were to make copy out of her indignation against New York – besides, it would sweeten the indignation.

Your California victory is admirable.[2] Our politics have been very confused – the Government behaved very badly over the strike, no one likes the Insurance Bill,[3] and the shadow of German enmity lies over everything.[4] Winston is an ardent Jingo, Lloyd George is becoming one; bigger and bigger navies seem inevitable, India is difficult,[5] and the Italian–Turkish war[6] is horrible and raises very complex problems for England, which is the leading Mohammedan power.

1. Lucy Donnelly had lamented that she had to teach a comparative-literature course.
2. California had allowed women to vote.
3. Lloyd George had introduced his National Insurance Bill which provided sickness and unemployment insurance, to be administered by private friendly societies under government supervision.
4. In June 1911, Germany had sent a gunboat to Agadir on the Atlantic coast of Morocco ostensibly to protect German interests there. The British saw it as a challenge to their naval supremacy in the Atlantic and the two countries came close to war.
5. Lord Curzon's years as Viceroy of India (1899–1905) had bequeathed many problems to the Liberal government – especially as a result of his partition of Bengal in 1905. A ferocious nationalist campaign, then at its height, succeeded in getting the province reunited in December 1911.
6. The Italo-Turkish war (1911–12) was for control of Libya, which Italy eventually achieved. Britain was not directly involved in the conflict, but her diplomatic position was difficult since she traditionally defended Turkey as a bulwark against Russia and yet would have liked to present herself as the defender of the oppressed peoples of the Turkish Empire and, though a friend of Italy, had no desire to see Italy dominate the Mediterranean.

Yeats, whom I have only met twice, seemed to me a snob and a very acute man of business. But I dare say he is interesting really.

I am very busy and very happy. I enjoy my young men very much. Only two stuck to my lectures to the bitter end last year, but they both got fellowships.[1] As only three fellowships were given, that was satisfactory. This year I have begun with about twenty, but they will no doubt diminish soon. I don't know when my shilling shocker will be out.

Now I must go to bed, as it is after one. Write again soon. I am *very* glad you are feeling so well, but sorry your friends are all away. It must be very lonely.

Yours affectionately
Bertrand Russell

Evelyn Whitehead's criticism of 'Prisons', and Alfred's indifference to it, probably cut deeper than Russell at first realized. Whitehead once said that Russell had the best analytic mind of any philosopher in history (*including* Aristotle). It was a sweeping judgement, but Whitehead was better placed than anybody to make it and there is no reason to suppose he made it lightly. Even though he had only read a bit of 'Prisons' he must have realized that this was work which betrayed Russell's best talents. For the non-credal religion that Russell advocates in 'Prisons' survives only because Russell rather self-consciously protects it from the rigorous criticism that was his trademark.

Yet Russell, quite characteristically, was unwilling to recognize that the task he'd embarked on with 'Prisons' was one that did not suit his talents. In this sense, the Whiteheads' criticisms did inspire him to redouble his efforts. As recently as the end of September he had told Ottoline of his plans for technical work in philosophy:

> [T]here have always been rival theories in philosophy on numbers of questions. ... In many of these perennial controversies, I believe there is not and never can be a jot of evidence for either side, but that by a further effort of abstraction one can arrive at something which both sides have in common, and which can be accepted as fairly certain. What is wanted for this is the particular kind of logical instrument which Whitehead and I have perfected.

But by December he was wondering if there was anything of a technical nature worth doing in philosophy.

1. C. D. Broad was one and E. H. Neville, a mathematician, was the other.

[181]

[34 Russell Chambers, London]
Wednesday, 13 December 1911
(I don't know what made me think
yesterday was the 13th)[1]

My Darling Darling

Your 2 dear letters in one envelope came this morning – I woke up for once before I was called, so I got up and fetched them out of the box – they were a great joy. Yes, you give me faith, not only or chiefly in my own powers, but in the things I fundamentally believe. All my beliefs are apt to grow dim at times, but you keep them burning. It will be sadly few days before Xmas, and not many more after if you are away till after the New Year. I have to be back at latest on the morning of Thursday 18th. Still that ought to leave at least a fortnight. If it is really fixed that you go to Oxford the 21st, I will go to my aunt then, and to the Whiteheads [the] 23rd. I am sorry you are tired again – I do hope it is not bad. I am glad you liked the 2nd thing I sent you.[2] I thought it was rather too pathetic, which is the fault those old writings most run to.

In spite of having slept so long in my chair I slept another 7 hours in bed, and I am not really awake yet. I have read a good deal of Ward,[3] and ordered 2 more fenders[4] – otherwise nothing has happened to me.

During this past year I have written 3 Paris lectures (of which 2 are published and the 3rd soon will be),[5] my shilling shocker, the Aristotelian paper, and 'Prisons'. Considering how much time has been taken up in lectures and proofs and seeing pupils, I don't feel seriously dissatisfied. But I have an uneasiness about philosophy altogether; what remains for *me* to do in philosophy (I mean in *technical* philosophy) does not seem of first-rate importance. The shilling shocker really seems to me better worth doing. It

1. His letter written the previous day had been dated '13 December'. He had mentioned in it that 13 December was his wedding anniversary and that Alys, to whom such things were important, would feel it very much.
2. Ottoline had referred to two unidentified manuscripts that Russell had given her.
3. James Ward's *The Realm of Ends* (1911), which Russell was reviewing for the *Nation*.
4. Presumably for the new flat. Ottoline helped Bertie furnish and decorate it. Ironically, in view of their efforts to keep their affair secret, Ottoline's friends immediately recognized her influence on its decoration.
5. 'Le Réalisme analytique', *Bulletin de la Société française de philosophie* (1911); 'L'Importance philosophique de la logistique', *Revue de métaphysique et de morale* (1911); 'Sur les axiomes de l'infini et du transfini', *Bulletin de la Société mathématique de France* (1911). It was the third paper that had not yet been published.

is all puzzling and obscure. For so many years I have had absolutely no choice as to work that I have got out of the way of wondering what is best to do. I think really the important thing now is to make the ideas I already have intelligible. And I ought to try to get away from pedantry. My feelings have changed about all this; I did think the technical philosophy that remains for me to do very important indeed.

I will try to write out what I think about philosophy; it will help to clear up my own ideas. All the historic problems of philosophy seem to me either insoluble or soluble by methods which are not philosophical, but mathematical or scientific. The last word of philosophy on all of them seems to me to be that a priori any of the alternatives is possible. Thus e.g. as to God: traditional philosophy proved him: I think some forms of God impossible, some possible, none necessary. As to immortality: philosophy can only say it may be true or it may be false; any more definite answer would have to come from psychical research. As to whether nothing exists except mind: philosophy, it seems to me, can only say that all the arguments adduced on either side are fallacious, and that there is absolutely no evidence either way. And I should say the same of optimism and pessimism. Except as a stimulus to the imagination, almost the only use of philosophy, I should say, is to combat errors induced by science and religion. Religion says all things work together for good: philosophy says this belief is groundless. Science leads people to think there is no absolute good and bad, but only evolved beliefs about good and bad, which are useful to gregarious animals in the struggle for existence; philosophy equally says *this* belief is groundless.

All this is rather dismal. But as a stimulus to the imagination I think philosophy *is* important. But this use is not so much for the technical philosopher, but rather for the man who wants to see his own special pursuit connected with the cosmos; therefore it is popular rather than technical philosophy that fulfils this need. This is fundamentally why I think it is more useful to write popular than technical philosophy.

There is one great question: Can human beings *know* anything, and if so what and how? This question is really the most essentially philosophical of all questions. But ultimately one has to come down to a sheer assertion that one does know this or that – e.g. one's own existence – and then one can ask why one knows it, and whether anything else fulfils the same conditions. But what is important in this inquiry can, I think, be done quite popularly; the technical refinements add very little except controversy and long words. I was reinforced in this view by finding how much I could say on the question in the shilling shocker.

I shall be interested to know what you have to say. Generally when we discuss these things I talk and talk and at the end you have escaped without saying anything. I shall make a list and put you through a Viva.

Tomorrow at 9 I shall come to Bedford Square unless I hear to the contrary. I hope you won't be nearly dead. Goodbye Darling. I can't tell you how I long to have you back.

Your loving
B.

Russell's enthusiasm for Tolstoy's conversion (letter 178) seems a little more ominous after this. Russell, of course, did prove to be a talented popularizer of philosophy; but while Tolstoy was impressive both as a novelist and a prophet, Russell's line of religious reflection in 'Prisons' was by no means so impressive as his logic.

Russell's growing conviction that he should write for a more popular audience had a number of sources. In part it was a reaction against the immense labour *Principia Mathematica* had involved – and still required as proofs arrived day after day. He may also have been influenced – a little jealously perhaps – by the cult status Bergson had acquired. He could smile at the enthusiasm with which Bergson's ideas were taken up even when they ran counter to the best scientific evidence of the day. He may well have hoped to propound a philosophy equally capable of generating enthusiasm among a wide audience, but one which was consistent with science. But by far the most important of his motives was his desire to share his work with Ottoline. That would be possible, he thought, if he gave up very technical work and if Ottoline could be brought to see that religious beliefs, like any others, needed the support of evidence and reasons and that the emotional satisfaction she derived from hers did not constitute either. Her religious attitudes, he thought, were fine and noble, but it was a mistake to attach to them religious beliefs which there was no reason whatsoever for thinking true. To do so was to indulge in wishful thinking, or muddle-headedness or even intellectual dishonesty. On this point it was difficult for Russell to be tactful. In 'Prisons' he had tried to accommodate Ottoline's position by building on the religious attitudes and avoiding the question of beliefs. And this, essentially, was why the book failed: all Russell's best talents lay in marshalling reasons for or against beliefs. If Russell was to avoid the sin of intellectual dishonesty himself, 'Prisons' had to confine itself strictly to attitudes. Attitudes could be recommended or not, but they could not, Russell thought, be argued for. But this left little to say in a book like 'Prisons', and especially little for a person of Russell's cast of mind.

In letters in November and early December, Bertie cautiously approached the question of Ottoline's religious beliefs. And then, when they met on 27 December, his tact failed him and he seems to have lost patience with her – accusing her of dishonesty in holding beliefs for which she had no intellectual justification. Ottoline was deeply hurt and Bertie was upset and contrite when he wrote to her late that night from the Whiteheads' country house in Lockeridge.

[182]

Lockeridge
27 December [1911]
night

My Dearest Dearest Dearest

I feel as if you would never believe me again when I tell you I love you and reverence you and feel myself deeply unworthy of you. I have upon me now the horror of a cruel action, of wanton destruction and ruthlessness. As soon as I had spoken I saw that what I had said could not be true and that I had given you a profound and needless pain for nothing when you were already unhappy. I believe honestly that the passion which culminated today has worked itself out and that I shall not sin in the same way again. But I don't feel any confidence that you will get over the hurt and the feeling that I may lacerate you at any moment if you speak sincerely of what is important to you.

My instinct has *never* felt what I said today, but my reason kept urging that it *must* be so and I couldn't see how to get out of it. Now I do see. It is difficult to me to understand a mind so genuinely unaffected by argument as yours; but the few words you said today helped me and I see now how I misjudged with my reason. O my Dearest don't give up the belief in the possibility of our sharing our spiritual life – and Dearest bear with me for the world's sake – we have great things to do together. I have been too fierce, too violent, too destructive – something of the cruelty of the ascetic has been in me – but Dearest these things will melt away – and they have to do with what prevents me from writing as I wish to write – it is all part of a sort of mental asceticism, which is bad like all asceticism.

Dearest I have been picturing you all the evening – proud, miserable, ill, joking with Mrs M.,[1] anxious about Julian, utterly alone in the world, feeling useless and a mere cumberer of the earth, considering suicide, longing for the rest which only death can bring. It wrings my heart – it is terrible. I have no power of bringing happiness to those who love me. And yet I long for you to be not unhappy; I long to bring you comfort, just to sit with you

---

1. Mrs Morrell, Philip's mother.

and help to bear your burden – I long that you should be able to lean upon me with the certainty that my heart yearns for you. I see and feel your tears and I have helped to cause them. – It has been a very unreal evening – I bore my part in the talk but it seemed a mere buzzing dream. – You cannot know how profoundly I long to relieve your loneliness. Ten years ago, it all began by my suddenly becoming aware of a great loneliness. For a long time I had absolutely no thought of self, and by patience I did at last make the loneliness less. With you I have not been unselfish – if I had, your loneliness would have grown less. Dearest you will find the future better if you can trust it.

This world is so full of pain and strife and destruction – there is only love – gentleness, sympathy – to make it bearable. I love the sorrowing race of mankind – but I have little to say to help – only courage and gentleness – and I fail sadly in both. Strange how tonight I have in mind the moment of my conversion when I first saw that love and tenderness are alone of real value. Then I forgot it. I forget it when I am too happy – I grow cold and intellectual – but in the depths I have never forgotten it, and tonight it wells up in me. I am filled with utter love and longing for service – to bring happiness, to bring relief from pain – oh if I could. I hate the furious persecutor in me – but he is terribly vital. I try to be kind in a common way – yet I do strangely little for others. I worship your devotion, your love, your tenderness, and I long to have that inward poise that you have. But that is not for me, I shall never have it while I am alive. Turbulent, restless, inwardly raging – I shall always be – hungry for your God and blaspheming him. I could pour forth a flood of worship – the longing for religion is at times almost unbearably strong.

O my heart how could you have thought I meant to cast you off – such a thing is utterly inconceivable – O my heart I long to hear from you – to know you are still alive, to know you still love me – but only time will make you trust me again.

I cannot bear to stop but I must. It is after 1.30. I hope you are asleep. I do understand the unhappiness you spoke of. It is not selfish – when one is not strong the world's misery is too heavy to be borne. Courage for a while – and Death will come without our hastening him. Goodbye. O Dearest believe in my boundless love, forgive me, and trust me if you can.

Your

B.

I must go on writing – it is impossible to do anything else.[1] I can already see

1. The next four paragraphs are written on a separate sheet of notepaper which was found

better how it is. You do not believe that reasoning is a method of arriving at truth; I do. That is the root of the matter. Reduced to that, it does not much matter. You are wrong in thinking it will crop up worse and worse as time goes on; hitherto I have never said the worst, and so it kept on growing. Things unsaid are poisonous in my mind. When once I have grasped fully how your beliefs are compatible with truthfulness I shall hardly wish them changed. But what I have done still makes me profoundly unhappy. I fear I have hurt you so deeply that you will always fear me. And I fear too that I have prevented you from trusting me again. You will not dare again I fear to seek sympathy with me when you are unhappy. You will live the rest of your life lonely, like the past. Yet I have it in me to give you sympathy and comradeship even in the things we don't agree about. And I should cease to hurt you as I understand better. It is love makes me hurt you and when I love most I feel most need to hurt you – I don't know why. That is *maladif* and will cease.

Do you remember in very early days I said I would give you the cold steel and you would know the fire of passion in which it had been tempered. Something like what happened today was then in my mind. When I am violent I am not immovable – things which are immovable in me are more quiet. You know that I have to contend against years of habit and the whole tendency of my work to understand your way of reaching your beliefs. I don't know what made me break out today. I think it was the pain of longing to agree with you completely, which is very intense and greatest when I feel nearest to you.

It made me miserable to see you so unhappy and to know I could never give you the real inward agreement, such as Mother Julian gave you. I don't believe it is possible for a human being to love more than I do. I am not nearly as much to you as I wish to be, and the pain of realizing it sometimes gives me a kind of frenzy. But I will learn patience – I will woo you afresh from the beginning – I will make you forget – I will be gentle – I *can* be gentle. O Darling you don't know how I long for you to have the love you should have. You have not yet the love you should have because in important things we disagree and because I have not enough freedom of sympathy and imagination to throw off professional habits. But there is one thing – I don't want you to think things because I do – I only wished you to hold all your

---

apart from the rest of the letter. Clearly they are a continuation of some letter and very probably of this one, but this last is not absolutely certain. The postscript, written the following morning, with which the letter ends was written in the margins of the first sheet.

opinions with the feeling they *might* be mistaken and ought to be open to examination. In that way I was afraid for a moment you misjudged me.

Forgive me. I hate violence even when I am violent, and most when it is towards you. Don't shrink from me and think I may hurt you at any moment. Goodbye Goodbye. You cannot believe the depth of my devotion. It rules my life. O do not fear me.

Your
   B.

Thursday morning

Darling your telegram has just come. Thank you Darling for sending it a 1,000 times. I feel this morning that I was excessive last night in grief and that all was less important than I felt. Still I am quite clear that I shan't behave so again. Now this must be posted. Goodbye Darling Love. I love you with all my soul deeply and absolutely.

   B.

Ottoline's reassuring telegram, followed by a letter, brought further explanations.

[183]

[Lockeridge]
Thursday night
[28 December 1911]

My Beloved Ottoline

Your dear letter reached me at tea-time today. Yes, my bigotry *is* unworthy – and half of me has no bigotry and wonders at the other half. Do you know that there is scarcely a word I disagree with in your confession of faith. The only practical difference is that things which both think possible but not certain seem to me rather less probable than to you. But otherwise I agree with everything you say. There are some great differences, but they are less definite. I don't think the case of music is analogous, because music does not involve beliefs and is neither true nor false. It is not love of religion, or caring for religious things, that I disagree with, it is the beliefs, which must be either true or false, though it may be impossible for us to know which.

What you say about the black spot which might ultimately spoil my love[1] is exactly the fear which impelled me to speak. If I were unable to overcome

1. The 'black spot' was Ottoline's fear that Bertie would find her dishonest in her beliefs.

the belief I expressed yesterday, I think you are right, it would not be good to go on. But today I seem to see quite clearly that I was utterly unjust in what I said – my *instinct* felt it unjust all along. I feel today no difficulty about that. I do most fully understand that you are quite truthful in your religion. But I do wish to share things of the intellect with you – it would be to me a very maimed relation if I did not keep on trying to make you understand things which I think very important. For instance I should want to talk about the difference between beliefs and tastes – between believing that there is a God and liking P. and me,[1] for instance – and why I think there is more need to find reason for the one than for the other. But I don't think you will find me so vehement again – I do hope not.

I think you don't quite understand why I make myself dry and cold when I want to think. You know that where human passion is involved – as for instance between you and me – one seems to see most clearly when feeling is numbed. I think the same applies to religious things.

Dearest it is *utterly* untrue that I despise you at the times when I am vehement. If I did, I should not attempt such extraordinarily painful sincerity. Only I can't bring myself to say painful things unless I first make myself cold and aloof.

I am very dead in feeling today after the passion of yesterday, but in thought I have been very much alive. I see that the danger of the black spot was real, but is past; the danger now is in our both acquiescing in reticence about intellectual things. To me in the long run that would be disastrous. I should begin to feel our relation frivolous. Therefore even if it involves labour and pain and some strife I cannot abandon it.

Dearest now I have finished all the business of exact statement. I cannot tell you Darling what a relief your letter is to me. What you call God is very much what I call infinity. I do feel something in common in all the great things – something which I should not think of quite as you do, though it is very mysterious and I really don't know what to think of it – but I feel it is the most important thing in the world and really the one thing that matters profoundly. It is to me as yet a mystery – I don't understand it. I think it has many manifestations – love is the one that seems to me deepest and that I feel most when I am very deeply moved. But truth is the one I have mainly served, and truth is the only one I *always* feel the divinity of. This has made me get things out of proportion and rather repress other worship in myself, so that I have grown starved and thin. I think if you can bear the pain you can help me by speaking of your beliefs when I am not argumentative. As

1. This was Ottoline's example.

you put them in your letter, though they go beyond mine I have no hostility to them. It is far better to find our agreements than our disagreements. But it will require a mutual effort. You *are* obstinate, just as I am vehement. When we have argued, neither you nor I have conceived for an instant the possibility that the other might be in the right. If we both made this effort we should get on better. If you felt that I made it you would not feel that I was despising you, and if I felt that you made it I should not be tempted to vehemence. When I speak of your not imagining that I may be right, I mean you don't imagine that perhaps your beliefs would be better if you altered them in my direction a bit.[1] But perhaps I am unjust in this – what you say about a personal God is against what I say. But the root of the matter is that I think we can each give the other something which will make us both richer. We have begun badly but it is not too late. – Now it is two o'clock so I must go to bed. Goodnight my dearest Life. I love you very deeply and our love *shall* produce great things.

Friday morning. My Darling Darling Your two dear letters came this morning. They are a great joy. I haven't time to answer them as I have had to come to the next village to telegraph. I do hope tomorrow will be possible.
  Don't be afraid of my *despising* your belief – I don't and never did.
  Darling I love you with all my being.
  Your
  B.

Bertie and Ottoline's religious problems were very much eased when they met again in January. But Russell continued to think about the status of religious claims and, as usual, began to come up with something interesting. He had already decided that religious language, if it was to be defensible, could not express beliefs but attitudes. In his effort to find some common ground with Ottoline, however, he had come to consider whether his theory of values could not be seen as just a different way of expressing Ottoline's religion, especially when the latter was pruned of its more theological branches which, in any case, Russell found it hard to believe she took seriously.
  Hitherto, Russell's ethics were largely derived from Moore, according to whom those items which were morally valuable possessed the property of goodness independently of whether we did in fact value them. On this theory, moral language expresses beliefs (asserting or denying that given items had the property of goodness)

1. Russell added in the margin: 'I see this is not true, but there is something more or less like it that is true I think.'

rather than attitudes. Russell was shortly to abandon this theory in favour of what is now known as an emotive theory of ethics according to which moral language expresses the emotions or attitudes of the people using it. This change is usually ascribed to Santayana's criticism of Russell's Moorean theory in his book *Winds of Doctrine* (1913). But the next letter shows Russell already moving towards an emotive theory. What Russell says in the letter about the value of things which don't exist is inconsistent with his theory of descriptions, *unless* an emotive theory of ethics is adopted. For the theory of descriptions held that all *statements* about what did not exist were false, while in the letter he says that the evaluation of some things that did not exist as better than some things that did was the basis of all rational action. To be consistent, therefore, he must deny that these evaluations involve statements about what does not exist. This is not to say that Russell had already embraced an emotive theory of ethics, merely that he realized that he faced a difficult problem if he continued to reject it.

Unfortunately, the beginning of term precluded further serious philosophical thought and Ottoline did not encourage this line of reflection. For the time being, Russell turned to other quasi-religious projects – a spiritual autobiography which is now lost and, disastrously, a novella, *The Perplexities of John Forstice* – in an effort to find common ground with Ottoline. The problems broached in the letter lay in abeyance until Santayana's criticisms stirred him up.

[184]

[London]
3 January 1912

My Darling
I didn't like to keep your maid waiting so I only wrote one line. Your letter made the impression that you were suggesting I should come, and I had to read it ever so many times before I saw you didn't. I long to talk and talk with you, and I long to hear you speak of your religion. I do most really feel that you can teach me a great deal that will be most precious to me – you have done so already and you will more and more.

I do love Vaughan's 'They are all gone into the world of light'.[1] He says

> And yet as angels in some brighter dreams
>   Call to the Soul when man doth sleep,
> So some strange thoughts transcend our wonted themes,
>   And into glory peep.

1. A poem by the religious poet, Henry Vaughan (1622–95). Russell quotes lines 25–32.

That is exactly the thing I feel. And the next lines too:

> If a star were confined into a tomb
> Her captive flames must needs burn there,
> But when the hand that lock'd her up gives room,
> She'll shine through all the sphere.

When I was talking today I put in more of my own theories than was necessary. What is plain is this: Man can imagine things that don't exist, and sometimes he can see that they are better than things that do exist: this is involved in all rational action, which is the attempt to create imagined goods. What is disputable is the status of things merely imagined, still more of things merely possible to imagine but not actually imagined. But this really doesn't matter except to technical philosophy. Some people say that the mere fact that one can *imagine* ideals shows that they exist somewhere – but if this were true it would apply to bad things too – the Devil would be proved by the same argument as proves God. The power of thought and thence of imagination is really the great thing – the senses are bound to the actual, but thought is not. Philosophers try to prove that whatever is best in our imagined ideals must somehow be actual. But I think their attempts are all dictated by bias, and would never have come to be made if they had been unbiased. Is there not the same reason to regard bad thoughts as promptings of the Evil One that there is to regard good ones as inspirations of God? Religion used to do both, and was then, I think, more consistent.

What we *know* is that things come into our lives sometimes which are so immeasurably better than the things of every day, that it *seems* as though they were sent from another world, and could not come out of ourselves. But our selves have strange hidden powers of good and evil – madness too will come as if from without, and make it seem as though we were possessed.

Religion, it seems to me, ought to make us know and remember these immeasurably better things, and live habitually in the thought of them – as you do, to a much greater degree than most even of the very religious people. I have hitherto only seen the greatest things at rare times of stress or exaltation. In the summer I lived with the vision – when I got back to Ipsden it faded because of my work. When it is strong, the kind of philosophical work I do seems not worth doing; and so when I have to do this work, the vision fades. That was why I hated going back to the work so much – it was like going back to prison. But if I could embody the vision in my philosophy, I should not have this conflict. For that, I must trust the vision when it is absent as well as when it is present. Hitherto I have always begun to doubt it when it faded.

What the vision seems to show me is that we can live in a deeper region than the region of little every-day cares and desires – where beauty is a revelation of something beyond, where it becomes possible to love all men, where Self as a separate fighting unit fades away, and where all common tasks are easy because they are seen as parts of what is greatest. It destroys the *bitterness* not only of one's own misfortunes but of other people's, at the same time that it makes it easier to help other people's and gives one a stronger impulse to do so. And it seems to show that even this life here on earth may be supremely good – that if men would cease their strife and greed, heaven might be here around us, in spite of illness and death and the whole tale of outward griefs.

Yet I have another vision, equally insistent, equally seeming like a revelation; in this vision, sorrow is the ultimate truth of life, everything else is oblivion or delusion. Then even love seems to me merely an opiate – it makes us forget for a moment that we draw our breath in pain and that thought is the gateway to despair. I don't see the slightest reason to believe this, yet recurrently the belief overwhelms me – quite as often when I am happy as when I am unhappy. It is this belief that often makes me frivolous – the world seems too terrible for seriousness.

> As those we love decay, we die in part,
> String after string is severed from the heart;
> Till loosen'd life, at last but breathing clay,
> Without one pang is glad to fall away.
>
> Unhappy he who latest feels the blow!
> Whose eyes have wept o'er every friend laid low,
> Dragg'd ling'ring on from partial death to death,
> Till, dying, all he can resign is – breath.[1]

Pessimism is really a form of self-indulgence, and loosening of one's hold, and a failure to care for what is important. The difficulty is to meet it with something equally serious, sincere, and fundamental. I think only religion can really do this; but those who have never known the despair can hardly know what religion saves us from. I don't think I could ever care very deeply or seriously for any one who didn't have sadness in the inmost depths. You

1. James Thomson, 'On the Death of Mr. William Aikman, The Painter'. Russell quotes the last eight lines, often printed as a separate poem.

seem to me to have just the same kind that I have – a nameless infinite sadness, the weight of all the sorrows of the world. It is that and your way of meeting it that make me feel a bond with you as deep as life, a spiritual union which is quite independent of passion. I sometimes wonder whether love can ever reach the same height with others as it does with those who meet out of the loneliness of a great despair. Dearest I feel we are only on the threshold of our common life – you will, I know, unfold to me more and more, and the years will draw us closer and closer, and I shall grow in the things you care for. I wonder if you know how utterly my life is changed since I have known you – I like to talk of past troubles and discords, to make you feel what I owe to you. Tonight, I don't know why, I feel no passion, but I feel unspeakably near to you in spirit – a strong abiding love, that holds within it all that I have ever tried to live for and all that has seemed noble in human life. If I were now to die, I should know I had had the greatest thing this world has to give.

Goodnight my Dearest. My whole soul is a prayer that all that is best may be yours.

Your

B.

At the end of February Ottoline went to Lausanne for a month to be treated by Dr Combe, the first of several such visits. Though supposedly a specialist on neuralgia, he cast his net widely and on this occasion operated on her nose. Soon after she left, Helen Flexner arrived, as expected, with Simon and their two children, a working visit for Simon and a holiday for Helen and the children. At the beginning of March they visited Russell in Cambridge for a few days. Russell was anxious about seeing Helen again as their previous meeting had not been a success and their friendship had never achieved the intimacy that it had had before Helen was married. Among other dangers was the possibility that she would find out about Ottoline. In the event, Russell found the visit a little trying, but not so disconcerting as he feared.

[185]

[Trinity College]
9 March 1912
Saturday night

My Dearest Dearest

I have very few minutes before the post goes. The Flexners duly arrived, and Isabel Fry,[1] whom I saw very little of owing to them. It was a delicious day, warm and sunny – I took them a little walk, and we met the Cornfords[2] and Rothensteins[3] – we shall go there to tea tomorrow. Then we had tea – Geach[4] came in, to see the wicked vivisector, also Ogden and an old gentleman named Wolstenholme,[5] with a flowing white beard – an amateur philosopher, a very lovable old man I think. I had only met him before at the Sorleys where both he and I were being respectable. He talked and talked about what philosophy could do and couldn't do, not very sensible, but very nice. The Flexners went away in the middle to 'rest' – I thought I should get a few moments' peace, but North turned up, having upset in a boat, got his head stuck in the mud, been half drowned, and incurred a debt of a good many pounds by smashing his boat. I hope he won't be the worse for it – he was determined not to stay away from a dance tonight that he had been looking forward to.

Then Moore came to dinner – he was very nice, but it was uphill work with him silent and Helen deaf and Flexner rather out of it – he is a specialist, quite uncultivated, though Helen has tried to give him a veneer. I like him very much indeed, and on his work he is very interesting, but he doesn't mix well in a general conversation. I am tired with talking loud – seeing people all day is tiring. I undertook to lecture 3 days a week the beginning of next term, and not at all at the end, as my two young men will have the Tripos, and I don't think I can lecture to the nun alone.

I am quite stupid from talking and being host. It is much more trouble when one is responsible for the entertainment. You would have laughed at the conversation with Wolstenholme. He said philosophy ought to be

---

1. Isabel Fry (1868–1957), younger sister of Roger Fry. She ran a progressive school in Buckinghamshire to which many of the Bloomsbury Group sent their children.
2. See letter 142.
3. William Rothenstein (1872–1945), the artist, and his wife, Alice. He was an old friend of Russell's.
4. George Hender Geach, one of Russell's students at Trinity. He went on to become a professor of philosophy in the Indian educational service.
5. Probably Henry James Wolstenholme (1846–1917), lecturer in German at Newnham.

concerned with life, at which of course I burst out against life and the paltriness of an outlook that never got away from Man – a first-rate avalanche. He mildly hinted that one ought not to think there was *nothing* but logic in the world – but I wouldn't hear of there being anything else. After a while I began to see I was absurd, and stopped.

But I simply can't *stand* a view limited to this earth, I feel life so small unless it has windows into other worlds. I feel it vehemently and instinctively and with my whole being. It is what has become of my desire for worship. But I despair of making people see what I mean. I like mathematics largely because it is *not* human and has nothing particular to do with this planet or with the whole accidental universe – because, like Spinoza's God, it won't love us in return. I wish I could get it all said so as to seem convincing.

Now this must go. Goodnight my Darling Love. I hope your nose is no longer hurting, and that they will have done good. Dearest, Dearest, I do love you and long for you. Goodnight my Beloved.

    Your

    B.

Many of Russell's letters to Ottoline contain references to Wittgenstein, almost all of them enthusiastic, but the discussion described in the next marks a turning-point in his appreciation of Wittgenstein's ability as a philosopher. Unfortunately, it is not clear what Russell took 'the most difficult point in mathematical philosophy' to be. The letter was written on the train as Russell travelled to Radlett, near Watford, to stay with 'Lion' Phillimore.

[186]

[In the train]
18 March 1912
Monday morning

My Darling Love

In a very full train it is not altogether easy to write, especially as it shakes terribly – but at the moment it is stopping. *Very* sorry you are so tired. How *beastly* your dinner sounds – Semolina – pshaw. I will stay with my brother till Wednesday if that suits you, probably I could get to London about 3 Wednesday afternoon leaving in the morning. I don't think it will do me good – it is not exercise[1] and I shall find the company oppressive.

1. Frank Russell was an ardent motorist. He was going to take Bertie motoring in the West Country.

Yesterday I lunched with a young law don named Hollond[1] whom I rather like. We got talking politics and I stayed without noticing the time till 3.45. Dons are timid – the company were liberals, but felt there was no knowing where this labour unrest would lead to.[2] So I gave a harangue on the beauties of unrest and revolution. I quite agree there is no knowing where it will lead to, but I think it will lead to a Better Society than we have now. Then Hollond and I went a short walk, then I had the Mirrlees's[3] and North to tea, then Geach, then just time to finish my proofs before dinner. After dinner I went to Bevan's[4] for a time, then addressed more envelopes to mathematical philosophers.[5] While I was doing this Wittgenstein came and stayed till after 12. We had a close equal passionate discussion of the most difficult point in mathematical philosophy. I think he has *genius*. In discussion with him I put out *all* my force and only just equal his. With all my other pupils I should squash them flat if I did so. He has suggested several new ideas which I think valuable. He is the ideal pupil – he gives passionate admiration with vehement and very intelligent dissent. He spoke with intense feeling about the *beauty* of the big book, said he found it like music. That is how I feel it, but few others seem to. Our parting was very affectionate on both sides. He said the happiest hours of his life had been passed in my room. He is not a flatterer, but a man of transparent and absolute sincerity. I have the most perfect intellectual sympathy with him – the same passion and vehemence, the same feeling that one must understand or die, the same sudden jokes breaking down the frightful tension of thought.

He is far more terrible with Christians than I am. He had liked Farmer,[6] the undergraduate monk, and was horrified to learn that he is a monk. Farmer came to tea with him, and W. at once attacked him – as I imagine, with absolute fury. He made of course no impression. Yesterday he returned

1. Henry Arthur Hollond (1884–1974); he had studied classics and law at Cambridge and was a Fellow at Trinity from 1909 until his death. He was Dean of the College from 1922 to 1950 and then Vice-Master until 1955.
2. The railway strike the previous summer had been followed by a dock strike in December, a general strike in Glasgow in January, a transport strike in March, and, most important, a miners' strike for a minimum wage also in March.
3. The parents of Hope Mirrlees (1887–1978), a poet and novelist. Hope studied at Newnham with Karin Costelloe and became Jane Harrison's favourite student and her lifelong companion. Her parents lived in the Whiteheads' old house in Cambridge.
4. See letter 77.
5. The next of the four-yearly international mathematical congresses was to be held in Cambridge in the summer of 1912. Russell was in charge of organizing the philosophical section and was writing to invite participants.
6. E. Farmer, a Trinity student; he got a second class in the Moral Sciences Tripos of 1913.

to the charge, not arguing but only preaching honesty. I wonder what will have come of it. He abominates ethics and morals generally; he is deliberately a creature of impulse, and thinks one should be. What he disliked about my last chapter[1] was saying philosophy has *value*; he says people who like philosophy will pursue it, and others won't, and there's an end of it. *His* strongest impulse is philosophy. I wouldn't answer for his technical morals.

When he left me I was strangely excited by him. I love him and feel he will solve the problems that I am too old to solve – all kinds of vital problems that are raised by my work, but want a fresh mind and the vigour of youth. He is *the* young man one hopes for. But as is usual with such men, he is unstable, and may go to pieces. His vigour and life is such a comfort after the washed-out Cambridge type. His attitude justifies all I have hoped about my work. He will be up again next term.

I lay awake ever so long and I ought to be tired but I am not. I have still my 2 books to review.[2] I must try to get them done before you come home. I won't *count* on you before the Friday but I shall *hope*. Some time next term I have to go to Cardiff to read a paper on Matter.[3] What date is least likely to be a nuisance? I shall have to fix it soon.

Not another moment. Goodbye Darling. I may have difficulty in posting at Radlett so expect another letter when it comes. Great haste. All love.

Your

B.

After leaving 'Lion' Phillimore's Russell went on a walking tour on the south coast. Without the Cambridge term, Wittgenstein, or 'Lion' to distract him, and with Ottoline still not home, he found, as he says in the next letter, that his patience and vitality gave out simultaneously. The last straw was when Ottoline, who had set out from Lausanne, decided to stop in Paris for a couple of days to have a dress made. To Bertie, it was incomprehensible, if she loved him as much as she said, that she could extend her absence for such a trivial reason.

1. Of *The Problems of Philosophy*.
2. One was F. C. S. Schiller's *Formal Logic*, reviewed in the *Nation* (18 May 1912). The other was possibly E. Belfort Bax, *Problems of Men, Mind, and Morals* (1912), which Russell reviewed in May. The review cannot be traced and Russell may have decided against publication.
3. The Philosophical Society of University College, Cardiff, had asked him to give a paper. He had proposed to speak on the philosophical implications of symbolic logic, but they preferred something less technical. The manuscript of the paper he wrote for the occasion, 'On Matter', is in the Russell Archives. It has not yet been published. He read it at Cardiff on 17 May.

Ottoline, needless to say, felt rather differently about it. In the first place, of course, the obsessive passion that Bertie felt for her was not reciprocated. Second, she was used to being able to go where she liked and return when she liked, without having to consult the feelings of others. She had been brought up to do so and it was the pattern of her marriage with Philip. She was not prepared to let a lover clip her wings. Third, her 'cure' with Dr Combe had been extremely gruelling, especially towards the end. He had burned her nose with electrodes and cut bits of bone from it, so that it streamed continuously and hurt her all day and all she could smell was burnt flesh. All this she bore with extraordinary fortitude and good humour. It is none the less not surprising that she did not feel up to travelling quickly back to England to resume her life, but preferred to spend some time in Paris to recover from her cure.

To be fair to Bertie, the impatient letter he sent her from his walking tour crossed with hers describing the gruesome details of Dr Combe's treatment. However, the arrival of her letter didn't entirely clear things up. Ottoline was convinced that she would have to break free from a love that was threatening to imprison her, while Bertie was torn between blaming Ottoline and blaming himself. On the one hand, he could not believe that her love was real if she felt it was a prison. On the other, he could not believe that his passion for her was as good as it ought to be if it imprisoned her. Frustrated by the delay in their reunion, he began to brood about the violence of his emotions.

In criticizing his paper 'The Essence of Religion', Ottoline had spoken in favour of desire. Bertie felt he had all too much of desire and that, in his case, it was too often a destructive force that had to be kept under control.

[187]

[On walking tour]
22 March 1912
Friday night

My Darling Love

I have been reading the beginning of *Endymion*[1] – it is wonderfully good, and as you say it has a cry in it. It sweeps away my pretence of being indifferent to beauty, but rather confirms me in thinking one ought to be. Visions of unattainable loveliness unnerve one and make it terribly hard to go on with one's job whatever it is. So much beauty – and Keats especially – rouses up in me the longing for personal happiness – when I am with you that doesn't matter, because the longing is satisfied unless you are ill or aloof –

1. By Keats.

but when you are away it makes it almost overmastering. One must have a certain austerity of desire to live a decent life, and beauty seems to sweep away austerity. That is what I am really thinking of when I talk against desire. You have mastered the desire for personal happiness to an extraordinary extent, without destroying the desires that ought to survive. To me it seems almost superhuman. I have tried for many years to grow indifferent to my own happiness, but quite in vain – I care about it just as much as when I was a child. At moments I rise above it, but not for long. If I could really rise above it, I could live much more freely, but as it is I must be always holding myself in check.

I think sometimes you think it is only peccadilloes I am afraid of, but it isn't, it is big violent crimes – murders and suicide and such things. I don't know what is the right way to deal with this violence in me – I know it is bad, but it is bound up with good things so intimately that it is hard to disentangle. I have a thirst for simple happiness – I had it at Marienbad – I have had many days of ecstasy with you, which is better, but different – in fact it is largely pain, and full of reaching out to something beyond which haunts human life as a dream, but probably is never attained; but of simple happiness I think there have not been many days except at Marienbad. It makes me gentle and takes away the violence and gives me rest while it lasts. You hardly believe me when I say I am often weary, because I am active – but I am active because of the inward goad, and I feel it would be heaven if that ceased. And the inward goad is desire born of the vision – personal and impersonal desire inextricably mixed. A hundredth part of the desire I have would be quite enough. But if I could diminish the personal part of it, that would be a gain. But I find I don't really want to – if I did, I shouldn't love you with the same intensity, and I wouldn't sacrifice an atom of my love for you for anything in earth or heaven.

Saturday morning. This morning's newspaper is bitterly disappointing. Asquith's refusal of the 5s. and 2s., and the chance that the Bill may be dropped altogether, are very disgusting.[1] If I had been a member, I think I should have got up and joined the Labour Party then and there. I gather it was not so much Asquith's doing as the doing of Liberal M.P's who announced that they would revolt if the 5s. and 2s. were granted. If Labour questions are going to be so much to the fore, obviously the Labour Party is the one to

1. On 19 March, the government had introduced a bill to enforce a minimum wage in the mines. The bill did not recognize the unions' demands, however, and for a while it looked as if the measure might be dropped altogether. It was, however, passed on 29 March and the miners went back to work.

belong to. At the Budget time I was much more Liberal than Labour, because I do think Land is the basis of everything. But now Lloyd George has turned Jingo, Winston has become a Statesman, and the whole crew would be better dead. Yet there is still Home Rule[1] – it would be too much if that were defeated again. And if the Tories come in we shall have Protection and war with Germany. It all looks black.

I am so sorry Dearest that you have been feeling depressed and caged. Yes I dare say it is loneliness, but also health partly isn't it? I am depressed too – politics, rain and cold, impatience, a bad night. I was kept awake a good while by toothache, and then I began to worry about your dress in Paris – I thought probably the dressmaker is poor and you want to help her – or something – and that you were trailing your coat – if so it was quite successful. My patience and vitality have given out simultaneously – I have kept patient by keeping busy and active-minded, now I am neither and I am gnawed by wild impatience. Don't let me pick a quarrel. I might, from mere tension. Today, if the weather clears, I shall go to Wareham – a rather longer walk than my other days. That ought to tame me a bit.

I should *love* to explain Part II of my Bergson paper to you if you would really like it[2] – there are few things I should like better. I am glad you liked the writing. Glad you spotted the joke. Darling I am *so* glad you like my letters. Yes, I have been *very* full of new life – it all comes out of you and love – love gives life, and with an effort one can turn the life to other things. I have been *much* more full of new life than before. I have had less conflict of intellect and feeling than usual.

In philosophical writing, one aims at a beauty of style which is not that of ordinary writing – clearness and force are the chief things – it wants to be very chiselled so as to have exactness. I thought my Bergson paper had succeeded in this, and I am glad you think so.

Darling I must stop. I can't think how I shall live through these next days, but I suppose they will pass somehow – it will be torture. I wonder what mood you will be in when you get home. Goodbye Dearest.

Your

B.

---

1. Irish Home Rule was still a Liberal Party policy. The Tories were implacably opposed to it and no other party but the Liberals could hope to get it through the House.
2. Bertie had written a long paper, very critical of Bergson's philosophy, which was published in *The Monist* in July 1912. He had sent the manuscript to Ottoline, who found part II beyond her and asked him to explain it.

Ottoline did not see Bertie immediately on her return from Paris. Their first meeting was on 2 April at Bertie's flat. It seemed to go well enough (to judge by Bertie's hyperbole in the next letter), but there was an undercurrent of unease left over from Bertie's annoyance at her stay in Paris. Although she had replied to his letter good-humouredly, Ottoline seems to have been more than a little put out by his expectation that she would return quickly to England to be with him. The underlying problem was that they loved unequally. Bertie's entire world could be set to rights by Ottoline's mere presence; the same was not true for her. Had it been, she would have rushed from Lausanne to rejoin him, as he, in similar circumstances, would have rushed to rejoin her. This difference made his love seem to her a constraint which could grow intolerable and she seems to have decided that she should try to keep him at a greater distance, though without giving him up entirely.

The 'St Paul's Day' incident referred to in the next letter occurred the previous summer when they visited St Paul's Cathedral. The exact nature of the problems on either side is not known, but it was one of a number of occasions on which Ottoline told Bertie that she needed solitude to deal with her problems. This made Bertie feel hurt and inadequate.

[188]

[34 Russell Chambers]
2 April 1912
Tuesday night

O my dear dear Love

I cannot tell you all the divine joy you gave me today. I have been in a kind of dream world ever since. The wonder of it was very like agony – as if I could hardly go on living after it. Very very great happiness does make me wish to die – as if death could make one dream through all eternity of the last divine moment when one lived. It was so swift and overwhelming at the last. Such joy is *really* an infinite thing – it is no use to say it is selfish or brief or anything of that sort – it is a revelation in a moment of all that life might be, of the world of light where even human souls can live – as if the hand of God suddenly raised me up from earth and set me among his angels in all the glory of heaven amid the mystic song of all creation in a vast universe of flaming splendour. O Dearest I try to tell you what is in my heart, but I cannot, I cannot. We are strangely poised between hell and heaven, both so near at hand. Indeed passion is of God – the unquenchable thirst for heaven – it is the power that drives us on to seek out good. We are exiles in this nether world, and all passion has something of home-sickness. Why I touch heaven in union with you I do not know, but I know it is so – the iron gates that shut the soul within its earthly prison open, and welcoming voices summon me to freedom. Never before have I seen so much of heaven as I saw today.

I have been reading over your letters of January (last year's letters are at Cambridge) – they are wonderful letters and very full of love. My trouble *lately* has been connected with the St Paul's day – the pain of that day went very deep. It was not, as you felt, that you had not sympathized with my anxiety – you really had, and anyhow that didn't affect me much. It was the discovery that I didn't know how to be any comfort to you in your trouble, but that your trouble demanded solitude. I understand better now, but at the time I hardly knew how to bear it. I felt unimportant to you, and that where you felt deeply you had to shut me out. I only say this now because I understand better and no longer feel as I did about it. It has been concerned in my unhappiness lately.

It doesn't do for me to relax discipline too much – the forces inside are too wild – some of them must be kept chained up. But there is no harm in that; I don't now need the degree of discipline that is killing, but only the degree that is wholesome. I had thought possibly now I might let all the dogs have an outing, but some of them are mad dogs and are not safe to leave at large. Our talk about passion today was interesting; I find so often in talking to you I see deeper into things than I ever have before, and it is easy to be very truthful with you even where truthfulness might well be difficult. Darling I hardly know what I said in all those mad letters I sent to Paris; if there were hurting things, please forgive me. It is love that makes me sometimes wish to hurt you; I hate myself for it, but the impulse is bound up with passion. Don't worry about the St Paul's day – I only say it because, as it is now ancient history, I felt I should like you to understand.

Goodnight my Darling.

Your

B.

Despite the impression given in the previous letter, there were also difficulties in their sexual relations. Bertie, after nine years of almost total abstinence, was once more very enthusiastic about sex. Ottoline, though she relished intimate friendships with men, had no very strong desire to go to bed with them. Whether this was from moral scruple or from lack of physical pleasure is hard to say, but, despite her numerous affairs, she seems always to have been a rather reluctant sexual partner. (The same was true of her relationship with Philip: from an early date they seem to have gone their own ways sexually.)

Early in April the question of sexual relations with other people arose once more, though their correspondence does not reveal how. Ottoline may have raised the possibility of being in love with two people at the same time – a present reality for her, but a useful possibility, she may have thought, for Bertie. Or Bertie may have reasoned that easing his sexual frustrations with someone else would make it easier to be less demanding on Ottoline. References in their letters suggest both ideas were explored. Though Bertie was prepared to concede that jealousy was an entirely bad emotion, he felt it was one he could not avoid. And he felt sure her passion for him would be weakened if he had a sexual relation (he could not admit the possibility of love) with another woman. 'I am inclined to think', he told her on 4 April, 'that jealousy would not be so devastating in people who had *never* thought of passion as exclusive, but in us, with our traditions and habits, it would make any at all satisfactory relation impossible unless it (the relation) was exclusive. I don't feel that about affection and tenderness, even when they are very warm, but I do about passion and any actual sexual relation.' In all this Ottoline apparently concurred. But as his frustrations mounted during the month, he returned to the idea to find Ottoline's opinion unchanged. He elegantly chided her double standard (24 April): 'Seeing that you, who have the whole of two men, would suffer greatly if you only had one and a half, you can perhaps imagine that it is hard to be content with a half, which is three times less than what would *not* content you.'

[189]

Liverpool Street [Station]
8.20. 29 April 1912

My dear dear Love

Yes, the end of our day was wonderful. In the spiritual region you do most fully satisfy me. But my lower nature sometimes yearns after the simple happiness I used to have at first. If I could get myself in hand as I did at the time of our summer crisis even that might return. The difficulty is, as I remember writing to you after the summer crisis, that one can't live always at the highest spiritual level, and at any other there are difficulties. However, tonight I am happy, because for the moment I have escaped from my prison.

I don't think you quite realize how rare and difficult what you ask is: I don't believe one man in a hundred would acquiesce in it. But I shall learn not to think about it in time. Only when, about a month ago, you told me I ought to realize your life in Bedford Square, you were suggesting all the most undesirable trains of thought to me. During this last week, I have written you a letter saying we had better part, and while you have been gone home to lunch I have resolved to tell you when you come back that things ought to end between us. But when I have seen you or had a letter from you, it has made me feel that all nonsense. Today, because I was tired, the feeling persisted; in fact I had practically made up my mind to speak. The whole trouble will recur; the only question is whether it will get worse or better. Quite at first, you were 'in love' with me; I think that ceased at the time of the summer crisis, I remember now the exact spot in the woods at Peppard where you said Studland seemed very long ago, and I remember just the stab of pain it caused me to realize how you had changed.

Dearest, whatever happens, and however I may go wild, I never lose sight of my purpose. So long as I feel you help me in that, the bond is absolute. The thing I am always struggling against is getting so tied to passion that my purpose becomes dependent on it. That has never yet happened to me – I have always worked steadily through every storm. But I have felt lately that without you I could not go on. I should like to think that untrue, but I am afraid it isn't. My courage is not what it once was. Ten years ago I met pain with the belief that it would remain high anguish. I didn't know the awful deadness that comes after. I am constantly now, and have been from the first, haunted by a terror of repetition, which I feel would be more than I could face.

Dearest be patient with me – it will be worth your while. My best and worst are very close together. When the worst comes out, it is likely the best will follow soon. I hate the prison-house of personal desires, but it is not easy to escape from it and retain any life at all.

The thing I was thinking of when I talked of another woman some time ago was not *so* shocking as you seem to have thought. I was thinking of a certain woman whom you don't know, who cares for me and for whom I have a very real affection.[1] I believe it would be for her happiness and would do her good. I only say this because I think you thought of worse things, and it is true they did cross my mind, but no more.

Our talk today has been very useful to me. I wish I could have fought it out alone. I have struggled with it for months, but it got worse instead of better. Sometimes I think we ought to give up everything sexual altogether. It may be we should get more of the best of each other that way. Only I doubt if I could stand it; I might find it necessary to break altogether. Then again I think sometimes it would be better if we met less often but for a longer time, with more freedom; if say once a month we could spend two days and nights together in the country. But I doubt if that would really be

---

1. This seems to have been Mildred Minturn Scott (see letter 130), who was writing very affectionate letters to him at this time.

better. Of course what makes most difference is when you *express* your love, like what you said about St Sebastian,[1] which has over and over again filled me with happiness since. I *long* to know what you think of me, how I strike you, what you feel about my virtues and vices, and all sorts of thing; but you have steadily refused to tell me one word, except the remark about St Sebastian and what you said today about the happiness of talking of spiritual things. (You have said something like that before.) If you can, you will always add to my happiness by telling me that sort of thing. I suppose you don't know how little you ever say.

Now we are nearly at Cambridge. I do *hate* having made your head ache. But at any rate it was not wholly a wasted day. Goodbye my Darling. You don't of course know the terrible intensity of my love, because only tremendous energy can give such intensity. But what you give me is infinitely precious, and does really foster and sustain my best. Goodnight my Dearest.

Your

B.

Though Bertie tried his best to be optimistic, their relationship continued to deteriorate. Through the Cambridge term he vacillated over whether he should break it off, but each time he came to the brink of deciding to do so a reassuring note from Ottoline would revive his hopes. Though she certainly wanted a cooler relationship with him, she was not at all prepared to let him go. And Bertie found it beyond his powers to break while there was the slightest hope of a reconciliation. Bound up, rather curiously, with this dilemma was another: that of deciding whether to return to technical philosophy. He had taken to writing fiction, in the form of a conversational novella, *The Perplexities of John Forstice*, which he hoped would succeed where 'Prisons' failed. Technical philosophy had lost its hold on his imagination. 'It worries me rather,' he told her on 20 May, 'having discovered that I have so little belief in philosophy. I did seriously mean to go back to it, but I found I really couldn't think it very valuable. This is *partly* due to Wittgenstein, who has made me more of a sceptic; partly it is the result of a process which has been going on ever since I found you. It may be temporary, and I rather hope so; but I doubt it.' But at times when he thought he should break with Ottoline, he thought also of returning to philosophy.

Ottoline's health remained a very persistent problem. She was planning to spend June on a second trip to Dr Combe's clinic, this time for treatment for her liver,

1. She had compared him to *St Sebastian* by the Italian painter, Andrea Mantegna. In fact there are two paintings of St Sebastian by Mantegna (one in Vienna and one in the Louvre); it is difficult to say which Russell resembled most.

despite the fact that the first trip seemed not to have produced much benefit to her nose. The liver treatment was less painful but equally appalling: a thirty-day course of doses of radium in milk. Since his work at Cambridge would be finished by the time she left, Bertie was hoping to go with her though he felt she probably wouldn't want him. By this time, following an especially disappointing meeting, he was in despair.

[190]

[Trinity College]
[30 May 1912]
Thursday night

My Dearest

After posting my letter to you, I saw North and Burns[1] and Dorward[2] and Geach, and talked to each about how he had done his Tripos; then I lectured to Wittgenstein; then I had Sanger to dinner (I love him very much); then an enormous crowd at my evening – I was very full of wit and kept them in fits of laughter – I have hardly ever been more gay. When they were all gone I walked out in the mist and moonlight – *very* beautiful. I do most fully and completely understand the way you feel, and no doubt I should feel the same way if I had the same kind of illness. I do not rage – it is inevitable, and it doesn't in any way lessen my opinion of you. It does lessen my love; I had to choose between ceasing to live and lessening my love, and with some hesitation I decided to go on living. Your love, though you don't think so, seems to me [to] have diminished steadily since Studland, and to be still diminishing. If I could face life without you, I would break; I shall try to learn to live without you, since if you go on in the same course it will soon be necessary. It is tragic, but nobody is to blame. I have little doubt that after some years of separation we could meet as friends, and our friendship would be the richer for our love in the past.

Out in the moonlight, I tried to exhort myself to remember other things – my work in the world, all that I wish to further, the young men for whom I have an affection, and to whom I wish to give a real initiation into the world of thought. But it had very little reality to me. My creative work, so far as it is important, is done. If you could have been different, I might have

1. E. B. V. Burns, a Trinity student. He got a First in part two of the Moral Sciences Tripos in 1912.
2. Alan James Dorward (1889–1956), also at Trinity. He got a First in part one of the Moral Sciences Tripos in 1912. He went on to teach philosophy at St Andrews and eventually became Professor of Philosophy at Liverpool.

done a new sort of work; but that hope is dead. I can probably weave what I have done into a connected narrative; the 'Free Man's Worship' only became a connected whole after the inspiration had left me; but I cannot do anything that wants fresh inspiration. And new ties, if I could form them, would not make it possible, because every fresh failure makes doubt harder to combat and more paralysing. The young men are really the only thing that strongly holds me to life. Moore does not give them quite what I do; besides, I love them. I have had a bad conscience this term, because I have rather neglected them for you. But they don't make a life. I feel that if we parted, little as I should intend it, the moment would come when in a sudden impulse I should put myself under a motor for the pleasure of feeling my backbone break. And if I avoided that, I should not avoid sexual crime, from mere desperation.

My Dearest, don't fancy that I have even the faintest tinge of feeling against you: the whole thing is Fate, and you can't help it. Only I suffer most profoundly. Ever since the letter you wrote on the anniversary of our meeting,[1] I have longed for death, even when things have seemed happy. It is your gradual inexorable withdrawal – like the ebbing tide – that keeps me over and over again at the very last point of agony. You flatter yourself in thinking you can imagine passionate love; as far as I have observed, you can't imagine it a bit. If you could, you would have known that letter would madden me. At first your vocabulary misled me, because it is more heightened than mine: the same words express smaller feelings.

I have lost the spring of life – I am weary of this world with its labours and sorrows. I want to lay down my head and sleep – to be done with strife and the terrible hope of happiness. I know this is cowardly; one ought to fight the fight to the end, and I suppose I shall really; but I have suffered so much, and endured such a long and solitary task. O Dearest, I cannot forget how different it would all be if you loved me; and till I have forgotten that I shall be weak.

I keep on thinking about the extract from your journal you once read me, wondering if you would ever get a really great love. It is profoundly tragic that now that it has come you can't meet it. I know you say you love me much more than you know or I know, but it is not passionate love, and if neither you nor I know of it, it seems rather ineffective. I think these last two months have given our love a mortal wound, but I am not sure; and in

1. The letter in which she told him that she didn't want him to meet her in Paris in March 1912. Thoughtlessly, she had mentioned in it that she might see Lytton Strachey and Henry Lamb there.

any case it will need time for me to detach myself. But I want to say this: Whatever may happen hereafter, I shall always worship your nobility and passion and gentleness and universal love; I shall always feel your beauty mystically; I shall always remember that I owe to you the greatest and most perfect and best happiness I have ever known; the times in the woods last summer will remain with me for ever to remind me what is possible even here on earth. And in full remembrance of earlier years, I can be quite sure that this memory will not fade. It may be that when all the storm is over, some sediment of wisdom will be deposited by the memory. I have not Alys now to make life sordid, therefore the pain of the future cannot be so horrible as the pain of the past, and cannot make it so necessary to put away all thoughts of beauty. If we part, there will be no bitterness on my side, nothing to spoil remembrance or take away the profound spiritual good that you have given me.

Now it is 2.30 and I must go to bed.

Friday morning.

My Dearest – Thank you for your two kind letters. I find I arrive at Lausanne at 7.10 in the morning, so I think I may as well get rooms for one night and have a bath and shave before I see you. If we find other rooms, I will fetch my things away, without waiting to spend the first night there. That is, if you do really want me to come. Take any books you like. I really have no choice in the matter. Shakespeare and Plato certainly. Carlyle's *Frederick* is very good in parts; the 1st Vol. I think is dull, and the last 3 or 4. The 2nd, 3rd, 4th, 5th I think are the best (in the 9 vol. edition).[1]

I leave at 10 or 11 on Tuesday, so I shall get the 1st post. I have no more to say now. I am sorry you are unhappy. But I can't pretend I am not, which is the only way I could prevent it.

　　Your
　　　B.

I will do anything you suggest about meeting you: meet you at Hotel Richmont or the Post Office or any place you like, at any time you suggest not before 9.

Friday night.

Darling Love I have still a few moments before the post, and I have had

---

1. Thomas Carlyle's *History of Frederick II of Prussia, Called Frederick the Great* (1858–65). Russell presumably meant the 10-volume Chapman & Hall edition (1893–5) which is the one in his library. Ottoline had suggested Shakespeare and Plato and had wondered about the Carlyle.

your little line. I will come to Lausanne. I thought probably you wouldn't want me. It will not be unhappiness to me I think. At any rate I am relieved that you wish to try. O Dearest my heart does ache so for you. It is so cold to come back to the old loneliness and despair. And you are so terribly what I can love. The Lord giveth and the Lord taketh away; and the Lord is some small poison from your liver.

I cannot learn not to love you. Wednesday morning we shall meet – Goodnight.

Your

B.

A paragraph, in which Russell quotes the whole of the final paragraph of his essay 'On History', has been omitted from the following letter. The passage in question can be found in *Papers*, vol. xii, p. 82.

[191]

[Trinity College]
1 June 1912

Dearest

Your letter has come. I don't know whether it is wise to come to Lausanne or not, but I know I shall come. This is not a decision of my will; I should come even if I decided not to. – You say you know what I feel; but at the very times when you say you love me, you prove by your actions that you don't. I know you are meaning to speak the truth, so I think you don't know what words mean. – I will try to take what you give me; at Lausanne the outward circumstances may make it easy to put up with its being so little. And perhaps I shall forget for a time how little it is. Dearest I haven't even the very tiniest resentment; it is Fate, no one can help it, you could not have foreseen it. And I am certain that by nature you are capable of great love; it is only physical exhaustion that prevents it. But meanwhile loving you is like loving a red-hot poker, which is a worse bedfellow than even Lytton's umbrella:[1] every caress brings an agony.

One can't transfer love to another person, as if it were a piece of luggage to be taken from one train to another. It takes me nine years to recover the freshness of feeling that is wanted for love. Nine years hence I shall be 49, and shall be too old for any one I could care for; even if they could care for me, I should wither their life by the depth of my pessimism and despair.

1. It is not known what incident this refers to.

Therefore nothing remains but frivolities. Of course I ought to be strong and live the 'quiet bachelor life' my cousin thought so nice. But apart from anything else, I must escape from memories – I have too many and they are too painful. I rule out drink and morphia and such things, because they would spoil my intellect, and if that were spoilt it would be simpler to die.

Don't think I don't realize your pain; I do, but I can do nothing to make it less. You will think me terribly self-absorbed, but that is only towards you. I am doing my work well, quite able to take an interest in others, talking well and gaily. Yesterday Wittgenstein began on Dickens, saying David Copperfield ought not to have quarrelled with Steerforth for running away with Little Emily. I said I should have done so; he was much pained, and refused to believe it; thought one could and should always be loyal to friends and go on loving them. We got onto Julie de Lespinasse,[1] and I asked him how he would feel if he were married to a woman he loved and she ran away with another man. He said (and I believe him), that he would feel no rage or hate, only utter misery. His nature is good through and through; that is why he doesn't see the need of morals. I was utterly wrong at first; he might do all kinds of things in passion, but he would not practise any cold-blooded immorality. His outlook is very free; principles and such things seem to him nonsense, because his impulses are strong and never shameful. I think he is passionately devoted to me. Any difference of feeling causes him great pain. My feeling towards him is passionate, but of course my absorption in you makes it less important to me than his feeling is to him. Oddly enough, he makes me less anxious to live, because I feel he will do the work I should do, and do it better. He starts fresh at a point which I only reached when my intellectual spring was nearly exhausted.

I told W. the story of Julie and then gave him one of her letters to read. He was much moved. I had represented Guibert as the cause of her misery. He said she was bound to be unhappy, since she could love like that. I had never talked with him before about things of that sort.

.   .   .   .

I will come and ask for your room at 9.30 on Wednesday. Goodbye.
Your
  B.

---

1. Julie Jeanne Eléonore de Lespinasse (1732–76) had run a literary salon at which *encyclopédistes* gathered. She is best known for the passionate and unhappy love letters she wrote to the Comte de Guibert, who did not love her and married someone else. Russell had been reading her letters with a good deal of sympathy.

Despite this inauspicious start, Bertie and Ottoline's time together in Lausanne helped mend their relationship. Bertie spent the mornings writing *Forstice* and in the afternoons they would read together or go for walks. They were much happier than they had been for a long time, and began to feel they were right not to part. Russell wrote her a note on their last night together in Lausanne.

[192]

[Lausanne]
2 July 1912

My dearest dearest Love

I must write one line this last night to tell you of all the love and joy that is in my heart. This month has been very wonderful – and you have borne with me in the most marvellous way: I do now feel very great confidence for the future – that has only come to me quite at the end. I really understand now all the things that made trouble – I have no grudges lurking, no devils ready to pop up their heads whenever I give them a chance. I do now believe that you care for me and that my love means something to you – it was hard for me to understand, because your way of caring is different from mine. Yes, it will be a great and wonderful treasure through years to come. You must not think now that I am full of demands which you have to resist. Dearest Love, I know that the communion in religious things which we have had lately, and which is the greatest thing in our love, will only be possible at times, because often I am quite dead to religious things; I wish it were not so, but you will know, won't you, that I am only dead for a time, and that they will revive? Except my love for you, it is the most passionate feeling I have, but it is so constantly checked and thwarted by reason that it cannot always come to the light of day. If I could really go on writing, it would be much more constantly alive.

Tonight I finished *Forstice* after a fashion, and then read it through. It wants changes, but it really is good; the best part of it is your part, *really*;[1] I am sure anybody would say so. I have much less doubt about it than I had about *Prisons* even at the time; it really is worth something, I feel sure. And I think it is only the beginning of many things. It is all due to you, my Dearest. Don't forget that, if times of discouragement come later. And don't think the world is full of people who could have done what you have done for me; for really it isn't.

---

1. Ottoline had written some passages towards the end of the novella. (The passages in question can be found in *Papers*, vol. XII, pp. 149–51.)

Darling, Darling, it would have been *madness* to part. Don't be too ready to let me go – our love really is sacred and not a thing to kill lightly, from trivial impatience. Goodnight my Beloved. I long to give you only good gifts – understanding, and unselfish love. And I have every hope. We are only at the beginning really – it will grow and deepen with the years. Goodnight, Goodnight, my Dearest Dearest.

The serene growth of love that Russell yearned for was not easy to achieve, and not always because of clashes between Ottoline and himself. Occasionally the past came back to haunt him, as on the following occasion at the end of July when he went to Covent Garden to see a performance of *Scheherazade* by Diaghilev's Ballets Russes, then at the height of their fame, and found himself sitting close to Alys. It was the first time he'd seen her since their separation and the event upset him deeply. His failed marriage still lay heavily on his conscience.

[193]

[34 Russell Chambers]
Wednesday night
[31 July 1912]

My Dearest Dearest

If I were you I wouldn't send those cakes to Mrs M[cGowan][1] as I shan't be here – it is most kind, but it seems hardly wise to have her meet your maids. Before, I have always been in when any of your maids came. I ought to have let you send them tonight only I was afraid I should be out.

Dakyns[2] and I settled to go to Covent Garden to see the Russian ballet. We got tickets and were just getting to our places when he said 'there's Karin'. I looked and saw Alys – looking radiant, seeing him and giving him a beaming smile. I turned and fled. He hadn't seen her, thought I didn't know where the places were, and hung on to my arm all the way out trying to stop me. We wandered out and had got into St Martin's Lane when Alys came along by herself, meeting us; I didn't see her till we were passing; she looked haggard and in torture – as she passed she gave me a look which was intended to pierce my heart, and did so. It spoiled Dakyns's evening for him. Her place was almost next to ours. I was very much upset, especially by the

1. Russell's housekeeper at Russell Chambers.
2. Arthur Lindsay Dakyns (1883–1941), a barrister. He was at Oxford for a while, where he was (so Russell said) the only person sympathetic to Russell's philosophy. Russell had been friendly with him for many years.

second meeting. I walked on a few steps and then had to lean against the railings for some time – but she was out of sight by that time. I brought Dakyns back here, and recovered very soon by talking metaphysics. At last we went out to a cinematograph to see if it bore out Bergson's philosophy, which it did.[1]

Darling I can't tell you how awful it was.

Your

B.

[194]

In the train[2]
Thursday morning
[1 August 1912]

My Darling Darling Love

I *was* glad of your little letter this morning. No, you certainly couldn't ask Bernard Holland[3] to post it! I wonder what you said about his poems, and how Virginia[4] showed her niceness. The cakes arrived before I had gone, so I gave them[5] as if from myself, which seemed best. I found she doesn't know your name. She said the maid had said they were from Lady Somebody but she hadn't caught the name, so I said 'Oh yes, that's all right.' Poor lady, she did hope I should say more, like my bedmaker[6] when she said you were very tall. But I was glad she didn't know your name.

How well I remember this journey after our agitating Xmas meeting – I remember writing madly, posting one letter at Reading and another at Marlborough.[7] What a curious madness it is to have an impulse to hurt

1. This was Russell's first experience of the cinema. According to Bergson, we experience motion as a continuous process but in thinking about it we conceive it as a series of successive states; similarly, in film the succession of static images is perceived as continuous motion.
2. On the way to Lockeridge to stay with the Whiteheads.
3. Bernard Henry Holland (1856–1926), a friend of Ottoline's who had been visiting her. He had been Secretary of State for the Colonies from 1903 to 1908 and held a number of other short-term political posts afterwards. In addition to voluminous works on the history of his family, he wrote poetry and edited the works of Crabbe. Blackwoods had just published his *Verse* (1912).
4. Virginia Woolf had been to visit with Lytton Strachey and had been unexpectedly pleasant.
5. To Mrs McGowan.
6. At Cambridge.
7. Letter 182 was written the same day, after the two written on the train.

where one loves – when I have hurt you, I mind your pain most intensely. I don't understand the impulse, but it is somehow a part of very intense passion. For a long time, I was so filled with passion that I had scarcely room for affection. Somehow at Lausanne your pride seemed less, you were more willing to explain things, you wore less armour. That made affection grow up, and has made everything much easier for me.

When I first saw Alys yesterday, I was very much struck by her good looks – she looked beautiful and not unhappy. The second time she looked old and tragic. I think she had only gone out a moment for air and solitude, and was going back. On reflection I think her look at me was not all tragedy, but also partly to see how I looked without my moustache.[1] Our eyes met before I knew she was there. She has a terrible hold on me still. Her power of making me suffer irritates me against her, but it persists all the same. There is *something* that never dies if one has cared deeply for a person. Somehow she holds my imagination still. In the days when I cared for her, I used to see her as a kind of free force of nature – she was at her best in very primitive things, bathing, paddling in streams, talking to children by the wayside – a sort of wind from the life of unconscious nature. And then I sophisticated her and twisted her and gave her standards that were artificial to her, and then lashed her for being insincere with them. And then her suffering was like the suffering of an animal – like a dog run over by a motor – with the same unbearable appeal. There is nothing for me but to forget her – only having lived with her so long, it is hard.

Now we are coming to Reading and I must post this. Goodbye my Darling Love. Tuesday I arrive Paddington 11.5. I long for it already.

Your

B.

Much of Russell's time during August was taken up with the International Congress of Mathematicians meeting at Cambridge. It revived some of Russell's interest in mathematical logic.

1. Russell had had a moustache since he was an undergraduate and it achieved a shape and size rather like Nietzsche's in its last years. Ottoline, however, didn't like it and Russell had shaved it off the previous December. 'The change in his appearance', Ottoline wrote, 'was astonishing. He at once ceased to be a Cambridge don, and emerged a mixture of Voltaire and an actor' (*Memoirs*, vol. II, p. 273).

[195]

[Trinity College]
Wednesday morning
[21 August 1912]

My Darling

Your dear letter reached me by 1st post and was *such* a joy – I hadn't thought it possible to get a letter so soon. I hope and expect that I shall want to come on the 29th, but I can't yet say definitely.

When I got home last night I found that Peano had come from London for the day on purpose to see Hobson[1] and me, and not finding me had waited 4 hours, but he was gone when I arrived. However I shall see him today and subsequent days. I shall be very busy – I have to take the chair for my Section, and make graceful remarks in opening the proceedings, and there will be endless people to talk to. I find it excites me and gets hold of me to think of seeing so many people interested in mathematical philosophy – my interest revives and the scent of battle stirs my blood. The love of power is terribly strong in me. I can't help reflecting that all these mathematical philosophers have different thoughts from what they would have had if I had not existed. But of course the real thing that makes an occasion of this kind feel important is the sense one has of scattered missionaries of truthful thought, each fighting a rather lonely battle, all coming together and finding encouragement in their common purpose. For the moment that feeling has swallowed up personal things altogether.

Goodbye my Dearest. I haven't time for more and I shall have to write mere scraps most days but I am full of love.

Your

B.

It was not, however, the logicians at the mathematics congress that persuaded Russell to return to technical philosophy, but the criticisms of Wittgenstein. The Cambridge term began on 11 October and Wittgenstein lost no time in coming to Russell the very first day to tell him what he thought of the article 'The Essence of Religion' which Russell had extracted from 'Prisons' and published in the *Hibbert Journal*. Russell was in the middle of a letter to Ottoline when he arrived: 'Here is Wittgenstein just arrived, frightfully pained by my *Hibbert* article which he evidently *detests*.' In another letter to Ottoline the same evening Russell explained why:

1. E. W. Hobson, see letter 165.

Wittgenstein was really unhappy about my paper on religion. He felt I had been a traitor to the gospel of exactness, and wantonly used words vaguely; also that such things are too intimate for print. I minded very much, because I half agree with him.

Where the Whiteheads' polite criticisms and evasions had failed, Wittgenstein's onslaught succeeded. Ottoline was conveniently away in Lausanne for another course of Dr Combe's radium and milk, and Russell once more took up technical philosophy. The emphasis in his letters to Ottoline was very much on exactness and precision. 'Wittgenstein's criticisms disturbed me profoundly,' he told her on 13 October. 'He was so unhappy, so gentle, so wounded in his wish to think well of me.'

Although Russell's mind was now turned back to what he did best, satisfactory results did not come easily. He started a paper called 'What is Logic?', dealing with the sort of fundamental issues about logic that he had been discussing with Wittgenstein. But within a week he was stuck and the paper was never completed. This work on the foundations of logic he felt inclined to leave to Wittgenstein, whom he now clearly thought of as his successor in that field. Russell was turning his attention to a new field, epistemology, and in particular the problem of the external world. He had treated it more or less conventionally in *The Problems of Philosophy*, but a good deal more sceptically in the paper on matter that he had read in Cardiff on 17 May. The task of overcoming the scepticism without abandoning the rigour which had led to it was what Russell was now attempting. In carrying it through he would be able to build on what he had already achieved in *Principia*: 'I feel', he told Ottoline on 29 October, 'that I really have got a method that gives more precision than there has ever been that things are built on. It is difficult to get people to see it, because philosophers are not trained to precision.' But it would be a large task – 'I have many years' work ahead of me' – and he dreaded 'the slavery of another big book'. None the less, the next day he was making plans for it.

[196]

[Trinity College]
Wednesday morning
[30 October 1912]

My darling Love

I was very glad of your dear letter this morning. I don't know why mine come Monday morning instead of Sunday night. – Yes, I know I was wrong when I said you cared more about 'states of mind' than about work. It wasn't really what I was thinking. I think it was an echo of the question how far one could live by love. Most work, however much love may approve of it, can't be inspired by love, but only by something much more impersonal, I mean an interest in *things* rather than *people*. And I was afraid of your finding me dry and unlovable in the moods in which I get technical work done. I shouldn't have been afraid if I had thought you could enter into what is positive in them, the actual interest in the subject, but I feared you would only feel what was negative. I am not afraid of that since our last days together, because you did really enter into the abstract interest then, I felt. It is so difficult to represent the essence of a thing when one can't talk about the details of it. I am enjoying being back whole-heartedly in the philosophical world. The time of half forgetting it has made things take their proper places – I see now where each thing fits, what is important and central, and what is more or less accidental. The whole scheme of things is vastly clearer in my mind than it was a year ago, and I feel I can go ahead to new problems with the feeling of a certain territory conquered.

The sort of thing that interests me now is this: Some of our knowledge comes from sense, some comes otherwise; what comes otherwise is called 'a priori'. Most actual knowledge is a mixture of both. The analysis of a piece of actual knowledge into pure sense and pure a priori is often very difficult, but almost always very important: the pure a priori, like the pure metal, is infinitely more potent and beautiful than the ore from which it was extracted. As regards the *mathematical* element in science, *Principia Mathematica* does the extraction very elaborately. But there are a number of other more elusive a priori elements in knowledge – such problems as causality and matter involve them. It is these that I want to get hold of now – I am only quite at the beginning – it is a vast problem of analysis, wanting tools that one has to make oneself before getting to work. It is very hard, to begin with, to make out what science really asserts – for example, what the law of gravitation means. Neither science nor philosophy helps one there – mathematical logic is the only help. And when one thinks one has found out what it asserts, one can't state the result so as to be intelligible to any one who doesn't know mathematical logic. So one's audience must be small!

The life of Lord George Bentinck,[1] which I have almost finished, interests

1. Benjamin Disraeli, *Lord George Bentinck, a Political Biography*; Russell's library has the eighth edition of 1872. William George Frederic Cavendish Bentinck (1802–48) was Ottoline's great-uncle and for a time a (minor) Conservative politician. He abandoned politics to devote more time to racing, but returned to oppose the repeal of the Corn Laws in 1846 by Sir Robert Peel, the Conservative Prime Minister. The Tories split on the repeal and Bentinck thereafter led the protectionists. In this he was helped by his protégé and adviser, Benjamin Disraeli ('Dizzy'). In 1847, however, he voted with the

me very much indeed – quite as much from the knowledge one gets of Dizzy as from what is told of Lord George. The chapter on the Jews is *very* interesting from that point of view – I had no idea Dizzy had such a passionate feeling for them. I was very much interested by the mixture of sincerity and insincerity – sincerity in praising the Jews, insincerity in praising Christianity. How he hates Peel!

Did you read the correspondence about the Chinese Loan in today's paper? Sir E. Grey comes out worse and worse the more one gets to know about that business.[1]

Dearest Love, you do indeed help me to feel the energy for new work, not only by your belief in work, though that is a very great thing, but also because when you make me happy you set free energy that would otherwise have to go into self-repression, and you give me new life and hope in every way, so that it seems possible to attack a new big task. What usually in the long run hampers men who think is a lack of buoyancy and vigour – they lose the *élan vital*, self-criticism paralyses them, and they fail in the sheer driving-force that clears its way through the jungle. I think the habit of abstract thought tends to produce a certain oppression and timidity that leads to failure. That is exactly what has happened to Moore – also to an elderly logician named Johnson[2] here, who has quite as good an intellect as I have, but has produced almost nothing – from failure of will and energy. In all those ways you help me more than I can say – that is what I mean when I say I feel young.

Now I must stop. Dearest, don't think being full of thoughts of work dims my love – it doesn't in the very least. I feel your spirit always with me, always an encouragement and a help. Goodbye my Darling Darling.

 Your
  B.

Liberals, led by Russell's grandfather, Lord John Russell, to admit Jews to Parliament. Disraeli was an assimilated Jew and devotes chapter xxiv of his biography to the issue.
1. A financial scandal, of a now familiar kind, concerning £11m in loans to China. Two British consortia had negotiated loans with the Chinese government with the apparent approval of the British Foreign Office. After the negotiations were concluded the Foreign Office tried to block the loans because it had secretly awarded a monopoly on such dealings to the Hongkong & Shanghai Bank. Sir Edward Grey, the British Foreign Minister, told the two competing consortia that he would intervene directly with the Chinese government to stop execution of the loans. The scandal had been developing since the beginning of the year, but on 29 October the British government took the now unusual step of publishing the documents relating to it. The *Daily News* carried the story on its front page on 30 October.
2. W. E. Johnson. See letter 97.

Since 1909 Harvard University had been trying to get Russell to visit. He had hitherto always put them off: while *Principia* was in press it would have been difficult for him to be so far away for an extended period and since March 1911 he had been anxious to avoid anything that would involve a long separation from Ottoline. By the end of 1912 neither of these reasons was so forceful as before. Two volumes of *Principia* were out and the third would appear in 1913, while his relationship with Ottoline had reached such a difficult pass that a prolonged separation began to look beneficial. Also important was his renewed interest in technical philosophy. So when, in 1912, Ralph Barton Perry, a Harvard philosopher and one of the six Realists, renewed the invitation for the spring term of 1914, Russell accepted. Russell and Perry had first met when Perry had visited Cambridge a couple of years earlier.

[197]

Trinity College
16 November 1912

Dear Mr Perry

I have very great pleasure in accepting your invitation to come to you next year (1914). I had to wait to reply until I had got leave from the College here to be absent. I have just learnt that they have no objection to my being absent during our summer term. I could not, however, sail much before the end of our Lent Term; that is to say, I could sail one of the first days in March. I gather from your letter that you could manage to start the courses, and let me take them up as soon as I arrived. If you think it very important that I should arrive earlier, I will make a fresh application to the Council here; but they feel − and I also partly feel − that in 2 terms I could give the bulk of my usual instruction here, whereas in a shorter time it would be impossible.

The financial proposals you make are quite satisfactory to me.[1]

Would it be possible for me to go some time to Columbia in case they desired it?[2] I do not know whether the lecturing you propose would fill all the 6 days of the week, or would leave a free day. If it would be inconvenient, I do not mind; I only wanted to know in case of being asked.

1. They had offered him £600 for his visit.
2. No doubt Russell was led to expect an invitation from Columbia by William Pepperell Montague (1873–1953), a Columbia philosopher and one of the six Realists, who was then visiting Cambridge. Although Russell went to Columbia to lecture at least once during his stay at Harvard, the sort of regular teaching engagement at Columbia which Russell seems to have expected did not materialize.

I wish to assure you how much I feel the honour of being asked to lecture at Harvard, and how much I look forward to getting to know your philosophy school, which is, I fully believe, about the best in the world.

Please remember me to Mrs Perry and believe me.

Yours very truly

Bertrand Russell

The plan was for Russell to give two courses of lectures: one on his earlier work in the philosophy of mathematics and the other on the theory of knowledge which would include the work he was just beginning on matter. He took his teaching duties at Harvard very seriously, as the next letter to Perry shows. In addition to his lectures at Harvard, Russell accepted an invitation from the Lowell Institute, a Massachusetts body devoted to popular education, to give their annual series of public lectures.

[198]

Trinity College

19 December 1912

Dear Professor Perry

Many thanks for your letter of Dec. 3. With regard to the date of my arrival, I think I ought to give very nearly two full terms to Trinity, and therefore I could not well leave before the beginning of March. My idea would be to take the first fast boat in March. If you had felt it *impossible* for me to carry out the programme starting so late, I might have asked the Council at Trinity for longer absence, but I think it would have been asking a good deal of them.

I do generally omit my two middle names, but in official documents it is well to put them in, as there is an Hon. Bertrand J. Russell (no relation) whom I have to be distinguished from. My position is 'Lecturer at Trinity College Cambridge.'

With regard to courses; I don't care whether the advanced course is called 'Logic' or 'Philosophy of Mathematics' – what I should say would be the same under either title. But perhaps 'Logic' better indicates its generality of scope. With regard to the more general course, I prefer 'Theory of Knowledge' to 'Philosophy of Nature'; but I assume I should have latitude to omit parts of the subject, and to treat other subjects that might seem to me relevant though not generally included. I think what one may call the 'Map' of Philosophy has got all wrong, and therefore my 'Continents' might not be quite the traditional ones. I am afraid there would have to be *some* overlapping of the two courses – e.g. I should have to talk about multiple relations[1] in both – but I would diminish it as much as I could. I think I should prefer to have both courses on the same three days, if there is no objection.

You ask whether I should like to give a few *public* lectures in Cambridge. But I gathered from your previous letter that I should probably be asked to lecture at the Lowell Institute, and in that case I should not, I think, care to give other popular lectures.

From what you say I gather that if (say) I were asked to go to Columbia one day a week, I could accept.

I should assume that the Intermediate Course had better be fully written out, and delivered practically as written – Is that right? The more advanced course, I suppose, had better be more conversational. Is that your view? Another point which has occurred to me is this: From my experience both as a pupil and as a teacher, I should say that really advanced teaching of clever people is best done in personal talk. I should be glad if there were some way of meeting the cleverer men individually and informally, not more than one or two at a time, when they felt so disposed, say by being known to be accessible at certain hours of certain days. Is this possible? In that way anything in my lectures which they disagreed with could be argued out.

Do you want a detailed syllabus of the lectures? I suppose not yet. If you do, could you give me the latest possible date? They will have to be quite different from the lectures I give at Trinity, and therefore the plan of them requires some thought.

I am looking forward with the greatest pleasure to my time at Harvard.

Yours very truly

Bertrand Russell

On the same day that he wrote to Perry, he told Lucy Donnelly of his plans.

1. Multiple relations were the basis of Russell's theory of judgement at this time. We shall hear more about them in 1913.

[199]

Trinity College
19 December 1912

My dear Lucy

Many thanks for your letter, which gave me a great deal of pleasure. You say you are anxious for news of me: there is a simple recipe, at all times, for getting it, which is to give me news of yourself.

Your letters always surprise me on the subject of my reputation in America[1] – I have not anything like that reputation in England. Yes, it gives me some pleasure to acquire reputation, but it remains rather cold and abstract when it doesn't reach the people one lives among.

I have accepted an invitation to go to Harvard in the spring of 1914. I shall be there March, April, May. My time will not be so taken up as to make it impossible to see you – particularly if you are ever able to get away to New York. I dare say I may lecture at Columbia some times. Will Carey admit me within the sacred portals of Bryn Mawr, or am I too wicked?[2] I am glad DeLaguana[3] likes my *Problems of Philosophy*, I feel myself that it is rather an achievement! I attained a simplicity beyond what I had thought possible.

My Aristotelian paper[4] was criticized rather severely, on two grounds, first that what I said had been said by many previous philosophers, secondly that it was obviously absurd, as all previous philosophers had proved. I myself was quite satisfied with it, and so were the people whose judgment I respect. After that I read a paper on Matter at Cambridge;[5] Prof. Montague (one of the 6 realists) was present, but I thought him an utter fool. He always gave one rhetoric in answer to simple questions.

I found Matter a large and fruitful theme, and I think very likely I shall work at it for some years to come. I have done the philosophy of *pure* mathematics, and this would be the philosophy of *applied* mathematics. I find myself *full* of ideas and projects and vast schemes of work – whether I shall have energy to carry them out remains to be seen. I feel as if I had just

1. She had told him that everybody in America was reading 'The Essence of Religion'.
2. Carey Thomas was still the autocratic president of Bryn Mawr and was unlikely to be sympathetic to Russell after his separation from Alys.
3. Theodore DeLaguana, a philosophy professor at Bryn Mawr.
4. 'On the Notion of Cause', Russell's second presidential address to the Society, delivered on 4 November 1912.
5. Russell had read 'On Matter' to the Cambridge Moral Sciences Club on 8 November. He told Ottoline that no one understood it but Wittgenstein (who had had the benefit of reading it beforehand).

discovered what philosophy is and how it ought to be studied. I look forward to setting forth my ideas when I come to America.

It *is* such a joy that you are so well and enjoying work. The feeling of getting through a great deal of work without utter exhaustion is delightful. For my part, I was worn out when Term ended, and went off for my usual medicine of a walking-tour,[1] but it has poured every day except one, so though I am rested I have not enjoyed it at all. For Xmas I go to the Whiteheads' in Wiltshire.

All you write about your Suffrage Convention[2] is interesting – but I wish you had said more about your speech and what it was about and whether it was a success. I am also interested and glad about Dorothy Lamb.[3]

I spent the summer in a wholly unsuccessful attempt to re-write *Forstice*, and at last I found I must put it aside and wait for fresh inspiration. Meantime I am busy with technical philosophy. There is a lot I must do there before I die, if I am to make the world understand things that I think I understand. All goes very well with me. Much love.

Yours affectionately
    Bertrand Russell

During Lent term Russell continued to think about matter. He had set himself a daunting task, as the following letter makes clear, and he never did carry it to completion. He was very thoroughly trained in physics – which had formed a large part of the mathematics courses he had taken at Cambridge – but his training had taken place before the revolution in physics at the turn of the century, a revolution that was still in progress in 1913. He started by reading some popular books on physics to get a general idea of the field and then read some heavier German material. (Unfortunately, he didn't bother Ottoline with authors and titles, so we don't know exactly what he read – though we know that he was talking about relativity in his lectures at Cambridge in 1913.) But for a while he didn't know how to proceed.

He was worried also about the size of the task he'd undertaken. 'I am nervous', he told Ottoline on 21 January, 'for fear Matter may prove too much for me. It is

1. In the West Country from 9 to 14 December.
2. Donnelly had just been at a women's suffrage convention at which she spoke. She did not say where it was held nor which of the several suffrage bodies in the USA organized it.
3. Dorothy Lamb was evidently at Bryn Mawr, though it is not clear in what capacity. Lucy Donnelly mentions her as if she might have been another Cambridge student visiting Bryn Mawr for a year, as Karin Costelloe had, but this is not certain. Donnelly described her as spirited, sincere and unconventional.

a difficult task, and my physical energy is not what it was.' He thought perhaps it was a task for younger people. But then in February the problem began to resolve itself. On 19 February he reported: 'I am groping my way to a new fundamental idea, which I half see, but not wholly; if I had it clear, the rest of the work would be easy. I find that by some obscure process I have come to understand the problems very much better than I did at the beginning of the term, which is a comfort.' Some of this advance had come, oddly enough, from reading William James's posthumously published collection *Essays in Radical Empiricism* (1912), especially the essay 'Does Consciousness Exist?' in which James denied that there was any such thing as consciousness. Russell did not accept this view, and argued explicitly against it when he started to write later in 1913. But James's views gave him a starting-point for his work on theory of knowledge which would, he hoped, be the preliminary to a philosophy of physics. By 23 February, he had laid out his plan of work, although he did not stick to it when the work actually came to be done.

[200]

[Trinity College]
Sunday evening
[23 February 1913]

My Darling

Both your letters, last night and this morning, were a *great* joy to me. It really wasn't in any way due to you that I felt you remote – it came entirely from myself. To do my work properly I have to absorb myself in it, and then it grows difficult to believe you really exist. And anxiety about the Whiteheads also had its share.[1] And I have been feeling old, in just the way you said you had. Altogether I got a mood of depression, but it is gone. Yes, I would much rather you came up Thursday. I suppose I mustn't ask you to stay Friday night too, and let me give you dinner. It would make more difference to me than you can well believe provided you were not unhappy and pre-occupied. But I fear you would be. That is one of the things I think about when I am worried or depressed, that all the circumstances which would make me really happy with you (if you didn't mind them) are impossible because they make you unhappy. But I am not worrying today. I see my way better and better as regards my work, though I don't think I shall be able to accomplish all I hoped to do – the task is too big, and there are too many preliminaries. But I shall probably be able to do the difficult part of the work, and leave the rest to others. This last week I have read

1. Evelyn Whitehead was once again thought to be very ill.

endless silly novels, which is the only way at certain stages of a piece of work. I find anything except novels not enough of a rest.

It was a lovely day today – North and I went out in the morning to the only nice wood near Cambridge (about 3 miles out) – it was quite warm and we were able to sit. He doesn't know how ill his mother is. Then I paid a call on W. E. Johnson (a logician) and his sister, an elderly sloppy would-be advanced woman with a moustache. He was ill so I only saw her (they are at home Sundays). He is very able, but lacking in vigour, and has published almost nothing.[1] His family make a cult of him, and talk as if having the ideas were everything, and writing them out a mere vulgar mechanical labour. It vexes me, because anybody who has ever written knows the intolerable labour of getting one's ideas into proper shape, long after they have seemed all right as mere thoughts. Universities are full of people who ought to write and don't – I always feel annoyed with them, and with people who minimize the labour of actually producing something. She said she feels annoyed whenever any of his pupils publish, because she thinks they are using his ideas. Family cults are always foolish.

But all this is horrid – I must have more charity. The Spirit has forsaken me – I have grown dry and dusty – but I can't help it if I am to get my work done. Forgive me and bear with me – it is not so underneath.

I get oppressed with all there is to do. I want very much to found a school of mathematical philosophy, because I believe the method is capable of bearing much fruit, beyond what I can ever accomplish. Then I want to get on with Matter – that wants first and foremost a fundamental novelty as to the nature of sensation, which I think I am on the track of – that will be the most important single idea involved. Then I must discover the truth about Causality – in the paper I read the other day,[2] I only showed that all current views are wrong, and I am quite at a loss as to what is right. Then I must reduce both ordinary dynamics and electro-dynamics to neat sets of axioms – this possibly I might get some one else to do for me. If all this were done, I could begin the actual carrying out of the work. But when I think of it all, and all the labour and fatigue and discouragement and wrong ideas that have

1. This second reference to Johnson's lack of vigour may suggest that Russell was pursuing a vendetta. It is, however, an illusion produced by the selection of letters. Russell seems to have forgotten that he'd already told Ottoline who Johnson was. It should be noted that Johnson, apart from some interesting papers in *Mind* in the 1890s, did publish a *Logic* in three (albeit slim) volumes towards the end of his life.
2. 'On the Notion of Cause'. There is no record of Russell's reading this paper to any group after he had read it to the Aristotelian Society on 4 November 1912. He did not read it to the Cambridge Moral Sciences Club, the most likely venue.

to be abandoned, my courage quails, and I wish some one else would do it. But no one I know could except Wittgenstein, and he is embarked on a more difficult piece of work. Ten years ago, I could have written a book with the stock of ideas I have already, but now I have a higher standard of exactness. Wittgenstein has persuaded me that the early parts of *Principia Mathematica* are very inexact, but fortunately it is his business to put them right, not mine.

It is a comfort to write to you about my work, although I know it can't mean anything very definite to you – but it is what makes me sometimes feel oppressed – also it makes it difficult to give as much thought and feeling to other things as I should wish to. At bottom, I am very happy about the work – it is only that there seems almost more than I can get done. And the oppression brings with it a great need of relief between times – that is why I have had to go back to silly novels. I am glad to have got my problem articulated – sensation (and consciousness generally) must be settled first, then causality. These are both manageable problems, not very vast. At first I only saw the thing as a whole, and it seemed all smooth and round, with no hook to catch hold of.

Dorelia[1] must be a strange person – it would have interested me to meet her. I am relieved to hear that she really did go. I am glad J[ulian] is in such good spirits.

When I can realize that I shall really see you Friday, I *long* to see you – I would much rather see you then than wait till Parliament meets, because then my term will be over and I can come to Cholsey.[2] When you and I are both absorbed in our respective duties, their absolute separateness makes you seem unreal – I realize that we met in the past, but the future is hard to believe in. But when I can realize it, I *long* to be with you – But my energies get so absorbed that very little is left over. I know you will understand because it happens to you – you will only wonder that I have not understood you better. And then I get a nervous dread – But that is all merely fatigue, and of no importance.

Now I must stop. Goodbye my Darling. I Love you with all my heart and I ache to be with you.

    Your
    B.

1. Dorelia John (1881–1969), the wife of Augustus John. By dint of much persistence Ottoline had become her friend and Dorelia was paying her a visit.
2. Ottoline spent much of the winter of 1912–13 at Breach House, Cholsey, in Berkshire, a house owned by Philip's sister.

Relations between Bertie and Ottoline were once again at a low ebb. The improvement which had been achieved at Lausanne the previous summer did not last, and by the end of 1912 Ottoline was once again finding Bertie something of a nuisance. His high seriousness exhausted her and made inordinate demands on her time and emotions. She had by this time struck up a new friendship, with Lytton Strachey, a far more frivolous companion than Russell. There was a playful eroticism in her friendship with Strachey, but no serious danger of sex – Strachey was much more interested in Henry Lamb, with whom Ottoline had still not broken though her relationship with Lamb was hardly less rocky than that with Russell. To Bertie she had made it quite clear that she didn't want to see too much of him and their meetings were now down to three a term. But they still wrote daily, for Ottoline found it easier to deal with him on paper than in person. From their letters one might well have concluded that their affair would soon be over, and indeed the possibility of breaking it off was frequently mentioned. But such a view ignores Bertie's desperate tenacity and Ottoline's reluctance to break finally with any of her lovers. In fact their relationship had achieved a curious equilibrium: As Bertie began to pull away, feeling that his love was hopeless, Ottoline would find the relationship more to her liking and be more affectionate. Thus encouraged, Bertie would press his case more ardently until another explosion from Ottoline would send him spinning away again.

Some of their misunderstandings have a comical side. On Friday, 28 February, for example, they had a meeting which, to judge by the next letter written immediately afterwards, produced a deep gloom in Bertie – notwithstanding his initial protestations of happiness.

[201]

[London]
Saturday morning
[1 March 1913]

My Darling Darling
    You were extraordinarily good to me yesterday, and it was a very happy day to me. I have had constantly, since last spring, Othello's words in my head 'O Iago, the pity of it'.[1] I have known it could all be right if I could get strife and insistence subdued. But I have felt I could only do that thoroughly if I gave you up. I could *now* give you up, without a fear that a moment's impulse would lead me to suicide, because of my desire to get on with work. You must really not think you are to blame when I am not happy – it is not

---

1. *Othello*, IV, i, 206.

so. It is the difficulty of serving two masters. If we parted, I should give up the attempt to have any serious human relations – keep all seriousness for work, and let the rest be recreation. That would be an act of fundamental cowardice.

I see that even if I behaved really well I could not make you happy, because I cannot give you some kinds of companionship which are necessary to your happiness, and because in some important ways I don't agree with your outlook on life – I don't mean that I don't agree with it for you, but only that I don't agree with it for myself. That was what I had to realize at Ipsden after Marienbad, when I had my Aristotelian paper to do. It would make it easier for me to feel rightly if I knew what I had to hope in the way of your happiness and also of your feeling towards me if I did learn to feel more rightly. I know that in quite early days you used to think well of me, because you used to say so. But that stopped with Logan's visit to Newington. Since then, you have only once said anything to show that you thought in any way well of me – the time, nearly a year ago, when you said that sometimes you thought me like Mantegna's St Sebastian. I really honestly do not know whether you think in any way well of me, or are only tied to me by a feeling of duty and loyalty to what you have undertaken. I do really try to live a decent life, but I don't find it easy.

Dearest please don't doubt that always you make me far happier than I should be without you. – I can't *tell* you how wonderful you were yesterday. I promise absolutely that unless something comes from your side to upset me I will trust you and feel sure that it will be a happiness seeing you and not be afraid of you. And on your side *please* don't let me make you feel old. Honestly, I *love* the things in you that you think I am critical of. I hate making you feel old. When Lucy Silcox[1] was with you, and you were bolder, I *loved* it. I do really not want to crush you. Goodbye my Darling Darling. I love you with an undestructible force as deep as life.

Your

B.

But this gloomy missive crossed with one from Ottoline saying that their day together had been altogether perfect. Russell received this the same day he had written. So in the evening he wrote again, in a much more cheerful vein, offering unconvincing explanations for his earlier misery and vowing, once more, to put the relationship on a better footing.

1. See letter 142.

[202]

My Darling Darling – only *one* moment, snatched from my uncle, to tell you of my great love and great happiness. Your dear dear dear letter just come is such a joy. When I wrote this morning my slow wits hadn't realized how happy I was. Coming down in the train I thought a great deal. I had a real vivid realization of how I have oppressed you and a real solid lasting determination that it shall cease. I hereby undertake that never again will I be oppressive to you even in my secret thoughts – if ever you see a sign, you need only remind me of this vow. If I criticize, it will be only genuinely when I think it may be a help to you. I will not be exacting or make demands or wish you different. And will you, in return, learn gradually to trust me, not to suppress what you call your frivolous side, not to be afraid to *demand*. I am going to begin the wooing of you all over again from the start! And I will never let myself think I have finished the process.

Dear Heart I do really love you enough to work miracles for your sake – time will show that I do.

My whole soul is a song of joy today – and of blessings on you.

Your B.

With technical philosophy now absorbing much of Russell's energy, Ottoline could afford to be more generous with her affection and at the beginning of March a new understanding between them seems to have been reached which lasted for several months. Bertie came to accept that he couldn't monopolize Ottoline's affections and that she could not love him as deeply as he loved her. At the same time the relationship became more Platonic, though by no means wholly so.

While this new arrangement was much more to Ottoline's liking than to Bertie's, she was not anxious to see him slide away from her entirely. There were occasions when she seems to have thought that he'd taken her advice about an intimate relationship with another woman too much to heart. On one of them Bertie had left her at his flat after a meeting to go and have lunch (followed by tea and dinner) tête-à-tête with Mildred Scott (see letter 130). Mildred had left Paris the previous year and settled in Britain. Her marriage was in trouble and she was writing very affectionate letters to Bertie. Bertie found her more interesting now than previously. On this occasion Ottoline took the opportunity before she left the flat to leave a very affectionate note for Bertie – saying how very happy she had been and telling him not to doubt her love.

Bertie was overjoyed to find it when he returned that evening. And yet, as so often when the relationship seemed to be picking up, he was unable to leave well alone and took the opportunity to try to clear up past difficulties. It is not difficult to believe an unacknowledged jealousy prompted Ottoline to leave the note. But, if we look for Bertie's hidden motives, he seems to have been self-destructively intent on picking their relationship to pieces. Ottoline complained in her journal a year later of Bertie's 'bitter criticism, a want of blindness to faults' (*Memoirs*, vol. II, p. 283). The problems he mentions in the next letter, written immediately on finding her note, may well have been discussed by them that morning, but her note itself gives no hint of them. It was, in appearance at least, a simple and affectionate love note. Bertie might have been happier if he could have accepted it at face value and replied in kind. On the other hand, there may have been an element of calculation in his account of his afternoon with Mildred Scott.

[203]

[Russell Chambers]
Saturday night
5 April 1913

My Darling Love

It *was* such a joy to find your dear little note when I got home, all the more because at first I thought there was none. When I found it I thought for a moment you must have come round on purpose, but on reflection I thought you wrote it this morning just after I was gone. Yes Dearest it *was* a happy moment this morning, and all these days have been very wonderful. I wish you didn't feel you ought not to have accepted me. I know it is my fault that you feel that, and that sometimes I have said so. But really it is not true. As it turned out, it would have been better to make the circumstances clearer to me, but that is a different matter. What you give is so rare and of such a quality that it utterly outweighs what you cannot give – it is only peevishness in me to pretend that it isn't so. It is natural you should feel it would have been better for me to care for a woman who was free, but there is much to be said against that. First; I should have had to leave Cambridge and give up teaching, and though I don't want to teach for ever, I think it is really important that I should teach for a time. I think America will be important, and that too would have been impossible. Then besides, the sort of submissive woman you picture to yourself would never have kept my affection, yet I should have been more bound than by any ordinary marriage.

I *know* you will keep my love as long as we both live – every day makes me more sure of it. Something in my inmost soul – something deeper than I was quite conscious of till I knew you – vibrates in response to you, everything that has to do with you is somehow important to me in the way that religion is important. What I say and think at times when I am not happy has nothing to do with this. Even pain that comes from you is like the pain of life itself – there is a quality in it that one would not forgo – I would rather have it than any happiness that a lighter nature could give me. What belongs to the most serious part of me can never be wholly happy, because I am not happy enough inwardly in that part, and I know I should give a great deal of pain to any one I cared for as much as I care for you. The only thing that could cure this would be religion – but I am so restless and prone to doubt that it is hard to get a religion that will endure – but if I ever could, no one could help me to it as you could. All that I have been saying is the most absolute sober truth. So don't let us say or think again that it was a mistake to let our love grow – that is really putting too much stress on mere easy happiness. You give me spiritual companionship except in my bad moments, and then I feel you a guide and a reproof. You keep me alive and seeking wisdom. And you give me times of such profound happiness as happier natures cannot give or feel. Dearest, Dearest, don't let my criticism depress you – it is merely the rough surface of a love and veneration which is deeper than I can ever tell you. I can't praise as glibly as I can criticize, because what I want to praise lies below the region to which words belong.

Mildred was feeling tired, so we lunched in her lodgings – dear Arthur had absented himself. Then we went out and got tea and dinner at restaurants. She told me about her marriage, but I doubted if she was quite frank. She professes to be still devoted to Arthur, and to find him a very good companion, but he wants liberty for amours, and she feels she couldn't stand that. She is a jealous passionate nature, and I feel sure she could never make a success of it. She says he has so far been faithful to her, and she is evidently very loath to let him go. She is much less insincere than she used to be, and I liked her and was very sorry for her. I was anxious she should not mistake sympathy for something else, so I made that *quite* clear – after that, I allowed myself to show sympathy more freely, and gave her a kiss of friendliness at the end. What makes one sorry for her is the way she has been humiliated. I think the marriage is sure to break up sooner or later, but it may last some time yet. She thinks of paying a long visit to America, leaving him to consider matters – she *says* he is anxious to keep her, but wants freedom. In theory one ought to agree with him, but he is such a worm.

I wish her wig was not so hideous![1]

Tomorrow I hope to finish my article on science in the morning[2] – then I go to Aunt Maude[3] to lunch, then tea and a walk with Desmond,[4] then supper with the George Trevy's.[5] So I shall have a full day.

Your flowers are much happier on my desk – they are so lovely and so full of you. It has been such a joy your being so well. Goodnight my Darling. My whole being is filled with love and joy.

Your

B.

During the spring of 1913 Russell continued to plan his next big work in philosophy. The problem of matter had receded somewhat, since he had come to think that it was necessary first to treat the theory of knowledge. This would start with the problem of sensation, as mentioned in his letter of 23 February, but would now extend far beyond sensation to deal with acquaintance, judgement and inference. The problem of causation, on which he had made a promising start with his Aristotelian Society address, had been shelved, since it depended upon the theory of probability on which Maynard Keynes was now working. Russell obviously hoped to have the results of Keynes's work before he applied probability theory to causation. For the time being the theory of knowledge dominated his thoughts.

At the beginning of May Ottoline went once more to Lausanne. This time Philip and Julian went too. Julian had been sick the previous year and had had to be operated on. In Lausanne, Dr Combe, ominously, diagnosed something wrong with her liver. Philip was treated for indigestion. Ottoline, this time, saw a new doctor, Dr Vittoz, a psychiatrist who taught techniques for eliminating unnecessary thoughts from the mind. On 5 May she had one last meeting with Bertie before her departure.

1. Mildred Scott's daughter, who was born in 1912, thinks Russell was mistaken about the wig, but that her mother may have dyed her hair too dark. (Information from Sheila Turcon.)
2. 'Science as an Element of Culture', first published in the *New Statesman* (1913) and reprinted in *Papers*, vol. XII, pp. 390–97.
3. See letter 23.
4. Desmond MacCarthy.
5. George Trevelyan and his wife (see letter 22).

[204]

[Trinity College]
Sunday night
[4 May 1913]

My Darling Darling

I *was* overjoyed to get your letter this morning saying you could see me tomorrow afternoon – I can't *tell* you how glad I am. The last two days I had been rather sad and listless, but today has been *quite* different – It seems odd that the prospect of an hour with you can so alter the whole aspect of the universe – but it is so. You must prepare yourself however for a dreadful blow! Thinking I shouldn't see you for 6 weeks, I have had my hair cropped quite short – it will horrify you, but I thought it would please all my relations tomorrow night.

The only thing that worries me is whether there is any chance of my carrying the infection of Mildred's influenza. I have arranged to lunch with her, so I can get home and even change my clothes – I really don't know whether the infection does carry in that way, but I should not like to give you influenza. I am going up by the 10 o'clock train. If you think there is any risk of your catching it through my seeing her, would you telegraph to me at Great Northern Station, Cambridge, and then I will telegraph to her to say I can't come. (I can see her on Friday.) *Nothing* would induce me to miss seeing you, but if you don't telegraph, I shall assume you think it is all right. I will reach my flat about 4, and hope for you soon – if I am to come to you, please send a line to my flat. There – that ends plans. Hurrah.

I have been bubbling over with delight all day – it has led to my doing a great deal of work – still sketching out my book on Theory of Knowledge. I have got the early part quite elaborately sketched, and the whole pretty full in my head. If I can write it while you are away it will keep me happy. I wish somebody would supply me with a perpetual succession of mild novels – I go to the Union[1] and fetch them, but I never know what to get. Some are too bad and some too good (if they are really interesting they take one's thoughts off work too much). Since the time at Churn[2] when I turned my thoughts back to work, I have had a number of fruitful ideas. This work is just what is needed before tackling Matter – in fact I can bring in the most interesting part of the problem of Matter. I have begun to think again that

1. The Library in the Cambridge Union.
2. Ottoline and Philip had spent the previous September in a remote farmhouse at Churn on the Berkshire downs. It belonged to her brother, Henry.

I may get Matter completely polished off before I die. If only I could sleep 8 hours a night, I could perform miracles.

Darling Darling I can't sit still for excitement thinking of seeing you again. I can't write about trivial things. I had no idea how much I was going to mind your going. But I don't mean to waste any time tomorrow the way I did last time. I will pour forth love and love and more love every instant. Goodnight my Beloved my Heart. All my soul is yours yours yours.

B.

On this occasion they had a good meeting. Even Bertie found little to worry about afterwards.

While Ottoline was away Bertie settled down to write his *Theory of Knowledge*. It was the middle of the Cambridge term and although he had complained in the past about the difficulty of getting original work done during term time he found no such difficulty now. With the outline of his work clear in his head it remained only to write it out. The book was to be a large one – 500 pages in print, he estimates in the next letter, though later remarks suggest that the final draft would be even larger – and he proposed to write it at the rate of ten pages a day, though, in fact, his daily average was rather better than ten pages. This was achieved despite a full load of lectures, meetings with students, discussions with colleagues, a busy round of visitors, his Thursday evenings, and a daily letter to Ottoline. Even though he expected to have to do some rewriting after the first draft was complete, it was, by any standards, a prodigious outburst of work.

Ottoline was still *en route* when Bertie sent news that the first chapter was nearly done.

[205]

[Trinity College]
Thursday afternoon
[8 May 1913]

My Darling Love

I have no letter yet from Paris, which hardly surprises me – possibly there will be one tonight, but I may not be able to write then because of my evening. I have got on with my writing – I find it all flows out, evenly and smoothly, properly arranged, with masses of detail that I hardly realized were in my thoughts. And what pleases me is that it is all so simple that Julian could understand it! No doubt it will get harder afterwards, but I have long thought that philosophers are obscure because they are confused, and that the subject can be made easy to understand, though not easy to do. I am delighted with what I have done, and if I can go on so it will be excellent. It is extraordinary the relief of getting it out.

I believe now I can go straight on till it is finished, without pause or obstacle. There will be an introductory chapter, which I shall probably leave to the last – the first substantial chapter, which I have nearly finished, is called 'Preliminary description of Experience.' Then I shall set to work to refute James's theory that there is no such thing as consciousness, then the idealist theory that there is nothing else. Then I shall classify cognitive relations to objects – sense, imagination, memory. Then I shall come on to belief, error, etc., then to inference; then finally to 'construction of the physical world' – time, space, cause, matter. If I go on on the scale on which I have begun, it will be quite a big book – 500 pages of print I should think. It is all in my head, ready to be written as fast as my pen will go. I feel as happy as a king. If I write 10 pages a day it will take 50 days – so it should be nearly finished when you come home. I want to do the popular lectures[1] while you are in London – it is such a help to be seeing you constantly for that sort of writing.

Nothing else has occurred to me. Did you see the suffragettes tried to blow up St Paul's and only failed by accident?[2]

I am afraid my letters will be dull while my writing goes well – it is a dream, a delirium, so that casual events grow dim. But my love does not grow dim – the thought of you never leaves me for a moment Dearest. I wonder how you are and where you are and whether J[ulian] is well and everything. You never told me what to give J. for her birthday. Goodbye my Darling. I love you with all my soul.

Your
B.

Ten days later he had passed page 130 of the book and was still going strong despite a round of visitors and meetings that would have prevented most authors from writing anything at all.

1. The Lowell Lectures he was to give in Boston. He originally planned to give them on 'The Place of Good and Evil in the Universe' but this was vetoed by the organizers since the terms of the bequest under which the Lowell Lectures were funded forbade lectures on religious topics. In the end he gave them on 'Our Knowledge of the External World'. They were the fullest statement of his thinking on the problem of matter at this time.
2. On 7 April a cleaner had found a bomb, wrapped in a WSPU newspaper, by the Bishop's throne in the cathedral.

[206]

[Trinity College]
Sunday night
18 May 1913

My Darling Love

Sanger is gone, after an early dinner – every one else is dining, so I am in peace. I have had a busy time – Sanger arrived at four yesterday, and except while I was lecturing I was occupied with him till bed-time. This morning he went across to Moore and I got on with my writing – in spite of him I am still 10 pages ahead of my average. Then I had Moore and McT[aggart] and Wittgenstein to meet him at lunch – Sanger likes Wittgenstein *very* much. I had some philosophical talk with Moore, which I very seldom have now-a-days – he is very good, and really helpful, in discussion. Then Tagore [1] and a Hindoo protégé arrived unexpectedly to tea – I liked Tagore much better than I had once – the saintliness was less aggressive. He was quite witty and amusing about America, where he has just been.

In the middle, Miss Stawell arrived, and I had two hours terrific discussion with her[2] – we were both utterly exhausted at the end, but she is coming back at 9 tomorrow morning to continue it. She hasn't much aptitude for philosophy, but she thinks so hard that it partly makes up. I found that I like her very much indeed. When Miss Reynolds[3] is not there, it is quite a different thing. I am exhausted with so much talking, all the more as the wish to be writing keeps worrying me the whole time. Happily Mildred is off to France on affairs of the school, so I don't have to move tomorrow. But next day I lunch with the Whiteheads.

What I am writing will all have to be re-written, I think; I am going ahead full steam, to get the skeleton done – then I can fill in at my leisure. I have more to say than I thought, and ideas that come later make earlier parts want alteration. I am surprised to find how much I have to say, and how clear the problems become. Probably by the time I really finish it it will be a great big book. But I shall write a popular Logic before I re-write this. I feel so bursting with work that I hardly know how to wait for the days to roll themselves out – I want to write faster than is physically possible. I haven't had such a fit for ages – it keeps me as happy as a king. It is

1. Rabindranath Tagore (1861–1941), the Bengali poet.
2. Melian Florence Stawell was a classicist at Newnham. She had come to discuss *The Problems of Philosophy* with Russell.
3. Probably one of Stawell's students.

delicious disentangling a complicated jumble of facts, and laying the separate ingredients side by side.

I am afraid you have been having a very bad headache and feeling very ill. I do hope you are better now. Has Julian enjoyed her birthday?[1] And what have you done with her today?

I am so immeasurably happier than I was a year ago. – Now this must be posted. Goodnight my Darling Love. All my love is with you every moment – my thoughts are *never* away from you for one instant. All my soul is yours my Dearest.

    Your
      B.

Eight days later, when he was probably somewhere past page 240, an unexpected blow fell.

[207]

Trinity College
Tuesday afternoon
[27 May 1913]

My Darling Love

Your *dear* letter this morning was such a joy. I am sorry I wrote such a wretched scrap yesterday, it was oppressively hot, airless and thundery without any actual thunder – I had a headache and had great difficulty in getting through my 10 pages – in fact I only finished them after midnight. Today it is rather better, and I think there will really be a thunderstorm, which would do good.

Wittgenstein came to see me – we were both cross from the heat – I showed him a crucial part of what I have been writing. He said it was all wrong, not realizing the difficulties – that he had tried my view and knew it wouldn't work. I couldn't understand his objection – in fact he was very inarticulate – but I feel in my bones that he must be right, and that he has seen something I have missed. If I could see it too I shouldn't mind, but as it is, it is worrying, and has rather destroyed the pleasure in my writing – I can only go on with what I see and yet I feel it is probably all wrong, and that Wittgenstein will think me a dishonest scoundrel for going on with it. Well well – it is the younger generation knocking at the door – I must make

1. Julian's birthday was 18 May – the same day as Russell's.

room for him when I can, or I shall become an incubus, but at the moment I was rather cross.

I am *very* glad Combe is pleased about J. and that you think she is better. Yes, I feel sure a sun-bath would cure you. I do hope Vittoz (is that his name?) will let you go by June 9 – I should like to be with you on June 16.[1] But if Vittoz does your nerves good, I shall owe him a debt of gratitude however long he keeps you.

Salimbene[2] came this morning – very many thanks. Also *Fortitude*,[3] which I have begun already. Thank you for sending it.

Tomorrow I shall perhaps go to London for the day to see the Whiteheads. Also I shall probably go there for next Sunday and Monday. I grudge the time taken from work, but it can't be helped. I shall still keep up to my average of 10 pages a day. North is doing his Tripos – he hopes to get a 2nd. He is utterly sick of Cambridge and longing to get away – he wants to be doing things more connected with his career.[4]

I am a little depressed about work, but otherwise cheerful. – Darling I *long* to be with you again – all my thoughts are *full* of love to you. I must stop as I am out and the thunderstorm is beginning. Much love and a thousand kisses.

Your B.

Russell's response to Wittgenstein's criticism was curious. On the one hand he seems to have recognized immediately that it was important, yet he did not at first see what was wrong. Nor did he stop or even pause with his writing to consider the problem. He continued with *Theory of Knowledge* until 6 June, when he finished the parts that had to do with acquaintance and judgement. Then he stopped, having completed 350 pages in thirty-one days, not because of Wittgenstein's criticisms but because of fresh difficulties he foresaw in dealing with inference. It was perhaps natural that he should continue writing while the fit was upon him. But it is harder to explain why he 'felt in his bones', as he said, that Wittgenstein was right before he had understood the objection. He must have had some vague sense of what the objection was and yet not had it formulated sharply enough to be able to tell whether a reply was possible.

Wittgenstein's objection concerned Russell's so-called multiple-relation theory of

1. Her birthday.
2. G. G. Coulton's *From St Francis to Dante* (1906), a life of the thirteenth-century Franciscan friar Salimbene.
3. A novel by Hugh Walpole (1913).
4. He was to become an engineer.

judgement, an unconventional theory that Russell had proposed as an account of truth and falsehood and of what he called 'propositional attitudes' like belief, doubt and understanding. Before *Theory of Knowledge* the multiple-relation theory had appeared in *The Problems of Philosophy* and *Principia Mathematica*. Wittgenstein, as was his wont, left no clearly articulated account of his objection and only recently has it been possible to say what exactly it was. It turns out to be an argument of the most extraordinary subtlety, the first true sign of Wittgenstein's genius and still one of his most penetrating pieces of philosophical work. What Wittgenstein was able to show was that Russell's multiple-relation theory of judgement was inconsistent with his theory of types, the lynchpin of the logic of *Principia*. Since the multiple-relation theory was an integral part of the theory of knowledge (on which, in turn, the proposed theory of matter was to be based), and since the theory of types had taken years of work, Wittgenstein's discovery was a devastating blow.

Wittgenstein sent a very cryptic account of his objection in a letter and by the middle of June Russell appreciated how serious it was and abandoned the *Theory of Knowledge* manuscript. (What remains of it is published as *Papers*, vol. VII.) This discovery overshadowed his reunion with Ottoline who was back from Lausanne somewhat earlier than expected. He went on to see Ottoline from a lunch in London with Wittgenstein and his mother. The mood engendered by Wittgenstein was not conducive to a happy meeting with Ottoline.

[208]

[Russell Chambers]
Thursday night
[19 June 1913]

My Darling

Here I am back from Tagore's lecture,[1] after walking most of the way home. It was unmitigated rubbish – cut-and-dried conventional stuff about the river becoming one with the Ocean and man becoming one with Brahma. Everybody thought themselves so earnest and had a look of fat spiritual exaltation. The man is sincere and in earnest, but merely rattling old dry bones. I spoke to him before the lecture – afterwards I avoided him. I had some talk with Mrs Shaw[2] whom I like; Mrs Rothenstein[3] was there, looking

---

1. He spoke on 'The Education of Indian Women' to the Indian Women's Education Association.
2. Charlotte Payne-Townshend (1856–1943), a Fabian whom Shaw had married in 1898.
3. See letter 185.

very unattractive; Sturge Moore,[1] looking rapt. Otherwise no one I knew
except a black I had met at Cambridge.

All that has gone wrong with me lately comes from Wittgenstein's attack
on my work – I have only just realized this. It was very difficult to be honest
about it, as it makes a large part of the book I meant to write impossible for
years to come probably. I tried to believe it wasn't so bad as that – then I
felt I hadn't made enough effort over my work and must concentrate more
severely – some instinct associated this with a withdrawal from you. And
the failure of honesty over my work – which was very slight and subtle,
more an attitude than anything definite – spread poison in every direction.
I am pure in heart again now, thanks to your divine gentleness and long-
suffering. And so my love goes out freely to you again. I must be much
sunk – it is the first time in my life that I have failed in honesty over work.
I have been creeping back towards a better frame of mind all these weeks,
but have only really achieved it today. Only yesterday I felt ready for
suicide – tonight I feel gay and happy – certainly honesty is the best policy.
I am sorry you found me so unsympathetic – I was in profound spiritual
trouble, and I feared love was leaving me. I didn't really know what was
the matter. As long as the talk was not about what was troubling me, it
seemed unreal and external. The disgust of human life that I have been feeling
lately is generally a sign of unrecognized sin.

When you feel as if I didn't want to listen to you, do please not feel
snubbed but persist. My mind is so slow in passing to a new topic, that I
often say something I had planned to say, after you have begun saying
something else, and before I have taken in what you say. This is not lack of
interest, but mere inertia, from the habit of getting immersed in a topic that
I get in work. And I will try not to notice your unintentional snubs. All you
told me about Vittoz today interested me enormously, and I agreed with
everything. – It is *such* a help to me when you will *tell* me what you have
to complain of – it is so baffling when you won't.

Goodnight my Darling. I feel as if you had called me back to you from
beyond the grave.

Your
  B.

---

1. Thomas Sturge Moore (1870–1944), G. E. Moore's brother. He was a poet, art
historian, and graphic artist, but best known for his poetry which Yeats, a close friend,
admired.

Though Russell took Wittgenstein's criticisms hard, he might have found some grounds for self-congratulation had he treated himself more kindly. The mistake he had made was, to say the least, not obvious. Russell had hoped that mathematical logic would bring a new exactitude to philosophy and in this he had certainly succeeded. Few, if any, previous theories of knowledge had been stated with enough precision and attention to detail to permit such a recondite refutation. This was the new style of philosophy Russell was advocating; he was its first proponent and one of its first victims.

Wittgenstein's criticisms upset Russell the more because of the emotional investment he had made in *Theory of Knowledge*. It was not just his next piece of work, but a refuge from his unhappy love for Ottoline and something like a consolation prize: if he had failed in love, at least he could still succeed in work. Wittgenstein had made him feel he had failed in both. He seems to have thought that his commitment to *Theory of Knowledge* had blinded him for a time to the force of Wittgenstein's objections. This seems to have been the 'failure in honesty' for which he berated himself. It was little surprise that his first meeting with Ottoline on her return was not the joyous occasion he had anticipated. The attitude required for Wittgenstein was incompatible with the attitude required for Ottoline. But if the first meeting was bad, worse was to follow.

[209]

[Russell Chambers]
[27 June 1913]

My Darling

This can only be one line in haste to say I am sorry, but I will try again. I mind the way I behave quite terribly. But don't think of me as reduced to a dangerous despair. I think we ought not to meet while my nerves are so overwrought. It is a great nervous strain, and it leads to my breaking down, which is bad for both. A few more scenes like today would put an end to things. I think I had better go back to Cambridge and not see you till I have myself more under control. It wears you out and makes me feel almost too ashamed to go on living. Perhaps when I feel saner you could come there for the day? It wouldn't matter in Vacation time. Don't think there is anything to hurt you in my going away – only a necessity to get myself under control. I have burnt the letter you left here. You didn't say if you were going to Southwold and if I should accept Lucy's[1] plan of staying near and meeting you. I should like that if you would. I don't see the future at

1. Lucy Silcox.

all clear tonight. I can't tell you how despicable I feel. But I have had much
to try me lately. Wittgenstein's attack – the difficulty of getting my lectures
done – the Whiteheads' troubles[1] – also a recurrence of what was troubling
me the St Paul's day – also, for purely unselfish reasons, an imperative need
to make money.[2] And my nature is easily depressed. The result has been that
doing my work and not committing suicide seemed as much moral effort as
I could make. But *I must* get myself in hand, and I will. Till then I am not
fit for you to associate with. It is an intolerable curse to have a capacity for
creative work. But really I am not quite and altogether a beast, though my
behaviour to you looks like it. I really am better in other ways. Now the
post is going. I love you out of hell – but I was *infinitely* more unhappy
before I knew you. I bless the ground you walk on and the air you breathe.
    Your
      B.

[210]

[Russell Chambers?]
Saturday morning
[28 June 1913]

My Darling
    Your little line this morning is wonderful. Your self-forgetfulness and
goodness are quite marvellous. Forgive these cold words – I am utterly
incapable of any feeling of any sort or kind today. Please don't think I am
hurt or angry or anything like that – I am only dead. It seems to me today
that we ought to part for good, because continuing leads straight to the
madhouse. Besides, a scene of such degradation as yesterday's makes it
impossible to stand spiritually upright in a person's presence again. Would
you mind if I talked about it to Mrs Whitehead? I want an understanding
outside point of view. I wonder whether some day you would talk with her.
I should like you to know that I am not *all* bad – that I *can* be unselfish, and
understanding, and sympathetic, where my madness doesn't come in. – I
know you must be very unhappy. But it is cold abstract knowledge. I am
not either happy or unhappy in the slightest degree. I suppose what is
happening is tragic, but I don't feel it so.
    Yesterday you thought I should make a mistake in parting from you, and

1. Whitehead had been quite seriously ill with flu.
2. Russell by now had no liquid capital. Not only that, but his bank account was often
seriously overdrawn.

you thought I was only hurt when I said the opposite. I am not hurt today, but full of clear vision. It seems to me all but certain that to save my reason I must part from you. Don't imagine I say this in anger, or that I shall plunge into reckless immorality. I only want to live quietly and work. It is not anger, but dedication, that prompts me. I have *no* anger. I think always you have been divinely patient and gentle. And I really don't now underestimate your love. We love each other, but neither gives the sort of love the other wants. Some time back, when I said I would win you, I decided to keep silence about my unhappiness, and to lie to you. I thought if in that way storms could be avoided I should in time become as happy as I said I was, and all would be well. But instinct is too strong for me. However I behave, nothing but insanity lies ahead of me if we go on. I haven't felt you the least cold lately – that is why I feel it is hopeless.

I'm afraid I can't make a letter reach you tomorrow. I will write tomorrow to Bedford Square. I come back here tomorrow. If you permit my talking to Mrs W. I will try to see her Monday or Tuesday. Forgive this dreadful letter. Nothing lives in me today except the fear of madness.

Your

B.

[211]

[Russell Chambers?]
Monday morning
[30 June 1913]

My Darling,

Your letter of Saturday night and Sunday has come. I think we ought to meet once more at least – I should not like the end to have been that flaming horror. I failed, as I constantly do, in reverence towards love – today that would not be so, and I could promise not to be too emotional. But if you feel you would rather not come again, don't fancy it will make things any harder for me. I am *very* sorry I worried you about Mrs W. – I hadn't the slightest wish to urge you to see her. – When I said I had lied to you, that was almost too strong – I had given you surface truth instead of fundamental truth, hoping the fundamental truth would change. What has just turned the scale has been the realization that you would *never* give *anyone* the sort of love that would make me happy, and that it is not *only* my bad behaviour that prevents me from getting more. But I can't make any final decision while my nerves are so queer – it is good of you to say I needn't. The only thing clear to me is that the physical relation ought to cease. And there is

some subtle unreality about my desires in that way now – they are so very
largely not desires for the thing itself, but for a state of mind in you; and in
the absence of the state of mind in you, the direct physical desire does not
exist in its proper form. I have only just understood this; it has been true for
a year.

I have a feeling of disloyalty in talking things over with Mrs W. I think
we must make our own decision, and then I can merely tell her. – My feeling
today is that if the physical side were cut away all would be well, and much
better than if there had never been anything physical.

Do *exactly* what you think best about coming this afternoon. It won't
upset me if you come, nor yet if you don't. I should like to say I mind the
pain I am causing you, but I can't truthfully – I don't mind anything at all
as yet. I suppose you are very ill and tired. But it all seems to me as if it were
happening to people in a book. Goodbye.

　　Your
　　　B.

It would seem impossible that things could ever be repaired after this extraordinary
cataclysm. With letters like these the danger of the madhouse, if the affair continued,
seemed real enough. Though Ottoline did go for the last visit Bertie proposed, they
agreed, not surprisingly, on a long separation. Bertie took himself off on a walking
holiday in Cornwall with Eric and North Whitehead and then for an even more
strenuous walking holiday with C. P. Sanger in the Alps (beginning in France and
ending in Italy).

　　Despite everything, their correspondence continued. On 1 July Ottoline ventured
a first, tentative letter. By 3 July, writing daily, she felt dreadfully lost without him.
Bertie replied, but for the first time since the affair began he did not write her daily
letters. Clearly he was now feeling the need of some distance. He told her that he
did not write much because he needed not to think about her too much. Ottoline,
worried no doubt lest she drive the country's foremost philosopher to the madhouse
and perhaps also by Bertie's apparent resolution to end the relationship, responded
with kindness and love. Her letters became more affectionate and a good deal longer
than they had been.

　　Although Ottoline's more affectionate letters produced hopeful, and sometimes
even joyous, responses from Bertie, he remained profoundly depressed. Near the
end of his alpine tour, she sent him an account of what she thought had gone wrong
between them: his criticisms had made it impossible for her to be spontaneous with
him; he demanded her entire devotion which it was impossible for her to give; their
'instincts' (by which they usually meant their sexual desires) clashed and this led

them to spend too much of their time together discussing their problems and feelings; he behaved like a don; his love had turned to grievance;... It was a long letter. Bertie, always apt to think that a clear statement of beliefs must improve things, had often asked her to say exactly what she thought was wrong so he could improve. This litany, however, drove him to the last extremity of despair.

[212]

Verona
Monday
[18 August 1913]

My Dearest Dearest Dearest

I have just got your letter – it is what I asked for and is all that is most kind. I am *utterly* and absolutely miserable – I find I *cannot* face life without you – it seems so bleak and dark and terrible. I know I should not go on with it long. Give me a chance Dearest to try again – and do go on trying to make me see that what you ask of me is reasonable. It is much easier to make a sacrifice when one's reason acquiesces. You cannot conceive how deeply I love you or how unalterably. But I do not always see why you cannot do things for me – for instance why you couldn't let me come to Lausanne this last time, or why you couldn't let me share your Italian lessons. In both those cases I thought you selfish, seeing the very great misery you caused – but I am really really willing to believe you were not, only it is hard to believe it would have done you as much harm to yield as you did me by refusing. You don't like explaining so I try to acquiesce without, and then things breed inwardly. My criticisms of you are hardly ever genuine – they are the result of thwarted instinct. I feel like a tree in a pot in an attic – roots pressed against the side, top against the ceiling, no room to grow anywhere. Somehow I never have an impulse – not even to read Spinoza – without its seeming wicked to have had it. I have only *one* genuine criticism of you, which is that at the beginning you said you and P. were only devoted friends which is not true. For the last year and a half this criticism has troubled me frightfully. I am afraid there is no hope of anything approaching happiness for me for the rest of life. I cannot face losing you and I cannot be content with what you give without a greater moral effort than seems possible to me. I have been going morally down hill for many years past and lately terribly fast. I think it ought to be possible to pull myself together. It would be much easier if I could get over the feeling that you have treated me badly, which is a feeling of instinct, but would yield to reason if reason is really against it.

The eye is *much* more to me than you think, only when I am with you I am always preoccupied – also I am terribly afraid of currying favour by exaggerating it.

There is absolutely only one way in which it is possible for me to go on at all – that is to make a supreme moral effort such as I made at Peppard in early days. I really *can* do this if I can see your justification! As things stand, it *seems* to me that everything that was to be said against John and Anrep[1] is to be said against you, and two extra things – one I have said in this letter, the other that they were productive and the people they used up were unproductive, whereas you are unproductive and I was productive. But if you could have the patience to help me out of the tangle I have got into, it would really be the best thing you could do for me.

My Darling my Darling my Soul calls to you out of the depths. I remember the woods at Peppard – I remember the wonderful wonderful days at Lausanne – quite lately the day at St Anne's Hill as wonderful as any – I remember the deep deep spiritual communion – O my Heart my Heart do help me to be good help me to love you freely and not to try to put you in fetters – O my Star my Light my Hope, do not let me destroy out of the world a precious and wonderful thing – I *know* deep down our love is a great great thing. I know it is madness to let it be obscured by trivial troubles. I know there is a great calm place and where we could live together in peace and perfect spiritual union – but the flesh is weak – O Dearest help me help me I call to you out of the tempest and the night. Life is hard for me – but I must try to live in the spirit and not in this wretched turmoil of self seeking. I have reached the nethermost pit of pain – Dear dear love don't let me destroy your love. Oh I love you I love you I love you – O help me Dearest have mercy on a struggling Sinner.

Do *please* write again soon – Albergo San Vigilio, prese Garda, unless I telegraph to the contrary. If I telegraph merely a town, address Poste Restante there. San Vigilio is near the town of Garda, and on the lake.

Goodbye. Goodbye. My utmost deepest love *and reverence* is with you *always*.

Your
   B.

Monday night
   My Dearest – I had to write in a hurry before, after reading your letter

---

1. Augustus John and Boris Anrep – two men who had exacted a gruelling devotion from their lovers.

only once. Now Sanger is gone to bed and I can write quietly. On re-reading your letter (which doesn't *hurt* me at all) I feel even more hopeless than I did at first. If *you* decide that we must now part, I shall bear you no grudge, and only feel that you have done what you had to do.

Since your letter came, everything has seemed strange and unearthly. I went to San Zeno,[1] where the beauty moved me infinitely. Sanger left me alone inside, and I found myself on my knees praying. I can't justify it, but it was a deep and sincere prayer – a prayer for strength to subdue my instincts. If we are to go on, I must give up wishing for companionship, or for any escape from loneliness, or for children – you do not know the depth of passionateness of my desire for children. As long as those desires exist in me, I cannot help instinctively resenting the fact that you would never satisfy them even if you were free and could. If I can conquer these desires (which unfortunately I let loose at the beginning of our relations) I should be then able to get great religious happiness from being with you. But I should have to become a saint to do that. Can I? I don't know. I have grown cynical about moral efforts and reformations. – We sat in the Piazza looking out on the Arena, and dined there – immense crowds of gay people listening to the band – many of them I loved from their faces, but they seemed separated from me by a vast gulf – I felt so utterly alone that I hardly could keep from calling to them that I too was a human being, and really one of them. This place has more moving beauty to me than any other except Venice – the river is quite wonderful – and many things.

You say you think at bottom I wish to part. No, not at bottom. Often the vision of a peaceful family life with a home and children comes before me and maddens me. But I know that is a dream. Even if we parted, I should always care for you too much to have a right to ask love of any woman I respected; for you hold the deepest depth of me, which no one else but one[2] has ever touched, and from which no one will ever dislodge you. Then

---

1. San Zeno Maggiore, a Romanesque church built in the twelfth century.
2. These two words, which Bertie inserted into the letter as an afterthought – in itself a remarkable concession to exactitude – are the more puzzling because we can't be sure to whom they refer. It is unlikely to be Alys because Bertie told Ottoline that Alys had never touched him as deeply as Ottoline had. On a number of occasions Bertie told Ottoline that she was his third love. Alys was evidently the first, and he never named the second. The most likely person is Evelyn Whitehead. It may seem odd that Bertie should have thought of Mrs Whitehead in his present supercharged emotional state, but less so if he is thinking here of the mystical experience which she precipitated in February 1901. That he should think of her now does not make it any less likely that his relations with her were always platonic.

besides: if the rest of my life is to be of any use, it must be in teaching, and for that I must avoid scandal. What I wish at bottom is to become a saint, and be able to bear your not giving more; then, as a reward, I should get the good of what you do give. But I really think you still don't at all realize how hard the thing is that you demand of me. You speak as if it were rare to desire another person's whole devotion, whereas it is normal; you differ from the normal in desiring *two* people's whole devotion. But forgive me – this is not the road to saintship! I must learn not to consider you morally at all, but to take you like the weather – sometimes propitious, sometimes not, but never to be praised or blamed, it is the only way.

I am sorry about the Don in me; he only comes out because of checked impulses. Of course my constant criticism has chilled you; I quite see that it must cease if we are to go on. – Now, my dear dear Love, I am in your hands. If you think me capable of doing better, after all these many many failures, I will try to conquer those instincts and put them right away, and make the best of what you can give. I am *quite sure* that is the right course if I can do it; and that any other course means absolute irretrievable ruin. It is very late, and I am worn out and dead in feeling – but I am less miserable than a few days ago, because I do wish to be good, whereas then I wished nothing. I must not wish to win back your love – if that comes, it must be without my thinking of it as possible. I want to say – God bless you – if I had the right. If we part, I shall always love you and wish all possible good to you.

　　Your
　　　B.

By the time Bertie returned to England he had received more of Ottoline's long letters, though none was quite so distressing as the one he had had at Verona. There was one waiting for him at his flat when he got home. In it she said that she felt she ought to remove herself from his life – she didn't want to, but she was causing him more pain than she was worth. None the less, another 'last' meeting was in the offing. By this time, however, Bertie was concerned not so much to woo her afresh as to deaden emotions which had become too painful to be endured. Signs of this appear in the next letter: in his talk of money and in the curious incident of Frau von Hattingberg (of whom we shall hear a little more later). At the very moment that Bertie was wailing most loudly that he had fallen over a precipice and was doomed, he retained enough self-possession to start looking for ways to climb back up.

[213]

Friday morning
[29 August 1913]

My Darling

Your sad letter was waiting for me when I arrived. There is not one word in it to *hurt* me – only the truest love – better love than mine has been. I think perhaps you are right, but I don't know. I don't know whether my love for you is still alive. It was at Verona, but when I came out from that time of sharp pain, I seemed to have lost the power of feeling about you. It may be temporary, but I can't tell. I am afraid it is not. And I am afraid that on both sides there are such walls of pain between us that it is hard to meet really. *Please* don't think I have *any* bitterness or criticism towards you – I see you now as I have always really known you – full of gentleness and unselfishness and divine love. But the sense of a personal relation is snapped – I feel you far away, like a person in a book. This has often very nearly happened before – it comes from lack of harmony in instincts.

I feel as if we ought to meet tomorrow, because I am so uncertain about everything, and because when I don't see you I get entangled in unreal nightmares. But if you think it needlessly painful, please telegraph, and I shall understand.

It is terribly hard to know the truth or to speak it. One thing that makes me think the passionate side of my love is dead is that I feel now, as far as I am concerned, friendship would be quite possible. But I don't know what you would feel about that.

The question of children in any possible future tie is not so simple as I think it seems to you. It would involve giving up teaching, which in itself is serious; and through that it would reduce my income to about £300 a year, which is meagre. So that I think it is hardly a serious possibility.

Dearest it is dreadful to write so coldly – it is the terrible effort to be true – and I am not the least sure it is the truth. I did feel it would be choosing the lower course while I loved you, and even if a woman would accept such a half-hearted affection, I did not feel it a thing to offer. But if passion ceased towards you, I should feel differently. My Dearest, it is quite terrible to give you so much pain – I have honestly struggled with my nature, but it is too stubborn. After Verona, I did at last make myself see truly and calmly – but to my utter astonishment, I seemed then to see that we ought to part. I distrusted that, but it was what came.

My dear dear Love, do not feel too much that you have failed – it is only true in part. There has always been between us a bond deeper than passion, and that will never be broken. I have learnt from you a very great deal that I shall never forget. I have seen a land of peace and I have found some kind of union of reason and vision. I cannot yet see the union of vehement action with vision, and yet the world needs vehement action.

But you have really really given greater breadth and richness and harmony to my mental life, and that remains in spite of passionate storms. I feel now that if passion were once for all shut out from our relation, what is of most value in it might remain.

As I write this letter, I am tortured by a sense of intolerable selfishness. But my prayer in Verona was not answered, and with things as they have been lately my work must suffer a great deal. But if I make up my mind not to look to you for instinctive things, the other things may remain. This is *really true* – on my side. You may believe it implicitly.

I had a curious sudden brief adventure the last evening of my stay at S. Vigilio – the evening before last. There was a solitary young German lady whom we all noticed and liked the looks of – at first she had an aunt with her, and then she was quite alone. She seemed lonely, so Lucy Silcox[1] invited her to join our expedition to Salò the day before yesterday to see the Martinéngo-Cesaresco gardens.[2] It turned out she had two children who were going to join her in a week. She may be a widow but seemed more as if she were separated from her husband. At the end of the evening I had an hour's tête-à-tête with her and liked her enormously. She is well-educated (has been at three universities!), very nice-looking, gentle but strong-willed. Her name is Frau Liese von Hattingberg. In saying goodnight I kissed her hand, and she appeared on the Veranda at 7.30 to wave goodbye yesterday morning. I don't suppose I shall ever see her again – the only importance of the incident is that I felt I could now give an affection worth having to someone else. I feel it shameful that it should be so, but so it is. It shows a great poverty of nature in me, and I wish it were otherwise.

Dearest this letter is difficult to write. I am haunted by the tragedy of things, and by reverence for what has been between us. It is very hard indeed to think of that ceasing, and it makes it difficult to be true. I honestly don't know what the truth is. If you feel you would rather not come tomorrow don't think I shall be hurt. I feel that at any moment I may wake as from a dream, and find love as burning as it has ever been. For my part, I would

1. At San Vigilio Russell and Sanger had met up, as they had planned, with Lucy Silcox, Melian Stawell and the obscure Miss Reynolds. They all returned to England together.
2. These were private gardens belonging to the Countess Martinéngo-Cesaresco, who was a friend of Lucy Silcox.

very much rather see you tomorrow, but it must be as you wish. I am a poor worthless creature – Goodbye.

    Your

      B.

The night Ottoline received this she wrote in her diary:

> Bertie has gone.... Such is man. There is nothing for me to say to him, but to open my hands and let the bird fly: which I have done.... I feel his letter tonight quite final, and that most probably I shall never see him again. Yes: I feel the poorer a great deal. But I don't think he loved me – only desired me. Love could not die like that. Desire could. (*Memoirs*, vol. ii, p. 284)

Despite what she wrote in the diary, Ottoline vacillated over the meeting: she wrote to say she would go; then wired that she wouldn't; then she wrote to say that she wouldn't go, but that he could come to her. Predictably, he went. Ottoline described the meeting (at Black Hall, Oxford, her mother-in-law's home) in her *Memoirs* (ibid.):

> The next day (August 30th) he came to Oxford to see me. He was hard and cold and old, as if all his soul had dried up, and kept saying that his love for me was dead. But before he went he quite changed, and all his love came back.

For the outcome she goes back to her journal:

> Since this crisis I feel happier and more at ease with him. I suppose what really comes between us is his passion and desire, and that upsets and frightens me, and makes me dislike him. What odd things men are!

Odd or not, in her letters immediately afterwards she was longing for their meetings, though circumstances conspired to keep them apart, since Ottoline would be away for September in Burnley.

While Bertie had been in Italy, Ottoline had met Joseph Conrad for the first time. He had made a great impression on her and she had urged Bertie to make his acquaintance. Russell had long admired his novels but would not have attempted to meet him without Ottoline's urging. On 10 September, armed with a letter of introduction from Ottoline, Russell went to visit him at his home in Kent. Despite their differences in background, work and politics, they became close friends. 'We shared', Russell said, 'a certain outlook on human life and human destiny, which, from the first, made a bond of extreme strength. . . . At our very first meeting, we talked with continually increasing intimacy. We seemed to sink through layer after layer of what was superficial, till gradually both reached the central fire. It was an experience unlike any other I have known. . . . The emotion was as intense as passionate love, and at the same time all-embracing. I came away bewildered, and hardly able to find my way among ordinary affairs' (*Autobiography*, vol. I, pp. 207–8).

[214]

In the train
Wednesday evening
[10 September 1913]

My Darling

Here I am on my way back from Conrad. It was *wonderful*. I *loved* him and I think he liked me. He talked a great deal about his work and life and aims, and about other writers. At first we were both shy and awkward – he praised Wells and Rothenstein and Zangwill and I began to despair. Then I asked him what he thought of Arnold Bennett, and found he despised him. Timidly I stood up for him and he seemed interested. Then I got him on to Henry James, and he began to expand – said he likes his middle period better than the novels from *The Golden Bowl*[1] onwards – attributes the falling off to the practice of dictating. Then we went a little walk, and somehow grew very intimate. I plucked up courage to tell him what I find in his work – the boring down into things to get to the very bottom below the apparent facts. He seemed to feel I had understood him; then he stopped and we just looked into each other's eyes for some time, and then he said he had grown to wish he could live on the surface and write differently, that he had grown frightened. His eyes at the moment expressed the inward pain and terror that one feels him always fighting. Then he said he was weary of writing and felt he had done enough, but had to go on and say it again. Then he talked a lot about Poland, and showed me an album of family photographs of the 60's – spoke about how dream-like all that seems, and how he sometimes feels he ought not to have had children, because they have no roots or traditions or relations. He told me a great deal about his sea-faring time and about the Congo and Poland and all sorts of things. At first he was reserved even when he seemed frank, but when we were out walking his reserve vanished and he spoke his inmost thoughts. It is impossible to say

1. Published in 1904.

how much I loved him. He spoke very nicely about you, and had been evidently *very* glad of your appreciation. He said he valued a woman's appreciation, as he had thought his novels were not the kind women liked. I realized as he spoke that he had hardly known any cultivated or intelligent women. His wife said you had promised to bring Julian some time, and she hoped you would. – You said you owed him to me, but I should never have got to know him but for you. It was poor Lucy Donnelly who first got me to read him – she gave me *Lord Jim* and the *Nigger*,[1] which was the first I ever heard of him. He is *wonderful*. Like all deep things, seeing him made my love to you more living and strong – it lives in that world.

Seeing Conrad has almost made me forget my visit to Bob,[2] which was very pale in comparison. It was pleasant and peaceful, as it always is, and I slept 9 hours as I always do there. Donald Tovey[3] was there, and poured forth information about music. I don't care for him – it seems to me he is choked by erudition and the desire to impart it – whatever fresh natural feelings he may have had about music seem dried up. He is agreeable enough, and it was nice hearing him play, but he is too academic and has little quality. Bob had nothing of interest to tell about his travels, except that he saw a lot of Tagore's relations and found that it is quite untrue that Tagore's poems are known and sung by the Bengal populace as Yeats asserts[4] – the relations say they are only known to educated people.

I am going to my flat now and I hope I shall find a letter from you there. I hope you are not very tired and don't have too much to do.

Yesterday morning Lucy Silcox came to breakfast with me, which was nice, though she only stayed a very short time. She said the German lady[5] had told her history, which is that her husband wants to marry another lady. But Lucy knew nothing of her feeling about the Greek God.[6]

Later (in my flat). Your dear little letter from the train was here when I arrived. – Of course I saw you still had the feeling of having been shut out,[7] but I felt I could dispel that soon. It all seems rather a foolish tangle, as it

1. *The Nigger of the 'Narcissus'* (1898).
2. Robert Trevelyan.
3. Donald Francis Tovey (1875–1940), the musicologist and composer.
4. W. B. Yeats makes this claim in his introduction to the English translation (1913) of Tagore's *Gitanjali*.
5. Frau von Hattingberg.
6. The 'Greek God' was a stranger on holiday in San Vigilio.
7. Ottoline had sent a very unhappy letter, saying she felt shut out from intimacy with him.

came from my feeling that you shut me out. We must try to have faith in
each other through tiresome moods – you have been *much* better about that
than I have. Dearest I am *quite sure* that I shall *always* cling to you in soul
and heart – it is a tie which is stronger than my will, stronger even than my
main purposes – and it would not be lessened if I had other ties – perhaps even
strengthened, because there would no longer be the pain of incompleteness in
instinctive ways. Instinctive desires unsatisfied, make me unkind and destroy
sympathy and tenderness, so I must keep them under – but nothing else will
suffer by that. I do need you Dearest – it is still very difficult to me to feel
that you need me – I got it so fixed in my feelings that I was not important
to you that I still find it hard to think otherwise. But I will try, and in time
I shall believe it if I am not wanting things you cannot give.

Now it is time for my train so I must stop. You were not the least horrid
about Mademoiselle.[1] Goodnight my Darling. Do write as much as you have
time for – it is such a long time till we meet again, and your letters are such
a joy.

Your

B.

For much of September, while Ottoline was in Burnley, Russell retired quietly to
Cambridge to write his Lowell Lectures. They were to be a relatively popular
statement of Russell's views on matter and the theory of knowledge. For them he
could build on the theory of acquaintance, the part of the *Theory of Knowledge* which
had escaped Wittgenstein's criticism. Russell held that perception gave acquaintance
with sense-data and that the problem of the external world could be solved by using
mathematical logic to construct material objects out of sense-data. The lectures were
published the following year as *Our Knowledge of the External World*. Russell said
that he found writing them unexciting, since they did not involve much original
work and the main difficulty was to make clear ideas he had already had. Still, after
the traumas of the previous summer, a quiet month writing must have been agreeable.

In his original plans for his book on matter, Russell had hoped to axiomatize
physics. The next letter indicates why 1913 was not a good year to attempt the task.
Niels Bohr (1885–1962), the young Danish physicist, had just devised his new theory
of the atom and had presented it at the meeting of the British Association for the
Advancement of Science at Birmingham on 7 September, at a high-powered session
devoted to the new quantum theory. On 17 September, Bohr was in Cambridge
and Russell had lunch with him.

1. Julian's French governess, who had had to be told off for laziness.

[215]

[Trinity College]
Tuesday night
[16 September 1913]

My Darling

Your dear long letter of yesterday has just come – I was *very* glad to get it, as it seemed a long time since Sunday morning, when I heard last. Very foolishly I had begun to think perhaps you were ill – but I won't again. I don't know your part of the country at all – except Manchester. I know nothing nearer than Kirkby Lonsdale, which I think *very* beautiful. To me the place is associated with Theodore's death – it was the first time I had been there. – I should feel *everything* that you feel about the football, including the enjoyment.[1] – It is a comfort to think of your having your mornings free – I hope Lady O'Hagan[2] won't prevent that. Yes, Plato is *wonderful*. But he is not intimate to me – I haven't enough urbanity for him. And I have begun to feel just a hint of the mediaeval prison-house in his authoritativeness and insistence on ethics as against science. Burnet's book made me feel this more.[3] But of course really he is about as great as any man who ever lived.

I am *very* glad your head is better. I am sending you Lectures III, IV, V, but I really don't think it is worth your while to do more than glance through them – they are difficult and I think wouldn't interest you.

I am *sure* I shan't think your reflections for J[ulian][4] 'bête' as you say – I am nothing like as critical of you *mentally* as you think I am and expected I should be. Your shyness about things of that sort is really unnecessary.

It is a pity Mademoiselle is so lazy. I wonder if it is true that she works when she is not having holidays; I also wonder if she is clever.[5] The little I

1. Ottoline had enjoyed going to a football match (*Memoirs*, vol. I, p. 250).
2. A Liberal supporter in Burnley who lent Ottoline and Philip her house on the outskirts of town for the month they would be in Burnley.
3. This was almost certainly John Burnet's *Early Greek Philosophy* (1892) which Russell refers to several times in *Our Knowledge of the External World*. Burnet says little about Plato in this book, but Russell was probably comparing Plato to the Pre-Socratics – especially his favourites: Parmenides, Zeno and Heraclitus whom Burnet discusses at length. Burnet did write another book, *Greek Philosophy from Thales to Plato*, in which he discusses Plato, but this was not published until June 1914 and there is no evidence that Russell read it before publication.
4. Ottoline was writing some 'reflections' for Julian's benefit.
5. Ottoline had said that she was.

talked with her, she seemed to me intellectually passive – wishing to be fed with knowledge, rather than to seek it out for herself. But I dare say I was wrong.

Since I began writing to you, Littlewood[1] has been here to ask me to lunch tomorrow, to meet 2 Danes and a German and his wife[2] – all four of them mathematicians. It seems one of the Danes has been reading a revolutionary paper on Physics at the British Association, and poor J. J. Thomson,[3] who has always been the very foremost in innovation, took the conservative line and was squashed (so they say) by an eminent German who agreed with the Dane.[4] The nature of matter has been changing about once a year for the last 15 years, but this change (from what Littlewood told me) is much more serious than any previous one. Physics is a most sensational science.

Thanks for sending me Molly's[5] letter. – I *love* hearing of all you do at Burnley – and it makes you seem not so terribly far away. It is a most *terrible* long time till we meet. I do wish you could have come here for a day during Vacation time, when there is no one about. I *long* to see you, but my instinct is against going to Burnley. I feel it would be a mistake.

My days here are so quiet that I have nothing to write about – I go out in the afternoon, I write my ten pages, and most of the rest of the time I play patience. Being free from obsessions is such a delight that I require nothing more to keep me happy.

Dearest don't think I am feeling remote or far away from you in spirit – somehow I seem to feel as if you did think so. I am feeling *very* full of love to you – real love and sympathy and longing for you to be happy. I wish we were not apart all this time while I am free from the horrors. But if I can keep so you won't find me so tiring, and perhaps things will be easier than they have been for a long long time. I hope so. I wonder what your inmost

1. John Edensor Littlewood (1885–1977), Cambridge pure mathematician. Much of his best-known work was done in collaboration with G. H. Hardy.
2. One of the Danes was Bohr. The other Dane and the German and his wife are unknown.
3. Joseph John Thomson (1856–1940), the experimental physicist, then Cavendish Professor at Cambridge. He had received the Nobel Prize in 1906 for the discovery of the electron, the first subatomic particle. Bohr had studied under him at Cambridge.
4. Bohr's biographer records the discussion at the British Association and reports that it was the chemist, George Hevesy (1885–1966), who defended Bohr's theory (R. Moore, *Niels Bohr: The Man and the Scientist*, London, 1967, pp. 68–70). Hevesy was hardly eminent at this stage in his career, though he became so.
5. Probably Molly MacCarthy. Ottoline doesn't mention it in her letter.

thoughts are. I do hope you are not unhappy. Goodnight my dear dear Love. I love you with all my soul.
    Your
      B.

Russell was much calmer as a result of the month's quiet work in September and perhaps also as a result of the meeting with Conrad. Conrad, he felt, was a man with the same tempestuous passions as himself, yet one who had managed a degree of self-discipline and control that Russell had been trying all summer to achieve. The beginning of the Cambridge term in October brought its own distractions with the arrival of new students and the return of Wittgenstein, who had been in Norway trying to solve the problems of logic. He had had some success and was determined to go back there as soon as possible to continue. Meanwhile, it seemed imperative to obtain a written record of what he had achieved so far. But getting Wittgenstein to commit his thoughts to paper was difficult. The result in this case was Wittgenstein's 'Notes on Logic' (posthumously published in his *Notebooks 1914–16* in 1961). The following letter explains how it came into existence.

[216]

[Trinity College]
[9 October 1913]
Thursday morning

My Darling
    Many thanks for letter and lecture, both duly arrived.[1] All goes very well with me. I will come up by the 8.30 tomorrow morning so that I shall be in my flat by 10. I had not realized you could manage to be so early as 10.45. I am in a terrific rush of work and excitement, which I *love*. Yesterday Wittgenstein turned up as I finished with you,[2] and was on my hands till near midnight, except a brief period when I had to deal with the prodigy.[3] You saw W's letter saying he wanted a means of preserving his work, and therefore wanted to *tell* me about it. I answered that I couldn't remember it that way, and he *must* write it down. Then his artistic conscience got in the way, and because he couldn't do it perfectly he couldn't do it at all. I tried

1. Ottoline had returned one of Russell's Lowell Lectures which she had been reading.
2. That is, as he finished writing to her.
3. Norbert Wiener (1894–1964), American mathematician best known as the founder of cybernetics. He had been an infant prodigy, gaining a Harvard doctorate at the age of eighteen with a thesis in which he compared Russell's logic with that of the German mathematician Ernst Schröder. He came to Cambridge to study with Russell. Russell thought that excessive praise had made him conceited, but came to like him more as he became more modest.

one method after another: he spent Tuesday at Birmingham dictating extracts from his note-book to a German short-hand writer; then there were newer things, and things not sufficiently explained. He said he would make a statement of them, and sat down to do it. After much groaning he said he couldn't. I abused him roundly and we had a fine row. Then he said he would talk, and write down any of his remarks that I thought worth it, so we did that, and it answered fairly well. But we both got utterly exhausted, and it was slow. Today he is coming again, and Jourdain's secretary (the one who is prettier than Waterlow's[2] bride) is coming to take down our conversation in short-hand. Mercifully Jourdain sent her this morning to borrow a book of mine so I grabbed her. It is early-closing day so no one can be got except as a favour. Tomorrow W. goes to London, and Saturday to Norway. Today in the middle I have to have Lucy Donnelly's young lady[3] to tea – she will give a breathing-space.

All this fuss suits me to perfection and prevents me from feeling impatience, or indeed anything except the wish to drag W's thoughts out of him with pincers, however he may scream with the pain. We walked out to Jourdain's to tea yesterday – it was nice there, but on the walk we were on each other's nerves. – The prodigy is disgusting, I don't know why; I hardly know how to be civil to him. The female prodigy (supposed to be the dearest girl at Bryn Mawr since Karin) is not disgusting, in fact seems totally colourless both for good and evil. What colourless creatures they seem beside Wittgenstein.

I have been looking at Lecture VII – it seems the easiest of them all, so I

1. Philip Edward Bertrand Jourdain (1879–1919), one of Russell's first students in mathematical logic: he had attended Russell's lectures in the winter of 1901–2. He suffered from Friedreich's ataxia, a form of creeping paralysis, which eventually killed him and which made it impossible for him to have a career as a teacher. None the less, he wrote voluminously on mathematics, logic, and philosophy and kept up a busy correspondence with most of the logicians of his day. (His correspondence with Russell was published by I. Grattan-Guinness, *Dear Russell – Dear Jourdain*, 1977.) He needed a secretary because his handwriting became almost indecipherable as his paralysis progressed. From 1911 to 1915 he lived in the village of Girton, just outside Cambridge.
2. Sydney Philip Perigal Waterlow (1878–1944), diplomat and member of the Bloomsbury Group. He had studied classics at Trinity and then gone into the diplomatic service, resigning in 1905 to return to Cambridge where he became a University Extension lecturer. His first marriage ended in divorce in the spring of 1913 and shortly afterwards he married Margery Eckhard. He returned to diplomacy during the First World War.
3. This was Helen Huss Parkhurst (1887–1959). She had studied philosophy at Bryn Mawr and Lucy Donnelly had recommended that she go to Cambridge to study with Russell – rather oddly, since her main interest was in aesthetics. She was the 'female prodigy' mentioned in the next paragraph.

think it should be Lecture II. Do you agree? Do you agree that the ones on Zeno and Infinity had better be postponed? I think everything can be grouped about the problem of the external world, and the difficulties kept till late. Tomorrow you can tell me what you think.

I am *very* happy and I am sure tomorrow will be *heaven*. W. makes me feel it is worth while I should exist, because no one else could understand him or make the world understand him. – Your letter hadn't seemed *cross*, only as if you had no power of feeling happiness at the moment. – Now I must stop. W. and Jourdain's Secretary will be here directly and then I shall have to start a fierce tussle with the combined difficulties of logic and human nerves. Goodbye Darling till tomorrow. I am so *full* of love and of joy in the thought of you.

> Your
> B.

In December, once term had ended, Russell went to Rome for a holiday. There once more he met Frau von Hattingberg with whom he had kept in touch since the previous summer through the useful device of some borrowed books. They were not – at least as yet – seriously interested in each other, but both were unhappily in love and found some comfort in each other's company as they tried to sort out their bruised emotions. Things might have gone more smoothly had not Ottoline and Philip been in Rome at the same time.

When Dr Combe, the previous summer, had found something wrong with Julian's liver his prescription, fortunately, was not radium in milk but a 'sun cure' at a sanatorium run by a Dr Rolier at Leysin. Julian had been sent there in October with her nurse, and in December Ottoline and Philip went out to see her. Afterwards they went on to Rome, leaving for Florence just before Christmas. Bertie found Ottoline more affectionate in Rome and afterwards she wrote warmly from Florence anxious for gossip about Frau von Hattingberg.

[217]

> Hotel Minerva, Rome
> Monday
> [22 December 1913]

My Darling

Your *dear* letter was here when I came in after lunch. Your letters express so much more of your love than you show when we are together, though this time you were much more expressive than usual. You need not be afraid of my plunging into things with my German lady. She does not excite me or make me lose my head, or much attract me physically. This morning I went with her and her children into the Borghese Gardens and then came home to a very scratch and uncomfortable luncheon at her place. She soothes my nerves and makes me feel happy and good – more or less the way Lucy Silcox does. I believe a friendship with her would be a great acquisition, but anything more would be disastrous, especially as she is prone to jealousy.

She has no servant, only a nurse, and at meals she is joined by an English husband and wife, the latter very vulgar. Her late husband is a professor of morbid psychology – in Germany his conduct does not deprive him of his post.

I wish I could be more content with what you give me. But the situation is against nature, and instinct revenges itself in all sorts of ways when one tries to ignore it. I know that whatever happens I shall never give to any one else the kind of feeling I give to you, the kind of feeling that has all the magic of western islands and all the passion of Beethoven. But it grows more and more difficult to me to forget enough to be really happy when I am with you. And thwarted instinct makes me self-centred and inclined to recklessness. I am sorry it is so – it would not be so in a more generous nature, but I think it would in any one capable of passionate love.

I wish I could write something else, but it wouldn't be true if I did.

I think tomorrow I shall go to Tivoli for the night but I shall come back next day. Goodbye my Dearest. Please forgive this letter – it is probably only a passing mood.

  Your
    B.

If Bertie was straying, as Ottoline's biographer says (Darroch, *Ottoline*, p. 123), it was not very far. On 27 December, after more affectionate letters from Ottoline, he was looking forward to seeing her again at Aigle in Switzerland on 2 January as he went back to England and she returned to Leysin. This meeting, however, was not a happy one, and they were once more close to parting.

Bertie got back to England bursting with new ideas. In his *Autobiography* (vol. i, p. 210) he says that on New Year's Day he hired a stenographer and started to dictate his Lowell Lectures. But on New Year's Day he was still on the Continent and in any case the Lowell Lectures, as we have seen, were written the previous September. What Russell did start work on as soon as he got back to Cambridge were his lectures for Harvard on the theory of knowledge. He had no need to prepare his lectures on logic, since these would presumably have been much like the lectures he gave at Cambridge, but he had been stuck on the theory of knowledge since Wittgenstein's attack the previous May. It seems he must have thought of some way through or around the impasse Wittgenstein had created. But since the lectures he prepared have not survived we cannot tell what innovations were involved. If he did think he had a solution to Wittgenstein's problems, it did not stand up since four years later, in 'The Philosophy of Logical Atomism', he was still stuck for a replacement for his old theory of judgement. Out of this spate of work came also a number of occasional lectures he would need for his American trip, an important article 'The Relation of Sense-Data to Physics' (*Papers*, vol. VIII, pp. 5–21), and several new ideas. One of these was that space had six dimensions (see *Papers*, vol. VIII, pp. 13–15), but it is difficult to identify the others without either the theory of knowledge lectures or the manuscript of the Lowell Lectures. He did alter some of the Lowell Lectures to incorporate the new ideas, but we have only the published book to go on and cannot date the innovations in it in the absence of the manuscript. Whatever the new ideas were, he was very pleased with them, and compared his burst of work in January with the one he had had in 1900 just after he discovered Peano.

|218|

Trinity College
Sunday evening
4 January 1914

My Darling

I am afraid you will get no letter from me till tomorrow – I am very sorry indeed, but I slept practically without stirring until my train was in the platform in Paris. There at the Gare de Lyon I met my brother, which delayed me – and when I got into the train at the Gare du Nord I was still in a lethargy. My brother asked me to dine with him in London, which I did, coming on here afterwards. My rooms looked very friendly and nice when I got home – it is a comfort to creep into one's hole. It is very quiet here – very few people are up.

What an odd *detached* thing the part of one's mind that does work is. I have done as much work today as I should usually do in a week, and I find myself intensely interested and very fit, in spite of travelling, a cold, and a fit of constipation which pills have failed to cure – not to mention all our troubles. The work-machinery seems to follow its own laws, and to exist in the same body without really belonging to the same person. For the moment, the sheer delight of clear vision as to the problem of matter makes the whole world look bright. It is odd: To see clearly after being long puzzled is one of the god-like things in life. I suppose what makes people philosophers is finding it intolerably painful to be puzzled and correspondingly glorious to see clearly. It is like surveying from a hill-top a country strewn with battlefields where desperate victories have been won against what seemed irresistible odds.

It really is a glorious thing to give understanding of things never understood before – to subdue a new province of the wild world to the empire of thought. It is worth being mad and hateful and filling oneself and others with pain if that is the price one must pay. Merely to write down what I have in germ in my mind about matter will probably take me the rest of my working life. I have a vast synthesis in my head, bringing together what had seemed discrepant facts from physics, physiology and psychology; and if I can fully succeed, it will be in the end as definite as the multiplication-table. It may turn out to be a better piece of work than any I have yet done. But it will want health and energy and a terrific driving-force. My work really is creative in a very high sense, because it consists in bringing scientific method and demonstration into regions where hitherto there has been nothing but conjecture. Forgive all this boasting – it is really the things I see, not my part in them, that I find intoxicating. After an interval, they are so much clearer and more solid – like things appearing in the dawn, growing more visible while one turns away. These big things make me ashamed of personal troubles – happiness and unhappiness seem small things beside science.

The effect of Conrad's letter has lasted,[1] and the feeling about work has intensified it. Everything that moves me deeply turns me instinctively to you. When I am really alive spiritually, I do not feel lonely, but I feel you with me, and the sense of distance diminishes – it is only in fatigue and discouragement and cynicism that I feel remote from you. If I could live always at my best, there would be no difficulties; but if by my act we part, I shall never reach my best again. The mistake I make is in wanting happiness. You *can* give me moments of unearthly joy, and also the very deep-down kind of happiness that comes of living by what is most serious; but in the circumstances you cannot give me ordinary daily happiness, and I cannot find it elsewhere without spiritual suicide. All this is horribly self-absorbed. It is not all that is in my mind, but of the rest I cannot speak.

Friday was dreadful. It would have been different if I had slept the night before. I was conscious of your pain, but too numb to do anything. You get an impression that I care more for Frau v. H. than I do. I think her warm

1. On his return, Russell had found a letter from Joseph Conrad praising 'The Free Man's Worship' very warmly (it is published in *Autobiography*, vol. I, p. 225).

friendship is all I *really* want; if I had *really* wanted more, I could probably have got it. But I didn't mind her not wanting to give more. I have great pleasure in being with her, but almost no wish for any physical relation. She is aware of all this.

My Darling, I fear you are very deeply unhappy. *Please* believe it is *all* my fault and not yours in any way. I have been feeling so *full* of love to you — feeling too late the power to break down the barriers and speak to your soul out the depths of my own — all that I ought to have said on Friday, but that was somehow frozen in me. I keep wondering whether you will still decide to part. I dare not hope that you will not. I cannot give you happiness or usefulness. I can only give you a great and terrible love — as great and terrible as life itself. Whatever you may do, that is yours for ever and ever. Goodbye Goodbye.

> Your
> B.

This letter crossed with one from Ottoline saying definitely that they ought to part. But by 8 January she was relenting and again no final decision was made. Russell's state of mind was now more independent of Ottoline than at any time since their affair began. His work continued to prosper and the satisfaction he gained from it could not be undermined by rebuffs from Ottoline. It was as if his intellect were an automatic safety device that had switched on of its own accord to absorb his interest and thus protect him from an emotional state that was too disturbing to be endured for long. Through January there is a curious, almost somnambulistic, quality to his letters: on the one hand, he comments in a detached way about his unhappy love; while, on the other, he reports on the progress of his work with relish. This was not quite the 'hard, intellectual mood' that he had often spoken about and that Alys had endured — that had been born of anger and puritanism, and would not return — but it was an effective protection against too much raw emotion. His affair with Ottoline had mellowed him; he was losing what Beatrice Webb had perceptively called his 'subtle absoluteness' (see page 249 above).

His enthusiasm for work received further encouragement by reports that Littlewood brought back from Göttingen of the interest of German mathematicians in his work.

[219]

[Trinity College]
18 January 1914
Sunday evening

My Darling Love

Your dear letter this morning was a great joy. I am glad my letter from the Athenaeum was all right – I was afraid it would be stupid from fear of my Uncle Rollo and Bernard Holland, who was also there but didn't see me.

I have made friends with a classical man named Stuart[1] – I have known him these 3 years, but only lately got to know him. In a sudden impulse I gave him *Forstice* to read, and he liked it. This morning I went a walk with him. He is not really very interesting, but he is nice and he is cultivated and civilized. I went another walk this afternoon, so I have done my duty in the way of exercise.

I am reading a number of the *Revue de Métaphysique et de Morale*, entirely on Poincaré. He certainly was a wonderful man. There are four articles, by a philosopher, a mathematician, a physicist and an astronomer, telling what he did in their various subjects.[2] There is no one in science now who is quite as eminent as he was. The French do put things delightfully. The physicist (Langevin) says: 'Au cours de nos conversations, pendant la semaine qu'il me donna la joie de passer seul avec lui en 1904, dans les vastes plaines de l'Amérique du Nord, au retour du Congrès de Saint-Louis (a philosophical Congress) j'eus l'occasion de voir avec quel intérêt passionné Henri Poincaré suivait toutes les phases de la révolution qui s'accomplissait ainsi dans nos conceptions les plus fondamentales. Il voyait avec un peu d'inquiétude ébranler, grâce aux instruments forgés par lui-même, le vieil édifice de la dynamique newtonienne qu'il avait récemment encore couronné par ses admirables travaux sur le problème des trois corps et la forme d'équilibre des corps célestes. Mais si son enthousiasme était plus réfléchi que le mien, il était, comme nous tous, dominé par la fièvre d'entrer dans un monde entièrement nouveau.'[3] It is just the same impression about physics that I got from the

1. Charles Erskine Stuart (1882–1917) got a First in the Classical Tripos of 1905 and became a Fellow of Trinity College in 1907 with a dissertation on the tragedies of Seneca. He was killed in the First World War.
2. The articles by, respectively, Léon Brunschvicg, Jacques Hadamard, Paul Langevin, and A. Lebeuf, were published in vol. 21, no. 5 (1913). The passage Russell quotes is from p. 702.
3. 'In the course of our conversations, during the week that I had the pleasure of spending with him in 1904, in the vast plains of North America when we got back from the St

Dane I wrote about last term. Physics is *the* science of the present day, just as biology was in Darwin's time. I often wish I were a physicist, but laboratories and experiments and mechanisms baffle me completely. It is strange how little ordinary educated people realize the world of science – it is a grave defect in our systems of education.

Littlewood went on the Vacation to Göttingen, the chief mathematical university of the world. From his account, they sound as superior to Cambridge as *La Nouvelle Revue française*[1] is to (say) the *Athenaeum*. It makes one's mouth water to hear how many good students they have, and what advanced lectures are attended in large numbers. Littlewood tells me that Hilbert[2] (the chief mathematical professor there) has grown interested in Whitehead's and my work, and that they think of asking me to lecture there next year. I hope they will. Germany (except Frege, who is not known) has hitherto been behindhand in mathematical logic, but if the mathematicians would take it up there, they would probably do wonders.[3] Littlewood also told me he met an American there who is going back to America solely to hear my lectures! Think of that! I shall be insufferable for a long time.

He found them all very jolly – great friendship between professors and students. He went specially to see a man named Landau,[4] the chief man in the *very* pure mathematics that Littlewood works at. They got up a plot to introduce a certain American to Landau as being Littlewood, and primed him with a speech saying he had seen through pure mathematics and now

Louis Congress, I had the opportunity to see with what passionate interest Henri Poincaré was following all the phases of the revolution which was then taking place in our most fundamental conceptions. With a little anxiety, he saw the old edifice of Newtonian dynamics, that he had recently crowned with his wonderful works on the three-body problem and the form of equilibrium of celestial bodies, being shaken, thanks to tools forged by himself. But if his enthusiasm was more reflective than my own, he was, like all of us, dominated by the excitement of entering a completely new world.' Unfortunately, the endless embedded clauses in the French, which Russell found delightful, do not fare so well in English.

1. An advanced French literary review founded in 1909. Ottoline had taken an interest in it and the new authors it published. The *Athenaeum* (founded in 1828) was much more staid in its tastes.

2. David Hilbert (1862–1943), Professor of Mathematics at Göttingen from 1895 and one of the most important mathematicians of the twentieth century. He published two books on mathematical logic and was the chief proponent of the philosophy of mathematics known as formalism.

3. They did.

4. Edmund Landau (1877–1938). He taught at Göttingen until the Nazis took power. His field was algebraic number theory.

only cared for applied; unfortunately Landau discovered the plot. German learned people are generally full of schoolboy pranks, and don't seem to suffer from nerves as ours do. I suppose it is beer instead of tea.

I feel so much calmer inside from having got a lot of work done. From the time I came here in 1910 until lately, I did not get any important new work done, and it worried me. Last June I hoped I was doing well, and then Wittgenstein reduced me to despair again. But this time I am *sure* I have done well. Worry about work colours all one's thoughts and feelings about everything, and takes the joy out of life. I know Wittgenstein will like the work I have done lately.

Very little more than a week now till we meet! What happiness it will be – I long to kiss you and hold you in my arms Dearest and pour out a flood of love – Goodbye my Heart. My thoughts are with you always.

Your

B.

Russell was very excited about the prospect of a visit to Göttingen. His visit to Harvard to convert the American philosophers to mathematical logic now seemed less important when compared to going to Göttingen to convert the German mathematicians. The First World War, of course, put paid to the visit, but the German mathematicians discovered mathematical logic without his help.

At the beginning of February Ottoline was consulting an English doctor to see if it was possible that she could have another child. It is not clear that she wanted another child: in seeking medical opinion she may have wished only to confirm that, for reasons that were no fault of hers, children really were one of the three things that Bertie wanted from her (as he had written from Verona and would repeat later in February) but couldn't have. The doctor's opinion was that there was absolutely no chance of another child and Ottoline communicated the news to Bertie in a note that sounded to him like a final goodbye, though it may not have been intended that way. He took the news hard.

[220]

[Trinity College]
Friday
13 February 1914

I had thought we should meet again, but from your letter it seems as if it would be useless pain on both sides. I am very sorry indeed that the Doctor's decision is what it is — it makes everything so useless. I should like to hope that after some time has passed we might meet again as friends, and try at least to save something. Would you mind letting me know if you would mind that, or if you would rather not. I should *like* to see you now — my whole impulse is to throw myself at your feet and implore pardon. But I feel we cannot really inwardly pardon each other, in instinct as well as reason — at least not yet. All life looks utterly blank to me.

Your
B.

[221]

[Trinity College]
13 February 1914

My Dearest

I can't bear that we should part with bitterness on both sides — it is too dreadful after what we have been to each other. I must try to make you understand and pardon what I have felt these days. It seemed hopeless to make you understand so I didn't try but I must try. I had no anger with you about the main thing   it hurt, but seemed right. Only I felt hopeless because of your not realizing it would hurt. The longing for children has grown and grown in me, and the pain of not having a child by you has been terrible. And from the very beginning I have felt pain because you didn't understand the things of instinct. When you spoke the other day, the bitterness of all the pain and hunger I have suffered became just too much and I couldn't bear it any more, and I lost all power to think of anything but anguish in connection with you. You have heart, but not understanding, and so over and over again without meaning it you hurt. I must break with you, or I shall be broken — and I must not be broken yet. Until now I had hoped you would come to understand and not hurt any more, but now I have lost that hope. You think I no longer love you and that that is why I break. That is *an absolute mistake*. I have no wish of any sort or kind to have anything to do with any other woman, that was only attempts to bear the pain — I break to save the spring of life and energy that I need. You don't know how I have been fighting to keep Hell under – it makes me precise and formal and cold but only because Hell is boiling and ready to burst out.

My Beloved, you have given me moments which no one else ever gave me or will give – and I have learnt some wisdom which will remain with me, and a breadth and freedom of thought that is your permanent gift to my mind. You will always always be more to me in my thoughts than any other human being. Do try to forgive me and to realize that other's natures are hard to understand. You felt I wanted to hamper your life – it was not that, but that I could only leave you freedom by going away – otherwise my pain would have destroyed your freedom. Goodbye goodbye – I bless you from the depths of my heart always always.

By now, however, it was Ottoline who was feeling deserted. What she wrote in her diary at the time makes one wonder whether she had read the letters Bertie had been sending her:

> For many months I have felt a dire loneliness that nothing will ever relieve. I seem to have tried everyone and found them all wanting, and yet I know the fault is my own. It is as if I were condemned to walk through life quite detached; quite apart from others, and not to enter their lives, never to arouse in others feelings of sympathy or affection, or a desire to give to me. At one time I seem to have plunged into others' lives – Roger Fry, Lamb, Lytton – but from some cause they all seem to have come to an end. (*Memoirs*, vol. I, pp. 251–2)

Bertie's name is conspicuously absent from the published list of failed loves, though Ottoline's biographer adds it (Darroch, *Ottoline*, p. 123), perhaps from the unpublished diary. Plainly it ought to be included.

Ottoline's loneliness no doubt prompted her to take up Bertie's suggestion of a final meeting, and the meeting proved to be as final as all the previous ones.

[222]

[Trinity College]
17 February 1914
Tuesday night

My Darling

The world seems strangely different since yesterday morning – I have never known such a quick and great change. It was your sudden outburst yesterday morning asking me not to give you up altogether that made the difference. You made me realize that it mattered to you – I had felt that at Leysin, and then I thought I had been mistaken. It is often very hard to realize – but when I do realize it, it makes everything easy and life full of joy. I am terribly sorry to have given you so much pain for nothing – and yet I still feel no one could have been expected to feel it differently from the way I did. You feel me terribly selfish – but it is easy for me to be unselfish when reason is on that side – only in what concerns you I often feel reason is on the side of selfishness – I dare say I am quite wrong to feel that, but I get the feeling that I must protect myself or be destroyed. However, I expect that is a delusion – but the sense of having to fight for my life makes me hard.

I perceive more and more that, whatever crisis we have, we shall always come together again. That being so, I must try to put out of my head the three things I want and can't have – children, daily companionship, and imaginative writing. I *could* make up my mind never to think of them, if my reason were convinced that I ought to.

I wish I could do something to relieve your sense of being remote from life – that sort of loneliness is a terrible suffering. I have it deep down – it is one of the terrors of living seriously – but I have more of a middle region where friends give something. It has been always a pain to me that there was not more companionship between you and me – I have felt over and over again that you deliberately thrust me out when I made any effort after companionship. Will you let me try in future to break down the things that make it difficult? It is very largely that you indulge your shyness, even when it hurts horribly and makes relations stiff and *difficiles*. I think, if you will try never to take anything I say about it as *criticism*, but only as trying to find out what makes constraint, something might be done – but perhaps it would make you too self-conscious. I think possibly you haven't realized enough that *little* intimacies and ease of ordinary talk are important. But it is *chiefly* shyness that makes you remote, I think – certainly with me it is – that, and shrinking from any invasion of your privacy. Don't you think so? And also the fact that your sympathy is intermittent, depending more on your mood than on other people's needs. I used to hope to coax you out of it, but it needs a gentler person. Lucy Silcox could do it I dare say, and I suppose Madame Anrep[1] does. It is stupid of me to write all this, because I see it must annoy you. Do tell me in reply what I *can* do to make you less remote from other people's lives. I should like to do something about it, and I know if you don't help me, whatever I try to do will only hurt you. But I do *really* mean well.

Mrs Whitehead had been reading *Chance*[2] and felt as I did about it. As she talked, I found myself taking your side – I generally agree very much more with you than with her about literature. She said there was less imagination than in some earlier books. I said Flora was well imagined – she said no, she was observed. She says Alys is very friendly with Molly MacCarthy, and I rather gather she (Alys) has been trying to make difficulties between her and Desmond for a long time past. It always used to be her favourite pastime to promote quarrels between husbands and wives, and I expect it is still. When she has succeeded, she turns round and blames them.

Dearest I felt your love yesterday as I hadn't felt it since quite early days. I had *no idea* you cared so much. If I could often feel it so, life would be full of joy. Passion in me gets frozen, but a moment's warmth from you brings it to life again. Goodnight my Darling. Don't imagine me unhappy now – I am not at all. I do hope your head won't be bad and that the injections will do good.

    Your
      B.

A long separation now could not be avoided, however, since Russell's trip to America was drawing close. He wrote to Lucy Donnelly about his plans.

---

1. The mother of Boris Anrep, the mosaicist. Ottoline had visited her in Paris.
2. Conrad's latest novel. Russell hadn't liked it as much as the earlier novels, but eventually seems to have come round to Ottoline's opinion (see letter 223).

[223]

Trinity College
20 February 1914

My dear Lucy

I was very glad to get your letter – it was a perfect age since I had heard from you. First as to plans: I sail March 7 on the *Mauretania*, so I suppose I shall land in New York quite early on Friday 13th (doubly unlucky date!), and go to Boston by the 1 o'clock train. I must get to Boston that night, as I lecture at Harvard on Saturday 14th. My address will be *Colonial Club*, Cambridge, Mass. I greatly look forward to seeing you. I don't think I can come during the Harvard Easter Recess as other plans have been made for me. (Perry has made my arrangements.) But I could come for some other week-end. I wonder if you and I could meet somewhere less far from Boston for the week-end of your recess? I am quite willing to give an informal talk at Bryn Mawr; the only question – and this applies to coming at all – is as to what Carey feels. I can't well come if she would rather I didn't. And if I come, is she going to see me or ignore me? I suppose she has been fed up with lies – I know both Mariechen and Logan have been spreading untrue stories about me. Otherwise her attitude seems unnecessary. I don't think it is what Alys would desire.

Unless you were happening to be in New York when I land would you let Helen know the time, on the chance of my being able to get a glimpse of her before I go to Harvard. But don't if you don't think it worth while. I shall be very much occupied while I am in America – I know a good many weekends I shall have engagements – so we must fix up things as soon after I land as possible. I want *very* much to see you – both at Bryn Mawr and, if possible, more quietly at some time. Please write frankly what you think possible.

I am sorry you are overworked, and also sorry you had such a painful experience with your Reader.[1]

Yes, I have read *Chance* – he gave it me! It is a wonderful book – Flora is amazing. I have seen Conrad just twice, but he is already one of the people in the world that I am most intimate with – I write to him and he to me on all the inmost things. He is quite wonderfully lovable. Poor old Bryce![2]

---

1. A Reader in Lucy's department at Bryn Mawr had had a nervous breakdown just before Christmas.
2. James Bryce (1838–1922), jurist, historian, and politician. He had been Regius Professor of Civil Law at Oxford (1870–93), then entered Parliament, and from 1907 to 1913 was British Ambassador in Washington. Lucy Donnelly had been reading one of his travel books: *South America: Observations and Impressions* (1913).

I feel your good opinion of him is touched by the romance of England.

Helen Parkhurst[1] has suddenly reached a new level in her work – she has caught on to the idea of thinking for herself instead of looking for the truth in books. I am afraid America will be shocked with her. Her own thoughts, as yet, are a little crude, but they *are* her own, and they are held with passion. My opinion of her has gone up very much. I congratulate myself, as I think it is due partly to the stimulus of belief in the possibility of new thought.

If you would like to have it, I will give you the MS. of *Forstice* when I see you. (I have a typed copy.) Since Fontainebleau I have never had a mood in which I could do anything to it, so it has merely lain in my drawer. At last, with great trepidation, I have decided to show it to Conrad and get him to tell me what to do with it.[2] This is in consequence of a letter he wrote praising 'The Free Man's Worship' in about the strongest terms in which writing can be praised.

At Xmas I went to Rome, but it rained almost every day, and I was glad to get home. Since then I have done an unspeakable amount of new work – my brain has been wonderfully fit. I shall pour it all out on America. I am reading a paper to a Philosophical Club in New York[3] of which poor Miller[4] (whom I remember from Bryn Mawr days) is secretary – I wrote it in the first days of the year, just after returning from Rome. It is 11,000 words and took me three days – don't tell them, or they will think it worthless, whereas it is one of the best things I ever did! I am giving a course of lectures here 'on our knowledge of the external world' at which I have a great crowd,[5] as they are semi-popular. I found they were taking every word I spoke as gospel, so I solemnly besought them not to believe anything I said, as I felt sure it was all wrong. So then they believed that too.

1. See letter 216.
2. Conrad gave his verdict when he met Russell in July. He was, not surprisingly, very critical and suggested a great deal of rewriting (see *Papers*, vol. xii, p. 127). Russell, wisely, abandoned fiction until he took briefly to writing short stories in the 1950s. The fact that Russell was giving the manuscript away suggests perhaps that, in keeping with his resolution in the previous letter, he was putting plans for 'imaginative' writing out of his head. Probably only a *very* favourable report from Conrad would have persuaded him to continue.
3. The Philosophical Club at Columbia University. The paper was 'The Relation of Sense-Data to Physics'.
4. Dickinson Sergent Miller (1868–1963). He was teaching philosophy at Bryn Mawr when Russell had visited in 1896 but since 1904 had been teaching at Columbia.
5. He told Ottoline there were 150 at his first lecture. These were, of course, the same lectures he was to give at the Lowell Institute in Boston.

Teaching is a difficult business. It is like Max Beerbohm's Walt 'exhorting the bird of freedom to soar'.[1] And the bird so seldom does – never unless he is foreign, and seldom unless he is a Jew. Do you know Blake's verse 'The only man I ever knew'?[2] In matters of intellect I often feel like that. I try to make people realize that there is a lot to be found out, and that anybody can find it out if they will free their imaginations and live boldly and adventurously; I try to make them feel that thinking is delightful, and that it is not impossible to build up the Cosmos from the very beginning, provided people can forget the authority of parents and guardians and the sages of former times. Reverence for the aims and minds of great men, contempt for their opinions and results, is what I aim at; to make people like them, not imitators of them. Revolution tempered by reverence – do you like that as a watchword?

I find that of all the men that ever lived, Heraclitus is the most intimate to me –

A bientôt.

> Yours affectionately
> Bertrand Russell

Russell's trip to America was the first time he had been anywhere as a visiting celebrity and he found the experience a bit overwhelming. He was kept extremely busy and, although he frequently lamented the lack of time for reflection, the rush of events did help save him from homesickness. He sent back a mixed bag of impressions in his letters: he liked American coffee, but was disgusted by the spittoons; he hated Boston, but enjoyed New York; he was overwhelmed by American hospitality, but found the atmosphere among the Bostonian middle class stuffy. Generally, he seems to have liked Americans who were not too Europeanized, though he was always apt to be offended if they departed too far from European ideals. On the other hand, he always spoke warmly of his Harvard students, though he was critical of their teachers and of the busy, specialized, businesslike temper of American universities. Generally, he thought the Harvard students were better, and the faculty worse, than those in Cambridge.

In fairness, it should be pointed out that the philosophy department at Harvard was in bad shape in 1914. In his *Autobiography* Russell noted with some amusement

1. A caricature of Walt Whitman by the English caricaturist and essayist, Max Beerbohm (1872–1956). It can be found in his collection, *The Poets' Corner* (1904).
2. The four-line poem is from the scattered verses in Blake's notebooks of 1807–9. It is on the painter Henry Fuseli and begins: 'The only man that e'er I knew / Who did not make me almost spew'.

that everyone he was introduced to made him the same speech about the three great losses to philosophy at Harvard: William James had died in 1910; George Santayana had left in 1912; and Josiah Royce had had a stroke, though he was still active in the department. None of these catastrophes, however, seems as important as the unremarked loss of C. I. Lewis, the department's one talented logician, who, as a young man in his late twenties, left Harvard in 1911 to take up a position at the University of California. The impoverished state of the philosophy department at Harvard was not unrelated to Russell's visit. For one thing, they needed someone to do the teaching. But, more important, they hoped that Russell might be persuaded to join the Harvard faculty permanently. Russell, however, had not the slightest intention of doing that.

Russell's time in Boston was made more pleasant by the presence of H. A. Hollond, the Cambridge law don (see letter 186), who was visiting the Harvard Law School. While Russell had a single room in the Colonial Club in Cambridge, Hollond was already established in a suite of rooms in Craigie Hall. Before long, Russell moved into Hollond's suite, for the sake of his company and to save money.

[224]

[Cambridge, Mass.]
Thursday
19 March 1914

My Darling

By this time I have begun to hope for a letter from you, but I have not yet got any letters from Europe. I am *longing* to hear from you – one feels terribly cut off here, not knowing anything of what is happening, not able to see you again for ages. Except when I am busy, I feel rather homesick – and I should feel more so but for Hollond. America produces a type of bore more virulent, I think, than the bore of any other country – they all give one exactly the same information, slowly, inexorably, undeterred by all one's efforts to stop them. On the other hand my pupils, as far as I have been able to judge, are very well prepared, much better (for my work) than at Cambridge; and several of them strike me as really able. They are a motley crew – Greek, Indian, German, Jewish etc. Yesterday morning I had them all in individually to talk to them, and liked most of them a good deal. I am having an evening for them, as I do at Cambridge; but it hasn't occurred yet. The teaching part of my time here is *delightful*; the classes are large and the men seem keen.

I am very busy, with teaching and seeing people, but the climate is invigorating and makes it easy to work. My first Lowell lecture was a failure.

There were 500 people, I was seized with shyness, I felt they couldn't like what I had to say and that it was foolish of them to come; so I didn't speak loud enough, and half couldn't hear. No doubt there will be much fewer tonight.

Last night I met Morton Prince,[1] who wrote about 'Sally'; he attacked psychologists vehemently, in a diatribe lasting about 30 minutes, because they don't take up his methods enough; Münsterberg[2] replied for about 15 minutes – all this at a dinner-party. M. Prince seemed to me genuine, though a bore.

President Lowell,[3] the head of Harvard, is an intolerable person – a deadly bore, hard, efficient, a good man of business, fundamentally contemptuous of learned people because they are not business-like.

I hope to sail on June 6 – I go to get my passage today, and I may have some difficulty, but my date was not fixed before. I *shall* be happy to get away – the people here are mostly dull. Darling I long for news of you – my thoughts are with you always and all my love reaches out to you every moment.

Your
B.

[225]

[Cambridge, Mass.]
Thursday night
19 March 1914

My Darling Darling

I can't possibly say what an *intense* joy it was to get your letter this evening and realize that you still exist in spite of the Atlantic and that some day I shall have escaped from this place and come back to your arms. Yes I remember very vividly the place where we used to sit in the mornings at Lausanne – *every moment* of our time there is minutely fixed in my memory –

1. Morton Prince (1854–1929), American psychologist. He was a Harvard graduate teaching at the Tufts Medical School in Boston. His work in abnormal psychology bears some comparison to Freud's. His most famous book, *The Dissociation of a Personality* (1906), was an early study of a case of split personality identified as 'Sally'. Psychologists at the time debated whether his work was genuine science or not – Russell became convinced that it was.
2. Hugo Münsterberg (1863–1916), American psychologist. He had come to Harvard from Germany in 1892 at the instigation of William James and since 1905 had been director of Harvard's psychological laboratory.
3. Abbott Lawrence Lowell (1856–1943), president of Harvard 1909–33.

I remember all the changing moods from day to day – single conversations almost word for word – it was the most *wonderful* time of my life – not quite so happy as some earlier times, but more wonderful – I suppose nothing nearly so wonderful will ever come to us again. Spiritually we starve and die, and pretend to make up for it by duties – it is all folly and self-deception really. My spirit yearns for you, and I have to lull it to sleep by work and activity.

Today at any rate I have had enough work and activity for any one. One has to shave in the bath-room here, and this morning another man was shaving at the same time, who turned out to be an Austrian economist, who at once began talking about Keynes,[1] Pigou,[2] etc. He had been trying to meet me for some days, but though we were both here, we had missed. We couldn't be *very* stiff with each other when we were both in pyjamas, but we did our best. He has a passion for England, and comes to Exmoor in the summer to hunt the stag.

Then I lectured at 9 and at 11, then, as usual, was introduced to millions of professors, all of whom said 'very pleased to make your acquaintance, Professor Russell'. Then I went into Boston and booked my passage home; I sail from *Montreal*[3] on Saturday June 6, and get home on Sunday 14th. Then I had a peaceful moment while Hollond and I had tea in his apartment, but it was brief, as the Austrian, who was just going, wanted to see me. When he went I had *just* time to go over my Lowell lecture tonight, in the middle of *constant* telephone calls (there is a telephone in my bedroom, which is rapidly driving me mad); when I got back from the lecture, I had to dictate an abstract of it to a reporter, and now at last I am free. The air is good and I sleep well, so I am less tired than I should be at home after such a day.

This is a regular American place – very dirty, disgusting food, windows *never* opened, spittoons distributed tastefully about the floor, hard efficient un-meditative men coming and going, talking in horrible American voices. Nobody here broods or is absent-minded, or has time to hear whispers from another world – except poor old Royce,[4] whom I like, though he is a garrulous old bore. Everybody is kind, many are intelligent along the narrow lines of their work, and most are virtuous – but *none* have any quality. Yes,

1. John Maynard Keynes had made an early impression on economists with his *Indian Currency and Finance* (1913). It is not known who the Austrian economist was.
2. Arthur Cecil Pigou (1877–1959), Professor of Political Economy at Cambridge.
3. Russell added as a footnote: 'I go West for a week's lecturing at the end of May.'
4. Josiah Royce (1855–1916), American idealist philosopher. He taught at Harvard from 1882 until his death. He earned Russell's respect by championing the use of symbolic logic in philosophy.

they 'make much' of me, but it gives me less pleasure than I thought it would.

Inwardly I am feeling very happy – our last days together were so divine. I have the restful feeling of being *inevitably* bound to you, in a way outside the control of will – by a deep tie which is not mere instinct, but something less fluctuating. I *long* for more news of you – how you are, how J[ulian] is, and everything. Goodnight my Darling Darling. All my love is with you – I wish this time were over – but it will pass some day.

Your B.

[226]

[Cambridge, Mass.]
Sunday morning
22 March 1914

My Darling Love

Your little line written in London before you started only reached me yesterday, after your letter from Lausanne.[1] The vagaries of letters from Europe are endless. I hope soon I shall get a letter from Leysin. So far I have only had one lot of letters from England, and they were mostly American letters which arrived too late. There was a telegram asking me to go to San Francisco in June – I was tempted, as they say California is very beautiful, and I feel I should die happier if I had seen the Pacific, like 'stout Cortez'.[2] I dreamed about the Pacific all night – its mere name is romantic to me. But on the whole I have decided against going. It would make me a month later getting to England, or 3 weeks at least, and it doesn't seem worth that.

Dewey (the third pragmatist, with James and Schiller)[3] has been here. I met him at lunch yesterday and then had a walk with him. To my surprise I liked him very much. He has a large slow-moving mind, very empirical and candid, with something of the impassivity and impartiality of a natural force. He and Perry and I had a long argument about 'I' – Dewey saw a

1. Letter 225 was the reply to the letter Ottoline had sent from Lausanne. From Lausanne she went on to Leysin to see Julian who seems to have spent the whole winter at Dr Rolier's clinic.
2. In Keats's sonnet 'On First Looking into Chapman's Homer', line 11.
3. John Dewey (1859–1952), the American philosopher and educator, is commonly thought of as 'the third pragmatist', but Russell's choice of the other two – William James of Harvard and F. C. S. Schiller of Oxford – is idiosyncratic. Most would choose James and Peirce; but Russell at this time evidently knew of Peirce mainly as a logician.

point I was making but Perry didn't – he is a good man but not a very clever one, as the country gentlemen said of Dizzy.[1]

Everything here is dust and ashes except the teaching, but that seems to me so well worth while that it makes up for all the rest. The young men don't seem to me to have the feebleness one associates with Americans, and there are many more of them than I should get at Cambridge. I enjoy the lecturing, and am looking forward to getting to know the young men. But I couldn't *bear* to be here long – it is a soul-destroying atmosphere – no patient solitary meditation, but quick results, efficiency, success – none of the lonely hours away from mankind that go to producing anything of value.

Monday morning. 23 March '14

No letter from Leysin yet – I expect there will be one soon. I long for news of you.

Yesterday Hollond took me to be with the famous Mrs Jack Gardiner, who made B.B's fortune.[2] Her house is arranged like an Italian palace, with a courtyard in the middle, and innumerable bits of actual Italian architecture torn from their setting. She showed us a few beautiful pictures, but not her gallery. She is a little wizened old woman, whose talk is a trifle foolish; but to my surprise I found she does really appreciate the beautiful things she possesses, and has a genuine delight in beauty, so on the whole I liked her. Her dress is not becoming to her years, and scarcely decent. She asked me to the Opera Wednesday.[3]

Then I had one of my pupils to dinner, a youth named Lenzen[4] from California – able, and *very* nice – I quite loved him. Obviously my coming is worth while from the point of view of teaching. – I telegraphed to San Francisco refusing, though not without some hesitations.

1. I think this is a reference to a *Punch* cartoon of Benjamin Disraeli, but I have been unable to identify it.
2. Isabella Steward Gardner (1841–1924), American art collector. Bernard Berenson made a fortune advising her on what to buy. Her house, Fenway Court, was willed to the city of Boston as a public museum.
3. They saw Verdi's *Aida*.
4. Victor Fritz Lenzen (1890–1975) had come to Harvard from California on C. I. Lewis's advice especially to hear Russell. He was not disappointed: 'To the students, Mr Russell was an almost superhuman person,' he wrote in old age. 'I cannot adequately describe the respect, adoration, and even awe which he inspired.' (Lenzen, 'Bertrand Russell at Harvard 1914', *Russell*, 1971.) Lenzen's field was physics and he returned to California to become a professor of physics at Berkeley. But he retained an interest in philosophy of science and he said that his book, *Causality in Natural Science* (1954), developed from an assignment Russell gave him forty years earlier.

Ulster seems very serious – it is hard to make out from the papers here.[1] I hope it will settle down.

Now I am going out to lunch so I must stop. My Darling my thoughts are with you always and I *long* for you – this distance is dreadful. All my love is with you every moment. Goodbye.

Your

    B.

[227]

In the train
Monday, 13 April 1914

My Darling

I can't tell you what a joy your long letter was that reached me on Friday – it was so *real* and so full of intimate things – it was the one in which you wrote about the depression you had had. Yes, I rather think one ought not to wish to be without those moods – they seem to belong with something of value. I do understand them most intimately – I think they are bound up with the real bond between us. But they are very terrible while they last.

I am on my way back from a week-end with the Flexners, which I greatly enjoyed. In this world of strangers, old friends become precious. There was none of that awkwardness with Helen that I felt 2 years ago at Cambridge, and Flexner is wonderful – he has a really beautiful intellect – clear-cut and masterly. New York seemed to me far less repulsive than Boston; it has pride of life, exuberant energy, a new form of self-expression – in many ways it is like the Renaissance. This morning Helen borrowed a friend's motor and took me through the business part of the town, and up to the top of the tallest sky-scraper,[2] which, incredible as it may seem, is really *very* beautiful as architecture – like an immensely magnified Gothic spire. There at last one sees the Americans not imitative, not insincere, achieving the honest temples of Mammon. The building is more than twice the height of St Paul's; from

---

1. A Government of Ireland bill, at last granting Ireland home rule, was before Parliament. It had been passed twice by the Commons but thrown out both times by the Lords, who despite their reform still retained the power to delay legislation. In 1914 it came up for the third and final time: if the Commons passed it this time, the Lords would not be able to block it. The problem now lay outside Parliament, for the Unionists, led by Sir Edward Carson, prepared for armed rebellion with plans for a provisional government if the bill were passed. The Liberals offered some degree of compromise, but also threatened to use the army to crush any revolt. The army, however, mutinied and in March 1914 civil war seemed possible.
2. Probably the Woolworth Building.

the top one has a view which is really marvellous: the whole town, the sea and islands, the inland country ending in hills as blue as Italy. It was the first moment of that sort of pleasure I had had in America. At last the weather has grown fine and fairly warm – till now we have had snow and rain almost continuously – there is hardly a trace of spring yet in the country.

Yes, Americans are *terribly* machine-made. They are only really nice when they are quite untouched by culture and retain the roughness of the people – and then they are generally so *terribly* rough that they are like porcupines. There is not a soul here I should mind never seeing again – except Helen and Lucy, and with them it is merely old times and memories of the glamour of youth.

I am glad about Alys. Mildred (who has been seeing her) gives a similar account. It is amusing that my brother's divorce comforts her.[1] When he heard of my engagement, he said 'We are always bad at choosing wives.'

Politics *were* exciting. How providential that Seely[2] finally went, and what a stroke old Asquith's taking the War Office! Do tell me what the feeling is now that things have settled down. Is there to be an election in the summer? And will the Liberals win if there is? And will the Tories agree on 6 years exclusion of Ulster?[3] It is all terribly interesting.

What you say about Nijinsky is really *terrible*[4] – I can't bear to think of it – it is horrible.

I don't believe you would escape your times of inner tragedy if you had

1. Ottoline had reported that Desmond MacCarthy had been seeing Alys and Logan and reported that Alys was very happy. The story that Alys was 'comforted' by Frank Russell's impending divorce from his second wife also came from MacCarthy, but no explanation was offered as to why she should feel that way.
2. The Secretary of State for War, J. E. B. Seely, had resigned after he'd given written assurances to the general commanding the mutinying British troops that they would not be called upon to suppress an uprising. The Unionists hailed this as a victory, and Asquith, the Prime Minister, had to deny that Seely's promise had the backing of the Cabinet. Seely then resigned, and Asquith took over his duties in the War Office.
3. Asquith's proposed compromise would have allowed the counties of Ulster to decide by plebiscite whether they wished to be excluded from the provisions of the Government of Ireland bill for six years.
4. Vaslav Nijinsky had been dismissed from Diaghilev's Ballets Russes. He tried to form his own company and develop his own repertoire. For this he had been offered an eight-week contract at the Palace Theatre, a variety theatre in London. The new arrangements were not a success, and when Nijinsky fell sick and couldn't perform for three nights, the management exercised its right to end the contract. The costs for properties, music, and salaries fell on Nijinsky. Though Nijinsky was by no means poor, Ottoline worried that he would break down as a result of the anxiety and disappointment. It was the last time he danced in England.

an outlet, though probably they wouldn't come quite so often. One has times of being dried up, and times when any other work in the world seems better worth doing than one's own, and times when *nothing* seems of any value at all, and human life seems a cruel vanity. I don't think these times can be escaped by fortunate circumstances. They are what one pays for being alive sometimes, which most people aren't.

All you say about Dorothy[1] is *most* interesting.

My entourage here is certainly horrid. In America everything is *messy* – table-cloths and knives dirty, no washing possible except in the bath-room, service sloppy and brusque. One's fastidiousness is offended at every moment. But think of my Greek pupil who earns his living as a waiter[2] – and Lenzen, German-Dane from California, who, I hear, writes long long letters about me to a young lady at Bryn Mawr, full (I am told) of passionate devotion.

Hollond loves them all, and I think will probably marry one of them (I don't know who). He is good and nice and kind, but quite without taste or any real distinction of mind. However, he is real and sincere, and I can't help loving his real goodness and unselfishness.

The time crawls on – more than a third of it is gone now. Darling I *shall* be thankful to be with you again. This time is just a long gap – My loving thoughts are with you every moment my Dearest Dearest.

Your

B.

1. This was possibly Dorothy Brett (1883–1977), a painter and member of the Bloomsbury Group. Both Ottoline's and Brett's biographers suggest the two did not meet until a few months later, but the evidence they cite is not conclusive. (See Darroch, *Ottoline*, p. 132; Hignett, *Brett*, p. 59.) Whoever she was, Dorothy, according to Ottoline, was supposed to be engaged to a young man at Oxford and had told Ottoline that Sapphism was very common among young women.
2. Raphael Demos (1892–1968), though of Greek descent, was born in Smyrna, Turkey. He educated himself by reading the books in a small library there. In 1913 he emigrated to the USA to further his education and enrolled at Harvard. He was, as Russell suggests, passionately interested in philosophy and desperately poor (he was in fact a janitor in a student residence, not a waiter). He went on to become a professor of philosophy at Harvard.

[228]

Low Buildings
Bryn Mawr, Pa.
20 April 1914

My Darling

Owing to being away I have no new letters from you since the one you wrote on the 7th telling about Mrs Wedgwood,[1] and the one in which you told of your visit to Downing Street.[2] I shall get letters Wednesday, but I couldn't manage it sooner.

The world seems more cheerful here, because the spring (or rather summer) has come. Thursday night, as I told you, was a snow-storm, on Friday warm, Saturday hot, Sunday broiling. Today there is a warm summer rain – I am sitting on a balcony watching the trees grow green under my eyes. It seems to make the place much more endurable.

I came here on Saturday ($8\frac{1}{2}$ hours from Boston), arriving late in the evening. I enjoy seeing Lucy Donnelly, but the other people here are very dreary – Lucy asked the local philosophers to meet me, but they were *ghastly* people. Lucy has a flat in a building wholly inhabited by the Faculty. She has made it nice with a nice chintz and old books – and many reminiscences of Logan, which are amusing to find here. Miss Thomas, the President, who (as you know) is Alys's cousin, refused to have me asked to give a public lecture here; but at the last moment she changed her mind, and I am coming back tomorrow to talk to their graduate students. I am rather glad, as I didn't wish to be *treated* as a wicked person even if I am one. Lucy tells me that Mariechen and Mrs Worthington[3] tell everywhere most pitiful tales of how Alys harries Logan filling the house with dreary women and children, never allowing him any peace, so that he has to have perpetual appointments with the dentist. Lucy says that Alys's relations here have come to the conclusion

---

1. Josiah Clement Wedgwood (1872–1943), the brother of Russell's Cambridge friend, Ralph Wedgwood (see letter 65), was the MP for Newcastle under Lyme. His first wife had left him in 1913 and Ottoline complained of the lies she was telling about him. His case played some role in reforming the divorce laws, since to get a divorce he had to provide bogus evidence by registering in a hotel with a woman as man and wife. As a result, he was the object of scurrilous attacks during his divorce case (though whether these stemmed from his wife is not clear). Once he had his decree, however, he made a public statement about the type of evidence required by the divorce law, the first time a public figure had done so.
2. Ottoline and Philip had had lunch with Asquith there and discussed the Irish situation.
3. Grace Worthington (see letter 72).

that the fault of the separation cannot be all on my side, in view of what Mariechen and Grace say.

I go from here to Baltimore for one night, then one more night here, then to Princeton where I stay with the widow of Hodder[1] (the man whom I think extraordinarily like Mirabeau).[2] She is a wicked woman, and all my other friends here have quarrelled with her, but I am not obliged to know this officially, and I am devoured with curiosity to see her again. (I saw her last in Paris in 1900, when she was still meeting Hodder on the sly, whenever she could escape from the eye of Miss Thomas.) She is the most perfect example of the sentimentalist I have ever met – she has turned her husband into a stained-glass saint, and avers that she lives only for his memory. She and Miss Thomas were passionate friends in youth, and went to Germany together when no women did such a thing. Miss Thomas has will, without intellect or taste; Mrs Hodder has both intellect and taste, with less will than I have ever seen in any one else. As long as they stuck together, they made each other respectively intelligent and virtuous, and Bryn Mawr prospered. (Mrs Hodder taught literature.) Then Hodder was engaged as a teacher here – after a time a woman turned up who said she was his wife, so he and she lived together. (She wasn't his wife after all, and he hated her.) Meantime he and his present widow had fallen in love with each other. This was the situation when Alys and I stayed with her and Miss Thomas in 1896. One used to hear Miss Thomas's fishwife scolding through any number of doors, hour after hour. After some years of this, he gave out that he had divorced his 'wife', and married the lady in question. Meantime he had wrought havoc with the morals of the girls, being a universally dissipated man – very brilliant, with a first-class philosophic brain. (He held then the general views I hold now but did not hold then.)[3] He smoked 70 cigarettes a day, and drank, and gradually wrecked himself, and died still young. It was a real tragedy, because there was first-rate material in him. He interested me more than any one else I met in America that time except William James.

Lucy is lecturing, which has given me time to write. I enjoy escaping from New England – it seems to me the most loathsome part of America, or perhaps it is only that a change eases the discomfort.

On Friday I spoke on Suffrage to a crowd of fashionable ladies in a Boston

1. See letter 141.
2. Honoré Gabriel Riqueti, Comte de Mirabeau (1749–91), French revolutionary and statesman. He led a dissolute life until the revolution of 1789 when he emerged as the popular leader of the Constituent Assembly.
3. Russell refers to his philosophical views, not his views on dissipation: Hodder was a realist at the time Russell was an idealist.

drawing-room – a futile proceeding. Mrs Jack[1] is the only woman I have met here who is not genteel – they all seem as if they ought to be governesses. Friday I dined with the Münsterbergs – *awful* people – and all their guests *horrors*. The ugliness of the faces along the table made me almost unable to eat – fat, stupid, complacent, without any redeeming trait of any sort or kind. I find myself *thirsting* for beauty to rest the eye – any kind of visible beauty. I did not know how much I should miss it. It makes me parched and dry. As I think of Cambridge Mass., I find I have an intimate horror of every corner of the place – it all screams at one, like living always with the screech of a railway-engine. Thank heaven half of it is over. – Goodbye my Darling. I feel more every moment how near you are to my spirit, and how empty the world would be without you. My deep deep love is with you always.

Your B.

I am glad about your health, but please tell me more.

[229]

503 Craigie Hall [Harvard]
11 May 1914

My dear Lucy

Ever since I got your letter I have been meaning to answer it – but here, when I get leisure, the sheer desire to do nothing overpowers me. I have by a little idleness got over the fit of spleen that came from fatigue after my trip. And my Greek pupil Demos, with whom I went a walk the other day, turned out to be so full of courage and of passion for philosophy that he really brightened the world for me. The spectacle of courage and high passion is the most consoling that life affords.

What you tell me of Mr Connor[2] pleases me very much – it is never a matter of indifference to me to get praise from people who are in earnest. I am amused that Miss Scott[3] considers it your fault that she was ill, but it is quite according to the rules that she should. It is the sort of thing that Spinoza would demonstrate by the geometrical method.

I have just been spending Sunday in the country at a lovely place with

1. Mrs Gardner.
2. A mathematician at Bryn Mawr who had been to Russell's talk there.
3. Another teacher at Bryn Mawr. She had missed Russell's talk through illness and complained about it to Lucy Donnelly as if it were her fault.

one of the philosophy instructors named Fuller,[1] an Oxfordized Harvardian, cultivated, full of the classics, talking as like an Englishman as he can, full of good nature, but feeble – quite without the ferocity that is needed to redeem culture. One of my pupils, named Eliot,[2] was there too – a very similar type, proficient in Plato, intimate with French literature from Villon[3] to Vildrach,[4] very capable of a certain exquisiteness of appreciation, but lacking in the crude insistent passion that one must have in order to achieve anything. However, he is the only pupil of that sort that I have; all the others are vigorous intelligent barbarians.

There seems to me every reason to expect that we shall manage to meet abroad in the summer. If the trip down the Dalmatian coast comes off, I should love it; but if not, we will manage something else.

Have you read the new Anatole France?[5] It contains one amusing scene, but is too much a repetition of previous books. The new edition of Blake by the Clarendon Press is worth looking at – it contains new things of some interest.[6]

Yours affectionately
Bertrand Russell

At length Russell's time at Harvard came to an end, and on Tuesday, 26 May, he gave his last two lectures and boarded *The Twentieth Century* express to carry him overnight to Chicago, the first stop on his lecture tour in the Midwest. To judge from his letters the leave-taking could not come too soon, but in the end he seems to have felt some genuine affection for the philosophers who had been his colleagues and students for the last two months.

1. Benjamin Apthorp Fuller (1879–1956), a historian of philosophy. Russell had been reading his book *The Problem of Evil in Plotinus* (1912).
2. The poet T. S. Eliot (1888–1965), then a teaching assistant at Harvard. Despite his lack of passion, he didn't do too badly. Eliot wrote a poem, 'Mr Apollinax', about Russell's visit.
3. François Villon, fifteenth-century poet.
4. Charles Vildrac (1882–1971), poet and dramatist.
5. Probably *La Révolte des anges* (1914), a satirical novel in which a group of angels, bored with heaven, try to amuse themselves in modern Paris and end up joining the Devil.
6. *The Poetical Works of William Blake* (ed. John Sampson, 1913). For Russell the most important of the newly published pieces was book 1 of *The French Revolution*, a long narrative poem of 1791 (the remaining six books are lost). It was an early example of Blake's 'prophetic' style and the most overtly political of all his poems.

[230]

In train to Chicago
Tuesday, 26 May 1914

My Darling

At last I have a breathing-space, until I get to Chicago tomorrow morning. I got a letter from you on Saturday, written when you had a howling cold – it was a dear letter though you seemed to think it wasn't. I have had my time filled, pleasantly, with all the people I had not seen enough of before. Saturday I went a long walk with Coolidge,[1] a mathematician who loves me because I recommended his book to the Clarendon Press; then I dined with the Perrys, who are both very nice people. I have persuaded Perry, and he has persuaded the other 'six realists', that logic is *the* important thing, and they are all going to try and learn it. That is one of the things I hoped to achieve here, so I am glad it has happened. Sunday Perry and I went off to the sea-side for the day (though Boston is on the sea, I had never been to the shore before) – we had a long peaceful day, talking, sitting on rocks smoking, and occasionally discussing philosophy amicably. The sea is much the same as in Europe, so it soothed my home-sickness a little. Yesterday Hollond and I went off for the day to see Mrs Fiske Warren[2] at a country place about 30 miles out. I had thought I did not want to see her (did you meet her at Oxford when she was sitting at the feet of Schiller and J. A. Smith?),[3] and had succeeded until then in refusing her invitations, but at last it became impossible, and to my surprise I enjoyed the day immensely. She seemed to me sincere, which I had not supposed before, and she is pathetically lonely after having got used to Europe (she is kept at home by some ear-trouble which Europe is bad for). – She has a lovely daughter, to whom Hollond devoted himself with gusto, though his flame is another Miss Warren (no relation). She also has a mother, who is all right except on re-incarnation. I liked Mrs Warren a good deal, and she was quite pathetically glad of a chance to talk about things that don't interest people here – philosophy, Blake, Chinese Art, etc. etc. They motored us back after dinner and then I had to pack and prepare my 9 o'clock lecture for this morning. I had two lectures

1. Julian Lowell Coolidge (1873–1954). The book was *The Elements of Non-Euclidean Geometry* (1909).
2. Gretchen Warren (née Osgood), wife of Fiske Warren (1862–1938), a Boston paper manufacturer and a single-tax reformer.
3. John Alexander Smith (1863–1939), an Oxford idealist philosopher. He became Waynflete Professor of Moral and Metaphysical Philosophy at Oxford. Russell had a distinctly low opinion of him.

this morning and got off by a 12.30 train – everybody *very* nice to me at the end. If I had stayed much longer I should have begun to feel it mean to desert them – they seem so grateful for the sort of thing I try to give, and so genuinely anxious to do their very best. There really is hope for the future here I think, as soon as the openings in business grow less good. I feel almost like a missionary who has converted a tribe of cannibals, and then left them to be eaten by their unrepentant neighbours.

This train is the grandest in America – it gets me to Chicago at 9.45 tomorrow morning.

It is hot at last – 87 in the train, and more outside. I rather like it. I am glad to see Home Rule is through,[1] without dramatic disaster so far. Is there to be a row between Asquith and Redmond[2] about the amending bill?

I hope your cold got better soon. Dearest, when you get this I shall be on the Atlantic and nearly home. It will be like coming to life again to be with you – this time has been a sort of long sleep with moments of uneasy waking. We will be *very* happy, won't we? Goodbye my dear dear love – I send you a thousand kisses and all my heart.

Your

B.

To Lucy Donnelly he gave a more diplomatic account of his stay in Harvard than the ones he had sent to Ottoline.

1. The Government of Ireland bill had now passed the Commons for the third time and the Lords were busy amending it out of existence. Though the Commons could ignore the Lords' amendments, Russell was overly optimistic about the chances for home rule. In this battle between the military and Parliament, the military won and the bill never became law. The First World War conveniently allowed the Liberals to drop the issue.
2. John Redmond, the leader of the Irish Nationalists. The Amending bill was the legislation which allowed the six years' exclusion of Ulster. Under the terms of the Parliament Act which now governed the relations between Commons and Lords, the Commons had to pass an Act unamended three times before the Lords were obliged to pass it. Hence the need for separate legislation to embody Asquith's compromises.

[231]

[In the train]¹
26 May 1914

My dear Lucy

Your letter duly arrived before I started for unknown addresses in the West. This morning I gave two lectures, and left Boston at 12.30 – everybody at Harvard has been amazingly nice to me – some of the philosophy department might well have been jealous or in some way ungenerous, but none were. And I liked the students to the last. On the whole, I think *very* well of what I have seen of Harvard. The only real objections to my mind are those it shares with all other universities here – the institution of the President and the Board of Overseers. The fact that universities are not self-governing makes the career of a teacher less attractive and respected than with us.

I quite agree with all you say about 'culture' – I do not like having to live among people who are without it, but I want it to be instinctive, not pedantic. I have got the new Blake, and read *The French Revolution* at once with the greatest interest. How strange that no one published it before. You can keep the mysticism and logic for ever.² I am glad you liked it.

My time has been terribly full, and will be in Chicago and Wisconsin, so train journeys are my only time for writing. My final impression of Harvard was good enough to moderate my future diatribes on U.S.

Do send a line to my Ship – *Megantic*, leaving Montreal daybreak June 6. Then I can answer on the ship, to Brown Shipley – if only Columbus had gone there, how much trouble he would have saved himself. Goodbye till we meet in the summer. This is a mere scrawl, but I am tired and hot.

Ever yours affectionately
Bertrand Russell

In Chicago Russell stayed with Dr E. Clark Dudley (1850–1928), an eminent surgeon and professor of gynaecology at Northwestern University. The invitation to stay there came from Helen Dudley, one of his daughters. Russell had met Helen Dudley at Bagley Wood some years before. She had studied at Bryn Mawr and then went

1. Written on Pullman Company letterhead.
2. Probably a typescript of 'Mysticism and Logic'; Helen Flexner had sent it to her. It was written during his burst of writing the previous January as a popular lecture for American audiences. He read it twice at Cambridge before he left and at least three times in the USA: at Greenwich, Conn., Wellesley College, Mass., and Madison, Wis.

on to Oxford to study Greek with Gilbert Murray, bringing with her a letter of introduction to Bertie and Alys from her teachers at Bryn Mawr.

After two days in Chicago, he was in the train once more, travelling further west to Madison, Wisconsin.

[232]

In the train, Chicago to Madison
Friday, 29 May 1914

My Darling

Your letter to Chicago reached me yesterday and I was very glad to get it. I am afraid this letter will probably be too late for tomorrow's mail but I hadn't one moment to spare there – Dr Dudley's house is 10 miles from the university so what with going and coming and luncheons and dinners I had hardly time to turn round.

I am very sorry P[hilip] is not well – I hope you are not really anxious. I wish I had seen Julian she must have been quite lovely.[1]

It was very hot in Chicago, and the natives complained of it but I rather liked it. Chicago itself rather pleased me – being on the lake makes the situation fine, and there is the same sense of bursting life as in New York – almost more so. The Dudleys turned out to be nice people – the father is a New Englander who has become a great Surgeon after appalling struggles with poverty in his youth – the mother is pleasant, and there are a number of daughters[2] who are civilized without being artificial and pedantic like eastern Americans. The one whom I had known at Oxford has developed a good deal since I knew her – she has written some poetry which is rather immature but has a really poignant quality – I liked her very much indeed. Probably I shall see her again as she is very likely to be coming to Europe for the winter. None of the people I saw in Chicago had the insincerity and high moral tone one associates with America – I expect the West really is better in that respect. I liked E. H. Moore,[3] the chief mathematician at the University, *very* much – and Dewey[4] comes from Chicago. I had seen Moore before, at Rome and at Cambridge, and had liked him then.

1. Ottoline had described how she had dressed up for her birthday party.
2. There were four daughters and a son.
3. Eliakim Hastings Moore (1862–1932), professor of mathematics at the University of Chicago 1892–1931, and a key figure in the American Mathematical Society.
4. Russell had seen Dewey several times during his visit and always spoke warmly of him. 'Dewey ... again impressed me very greatly, both as a philosopher and as a lovable man,' he had told Ottoline on 24 April. Their later relations would be more controversial.

It is exhilarating to feel the time here so nearly over, it makes me like everybody better than when I had months ahead of me. I will write once again, from Ann Arbor, and that will be the last letter. If you are away for the week-end of June 14, will you leave your address for telegrams, as I will telegraph when I know when I am likely to arrive. I dare say it won't be till Monday 15th.

It is rather a blow that Alys and Logan are coming to London. I suppose she no longer minds the prospect of meeting me, but it will be an anxiety.

I am very tired, longing to be done with lecturing and meeting new people – mercifully I have only three more lectures now. They are paying me £60 for this western trip, so I felt bound to do it – and it is certainly interesting seeing new places, but it will be more of a pleasure in retrospect than at the moment.

How interesting about Parnell – I must certainly read it.[1]

Will you send a line to the ship (*Megantic*) at Liverpool, to greet me when I land? It will be *heaven* to be together again – Goodbye my Darling. My love is with you always.

   Your
   B.

Part of the reason for Russell's cheerfulness in Chicago was the pleasure he'd taken in Helen Dudley's company. She was then twenty-eight and struggling to become a writer. She had met him at the station and Russell wrote in his *Autobiography* (vol. I, p. 213) that he 'at once felt more at home with her than I had with anybody else that I had met in America. I found that she wrote rather good poetry, and that her feeling for literature was remarkable and unusual.' She was lonely in Chicago and yearned for access to a literary and less provincial world. Russell found her 'passionate, poetic, and strange'.

On his way back from Madison, Russell spent a second night at the Dudleys' home and this night he spent with Helen, while one of her sisters mounted guard outside the door. This was an 'adventure' of the sort that Bertie and Ottoline had often discussed hypothetically. But it had some serious ramifications, for Bertie and

1. Charles Stewart Parnell (1846–91), the Irish nationalist leader. His political career ended in scandal in 1889 when William O'Shea sought a divorce from his wife, Katherine, on grounds that she had committed adultery with Parnell. No defence was offered and Parnell and Mrs O'Shea got married shortly after the divorce was granted. In 1914 Katherine O'Shea brought out a biography of Parnell, *Charles Stewart Parnell, His Love Story and Political Life* (2 vols.), which included his letters to her. Ottoline had told Bertie of its publication.

Helen agreed that she should follow him to England where they would live together and even get married if Bertie could obtain a divorce. Bertie took the first opportunity to inform Ottoline of this remarkable development.

[233]

In the train between Chicago and Ann Arbor
1 June 1914

My Darling

This is the last letter before I sail – thank heaven. I am *longing* to be with you again my Dearest.

When I started, I assured you I should not have any adventures here, but I have had one, a rather important one, though not one that strikes me as in any way regrettable. The more I saw of Helen Dudley, and the more I read of her work, the more remarkable she seemed. Yesterday she and I spent a long day in the woods together and I found that I care for her a great deal – not with the same intensity or passion as I feel for you, but still very seriously. I told her I cared for some one else with whom I would not break, but she did not mind that. It ended by our spending the night together – and she will come to England as soon as she can – probably in September or late August. I do not want you to think that this will make the very *smallest* difference in my feeling towards you, beyond removing the irritation of unsatisfied instinct. I suppose it must give you some pain, but I hope not very much if I can make you believe it is all right, and that she is not the usual type of American. The whole family are extraordinarily nice people. The parents have the morals of their generation, and will suffer greatly if it becomes necessary for them to know – but her sisters all sympathized (seeing something was going on), and it was by the active connivance of a married sister that we got time alone yesterday. I am bringing a play of hers with me, which will tell you more about her than my description.

She is 28 – not good looking – her mouth, and still more her nose, very ugly – her eyes an unusual brown, Chinese-shaped, very interesting – her figure good. Her face shows great intensity of feeling and a good deal of suffering. She is very passionate, very full of creative impulse, *absolutely* sincere, and without a hint of sentimentalism. I found her withering, like a flower in drought, for want of love and understanding and friends who cared for the sort of thing that makes her work. The impulse to foster creativeness was first aroused, and the rest followed. She cares for me, as far as I can judge, up to the full limit of a generous and lonely spirit. I am sure my judgment of her is right, and not merely because I have been away from those I care for. The only really doubtful question in my mind is whether to keep the matter secret or not. For the moment of course it must be secret.

My Darling please do not think that this means *any* lessening of my love to you, and I do not see why it should affect our relations. I do mind most intensely giving you pain, I do indeed. I long to be with you and to make you *feel* that my love is absolutely undiminished. The impulse that came over me was like the impulse to rescue a drowning person, and I am *sure* I was right to follow it. And now Darling goodbye until we meet – and do not let this prevent the happiness of meeting if you can help it. My deepest most intense devotion is with you always.

Your
B.

Bertie's letter to Ottoline telling her about Helen crossed in the post with the letter Ottoline sent to Liverpool to greet him on his return. In that letter, written on 11 June, she told him that she wanted their relations henceforth to be platonic. The next day she had received his letter about Helen and wrote again. In this letter she said that she hoped he would be happy with Helen and that they would be able to live openly together. However, she thought it best if she did not see Bertie again because she didn't want to come between him and Helen, though she would still like to write to him. This was not the outcome Bertie had anticipated, but his reply to it was probably not what Ottoline anticipated either. For he seemed only mildly disappointed about the termination of their meetings and even expressed some doubts as to whether he would be able to write to her for a while once Helen had arrived.

[234]

Russell Chambers
Sunday
[14 June 1914]

My Darling
Your letter to Liverpool reached me this morning and now I have your letter about Helen Dudley. I am very unhappy in your suffering – I feel you are suffering very much. I am afraid my letter telling you was horrible – I need your forgiveness and I cannot help a deep sense of shame. But it was not a light impulse that took me to her. I have had time to think it over in solitude, and I know it is a very real and serious thing. I felt some longer

trial of each other was necessary before taking any open step, but I should certainly want it to be public as soon as we felt sure – the hesitation has been on my side, because I have been rather troubled by the responsibility, and also by the loss of my teaching, which is a serious matter.

It had not occurred to me that you would think it better not to meet. I should not for one moment have thought you were *angry*.[1] You say it is better for *both* our sakes. I do not know what is best, but I cannot ask you to see me if you think it better not. The whole world seems a maze of pain. The sea the last two days was beautiful beyond belief, with the rare gentleness of fierce things. I feel I do wrong to offer to any one a soul so ringed round with a fire of pain – but in happy moods I forget. Dearest, I shall never thrust you out of my heart – there is something, beyond passion, absolutely and forever indestructible in what you give me. You must decide everything as you think right, but it cannot be right that we should lose each other altogether. For the present, let us at least write – but I believe in the first times with her I might find it hard to write. Afterwards, if any sort of friendship between you and her were possible, it would be good – but those things are difficult.

At present I am harassed by practical problems – when and how to leave Trinity – the necessity of telling the Whiteheads, which I dread doing more than I can say. I don't think you need fear that you would come between – the impulse is too deep and strong for that. – I am crushed to earth by your goodness, my Darling. Forgive this letter – I can't write differently.

  Your
    B.

She may come in August but it is still uncertain.

Had this plan been kept to things might have run a lot more smoothly. But by now Ottoline was having second thoughts about giving up the meetings and in notes written on 14 and 15 June told him that she was longing for a meeting even though she thought it weak to do so. Bertie was unable to resist this and on 15 and 16 June she visited him at his flat. The outcome now was even less what he had anticipated than her earlier decision not to meet.

1. Ottoline had assured him she was not.

[235]

[Russell Chambers]
Tuesday night
16 June 1914

My Darling Love

All day I have felt so strangely happy and light-hearted – it was so *divine* while you were here, my Dearest. I did not in the least foresee that it would be as it was. My Heart, I cannot lose you – it was that that made the pain, though you thought the pain was 'worked up' – but for the moment I doubted if I had any right to try and keep you – but I really have. As soon as I feel that I need not lose you, I begin to feel more at ease about the other – but if it meant losing you, it would not be a success. I really don't think it is unduly selfish towards her.

It is so *divine* when I cease to *fear* you. Yesterday I was in an agony of fear the first half of the time – today it all seemed easy and natural. I wonder why it is so often impossible for us to be easy with each other – it is the conflict of instincts I suppose.

Don't think I want or intended to go against what you wrote in your letter to Liverpool – at the moment the impulse was overwhelming, but it was quite unforeseen, at least on my side. Dearest I shall never care for any one else with the poignant intensity with which I love you – but I suppose a feeling like that is hardly made for daily life – it seems too wild and fierce. And when I try to tame it, I cannot express anything.

Your lovely flowers are *such* a joy my Darling. I didn't half thank you enough for them, but I was so taken up with you that I couldn't really attend to them.

Was it next Tuesday you said? Lady Sheffield[1] has asked me to dinner on Thursday 25th, I suppose to meet Cyril Asquith;[2] so if you haven't yet written to ask him, there is no need – not that I should dislike meeting him first at Bedford Square, but we should both be shy.

Goodnight my Darling Darling. My heart is filled with love to you.

Your

B.

Let me know what time to come please.

1. Probably Mary Stanley, the wife of Russell's uncle Lyulph Stanley, who was fourth Baron Sheffield.
2. The son of Herbert Asquith, the Prime Minister.

It seemed as though their relationship was transformed. Their meetings went smoothly (with Ottoline for once taking the initiative in suggesting them), her letters were full of affection, sexual relations were resumed, things between them were better than at any time in the last two years. It was ironical that just as Bertie seemed in prospect of achieving with another woman the sort of day-to-day happiness that had eluded him with Ottoline, Ottoline began to offer him some of the things that previously she had refused. The two developments were not, of course, unconnected; though it would be wrong to jump to the conclusion that it was jealousy *alone* that galvanized Ottoline into action. She had long wanted a less demanding relationship with Bertie and, now that his thoughts were at least partly taken up with Helen, she had got one. Without the pressure of Bertie's most insistent and desperate emotions, she quite likely found it easier to be a congenial lover. There was also the matter of Bertie's breath. In his *Autobiography* he tells us that he had been suffering from pyorrhoea, which made his breath offensive and caused problems in his relations with Ottoline. (The matter is alluded to discreetly in their correspondence.) In America Bertie had been to see a dentist and the pyorrhoea was now cured. But the imminent arrival of Helen Dudley was probably the major factor. The possibility of losing Bertie completely seemed real and Ottoline, who had felt lonely in February when Bertie's fanatical ardour began to cool, would doubtless have felt lonelier if it had been transferred to Helen.

In his *Autobiography* Russell could describe these events with some advantages of hindsight:

> Ottoline could still, when she chose, be a lover so delightful that to leave her seemed impossible, but for a long time past she had seldom been at her best with me. I returned to England in June, and found her in London. We took to going to Burnham Beeches every Tuesday for the day. . . . Ottoline was at her best. (Vol. I, p. 213)

In her letters, at any rate, Ottoline did not demand that Bertie choose between Helen and herself. But Bertie himself felt obliged to choose and, given his promises to Helen and his terrible desire to continue with Ottoline as long as any barely tolerable relationship with her seemed possible, it was not an easy choice. Ottoline's new mood produced a reappraisal of Helen. Bertie found himself 'less fond' of her than he had 'tried to persuade' himself that he was; he had even overestimated her writings (to Ottoline, 22 June). He began to hope that she might not come or that she would come and quickly lose interest.

[236]

[Trinity College]
23 June 1914
Tuesday night

My Darling

The whole day till now I have been seeing people – Karin, Margaret,[1]
Veblen,[2] my brother – and all the time I have been thinking. The chief thing
I have been thinking about is how to make you understand what is your
importance to me – but I suppose it is useless to try to make you understand
that at this date. However, I will try.

The root of the whole thing is loneliness. I have a kind of physical
loneliness, which almost anybody can more or less relieve, but which would
only be fully relieved by a wife and children. Beyond that, I have a very
intense and terrible spiritual loneliness. You and the woman I cared for many
years ago[3] are the only two human beings who have touched that in
any way. I have dreamed of the combination of spiritual and physical
companionship, and if I had had the good fortune to find it, I could have
become something better than I ever shall be. But both in your case and in
the other, physical instinct was left unsatisfied, and its insistence interfered
with the real spiritual companionship, until it had been got under. I wish I
could explain to you what I feel about spiritual companionship. Most people,
even when I am very fond of them, remain external to me. Alys, even when
I was most in love with her, remained outside my inner life. H[elen] D[udley]
would never touch it. What I get from most of the people I like to be with
is escape from the inner life, which is too painful to be endured continuously.
But what I get from you is an intensification of it, with a transmutation of
the pain into beauty and wonder. But owing to the weakness of your physical
instinct I fail to get this as long as I am starved physically. If you could
believe it, I could really have a much better relation with you (if your nature
permits it) if I were not dependent wholly on you for what it is hard for
you to give. If H.D. finds my keeping up with you intolerable, I shall part
from her. I am sure this is right, and that anything else would lead to an
unspeakable tragedy.

Physical instinct, at least in me, is not satisfied by the physical act alone,
but cries out for constant companionship, especially in the night.

1. Margaret Llewelyn Davies.
2. Oswald Veblen (1881–1960), a professor of mathematics at Princeton then visiting
Cambridge.
3. This was probably Evelyn Whitehead. See letter 212.

With most people, the basis of my relationship is sympathy – by living in their world, I escape for a time from mine. But with you it is different – that is why I am not sympathetic with you. Except where sex comes in, I do really live a very unselfish life – much more so than you know. But I do find sex too strong for me.

Dearest *please* don't despair or think that you have grown unimportant to me. Thwarted instinct makes everything contorted and difficult, but indeed if the tie between us were severed it would be spiritual death to me. Oh my Ottoline, do please believe this. And if we are apart for a time, do please believe that it is *only* for a time, and that *nothing* can *ever* take your place in my spirit. You don't know in the least what you are to me. There has been so much constraint in our relations for two years now that I find it hard to tell you what you are to me – the need of self-control paralyses expression. I am not asking you to see me now more than is for your happiness – that is not the important thing. The important thing is that you should let me still live in your spirit, and that you should not imagine you will ever become unimportant to me. And *please* try not to think I am insincere – it puzzles me and makes me doubt what is most true. I have written this letter in a cold precise way, in hopes of making you believe me, and because I want to be quite exact. Dearest I *need* you most profoundly and unalterably. Goodnight my loved one. I feel you a comrade in difficult battle, and without you it would be very hard.

Your B.

Ottoline's only comment on this was that she was relieved he had got things clear in his mind. But this, despite his 'cold exact' statement, was far from the case. At this time it would still have been possible to write to Helen and tell her not to come. But Bertie was still taking at face value Ottoline's disavowal of jealousy. If Helen could give him the physical satisfaction and companionship he longed for, perhaps this would make it easier to continue a spiritual relationship with Ottoline. What Helen might feel about all this was not known and it was rapidly becoming too late to find out, because she was now set to travel to England with her father early in August.

[237]

[Trinity College]
11 July 1914
Saturday night

My Darling

This can't go till tomorrow night, but I want to write *now*. It is because of what you said about not foreseeing the future. A great deal of the future is dark to me, but not what concerns my feelings towards you. I *know*, without any doubt, that you have, now and always, more *importance* for me than anybody else can have. This will not cease; and if anything destroys your love for me, or makes it impossible for you to show it, I shall never get over the sorrow of it. I know now that it is absolutely necessary for me to have a tolerable life apart from you, and it is necessary for the happiness of our love; and this will mean that there will be times when I shall seem absorbed elsewhere. But they will be like the times when I don't think about work, which don't mean that I am tired of philosophy. I know that when H.D. first comes, if I go away with her, it may *seem* for the moment as if you had grown less important to me; but I know that will only be a superficial appearance, and won't even *seem* so when I see you again. I know too that there is no chance of any success in my relations with her unless you and I can remain as we are. If it makes any estrangement between you and me, I shall infallibly feel a grudge against her.

That is one reason for not coming quickly to any decision about her, because I should have to break with her if she turned out to be incompatible with you.

You were wondering at my being so happy. It is partly that I have found a way of not asking too much of you, partly that I don't have to face the horror of holidays – last summer with Sanger, and the days in Rome after you were gone, were so dreadful that the mere prospect of such times had become a nightmare. If I could always work, things would have been bearable, but holidays were necessary and yet a torture. Partly too I am happy merely from the feeling of good work done – my happiness depends enormously on how my work has been going.

It is all quite simple really: I love you as I shall never love any one else, but the situation is full of pain, and only endurable by finding ways of distracting my thoughts from you when you are absent. Work is enough when I am working, but I can't always work, and if I have no other distraction I am tempted to work too much, which spoils the work. What I do want you to believe and realize is that there is no *inward* unfaithfulness –

there is merely a need of some way of making the situation bearable. I used to hope I could do it by discipline but *I* can't; I think this way I can, if *you* can bear it. And I feel you can bear it if you really *understand* it. You have been generous about it almost beyond belief, but I want you really to understand too, because I think then I won't be so painful to you.

I *am* worried at times, terribly; what worries me is the doubt whether I can give H.D. enough affection to make her life bearable. I certainly cannot if I depend upon her alone, but I think if I still have you I can. She loves me very intensely and passionately – I have towards her a great tenderness, and a great desire to develop her best. But I feel no passion, and if she came to care for some one else that seemed capable of helping her, I should be glad – not only reasonably, but with all my instincts. All that is good in my feeling for her is like the feeling I have for my pupils – a mixture of philanthropy and desire for production – not pity, but also not passionate love. What is selfish in my feeling is not passion, but longing for companionship – which many others could satisfy, but which I could only indulge with a good conscience where I can be of real use, as I can in this case if I can avoid tragedy; and to avoid tragedy the one and only thing necessary is to keep inwardly happy. It is all rather complicated. I wonder if I have made it clear. I know that every word I have written is *exact* truth the bottom truth, without any muddle.

Dearest I cannot tell you the agony and sharp stab of my love for you – it is really a great and terrible thing – do please *believe* that it is always almost more than I can live with, a scorching flame lighting up all the splendour and terror of the world – and if I find ways of not being utterly burnt up, it is not for want of love – Goodnight my loved one, my Ottoline, you cannot know how my soul lives in you.

[238]

In the train[1]
29 July 1914
Wednesday morning

My Darling Love
I cannot tell you how full of happiness I feel or what complete joy it is now when we are together. It all seems so easy and natural there is not a trace of the constraint which had grown up. And it is such a relief to find oneself thinking and talking of all sorts of things, instead of being always

1. Bertie was travelling back from London to Cambridge.

preoccupied with our relations to each other. I thought at first it was due to H.D. but I don't think so now. I think it is much more due to my teeth being all right. However, I don't think H.D. will do any harm between you and me, and I think her existence is in a way a safeguard for the future. Otherwise I feel I might in time again begin to demand too much. Now, whatever happens, I don't believe I shall. And all the things you didn't like in me will not show themselves again if things work out as I expect. All the insistence and vehemence of physical desire ceases when there is response – it takes its place, and no longer blots out the horizon. And it is infinitely easier to bear not seeing more of you when we are so perfectly happy while we are together. For the first time since our difficulties more than two years ago, I feel really happy inwardly, not merely happy at moments when I can forget painful things. I am really regretful that H.D. will interfere with our day the week after next. But I know in the long run it is a good thing that it should sometimes be owing to me that we don't meet.

I think as things will not be open with H.D. it is sure to be temporary. She will dislike the situation, and come to prefer some one else. I hope so.

The war and risk of war is quite awful. I try not to realize it – the horror of it is too great. As regards home politics I suppose it may make things easier.

Now we are arriving. Goodbye my Darling. I cannot tell you how deeply and unalterably I love you or how profoundly you make me happy. I do feel that you give me what I most long for and what no one else I have ever known could give me.

I *loved* our moment this morning.

    Your

      B.

Russell's world had become strangely smaller since his affair with Ottoline began. He still kept up with political events and remained in touch with numerous people who were active in them. Yet, since the advent of Ottoline, politics had not been at the centre of his attention. He was still involved in the campaign for women's suffrage, though no longer very actively as he had been from 1906 to 1911. The period from 1910 to 1914 was one of the most dramatic in British political life. The reform of the Lords, the introduction of National Insurance, the use of the strike as a political weapon by the working class, the Irish crisis, were all events which were mentioned only cursorily in his correspondence, though, before Ottoline, they might have absorbed his entire attention. Even technical philosophy had had to fight for his attention over the last four years.

Reading his letters over this period one has the eerie feeling that war was creeping up unnoticed even on someone as attentive and well-informed as Russell. It is true that in earlier letters there had been occasional remarks about the danger of war with Germany, but this was a danger, Russell thought, that was contingent upon a Conservative victory at the next election. That the Liberals would take the country to war with Germany was something he hadn't considered remotely likely until, as in the previous letter, he suddenly realized how real the danger was.

The European situation by the end of July 1914 was very serious indeed. On 28 June Franz-Ferdinand, the heir-apparent to the Austro-Hungarian throne, had been assassinated by Serbian nationalists at Sarajevo, the capital of Bosnia, a Serbian province annexed by Austria–Hungary. On 23 July Austria–Hungary delivered a forty-eight-hour ultimatum to Serbia which would have meant in effect that Serbia ceased to exist as an independent country. Serbia capitulated to the ultimatum except on two points which it wished to put to international arbitration. Austria–Hungary would not allow any compromise and mobilized its armies. At this stage all the European powers, bound to each other by mutual defence treaties, found themselves drawn into the dispute. Germany was obliged to stand behind Austria–Hungary; and on 30 July Russia mobilized in defence of Serbia. Germany demanded that the Russian mobilization be stopped. When it was not, Germany declared war on Russia on 2 August. By this time, events were out of political control and were being determined by military priorities. German war plans made it necessary for them to fight France before they could fight Russia. So on 3 August Germany declared war on France, and the next day launched an attack on France through Belgium. At midnight, Britain, bound by a secret defence treaty to France, declared war on Germany. For Russell the realization of these events was like waking from sleep to nightmare.

Meanwhile, as inexorably as the European armies were taking the world to war, Helen Dudley was setting sail from New York. It seems, from the next letter, that Bertie had made some attempt to warn her about the change in his relations with Ottoline. His letters to her do not seem to have survived, so we do not know what he told her. Whatever warning was sent, she did not heed it.

[239]

My Darling

I was glad of your telegram. I will come up tomorrow afternoon. Will you send a note to the flat to let me know what time you are free.

I suppose this is the greatest misfortune to mankind since the Napoleonic wars. It is strange how it obliterates things – a week ago at the Hammonds',[1] life seemed happy and gay – it seems to belong to another world, a dim dream of long ago. I am fixing some things in my mind, which I forgot during the Boer War: not to hate anyone, not to apportion praise and blame, not to let instinct dominate. The force that in the long run makes for peace and all other good things is Reason, the power of thinking against instinct.

I find Goldie was disgusted with Roger.[2]

The little thought I can spare from public events is spent worrying about H.D. She has argued herself back into happiness and the belief that all will turn out as she wishes. I feel now an absolute blank indifference to her, except as one little atom of the mass of humanity. I simply *cannot* act as I had intended. I fear I shall break her heart – but the whole affair is trivial on my side, and just now I cannot play at things. If I had even the faintest hope that she could understand, I might come to care for her seriously; but I know she will think it monstrous to forget her because of public things. This day week I must face her. Perhaps by then my mood will have changed. Obviously one will have to grow reckless in order to endure life.

I wonder what became of the Conrads.[3] They were going to a place exactly on the frontier between Russia and Austria.

---

1. John Lawrence and Barbara Hammond, British historians. They had recently published the first volume of their important trilogy on working-class life from 1760 to 1832, *The Village Labourer* (1911); the other volumes were *The Town Labourer* (1917) and *The Skilled Labourer* (1919).
2. It's not clear why G. L. Dickinson was disgusted with Roger Fry.
3. Joseph Conrad, his wife and their children were visiting a friend near Cracow, the town in which he had grown up, just inside the Russian zone of Poland. They had set sail for Hamburg on a British ship on 25 June. War broke out after they had reached Poland but before they reached the Russian zone. They fled to Zakopane, a small town near the Slovakian border, and eventually escaped back to England. Their adventures are described in Roger Tennant, *Joseph Conrad* (New York, 1981), ch. 25.

My thoughts cling to you in these times. The pain of it all turns me to you more and more.

Your

B.

[240]

[To Margaret Llewelyn Davies]   Russell Chambers
Monday
[August 1914]

My dear Margaret

You were right about the Liberals. I have done with them. I had never believed anything so frightful could happen. I *feel* as if it meant an end of all happiness for the rest of our lives – but perhaps in the end the forces making for peace may be strengthened – perhaps we shall emerge into a saner world. Anyhow everything has to be begun afresh – old fixed points are gone. I feel it *utter madness* for us to join this war. I try to fix my thought on the future – the present is too unbearable.

Yours affectionately,

B. Russell

Appendix: Granny to Bertie

The following letter to Russell from his grandmother was written immediately after the crisis of June 1894, when he and Alys were led to believe that if they married their children would likely be mad. It was written while Russell had been packed off to North Wales on a holiday with Eddie Marsh and away from Alys. The letter illustrates the extraordinary skill with which Countess Russell manipulated her grandson. The first page of the letter is numbered 'IV', but it is not clear what series of letters this refers to.

Pembroke Lodge
5 July 1894

Dearest Bertie

I like to think of you among mountains and burns and out all day long in this glorious weather – and only dread too much walking which would spoil all the good I hope for you and which your looks told me that you needed. I hope N. Wales comes up to your expectations, and that Scotland will be your next holiday. Tell Mr Marsh with our kind remembrances that I hope he will keep you in order and insist on there being the right proportion of laziness and activity in your days.

Here all goes well. On Tuesday evening about 9 o'clock we were surprised by the sudden announcement of 'Mr and Mrs Frederick Berney' – they had cycled down as usual – and after tea and chat they cycled back. No other visitors since you went and Mimi gone yesterday, so Auntie and I are in our normal *tête-à-tête*. She now gets up to luncheon and sits up till bedtime, so that only our breakfasts are solitary.

We think a very great deal of you, my Darling – you are going through a great trial, and my heart aches for you – but your natural uprightness will with God's help bring you through it all the better and the nobler man. We have seen how Uncle Rollo has borne many a hard and bitter trial, some that you know of, some that you don't, and now he has been raised and strengthened and hallowed by sorrows which would have made a weaker mind sink and despond – never be afraid or ashamed, my Child, to let out everything to us three when you feel the wish to do so – the love of 22 years only strengthens in your day of need. But while I wish you never to dread giving us pain by unburdening yourself to us, I also earnestly hope that you are as far as possible detaching your mind from the one subject and bidding it range over others and refresh itself in the peace and beauty and grandeur of all around you – and that you and Mr M. converse on all things cheerful and interesting in this wondrous world – and dwell on all its brightness and its hopes rather than on its sadness and its disappointments. Oh my boy! we foresaw the likelihood of this trial to you and did so long to save you from it – Goodbye and God bless you, My Boy, your ever loving

   Granny

You'll like to hear that my old foot is much better.

Bibliographical Notes

The standard biography of Russell is Ronald W. Clark's *The Life of Bertrand Russell* (London, 1975). Alan Wood's much older and less critical *Bertrand Russell: The Passionate Sceptic* (London, 1957) is still worth reading, however, since Wood had the advantage of knowing Russell. Two new biographies are currently being written: one by Caroline Moorehead and the other by Ray Monk. Russell left many autobiographical writings: *The Autobiography of Bertrand Russell*, 3 vols. (London, 1967–9); *My Philosophical Development* (London, 1959); 'My Mental Development' in *The Philosophy of Bertrand Russell*, vol. 5 of *The Library of Living Philosophers*, ed. P. A. Schilpp (Evanston, Ill., 1944). Many of the pieces in *Portraits from Memory* (London, 1956) are also autobiographical.

There is no good introductory survey of Russell's philosophy. Ronald Jager's *The Development of Bertrand Russell's Philosophy* (London, 1972) comes closest to being comprehensive. But for a quick introduction to the main themes of Russell's philosophy in the years covered by the letters in this volume, John Watling's brief *Bertrand Russell* (Edinburgh, 1970) is hard to beat. Russell's career as a student at Cambridge and his philosophical work up to 1898 is discussed at some length in my *Russell's Idealist Apprenticeship* (Oxford, 1991). The specialist literature on Russell's philosophy is vast (and improving). See, for example, the recent study by Peter Hylton, *Russell, Idealism, and the Emergence of Analytic Philosophy* (Oxford, 1990). Russell's political views are chronicled by Alan Ryan in *Bertrand Russell, A Political Life* (London, 1988). Articles on all aspects of Russell's life and work are published in *Russell: The Journal of the Bertrand Russell Archives* (quarterly 1971–80; twice yearly since 1981). (This journal is cited as '*Russell*' in my notes.)

Russell's own writings (apart from letters and his published books) are being published in *The Collected Papers of Bertrand Russell* (London, 1983 onwards). Seven volumes of a projected thirty have so far appeared. (These volumes are cited as '*Papers*' here.) Each volume contains a useful chronology of the main events in Russell's life during the period covered by the volume; and each paper is accompanied by a commentary describing what is known of its composition and publication. Several collections of Russell's letters to particular correspondents have been published, most notably the following: those to Jourdain in I. Grattan-Guinness (ed.,) *Dear Russell – Dear Jourdain* (London, 1977); to Frege in Gottlob Frege, *Philosophical and Mathematical Correspondence* (Oxford, 1980); to Wittgenstein in B. F. McGuinness and G. H. von Wright, 'Unpublished Correspondence between Russell and Wittgenstein', *Russell*, vol. 10, no. 2 (1990); to William James in *William James, The Meaning of Truth* (Cambridge, Mass., 1975), appendix IV; to Joseph Conrad in Edgar Wright, 'Joseph Conrad and Bertrand Russell', *Conradiana*, vol. 2, no. 1 (1969); to H. Wildon Carr, in Michael Thompson, 'Some Letters of Bertrand Russell to Herbert Wildon Carr', *Coranto*, vol. 10, no. 1 (1975). Russell's correspondence with Louis Couturat is being edited by Anne-Françoise Schmid. Russell's letters to Helen Flexner and Lucy Donnelly were compiled in a PhD Thesis for the McMaster University English Department by Maria Forte, 'Bertrand Russell's Letters to Helen Thomas Flexner and Lucy Martin Donnelly' (1988). Russell also included many letters in his *Autobiography*.

Four journal articles about particular aspects of Russell's life covered by this volume are worth noting: on Russell's visit to America in 1896 see William M. Armstrong, 'Bertrand Russell Comes to America, 1896', *Studies in History and Society* (1970); on the free-trade campaign see Richard A. Rempel, 'From Imperialism to Free Trade: Couturat, Halévy and Russell's First Crusade', *Journal of the History of Ideas* (1979); on his efforts for women's suffrage see Brian Harrison, 'Bertrand Russell: The False Consciousness of a Feminist', *Russell* (1984); on his visit to Harvard see Kirk Willis, '"This Place is Hell": Bertrand Russell at Harvard, 1914', *The New England Quarterly* (1989).

Books have been written about two buildings which appear briefly in Russell's letters: Cynthia Gladwyn has written on *The Paris Embassy* (London, 1976), and Margaret Keynes on Newnham Grange and 'The Old Granary' in *A House by the River* (Cambridge, 1976). Gladwyn's book is worth reading for its account of Dufferin's years as British Ambassador, and Keynes's gives an interesting account of the Darwin family in Cambridge.

There are many books on Russell's family. For a brief family history see Christopher Trent, *The Russells* (London, 1966). For Russell's parents see *The Amberley Papers*, 2 vols., ed. Bertrand and Patricia Russell (London, 1937). John Prest's *Lord John Russell* (London, 1972) is a political biography of his grandfather. For Granny see the biography based mainly on her correspondence and diaries by Desmond MacCarthy and Agatha Russell, *Lady John Russell, A Memoir* (London, 1910). There is no biography of Frank Russell, though one would be worth writing (preferably by an expert in turn-of-the-century marital law). There is, however, Frank's (rather unrevealing) autobiography, *My Life and Adventures* (London, 1923). *Recollections of Lady Georgiana Peel*, compiled by her daughter Ethel Peel (London, 1920), is a memoir of one of Russell's (less interesting) aunts. A more interesting aunt from his mother's side of the family is portrayed in *Rosalind Howard, Countess of Carlisle*, by Dorothy Henley (London, 1958), for which Russell wrote an introduction. For the Stanleys in the mid nineteenth century see Nancy Mitford, *The Ladies of Alderley* (London, 1938).

The best account of Alys Russell and her family is Barbara Strachey, *Remarkable Relations* (London, 1980). Barbara Strachey and Jayne Samuels also produced a book on Mariechen, *Mary Berenson, A Self-Portrait from her Letters and Diaries* (London, 1983). For Berenson himself, see Meryle Secrest, *Being Bernard Berenson* (New York, 1979), and more fully Ernest Samuels, *Bernard Berenson*, 2 vols. (Cambridge, Mass., 1979, 1987). Logan Pearsall Smith's memoirs, *Unforgotten Years* (London, 1938), are good for his early years, but tail off later.

Ottoline Morrell left two volumes of posthumously published memoirs: *Ottoline. The Early Memoirs of Lady Ottoline Morrell* (London, 1963), and *Ottoline at Garsington. Memoirs of Lady Ottoline Morrell 1915–1918* (London, 1974), both edited by Robert Gathorne-Hardy. Much material about her affair with Russell is printed, out of chronological order, in an Appendix to the second volume. The only biography of Morrell so far available is Sandra Jobson Darroch's *Ottoline. The Life of Lady Ottoline Morrell* (London, 1975), but a new one is being written by Miranda Seymour.

Biographies are now available for many of Russell's friends. For Whitehead see Victor Lowe, *Alfred North Whitehead. The Man and His Work*, 2 vols., the second edited for publication after Lowe's death by J. B. Schneewind (Baltimore, 1985, 1990). For Moore see Paul Levy, *Moore. G. E. Moore and the Cambridge Apostles* (London, 1979), and Tom Regan, *Bloomsbury's Prophet. G. E. Moore and the Development of His Moral Philosophy* (Philadelphia, 1986), though neither is a biography in the conventional sense and Levy is very inaccurate about Russell's relations with Moore. The only major biographical work on McTaggart is G. L. Dickinson's dated and diplomatic *J. McT. E. McTaggart* (Cambridge, 1931). John McCormick's excellent biography, *George Santayana* (New York, 1988), is useful also for its account of the Harvard philosophy department just before Russell visited it. (For this last topic, however, Bruce Kuklick's *The Rise of American Philosophy: Cambridge, Massachusetts, 1860–1930*, New Haven, 1977, is the definitive source.) Whitehead, Moore, and Santayana, together with C. D. Broad, have volumes devoted to them in *The Library of Living Philosophers*, edited by P. A. Schilpp, each volume containing an autobiography and several (now somewhat dated) articles on their philosophical work. Santayana also left a separate autobiography, *Persons and Places*, 3 vols. (New York, 1944–53). Wittgenstein didn't get a Schilpp volume, but there are now two good biographies of him: B. F. McGuinness, *Wittgenstein. A Life* (London, 1988), of which only vol. I has appeared so far; and Ray Monk, *Ludwig Wittgenstein. The Duty of Genius* (London, 1990). For Russell's early relations with Wittgenstein see Kenneth Blackwell, 'The Early Wittgenstein and the Middle Russell', in I. Block (ed.), *Perspectives on the Philosophy of Wittgenstein* (Oxford, 1981).

Among Russell's non-philosophical friends Gilbert Murray is now well served by Duncan Wilson's *Gilbert Murray* (Oxford, 1987) and by his own *Unfinished Autobiography* (London, 1960), to which Russell and other friends contributed chapters. The lives of Helen Thomas and Simon Flexner up to the time of their marriage are chronicled in a dual biography by their son, James Thomas Flexner, *An American Saga. The Story of Helen Thomas and Simon Flexner* (Boston, 1984). Jane Harrison is less well served by Sandra J. Peacock, *Jane Ellen Harrison. The Mask and the Self* (New Haven, 1988). For Eddie Marsh see his memoirs, *A Number of People* (London, 1939), and Christopher Hassall, *A Biography of Edward Marsh* (New York, 1959). For the MacCarthys see Hugh and Mirabel Cecil, *Clever Hearts. Desmond and Molly MacCarthy: A Biography* (London, 1990). There is no good biography of Sydney and Beatrice Webb (Royden Harrison is writing one), but in the meantime *The Letters of Sydney and Beatrice Webb*, ed. Norman MacKenzie, 3 vols. (Cambridge, 1978), and Beatrice Webb's *Diaries*, ed. Norman and Jeanne MacKenzie, 4 vols. (Cambridge, Mass., 1982–5), are especially useful. Beatrice wrote an autobiography for both of them, *Our Partnership* (London, 1948). G. L. Dickinson seems to be passing into oblivion. The main work on him is still E. M. Forster's memoir *Goldsworthy Lowes Dickinson* (London, 1934), though his *Autobiography* (London, 1973) appeared not too long ago. The best source on Ivy Pretious is the autobiography of her son, Hallam Tennyson, *The Haunted Mind* (London, 1984). Mary Sheepshanks, long neglected, now shares a biography with Flora Mayor in Sybil Oldfield's *Spinsters of This Parish* (London, 1984). Much, of course, has been written about Joseph Conrad, but see Frederick R. Karl, *Joseph Conrad: The Three Lives* (New York, 1979) or Roger Tennant, *Joseph Conrad* (New York, 1981).

Finally, there are those friends of Russell's who still languish in undeserved oblivion. There is no biography of C. P. Sanger, whose contributions to the history of his time were significant but largely unmarked. Nor is there a book on the Llewelyn Davieses, though one could well be written on this exceptionally interesting family. Sylvia and Arthur Llewelyn Davies, however, appear in biographies of J. M. Barrie, for Barrie was in love with Sylvia and looked after her children when she died a few years after Arthur – the children were the inspiration for *Peter Pan*. Chapter 4 of Andrew Birkin's *J. M. Barrie and the Lost Boys* (London, 1979) is devoted to the Llewelyn Davies family.

Index